THURBER

THURBER

A Biography by
Burton Bernstein

Illustrated with drawings
and photographs
by James Thurber

LONDON
VICTOR GOLLANCZ LTD
1975

All the writings and drawings by James Thurber are protected by copyright and used with the permission of Helen Thurber and Rosemary Thurber Sauers.

The excerpts from A Note on the Drawings in This Book from *Is Sex Necessary?* on page 188 and the Introduction to *The Owl in the Attic* on page 193, both by E. B. White, are protected by copyright and used with the permission of the author.

The article by E. B. White on pages 504–505, © 1961 The New Yorker Magazine, Inc., used with the permission of The New Yorker Magazine, Inc., and the author.

The poem "Anger Is, Anger Was" by Mark Van Doren on page 380 is protected by copyright and used with the permission of Dorothy Van Doren.

The excerpts from the Introduction by Dorothy Parker to *The Seal in the Bedroom* on page 205, copyright © 1963 by James Thurber. Published by Hamish Hamilton, London.

Printed in Great Britain by
Lowe & Brydone (Printers) Ltd, Thetford, Norfolk

For Karen and Michael

Foreword

Never get into biography, it throws too harsh a light on the prevalence of lunacy.

—James Thurber, in a letter to Roger Angell, July 2, 1959

Thurber's warning came too late. I was already hard at work on the authorized biography of James Thurber when I ran across my subject's bitter injunction. At several points along the way towards this publication, I almost agreed with him. Often, I asked myself how I ever got into all this.

My relationship with Thurber began, I suppose, when I was old enough to read anything more formidable than the Mystery Boys series, roughly thirty-five years ago. There were a few Thurber collections around the house and my family subscribed to the *New Yorker*. At first sight, I was enchanted by his writing and drawing. I found myself laughing out loud in a spasm of identification with the absurd, the same peculiar way I laughed at, say, Vic and Sade on the radio. Through the years, certain Thurber lines (usually cartoon captions) grew into everyday shibboleths with family and special friends—for instance, "Perhaps *this* will refresh your memory" and "It's Parkins, sir; we're 'aving a bit of a time below stairs." Thurber was for me more than mere entertainment; he became a masterful instructor in the writing and celebration of humor.

During the winter of 1948, my brother and I were driving through a snowstorm in search of a new Connecticut skiing area we had heard about. We stopped at a fine old white Colonial house in Cornwall to ask directions and we were greeted by a slender, pleasant woman who gave us all the information we required (the new skiing area was just down the road). I noticed some unmistakably familiar drawings on the walls, and I asked the woman if she was a friend of James Thurber. She was not only his friend but his wife—Helen Thurber. Soon, her husband came downstairs from his workroom to join us. The tall, angular, almost blind man feeling his way down the stairs was so different from what I had imagined him to be. It was a singular thrill to meet and talk with him. He later showed us the strange equipment he needed to produce his drawings, with the negligible vision remaining to him. The story of this chance encounter made me a hero in certain circles of my high school, and I was more enchanted with Thurber than ever.

I met Thurber a few times after that on Martha's Vineyard and, during the late 1950's, in and around the *New Yorker*, where I had become a staff writer. There was a marked difference in the man and, of course, his writing—an unsettling sense of tragedy seemed to hang about him. With his death in 1961, it occurred to me that Thurber would be a grand exception to the conventional wisdom that biographies of writers are superfluous. He would be an engrossing subject for an unfettered biography by somebody someday.

In 1970, I was approached by Dodd, Mead to write the authorized biography of Thurber. Access to his papers and letters and the cooperation of his family and friends were promised. As an occasional book reviewer, I was perhaps more aware of the stigma attached to the term "authorized biography" than most. I told the publisher I wouldn't be interested unless the Thurber estate—that is, Helen Thurber—would allow me sole control over the final manuscript. Helen consented, legal agreements and contracts were signed, and I began work in early 1971.

Helen was more open and cooperative than I had dreamed possible. First of all, she had efficiently organized Thurber's vast files of letters and papers, thus making my research infinitely easier. (As an inveterate letter writer in spite of his blindness, Thurber relied on dictation to thorough secretaries for much of his life, all of whom dutifully kept carbon copies of his correspondence. His blindness, ironically, thus simplified his biographer's work.) In our long and, I'm sure, painful interviews, Helen held nothing germane back, nor did she encourage any of my other interviewees to censor their statements. For three years, she was a model source and, in a way, collaborator.

When I finished my final draft of the biography, I presented her with a copy for her emendations and comments, in conformity with our agreement. Her emendations were comparatively few but her comments were numerous. The gist of her complaints was that I had treated her husband's life in too negative a fashion. I am sorry she felt that way. What I did was simply take the facts as they were revealed to me from letters, personal papers, published matter, interviews and, with a minimum of preconceptions and using Thurber's own words as much as possible, set them down. In biography—a more profound form of journalism—patent truth can have no surrogate.

No one knew this better than Thurber himself, who had his own difficulties with work in that enervating field. Indeed, on April 25, 1952, he wrote E. B. White, after the biographical *The Thurber Album* came out: "I am going to write about imaginary people from now on since real ones take too much out of me." And apropos of his biography of Harold Ross, *The Years with Ross*, he wrote his July 2, 1959, injunction to Roger Angell. However, his own brand of autobiography was his pleasure and his forte—the wild flowering from a seed of truth. Yet, so much of his own life was in direct contradiction to his fictional autobiographical life that it can be said most of his reminiscence dealt with "imaginary people." But what an imagination created those people!

Here, then, is the authorized, if not approved, biography of James Thurber. A large share of credit for its existence goes to Helen Thurber, and to the following persons I would also like to offer my gratitude for their help and cooperation:

Larry Adler, Roland Algrant, Rose Algrant, Roger Angell, Ellen Bernstein, Walter Bernstein, Lewis Branscomb and his staff, Gladys Brooks, Jeff Brown, Dr. Gordon Bruce, Truman Capote, Robert Coates, Hyman Cohen, Louise Connell, Whitfield Connor, Mr. and Mrs. Malcolm Cowley, Dr. Virgil Damon, Mr. and Mrs. Peter De Vries, Edward Dodd, Candida Donadio, Ellen Dunham, Louis Forster, John Fullen, Mr. and Mrs. F. R. Ted Gardiner, Milton Greenstein, John Gude, Hamish Hamilton, Julie Hayden, Susan Lardner Hellerman, Leo Hofeller, Ann Honeycutt, Ralph Ingersoll, Armin Landeck, Kenneth MacLean, Faith McNulty Martin, Ralph McCombs, Patty Gardiner McGuckin, Thomas Meek, John Duncan Miller, Frank Modell, Howard Moss, Carmine Peppe, James Pollard, Neil Rolde, Richard Rovere, Rosemary Thurber Sauers, Nora Sayre, William Shawn, Marc Simont, Helen Stark and her staff, Mr. and Mrs. Donald Ogden Stewart, Donald Ogden Stewart, Jr., Haila Stoddard, Robert Thurber, Robert Tibbetts, Paula Trueman, Mr. and Mrs. Mark Van Doren, Elfride Von Kuegelgen, Richard Watts, Peter Weed, R.E.M. Whitaker, Mr. and Mrs. E.B. White, and Elinor Wright.

Also, thanks are due to the Beinecke Rare Book and Manuscript Library at Yale University, the Cornell University Library (E.B. White papers), the Newberry Library (Malcolm Cowley papers), the New York Public Library, the New Yorker Magazine Library, and the Ohio State University Library (James Thurber Collection).

Contents

Contents

PART 1

Innocence

CHAPTER 1

"The score was 4-1 in favor of me."

Columbus is a depressing place. The All-American City, as it likes to call itself, is exactly that: a homely mélange of all America's late-twentieth century problems. Grotesque shopping centers sprout with the predictability of goldenrod in August; the old inner-city single-family frame houses seem to decay before your eyes; the whites flee from the blacks' siege of the city's core to the instant, overpriced suburbs, where all the lawns boast precisely the same shade of green; the once sedate Ohio State University campus is in a thrumming fettle of rush-hour traffic, as its generally undistinguished 45,000 students spend far too much of their time simply hunting for parking space; and, as Betty Garrett, a reporter for the Columbus *Citizen-Journal*, wrote, "Babbitry is alive but unwell here."(1)

Like so many other All-American cities, Columbus was once very different. At the turn of the century it was "just an overgrown country town, a walkabout place where everybody knew everybody else," in the words of a city elder.(2) With one-fifth of its present-day population, with blacks pretty much in their place, and with Babbitry not only alive but well and heartily admired, Columbus, the state capital and home of the Ohio State University, was not a bad city to be born and brought up in, if you had the right kind of parents. James Grover Thurber described it, in one of his relaxed, nostalgic moments, fifty-six years after his birth in Columbus on December 8, 1894:

I went back to Ohio last year, to the town where I was born in the middle of the tranquil old decade that considered itself such a devil, the 1890's, with its flamboyant Teddy Roosevelt and its gaudy Oscar Wilde, the diavolos, the wood-burning sets, the euchre and pedro parties, the leather cushions with Indian heads on them, the noisy bamboo portieres, the Turkish corners in living rooms, the pug dogs, the brightly enamelled bicycles, the books of Stanley Weyman and Owen Meredith, and such daring songs as "After the Ball," "Gypsy Love Song," and "Down Where the Wurzburger Flows."

I was just six at the turn of the century, but I remember the Columbus, Ohio,

/ 3

of those somnolent years as fondly and sharply as a man on a sinking ship might remember his prairie home and its dangers no greater than gopher holes or poison ivy. In 1900, Columbus hadn't had a serious threat to its repose since Morgan's Confederate raiders insolently approached the city during the Civil War. There was a lot of picnicking and canoeing and cycling, and going for hikes in the woods on Sundays in spring, the men in boaters and bright blazers, and the women in shirtwaists and skirts. The men got up baseball games, and the women looked for white violets and maidenhair ferns to take home and transplant. People liked to sit on the wide verandas on the hotter Sundays, the men with their feet up on the balustrades, reading in the sports pages about Corbett and Jeffries, Maud S and Star Pointer, Cy Young and John McGraw. The women sat more decorously, reading *The Lady of Lyons* or *Lucile,* and the children, sprawled on the floor, eagerly followed the comic adventures of the Katzenjammer Kids, Lulu and Leander, Happy Hooligan, Foxy Grandpa, Buster Brown, and Alphonse and Gaston. A couple of young men named Orville and Wilbur were thinking about the laws governing the sustained flight of heavier-than-air contraptions, but people were more interested in the cakewalk than in the gas engine . . .(3)

The only hitch in this idyllic setting for an American humorist's birth, in the Mark Twain tradition, was that Thurber's immediate family ran against the 1890's grain. The Thurbers were eccentrics—not simply the lovable, slightly daft characters Thurber fictionalized in *My Life and Hard Times* nor the proud pioneer-individualists of *The Thurber Album,* but certifiable eccentrics of a stripe only the British, perhaps, could fully appreciate. His family wasn't congenitally peculiar; it just worked out that way.

Take, for instance, Judge Stacy Taylor, his step-great-grandfather on his mother's side. Stacy Taylor was a restless Virginian of English stock who struck out for the other side of the Alleghenies in 1826, finally settling in St. Marys, Ohio. He made his fortune trading furs with the Wyandots, Ottawas, and Senecas and read law at night with a lit candle balanced on his chest. Judge Taylor could also recite all the poetry of Robert Burns by heart. He became an established jurist, a state legislator, and a man of some means by the time he took for his third wife Lizzie Bell Matheny, Thurber's great-grandmother, in 1853. (Her first husband, John Matheny, a pious Ohio farmer, drowned in the Hocking River when Katherine Matheny Taylor Fisher, Thurber's grandmother, was only seven, and thus he took a poor second place to Judge Taylor in family lore.)

A neat complement to Judge Taylor was Jacob Fisher, Thurber's other maternal great-grandfather. Jacob was one of eleven children of

Michael Fisher, who pioneered to lands along the Scioto River, south of Columbus, at the end of the eighteenth century. (Like Judge Taylor, he was a Virginian of English stock.) Jacob became a local legend, a giant of a man whose feats of strength and combat served to back up his deeply held political and religious beliefs (he was anti-Andrew Jackson and pro-Methodist). But what astounded his contemporaries most was the man's odd sense of fairness. He fought murderously, but made it a point to heal the wounds of his adversaries, never holding a grudge. He was the first man in Franklin County, Ohio, to sit down at table with a Negro, explaining to his disturbed fellow church-goers, "If a man's good enough to work for me, he's good enough to eat with me."(4) He was ardently for Lincoln in the Civil War and tried desperately, but vainly, to join the Union Army, although he was fifty-three when Fort Sumter was fired upon. In short, Jacob was strange stuff for his time and place. When he died at seventy-seven, he was survived by six of his thirteen children, thirty-two grandchildren, and six great-grandchildren, all of whom were in total awe of the man. This awe, however, was by no means reciprocal. "Goddam it," Jacob reportedly said after seeing a puny newborn great-grandchild, "the next generation of Fishers is goin' to be squirrels."(5)

In any case, the offspring of Jacob continued to be squirrelly. Jacob's son and Thurber's maternal grandfather, William M. Fisher, "walked the thin line between eccentricity and insanity."(6) Thurber, in *The Thurber Album* piece called "Man with a Rose," described his grandfather as an incurable egocentric, given to announcing in public places, "I am William M. Fisher, of Columbus, Ohio," capping all his teeth with gold, regularly clamping a red rose in his mouth like a cigar, and having his photograph taken every chance he could get. William was the physical and spiritual opposite of his father, Jacob. He was a city boy at heart, whose tastes ran to good food, plentiful drink (in spite of his severe Methodism), mercantile gain, the Republican Party, and, most importantly, Ulysses S. Grant, about whom he was obsessive. However, as the son of a legendary man of strength, he tried often and unsuccessfully to emulate his father's reputation as a brawler. "As far as we know, he never actually hit a man, but he was forever swinging his rather short and far from swift right arm," Thurber wrote of him. "If one of his grandsons got hurt while he was around, he would shout proudly, 'Show your Fisher, boy, show your Fisher!' "(7)

In truth (although Thurber only hinted at it in "Man with a Rose"), William M. Fisher, of Columbus, Ohio, was a coward, a bully, and a sadist, as well as "probably committable."(8) For all his love of General

Grant, William couldn't see his way clear to joining the Union Army, which his father so dearly wanted him to do. William paid a substitute to wear the blue for him and settled for the Ohio Home Guard, a humiliation for old Jacob.* Young William disliked the brutal labor on his father's farm, leaving it in his twenties to work as a grocery clerk. Flamboyant and ambitious, he became the founder and owner of the William M. Fisher Company, a wholesale fruit-and-produce commission house, which is still in business in Columbus as the William M. Fisher & Sons Company. He bought a huge two-story brick house with four porches on Bryden Road, in what was then the fashionable outskirts of Columbus and is now the heart of a black neighborhood. It was this house that served as the center for Fisher–Thurber family life.

This coarse, swaggering man perversely took for a wife a sweet, delicate, kind lady named Katherine Matheny Taylor, or "Aunt Kate" as she was known to legions of relatives and friends. While her husband was grasping and selfish, Aunt Kate was neighborly and generous, habitually giving away baskets of the William M. Fisher Company's finest produce to the penurious half of Columbus. Frequently, she would enclose discreet checks in the baskets. Her husband didn't approve of such uninhibited charity. "Who's she looking after now?" he would say, whenever she was absent from the house. She was a devoted, if often embarrassed, wife and a loving mother and grandmother, as well as the "acknowledged head of the far-flung family" during the regular reunions in Sugar Grove, Ohio.(9)

Aunt Kate's benign conventionality marked her as the odd one in the family, for her myriad Matheny and Taylor relatives were cast as certifiables. As Thurber read the roster, there were, for example: "Aunt Lou, who wrote poetry and believed that everything was for the best; Aunt Melissa, who knew the Bible by heart and was convinced that Man's day was done . . . Aunt Fanny, plagued in her old age by recurring dreams in which she gave birth to Indian, Mexican, Chinese, and African twins . . ."—and one of Thurber's favorite Ohio creatures—"Aunt Florence, who once tried to fix a broken cream separator on her farm near Sugar Grove and suddenly cried, 'Why doesn't somebody take this goddam thing away from me?' "(10) Then, too, there were the likes of Aunt Ida Clemmens, a loony mystic who smelled dire conspiracy in such disparate phenomena as the sinking of the *Titanic* and the invention of

---

*Thurber's family was touchy on this subject. While he was researching "Man with a Rose," Thurber wrote them, on December 22, 1950, "I will emphasize Grandpa's essential work as farmer during the Civil War and the fact that sending substitutes was common in such cases."

electricity, and perhaps the queerest of the lot, Aunt Mary Van York, a wisp of a woman who survived till ninety-three mainly on a diet of an estimated two hundred thousand pipefuls of vicious Star plug chewing tobacco.

It was only fitting that Thurber's mother was the namesake of the redoubtable Mary Van York. Mary Agnes Fisher—or "Mame," as practically everybody called her—was the first of six children born to William and Katherine Fisher, in 1866. She lived to be eighty-nine years old, and during much of that span she was famous as the prototype, for millions of readers, of the Thurber Eccentric, Female Division. Even as a child, she was effusive and uninhibited, in spite of (or perhaps because of) her father. She grew up in Columbus with her eyes set on the stage, but nice Methodist girls of substance didn't hurl themselves into the godless world of theatre. Even the amateur theatricals she attempted in high school were frowned upon. At one point, she tried to run away from home and Columbus for the thespian life, but she was caught just in time by her parents. So young Mame took to play-acting about the house, or, for that matter, in front of anyone who would pay the slightest attention to her. This developed her natural sense of mimicry and infatuation with the practical joke. Thurber wrote in "Lavender with a Difference," his paean to his mother in *The Thurber Album:* "Deprived of a larger audience, the frustrated comedienne performed for whoever would listen, and once distressed a couple of stately guests in her father's home by descending the front stairs in her dressing gown, her hair tumbling and her eyes staring, to announce that she had escaped from the attic, where she was kept because of her ardent and hapless love for Mr. Briscoe, the postman."

Later in life, she committed practical jokes that became a part of Columbus folklore. When dog-hating Aunt Mary Van York came for a visit, Mame gathered together in her cellar all the neighborhood mutts she could corral. She asked Aunt Mary to help her out by feeding the family dogs, but when the cellar door was opened, eighteen famished canines assaulted the poor woman. There was bedlam, and Aunt Mary never returned for another visit. Mame also masqueraded as an avid buyer of a neighbor's house that was up for sale, and intoxicated the seller by upping all his suggested prices for the house and its furnishings. One of her finer moments in prankishness came when she borrowed a wheelchair at a faith-healing meeting, rolled down the aisle, suddenly stood up, and proclaimed that she could walk. With hallelujahs sounding about her, she fled on foot as the owner of the wheelchair recognized his property.

This streak of pixyish rebellion against the formidable House of Fisher and Victorian Columbus quite naturally extended to her romantic attachments. The eligible and attractive Columbus maiden kept a diary guaranteed to shock. The diary is no longer available, unfortunately, but one entry in it, for May 14, 1888, came to the attention of her second-born son, who used it in "Lavender with a Difference." The entry read: "Went over to Flora's to talk over yesterday's visit. I tell you that Ira D. is cute, but I do not like him very well—he is a perfect gentleman, only he will insist on kissing me every time and I will not allow it. I can truthfully say I never kissed a fellow in all my life but once, and that was Charlie Thurber at the depot a few years ago."

Most likely, the Fishers would have far preferred their spirited daughter to lavish her kisses on Ira D.—or almost any white Protestant gentleman—rather than Charlie Thurber. Charles Leander Thurber, though certainly a white Protestant gentleman, was not William M. Fisher's idea of the perfect son-in-law. For one thing, he was not from Columbus, or even Ohio, but from the definitely less civilized Indianapolis, Indiana. His family background was at best hazy, at worst eyebrow-raising. Most discouraging of all for the Fishers was the certain knowledge that Charlie Thurber was merely a hard-working but unambitious political clerk and would undoubtedly die a hard-working but unambitious political clerk.

The first Thurbers were from Boston and Providence—that is as far back as anybody has been able to trace them, although some highly speculative genealogical research turned up the usual comforting information that the first Thurber to arrive in America was an "English gentleman"—and the next authenticated data reveals Charles Thurber's father, Leander Thurber, heading west for California and gold. He rode no farther than Indiana, where he married a local girl named Sarah Hull and, in effect, her spinster sister, who had no other place to live except with the newly wedded Thurbers. Here is where the Thurber family history gets particularly murky. There was whispered reason to believe that the spinster sister was the real mother of Charles Thurber, having ceded, for propriety's sake, the newborn baby to her married sister and the rightful father. (Many decades later, after her husband's death, Mame Thurber tried unsuccessfully to trace the Thurber family history in Indiana to see if the bastardy theory had any truth to it, mainly for her own amusement.) In any case, shortly after Charles Thurber was born in 1867, his father was thrown from a horse and died, leaving his widow to provide for her son-of-record and sister. She barely scraped by as a school teacher, until at last she deteriorated mentally and physically. The sister, meanwhile, was not too well herself, and young Charles, still in short pants, took on the burden of support by selling newspapers in Indianapolis. He was attracted to the law and the stage (the latter attracting him, in turn, to Mame), but both careers were out of the question for the impoverished boy with the sickly mother and aunt. He somehow completed the eighth grade and landed various clerical jobs, thanks to his devilishly good memory and aptitude for language. He was painstaking in his vocabulary, spelling, and calligraphy, way beyond what his formal schooling would indicate.

Politics, a kind of compromise, or amalgam, of the law and the stage, fascinated him. He was a fervent Republican and partisan of James G. Blaine, and by the time he was seventeen and had met Mame during a trip to Columbus, he was already marching in anti-Grover Cleveland parades.

The following love letter* to his intended gives some idea of his writing style, his meticulousness, and, for a young man who was to immerse himself in politics for the rest of his life, his marked lack of political acumen:

Indianapolis, Ind.
Wednes. Eve
Oct. 29, 1884

Dear Mamie:—

Your welcome little letter received. The omission of the word "Friend" is certainly compensated for by the appearance of the adjective as above. I know that I can assume the friend to be true.

My letter could appropriately be a copy of yours, for "Politics" is here, as in Columbus, and I guess everywhere else, the main and almost only topic discussed...[Unclear]... When you answer this, Blaine will be the President-elect, unless you are prompt. Remember this and see how good a prophet I am.

Pearl and I, with a merry crowd of young folks, attended the opening of a new Roller Rink last night. Our pleasure . . . [Unclear] . . . caused by tripping on someone's skates, and we have about concluded to change our amusements from rinks to theaters, etc. hereafter.

Allow me to return many . . . [Unclear] . . . likeness of yourself, enclosed in reciprocation for the one "inflicted" upon you. The picture looks just like the charming little miss it represents, if you will permit me, it a little mis(s)-represents her, in not being quite so—(well, I'm so far away it will be safe to say it—and "honor bright" too) pretty.

My mother went to Grandma's in Providence, R.I., leaving here the 8th inst.

---

*All letters are intact with regard to spelling, punctuation, and usage except when the letter writer's typographical errors have been corrected to avoid confusion.

She will remain until after Thanksgiving, I guess. She passed through Columbus, but . . .
[Rest of letter incomplete]

By 1888, still wooing Mame by mail and occasional visits to Columbus, he received an appointment to the staff of the Indiana governor's office, where one of his colleagues was the considerably more ambitious Kenesaw Mountain Landis, later a jurist and baseball commissioner. Another friend was Alvah Currie, also an Indianapolis lad, who made it big in the other field Charles Thurber had interest in but no real chance at—the stage.

Indianapolis, Ind.
Sunday, Feb.2/90

My Dear Mame,
   My joy, my hope,
     my pride,
      and mine
       only:—

Wonder how Mr. Poe would like the above for a beginning? You might ask him what he thinks of such headlines. Of course the genial, good natured Auditor has doubtless had more experience in this line than I, but I seriously doubt whether he ever crowded more happiness in five days consecutively than did I from December 25th to 29th, 1889. Tell him that time will gradually obliterate my bashfulness but that it can never remove my happiness, though my love for you will accumulate with the days.

Your pictures arrived yesterday. I wish you had not stipulated the return of either for I would like to keep them both. It's Hoosier, you know, to want everything in sight, and sigh for the unseen. But, of course, you are always to have your way, so I will say that I like the one with the tablet the best. While you are too much in the shade, the side view of your face is decidedly pretty. In general, I like that picture better than the other. The other, however, shows your face more clearly and in that respect is superior. You did not say when to return the rejected photo, so I will hold them both awaiting your orders. As I said before, I would like to have them both, but your pleasure will govern that. I frankly agree with you girls in thinking that you could take better pictures. These are good but the subjects thereof could appear to better advantage on paper, I am sure. Accept my thanks for them. I will not make the thanks in eloquent terms until I hear from you as to the disposition of both of them.

While I am engaged in returning thanks, it affords me great pleasure to sincerely thank you for the kind invitation to dinner and lunch. I will be pleased to accept for next Sunday should circumstances permit. I hope to be in Columbus next Sunday. I am very anxious to see you again. There are many things I can talk with you about that limited time will not permit me to write. As soon as I am certain that I can come I will inform you. Of course, I am trying to secure a trip pass as before. The gentleman whom I wish to see on the subject is, or was last week, out of the city. I will try to see him to-morrow and arrange everything to leave here next Saturday evening. I will have all day with you and I know it will be a happy one for us both.

I have been very busy lately. I have adopted a new plan for making the days longer. It is quite successful: I get up earlier. I tell you there's a good deal in that.

Book and Griffin are both in Kansas on Sons of Veterans' business. They are combining business with pleasure, you may be assured. Both have relatives and friends out there.

I have received a great many personal letters recently. You are the only young lady, I will say, who makes life happier by writing to me. One's enough. Now please don't misinterpret that remark. One is enough when she is the right one, as in this case.

Yesterday I heard from Ed Harvey, now in Helena, Montana. It was the first letter I have received from my old chum for a very long time. He is prospering and happy in the Wild West. Says he wouldn't be contented here again.

Also received letters from Curry and Darrow lately. Everything is lovely with them. Alvie asks: "Have you had it?" From Michigan comes the same old story —"La Grippe."

I heard Rev. A. A. Willits lecture here in Plymouth Church some years ago. I liked him better than Mark Twain. His subject was "The Secret of a Happy Home." I know "The Model Wife" must have been a magnificent lecture. Have never heard that one, but it's unnecessary. I'll have a model wife of my own some of these days.

"Lord Chumley" will be here soon. I want to go to that play. Have you ever seen it? "The Wife," which you mentioned in a recent letter, was here during the early part of the season. I did not go. It made a hit here, I remember.

Poor James Whitcomb Riley! He is, it seems, on the down track. It is a pitiful thing for so bright and lovable a man as he to become such a slave to drink. This is his home, you know, and he is loved here by everyone. He is our Hoosier Burns. I hope he will brace up and be a man yet.*

I was expecting company to-day—(Armand, Charley Weis, Will Jordan and others)—at home, but I left after dinner to come down to the office to write to you. We had a late dinner, so I will have to bring in the concluding chapter soon and go home to receive my callers. We boys are to have a little party of our own next Tuesday evening. No girls need apply this time. Rous & Weis are hosts. I am one of the invited guests.

---

*Thurber wrote in "Gentleman from Indiana": "It was a matter of early awe to me that my father knew most of the Riley poems by heart and could actually recite all of 'An Old Sweetheart of Mine.' "

I don't believe I have told you of the "Dickens Social" to be given at Plymouth on Valentine's night. I am cast for "Mark Tapley," one of my favorite characters. Am reading "Martin Chuzzlewit" in spare moments to be prepared for the ordeal. Am also reading Hamlet, and, I may add, the daily papers—Like you I fancy a 72 hour day might be a good idea. —Still, as the burglar said, "we must take things as we find them," and stare bravely the probabilities of soon having instead an 8–hour day.

I am almost counting the hours until 7:15 next Saturday evening when I hope and expect to board the train bound for Columbus to again see and kiss and hug, of course, the dearest and sweetest girl in all the universe to me.—

Wonder how Mr. Poe would like to read the above and hear me assure you that I am

Yours regardless of death and taxes!

Charlie

And so, after a whirlwind courtship of more than eight years, Charles Leander Thurber and Mary Agnes Fisher were married in a Methodist church near William Fisher's mansion in 1892. According to a local newspaper account, it was "one of the neatest and pleasantest" weddings ever witnessed in Columbus, with "numerous and costly" wedding presents. Charles, of course, moved to Columbus, and soon after the nuptials he changed his middle name to Lincoln, at his wife's suggestion. It was one of her grander practical jokes.

We read most of the reviews [of A Rage to Live] and the various summaries printed of the score. It is amazing how the 50–50 ratio kept going. This happened to "Madame Bovary" in France, to Shaw's first plays in England, and even to "Alice in Wonderland" which was not even reviewed in Punch the year it came out. Later a Sir Hobart Gill took a crack at it, referring to the text as "those nonsensical legends for the superb Tenniel drawings." The night I was born, December 8, 1894, César Franck's D-minor symphony had its world premiere in Paris. Fifty percent of the audience cheered at the end and the others booed, tore up auditorium seats, and fenced the other side with walking sticks. The piece is now known as "The keystone of modern symphonic music." At 245 Parsons Avenue that night, the score was 4–1 in favor of me.

—Letter from Thurber to John O'Hara, October 29, 1949.

The Fishers in 1892 were people of property, pillars of the community, leaders of the Columbus business, religious, and social worlds. Their eldest child, a lively girl of twenty-six, had married a nobody of twenty-five, a political clerk of doubtful parentage from Indiana, who was patently no match for the rough-and-tumble machine politics of turn-of-the-century Ohio and who seemed to be content only while solving newspaper-contest puzzles. The obvious solution to this potentially embarrassing quandary was for William Fisher to take the young man into the family firm and squeeze him into that fabled make-work job designed for the milquetoast son-in-law. However, William M. Fisher was no ordinary rich father-in-law, just as Charles L. Thurber was no ordinary milquetoast son-in-law. Fisher did offer Charles a job with his flourishing commission house, but it was a menial one—totting up inventories of grapefruit, which Fisher had introduced to the Midwest—hardly a challenge to an intelligent clerk who had worked in the Indiana governor's office and who prided himself on his penmanship, spelling, and grammar. With pride hurt, Charles turned down the job flat and started looking for a position, any reasonable position, in Ohio politics. By 1893, with his wife already pregnant, he at last found work as a clerical drudge for the State Republican Executive Committee. In many ways, he was just what the politicos were looking for: Charlie Thurber was diligent, didn't ask questions, was scrupulous in his stenography, could write passable speeches, brought in some contributions, and, luckiest of all, he was honest—so honest, in fact, that he never expected to get paid off. (As Thurber wrote in "Gentleman from Indiana": "He was easily the most honest man I have ever known.") By the time William Fisher Thurber (named after his grandfather) was born in 1893, Charles was the secretary to the Chairman of the Republican State Committee, at a salary low for even 1893.

Fortunately for the budding Thurber family, Mame had been given Fisher Company stock by her father, as a kind of combination wedding present and dowry. They managed to get by with that extra income, scrimping all the while, accepting checks and food baskets on the sly from Aunt Kate, and entering newspaper contests with a hungry eye on the grand prize, although Charles rarely did better, at that stage of his life, than sixth place, or about seventy-five dollars in winnings.*

William Fisher Thurber was a chubby, robust baby and something of a caution. His grandfather was proud of this first grandchild, his namesake, and, by all accounts, heaped attentions on him. By the spring of 1894, he expressed his pride with more largesse; he bought the Thurbers a small, two-story house on Parsons Avenue, in Columbus's almost fashionable east side. Mame was quickly pregnant again, and a house of

---

*"Over a period of fifty years, he won a trip to the St. Louis World's Fair, a diamond ring, a victrola, two hundred dollars' worth of records, and many cash prizes, the largest, fifteen hundred dollars, as first prize in a proverb contest."(11)

their own was welcome. They would never have a house of their own if it were up to Charles. On Saturday, December 8th of that year, another son was born.

. . . James Thurber was born on a night of wild portent and high wind in the year 1894, at 147 Parsons Avenue, Columbus, Ohio. The house, which is still standing, bears no tablet or plaque of any description, and is never pointed out to visitors. Once Thurber's mother, walking past the place with an old lady from Fostoria, Ohio, said to her, "My son James was born in that house," to which the old lady, who was extremely deaf, replied, "Why, on the Tuesday morning train, unless my sister is worse." Mrs. Thurber let it go at that . . .

That was how Thurber described his entrance into the world fifty years later in his Preface to *The Thurber Carnival,* one of the funnier and more telling pieces he was ever to write. "The infant Thurber," he went on in the Preface, "was brought into the world by an old practical nurse named Margery Albright, who had delivered the babies of neighbor women before the Civil War. He was, of course, much too young at the time to have been affected by the quaint and homely circumstances of his birth, to which he once alluded, a little awkwardly, I think, as 'the Currier and Ives, or old steel engraving, touch, attendant upon my entry into this vale of tears.' Not a great deal is known about his earliest years, beyond the fact that he could walk when he was only two years old, and was able to speak whole sentences by the time he was four."

The only provably erroneous statement in this autobiographical fragment is the street number of the Parsons Avenue house; it was 251, not 147 (or 245, as Thurber wrote O'Hara)—an outrageous mistake for a man who boasted of, and often possessed, total recall. The mention of the practical nurse, Margery Albright, was more than incidental charm. Aunt Margery, as she was known to her clients, was a woman of considerable and lasting effect on Thurber; indeed, at one point in his youth she took on more of the qualities of a mother than his real mother did. Not only did she deliver the infant James without the aid of Dr. Dunham (who arrived at Parsons Avenue too late; "You might have spared your horse," she told the doctor. "We managed all right without you."), (12) but she delivered him from countless childhood menaces in the years ahead. Aunt Margery was worried about Thurber from the first. "He has too much hair on his head for a male child," she said to Dr. Dunham. "Aint it true that they don't grow up to be bright?"(13)

Since the second Thurber boy arrived in a house given by William

Fisher, and from the womb of a Fisher daughter, and even delivered by the Fishers' practical nurse, it fell on the patriarch Fisher to supply the name. His very own was pasted onto the first Thurber boy; for the second, he decided to pass on the name of one of his best friends, James Grover, a Columbus Methodist minister and the first city librarian, whose reverential portrait hung in the Fishers' Bryden Road parlor. So it was James Grover Thurber.

James Grover—or "Jamie," as he was called by his family from the start—was a thinner, cuter, more fragile boy than William. Through the clarifying lens of retrospection, early photographs of him seem to show a sensitive, even sickly child, but there is no record of any parental complaints of colic or hyperirritability. Not a great deal *is* known about his first years; he probably could walk at two and speak whole sentences at four, as he said.

In 1896, a third son, Robert, was born to the Thurbers, and his arrival completed the Thurber family. Robert, by his own admission, received most of the attention as the baby in the house. ("As a result, I was the closest to my parents," he said, "although they didn't play favorites.") During the previous year, while Mame was pregnant with Robert, Charles Thurber lost his job as secretary to the Chairman of the Republican State Committee. "There were usually gaps of several months between my father's jobs," Robert recalled. "It just meant we had to scrimp all the more." However, at the end of 1895, Charles luckily caught the attention of Asa S. Bushnell, a Springfield, Ohio, heavy-machinery manufacturer who ran successfully for governor.

"My Dear Sir:—" wrote Governor-elect Bushnell to Charles Thurber on December 27, 1895. "I beg to acknowledge receipt of your favor of the 24th inst. and assure you that I am greatly pleased to have you accept the appointment as Correspondence Clerk in the Executive Office and I am sure that you will fill the place to the best of your ability and be a credit to the administration.

"Hoping that the sickness in your family, which prevented your writing, is now a thing of the past and that you had a 'Merry Christmas', I remain,

Yours very truly,
Asa S. Bushnell"

Scratching out his living with another poorly paid clerkship, Charles provided for his family, with a little more reluctant help from his father-in-law. In 1898, he sold the Parsons Avenue house and bought the second house the Thurber family ever owned outright in Columbus— a brick three-story structure in what was then the sticks of Columbus,

921 South Champion Avenue. This was Jamie Thurber's favorite boyhood place, full of wondrous happenings:

. . . No. 921 South Champion Avenue is just another house now, in a long row
of houses, but when we lived there, in 1899 and 1900, it was the last house on
the street. Just south of us the avenue dwindled to a wood road that led into
a thick grove of oak and walnut trees, long since destroyed by the southward
march of asphalt. Our nearest neighbor on the north was fifty yards away, and
across from us was a country meadow that ticked with crickets in the summertime and turned yellow with goldenrod in the fall. Living on the edge of town,
we rarely heard footsteps at night, or carriage wheels, but the darkness, in every
season, was deepened by the lonely sound of locomotive whistles. I no longer
wonder, as I did when I was six, that Aunt Mary Van York, arriving at dusk for
her first visit to us, looked about her disconsolately, and said to my mother,
"Why in the world do you want to live in this godforsaken place, Mary?"
Almost all my memories of the Champion Avenue house have as their focal
point the lively figure of my mother. I remember her tugging and hauling at
a burning mattress and finally managing to shove it out a bedroom window onto
the roof of the front porch, where it smoldered until my father came home from
work and doused it with water. When he asked his wife how the mattress
happened to catch fire, she told him the peculiar truth (all truths in that house
were peculiar)—that his youngest son, Robert, had set it on fire with a buggy
whip. It seemed he had lighted the lash of the whip in the gas grate of the
nursery and applied it to the mattress. I also have a vivid memory of the night
my mother was alone in the house with her three small sons and set the
oil-splashed bowl of a kerosene lamp on fire, trying to light the wick, and herded
all of us out of the house, announcing that it was going to explode. We children
waited across the street in high anticipation, but the spilled oil burned itself out
and, to our bitter disappointment, the house did not go up like a skyrocket to
scatter colored balloons among the stars. My mother claims that my brother
William, who was seven at the time, kept crying, "Try it again, Mama, try it
again," but she is a famous hand at ornamenting a tale, and there is no way of
telling whether he did or not . . . (14)

The South Champion Avenue period was the only truly joyous time
of Thurber's childhood. He and his brothers were enrolled in the Ohio
Avenue elementary school, and all of them did well there. The three
boys, close together in age, fought a lot ("I instigated the fights," Robert
said. "William was quiet and Jamie was the peacemaker, but I was the
pugnacious one"). By and large, it was a good time for growing up. One
of Thurber's first memories was accompanying his father to a Columbus
polling booth, in 1900, where the loyal Republican cast a loving vote for
William McKinley.

. . . It was a drab and somewhat battered tin shed set on wheels, and it was filled with guffawing men and cigar smoke. . . . A fat, jolly man dandled me on his knee and said that I would soon be old enough to vote against William Jennings Bryan. I thought he meant that I could push a folded piece of paper into the slot of the padlocked box as soon as my father was finished. When this turned out not to be true, I had to be carried out of the place kicking and screaming. In my struggles I knocked my father's derby off several times. . . . It remains obstinately in my memory as a rather funny hat, a little too large in the crown, which gave my father the appearance of a tired, sensitive gentleman who had been persuaded against his will to take part in a game of charades . . . (15)

These comfortable South Champion years ended with a decline in the political fortunes of Governor Bushnell in the 1900 elections. Charles Thurber was out of a job again. It wasn't until 1901 that another appointment worthy of his talents offered itself—a position as secretary to the congressman from his Ohio district. The catch was that he would have to live in mysterious, far-off Washington, D. C. So the pleasant South Champion Avenue house was sold and the Thurber family moved to Falls Church, Virginia. It was summer and too hot for Mame to live right in humid Washington.

The tree-shaded, broad-porched house the Thurbers rented in Falls Church for the summer was at 319 Maple Avenue, a site now occupied by a row of town houses called James Thurber Court. On December 26, 1958, Thurber wrote to an inquiring Washington acquaintance, Elizabeth Acosta, about his years in Falls Church:

. . . Many of the memories of Falls Church are as vivid as last year's. Our house was, I am now convinced, the middle one, the so-called Nicholas house. I remember distinctly my father turning a corner, on his way home from work in the evening, and walking down the street swinging a Malacca cane—every man in Washington had one that year.

It was in the Falls Church house that we had the colored maid who served dinner in her bare feet and burned her finger in the steam of the kettle so that she could try out the salve she had bought at a travelling medicine show, complete with banjos and ballyhoo, that visited the town. Our garbage was collected by an ancient white-haired negro, not more than five feet tall, whose two-wheeled oxcart was pulled by a brace of oxen. His appearance never failed to enchant us boys, for he was not only out of the South, but out of the past, even out of fiction, as remarkable as old Uncle Tom himself.

It's odd, too, that you would mention the Benéts, for they, Bill, Steve, and Laura, lived only a block from us in Washington in 1901. Our winter house was at 2031 I Street . . .

I remember very well that two new expressions fascinated my even then word-loving mind, "so long" and "hot dog." This was the era, too, of "In the Good Old Summertime." I remember my father took me to hear Senator Beveridge speak in the Senate and introduced me to Peary one day in an elevator. He also took me to a baseball game and afterward we visited the players in their dressing room. The one whose name fascinated me was Unglaub, the first baseman. (My secretary just now tells me Unglaub means "disbelief" in German.) The Senators were pretty unbelievable then (why doesn't God send them another Walter Johnson?) and I remember a story told at table by George Mervin, then covering Washington for a Cleveland newspaper. It seems the shortstop picked up a grounder and threw out the runner, after having made a dismal series of errors in previous games. "Extra, Star!" cried a youngster in the bleachers . . .

I always think fondly of Washington and Falls Church, and have enough memories of both places, most of them fond, to fill a book . . .

Most of the memories may have been fond—they were, after all, away from the Fishers and well enough off to afford both summer and winter rented houses *and* a Thurberesque colored maid—but at least one memory was haunting and hideous. On a hot Sunday afternoon in their first Washington summer of 1901, while Charles was off on a short fishing trip, the three brothers were playing a version of William Tell in the backyard of the Maple Avenue house. Jamie and William both cavorted with homemade bows and blunt arrows, and Robert watched them take turns trying to shoot each other in the back. As Robert remembered it: "Jamie said it was his turn to be the target, so William told him to stand up against the house. William took an awful long time getting his bow and arrow adjusted, and just when Jamie turned to see what was going on, William shot and the arrow hit Jamie smack in the left eye. Jamie said years later that we all threw up together, but as I recall it, he didn't even cry out in pain. No throwing up. Nothing. When my mother saw what happened, she didn't know what to do. She had been fooling a bit with Christian Science—the Fishers were Methodists and so were we, but mother was fooling with Christian Science and other things; she wanted to try all the religions, I guess, just in case— anyway, she may not have taken Jamie to a doctor right away, or to the right doctor. I think when my father came home, they took Jamie to a local doctor, who didn't recommend having the eye removed. It was a long time before the blind eye was removed, and that was why the good eye went bad.

"The rest of that incident is pretty vague to me, but I don't remember Jamie ever being bitter towards William, then or afterwards. But William, it bothered him a lot. In later years, Jamie was bitter about his eye not being attended to right away. He blamed his parents, I think, more than William. But as he often said, 'I could have been the one who shot out William's eye. I had a bow and arrow, too.' Jamie never blamed his parents directly, if you know what I mean."

William has said of the disastrous summer Sunday afternoon: "I've had a lot of tragedies in my life but that was the worst . . . . And if they'd have taken him to Washington to an eye specialist, they could have saved his eye. But instead of that, they went to one of these country doctors that said that it would be all right. . . . But that was a shock I never got over, and I look at it this way: sometimes things like that happen and are a blessing in disguise. In other words, he was not able to serve full military duty during World War I and if he hadn't, why, he might have been killed in the war. . . . When you lose one faculty, the others develop. And then you look at it from the benefits he received from it, why, it probably was a blessing in disguise in a way. . . . I suffered more from it than he did because that's something I never got over. But it was an accident. Accidents happen all the time."*(16)

It was indeed just an accident, but an accident that was to fill various Thurbers with grief, guilt, remorse, and horror all their days. For Thurber himself, it was the first and most crucial trauma of a trauma-laden life. Helen Thurber, who lived closer to the results of that trauma than anybody else, corroborated Robert's feeling that Thurber harbored no consuming grudge against William. "Jamie only got mad when William would boast about his twenty–twenty vision years later," she said. " 'Why does he have to keep talking about his damn eyesight?' Jamie would say. Now that I think of it, Jamie never invited William to his house, although he supported him for most of his life. I guess Jamie couldn't bear having William around too much, as a kind of constant reminder. There was naturally some resentment. As for his mother, Jamie blamed her for not taking him to Dr. Burnett [Dr. Swann Burnett, a noted Washington eye specialist] sooner, so the eye could be removed. She was in one of her Christian Science periods then, which didn't endear Jamie in later years to Christian Scientists, or to any

---

*In an August 27, 1946, letter to his friend and eye doctor, Gordon Bruce, Thurber wrote: "A psychiatrist acquaintance of mine asked me recently if the brother who shot the arrow had ever married, and when I said he had not the psychiatrist said that this was to be expected. The human being is indeed a complex creature . . ."

William Thurber was married for the first time in 1963, at the age of seventy. Robert has never married.

religious people, for that matter. The general practitioner his parents did take him to was, of course, an idiot."

By not removing the irreversibly injured and sightless left eye, the local Falls Church doctor laid the groundwork for a phenomenon called "sympathetic ophthalmia"—inflammation to the uninjured eye because of the transfer of poisons from the injured eye. Since the development of cortisone, this syndrome has all but disappeared; cortisone negates the effects of the destructive chemistry of the bad eye on the good eye. But even before cortisone, immediate removal of the diseased eye would have prevented sympathetic ophthalmia. The gradual deterioration of sight in Thurber's right eye to total blindness in the late-1940's probably would not have occurred if Dr. Burnett had been allowed to excise the damaged eye in time. Several weeks after the accident, the left eye was finally removed and a glass eye fitted, but the right eye was already inflamed. By what Thurber later deemed a miracle, he was able to see well enough out of that chronically afflicted right eye to read, write, and draw for another forty years, and to see cloudy images for almost fifty.

With a dead, cosmetic left eye, a barely functioning right eye, and a bruised future, the six-year-old Thurber was not sent to grade school in Washington during the 1901–02 term. Instead, he stayed at home and watched his boyhood slip from him. The following September, he entered elementary school, but by early 1903 Charles Thurber's tenure as a federal civil servant was abruptly over, and there was no place to go but back to Columbus. Considering what had happened in Washington, it was a relief.

CHAPTER 2

Teacher's Pet

Back home in Columbus, jobs were not easy to come by, even for a clerk who had recently been connected with a congressman, a congressional committee, and the Department of Justice. Apparently, William Fisher was still not impressed enough with his son-in-law to offer him a more substantial position in the family business. The fact that he brought home a half-blind son didn't raise Charles's standing, either. "Accidents will happen" was the unconvincing explanation in Columbus.

So Charles Thurber did his newspaper-contest puzzles, visited with cronies in the corridors of the City Hall and the State House, and, for a short time, had some vague connection with the Underwood Typewriter Company. (He kept a sample Underwood at home, and young Jamie learned to operate it. Thurber was proud of his typing ability for the rest of his life; it was just about the only machine he ever mastered.) After several months, Charles found a job as a recording clerk in the Ohio Senate, when Warren G. Harding was lieutenant governor. (Harding was a family hero until well into his presidency.) The Thurbers lived in a large boarding house called the Park Hotel, and it was there that Charles fell ill in 1904 with what Robert Thurber described as "brain fever." As the sickness, probably connected with influenza, worsened and lingered till the beginning of 1905, the family was invited to move into Grandfather Fisher's Bryden Road mansion, where Charles could be looked after in the inimitable Fisher fashion:

. . . I remember the time in 1905 when the doctors thought my father was dying, and the morning someone was wise enough to send for Aunt Margery. We went to get her in my grandfather's surrey. It was an old woodcut of a morning. I can see Mrs. Albright, dressed in her best black skirt and percale blouse (she pronounced it "percal"), bent over before the oval mirror of a cherrywood bureau, tying the velvet ribbons of an antique bonnet under her chin. People turned to stare at the lady out of Lincoln's day as we helped her to the curb. The carriage step was no larger than the blade of a hoe, and getting

Aunt Margery, kneecap and all, into the surrey was an impressive operation. It was the first time she had been out of her own dooryard in several years, but she didn't enjoy the April drive. My father was her favorite person in the world, and they had told her he was dying. Mrs. Albright's encounter with Miss Wilson, the registered nurse on the case, was a milestone in medical history—or, at least, it was for me. The meeting between the starched young lady in white and the bent old woman in black was the meeting of the present and the past, the newfangled and the old-fashioned, the ritualistic and the instinctive, and the shock of antagonistic schools of thought clashing sent out cold sparks. Miss Wilson was coolly disdainful, and Mrs. Albright plainly hated her crisp guts. The patient, ganted beyond belief, recognized Aunt Margery, and she began to take over, in her ample, accustomed way. The showdown came on the third day, when Miss Wilson returned from lunch to find the patient propped up in a chair before a sunny window, sipping, of all outrageous things, a cup of cold coffee, held to his lips by Mrs. Albright, who was a staunch believer in getting a patient up out of bed. All the rest of her life, Aunt Margery, recalling the scene that followed, would mimic Miss Wilson's indignation, crying in a shrill voice, "It shan't be done!" waving a clenched fist in the air, exaggerating the young nurse's wrath. "It shan't be done!" she would repeat, relaxing at last with a clutch at her protesting kneecap and a satisfied smile. For Aunt Margery won out, of course, as the patient, upright after many horizontal weeks, began to improve. The doctors were surprised and delighted, Miss Wilson tightly refused to comment, Mrs. Albright took it all in her stride. The day after the convalescent was able to put on his clothes and walk a little way by himself, she was hoisted into the surrey again and driven home . . .(1)

Charles recovered from his brain fever at the Fisher house, but Jamie grew increasingly unhappy there. Indeed, he could hardly wait to get beyond the massive front door in the morning. "The main cause of it was my grandfather," Robert said. "Sometimes he would be drinking a little and he'd like to be free with his hands, push us around. During those times, he went for Jamie first and would grab his wrist and squeeze till he heard Jamie cry out. He didn't like Jamie 'playing the fool,' as he called it. And, of course, Jamie never liked Grandfather."

The Fishers were almost as unhappy as Jamie was over the Thurbers' moving in. With an invalid and three squabbling young boys, something had to be done to ease the tension. The family hit upon a typically unorthodox solution: Jamie, who had a strong attraction to Aunt Margery, would be farmed out to her as often as possible, and then maybe there would be some peace and quiet around the Bryden Road house. "From 1905 to about 1910," Robert recalled, "Jamie went to Aunt Margery's at least three or four times a week, and sometimes he'd stay there straight for weeks at a time. Aunt Margery was a second mother to him.

Also, he liked her daughter Belle and all the weird boarders she had in that poor house of hers. I think Jamie's first writing ever was a poem he wrote called 'My Aunt Margery Albright's Garden at 185 South Fifth Street, Columbus, Ohio.' He may have been hurt at first for being sort of sent away from his real family, but after a while it was a treat for him just to get away from the Fishers—not a very sentimental bunch. He felt at home at Aunt Margery's, poorness and all. I doubt if there was more quiet around the Bryden Road house, though. William and I still fought a lot, as I remember; we were both athletic, high-spirited boys."

Helen Thurber noted about this period of her husband's boyhood: "I could never understand what Jamie saw in Aunt Margery or her household. It was a miserable, filthy place. I went to call on her once with Jamie, after we were married, and I came back to our hotel with bedbugs on me. But Jamie was devoted to her. I don't think he was as devoted to his own mother as a boy. By the time I knew him, he adored Mame, though, and gave her all the credit for everything he was or became, especially his sense of humor. Of course, she was good literary material for Jamie, too. He tended to think of many people as material for his writing, and he appreciated them for that. The same was true for Aunt Margery."

Thurber lovingly described the household of the lame, chunky "natural nurse," who said "naushy" and "tishas" and "gangrum":

. . . Mrs. Albright and her daughter were poor. They took in sewing and washing and ironing, and there was always a roomer in the front room upstairs, but they often found it hard to scrape together ten dollars on the first of the month to pay Mr. Lisle, a landlord out of Horatio Alger, who collected his rents in person, and on foot. The sitting-room carpet was faded and, where hot coals from an iron stove had burned it, patched. There was not hot water unless you heated it on the coal stove in the dark basement kitchen, and light was supplied by what Mrs. Albright called coal-oil lamps. The old house was a firetrap, menaced by burning coal and by lighted lamps carried by ladies of dimming vision, but these perils, like economic facts, are happily lost on the very young. I spent a lot of time there as a child, and I thought it was a wonderful place, different from the dull formality of the ordinary home and in every difference enchanting. The floors were uneven, and various objects were used to keep the doors from closing: a fieldstone, a paving brick that Mrs. Albright had encased in a neat covering made of a piece of carpet, and a conch shell, in which you could hear the roaring of the sea when you held it to your ear. All the mirrors in the house were made of wavy glass, and reflected images in fascinating distortions. In the coal cellar, there was what appeared to be an outside toilet moved inside, miraculously connected with the city sewage system; and the

lower sash of one of the windows in the sitting room was flush with the floor
—a perfect place to sit and watch the lightning or the snow. Furthermore, the
eastern wall of Jim West's livery stable rose less than fifteen feet away from Mrs.
Albright's back stoop. Against this wall, there was a trellis of moonflowers,
which popped open like small white parachutes at twilight in the summertime,
and between the trellis and the stoop you could pull up water from a cistern
in the veritable oaken bucket of the song. Over all this presided a great lady,
fit, it seemed to me, to be the mother of King Arthur or, what was more, of Dick
Slater and Bob Estabrook, captain and lieutenant, respectively, in the nickel
novels, "Liberty Boys of '76." . . .(2)

Even perfectly sighted, Thurber would most likely have been a different sort of child. While he was engrossed by sports, he leaned towards
books (albeit nickel novels), words, and drawings. But with an insecure,
to say the least, home life and seeing the world solely through an
inflamed right eye, he was lucky to survive—especially since the elementary school he attended was Sullivant School. An ancient (even in
the early 1900's) three-story brick edifice, Sullivant School was located
in a tough, mixed, working-class section of Columbus, and most of its
pupils were indicative of the neighborhood. Thurber was a year behind
in his schooling, because of his missed school year in Washington, but
that was nothing compared to his Sullivant classmates:

. . . I remember always, first of all, the Sullivant baseball team. Most grammar-
school baseball teams are made up of boys in the seventh and eighth grades,
or they were in my day, but with Sullivant it was different. Several of its best
players were in the fourth grade, known to the teachers of the school as the
Terrible Fourth. In that grade you first encountered fractions and long division,
and many pupils lodged there for years, like logs in a brook. Some of the more
able baseball-players had been in the fourth grade for seven or eight years.
Then, too, there were a number of boys, most of them colored (about half of
the pupils at Sullivant were colored), who had not been in the class past the
normal time but were nevertheless deep in their teens. They had avoided
starting to school—by eluding the truant officer—until they were ready to go
into long pants, but he always got them in the end. One of two of these fourth-
graders were seventeen or eighteen years old, but the dean of the squad was
a tall, husky young man of twenty-two who was in the fifth grade (the teachers
of the third and fourth had got tired of having him around as the years rolled
along and had pushed him on). His name was Dana Waney and he had a
mustache. Don't ask me why his parents allowed him to stay in school so long.
There were many mysteries at Sullivant that were never cleared up. . . .

I don't suppose I would ever have got through Sullivant School alive if it
hadn't been for Floyd. For some reason he appointed himself my protector, and

I needed one. If Floyd was known to be on your side, nobody in the school would dare be "after" you and chase you home. I was one of the ten or fifteen male pupils in Sullivant School who always, or almost always, knew their lessons, and I believe Floyd admired the mental prowess of a youngster who knew how many continents there were and whether or not the sun was inhabited. Also, one time when it came my turn to read to the class—we used to take turns reading American history aloud—I came across the word "Duquesne" and knew how to pronounce it. That charmed Floyd, who had been slouched in his seat idly following the printed page of his worn and pencilled textbook. "How you know dat was Dukane, boy?" he asked me after class. "I don't know," I said. "I just knew it." He looked at me with round eyes. "Boy, dat's sump'n," he said. After that, word got around that Floyd would beat the tar out of anybody that messed around with me. I wore glasses from the time I was eight and I knew my lessons, and both of those things were considered pretty terrible at Sullivant . . . (3)

The writer Donald Ogden Stewart, a Sullivant classmate, recalled the old days as a time of more or less constant fighting. He remembered seeing Thurber first while Stewart was "hitting 'Beans' Horne in the stomach," behind the school's outdoor toilets during one recess period.* (4) Thurber was perforce an observer, not a participant. He attempted to play "baccy ball" (a sort of peggotty game with a stuffed Bull Durham sack and an old broomstick) and the more formal sports of baseball, football, and brawling, but he simply didn't have the necessary physical equipment for them; besides, the other boys were afraid of hurting the "blinky," as he was inevitably called by some kids and occasionally himself. But he had an excellent memory for batting averages and team rosters, and relished watching such future sports stars as Billy Southworth, Hank Gowdy, Billy Purtell, Chic Harley, Allen Thurman, and Raymond (Fike) Eichenlaub compete on various Columbus athletic fields, particularly the hazardous lot near the Blind Asylum just behind the Fisher mansion.

Young Thurber had friends and was not helplessly shy (considering his problems), but he daydreamed and kept his thoughts to himself. One of his Sullivant teachers believed he might be deaf because of his tendency to distraction. "He's so nervous," complained his sixth-grade teacher, Miss McElvaine, to Mame Thurber, "that when I call on him

---

*According to Helen Thurber, Stewart once told her husband in London that he became a Marxist when he was beaten up by a bully at Sullivant and suddenly realized what it was like to be persecuted. Thurber—who remembered Stewart as the kid who always owned the ball—replied, "But Don, you *won* that fight."

to recite, his Adam's apple rolls around so wildly he can hardly speak."
(5) He blushed easily, especially when confronted by such lovelies as
Eva Prout, a third-grader and child vaudevillian Thurber deified for an
embarrassingly long time after the third grade, and Elsie Bierbower, a
curly headed cherub who later became the actress Elsie Janis, sweetheart of the A.E.F. There were other mind-etching people, too:

> . . . once, in the 5th grade at Sullivant School, Miss Ferrell, teacher, she had
> a Xmas concert and Eva Prout, my girl, sang "Slumber Boat" and "Sing Me to
> Sleep" and others sang similar songs;—"Silent Night," etc., got into it and in
> the end Miss Ferrell called on a tall yella gal whose name I remember after
> all these 32 years was Almeda, and she asked Almeda to sing—so Almeda gave
> us In the Shade of the Old Apple Tree with something of that plaintive, sure,
> easy individuality . . . that simple song was therefore a touch of that black
> shining glory that never quite illumines the brow of the lovely white race. So
> I've never forgotten Almeda. She probably died years ago in a Long Street
> cuttin' scrape . . . (6)

His marks at Sullivant were unexceptional but never below "F" for
Fair. At the age of seven, he had become interested in drawing. His
earliest effort shows a sketch of a tree, looking for all the world like any
seven-year-old's sketch of a tree, straight bare branches and all. Another
drawing, a combination pioneer and Civil War battle-scene—with captions reading "Hard Job," "Easy now," and "Durn"—at least gives some
hint at later Thurberian forms, especially in the unsteady lines depict-
ing soldiers and axe-swingers. But it was in the fourth grade at Sullivant
that a teacher, Miss Ballinger, told him he had a definite flair for art.
Thurber described the moment of mixed emotions in a letter to Mrs.
Rachel Rowe Macklin, a Columbus woman, in June, 1959: "My teacher
in the 4th grade at Sullivant School once brought a white rabbit to class
and held it in her arms while we drew pictures of it in pencil. She
thought mine was the best but made the mistake of asking me to stay
after school the next day and draw it again, with just her and me and
the rabbit in the room. The results were nervous and deplorable. I
never drew after that with a woman or a rabbit in the room."

The Thurber family thought William was the son with artistic talent.
William would carefully copy in pen and ink Charles Dana Gibson
drawings, which Mame and Charles took for original William Fisher
Thurbers. "Don't bother William with your scrawls, Jamie; let him get
his work done, he's going to be the artist," Thurber quoted them as
saying.(7)

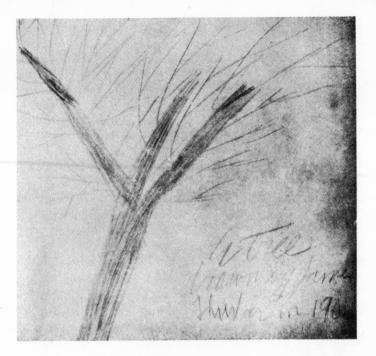

Early drawings

About the time Thurber finished Sullivant School and the sixth grade in 1907, his family either voluntarily moved or was evicted from the Fishers' Bryden Road house to a shabby rented place on South Seventeenth Street. Charles's job as a recording clerk in the Ohio Senate had lapsed, and he was in the midst of one of those between-jobs gaps. However, this particular gap was to last for almost two years. There is some evidence that the Fishers—at least, Grandfather Fisher—disowned the lot of them. Ralph McCombs, a childhood friend of Thurber, recalled that the split widened between the two families because of class and money. "The rich Fishers didn't want the poor Thurbers around," McCombs said. "It was the typical poor-relations story. Everybody in Columbus knew about everybody else in those days, so the Fishers pretended the Thurbers weren't really a part of their family. Charlie Thurber, as far as old man Fisher was concerned, was a complete nonentity, a nobody, just like Walter Mitty. I always saw a lot of Charlie Thurber in William and Robert—no drive, no ambition, nothing to make you remember them. James took after his mother, I guess, especially in his adult years when he became a non-stop talker and general show-off. But when he and his brothers were at the Douglas School, where I first knew them, they were certainly scruffy boys, every bit the poor relations."

At Douglas Junior High School, where Thurber completed the seventh and eighth grades, he came into his own. Still basically quiet, nervous, and shy, he nevertheless warmed to the less violent atmosphere of the school, and his exceptional intelligence became apparent to teachers and students alike. It was there that he discovered his glass eye was more than a handicap; it was an object of wonder for squealing girls and open-mouthed boys, whenever he removed or tampered with it. What with one triumph and another, he won an appointment as a writer of the Class Prophecy for the eighth-grade class of 1909. The Prophecy is an unremarkable document, following that weathered format in which every student's name is mentioned in an original saga set in the indefinite future. In Thurber's eighth-grade future, Harold Young (who must have been the most clever lad at Douglas) invents a " 'Seairoplane' that travels in the water as well as thru the air and on land." The entire class is invited to ride in it on a tour of the United States and Mars:

... One day, as we were sailing easily along, Harold came rushing out of the engine room with dishevelled hair and bulging eyes. We asked him what on earth was the matter. For answer he pointed to a piece of rope that had caught in a part of the machinery that was situated on the farthest end of a long beam, which extended far over the side of the Seairoplane. Then he said, "unless that rope is gotten out of the curobater we will all be killed." These awful words astounded us and we all became frightened at once. Suddenly amid all of our lamentations a cry from Harold was heard and we all looked up. What was our surprise to see James Thurber walking out on the beam. He reached the end safely and then extricated the rope, but when he turned to come back his foot caught and he pitched head foremost towards the deck. His unusual length saved him for he landed safely on the Seairoplane. We were all very joyful that the terrible crisis had been safely passed and afterwards learned that James was a tight rope walker with Barnsells and Ringbaileys circus. . . ."

Thus, Walter Mitty was born as "James Thurber" in the restless imagination of a one-eyed, sensitive boy of fourteen in Columbus, Ohio. It was true: He never wasted a word; he used everything, sooner or later.

Things picked up a bit for the Thurber family by September, 1909, when Jamie entered East High School, the most prestigious of Columbus's secondary schools. They were still living on Fisher handouts (more and more sub rosa) and Fisher stock, but then Charles wangled a job with his old employer of fifteen years before, the State Republican Executive Committee. He was back where he had started as a young, newly wed clerk, but at least it provided a regular, if small, income. Mame and Charles had a close circle of friends who formed a club called "The Frioleras," at whose gatherings they all shared an appreciation of practical jokes, mostly contrived by Mame. Robert and William were showing promise on the baseball diamond, even entertaining thoughts of professional careers. (William gave up any professional hopes when he developed thyrotoxic goiter as a junior in high school, a disease that was to strike the other two brothers even more severely, as well as one out of every three Ohioans.) And Jamie was almost blooming. "By the time he was in high school," Robert said, "Jamie stayed with Aunt Margery much less. Even so, he wasn't around home as much as William and I were. He was quiet about where he went. We knew he was always thinking, but we never knew *what* he was thinking."

Thomas Meek, a friend of Thurber for many years, remembered him in high school as a "studious and sometimes withdrawn type, a kind of loner. But he wrote much better than the rest of us, and that made the teachers love him. He was, without a doubt, their favorite. He was constantly drawing and then throwing the drawings away, as if he had no further use for them. I believe it was his family that made him different, more than his half-blindness. They weren't at all like, for instance, my family. Why, Jim's brothers were even more eccentric than Jim; they were practically recluses. The mother was the powerful figure, a great talker who held them all together. The father was, well, Walter Mitty, dreaming of what might have been."

As the teacher's pet of East High, Thurber elected to take the Latin Course (a Science Course, a General Literary Course, and a German Course were offered for the less intellectual), which stressed the humanities and composition besides a rigorous study of Latin. Almost fifty years later, on April 22, 1959, Thurber wrote to his Latin teacher, Miss Daisy Hare, ostensibly about a mistake in Latin he had made in a piece called "Midnight at Tim's Place." He took the opportunity to reminisce about his high-school days:

. . . I often wonder what became of the pretty Miss Gallen, Miss Stewart, Miss Farrell, Miss Lemert, Mrs. Guild, and Miss Gordon. I am just a woman teacher's pet, and when I was assigned to Mr. Huesch's algebra and geometry class, I asked to be reassigned to Miss Gordon's instead, and she seemed to be pleased by that and took me in. Mr. Huesch's shoes squeaked and it got on my nerves . . .

P.S. When I was in your first-year Latin class there was that odd boy, Charles Justus, who could never pronounce "nauta" correctly. He always said "noota," and I remember a flamboyant colored boy who once said to you in class, "I do not believe I comprehend your stipulation." . . .

And in a chronology of his life he set down to aid *Time*'s editors for a July 9, 1951, cover story, he recalled more of his East High days:

. . . Only low grade I got was in Physics. Developed my own system of computing rate of momentum and after I demonstrated it on the blackboard, Professor Hambleton said, "You would go from New York to Boston by way of Detroit." . . . Was greatly disappointed not to be made editor-in-chief of the high school magazine, "The X-Rays." Found out some years later my mother had asked principal, John D. Harlor, not to give me this post because of my eyesight . . .

Thurber was the logical candidate for editor of the *X-Rays*. Both at home and in school, he would idly write imitative stories for his own pleasure, and Mame once said that he "buried himself in books, read almost everything, and took very seriously some of the Victorian writers, like Meredith and Henry James."(8) However, the *X-Rays* did print, in May of 1913, Thurber's first published story, "The Third Bullet," a dogged effort showing infinitely more Zane Grey, nickel-novel, and O. Henry influence than Meredith or James. A potpourri of solecisms, misspellings, and banalities, "The Third Bullet" evinces not the slightest clue of literary promise; indeed, another piece in the same issue, "The Muffler Cut Out," a humorous tidbit by Everett McFadon (who took the Science Course) is far more appealing. Thurber's first story deals with a wronged man named (and this is not without significance) Harding, who gets the jump on his false accuser in the middle of a desert. Harding allows the villain ("Bill Sherring, the quickest gun man in Texas") to duel with him fairly, rather than just to shoot him down in cold blood. Sherring fires several bullets, the third's impact revealing the presence of gold in a rock near the hero. With an absolving confession signed by Sherring and the promise of immense wealth, Harding is the moral and material victor, as Sherring is permitted to slink away over a sandy knoll. The following scrap of dialogue will suffice to illustrate Thurber's earliest prose style:

"Going to die? You don't mean you are going to kill me here in cold blood? Good Heaven, Harding, you wouldn't murder me! I tell you, Harding, it was all a mistake, all a mistake!"

"No," answered Harding, "I won't kill you in cold blood. Don't judge others by your own low standards, Sherring, I always play fair, you know that, tho' it goes hard when you are dealing with a cur like you!"

Thurber was just a high-school senior when he wrote "The Third Bullet," but he was eighteen and a half years old—an age at which Byron had published his first volume of poems, *Hours of Idleness.*

There was one other western yarn Thurber had written in high school, "How Law and Order Came to Aramie." It is, if anything, less promising than "The Third Bullet," chock full of carefully phoneticized dialect. Apparently, the editors of the *X-Rays* were unawed, because it exists only in manuscript, in Thurber's neat handwriting.

Thurber was not active in extracurricular activities at East High. There weren't many school functions—outside of the usual proms, class plays, and class days—and Ruth Young White, a classmate, remembered him as being "a very good student" and little else.(9) Talent in sports was what made memorable classmates, and the students' collective adoration went out to the redoubtable Chic Harley, a titanic football player for East High and, later, Ohio State. Brainy Jim Thurber was by no means immune to this adoration; in fact, he retained it longer than most. A decade later, when he wrote his Sunday half-page, "Credos and Curios," for the Columbus *Dispatch,* he devoted generous space to extolling Harley and the old high-school games:

... The hush that fell in the week before the North game, working up to rallies and songs and speeches and proud boasts, with a great undercurrent of unmentionable fear, made life worth living in a painful, bitter-sweet sort of way. It was the terrible, keen enjoyment of a man dicing for his life. Nerves are never strung so high, hearts never break so often or with such a sad whanging note as when one is in his teens and high school.

On the day of the game the orange and black of East blazed out defiantly against the sullen, more impressive maroon and gold of North. There was something unbreakable, masterful, ineluctable in maroon and gold, something gay and brave as youth, and as finely futile, in orange and black ...

In his senior year, Thurber took it into his head to run for class president. He had some stiff competition in the person of an unscruffy rich kid, but, according to Robert Thurber, it was this very difficult challenge that made him want to win. He won. He also was graduated with honor (which meant that he did not have to take examinations in the Latin Course), and he delivered the President's Address at the Class Day Program, just after a choral rendition of "If With All Your Hearts," from Mendelssohn's "Elijah." It was certainly his finest moment in eighteen and a half years, and his classmates sensed that his accomplishment seemed all the sweeter because he was handicapped—rather like a school's only graduating Negro being chosen the valedictorian.

At various times during his high-school career, Thurber held various jobs. This was one reason he was not at home as often as Robert and William were, another being he was less sickly. He worked for, by turns, the Buckeye Steel Castings Company, a cigar store, the Central Ohio Optical Company, and, during one summer, the State–City Free Employment Agency. Young Thurber also found time to attend Miss Naddy's Dancing Academy, probably in preparation for the senior prom. Helen Thurber described the event (from years of hearing it as one of her husband's choice party recitations) in her Foreword to the posthumous Thurber collection, *Credos and Curios:*

... I will never forget the picture of that dancing class, over a bowling alley very much on the wrong side of the tracks, and so delightfully different from the prim, white-gloved school where I learned to one-step. At Miss Naddy's (forgive me if I misspell her name—I have only heard it spoken), most of the male students smoked cigars and packed guns, but their teacher was pretty tough herself, and never daunted. "All right, now we'll try another moonlight waltz," she would yell, after three previous attempts by candlelight had failed, ending in what could hardly be called waltzing, "and this time I want you guys to stay out from behind them palms!" ...

There were even seedier exposures to the hard world of adult Columbus. In a March 8, 1938, letter to John McNulty, Thurber described
some, also giving a new insight into the ever-arresting Fisher clan:

. . . as the brakemen on the Pennsy used to say over at Taylor and Mt. Vernon
avenyahs: "I got a blue suit with a red stripe into it," they'd say. Did you know I
used to work behind the counter of a cigar store over there? There was a Pennsy
calling station in the back of the store, run by a little gray-haired guy who wore
gold collar buttons, front and back, but no collar. He'd phone Calloway and say
"You're going out on Number 197, at 3.15." Then he'd phone Jennsen and say
"You're firin' 197, at 3.15. Calloway drivin'." The place was usually full of firemen
and engineers a-spinnin yarns. One fireman was the roller skating champion of
Port Clinton, Ohio, which had the highest syphilis rate in the state at the time.
My uncle Kirt got the syphilis there the first time. Kirt had all the known
venereal diseases at one time, including a couple that the doctors only knew to
nod to, from the farther Hebrides and the Western part of Cuba—and what my
aunt Margery Albright when she was 80 used to call the 'blue boars', scaring me
to death. That was when I was only 12 or 13 and had heard from a boy named Karl
Yoakum that if a man made love to a girl he always got the 'collapse'. What with
the collapse and the blue boars it is a god's wonder I did not retire to a monastery
when I was in my teens. Kirt died of his unprecedented complications when he
was only 38 or 40. Up to the last, my mother says, he wouldn't let the surgeons
take off his whats-its-name. 'That's my friend,' he told Dr. Wilcox. Dr. Wilcox
replied that it was his worst enemy. 'But awful good company,' says Kirt, who had
a dry humor. In his last years, Kirt used to sleep with the colored women at
Smokey Hobbs, a fact my sainted grandmother died in blissful ignorance of. The
Fisher boys were never what you could call choosy about their tail, as old Mrs.
Albright once called it. Let's see, where were we?
   Oh, yeh, the cigar store. Well, it was run by a man named Una Soderblom and I
worked there after school when I was a senior in East High school in 1913. That
was the year of Row, Row, Row and In My Harem, and I Lost The Sunshine and
Roses and Snooky Ookums and the Gaby Glide. I hadn't seen Una Soderblom, a
little, small-footed blond guy, since 1913 until my brother and mother took me
over to call on him last year. He lives out across from Douglas school and is dying
from an incurable disease that eats up your bones and was braver about it than I
would be with the mumps. He was just the same after 25 years, except that he was
dying. We sat around and talked about it as if it were a poker game in which he
held only a pair of trays. I had never liked the guy much when I worked for him.
He once thought I stole pennies. But he was a fine fellow, after twenty-five years,
and I liked him. I had mentioned his name once in a New Yorker story and his
wife had seen it and somehow she knew my mother, because she clerks in the
Woman's Exchange and my mother sooner or later talks about me to everybody,
particularly to women who have sons around my own age who my mother figures
haven't done as well as I have, a fact which she feels called on to take up with
these women, in a nice way. She tells them that there's everything in the way a

boy's brought up and who his mother is. Mary-Tact, they call my mother in the neighborhood. *Now,* where were we? Oh yeh, Kirt.

Kirt was the youngest of the Fisher boys, all of whom were strange. Grant died of a knee disease when he was 48. Like Kirt, he was buried in a hard collar. Willie is the only survivor. He does nothing now, my mother tells me, except wind clocks. And lie down in the backyard on warmish days. Life has closed in on him, and has him against the wall with a clock key in his hands. My mother views this extraordinary narrowing down of Willie's activities with a scientific detachment. She never liked Willie much, and once threw a cup and saucer at him. This was the year that "Underneath the Stars" came out. Kirt could ride a bicycle with his head on the saddle and his feet in the air, a position that was not half as bad for him as when he was prone. He was prone everywhere from Front Street to Seventh Street most every night. We never liked Kirt when we were kids because he was severe, but we liked him as we grew older. I remember William and I once had lunch at his house and William put butter in his coffee cup (his own). "For God's sake, Bessie," says Kirt to Bessie, "Hide the eggs!" Bessie was his wife. She insisted on marrying him even after he told her he was the clinical wonder of all the venereal specialists in the Middle West. "I don't care," she said. "I will throw myself over a cliff if you don't marry me." "Well, Jamie," says my mother. "She not only married him, she buried him." Bessie was a great gal. Kirt without sex was better than any other man with sex, to her. And so it goes . . .

But it is fairly safe to assume that, during his teens, Thurber was a wide-eyed and -eared observer of Midwestern sexual rites, not a participant. As he himself often said, "I was a late starter."

In 1912, with his unerring knack for standing firm on the losing side, Charles Thurber resigned from the Taft-backing State Republican Executive Committee and threw in his lot with Teddy Roosevelt, becoming the Secretary of the Progressive Party's State Campaign Committee. He worked night and day for the Bull Moosers, raising funds, entertaining visiting politicos, writing speeches, running the Columbus office in the Harrison Building, all because his beloved regular Republicans had demonstrated that they were not virtuous practitioners of good government. Of course, on Election Day, 1912, good old Charlie Thurber was out of a job again, having nothing more to show for his pains than extreme disillusionment, "six dozen yellow Mongol pencils, a few typewriter ribbons, and several boxes of stationery."*(10)

---

*Actually, Charles Thurber stayed with the remnants of the Progressive Party through the state elections of 1914, when he worked for the unsuccessful gubernatorial candidacy

Helen Thurber said of Charlie's Bull Moose disaster, "It was one of the few times that Jamie showed true pride in his father, for being a rebel and idealist in 1912. But Jamie loathed and distrusted politicians, bureaucrats, and especially Republicans because of what they did to Charlie." However, on the night of the 1912 election, young Thurber was anything but angry. He was abrim with the excitement of the moment, so much so that one suspects it made him want to accept the challenge of running for class president of East High. In any case, he wrote a school theme about it called, aptly, "Election Night." It was easily the best writing of his teens, and it is noteworthy that his best writing was straight journalism, so to speak.

ELECTION NIGHT

The Presidential election this year was an event which has been looked forward to for the last two or three years, discussed in detail, and debated from every angle all over the nation. Accordingly excitement was at a fever heat in Columbus as elsewhere last Tuesday night when the fate of the candidates hung in the balance. From early evening until late at night and even into the "wee sma'" hours of Wednesday the city, and High Street especially, was a scene of great action and irrepressed excitement. A mighty crowd thronged the sidewalks brilliant with the myriads of electric lights strung along the thorofare in blinding array.

Everybody jostled everybody else, but all in a spirit of hilarity and good feeling; at least before the election returns counted out all but the winning man.

At several of the busiest corners results of the poll in various states were being flashed upon large screens placed so all who cared to, could stop and see "who was winning." As the night wore on these places became black with people who shouted themselves hoarse with more or less volume as bulletins to the effect

---

of James R. Garfield, a Cleveland lawyer and the son of President Garfield. All that he was left with after that campaign was a letter reading:

Nov. 4, 1914

My dear Mr. Thurber:

I thank you most heartily for all that you have done during this campaign. It has been a good fight and none of us need feel any regret that we made it. You have had a difficult and trying task and have made many friends by the way you have conducted our headquarters.

With best regards,

Sincerely yours,
James R. Garfield

that "Wilson is ahead in New York" or "T. R. leads in Illinois" or "Taft had carried Cincinnati" were thrown upon the screen.

At the newspaper offices the eager people were acquainted with "how things were going" by virtue of verbal returns shouted out by men with megaphones, who, when they raised them to their lips after studying the slips of paper thrust into their hands by coatless and dishevelled assistants, stilled as by magic the anxious murmurings of the waiting crowd that hung on their every word.

Large numbers of people besieged the different political headquarters where the wires were being kept hot and the incessant clicking of the receiving instruments was all that broke the silence until some headquarters attachee in measured tones gave out the word received, showing neither sign of triumph or defeat as is the way with veteran politicians.

As ten o'clock rolled around and it was established beyond a doubt who was to be our next president pandemonium reigned in the street. Millions of horns kept up an incessant and strident song of victory. One could scarcely force his way thru the struggling pushing throng and at best emerged with a mouthful of confetti and a pair of ringing eardrums.

Wide mouthed newsboys and uniformed messengers slipped easily thru the mass of humanity, the former shouting "Election of Wilson!" and the latter hurrying on various missions to political headquarters, newspaper offices, leading politicians rooms etc.

A Presidential election comes but once in four years and the people evidently try to become inoculated with enough enthusiasm and celebrating to last them until next time. If one can judge by the general actions of last Tuesday night they not only succeeded but should have enough left to give them a fair start Tues. night Nov. 5 1916 toward another night of hilarity. There certainly was a "hot time in the old town" that night. And the reason was Wilson—that's all!

James Thurber

(To which the teacher added: "Very good, James. You sometimes use quotation marks where they are not needed.")

By 1912, the family had moved to 77 Jefferson Avenue, a substantial improvement over the last rented house. They lived there till 1917. Thurber later fictionalized this address in *My Life and Hard Times* as 77 Lexington to protect the innocent, because it was the house of "The Night the Ghost Got In." He once wrote to Bill Arter, of the Columbus *Dispatch*, in answer to an inquiry:

. . . I deliberately changed the address for the simple reason that there *was* a ghost. . . . The family who lived in the house ahead of us moved out because of the strange sounds, we found out later. A corner druggist near the house, to whom I related my experience, described the walking and the running upstairs before I could describe it myself. They were undeniably the steps of a man, and it was quite an experience to hear him running up the stairs towards us, my brother and me, and to see nothing whatever. A Columbus jeweler is said to have shot himself in the house after running up those steps. This is the only authentic ghost I ever encountered myself and we never heard it again. . . . I didn't want to alarm whoever might be living there when I wrote the story. I think it was a music school for girls. . . .

The house, in fact, became the Wallace Collegiate School and Conservatory of Music during the 1920's, and a ghost was never seen or heard from again by any occupants. It was at 77 Jefferson, too, that Thurber and his brothers drove their father to the edge of madness by playing the Victor record "No News, or What Killed the Dog" over and over.

Dogs were more important than most creatures, real or occult, in the Thurber family life, as they were in James Thurber's artistic life. There was, of course, the South Champion Avenue residence that was either on fire or full of dogs, to say nothing of rabbits, chickens, and guinea pigs. (It was while Charles Thurber was trying to fix the snap lock of the rabbit pen that he contrived to imprison himself inside the cage for three hours with six Belgian hares and thirteen guinea pigs, squatting all the while. Mechanical feats were not Charles's forte; the failing was a hallowed trait in both the Thurber and Fisher clans, and one that James Thurber parlayed into a literary fortune.) The dogs were giants in those days, and a grand procession of them became part of American canine lore, thanks to *My Life and Hard Times* and the collection called *Thurber's Dogs:* Muggs, the formidable Airedale . . . Rex, the sterling bullterrier, raised from puppyhood . . . Scottie, William Fisher's Scotch collie. Two of them moved Thurber to poesy during his high-school years:

To Scottie and Rex
A Tribute by James G. Thurber

Somewhere beyond the brightest star,
That's always a-shining up there so far
There's a heaven that no good life will bar—
A heaven where Rex and Scottie are.

The two best dogs that have ever been
Steadfast and true through thick and thin,
Innocent of human crime and sin,
Some canine paradise has let them in.

Faithful and good and staunch and fine
As good as the best, if they were canine,
Scottie and Rex, old pals of mine,
Surely some Elysium bright is thine.

I like to think it's a glorious hall,
Where a doggie knows no sorrow at all—
Where Scottie is chasing a pearly ball
And Rex is jumping a golden wall.

"Jamie loved Rex," Robert said, "but he didn't like Muggs at all, although the Airedale was crazy about him. He simply didn't like Airedales. I did, but Muggs was a one-man dog. My parents were crazy about all of them." Favorites or not, Thurber in later years spoke and wrote often about his boyhood dogs. They were more tangible aspects of his childhood, in many respects, than some of the humans around him.

A bookish, sensitive lad who thought loosely of being a writer, who was president of his class at the city's best high school, who won high grades and smiles from all his teachers, should have had his sights set on an Ivy League institution, or at least on a good Midwestern private college. Not so young James G. Thurber. For one thing, the Thurber family was, in 1913, generally incapable of mustering the train fare to the East, let alone tuition and board—without, that is, selling off the remaining life-sustaining Fisher Company stock. For another thing, Thurber was a peculiarly unambitious eighteen-year-old. His partial blindness and his insecurity in personal and family matters certainly contributed to this lack of verve. But no higher education at all would have put him on a dangerously parallel course to his father's life (Jamie had indeed already worked as a clerk), and, ambition aside, that was the last course he wanted to follow. Then, too, there was his nagging intellectual curiosity, that strange concern with words and ideas. The answer to this dilemma was—and it was not arrived at until the late summer of 1913—to enroll at the tuition-free, land-grant Ohio State University, a forty-five-minute streetcar ride from 77 Jefferson Avenue. He would be a townie among 4,435 students, most of them farm boys and future small businessmen. His just-under-the-wire application was approved on September 10, 1913; on September 17, he entered the College of Arts, Philosophy and Science at the Ohio State University as one of a small army of freshmen.

Then as now, O.S.U. was at heart a football-and-fraternity school, with occasional starbursts of talent from its faculty and student body. It had, as it still does, an undersized library, an undiscriminating admissions policy, a heavy emphasis on agriculture and engineering, and a view of life in keeping with its geography. Ludwig Lewisohn, the German critic and novelist who taught there about the time Thurber registered, wrote with fearless accuracy of its rampant philistinism, in his autobiography *Upstream:* "It is, as a matter of fact, considered rather bad form among them [the students] to show any stirring of the mind." And Thurber himself, one of O.S.U.'s most distinguished non-athletic sons, was later fond of quoting Professor Joseph Villiers Denney's précis of the institution: "Millions for manure but not one cent for literature." Thurber was sometimes at his funniest when describing in semifictional truth his alma mater:

. . . Ohio State was a land grant university and therefore two years of military drill was compulsory. We drilled with old Springfield rifles and studied the tactics of the Civil War even though the World War was going on at the time. At 11 o'clock each morning thousands of freshmen and sophomores used to deploy over the campus, moodily creeping up on the old chemistry building. It was good training for the kind of warfare that was waged at Shiloh but it had no connection with what was going on in Europe. Some people used to think there was German money behind it, but they didn't dare say so or they would have been thrown in jail as German spies. It was a period of muddy thought and marked, I believe, the decline of higher education in the Middle West . . . (11)

The courses Thurber signed up for in the first semester of his freshman year were Medieval European History, American History (taught by Arthur M. Schlesinger, Sr., who, like Ludwig Lewisohn, was an open critic of O.S.U., though less acerb), Latin, General Psychology, English Composition, and, of course, the required Military Science and Tactics and Gym. His subject schedule for the second semester was pretty much the same. Three of these courses had a significant influence on Thurber—Psychology, English, and Military Science.

One day, in his General Psychology class, taught by a Viennese professor named Albert P. Weiss, a memory test was given. After a thousand-word article was read aloud, the students were instructed to write down everything they could remember from the article. Thurber scored an astounding seventy-eight per cent, and a week later he could still recall about half of the article's facts. Professor Weiss and Thurber's classmates were more amazed than Thurber was. He knew he possessed a good memory, but now this test seemed to point towards something he liked to term "total recall." He told an interviewer in 1957, "My mother had total recall, too. She could remember the birthday of a girl I was in love with in the third grade. So can I. October 9."*(12) But total or not so total, Thurber's sharp memory was to serve him well in his journalistic career and, more importantly, in his writing after blindness. As Helen said, "That fantastic memory saved his life."

Professor Weiss's psychology class was significant, too, in that Thurber's only extant college notebook was a product of that not always gripping session. Its author described the contents in a piece called "The Notebooks of James Thurber":

... The first few pages are given over to a description of the medulla oblongata, a listing of the primary colors, the score of the Western Reserve–Ohio State football game that season, and the words "Noozum, Noozum, Noozum." (I figured out this last entry after some thought. There was a young woman in the class named Newsome, whom Dr. Weiss always called Noozum.) The rest of the pages contain a caricature of Professor Weiss; one hundred and thirteen swastikas; the word "Noozum" in block letters; the notation "No William James in library"; an address, 1374 Summit Street; a memo: "drill cap, white gloves, gym suit. See G. Packer. Get locker"; a scrawl that seems to read "Orgol lab nor fot Thurs"; and a number of horrible two-line jokes, which I later contributed to the *Sundial*, the university monthly magazine. Two of these will more than suffice:

1. HE: The news from Washington is bad.
   SHE: I thought he died *long* ago.
2. ADMIRAL WATCHING ENEMY SINK: Who fired that shot?
   MATE: The ship's cook, sir. He got the range and stove in her side. . . .

The English Composition course concentrated on paragraph writing, a form of folksy, lightweight editorializing very popular in America then. Paragraphing was brought to the point of near-art in Columbus by Robert O. Ryder, the editor of the *Ohio State Journal* from 1904 to 1929. Thurber worshipped from afar the master paragrapher and imitated his style shamelessly in some columns called "Sidelights" he wrote in 1914 and 1915 for his old high-school magazine, the *X-Rays*. One of Ryder's pithiest and most famous lines on the *Journal*'s editorial page

---

*Thurber claimed even grander memory feats. He later said that given any two consecutive lines of *The Great Gatsby*, which he had read only one, he could state on what page the lines occur and approximately where they were placed on the page.

was: "A woman is either hearing burglars or smelling something burning." It is a line that could have been written by the adult Thurber. The youth Thurber's emulation ran to this sort of thing: "A lady asked a doctor if eating soap is bad for a child. So long as he doesn't get to associating with rough towels, no."

Thurber was quick to give Ryder a good deal of credit. "The man who first inspired me to write humor and whose memory I greatly revere," he wrote Harvey Breit, on November 25, 1949, "will probably not be known to you. He was the late Robert O. Ryder, the really great paragrapher of the Ohio State Journal, who died in the 1930's. He is often mentioned by other great admirers of his, including John McNulty, Frank Sullivan, Joel Sayre, and Donald Ogden Stewart. . . . I rate him among the great American humorists from Twain to Andy White." He meant it, too; one of the longest and most excessive chapters in *The Thurber Album* was devoted to Ryder.

Chances are that Thurber chose the paragraph-writing course because he wanted to be, at that tender point in his life, another Robert O. Ryder. He tried very hard to be just that, as a writer and editor of the O.S.U. magazine, the *Sundial*, and later as the author of his Sunday *Dispatch* half-page, "Credos and Curios." In one of the first "Credos and Curios" columns he wrote in 1923 was this paragraph:

Every now and then we see Bob Ryder, the man who sends truly great paragraphs ripsnorting, ricocheting and non-stop dancing down the corridors of time, in a certain excellent but salady restaurant, and, having in mind his abdominal troubles, we always feel like taking him aside in a brotherly way and saying, lay off the minted marshmallow cocktails, the steamed fig pudding with vanilla sauce and the fruited meringue balls.

Military Science and Tactics (or just plain "drill") had a penetrating effect on Thurber. O.S.U. required at least two years of drill, five days a week, for each male student, provided he was healthy enough to walk. Thurber was healthy enough to walk, but while he had an interest in, even a fascination for, Civil War lore, he hadn't the simplest talent for military endeavors. He later said, "I seem to remember that 'Squads right about, and squad right front into line' did the damage."(13) The source of that damaging command was Captain Converse, the despised and feared commandant of the university's cadet corps, who singled out that poor half-blind townie Jim Thurber as the object of his special wrath. "You're the main trouble with this university," he reportedly shouted at Thurber on the drill field. "Either you're a foot ahead or a foot behind the company." The fine irony of the difficult Thurber–Converse relationship was that the Captain was half-blind himself. He lost an eye while participating in some Indian fighting after his graduation from West Point in the 1880's, but instead of being sympathetic to Thurber on that account, he was doubly severe; he felt that if he could drill an entire corps with one eye, Thurber could certainly follow simple orders with one eye. (It was bruited about the campus that the Captain could see more with one eye than most people could with two.) "Jamie hated that drill," said Robert, who, with William, also attended O.S.U. for a brief period. "He especially hated old Converse—a real disciplinarian, sort of like our grandfather. He had a patch over his bad eye and he swaggered a lot. Jamie called him 'Pussyfoot'—not to his face, of course—and he did a pretty good imitation of him around the house."

When the humiliation of daily drill proved too much for Thurber, he wouldn't show up for it. As a result, he was forced to take drill during each of the five years he was technically registered at Ohio State, without ever actually fulfilling the requirement. However, Thurber ultimately got even with Captain Converse; he used him as the model for the idiotic martinet, General Littlefield, in the *My Life and Hard Times* piece "University Days"—a sweet, secret revenge in 1933, perhaps, but no help to a tortured youth in 1913.

And tortured he was. He had been a something at East High School, but he was a nothing at Ohio State in his freshman year. Most of his coevals hardly remembered his being there at all, unless they happened to witness his feat of memory in Professor Weiss's psychology class or his humiliation on Captain Converse's drill field. Charme Seeds, a member of the O.S.U. class of 1915 and later one of Thurber's infatuations, wrote charitably in the April, 1930, issue of the *Ohio State University Monthly* that Thurber as a freshman was "a tall, worried lad." He felt lonely and lost on the enormous campus, and covered up this insecurity by telling family and friends that he was bored with his courses. He had barely begun his first year when he suffered a devastating defeat. Mildly rushed by only one fraternity, Chi Phi, Thurber was finally blackballed, and at an institution like Ohio State that was akin to a terminal case of leprosy. To make matters worse, his best high-school friend, Ed Morris, was accepted by the Chi Phis and promptly dropped Thurber as a pal. So on top of everything else, Thurber was a deeply hurt young man. He wandered about the campus, orphan-like, ignored, or, in the words of his classmate Ralph McCombs, "without manners or any trace of sophistication." What with one indignity and another, it was almost more than Thurber could bear. As it turned out, he couldn't bear it.

In the fall of 1914, after a summer of odd jobs and more loneliness, Thurber registered for a full slate of courses at O.S.U., and he may even have had some intention of completing them. But from the outset of the 1914–15 academic year, he rarely went to class and didn't pass a single course. To all intents and purposes, he dropped out of school, in the close manner of the young Thurber—without telling a soul. It seems incredible, but none of his acquaintances nor any members of his family knew at that time that he was not attending O.S.U. regularly. It may be an index of how easily Thurber blended into the wallpaper in those days.

His brother Robert had this to say about the lost school year: "I didn't know until recently that Jamie missed a whole year at college. It just shows how clever and tight he was. He never talked about it to me or anyone. I remember seeing him leave every morning for the campus, and I used to see him there myself that year, but I didn't know he wasn't going to class. He was awfully withdrawn then. He felt kind of put down by the college people. My guess now is that the way he spent his time was either to go to the library and read, or to head downtown and see a silent picture show. He loved movies, always did—Charlie Chaplin, Civil War movies, Westerns, anything. He was quite an actor himself, when the mood struck him."*

The most startling aspect of Thurber's lost academic year was that his parents never inquired about his work at school—to say nothing of his hopes and dreams—and consequently they never discovered that he was an outrageous truant. An explanation might be that, as Robert suggested, Thurber somehow tricked them into thinking he was at school by acting as if he were. But he wasn't *that* good an actor. Most likely, the truth was that Mame and Charles Thurber were content to

---

*On May 31, 1919, he wrote Robert from Paris, where he was a code clerk at the American Embassy:

". . . *Old Davy Griffith's Intolerance is running at the Salle Marivaux here, and I guess I will have to sweep my optics at it. It is awfully funny to read the advertisement for movies in French,—they have Douglas Fairbanks and Mary Pickford and all the other well known stars here often, and the French seem as strong for them as the Americans. They are especially in favor of Wild West plays, it seems. Bill Hart's mean look and gun stare and shoot around here often, also. I remember one picture advertised as "Le Roi de Ranch" or something of the sort,—French for words that can be translated, and just the plain English word for those that can't, make the signs very funny some times.*

I have only been to one movie since I came over, strangely enough, for you will recall me as an almost everyday frequenter of the palaces back home. On that one occasion I went with one of the fellows to the Gaumont Palace, the world's largest movie house." . . .

let their moody, handicapped, uncommunicative second son remain that way. They had their own problems, not the least of which were their other two sons.

But foremost among the parental troubles was the lack of a regular, paying job for the breadwinner. By late 1915, Charles had lined up a position as a cashier of the Municipal Court, a minor but nevertheless steady post. (He held that job till 1923, marking one of the longest periods of employment in his erratic career.) He was also putting in some long extracurricular hours in behalf of the senatorial candidacy of Myron T. Herrick, a former governor of Ohio and ambassador to wartime France, who wanted to make a bid for public office in the 1916 elections. Herrick lost, as almost all of Charles Thurber's political heroes had a way of doing, and, once again, just about the only reward Charles received for his toil was a duly signed letter of thanks:

July Twenty Nine
1916

Mr. Charles L. Thurber,
Municipal Court Clerk's Office,
Columbus, Ohio

My dear Mr. Thurber:

Mr. Gongwer has advised me of the splendid work you have done in my behalf and I take this opportunity to thank you and to acknowledge my indebtedness to you.

I have been deeply gratified by the splendid help given me by volunteer workers in all parts of the state and I count you as one of the most effective of these.

I believe I will receive a substantial majority at the primaries on August 8th but whatever the result may be I shall always hold in pleasing memory your activity in my behalf.

With kindest regards, I am

Very truly yours,
Myron T. Herrick

Perhaps it was the example his father set of tenacity under almost no pressure—or, more likely, it was just that he couldn't think of anything else to do. Whatever the case, James Thurber returned to O.S.U. for another try at higher education in the fall of 1915. He was, in effect, beginning his sophomore year, as a neurotic lad of almost twenty-one. He took English courses, an elementary French course, and experienced his usual difficulties with drill and Captain Converse. He also tripped over a whole new stumbling block—Botany. Thurber, as man and boy, was more mystified than most by the sciences. He was bored by all the sciences, and often said in the following years that the only subjects that interested him at college were literature, English, and history. Having just one functioning eye didn't enhance his scientific curiosity any, especially when it came to the use of the microscope. A more or less accurate picture of Thurber's trials in Botany turned out to be one of the most brilliant episodes in "University Days," from *My Life and Hard Times:*

I passed all the other courses that I took at my University, but I could never pass botany. This was because all botany students had to spend several hours a week in a laboratory looking through a microscope at plant cells, and I could never see through a microscope. I never once saw a cell through a microscope. This used to enrage my instructor. He would wander around the laboratory pleased with the progress all the students were making in drawing the involved and, so I am told, interesting structure of flower cells, until he came to me. I would just be standing there. "I can't see anything," I would say. He would begin patiently enough, explaining how anybody can see through a microscope, but he would always end up in a fury, claiming that I could *too* see through a microscope but just pretended that I couldn't. "It takes away from the beauty of flowers anyway," I used to tell him. "We are not concerned with beauty in this course," he would say. "We are concerned solely with what I may call the *mechanics* of flars." "Well," I'd say, "I can't see anything." "Try it just once again," he'd say, and I would put my eye to the microscope and see nothing at all, except now and again a nebulous milky substance—a phenomenon of maladjustment. You were supposed to see a vivid, restless clockwork of sharply defined plant cells. "I see what looks like a lot of milk," I would tell him. This, he claimed, was the result of my not having adjusted the microscope properly, so he would readjust it for me, or rather, for himself. And I would look again and see milk.

I finally took a deferred pass, as they called it, and waited a year and tried again. (You had to pass one of the biological sciences or you couldn't graduate.) The professor had come back from vacation brown as a berry, bright-eyed, and eager to explain cell-structure again to his classes. "Well," he said to me, cheerily, when we met in the first laboratory hour of the semester, "we're going to see cells this time, aren't we?" "Yes, sir," I said. Students to right of me and to left of me and in front of me were seeing cells; what's more, they were quietly drawing pictures of them in their notebooks. Of course, I didn't see anything.

"We'll try it," the professor said to me, grimly, "with every adjustment of the microscope known to man. As God is my witness, I'll arrange this glass so that you see cells through it or I'll give up teaching. In twenty-two years of botany, I—" He cut off abruptly for he was beginning to quiver all over, like Lionel

Barrymore, and he genuinely wished to hold onto his temper; his scenes with me had taken a great deal out of him.

So we tried it with every adjustment of the microscope known to man. With only one of them did I see anything but blackness or the familiar lacteal opacity, and that time I saw, to my pleasure and amazement, a variegated constellation of flecks, specks, and dots. These I hastily drew. The instructor, noting my activity, came back from an adjoining desk, a smile on his lips and his eyebrows high in hope. He looked at my cell drawing. "What's that?" he demanded, with a hint of a squeal in his voice. "That's what I saw," I said. "You didn't, you didn't, you *did*n't!" he screamed, losing control of his temper instantly, and he bent over and squinted into the microscope. His head snapped up. "That's your eye!" he shouted. "You've fixed the lens so that it reflects! You've drawn your eye!" . . .

He had his difficulties with Botany during the first semester of 1915–16, but they were mere nuisance raids compared to his continuing battle with Captain Converse, on and off the drill field. Soon, Thurber fell into his old habit of ignoring drill altogether. In February of 1916, Thurber received the following letter from the O.S.U. administration:

February 4, 1916

Mr. J. G. Thurber
77 Jefferson Avenue
Columbus, Ohio

Dear Sir:—

I beg to advise you that the President has protested your registration for the second semester of the current year owing to your continued absence from Military drill. The registering officers have been instructed not to register you except upon written authority from the President.

Yours very truly,
Executive Clerk

Not terribly upset by this disciplinary action, Thurber waited four days before he called President William Oxley Thompson's secretary and agreed to see Captain Converse about his truancy. He had an eyeball-to-eyeball, as it were, confrontation with the Captain, and shortly thereafter another communication was sent out noting: "Protest withdrawn. Mr. Thurber allowed to register, having agreed to attend to military drill." Thurber, however, didn't live up to his side of whatever bargain was struck with Converse. He received no credit for the second semester, apparently spending most of that term, once again, in the library or the downtown movie palaces. And, still, his family wasn't privy to his activities. It took the personal intervention of President

Thompson, a kindly but uninspiring Presbyterian minister, to reinstate Thurber in the fall of 1916. "W.O.T. reinstated me on his own, without any letter from Converse," Thurber wrote an Ohio State friend decades later. "The great Thompson said to me, 'Don't let the military get you by the neck.' "(14)

Thurber made another stab at his elusive sophomore year. He was going on twenty-two.

CHAPTER 3

Regular Guy

William Oxley Thompson probably didn't realize it at the time, but his reinstatement of James Grover Thurber was a signal service for both James Grover Thurber and American letters. Crucial, fateful strokes abruptly changed the course of Thurber's life from boyhood to old age—more so, it would seem, than with most people—and President Thompson's action was the first truly positive stroke. Had Thurber not taken advantage of Thompson's kindness and not made a fourth attempt at acquiring a higher education, he very likely would have followed in his father's shallow footsteps, ending his days as a dimly recollected clerk. He was, after all, bright, like his father, but, also like his father, lacking in initiative. While he had more of his mother's spirit than his brothers inherited, it was usually lurking beneath his stumbling indirection. His good luck in the fall of 1916 was that President Thompson was a benevolent, flexible Presbyterian, not a rigid man of the cloth determined to back up Captain Converse. Thurber desperately needed that fortuitous push, and it was an indication of how his luck was running that year when a second blessing almost immediately visited that gangling, scruffy frame. He met Elliott Nugent.

Thurber had plunged into his studies with a full schedule of courses: American Literature, Nineteenth Century Poetry, Journalism, Political Science, and Economics. In the American Literature course, the instructor read aloud to the class a theme entitled "My Literary Enthusiasms," a flip critique of contemporary nickel novels, without mentioning the author's name. Elliott Nugent, who was the antithesis of the student Thurber—which is to say, handsome, athletic, poised, even a professional actor and the son of playwright–actor J. C. Nugent—was amused by the theme and he asked after class who had written it. Thurber sheepishly confessed that he had. Elliott Nugent said in his autobiography, *Events Leading Up to the Comedy*, that their friendship "ripened slowly," for Thurber, while he impressed Nugent with his sense of humor, "was lank, not exactly well dressed in what was the collegiate fashion of 1916, and was inclined to give a rather limp hand-shake when introduced." Furthermore, Nugent noted, "there was evidently something wrong with one of his eyes, as it did not always look in the same direction as the other one."

But their friendship did ripen. "Nugent cleaned Jim up a bit," as their classmate Dr. Virgil "Duke" Damon put it. He got Thurber a haircut, a new blue suit, and he even got him into his posh fraternity, Phi Kappa Psi. According to Dr. Damon, who was also a Phi Psi, "Jim was considered an oddball by the brothers, but Elliott, even though he was an actor from a theatrical family, was one of the boys. To be truthful, Elliott had a problem getting Jim into the fraternity. None of us knew much about his background or his folks. We were never invited to his home, for instance. It was like he pretended he didn't have a family. But Elliott went to bat for Jim as a great genius and got him in. Jim went through hell week in good spirits, even though he was several years older than most of us who were doing the helling. He tried to be a regular guy." Ralph McCombs concurred with this description of the reborn sophomore, and added, "Nugent completely made Thurber. I think he even paid his fraternity fees."

Helen Thurber said her husband gave proper credit to Nugent for his collegiate renaissance. "Deep down, Jamie was a terribly gregarious boy, even kind of rah-rah," she said. "But it never had a chance to come out during those early years at Ohio State, until Elliott took him under his wing. Elliott recognized his abilities and didn't ignore him as a person. It was always very important for Jamie to be recognized."

Magically, the shrinking, sullen young man turned into something approximating a real student, determined to wring every useful drop out of Ohio State. His bent was towards writing—specifically, journalism—in good measure because of Nugent's influence. Under that influence during the 1916–17 school year, both he and Nugent worked hard as reporters for the *Ohio State Lantern*, the university newspaper, writing straight, unsigned news stories. The following year, they were both made issue editors of the paper. Thurber was in charge of the Wednesday edition, while Nugent brought out Thursday's. They played the newspaperman role to the hilt, even staying up late at Marzetti's, a professional reporters' hangout on High Street, smoking, drinking, and talking with the big boys. James Pollard, who was a co-worker on the *Lantern* and later became Director of the O.S.U. School of Journalism and the University Historian, remembered Thurber as "a good and serious editor. As a reporter, he was nuts on accuracy."

But it was on the *Sundial*, the O.S.U. monthly humor and literary magazine, that Thurber found his most comfortable niche. Ruth Young White, a classmate who was part of the small but active clique of Ohio State writers, said, "I think that we considered him as the most talented man on the *Sundial* staff. I think we really regarded him more as a *Sundial* man than we did as a *Lantern* man because he was not as good at straight reporting as he was at satire and humor and that sort of thing."(1) In his 1917–18 academic year, he was selected Editor-in-chief of the *Sundial*, and, as a small repayment for services rendered, Thurber appointed Nugent his assistant. The literary quality of the *Sundial* was poor, without even the naughtiness of its contemporary college magazines. Thurber described it in a November 11, 1950, letter to Edward Spencer, Chairman of the *Princeton Tiger*, who had invited him to speak at a staff dinner:

. . . I was editor of the Ohio State Sun-Dial* in 1917–18 but we had no such elaborate setup as you have. My chief assistant editor was Elliott Nugent and there were three or four others, but most of them went to war and I wrote three-fourths of the material myself, which was pretty bad, and filled up many pages with my so-called drawings, which were very much the same then as they are now. The Sun-Dial goes back only forty years and one of its first editors was Gardner Rea. . . .

I was lucky enough to have the services of a Cornell Widow artist who was taking officers training at Ohio State. I still remember that the longest piece of mine to be reprinted in the old Life in those years was mistakenly credited to the M.I.T. magazine. Then, as now, the magazine was notable for mistakes and the nice sonnet by Nugent lost its final line, for which was substituted a sentence from another piece like this:

" 'If that is all you want,' she said, 'I am going home.' " . . .

I showed about as much promise as a writer thirty-two years ago as I did an artist and I am willing to pay enormous sums of money for old copies of the Sun-Dial if people want to blackmail me with them. The magazine had the virtue of being clean so that the censors never bothered us, but it had the fault of being pretty dull and full of incredible puns. . . .

I haven't seen the Sun-Dial much in thirty years, but I remember one copy in which the editor said that Wilbur Daniel Steele is a better writer than Ring Lardner. This proved that Ohio State still turns out wonderful football teams.

I suppose I still could go back and get out a Sun-Dial in the old tradition. Let me see.

HE: "Have you read 'How Green Was My Valley' "?
SHE: "No. How green was it"?

---

*Thurber's spelling.

Thurber's 1950 He–She joke was only slightly worse than his *Sundial* output. Take, for example, this 1917 Thurber observation: "I go down blind alleys. I ride the stars. A man and his dog and myself. And the world is not so bad after all. I have a sense of humor."

Or his paragraphing, à la Robert O. Ryder: "Happiness is the coffee that conceals the castor oil."

Or his romantic poetry (inspired by his child love, Eva Prout):

> I held her in my arms,
> This one at present dear,
> And there came from out the past
> Your vision clear.
>
> The human touch is strong,
> But close and warm as faith
> Clings the memory of you,
> My sweetheart wraith.

Or—and here, at least, is some sense of Thurberian nonsense—his light verse:

> Once upon a time,
> I forgot now when
> I heard a father growl,
> Growl, "Go, my son, and shoot me an owl—
> Shoot me an owl."
> And answered the son,—
> I forget just when,—
> The son the father had,
> Had, "Oh, my father, it's too bad,
> Indeed too bad."
> Just what he meant
> I forget me now,
> But I knew it once,
> I forget it now—
> No. By Jove, I have it sure,
>   And four more lines to boot,—
> He meant that in the neighborhood
>   There were no owls to shoot.

Even while putting out the *Sundial* almost single-handedly, as his healthier colleagues marched off to make the world safe for democracy, Thurber, savoring his sudden campus eminence, had time for literary pranks:

... I just remembered how I plagued Edith Cockins when she acted as censor of my Sun-Dial. I hated censorship, and I didn't use any dirty text or drawings, anyway. But I submitted for her approval the famous Housman lyric containing these lines:

> Yes, lad, I lie easy
> I lie as lads would choose,
> I cheer a dead man's sweetheart,
> Never ask me whose.

It was promptly and sternly rejected, to the vast amusement of W.O.T. and my favorite English professors . . . (2)

Thurber also made his first stab at drawing for the *Sundial*. Derivative and very Art Nouveau, his pen-and-ink *Sundial* sketches, however, give more of a glimpse of ur-Thurber than his attempts at written humor. But only a glimpse. By and large, the *Sundial* drawings show atypical attention to detail, careful inking, and mechanical crosshatching. As Thurber wrote to his close friend and classmate Herman Miller, in an undated (probably 1940's) letter:

... It is true, of course, ... that I used to draw in Caesar's Commentaries and also illustrated the Manual of Arms at Ohio State (usually with pictures of Mutt and Jeff.) . . . I did pictures for the Sun-Dial when I was editor because all the artists went to war or camp and left me without any artists. I drew pictures rapidly and with few lines because I had to write most of the pieces, too, and couldn't monkey long with the drawings. The divine urge rose no higher than that. In those years, I was absolutely uninterested in the art, not only of myself, but of anybody else, from anybody else to myself . . .

Hidden in some of Thurber's *Sundial* art work, though, are the spareness of line, the boneless limb, the mere speck of a feature strangely familiar. And there, too, is the definite beginning of wit, much more evident than in the writing. For all the later artist's self-deprecation, Thurber's first published drawings make one actually smile. There is a grain of originality in all the imitation.

Following the heady example of Nugent, Thurber joined everything in sight, except the football team and the short-lived avant-garde literary magazine, *Sansculotte*. Thurber was strictly establishment. He diligently went to football games and madly cheered on to new glories his high-school friend Chic Harley. Nugent introduced Thurber to The Strollers, the O.S.U. dramatic society; a select sub-fraternity of hearties called Bucket and Dipper; an even more discriminating (seven members in 1917) literary group of students and faculty members called La Boheme, which occasionally met for dinner and thrashed out pressing intellectual questions; and Sigma Delta Chi, the honorary journalism fraternity. Then, honor of honors, both Thurber and Nugent were "linked" for Sphinx, a tony senior society reserved for the biggest men on campus.*

Nugent uncovered Thurber's secret love of performing when he coaxed him into joining The Strollers. Both friends appeared in The Strollers' 1918 production of Arnold Bennett's *A Question of Sex* (a hazy question for Thurber then), and Thurber was infected by the stage bug, never to be cured. Nugent wrote in his autobiography that his friend "was naturally a good actor and retained a spark of ambition along those lines," but Ralph McCombs said that "Jim couldn't act worth a damn but Elliott somehow made him perform without mumbling too much." Still, Thurber was at long last liberated from himself, so liberated, in fact, that he gained a reputation as something of a campus cutup.

"Jim was easily the funniest man I've ever known," said Dr. Virgil Damon. "He could kill me with a line or an imitation, especially when he mimicked Captain Converse and all the drilling. He'd forever be putting on impromptu skits at the fraternity house. He really broke me up. He looked so naturally comical, with that blank stare and that tall body and unusual clothes, sort of like a court jester. He couldn't hold his liquor too well in those days, but he sure was funny."

Another old fraternity brother, Thomas Meek, agreed. "Thurber was an obvious big talent for Ohio State," Meek said, "just like Nugent. I think he gave Nugent the idea for his play *The Poor Nut*, which Elliott wrote in college and later opened in on Broadway. They both went out for track, just like *The Poor Nut* character. But even while Jim amused us with his jokes and charm, even while he was trying so hard to be a regular guy, there was a conflict in him. You could feel it. He wasn't ever a complete fraternity man because there was an antisocial streak in him. He had other interests and leaned towards what we used to call 'the masses.' He hated Republi-

---

*In his autobiography, Nugent described how, on Link Day, Thurber had vanished, fearing that not even his new popularity would get him linked. When his name was indeed called, he suddenly appeared from behind a bush and proudly assumed the highest station of his young life.

cans—and we were all Republicans—because, I suppose, of what they did to his father. He amused us, but he was a little odd. He didn't have many close friends."

Thurber participated in such regular-guy activities as standing watch on the fraternity-house roof to protect Phi Psi from marauding Betas

Sundial *sketches*

and Sigma Chis. He also wrote risqué verse, the better to slay the brothers at the Phi Psi house. One effort went like this:

> Don't never pinch a bulldog's balls
> Even though you're clever;
> For when he runs fast ass he hawls—
> He'll tear you shirt from overalls;
> Don't never pinch a bulldog's balls
> Even though you're clever.

There was something in him, a smidgen of sensitivity amid all that frivolous convention, holding him back from being an utter Joe College. Helen Thurber thought the fraternity life at Ohio State was a phase "he lived down." He wasn't above singing college and fraternity songs with his cronies years later, but, Helen said, "I always felt he sang them a little ironically—not the way he sang 'Who' or 'Bye Bye, Blackbird.' " Also, his social life during his O.S.U. renaissance was less than the norm. He liked to ridicule his collegiate gaucheries, such as knocking the fruit salad onto the floor during the Phi Psi May Dance of 1917, but at the same time, his lingering shyness and clumsiness must have been painful. He wasn't exactly every comely coed's dish of ice cream.

Thurber's amorous encounters up to his last year of college were at best stunted. He held a smoldering torch for Eva Prout, his third-grade love whom he had last seen in the eighth grade before she left Columbus for a career on the stage. They had written newsy letters to each other during Thurber's high-school and early college years, but their romance was to remain basically epistolary and ludicrous. His only other noteworthy attachment was with a popular coed named Minnette Fritts. As Thomas Meek described her, Minnette complemented Thurber's timidity towards the opposite sex "by being a good listener who put up with Jim's peculiarities." Thurber fell for her—although she had a reputation as the college widow and the competition was strong—and he took her to dances and on long walks along the Scioto whenever she was available. By all accounts, Thurber barely rounded first base with her, although at one point in 1918, they had an "understanding." Meek used to take her out, too, during that same period. "We'd compare notes," Meek said. "After Jim became famous, he'd say when we had a few too many that 'Minnette only loved us.' And then I'd answer, 'We were the only ones left at Ohio State to love.' " While there was release, finally, for Thurber's talent, intelligence, and personality at college, there was, alas, no release for his loins. Sexually, as in everything else, he was a late starter.

The intellectual flowering of Thurber led him to the best the university had to offer in the arts and humanities. He took all the English courses he could carry—Nineteenth Century Poetry, American Literature, the Short Story, the English Novel, Shakespeare, Versification, plus more courses in journalism, political science, and economics, while still trying to satisfy his drill and gym requirements. It was in the English courses that he distinguished himself, thanks in great part to three professors who had such a tremendous effect on Thurber's career that he devoted a chapter of *The Thurber Album* to each of them.

The first and most influential of these mentors was Joseph Russell Taylor, whose specialty was the Romantic and Victorian poets and novelists. Inspiring his students with pronouncements like "A straight line can also be the dullest distance between two points,"(3) Taylor gave Thurber his first real taste for Henry James, a savor that was to last him for most of his life. The professor himself was something of a James character—hypersensitive to beauty, enthralled by subtleties, and a worshipper of the female. He was also a painter, who, before Thurber's time at O.S.U., had encouraged the pursuit of an artistic career by a young student named George Bellows. As far as is known, he never encouraged Thurber to continue his drawing, but he did stimulate an appreciation for Henry James (Taylor said of *The Wings of the Dove:* "If you can't make anything at all out of the first hundred pages, don't let it worry you."),(4) George Meredith, the Tristram legends, A. E. Housman, and Joseph Conrad (whom Taylor concluded was "Henry James in the waste places.").(5)

Professor Taylor was Thurber's (and a thousand other O.S.U. students') first exposure to a bona-fide aesthete and intellectual. The effect of such a man on a budding aesthete and intellectual is incalculable. Perhaps even more significant for the future writer, Taylor set up the literary ground rules that impressed Thurber all his days: "Art is revision" . . . "You can't get passion into a story with exclamation points" . . . "The only taste that is false is that which does not change" . . . "Nothing genuine need fear the test of laughter."(6) Thurber never had much of a personal attachment to Taylor; the professor dwelled in too lofty an ivory tower for the aging Phi Psi lad who was trying so hard to make a go of it as a regular guy. But, as Ralph McCombs pointed out, "Taylor planted seeds in all of us that blossomed into love for good literature."

Joseph Villiers Denney—Shakespearean scholar, Dean of the College of Arts, fighter for academic freedom—was Thurber's idea of what a professor should be. He exerted less intellectual influence on Thurber than did Professor Taylor, but he was far more attractive to him as a person. For one thing, he was a man of wit and humor, the "imp of the faculty," as Thurber called him in *The Thurber Album*. His mots are still repeated on the Ohio State campus (or, at least in the Faculty Club). He perfected a studied absent-mindedness fully befitting his position as the President of the American Association of University Professors. "Jamie liked Professor Denney best of all his teachers," Helen Thurber said. "He amused Jamie and was the source of some of his better imitations at parties. Actually, so were his other professors, but he did Denney with more love. Jamie later tried hard to get Denney's books published, without much success."

Denney was a scholar's scholar, who, by all rights, deserved a more cerebral institution than Ohio State. He was the author of the "Millions for manure but not one cent for literature" line that so titillated Thurber when he was chronically ambivalent about his alma mater in later years. Nugent and Thurber used Dean Denney as their model for the liberal, unhysterical Dean Damon in their 1940 play, *The Male Animal*—which, of course, dealt with academic freedom at a state university indistinguishable from O.S.U. During the McCarthy days of the early 1950's, when Ohio State was suffering from academic costiveness more than most universities, Thurber wrote about the long-dead dean:

. . . Joseph Villiers Denney, through all this, must have turned restlessly in his grave. Ohio State, trapped somewhere between Armageddon and Waterloo, needed him and his strategy of reason and his tactics of friendliness, and all the armament of his intellect and his humor. But he wasn't there, and there was nobody to take his place . . .(7)

It is a measure of Thurber's devotion to the man and what he stood for that Thurber, ill and weary, went out to Columbus in April of 1960 to take part in ceremonies dedicating Denney Hall as a new College of Arts building. He wrote a speech, delivered by Helen, in which he said of Denney: "He cast a light, and still does—the light of learning, of scholarship, of laughter, of wisdom, and that special and precious light reflected by a man forever armored in courage."

While Professors Taylor and Denney were misplaced in the Ohio State milieu, Professor William Lucius Graves, the third academician in Thurber's college life, was made-to-order for the place, if not made-to-order for Thurber. Billy, as he was known to everyone, was a boy–man, a professional Beta Theta Pi to his last hour on earth, a polished and popular instructor in second-rate literature, a sympathizer of Fascism, and, probably, a raving homosexual. The last characteristic definitely wasn't made-to-order for O.S.U. and Columbus, but it was generally overlooked at dinner parties and fraternity bashes where Graves's charm at the pianoforte and in quasiliterary badinage was highly appreciated. He was, quite apart from his teaching talents, a fascinating subject, which was really why Thurber devoted an entire chapter of *The Thurber Album* to him. His intellectual value to the young Thurber, however, was in setting a negative example. By his conscientious instruction, he taught Thurber precisely how *not* to write and who *not* to revere. Graves taught the Short Story course, a subject Thurber was avidly interested in, and, since it was the only Short Story course available, Thurber took it. He received a deferred pass because he hadn't turned in enough stories based on Graves's ready-made outlines in the Fannie Hurst/ Gouverneur Morris/ Richard Harding Davis styles Graves encouraged, even forced upon, his young fictionists. Just as Professor Taylor had laid down the ground rules for good writing, Professor Graves laid down the ground rules for bad writing. It is to the everlasting credit of James Thurber that he was able to learn both lessons and make the careful distinctions.

Ralph McCombs was also in Graves's class with Thurber and Nugent, and remembered that the three of them sat in the back of the room whispering nasty remarks about the professor. "I suppose he was a good teacher," McCombs said, "but an odd one. He lived mainly for his old fraternity and his old mother. He was easy for us to parody, being so sissified and all. At the end of his life, he made the dreadful error of marrying a girl student, as if he was showing the world that he could do it. He had a great influence over many students, but not, I think, over Thurber." As Thurber wrote Dorothy Canfield Fisher, the daughter of a former O.S.U. president, on July 20, 1951: "I always liked Billy, in spite of his eternal boyishness and what I considered his rather mediocre treatment and understanding of the short story and his formal and unimaginative approach to writing." On August 23, 1951, as he was finishing up his chapter on Graves, Thurber wrote Elliott Nugent:

. . . I was astounded to discover that Billy was a vehement pro-Nazi in his late sixties, a hater of Britain and France, and a violent admirer of Lindbergh. He got married about the same time to a woman of identical views, lost a lot of friends when he wrote his political ideas in the Lantern. Professor Leighton answered him at length. I'm also quoting from "The Miracle of Brotherhood," a creampuff he wrote for the Beta magazine. He remained a pledge all his life. The strange case of Billy Graves. . . .

Of the three chapters in *The Thurber Album* about old professors, the one on Graves is a masterpiece of damning praise. The irony was, after it appeared in the *New Yorker* under the title "B$\theta\pi$," Thurber received a letter signed by a dozen members of Graves's fraternity saying that they appreciated the piece about their hero.

All three of the influential O.S.U. professors had a definite prescience about their on-again-off-again protégé James G. Thurber. Each of them separately told another student that Jim Thurber was the one who would make a lasting mark in literature.(8)

CHAPTER 4

The Aging Lad

As second-semester classes were drawing to a close in May of 1918, Thurber took a long, hard look around and, for all his social and academic successes of the past two years, he found his situation discouraging. Almost every able-bodied young male friend was off to the trenches (or, in a few cases, the skies) of France; Elliott Nugent was awaiting orders to report for Naval training; even some of the coeds were in the Red Cross, serving doughnuts to doughboys. And there was Thurber, once again at loose ends, living with his parents at 56 North Grant Avenue (they had moved to a less expensive rented house), still in Columbus, Ohio, U.S.A. Besides these depressing circumstances, there were other unassailable facts about himself to ponder: He was twenty-three and a half years old; he had only completed eighty-seven hours credit at O.S.U. out of a hundred and twenty needed for a degree, which is to say he was still a junior after five years of college; he had precious little heart left to satisfy his science, foreign-language, drill, and gym requirements; he was still half-blind, ungainly, and technically a virgin, not quite bold enough to take advantage of the sudden decrease in the local young-male population; and he was bored to tears with his, by turns, cloying and distant family. Thurber decided to quit college, perhaps for good, without getting a degree. It was another watershed moment.

Thurber was no likely prospect for cannon fodder, but he was nevertheless a patriotic man, intrigued by the Civil War and imbued with the anti-German sentiments rife in Columbus over the past four years (the life of Ludwig Lewisohn was made miserable during the war and the teaching of German was abandoned at Ohio State). But with his recent encounters with the military still fresh in his mind, he was relieved at being declared ineligible for combat duty by his local draft board.*

---

*One of the most Thurberian and hilarious pieces he ever wrote was "Draft Board Nights" in *My Life and Hard Times*, in which he fantasizes being called up for a physical so many times ("twelve or fifteen") by his draft board that at last he joins the doctors'

Thurber wanted to help in the war effort, but far away from Columbus. The governor of Ohio provided a neat excuse for Thurber to leave school with impunity, even before his classes were completed; under a proclamation of May 14, 1917, students could be excused early from studies for military duty or war work without penalty to their academic credits. As far as Thurber was concerned, it was only a formality, since he had little intention of ever returning to O.S.U., but it was a good formality. What he needed next was some interesting war work, out of town. He learned that the State Department was recruiting qualified trainees for code-clerking. They would be trained in Washington, D.C., and then the lucky ones would be assigned to embassies around the world. It is significant that Thurber chose a clerical job, albeit a more brainy variety than any his father had ever done. In fact, it was Charles Thurber who found out about the code-clerk program and used whatever political influence he could muster (mostly from Sloane Gordon, a newspaperman and friend of congressmen) to have his son accepted as a trainee. The accommodating O.S.U. president, William Oxley Thompson, helped out by writing a not entirely accurate letter of recommendation to the Hon. Breckenridge Long, Third Assistant Secretary of State:

14 June 1918

Hon. Breckenridge Long,
Third Assistant Secretary of State,
Washington, D. C.

Dear Sir:—

Permit me to direct your attention to the following statement concerning Mr. James G. Thurber, who desires consideration for position in the diplomatic service as an embassy clerk or in such capacity as he may be able to serve.

Mr. Thurber has recently been rejected by the District Board for regular enlistment and assigned to Class I—clerical, the reason being the loss of the left eye when 6 years of age, through an accident with a bow and arrow by his brother. His desire, therefore, is to serve in the class to which he has been assigned by the District Board.

In support of this desire permit me to say that Mr. Thurber will be 24 years of age next December; is a graduate of East High School, Columbus, Ohio; a

---

examining line. He is completely accepted by the other doctors as "a good pulmonary man" and passes the war happily examining the draftees by making them hold their breath and say "mi, mi, mi, mi." Actually, Thurber was rejected after one quick physical because of his lost eye. (On May 20, 1946, he wrote Dr. Saul Rosenzweig, a psychiatrist acquaintance who enjoyed analyzing Thurber's work, of his relief at being rejected by the Army; he went so far as to say that artists should never be drafted.)

member of the junior class in the Ohio State University, and was selected by the Sphinx Society as a member, which selection may be taken as the student judgment as to his all around quality and standing as a student. In his education Mr. Thurber has pursued courses in American and European History, the foundation courses in Economics, and also in the Department of Political Science. He has given special attention to the study of English and also the courses in Journalism. He has made a creditable record through the three years in the University, and I am pleased to commend him for favorable consideration to any position for which his education and personal qualities would qualify him.

Very truly,

William Oxley Thompson

Armed with his recommendations, some cash from the *Sundial* profits, and his father, for bureaucratic guidance, Thurber went to Washington on June 21, 1918, to snatch a morsel of adventure. A week later, he wrote Elliott Nugent, who was still awaiting orders from the Navy in his hometown of Dover, Ohio. This letter, the first of an extraordinary and revealing series of soulful effusions sent during his code-clerking days, read:

Friday, June 28, 1918

Mr. Elliott J. Nugent
Dover, Ohio

My dear old confrere, Nugey:

Time has not yet served to efface your blonde handsomeness from my retentive memory, old keed. I have been in the capitol of our lil old nation just one week today, and every now and then I spare a moment for reminiscence on the college days etc. Sounds like the mournful words of one bidding adieu to his youth, doesn't it? Well, not youth exactly, Elliott, but certain of the haunts and pastimes and ways of things connected with youth, such as the "keen, bitter-sweet days, blazoned against the night." For there you are in the navy, and there everyone else is in the navy except the misguided few who are trench food. And here I am in Washington intent on vieing with the whole darn enlisted bunch in the matter of ultimate distance from Ohio State attained. When I think of the old institution with its rich gallery of imperishable pictures by Memory, I can see now only a drab chromo of the well known Duke of Medina, studying in a far corner, a solitary figure in the old Phi Psi Castle. That is my vision of next year.

I am not going back, Nugey.

If you have tears of joy or regret or whatnot, prepare to shed them.

Nugget, old fella, I am promised a place with an American Embassy, told that I can begin preliminary work in the State Dept here in a few days,—to last a week or 10 days—and then go over. Furthermore and best surprise yet, it is almost a certainty that I will be assigned to Berne, Switzerland, where the well known Bernie Williamson is.

We came here with some good letters, especially 2 personal notes to Pomerene's* secretary from some mutual friends of his and my dad's—newspaper fellows with a drag. We were then sent to the office of the 3d assistant Sec'y. of State where a dream of a brunette, just my type and not over 27, quietly informed us that she had charge of those appointments, that there was an opening and that I could have it, after my papers had gone thru the necessary channels. The Hague was the place. Then I mentioned about Bernie, whereupon she gave me another smile (there were several) and said she would very gladly shift the 6 or 8 fellows who were listed for Berne over to other places, and give that to me. It was all so quick and miraculously easy that I am dazed yet. The only ways I can account for the speed and certainty of her words is (if youll pardon me and likewise God save the mark) that the lady was impressed with me. Pomerene's Secretary told us we could be certain of a place but might have to wait 6 months or a year as Pomerene himself had 4 recommendations in ahead of mine. And there are several other senators whose influence to stimulate appointments is assiduously sought, you know.

Of course, something may happen to queer me yet, or at least to hold me off a while. Certain democrats back home are not exactly willing to die for my father at the drop of a headgear, and a relay back there of the word might start a reflux or something. We had newspaper influence for the most part on this thing. I have been surprised and pleased to find out that political pull under the present regime here is not the *sine qua non* it was wont to be . . .

I hope this finds you in Dover, because I am counting on your being as yet off the bounding deep. I want a final vis a vis, you know. The way I have doped it out, I will be back in Columbus for a week before I go over, somewhere around the 10th, 15th of July. I will let you know as soon as I find out more definitely, and what I mean is, I want you to run down to Columbus for a few days and say hello, drink a white-grape juice highball, listen to Sammy Stewart play his version of the "Moment Musicale", let me kiss you on the cheek, say "au revoir, cheero, till we meet again, Kismet, god-speed, Lord love you" and depart, each his own way, for a brief space.

That about covers my present status and my prospectus, I guess. As far as things else go—in Washington—the phrase "historical interest" describes my daily life in a nut-shell. I have seen more "here lies," more "This was builts", more "in the original handwritings" and that sort of stuff here than I imagined existed. But my dear fellow much of it is really interesting with a punch. And one can trust the relics, in the Library of Congress to be authentic. It is only when one discovers, after adding up on his fingers the various individual ones he has seen,—that Booth wore six spurs on his right boot the night he shot Lincoln, that one loses some zest. That is more or less a fanciful illustration,

---

*Senator Atlee Pomerene of Ohio.

however. In the Congressional Library we saw the original draft of the Gettysburg Address. It contains on the first page 6 or 8 changes—additions or erasures. One line is like this, if I can remember it: "as a final resting place for those who here etc." You see even the wonderful grammarian Abe had to moil and toil a bit with his Mss. Also the original draft of the Second Inaugural, with the famous words staring up at you in Lincoln's own pen-script "With malice towards none, with charity for all."

Countless other things of a similar nature. If you have never seen Washington, do it before you get sunk. Historical interest is all very good, I might add, but sentimental attachment knocks it cold. Imagine my sentiments upon seeing, after 15 years, the old homestead here, the old corner drug store where we spent the hoarded nickels, and a tall, whistling youth striding by that was an 8 year old kid playmate o'mine. It sure has been an enchanting week, and what with my prospects and all, it well overbalances the shooting up of old John Sundial money.

Which reminds me I gotta scrape together some coin of the Rellum before I sail, and mail it to Chubby. But that should be easy. $2000 a year I will get, you know.

My eyes are beginning to "get" me and I'm going to end this history. Wish I had me trusty Underwood by my side.

I aim to write you much more very soon, as there is much more to report especially one certain topic that I wont touch on 'till I can finnish (sic) it at a setting.

Address me care this hotel, and please, Nugey, *have a heart* and write me much and soon. Dad goes back tomorrow and I will be like a painted ship upon a painted ocean. Another phrase from that same poem will fit here too. "Water, water everywhere—" Washington is bone dry. The only thing I've seen in the way of liquor here is the law. Papa asks me to add his best regards and luck.

Now, please, old rounder pal o'me' yout', *Write me quick*. I want to know how much more time you get before they sink you etc.

Yours in Phi Psi
Jim

One of the 8 memorial trees at Mt. Vernon is an Elm planted March 19, 1902 by Phi Káppa Psi. The Sigma Chis also have one,—the other 6 planted by prominent societies and famous men.

Thurber won the cryptographer job and joined a class of sixty young men, among them Stephen Vincent Benét, for what turned out to be more than four months' training in encoding and decoding at the State Department. As far as codes were concerned, James was his father's son; brought up in a household headed (at least in name) by a practically full-time puzzle-solver, Thurber took to the challenge of cryptography with zest. It further stimulated the deep fascination for words that was both to excite and torment him throughout his life. He was an "excellent" code clerk, said Stephen Vincent Benét later, "and rapidly became an expert at solving difficult and improbable messages. He can still talk in Green Code, when necessary."(1) (Thurber also *wrote* in Green Code, one of five basic codes in use by the government at that time. The characters named Golux, Todal, Hagga, Pivir, Ninud, and Nadal in his adult–child fantasy *The 13 Clocks* were all Green Code ciphers.) Also, Thurber appreciated the idea of codes, the secrecy, the mystery, which later attracted him to Houdini and his works. He read books on cryptography, apart from his State Department curriculum, but his interest in the mechanical aspects of the craft waned after World War I.

With time on his hands, he gravitated towards working newspaper-men of the Washington press corps, and he ate, with relentless regularity, every night in the Post Cafe, a fourth-estate hangout where he felt safe and among friends. He later wrote about that restaurant:

> . . . Some of our most memorable meals were eaten there, and some of our fondest memories name that place as home. There was a genial fat Southern negro cook, wonderfully called George, who put out such soups as may not be discovered anywhere else in America. There was remarkable coffee, such as you find at intervals of not less than 700 miles in a trans-continental tour. And there was a genial, tranquil Washington air about the place. . . . To the old Post Cafe we shall sometime indite a lyric and if the lines are one-half so lovely as the inspirational reminiscence out of which they shall be born, it will be a pretty piece and a lasting one . . .(2)

His elite station and his fellow trainees—mostly well-born Ivy League graduates, like Benét (Yale, 1919)—pleased him, too. He lived at inexpensive rooming houses, studied hard, and wrote long letters back home. The Ohio State verities of pedestalism for most women, unswerving loyalty towards one's fraternity brothers, and high thoughts whenever possible kept him sexless in Washington. Physically, he was liberated from Columbus, university, and family, but he was loath to make the most of it. This romantic, adolescent catatonia (eerie in an intelligent, sensitive man of almost twenty-four) was amply demonstrated in his letters to Nugent, who assumed the disparate roles of father, mother, brother, and confessor—all the life supports, in effect, Thurber never had.

July 16, 1918

Dear old Pythias:

So a pair of Brown Eyes has wooed you away from old John Typewriter and allowed me to pine and waste away worrying about just what sector of the sea had embraced your sunken form. No, my dear Nugey, in all our many lil talks over the W. K. Omars; you never told me a word about the love that came but once, and then perhaps too soon. "You rascal, you damned old rascal," little did I reck that your bosom treasured also a youngster love affair that you never quite forgot. "Also", advisedly, because the Romance of me life is, too, just such an affair as our well-meaning parents laugh to scorn, only I was not quite so precocious as to play Lothario at the callow age of knee high to a duck. Mine was one of the legended "school boy and girl" affairs. I played 15 opposite her 14 in the drama "The Seventh Grade," and ten years have passed, friend of me college days, and I love her yet. Surely I told you, if only briefly, the plot of the piece. My eccentric memory for the trivial calls up a scene in your handsome Phi Psi rooms, you lolling in your upper berth, I dragging on a Piedmont, just abaft the picture of the Rocky Mounts there on the mantelpiece, when I spilled the tale. Your own story of Her Return after many years, gives me quite a pang. You're a lucky, lucky dog, you blonde sea-going mop of a ensign, you. The story of my youthful affaire dem herz is too long to rehearse, but, oh boy, I wish a certain pair of Brown Eyes would come back where I could dream life's sweet, sweet dreams agazin' into 'em again. She is the One Girl, old keed, but I guess the long and attenuated Jimmy is out of luck. However, I'm going to play one last long chance before I try the impossible method of forgetting and, quite crudely, giving the rest of the world's women a chance. I once wrote this wonderful girl a letter, 7 years after we parted back in the grammar grades,— or three years ago. I was lifted aloft to places where cherubin twitters by a 12 page answer from Colorado Springs asking me to write again which I did in a way that set me back 8 cents for postage of the Rellum, addressed, as she requested, care of her sister 203 Underwood St., Zanesville, Ohio. No response. And, quite like the lackadaisical Thurber, I let it ride from thence to nownce. She was beautiful as the Helens of Poe and Troy, graceful as Endymion etc. etc. since it's too hot to reach for classical similes. But her voice, Nugey, her voice! Keats' nightingale. Darn you, I told you she used to sing that song to me about "Love, I am lonely." At least you recall my persuasion of the Nugent rendition of it a la like, of a quite often frequency, back in the college days. Hence, the stage for her. But she had ruined John voice when young. Thence, the movies. Thence, vaudeville. Now, Lord only knows. Ask your dad if ever in his theatrical circles he saw or heard of a certain little Dream named Eva Prout.

But, Nugums, I rave,—where is the Blasety of yesterday! And now I'm going to tell you how I lost my mind. You remember The Minnette? Right, oh. And, of course, the whole situation, in all its circumlocutions, appanages and ramifications. Nugey. I'm a damn fool. Not that you didn't know, merely to refresh your memory. Of course, as you know, I at one time,—and still—was rather attracted by the Fritts. You also recall the Dampers de Ardour you flung. Also, very confidentially, I stuck away, quite altruistically, because of a Mullie appeal with tears in his eyes. Not to be mentioned, of course. The Phi Psi Xmas dance was my first and only date. Until a week before I left.

Columbus, that week, heaved a huge Win-the-War parade. Thousands

thronged the main travelled marts. In this vast crowd I upheld the basis of all
O. Henry stories, by meeting Minnette. A date was inevitable. We saw Marguer-
ite Clarke in "Prunella", which, by the way, I liked very much,—hope you saw
it. Took her in old John K. Reo, eats at Marzettis, 1.15 A.M. Date two nights later.
Karl Finn, Tom Meek out of luck. Moonlight, Reoings along the Scioto; in brief,
all the old paraphernalia and stage drops. And, deus ex machina, the Thurberian damn temperament or lack of balance. Oh, well, hell, Nugget, it's gone
pretty damn far and I only wish I could hope for a repetition of the Minnette
engagement history. But a little hunch informs me I'm in, that's all. I don't know
what she wants, unless it's my P.K.P. pin, surely not my Sig Delt Chi decoration.
At any rate, I'll never be able to get back home with the suit-case I brought
here, on account of Minnette's loving letters taking up so darn much space.
And, Nugey, like a damn fool, I can't retrench or nothin! I haven't the heart to
appear less amourous than I was during the moonlight madness of those few
dates. I like Minnette very much, more than any girl at school by far, as you are
aware; she used all her tricks them nights,—and, there you are,—or, rather, old
thing, theah I am, don't you gathah? I think that we are engaged. Go ahead,
you blonde Don Juan, and laugh your head off! Now I could learn to love the
kid, and I'm sure that as married couples go, we would be domestically out
there. But, Nugey, the blow that cools James is the Hope that Spouts eternal
about the One Girl. Someday, somewhere I'll find her. I've quite an O'Henry
philosophy and Faith. Oh, quite. I'm positive that me and the Eva are Hero and
Leonidas, or Heroine and Alexander or whoever it was, those eternal destined
lovers, that swam the Halcyon. "Two shall be born" etc. The drift is yourn, I
presume. . . .

But Time and Change now whet their papiers and run the rest of the cast into
separate wings where the forgetting is good, and, I hope, the suitability of
affection is rife. For, dearest old Fellow, I have formally been appointed to the
American legation at Berne and have accepted. Got the official letter here
Friday, and am awaiting draft release and required Birth Certificate so that I
can begin my "several weeks" course of instruction in the State Dep't here. The
appointment is "duration of the war.". . . I expect to be here "in training" at
least 2 weeks, maybe 3, possibly 4. Then home for 5 days or a week. That means
Columbus about the middle or 3rd week of August—and you may be called the
first, or thereabouts. Pardon me if I appear to quoth "Hell's Bells!" However,
I am using "silent unity thought control" and thus assuming the delay of your
call, so you can bust a bottle or three into me in the old "town of the Spree and
home of the Graves" (clevah rascal, this bird Nugent, with his droll parodies on
the-aw-Star Sprinkled Decanter—law) and surely by that time you and Brown
eyes will have come to some sort of a something or other that will make for the
temporary abeyance of Romes in favor of Pythias with a Columbus-bound
suitcase. T's not for the world would I press Damoniacal claims resulting in the
abortive cessation of Pythiaspirations towards Romeogling Brown Eyes. Oh,
revah. I hope, my dear Nugey, that you do not take merely a poet's desire for
a lyric in your case with the old love. I might wish for your philandering to

cease, except that I want us both to be free to fling a few twosome parties when this man's war is over, without having to dodge friend wife to arrange them. Marriage is all right in its place and time, but the Paldomain of Men must not be jeopardized for a mere—a mere quibbling of matrimony. I demur. Sounds like Isle d'Amour. But please be good and sincere with Brown Eyes, thus not emulating me, I take a keen   —this space reserved for a word that escapes me(—you know, it means taking an interest by proxy—what the heck is the word,—all I can think of is "atavistically" which it aint)—interest in the affair. I really should shoot myself at sunrise, but moonlight and Minnette and 15 gals of gas leads the way that madness lies. I wouldn't dare show you the answers I send to her letters, simply because I believe I have compromised myself so that I cant get out of it, without being of the genus mucker or cad. I thought of course she would play around and toy a bit and let it go. Perhaps she yet will. But Nugey, her letters don't sound like it, and, if I lost on my chance that she would play with me as the rest, no matter what was said, I'm willing to pay and act the gent. She is really a fine girl, and of all the kisses I have ever kissed none can compare to the peculiar quality of hers. Like nothing so much as frozen roses on an August night. The crux of the thing is she seems to count them not berries, but trysts. And my line somehow or other couldn't, with her, follow the safe and sane drive for mere berries. She used lots of tricks, but I'm afraid she has decided she now has the One & only case, and I believe she decided that since I left. I think she was willing for a while to let our respective lines go cum grano salis, but now finds her heart was really on her lips. Gawd help me. I either want to be saved, or—garçon, a love potion, queek! . . .

Please answer soonly and at your usual delectable length and with the unfailing Nugentian style, which, I can't refrain from telling you, my love, makes the institution of correspondence something worth the living and writing for. . . .

It's now 1.17 so good night, laddie, and when you write, you old DonjuanlothariapythiasRomeoCyranodebergerackberrygatherer,—give me from the store of your experience and knowledge of sex problems and 5 part movies, some advice. But for God's sake keep my confessions to your ain self,—Love towards you, Nugey,

Jim in old Phi Psi forever.

One wonders what Nugent, the urbane professional actor, made of this slobbering protégé of his. Here was Thurber in a quandary of his own devising: in rapturous love, on the one hand, with his "sweetheart wraith" who barely existed outside his imagination, and, on the other hand, in over his head with the teasing college widow. Even for those innocent years, it was a letter that one would have been surprised to receive from anybody older than eighteen, except for the few flashes of humor and lyricism.

Thurber's romantic predicament inevitably grew worse. Minnette kept writing "loving" letters and Thurber responded in kind. "Really I do like her very, very much, because she is to me, I am positive, what she has never been to any of the other luckless lads," he told Nugent in an August 25, 1918, exudation from Washington. "I mean she has done with trifling, jipping et al and she's mine for life." But he also sent off "one regular Thurberian masterpiece" to his childhood sweetheart wraith, hoping that she would answer. ("Let me whisper the heroine's name—Eva Prout—*Eva*,—sweetest name in John World," he wrote Nugent. "Oh lady, lady and, as it were, oh, Boy.") Eva indeed answered, from her home in Zanesville, Ohio, where she had retired from her stage career. She invited Thurber to visit her there, and she spoke of a mutual friend, Gleeson McCarty, who had nice things to say about Thurber. ("Now, you see, when I was a bit of a lad in grammar grades and short pants I was a wreck—teacher's pet—grind—nothing for whose memory the Eva would fall," Thurber confided to Nugent. "Gleeson is strong for me. He has handed her a nice line that I am really not an ass at all. Gleeson thinks, in fact, that I'm out there. He has told her that I'm worthy of the name 'Jim'. She believed me a regular 'James' . . . I'm going to pledge Eva Phi Psi. I can't help what happens. I just feel it coming, big and sure as Destiny. For 10 years I've never absolutely in my subconscious mind given up hope.")

Thurber expected soon to go to Ohio on leave, first visiting with his family at the latest rented house on 330 East Gay Street in Columbus before "the halcyon days to come in Zanesville with the One and Just One." Meanwhile, he learned of Minnette's enlistment in the Red Cross. Somehow, he missed Minnette's broad hints that she had no intention of marrying him. Her enlisting in the Red Cross was not the act of a wench bent on matrimony. Perhaps Nugent, in his letters full of "satire and sympathy," alerted him to this. In any case, Thurber was basking in the cool glow of a suddenly materialized dream woman and the extreme honor of being termed a regular guy—a "Jim"—by no less a personage than Gleeson McCarthy, a mutual friend of Eva Prout! However, his leave was delayed, which didn't ease his quandary any.

Sunday, Sept. 15, 1918

Dear Bringer of Wisteria into Waste places:

. . . The well-meaning folks o'mine did not forward your letter till yesterday, since they have been expecting me home every day, and since I have been expecting the same thing and so advised them even two weeks ago to be wary of sending important advices and missives to me here. Six weeks is the average stay of one in my position of trust and responsibility in this lovely, languorous war capital, and I am now in my ninth week. However, no definite visit here is stipulated and length of dolce far niente in this tranquil, dreaming world-conflict burg depends on many things, such as tall ships that sail amain, for instance. I am very confident of heying ho for home this week, however, and since my mother informs me that you are in Columbus and at the dear old Phi Psi house and are probably to be there till Friday, I am going to make every effort to get away before then. But I am at the mercy of a very clam-like department whose officials merely answer one's questions: "hist, all in due time". . . .

My long stay here prevented me from giving a goodby grip to one of me oldest pals, 1st Lieut. Ed. Morris,* who is inter-seas now, France-bound. And surely the saturnine God's reign's over, and dates and connections will work out nice in our case. Otherwise I hold a brief for Sherman. But should the times and dates be out of joint, never forget that long, long trail and the halcyon days to come after the last requiem is howled over Kultur, and gun-steel is converted into pruning hooks, ploughshares and steins once more.

All the foregoing was done in febrile haste, because I have been cursing preliminaries that must be did before I could comment with many a rhapsody and possibly a rhyme upon Things Other, especially Only girls—not *merely* girls, but oh boy, *Only* Girls.

I have always thought only two pins should be worn, if one is to be correct, —and happy. And the black and gold of the little old shield is charming against Chiffon or georgette crepe; lots charminger than staring from the flare of The Nugent Shirt or the dull brown glow of the Nugent Vest of Arnold Bennett fame. But in less consular language, Nugey, old fidus Achates, it *is* a glad world. My only regret is that only one girl can have the all of Elliott, for lots of girls are also deserving of the best old John World has to offer. So much for my lone regret, now for my only doubt: as I recall the Nugentish pearls anent Woman, (God bless her but watch her) promiscuity of playing around was a stressed note and heart-whole and fancy-free was a motto. Also, of course, I remember the qualifying rider as to the eventual anchorage in some Only Haven of Love, but so remote a time did you make this seem to be, I quite definitely had placed you among the Lotharios of the World and dreamed not, therefore, of such a sudden proselyting to the little circle of the Romeos. However, I really do not doubt greatly, for I realize what an iconoclastic thing a girl's voice is and how simple it is for the mere curve of a girl's cheek to smash the philosophy of a young lifetime. Still you did seem, you will please admit, quite adamant to these tiny but potential smashing qualities. Therefore I will only dismiss my last bit of doubt say two months from now, having, for one thing, a memory of how eternal the Rocky Mounts are not, and yet how for two weeks or more a certain Phi Psi believed them a staunch stairway to old John Eternity. That's not quite

---

*Morris was the high-school friend who snubbed Thurber after being pledged by Chi Phi at O.S.U.

fair, however, as I believe during that time old John Phi Psi pin still gleamed from the dusky brown glow and the silk flare, quite immutably. The average girl is always either an actress off stage or a girl "made up", or a mixture or vice-versa or what not. Only she never says which, leaves it to you to find out whether you have dashed into a movie scene or otherwise. Possibly she doesn't know herself. . . .

Regards n' everything to whoever of the lads are there, if any. Don't even know when State opens this year; if it opens. Afraid to learn of prospects.

O tempora, O mores, o hell

Jim

Here is the first recorded instance of Thurber's bemused astonishment at womanhood: "How simple it is for the mere curve of a girl's cheek to smash the philosophy of a young lifetime." Amid all the mawkish naïveté of his adolescent love troubles, he had somehow begun to study the female as an object of inscrutable wonder, a study culminating in the creation of the Thurber Woman. Maybe he was just starting to wise up.

October 15, 1918

Dear Nugey:

. . . I have a bet with a bird here that the next bit of Hell to take place will be the entire destruction of that region west of the Mississippi by floods,—he bets the next thing will be the spread of painters colic among all the little babies of the world. But it was two days ago that I made the bet and now I feel I should have said the next holocaust, cataclysm and hellsbelling would be the entire disappearance of water from the world or the unputdownable uprising of maniacs, or yet the conquest of Ohio by the Bolsheviki. What is your pet hunch? There aint no use dodging the mournful truth that times aint what they used to be. However, being by nature an oculist, I mean optimist, I see the faint flush of the dawn of a newdick, I mean a new day, thru' the blackness of the pit from pole to slav, I mean from pole to pole. You mentioned Mary Flu in your letter, —(I refuse to call it John) Well, here's hoping Dover doesn't get in bed with it as badly and thoroly as Washington. All one sees here is nurses & hearses and all he hears is curses and worse. And such a heroic thing to pass out with,— Influenza! dying of influenza in these times of brave, poetical deaths. Allan Seeger was a lucky bird. I imagine him writing: "I have a tryst with influenza, at daybreak in some pest-house ward". I'd just as soon go with house-maid's knee. However, fear no fears for the J.G.T. I am in chipper condition with the correct psychological attitude of chestnuts and baseballs towards all flu. The influx of Enza will have to select a clever rapier and twist an adroit wrist to pink me, altho' I am in the pink of condition. To get my mind off the measured tramp of jazzless bands here, to forget the persistent odor of floral wreaths to hear not the thud and scrape of the spade and to shut my ears to belated eulogies over Yoricks, I am writing a novel. No, not a regular one. My novel is very novel. It is called "The Wine Seller" and is similar in style to a piece of junk I wrote two years ago for a great pal of mine with lit'ry leanings albeit he has a wife and two marriagable datters. That venture was "The Salt Seller",—so this present "book" is the second in the list of the six best sellers. To write a novel of this sort, one begins with no plot at all, and gradually loses the thread of the plot as he goes along. Settings are subject to change with or without notice. Slang and puns are allowed, character limning is banned, Billy Graves gets gray hairs, Joe Myers swallows a stogie and all is ready for the reviewer. Briefly the lack of plot of this famous novel is this:

Chap I

The king is bitten by a beetle. The royal ankle swells and gets all kind o' green sort of. This worries the queen, because she dislikes green. As she tells the King in one of the books most charming passages:

"Lookit, green may rime with queen, but it doesn't chyme with my propensities anent colors befitting the wallpapers of royal bedchambers. You must sleep, therefore, with the seneschal."

"Royal robertchambers!" howls the King; forgetting for the nonce that Robert Chambers wasn't born yet. (The scene is laid in 1603.—There is a ghost in it, too, but that isn't laid till 1605. No cornerstones are laid.)

The Chamberlain, the Premier and the Duke of Mixture are called in, the latter rolls in wealth, has a powerful drag, and his job is a pipe. The King holds a star-chamber session with them in the sun-room. It is night and there is a moon. The Chamberlain suggests calling the Royal Doctor. The King says he's called him all the names he knows already. The Premier suggests shooting the beetle at sun-rise to which the King offers three objections: 1. there is in the whole realm no handkerchief small enough to bind the beetle's eyes, 2. this especial beetle has no eyes, 3. immediately upon biting the king, the beetle made good his escape. The Duke then puts in his oar and suggests that the King try abdication. (The Duke is next in line for the throne). The King whispers in the Chamberlain's ear to get a medical dictionary and see what "abdication" is, but in order not to show his ignorance to the duke he receives his suggestion very kindly, says it may be just the thing and promises to think it over. The Duke twirls a satisfied mustache end. In this chapter there is also a duel between two courtiers who get into an argument as to which is correct, "bit by a beetle" or "bit with a beetle". The Royal grammarian endeavors to prevent the duel by telling them they are both right in a way, but that the generally accepted form is, "bitten at the hands of a beetle". "What do you think it is, a clock?", demands one courtier, and the duel goes on, the weapons vases at twenty paces.

This is as far as I have developed the wonderful thing yet, but in the next chapter, the royal palace is besieged by the noted bandit leader, Purple Jake and his wild band. Purple Jake's lieutenant is the profligate and evil Earl of Pongee and Madras, a former court favorite, whose banishment had taken place 6 months before at the behest of the queen who complained to the King that the Earl had up and hit her with a croquet ball, during what she supposed was going to be a friendly game in the Palace Gardens. The Earl, eager for revenge, eggs Purple Jake to the attack on the palace, telling him he knows the secret panel where the royal jewels are concealed.

There is a wonderful heroine, and of course a wonderful hero, yet to appear, the latter none other than the Wine-Seller,—altho' events finally show he really isn't a mere wine-seller at all. You can see at a glance that I have written the Great Armenian novel. But enough of the plot has been told to put you in a position to steal the thing and win an unjust fame, so I will try to get your mind off of it.

There is one sure way: only girls,—nothing else. Boy, you wrought a great longing in me soul with your wide panorama of a world for two with Christmas Cows in the dim offing. Such a mixture of Corot and Shelley naturally would ruin one who for months has been able only to live in dream worlds for two, and see with his minds' eye visioned Christmas cows. First I built an August world for two, "a silver chime, a golden sphere", but as you know, Fate rolled up the corduroy sleeve of his hairy right arm and heaved a brick. Then a September world of cool white stars at night and warm, dreaming suns at noon. Again the corduroy preliminaries. So like the persistent spider I fashioned an October world for the Eva and me. October burning on the far hills at daybreak, October flaming all the ways at noon, October smoldering in the purple vales at twilight, October ashes red beneath the moon at night. Blooey, is the song of the Brick as it nears my frail October world, faster and faster.

But one of these worlds will outlive the strong arm of old Percy Mike Fate, and one of these days, one of these days!

I see her mostly in blue, dark blue, with just the right dash of real red. She has,—oh, Nugey, she has the most won'erful dark, glossy chestnut brown hair ever in old world, ever in old world. I see it rippling down, a shimmering cascade over that deep Blue. I have always had an almost irresistible desire to hug every pretty girl who has dark brown hair and wears one of those neat dark, navy blue suits. I'm afraid in this case it will really be irresistible. I imagine I will have to do something crazy and sudden, anyway, for time will be brief, too damn brief. Boy, cant you see the lil golden shield, the greatest pin in the world, gleaming richly and austerely and yet debonairly from the folds of that Blue?

Speaking of Phi Psi,—to digress a moment—John Davis, America's new ambassador to Great Britain is a Phi Psi. A recent issue of "Life" says: 'His social and scholarly achievements are attested by his membership in Phi Beta Kappa, Phi Kappa Psi, Masons and Elks" In which we have the falsity proved of "once a Phi Psi, never a Phi Bete". It's a great old bunch, Nugey, and till the stars grow dim on high it will continue to be.

I couldn't manage to finish this letter at the first setting—in fact it is now two days later so this represents a pleasurable task of three days. In that time I have received the news of the death of my grandfather,—mother's father—Tuesday. The end was long expected so comes as no shock. He has lingered near death for over two years.

My dad also enclosed a cut of the dear Minnette from the Ohio State Journal, which says she received her call for Red Cross training last week and leaves this week. It fails to say for what place she leaves. The letters of Minnette and I have dragged horribly—as to oftenness—in the last month,—but when we do write we are as deep friends as ever—much more than friends. My folks are very strong for her, indeed I received some weeks ago a very remarkable letter from my father full of mellow advice, including the injunction that I do or say nothing to jeopardize my relations with Minnette and be not too sure of the felicity of things Eva. Letters forwarded via home drew from me a partial statement of feminine entanglements. The folks of course remember very clearly my terrible schooldays case on Eva, and it seems the fact that Eva's past and present are more uncertain than Minnette's calls up maternal fears. I have reassured home of my luck in handling the situation so far.

I have not heard from M. for about 12 days. This is the longest delay she has allowed except the last letter I got came after an almost equal delay. Before that we wrote twice a week almost. However, her last letter was warmly cordial and nice as ever, and my answer was too. I cannot understand why she hasn't written me about her call and where she is going and so forth. Really, I worry about it. It is useless for me to laugh Minnette from my thots. Sincerely, Nugey, I never have—and I never can. As time goes on I admire her and yes, damn it, love her more. Perhaps my expedition to Zanesville will——but I can't believe it will. What to do with Minnette, I don't know. Do not be surprised if, years from now, I become even more deeply serious about her. I believe I told you she understands about Eva—that I confessed completely and straightened everything up, and of the wonderful clever letter she wrote me. I can't but believe Minnette cares a lot for me, but the situation is not now "gone too far." It is simply that, if I allowed her to, she could care enough after awhile to hurt. Perhaps I shall find it nearer to my heart after all to allow her to, without any hurt. The thing is the same with me as with her—I could care very very much for Minnie. Given a few more moons and a little more less-distance between and all would be wildfire. . . .

Heavens alone, I believe, know when, if ever, I shall leave here. I am totally resigned to permanency. Eventually, is all I can say. It may be months. I have no hunch now that it will be before November. And I am even building a December world for two already. The cold information via Journal type about Minnette's going and the lack of word from her, altho' she knew it 10 days ago, not only hurts a bit, but makes me realize I like Minnette. So we'll close with her name instead of Eva's. Minnette. This time. Of the future? Lawd, I live by the hour, really. I have had so many worlds of various kinds bricked that I believe I don't care to dream wholesale nice dreams any more. Sort of carry on, see it through and grin occasionally. For Heaven's sake don't quit writing muh, whatever plague sets in next.

Awfully glad The Girl knows me. Of course I know her, too, not merely because of your wondrous pen dreams, but also because I long ago pictured for myself just what the Nugget Only Girl would be, and I'm sure I'm right in every detail of charm and wonderfulness. I sincerely hope—and believe that Some Sunday Morning when Everything is What We Dream of again, the two only girls and you and I will put on the Worlds Most Great Party. Someplace where skys are blue and suns are golden and there are Christmas cows in the far, enchanting distance.

Immutably thyne,

Jim

Although written only a month after his last outpouring to Nugent, the October 15th letter showed a miraculous maturing on Thurber's part. He was afflicted with incipient *Weltschmerz,* a condition that was to dog him off and on all his days. True, it was inspired by the dreadful influenza epidemic of 1918 (which he nicknamed "Mary Flu"—his mother's given name—since "I refuse to call it John"). His worldly sorrow even moved him to a rather felicitous poetic line: "All one sees here is nurses & hearses and all he hears is curses and worse."

To get his mind off disease, war, sex, and death, he changed in even a more momentous way. He wrote humor—not *Sundial* paragraphing, He–She jokes, fraternity-house skits—but real, original humor. Suddenly, Thurber was funny, Thurber was Thurber, as if by a wayward muse's visitation. His "novel" (he never made much more progress with a genuine novel than he did with *The Wine Seller*) is a nice touch of nonsense, for all its easy puns. There is a seemingly effortless flow to its bits and pieces, which found their way into the fairy tales and adult–child fantasies he loved to write decades later. They were crowded with bilious kings, evil dukes, bumbling royal doctors, and fair heroines. To make a case that this lark is prophetic of *The White Deer, Many Moons, The 13 Clocks,* and *The Wonderful O* is simply to know that Thurber never wasted a literary thought or word. He used everything, sooner or later.

But then, despite this flight, Thurber fell abruptly back to mewling about his dreary girl friends and his fraternity pins. It is difficult to believe the same young man wrote these two lines in the same letter:

"There is in the whole realm no handkerchief small enough to bind the beetle's eyes."

and

"Boy, can't you see the lil golden shield, the greatest pin in the world, gleaming richly and austerely and yet debonairly from the folds of that Blue?"

But that was James G. Thurber in 1918.

It is also interesting to note how Thurber took the news from home. That he displayed little grief over Grandfather Fisher's death comes as no surprise. What is surprising is that his father went to the trouble of writing his code-clerk son "a very remarkable letter," actually offering advice and a personal opinion on Minnette Fritts vis-à-vis Eva Prout. Perhaps physical distance from their son made it somehow easier for Mame and Charles to communicate with him.

CHAPTER 5

The Battle of Paris

In October of 1918, just a month before the Armistice, Thurber and a dozen other Clerks, Code, Grade B, received their sailing orders for Paris. Thurber was originally assigned to the American Embassy in Berne, Switzerland, but a severe outbreak of flu there and an urgent request for code clerks at the Paris headquarters of the American Peace Delegation, in the Hotel Crillon, changed all that. It was a lucky break for him.

His final security clearance consisted entirely of being called to the office of a Mr. Shand just a week before sailing and answering yes to the question, Were all your grandparents born in the United States? ("In 1918, Americans naïvely feared the enemy more than they feared one another," Thurber pointedly observed thirty years later in a piece called "Exhibit X.") Having passed the loyalty test with flying colors, he was given a four-day leave before shipping out from Hoboken, New Jersey, on the S.S. *Orizaba*, a passenger ship converted into a troop transport. His leave was spent, naturally, in Columbus, where, for perhaps reasons of time, he made no effort to see Eva Prout, Minnette Fritts, or Elliott Nugent, who was at the Great Lakes Naval Training Center for a short stay in the U.S. Navy. He did see a great deal of his family, which helped him pack a trunk and suitcase. Mame placed generous quantities of Hershey bars in the folds of various apparel as survival protection against wartime famine. She also warned him, obliquely, about those French girls. On the last day of his leave, a snapshot was taken of him, which he described in "Exhibit X":

. . . The subject of the photograph is obviously wearing somebody else's suit, which not only convicts him of three major faults in a code clerk—absent-mindedness, carelessness, and peccability—but gives him the unwonted appearance of a saluki who, through some egregious mischance of nature, has exchanged his own ears for those of a barn owl. . . . His worried expression indicates that he has just mislaid a code book or, what is worse, has sold one. . . . This man could even find some way to compromise the Department of Agriculture, let alone the Department of State . . .

Fortified with sound maternal advice and Hershey bars, the owl-eared saluki went off to war—or at least the last ten days of it. The captain of the *Orizaba* had no sympathy for civilians travelling on his military vessel, and Thurber literally had to talk his way aboard, since the State Department had neglected to visa his special diplomatic passport. He wasn't able to talk his trunk and suitcase onto the ship, however, and he spent the twelve-day voyage across the Atlantic (the captain zigzagging to avoid the last U-boats) with only the ill-fitting clothes on his back and what garb he could borrow from his friend and fellow civilian code clerk, Edmond Corcoran. The crossing was rough as well as tense. Thurber had bought a box of San Felice cigars before sailing, but he was unable to smoke them because he was seasick the whole twelve days. Not so Edmond Corcoran, who was in and out of their stateroom, singing, joking, and smoking Thurber's cigars. At last, the torture ended, and they arrived at Saint-Nazaire two days after the Armistice was declared.

. . . What I saw first of all was one outflung hand of France as cold and limp as a dead man's. This was the seacoast town of Saint-Nazaire . . . . I was only twenty-three then, and seasick, and I had never been so far from Ohio before. It was the dank, morose dawn of the 13th of November, 1918, and I had this first dismal glimpse of *France la Doulce* from the deck of the U.S. Transport *Orizaba*, which had come from the wintry sea like a ship out of Coleridge, a painted ship in an unreal harbor . . . . Saint-Nazaire was, of course neither dead nor dying, but I can still feel in my bones the gloom and tiredness of the old port after its four years of war. The first living things we saw were desolate men, a detachment of German prisoners being marched along a street, in mechanical step, without expression in their eyes, like men coming from no past and moving toward no future. Corcoran and I walked around the town to keep warm until the bistros opened. Then we had the first cognac of our lives, quite a lot of it, and the day brightened, and there was a sense of beginning as well as of ending, in the chilling weather. A young pink-cheeked French army officer got off his bicycle in front of a house and knocked on the door. It was opened by a young woman whose garb and greeting, even to our inexperienced eyes and ears, marked her as one of those females once described by a professor of the Harvard Law School as "the professionally indiscreet." Corcoran stared and then glanced at his wristwatch. "Good God!" he said. "It isn't even nine o'clock yet."(1)

That was how Thurber remembered his landing in France from the perspective of 1957, but it had a trenchant feeling of truth to it. The virginal Ohio lad, smitten with Jamesian Francophilia, with visions of Mme. de Vionnet dancing in his head, came abruptly face-to-face with real life, with war, with unJamesian dolor. The premier order of business, after the cognac, was to acquire some kind of wardrobe, since his trunk and suitcase were still lost. Upon arriving by train in Paris, he went straight to the Galeries Lafayette, where he blew five dollars for underwear; then it was on to a shop called "Jack, American Tailor" for a suit that "might have been made by the American Can Company."(2) He indulged himself with the purchase of a cane, but he couldn't bear the grotesque spectacle of himself in the only hats available, despite the raw Paris winter.

Thus unequipped, Thurber sallied forth to report for duty to the formidable Colonel Edward House at the Hotel Crillon, where he had been instructed to appear. A subordinate, "who plainly regarded me as an unsuccessfully comic puppet in a crude and inexcusable practical joke,"(3) said heatedly that Colonel House did not want so much as a single code clerk, to say nothing of a dozen. What Colonel House desperately needed was a dozen code *books*. Thurber later figured out what had happened: Several weeks earlier, the Colonel had sent a coded cable to the State Department in Washington requesting a dozen code books for the American Peace Delegation headquarters. The cipher groups for the words "books" and "clerks" were apparently too similar to escape garbling, and the result was that a parade of code clerks kept turning up on Colonel House's doorstep.* Thurber was summarily dispatched to the chancellery of the American Embassy, at 5 rue de Chaillot, with the rest of the unwanted clerks. Years afterwards, he wrote to one of his Paris colleagues, R. Henry Norweb, who had praised "Exhibit X":

. . . I decided to leave out of my piece, out of love and loyalty, the story of the first time Jefferson Caffery got a look at a big batch of those clerks who should have been books. One was cross-eyed and lame, one was a hunchback whom we called Judge Cooper, one had a bad left arm, and Caffery must have believed that they represented the bottom of the barrel of American manpower . . .(4)

In due time, Thurber settled into a routine of long hours of work at the chancellery and some wide-eyed sightseeing. He lived and took most of his meals in a humble pension near the embassy, also eating

---

*According to Thurber, most of the diplomatic codes in 1918 were quaint leftovers from President Grant's day, intended to conserve words and telegraph costs rather than to confound an enemy. The Germans laughed at the Americans' pitiful attempts at cryptography, and the Japanese actually returned a missing code book, neatly wrapped, to an American embassy because they were either finished with it or already had one.

occasionally at an Army mess in the basement of the Crillon. Food prices in Paris immediately after the Armistice were wildly inflated; fried eggs, for instance, ran to as much as a dollar apiece. It wasn't such a bad idea, after all, for Thurber's mother to pack Hershey bars in his luggage, if only he had his luggage. (When his trunk and suitcase finally arrived in Paris the following April, the Hershey bars had melted nicely over his clothes, coloring them an unpleasant dull brown.)

The American ambassador then was William G. Sharp, an uncharismatic Ohio businessman who had replaced, quite early in the war, a very charismatic Ohio politician named Myron T. Herrick, for whom Thurber's father had worked so hard in the unrewarding 1916 Ohio senatorial race. Thurber was first amused and then embittered by Herrick's talent for publicizing himself as the great wartime ambassador, part of Thurber's resentment springing from Charles Thurber's treatment by Herrick. He later wrote two critical articles about Herrick and mentioned him derogatorily in other pieces; Thurber could hold a grudge, if he wanted to. He wasn't so keen on the other Ohioan, Ambassador Sharp, either. He wrote in 1948 to a Paris colleague:

... There was also the time that Ambassador Sharp handed me a telegram one night which began en clair and then said, still en clair, "The rest of this message is in our new A-1 code." I disobeyed orders on that and sent it all in code. I remember talking to Representative Black of Ohio many years ago and asking him why Sharp had ever wanted to be a diplomat. Black said, "I guess every little boy dreams of being an engineer or an athlete when he grows up but Sharp was born with the desire to be Ambassador to France—why, God only knows." . . .(5)

Thurber's creeping progress into adulthood was enhanced by his shy immersion into *la vie Parisienne,* but for him it was like entering a cold shower. He arrived in Paris just after the Armistice, when "her heart was warm and gay" once again. In fact, as Thurber later wrote, "there was hysteria in its beat . . . the kind of compulsive elation psychiatrists strive to cure." He went on:

Girls snatched overseas caps and tunic buttons from American soldiers, paying for them in hugs and kisses, and even warmer coin. A frightened Negro doughboy from Alabama said, "If this happened to me back home, they'd hang me." The Folies Bergères and the Casino de Paris . . . were headquarters of the New Elation, filled with generous ladies of joy, some offering their charms free to drinking, laughing and brawling Americans in what was left of their uniforms. At the Folies a quickly composed song called *"Finie la Guerre"* drew a dozen encores. Only the American MP's were grim, as they moved among the crowds looking for men who were AWOL, telling roistering captains and majors to dress up their uniforms. Doughboy French, that wonderful hybrid, bloomed everywhere. *"Restez ici* a minute," one private said to his French girl. *"Je* returny *après cet* guy partirs." . . .(6)

It was all a far cry from fraternity dances and late nights at Marzetti's, and the tentative, sensitive Thurber grew to like it, once he had put his foot in the water. He was free at last, free to be a regular guy with class in Paris, France. Of course, he was cagey about his newly liberated self with the folks back home. He made a lot in his letters of the local newspaper clippings and gossipy tidbits Robert kept sending him, especially since he was worried about Robert, who was still suffering from a chronic case of Thurber "nerves," consumption, and toxic thyroid. Right after an imperfect thyroidectomy, in which too much tissue was removed causing him to be permanently depleted, Robert barely survived an appendectomy in the same hospital. His athletic plans were crushed, and, as it turned out, so were most of his other dreams. Thurber, in one of his first letters home from France, wrote Robert personally on impressive American Embassy stationery:

March 18, 1919

Dear Old Thurber:

I am awaiting further clippings—and also a letter from you and dear Old Bill. I am addressing this letter to you because I want to send you the enclosed check for 10 beans.* I understand you are about to have six or eight more cuttings to add to your collection. As a ball player, you are quite a patient. But I sure hope you will be all fixed up when this arrives,—and for Heaven's sake sign the pledge never to get anything else the matter with you. Of course you couldn't possibly get anything new, but stick away from relapses and lay off of setbacks. Decline to go into declines—and refuse to be flung amongst the refuse. . . .

Don't infer that I mean for you to use the $10 for to pay any bills with. It won't go very far but fling yourself a little party, and write me a letter, using the remnants of the 10 seeds to buy a stamp with. William is able to work, and you aint just yet,—so you can probably use the few bones.

I would ship you more now, but living is terrible high here now—and furthermore I feel I just gotta see Paris and that does take the money. Also I have made three trips to Northern France,—Reims, Soissons and Verdun—and R.R. fare is steep,—but boy, oh, boy it was worth it. I seen things. I am writing accounts of

---

*Probably the first of a lifetime of checks from Thurber to various members of his family. In later years, when the Fisher Company stock was all sold, he was their main support—just as Mark Twain had been for his deficient family.

my trips and will mail them home soon as they are finished.

Picked up a few souvenirs,—no helmets altho' I saw beaucoup. There'll be more helmets back in America after all the boys get home than will be left in North France and Germany and Belgium together. The few things I picked up are more interesting than mere helmets, which at best are chunks of heavy iron. At Fort Douamont—5 miles from Verdun—I bought a pretty vase hammered by hand out of a French 75 shell case. I picked up some Allied propaganda— in German—from the wreckage of a plane near Soissons. I got near this place an Algerian soldier's service record with two bullet holes through it.

When I get home I'll have you all draw up around the fire in a semi-circle to listen tensely to my tales of action at the Front. . . .

Now use this money for some damn fool purpose. Don't use it to defray expenses or buy nails to fix the back yard gate.

I'll send you some more pretty soon.

Mamma's first letter telling about "our dog" must have been de-railed. First I heard about him was her last letter telling me the names you were considering and asking me to suggest some. What brand of animal is he? Collie, bull, Florida wine Spaniel, Iceland Seal terrier or what? Anyway, he'll probably always con- sider me as an intruder when I get back. Show him my picture, let him sniff an old suit of mine and tell him the story of my life.

I'll write William and You a special letter soon as I can.

Keep the Home Fires Burning.

> Always
> Your Bro
> Jamie

But to Nugent, recently discharged from the Navy and back at Ohio State, he wrote with more truth and zeal. Just two days after his March 18, 1919, letter to Robert, Thurber composed a long, painful, contradic- tory gush of lyricism, chauvinism, and banality, betraying a conflict well at work on his innards. He made it clear that he appreciated his free- dom and independence in "pagan" Paris, lording it over Ohio-trapped Nugent with faulty French and romantic place names. In diary form, he detailed the blossoming of the *marronniers* in the Tuileries, the charm of his pension, picturesque scenes along the Seine, the colorful mix of people in the Paris streets, and his trips to the grim battlefields of Château-Thierry, Soissons, Verdun, and Reims, where he acciden- tally tripped a booby trap while climbing over some barbed wire at the deserted trenches ("There wasn't much of an explosion—a sharp report like a pistol—and no pieces of the stuff fell very near . . . But I'm admitting herewith quite frankly that I was scared bad . . .").

Yet, through all the romantic-heroic writing ran a streak of abject homesickness for virtuous, clean America and its virtuous, clean women. A letter and snapshot sent from Eva of Zanesville threw him into a moralistic dither of adulation for the American female:

. . . Nugey, she is a Princess of Youth, and the Apotheosis of the American Beauty. . . . The clear, sweet, beautiful eyes of an American girl. And there is nowhere in all the world their equal. I mean, not selfishly *her* eyes,—but eyes like them,—eyes like the eyes of American girls. And I have seen beaucoup eyes of girls from other lands. . . . The A.E.F. in France has learned to respect American womanhood, to revere,—to worship the clean, fine morals of American womanhood, to idealize American girls,—and to worship them with a fire that burns brighter and steadier than ever before,—and that will never die down. Things they have seen and heard and felt here, these American boys, have not added fuel to any base fire, or kindled any new and regrettable flame. And they never will . . .

However, there was the seductive female Paris haunting the priggish Thurber, as she would continue to haunt him till he left France, a year after this letter was written:

. . . It's a wonderful place to study in. And you don't have to go to the Sorbonne or the Ecole des Beaux Arts. Every one is a school. Every museum a college—and the whole of Paris a vast university of Art, Literature and Music. So that it is worth anyone's while to dally here for years. Paris is a seminar, a post-graduate course in Everything. . . . She is pagan,—with a pagan love of beauty—but with a pagan "love" of women also. . . . One thing is sure sure. I gotta get back pretty soon, and make a few decisions, or I'll be quite thoroly S.O.L. . . .

He regressed to puritanical inanities at the very thought of Zanesville and home; he even seriously considered going back to Ohio State. It could have been a letter written by the young Richard M. Nixon.

The Paris vs. Columbus conflict popped up, less emotionally, in more letters to Robert, who, during his long convalescence, continued to send what Thurber called his "letter-newspaper-history-dissertation-drama and comedy" missives about Ohio. On April 9, 1919, Thurber answered him:

. . . As to myself, if I care to stay I could probably be here till Fall, maybe later. Again, if I wish to go back, I could no doubt leave here most any time. There are all kinds of fellows here to handle the work, and 3 or 4 of us could be spared anytime. Often I decide to go home soon as possible but then I re-decide that as long as I am in Paris and have the chance to stay, I ought to do it, as time spent in Paris is time not wasted, by any means. It is always interesting, and a wonderful field for study, of all kinds.

James and William Thurber, 1897.

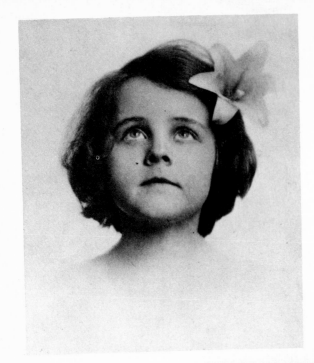

Eva Prout.

Grandfather William
Fisher.

James and William Thurber, 1897.

Aunt Margery Albright in her garden.

James Thurber, age 12.

Charles Thurber, as a
young man.

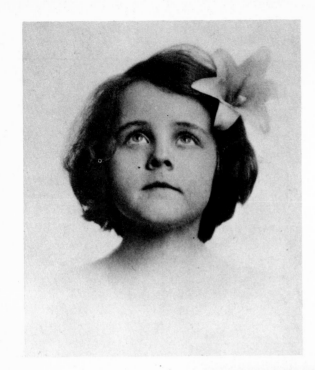

Eva Prout.

Grandfather William
Fisher.

Family portrait, 1915. Top: William, James, Mame. Bottom: Robert and Charles.

Sun Dial Board, 1916. Elliott Nugent is on the extreme left of the front row; Thurber is on the extreme right.

Minnette Fritts, as a
"Rosebush" girl.

Althea Adams, as a
"Rosebush" girl.

Muggs.

Thurber, as a young *Dispatch* reporter.

Althea and Thurber, newlyweds.

Daughter Rosemary and poodle at Newtown.

Thurber, 1936.

Thurber and Helen, newlyweds.

Thurber and friend.

Thurber and Helen in Bermuda with the Williamses, 1936.

Algonquin, 1938.

Left: Relaxing in Bermuda.

On a boat off Bermuda, 1940.

Opposed to this slant, however, is Home and the U.S.A.—and the boys-*and* the girls. Every now and then these factors swing uppermost in my mind, and I think I have seen enough of Paris. Because, on final analysis, there are more things to go back for, than to stay for. My heart is in Ohio. And there's no use trying to make-believe I am, or could be perfectly satisfied to stay here very much longer. I guess you all know back there how greatly the A.E.F. wants to go home. And I've naturally absorbed the A.E.F. spirit. All they talk about is the Statue of Liberty. You hear, on all sides, "My Alabama", "Me for Old Illinois", "Oh You Lil Old New York." And the most popular songs are "Homeward Bound" (which is sure class) and "When Are We Going Home?" a song written by an Ensign over here. . . .

Now for a piece of good news—especially for Mamma—yesterday afternoon I received a long, official envelope from the Army authorities at Hoboken Piers. MY SUITCASE IS TROUVE! And it is now nearing Brest, aboard the U.S.S. Agamemnon, and will be forwarded, by official orders, right up to the door of the Embassy. Six cheers! Bonheur! C'est joli! And one big worry is vanished.

Received papa's letter, one from Mamma—William's also, as I mentioned before—and one from Mrs. Botimer. I realize how busy papa is, and tell him not to feel at all that I do not understand it. Ca ne fait rien, to use a famous French phrase. I know he would like to write more, but Lord knows he has enough other things to keep him busy. . . .

Paris vs. Columbus was a nag. In a May 31, 1919, letter to Robert, his mood of indecision helped fuel his chauvinism (rapidly swelling to racism) and even allowed for a few cracks about his parents:

. . . Mamma writes that papa is still an earnest advocate of putting his family to bed early, doubtlessly tucking them in securely also, and so I assume that you are getting your rest, which ought to help you recuperate in good shape.

Your very clever dialogue of the O.M. [old man] learning to crank the machine, since he might as well learn then, was one of the funniest things I have had the good luck to have come over to cheer me up, your final touch about the use of the brush to calm the Thurberian temperament was true to life, all right. I suppose by this time he has tried, tried again, and is now one of the world's swiftest and surest, if not indeed, fanciest, crankers of machines. . . .

The most recent piece of news with me, however, happened today. The little French garcon who guards the Embassy door, that is the porte to that inner sanctum known as the code room, came in and informed me that one demoiselle Americaine wished to see me. I couldn't imagine who, but I hurried out all eager to see. An extremely pretty and bright looking American girl was standing there, in the well known trim gray uniform of the Rouge Croix. I recognized her face at once but couldn't place her, and she had to tell me that she was Charme Seeds and that she had heard I was at the Embassy and had also heard a word or two about me in State, and thought she ought to come up and pass the time of day and one thing another. I had never met her, but of course had seen her quite a bit, as she is very famous at State, and was one of the most popular girls in the whole doggone campus in her day, and is yet for all of that. So I grabbed the afternoon off and we buzzed out to her place, a Red Cross Hotel in the Latin Quarter, and there we had tea in a very pretty garden, and cakes and marmalade and a long talk about people at State and things back on the old campus in general. . . .

Yesterday I went out to the cemetery of Suresnes, about six miles out of Paris, where a great many American boys are buried, and where one of the finest services was held. It was surely a thing not to be missed. There were oceans of flowers, and a very impressive honor guard of American and French soldiers, drawn up for no less a personage than the President of the United States who delivered a fine address, not a word of which I could hear however, since the closest I could get to him was jammed up on a hill at his back among about nine million doughboys and two thirds of the rest of the American war workers in France. French and American bands played,—the Star Spangled Banner and the Marseilleise, (spelled very uniquely I think) and then Chopin's Marche Funébre, and ending up with about as fine and touching a note as music is capable of,—the sweetly sad tones of Taps floating across the flower shrouded wooden crosses; the bugle call was played by a fine looking American bugler, and somehow it left an impression that will always stick.

My very best as always to everyone, and tell mama and papa that I am sorry that cablegram of mine had to float in at such an ungodly hour and ruin the paternal rest. I was sorry after I sent it that I hadn't put a date on it, because it occured to me after it had been sent up and put on the wires that you all might never be able to figure out what on earth it meant, and it might even scare you into believing that it was my final word of parting before I took a Brody into the Seine or something.

No such prospect contemplated however, and hoping you feel the same about the Scioto, I remain,

forever,

yours,

Jamie.

Thurber's budding racist feelings, which were probably more of a symptom of his geographical and emotional quandary than any serious belief, flowered in a June 25, 1919, letter to both of his brothers. He had been attending the Inter-Allied Games at Pershing Stadium, in Porte Vincennes, whenever he could get time off, and finding common ground on which to communicate with his sports-crazy siblings, he wrote a lengthy and rich description of the competition, dwelling rather crudely on what he considered national traits:

. . . The Arabian sabre combat was very wonderful as far as cleverness in flailing a sharp weapon right in a brother's face without clipping off a nose or a cheek, but it was so darn funny in the various dances ala Al Jolson and "no news for the news man" which they would suddenly waft into, away from each other, just when the give and take was at its roughest. The Americans in the stands were tickled to death and cheered and applauded, so that the Arabians thought they were getting by wonderfully, whereas the Americans, and most of the other onlookers for that matter, were overlooking the marvelous hand and arm work because the la dee da Pavlowa accessories were so killing, so to speak. The camel race was picturesque all right with true sons of the desert riding real ships of the desert, but the old boys weren't much at taking a curve on high, being content just to keep on going, across lots, toward the exit. Finally two of them ended up with a fairly close finish, a pacin' fool defeating a trottin' bird. . . .

The next event, a burly Frenchman beat up a lil son of the sunny slopes about as high as the Frenchman's stomach. All the Italian did was to crouch low and cover his face with both gloves, while the Frenchman stood above him, one hand resting on the Dago's back and the other continuing to pound the lil bird on the gloves, with the even stroke of a pendulum, until the gong rang. After 2 rounds of this comedy, the Italian delegation pulled out. Every now and then during this fight the dago would jump away run around the ring and fling a wild right swing at Friend Frenchy, missing him by not more than 2 feet and a half, and completely turning around in the effort. The 3d bout, Al Norton of America and a Canadian named Herskowitz or something of the russiansort, was naturally the best of the afternoon, more science, skill, cleverness, and variety of swings and blows. . . .

When ever there is anything to celebrate here and often when, like a negro parade, there is no call whatever for celebration or parade, the Americans always do the most and the loudest and the fastest and the peppiest stunts of all the rest put together. The ones who run a close second to them are the French girls. An American is seldom seen on the Boulevards or anywhere else without his lil francaise along, and they have taught the gals all the well known yells and songs and whatnots with which to make revelry by night. So the other night they were out and at it again. There were also contingents of Frenchmen parading and singing, but in a more reserved and genteel fashion. British and Canadian soldiers, especially the Canadians are pretty Americanese when it comes to making a noise, and when the Australians were here in goodly number they could hold up their end too. Of all the nations of the earth, the Yanks easily lead in the matter of pep and enthusiasm, endurance and gogettem stuff, however. They are also craftiest with the right swing. . . .

You will observe that in all five heats of the 200 meter dash, the only English speaking runners entered in each event took the first places every time, . . . where only one was entered he won, where two were in it, they got first and second, and where three were entered they took first, second and third. The Anglo Saxon stuff gets there. . . .

As his first spring in pagan Paris wore on, his impalement on the horns of his private dilemma grew almost comically painful. Now, an added inducement either to stay in Europe or return to America (depending on how it influenced him from moment to moment) was the grating knowledge that Elliott Nugent—four years younger than twenty-four-year-old James Thurber—had returned to O.S.U. and received his degree. Also, Nugent showed good promise for a theatrical career. He was at once an object of admiration and envy—and very heavy competition. It was as if they were back in their early undergraduate days, with Thurber as the scruffy unknown and Nugent as the big man on campus. About all Thurber could do between bouts of vacillation was try to make himself sound like a heedless man of the world:

> American Embassy, Paris
> The Greatest City in John World
> June 11, 1919

Dear old Nuggett:

... Heaven's only knows where this missive will find you, for by the time it reaches the only shore you will be through forever ... that is as far as burning the midnight cigarettes goes, ... with Ohio State. Thank your lucky stars and the way things are arranged, however, that the memories and the places and people to go back to will last quite a long while yet, and that letters can still be carried ... if written ... and that railroads still bring to ends journeys that culminate in lovers and friends meeting etc. etc. the et ceteras to suggest a million other nice things about college futurity that, due to a real mean and sultry day, I can not locate the proper juxtaposition of letters on this keyboard, to describe. You know, without my elaborating on the theme that I would sure have admired to have been back on the campus with you for the final fling, which is a subject that I wont go into at length, being bitter sweet with the accent on the ante penult, or proscenium, or whatever it is that "bitter" plays in the bifurcated expression referred to. What I mean is, that I am all low because I didn't get back for a few final parties, a few final wee sma hour chats thegither, a few more consumings of the beaucoup (French for countless) midnight Omars. But that is neither here nor there; rather, it was there and not here, which is even worse. However, let us grin broadly at the vast expanse of silver almost obliterating yonder cloud bank, and reflect that there are other places than Phi Psi corner rooms to talk and smoke in, even if not quite so nice, and that also, we will be going down the way to old John corner room together several times yet again before we resign as mondaines here below. And ruminating thus, he suddenly exclaimed happily "Sappy life, oh sappy life."

Reverting for a few more minutes and sentences to the fini of this last fiscal semester on the campus, I presume that as far as inheriting the yellow parchment with the ribbon, and getting away, making off with, or slipping over all the necessary codicils, corollaries and ramifications of said legacy, you have come off with the palm, the green beaver, the azure riband, and flying colors. But that of course, important as it is, isn't half so weighty or lasting a matter as the playing around you did the last few weeks of them college days and nights, including strolling, in all its several aspects, but particularly Earnest's Importance as Such. Clippings have already come to me, via my young brother, from the Journal and Citizen, setting forth the annual triumph of the OSU boys and girls, and although both these reviews say real nice things about you . . . I liked especially the parenthetical expression of this Daisy Somebody or other telling the world that one can invariably look for the crafty putting over of mean lines from you, or words to that effect . . . but as I started to say, although these critiques are really good, I am sure they were not half strong enough. I desire to go on record as expressing myself as being very regretful that such a trivial matter as some nine billion odd square miles of water and a few other elements, so to speak, of equal triviality and extent, kept me from splitting a palm, straining a neck and opening wide an appreciative and admiring eye on the occasion of that most nervous dreaded and at the same time most tranquil and happy affair in the world, le premier soiree. . . .

I appreciated and liked very much your poem yclept "The Two", as I suggested, or made a veiled allusion to in the preamble of this melange of words and ideas, mostly words. I have showed it to quite a few persons who have been enchanted, may I not say? One of these was a Red Cross girl whom you do not know, but who has a penchant for Browning and poetry in general; and she pronounced the last line of the last verse as very fine. Please dont get funny, at this point, Nugey, and suggest with a cynical smile. . . . . but you will already have done so. Allow me to state that that isn't the point at all, she liked the imagery of "tall dreams that fade out". As you say, I shall doubtlessly become, before I die, the world's greatest authority on Nugentiana, if indeed, as you say further, I am not already that. Another person to whom I showed the poem was a Red Cross girl whom you do know. . . . Nugent meet Miss Charme Seeds . . . Yes, its quite an interesting little story that hangs thereby. You know I had never known Charme Seeds when I was in school . . . I remember your once telling me in a shocked and grieved tone of voice that I was missing a large part of State by not doing so. . . . if it wasn't you, then, it was someone else, but my memory seems to recall the recollection that. . . . however, let us on with the story hanging thereby. Charme has been here since April with the Red Cross . . . I was going to say in the uniform of the Red Cross, but she has the smartest and cutest and most irregular way imaginable of not wearing the regulation uniform. . . . she prefers a rakish little blue toque set ala Martha Hedman's hair, over a large slice of forehead, to the simple and plain sailors of the rules in the book. Then of course the wide and cool and sweet looking Buster Brown collar that ever made her famous, or which she made famous, I dont know which. So that about all the Red Cross rules, regs and bylaws carried out in her vetements is an enamel Red Cross insignium pinned against the dark blue of her toque, and I fear it is worn more for the indubitably Charming effect than because of a quaking before the Board of Discipline, room 119, Hotel Regina, Rue de Rivoli. But let us get back to the main travelled road. Charme met Buzz Speaks on the boulevards here, about ten or twenty days ago . . . or fifteen or thirty . . . the ability to hit within two days of the exact time escapes me just now. Buzz, however, had heard through that prolific and untiring writer to Phi Psis in Phoreign Phields, M.Hugh Bennett, that I was attached, as I always put it, to the embassy here, and so one day she came up, and I was summoned to the door and we met. And since then we have had tea and marmalade and cakes in the pretty court garden of her place in the Latin Quarter, one of the famous Duck Dinners at the Tour D'Argent, the famous restaurant opposite Notre Dame and the place where Strether and Madame de Vionnet dined together, if you have as yet read M. Henry James' "The Ambassadors". And tomorrow night we hear a concert in concert. And life goes on fine and gay and . . . ahum . . . extremely expensive, in Oldgayparee. Buzz himself didn't drop around until after Charme did, but he drifted in a few nights ago, big as a house and strong enough for two . . .

I really must admit that I dont exactly and absolutely know what I want to do, either now or in the near future. I have arrived, or have been arrived, at that point in one's life which is extremely disturbing and full of hopes and fears and doubts and one thing anothers in wild profusion. I have a deep and sneaking feeling that I should return and finish school for the purpose of wearing the initials after my name and a few other reasons, and I guess that is the sensible thing to do, so the chances are that I wont do it at all, . . . unless someone "comes out" for me, as H.J. always says for coming over.

I must admit that Paris is going to be a very hard place to leave. It is all that dear old Henry said of it, just as wonderful just as charming. There is surely no other place in the world where there is such a variety of things that interest or amuse or instruct or enthrall. Why, it is going to be hard just to leave the concerts in the Tuilleries garden where a symphony orchestra plays beneath the acacias, plays Madame Butterfly and Thais, all the prettiest songs from the finest operas, . . . where the moon comes up over the Louvre that reaches its old gray arms towards you invitingly and a bit menacingly, like all old Paris buildings. And in the intervals, the plash of the fountain in the wide purple tarn, the witching glow of the near rose garden in the moonlight. I took Charme there last night. And we had a real nice time, I aim to state. Dauphine terrace in the Bois de Boulogne with almost equally as good music and exactly as fine a moon, and chestnut trees as tall and whispering as the acacias, . . . and ice cream or citronnade or biere or port, as your inclination may be. I dont think that some of these things would ever tire, and yet of course one must snap out of them eventually and the sooner the better in many respects I know. And yet, it's a long life, and one can really not get too much Paris if he only stays away a year or. . . .

On the other hand, I have to get back and get at something. It is impossible to get a perspective or a determination over here. All that is Paris militates against determinations and decisions, and for that reason it isn't any too good for one in a sense.

Then there is Zanesville and everybody of which, my dear Cassius, you are not the least. There is a long long pull exerting itself from Gay street, and a darn strong yank coming from Tenth avenue. And I suppose, that coupled with real good sense, they will get me back by the first of September at the latest. Another element that may enter into the scheme and play the deus ex machina and the heavy lead etc is the fact that things are rapidly closing up over here, work is subsiding mightily and the chances are very great that all but one or two of the older men will be sent back, and I am not one of the older hommes.

I suppose I will have decided it for certain one way or another by the time I get your answer deciding it another way for me; anyhow I want that answer, and the best way to get it is to ship this letter. Hence, (not being a German) I will sign.

Forever & Forver & frever,

Yours, Nugget, yours,
Jimmy

Nugent's star continued to rise, with frightening implications for Thurber's own unbegun career. After some grudging, slightly green congratulations in a September 24, 1919, letter to "old Laurel-wreathed Elliott," Thurber spoke weakly of his own professional plans. Suddenly, he, too, was coincidentally involved in dramaturgy—"a one-act play or so"—but his lack of confidence in his talents was widened by Nugent's initial success. He had the honesty to admit that "my range doesn't naturally reach beyond the skit sort of thing, and that if it ever does emerge above that level, it will have to be pushed with strenuous efforts. As a matter of real fact, Paris has shown me that I may have known considerable of the tricks of the writer's craft as an omniscient student of the OSU college, but that when you drift beyond the confines of old John Campus you find that there is considerable expanding has to be done. What I mean is, I am a bit shaken in old Samuel Confidence which is the most totally destructive thing imaginable . . . For I have never had a natural invisible supply of supreme confidence or even of transcendental courage, and it keeps me concentrating and gritting the molars every now and then to keep the manufacturing plant going . . ."

But then, as if to demonstrate to Nugent who was potentially the more sensitive writer after all, he launched into a rich, lyrical Baedeker of his excursions through Normandy—"She of the chimes, the tears, and the apple blossoms. . . ." And as for Paris: "It's a great life, in many ways, a great life, this Paris affair, so utterly darn different from American ways of going at things and getting places that it completely baffles attempts at perspective at times. . . ." The message to Nugent was clear: Watch out, Elliott! I may be a slow starter, but I'm coming on.

At long last, in the fall of 1919, just before his twenty-fifth birthday, Thurber jumped unclothed and unencumbered into the cold shower of Parisian debauchery. He must have been the very last American in France to do so. His scrupulously guarded virginity, hidden for so long on that same lofty pedestal where American Womanhood dwelled, was surrendered to a semi-professional demimondaine, a Folies Bergères dancer named Ninette, and was continued with yet another. The "first step aside," as he put it in an almost offhand confession of the cataclysm, set him on a downward course of guilt-ridden indulgence. He tried to make light of the whole thing:

. . . The whirl when once it whirled went whirling so fast that I saw it as a reason for whirling home. Ninette told me once in the privacy of her cute Montmartre apartement, "Jeemy, at zee step which you step, you must last about two weeks." "Ah, non, ma cherie," I returned, lighting a Pall Mall from a huge red box of them which I had given her, and offering my glass for some more of her fine Porto, "Ah, non, vous vous trompez, you are very wrong, at this pace I will last all of ten days." Voila . . .

I have no regrets, fortunately, but I will say that I can't see it except as a passing experience once in—or twice in—a life-time, providing there is no One Girl. I mean if there isn't One Girl, why then say six or eight passing experiences or nine or ten or . . . hell. The genus known as Gash Hound intrigues me not. Nor does it suffocate you with enthusiasm, either. But what have you to say as to how long your pace would have lasted? Come to think of it I never had your statement that you hadn't hunted forbidden berries long ago, but I at least imagined you hadn't. I don't believe I ever told you I got as far as Paris all right, either. It seems to have been a thing which we naturally didn't consider worth the time for discussing. And God knows it isn't . . . .(7)

Not worth discussing indeed! Thurber was so tormented, almost destroyed, by his first steps aside that he suffered an acute attack of "nerves," as the Thurbers tended to call mental collapse. It tied his tongue and his psyche in knots, and he withdrew into a dark silence from family and friends, even the beloved Nugent.

Thurber had cleared his strangely prized Victorian barrier and become an adult man, his affairs complicated by his feverish love–hate for Paris. Some of this torment came out in a short story he wrote at the end of his life called "The Other Room." The telegraphic, Hemingwayesque tale concerns an aging American World War I veteran revisiting Paris and telling some other Americans in a bar about his first encounter with a sympathetic cocotte.

. . . "I remember walking along the Champs-Elysées," he began finally. "I never could pronounce it right." He was correct about that, but none of us pronounced the words for him. "Then, there was this girl, this French girl. She wasn't any older than I was. She spoke English, though, and was I glad for that! Well, we sat out in front of the Café de la Paix. We drove there in a taxi. She said she thought I didn't look very well, and she said she thought I should have something to drink. And so we had a couple of drinks. Then she told me about herself. She came from some place in Southern France, and her father was a drunkard, and used to beat up the family on Saturday nights, so she ran away to Paris, and got some work in a garment factory, but all they gave her was a few francs a week, and she saw all these other girls in fur coats and things, and so she took to—well, making the boys feel better, she called it." . . .

As did the American vet in the story, Thurber tried to look up the first girl during a later visit to Paris. She had left France after the war with a doughboy, married him, and lived miserably in the Middle West, until, having had enough of the New World, she returned to France without her husband. She somehow got hold of Thurber's address while she was in America and asked him to send her some books in French, which he did. Coincidentally, the other woman in Thurber's Paris life also married an American and followed him to the Middle West, but Thurber never heard from her again.

Finally, the distraught Thurber—a casualty of the Battle of Paris, from self-inflicted wounds—returned home, with the stragglers of the A.E.F. The Paris vs. Columbus dilemma he had agonized over for so many months was, in a way, resolved for him. His headlong plunge into the Parisian fleshpots, his consequent guilt and depression and "nerves," and the last demobilization of Americans, civilian and military, left him with little choice but to go back. On February 14, 1920, he sailed for America at government expense, sharing a stateroom with Alfred Goullet, a famous six-day bicycle racer. He returned disturbed, uncertain of his future, in a crisis of confidence, but at least and at last an adult male who had tasted something of life outside Columbus.

As he wrote thirty-seven years later:

. . . When I finally sailed back home, sixteen months had elapsed since the Armistice, and the Brave New World was taking on its disillusioning shape. Theodore Roosevelt had died in 1919, which marked in its way the end of an era, and Woodrow Wilson had come down from his dizzy pinnacle of fame and hope, and was on his way to his own dismayed and frustrated end. Before long a celebrated room was to be filled with smoke out of which a political magician named Harry M. Daugherty would produce the shadowy figure of Warren Gamaliel Harding and the misleading motto of "Return to Normalcy" in a period of flagpole sitting, nonstop dancing, Channel swimming, ocean flying, husband murder, novels of disenchantment, and approaching financial chaos. I reached New York still without a hat. It was March and blustery in New York, and one of the first things I did was to buy one. It fitted my head, and seemed to my repatriated eye extremely becoming. It wasn't until later that day that I looked inside the hat to see the mark of the maker. I quote from a piece I wrote in 1923 for the Columbus, Ohio, Sunday *Dispatch:* "Something inside the crown caught my eye. I looked more closely. *'Fabriqué par Moissant et Amour, 25 Avenue de l'Opera, Paris,'* it said."(8)

PART 2
Sophistication

CHAPTER 6

"We want to be a literatus when we grow up." (1)

Thurber came home from the wars with his fraternity pins still intact, but with brooding guilts, a somewhat worldly view, and a bad case of trench mouth. He directly moved into his family's rented house at 330 East Gay Street, and while the sight of the fraternity pins was reassuring to his parents, the brooding guilts, worldly view, and trench mouth gave them a nasty scare. What had Jamie been up to in sinful Paris? Robert, who had commenced a lifetime of recuperation at home, remembered his hero brother as a changed man. "Besides the trench mouth, which pained him a lot, Jamie got a kind of experience," Robert said. "You could see that right away. He was so independent. He talked to Mother and Dad like an equal, and they were a little surprised, I guess. He was jumpy and moody, but he seemed to know what he wanted to be—a writer of some sort."

It wasn't all that easy to be a writer in 1920 Columbus. A newspaper job was the most practicable answer, but even if he could get one, the pay was notoriously low and the work was usually dreary. There was, too, the possibility of free-lance writing, but that took a greater measure of self-confidence than he possessed at the moment. Meanwhile, he had to earn his keep at East Gay Street. His father was still an underpaid Municipal Court clerk and medical bills for Robert were eating into the remaining Fisher Company stock. The trench mouth cleared up but the case of "nerves" took longer to heal. A trip to Zanesville to see, at long last, The One and Only Eva Prout eased his nervous condition but it sent him into new spirals of confusion. The confusions all came out in another gush to The One and Only Confidant:

Friday, March 25, 1920

Dear old Guy o' mon coeur:

... First of all, concerning myself, I wish to speak of plans, or such plans as I have, for my future. Naturally I am still a bit unsettled and uncertain yet, and things are somewhat nebulous and a trifle worrisome. You see I am not in tres excellent condition, having had a very bad time of it with nerves in Paris, —which is a hint of the silence story—untold yet by the way—but out of that life into a new routine altogether I am picking up wonderfully. The ocean trip in itself was a wonder worker, and home and the way spring comes up Ohio ways, are keeping up the good work, ably assisted by Fellow's hypophosphites and new mental orientation. Perhaps I touched on this in my letter from Phi Psi Castle, if so I will just suggest the story again,—and tell it fully in another letter devoted solely to that, for it is long, unsolved and not uninteresting.

Your second letter shows me that you believe I am in school, but I aint. I got back too late for one thing and I didn't feel up to it for another, and there are also family complications,—the sickness of my younger brother and things financial. However, all is a bit rosier than when I hit home, and I believe everything will turn out fine and bien tranquil.

As to plans, I don't yet know, I am certain that very soon I will start out as you have on the old road of life, which in my case can mean but one thing, writing. It must mean that, win or lose, fail or prosper. But I intend to hit it hard and consistently and go in for the big things, slowly, perhaps, but surely. I have of course no assurance of success, even of ability beyond the outer rim of mediocrity, but I have the urge, the sense of what it is and means, and a certain vague confidence which will grow, I believe, as I grow and work.

I was, as you know, low in spirits and confidence over there at times, but I broke that and the victory was sweet. I grew up, at least, and became a man, oh, much more of a man than ever your erratic and youthful but willing dreamer of a Jamie ever was. I'm not saying I'm anything fine. I'm not. It's still a fight to down certain weaknesses, but an easier fight. I am more sure of myself, older, wiser and I've felt the bumps out there beyond the border of the campus, in the center of the cruel old world, damn her, sweet and beautiful always, too!

But the course is yet incompleted. I've much to learn, much steadiness and stability to gain. . . . Certainly I am not the ineffectual boy of Washington days. It's hard to recall them, but I was just a boy then. Minnette is next to you a wonder at understanding. I don't believe you know how good at it she is. If not, believe me, she has a quick sense for values and a sure finger for the right spot, be it strength or weakness. . . .

Which means that pure sentimentalism prevailed for the past few hours after being with her. Even then, tho, I subconsciously knew that I would have had it no other way, that with her there could never have been, first, love, or even passion, that I realized in Paris it was,—our affair,—as far as love goes,—a thing of May dances, College days and June nights. I believe she knows that she also felt that way when I was gone. The factor that threw me off, that lay behind my plaint to you—was merely the mistake I made of trying to stretch—or narrow—a wonderful friendship to cover an impossible love affair. I see now, —I saw immediately that ours is a fine friendship,—a thing of understanding, sympathy and perfect communion,—and in a boy's way, at first contact,—it seemed she should have been the One. It wouldn't have been a failure as a marriage, rather a great success,—but while we would have builded always a completer perfection of life and helpfulness and content, there would surely ever have been the worst lack of all,—love and the basis for love of the sort that surpasses reason, successful mating, eugenics of intellect or what-not. I will venture the venture to you that even she was a trifle erratic and youthful just after our first meeting. I will venture that though she too had reasoned it out and seen it clearly and sanely, the sudden sweeping of everything in our past and present and possible future into that meeting, each uncertain of the others attitude, left her for the time flustered and out of mental breath. To see the sense of this, realize that for a certain while in 1918 we called each other beautiful titles and had an air of letting the rest of the world go by. And never quite will certain memories leave either of us,—they may dim or grow fearfully bright still in this life—who knows,—but that will merely be the trickery and magic of distance, time and what-might-have been, the three most romantic things in life—and what soul is cold enough or sensible enough, to present always a duck's-back armor to their occasional cascade? Dites-moi!

But "People" will never have the chance to "talk". For if ever there was a safe, a fine friendship in dangerous waters, it is mine and hers. Why, we would always do the Henry James thing—the Strether thing—playing souls against hearts,—reason against emotion, no matter what the ache, and who knows what situation the tragicaster time may yet have up his sleeve, and cackling over?

In our second talk we walked about the campus. The dialogue was good. Nugey, it isn't easy to let convention take such a dolly dialoguer out of one's life. It isn't terribly comforting to feel that I know her better than anyone else does, —that our plane is a thing Tommy Meek, Carl Finn and any other never reached, nor even to feel that, with any other girl there can not for a long time be the same plane built up for me, and to wonder what plane, maybe, I must compromise on.

Somehow when Minnette and I are together we walk at once into the cool places of H. James' old churches, or into the clever, clear gardens of his best communions. There is an art and a peace in the thing that I feel like a tangible and exceedingly fine thing. And she does, too. She counts me her Great Friend, —of my sex—I count her my Great Friend of her sex. She said suddenly "Jim, you'll be coming to talk with me when we're sixty!" A lot of it is in that sudden sentence. Damn it all, we "get" each other and by each successive "get" there is an increased sense of a fine proportion in things. I leave her with horizons raised and doors opened. And with each successive time, all idea of love or marriage fades. It simply isn't there. I think, even, we take glad breaths at what we found by losing all the impossible things that hampered us, and we sigh because "People" would say we cant leave our cake uneaten and still have it. And, of course, we cant. To have her companionship it would mean marriage, the way things are done. Now do you see her sudden leap ahead to sixty? It's quite the thing old Henry would have a Maria Gostrey call "ah, wonderful!" But enough of this, except to say that the original basis we built up in Washington letters, Joey Taylor references, and much in-between-time thought. It was always there, only what a hell of a time we had keeping it in those parlous days of pretty titles!

Anyway, I'll never know the right answer to sex and marriage, sense and mirage. Will you, old dear?

And so, naturally, to Eva. And already my firm intention of telling you my "plans" is side-tracked. But this is necessary, too, and I better get it out of sight down the right of way first.

Eva, the Girl of Dreams,—the perfect foil for the other girl, this one of reason and H. James and all. Eva, the Girl I felt I would love, awfully, and without any cause or any need of cause, without any thought about communion, understanding or reason. The Girl heroine of movie stories, and "Prince Chap" plays and pipe-dreams, the girl one's heart yearns for and the devil take Joey Taylor's neat philosophy and H. James' cool churches! The girl of Browning gondolas, of Lee Robert's songs, of Douglas Fairbanks fifth reels and of Harold McGrath's novels. The one, after all, we marry.

And now, the mood of my other letter gone, and looking at the canvas from the middle of the room, I can deal with her fairly, too. Letters and thoughts since seeing her have done wonders. I love her, always have, always will. I loved her when I saw her. There were the "rapid heart-beats" and all. I sat and stared at her as I never sat and stared at anyone. I didn't give one damn at first about talking. I didn't know what I said or what she said. It's simply when I snap out of that into the other and opposite tete-a-tete that I wonder and think and write lots to you.

I don't know what it is, or was to begin with, but there was the same sensation after eleven years that I had when, as a kid, I told her good-bye, pulled my cap to pieces, and felt an ache and an urge in my heart too old for my years, but too eternal and atavistically strong ever to be classed as "puppy love" or any other thing. She was the One Girl. And I felt it again, that unexplainable thing. When sitting opposite her, after dinner in her home, we were for the first time solidly alone. I wanted her. That's all. And I always will, and I have the courage of that fine "want". I have the faith of it. Oh, man, it's bound to be good. I see quickly, and she is fine,—she has depths, she has poise and sense, cleverness and stability and all. And, from her letters since then, I have great hopes.

There is a handsome Beta with a D.S.C. I mean there was one. My letters—which is me—ruined him. And, god help her, she likes me in person! Now what do you think of that? Why darn it all, the finest letter she wrote to me in all of the time was one she sent after she had seen a recent picture of me. That letter I answered November 28th.—my first letter to her since April 20th. She answered my "explanation letter" so that I got it February 6th. I sailed February 14th. But thats just a part of the past dates play. Furthermore, her first letter after my visit was all the old ones were and more too, and today's letter from her is more yet. And mine are too. I give myself credit for a lot of sense, yet, and restraint, but the Lord knows I've been reticent and long-circuited so many years!

She is coming here a week from to-day for the Follies—and as she put it in today's letter—"to see you and the Follies". Step down, brother Ziegfeld!

Now, with a handsome Beta out of it,—doubtlessly a perfect foil for me—a direct opposite in all ways—isn't it a nice story?

I'll finish this tomorrow. It's 12.30 and a part of my program is early to bed for a while.

Well, up again, old kid, and immediately after the hypophosphites and the lunch, I begin on you again. And since it is no longer night, but practical day, I'll speak now of plans.

Very greatly I want to go back one more year to school, for the express purpose of amassing knowledge on certain courses, and with the determined intention of letting much of the rest of the campus world ride past.

After that—well, it will then be square up to me to say, finally, "hello, world." Meanwhile, I am going to rent a nice Underwood and try out a few things, while I am getting over the remnants of nerve-fog and physical near-wreck. After that I will have to take on something inconsequential but with money in it for the summer, and maybe, if the Purple Gods rule or if Saturn is in Taurus,—or what ever does it—maybe for longer with the necessity also of giving up graduation, —which of course I can do with no terrible blow to me or my career.

Somehow I can't accomplish much here at home, since never have my folks understood me, altho' they have always sympathized and helped wonderfully....

Unshakably yours,

Jim

There is no question that Thurber was being overwhelmed by the rarefied, convoluted influence of Henry James. He had long fancied himself as a finely wrought, hypersensitive Jamesian character caught up in a difficult, immoral world, but now—disjointed, finding contradiction at every turn, still torn between loves—he used James as the premise for colossal rationalization. In another outpouring to Nugent, written just ten days later, he managed to entangle himself even more in a Jamesian web, but he cleverly used Jamesian logic as a noble means of escape:

April fourth
1 9 2 0

My dear Old, better 'old, gold Nugget:

... Have I mentioned to you that Henry James has now become my greatest enthusiasm along lines literary? He always was a big card with me, especially in Joe Taylor days, but I cultivated him extensively in Paris, becoming possibly the world's greatest authority on "The Ambassadors" which I bought over there for $5 in the N.Y. Edition and perused many times with increased interest, since I was right amongst his places and in the atmosphere, and no one can enjoy it to the farthest ultimate who does not know Notre Dame, Le Tour D'Argent and the Boulevard Malsherbes. Perhaps it is my deep interest in him and his art and his philosophy and his orientation which makes the M.Y.F.P attraction never the less, for she not only can talk him with me but she has always appealed to me as having many of the elements of his ladies, tho' I quite concur in your earlier statement that she is not a Madame de Vionnet and never will be. Still I can't help but know that she has a—what I might call—"depth of charm" and a scope of manner and a princess quality of bearing and a poise and reserve in dialogue which is so far above the average American girl of these twelve cylinder, jazzomarimba days that it is refreshing like the drift of May roses across a base-ball field. (If anyone should ever wish to compile my letters after I am famously dead, and should call upon you to furnish the most of them and of me, I fear you would have to censor and expurgate with a free wrist movement) In order to keep a certain tendency to campus brief style out of this letter I will have to stick to one subject till it is written out, or I will be fade-outing and cut-backing like a Griffith fillum run sideways thru a magic lantern. Therefore I will get the Girl element first off my mind, tho' it remain forever on my shoulders.

The day before Spring Vacation began I called Minnette and we met at Lazurus where she went shopping, and there was a most interesting two hours in the nice lil Tea Room on the Fifth. There was between us, besides the fine understanding, a flat cut glass dish of sweet peas, my favorite flowers. The orchestra was playing things from a few of my favorite operas "Manon", "Boheme" and "Lakme." It was really nice. Then we walked up to Long and High to get a car and one not being there we kept on walking. When we next looked up, we were ten steps from Hennicks and I was in two street car tickets. She left the next day for Chicago and Hubby. Have I yet flung diatribes at you anent the Fish? The Fish as you know are the riff-raff, the hoi-polloi, the 5500 of the 7000 at State, the 200,000 of the 200 and odd thousand in Columbus, sometimes known in an anti-Kipling sense, as "They" or more popularly called "People". Having gone to France an aristocratic democrat and returning a democratic aristocrat I have lost none of my antipathy,—it's even stronger. The connection is, I fear the Fish. I mean I am afraid I must forego further beautiful talks with the Minnette,—for her sake. They dont talk yet, but I'm so gosh damned sure they will.

Friday, three days after Minnette left, Eve o' Zanesville came down for the Follies avec sa famille, and I had her and her wondrously good looking mamma out to my home, where she met the family of Thurber. Eve and I had but a very few minutes together this second time, not enough to make any progress towards knowing each other than before. It will take so many visits to establish a basis. One of the changes in me since 1918 is that at that time I didn't give a damn, in her especial case, for a basis. Moonlight and Honeysuckle was all I wanted—with her. Now it is different. I want the biggest basis of all. Whether it is there or not I dont know. But I think there is a basis for a basis. I have found this out that Eve never in her life bumped up against or associated with a personality just like mine or with a man of my interests and enthusiasms and my change of gait. I know that she is a bit puzzled, vastly interested, in a way fascinated and most of all half-eager and half-afraid about her own ability to find my plane. It is, as I say, a new field altogether for her, for she never went to college, has no idea then of that life, and about all we have at the start in common is I believe a mutual interest from some unknown source and a common playground in an affection for things of the stage. She still yearns for the stage a bit, but the call of home and happiness is strong too,—she is balancing between the little comforts of folks in Zanesville and the call of the New York existence. That she has talent I am positive,—in fact I have told you that she got as far as a principal at the Winter Garden five years ago and the offer of a contract with Roscoe Arbuckle in the movies, and that she left everything then at its peak and went to Zanesville to recuperate from nerves and has been there ever since. I forgot to tell you that in her book of autographs there is one written by your father,—or I guess I did tell you that.

Another thing, she is evidently not very strong, and her nerves seem to be mated with mine in many ways, which is a discomforting reflection. I have fine reason to believe that she hates the idea of marriage because she and her mother have decided it wouldn't do for her to have babies,—that is, an uncanny seventh sense of mine tells me that—but I am sure that she loves the lil things, les cheres enfants,—just as I do; but you see I myself had arrived at the determination never to bring any children into this old vale to inherit the Thurber nervousness which is sure constitutional if anything ever was, the three of us brothers having had a double heritage of it, and before I believed Eva felt that way I had decided that I would never marry either, if the girl did want children; so I suppose after all this phase is what you might call "everything coming out all right",—I suppose you might, but it seems a form of hard lines or something like that.

However, here I am living in the cottage and everything and we may never get that far at all. In fact I met a girl at Wurlitzer's Victrola store to-day who hasn't faded yet, but may to-morrow morning, and then I ran into Marion Poppen on Broad Street today, she all bodiced up with a corsage of sweet peas. You never knew I long had a silent case on her, did you, in days when she seemed to be engaged to a ChiPhi?

There is no use in denying that, after all, this Eva girl is *not* the girl of all my dreams, that I really did manage through the years to build up a glittering image based upon a pretty little Bob-haired girl, an image which was so wonderful that she couldn't, I suppose, live up to it. And since she couldn't, there is still what Henry J. would call a "drop", something big has gone out of my life. Maybe after a while something bigger will take its place, but the little princess of mine who played about willow trees on Yarrow is still there. I have never found her,

I never will. There's something in this story of mine that would have delighted old Henry who loved to play with psychological and social and imaginative difficulties. And he would have seen in it as you do something higher than emotionalism and stronger than fancy and sincerer than sentimentalism, something rather wonderful and big. He was a connoisseur of special cases,—the things that happen to most of his "poor, sensitive gentlemen" could not have happened to more than one in a million,—take his collection including "The Jolly Corner" "The Friends of the Friends" "The Altar of the Dead" the "Beast in the Jungle",—frail, too greatly attenuated too impossible the average person would say in some disgust, but of a pure type with mine, in uniqueness of experience and quality of thought. I wont let it take up all of my life or warp my perspectives, but It must always be bigger to me than most things, I am formed not to be able to let career or business become more to me than friendship and love. I am, I am proud and at once miserable to say, a follower after the great God James. I mean Henry James. Funny, before him, before I knew him my greatest most personal interest was in Edith Wharton who is admittedly a sitter at his feet and is nearest like him than any other writer alive or dead and gone. It was a great discovery to me that she was not the ultimate that I still had before me the exquisite pleasure of the Master. Joe Taylor and I when I saw him at his home had quite a James talk fest, for he is also more for H.J. than for any of the rest. It just means that I am of that particular character and being,—it has more drawbacks and heartbreaks than any other type. Imagine, then, this for a story: a person whom one knows and actually loves at 14 and who then has a nice absence of 12 years. During that time there was never actually one day when I didn't add at least a splinter to the image of what she was growing to be. The thing became finally a real person, more real to me, you know, than most of the actual millions of persons alive. I had much to go on. I will say this, that she hasn't in many ways carried out the promise she had, hasn't become the shining person she had the spark for. As a kid she was beautiful, charming, clever, wonderful. She was the most popular little girl in Columbus, she was sincerely called the Second Elsie Janis, she became so well known that Keiths made the hit of its existence when they billed her above the headliner when she was 14 as a special added attraction. You couldn't see across the mountain of roses that were heaped on the stage. That was what I had to build upon together with an unusual love for her which began some months before she became so well known. Her contralto voice, had it not been ruined by so much singing then, would have been the greatest ever heard in this America. It would have been on a hundred Victor records. The sound of her singing "Slumber Boat", "My Rosary" and "Sing Me To Sleep" will never cease to come to me. At that time I had no stuff at all, myself. There you have the fully capable start. Now the middle.

I built up on those things. It became a deep thing with me. Why, four years ago I could get my heart to rackety-cooing over my fancies. Her letters came along then, and did nothing to lessen the corruscation of light around her name. They had just the charm and repression and a certain peculiar style which added an imaginative fuel.

And then finally I go to see her. She is not so pretty as she was, not so beautiful as I had been sure she would be. She has flashes of aspect that are what she was attitudes that for the moment are my dream,—then they go. For the most consistent part, she isn't the physical Dream, then. Her ability hasn't progressed as I believed it might, as I know it could have. She was radiant. She is appealingly clever now. Her wonderful voice is gone. Why, it's the voice,—even her speaking voice of a total stranger to me. It amazes me. I have dreamed for twelve years of that voice, as it was, a rich, thrilling tone full of pulsating reaches and Ruth Chatterton innuendoes. That is all gone. She has charm and sweetness and poise, as I told you, and a certain note of things broader and deeper than the floss and flatness and shallowness of the average University girl. But she hasn't attained what I felt she would, a colorful depth, a radiant personality. There is just one thing that she has improved in, and idiotically enough, it is the one thing that I kept myself from building castles in the air about,—she is infinitely more "sisterly" more full of a comfy, home-like, rose-garden sort of sweetness than I had ever believed she could be.

There you have most of it. Here's the story, the punch. How could I ever love a girl who fails after all in being the person that I have come to worship as few damn fools have ever had the chance to worship, AND how can I help but love the girl who, whatever else, is after all the girl of the dreams, as little like them tho she may be; isn't she despite everything the Girl; if I gave her up, could I ever see anyone else; wouldn't it resolve itself into a flare-back for good to the dream of a person who isn't? Supposing I found a girl who looked like talked like was like the Dream creation,—everything exactly as I would have it— wouldn't the killing lack there be the fact that she wouldn't be the girl even tho she was the girl? Ha, my dear Watson, I have you cornered! All right, then, how could I live with the real girl who would be the most acute reminder always of what might have been, if I finally decide she isn't as much like any phase as she should be. Damn it, its metaphysical! I can lapse back into my chair, light a skag and picture two Evas as clearly as I can picture two Phi Psis. Maybe you can decipher the dilemna. At least you will see, if you give enough weight to that interim of 12 years of practically unremitting memory, that it is a darn big affair. Here's the best concrete example, set and staged, that I can give you. I had in Zanesville mentioned Minnette to Eve. Recently Minnette has been made one of the eight candidates for May Queen. When Eve was out here she mentioned that fact. I had completely forgot that I ever told her a thing about Minnette. So I said, very surprised, "Why, how did you know about her?" Now, if at that moment she had suddenly said she also knew about Eva, I would have had flash into my mind my Dream Eva, and I would have said "Why how did you know about her?" she is that unlike, some moments. Finis.

I'm not saying she isn't a wonderful little girl. If I had met her for the first time I would have been crazy about her, I think. But she isn't the girl who of all girls has the strongest hold on my heart. So here's the punch for a second story: if she veers into the tack of trying to become that one she'll have just as hard a task as she would by hitting off starboard and becoming so utterly unlike the other, but so fine in her way, that the other one will vanish. Watson, you better try a bit of the cocaine yourself tonight. The End.

Brother, there was a La Boheme meeting a few nights back. There were a few knights back, a few of the old ones. Andrews and Louis of the faculty, McCombs of the gang. Anderson, Phi Psi, is a member and Chamblin is to be taken in. McCombs musical play "Taint So" done for the first Scarlet Mask production was very good. His situations and plot were well done, his lines were poor, the music was fine, there were one or two clever scenes and one or two good musical-comedians.

Carson Blair was in Columbus over Easter and tries to get me to go into advertising work in Detroit where Mully and he are both in that line, with different firms; Carson is making very good with Burroughs. I am still unsettled. I want to go back to state and intend to, if possible, but I have to do something pretty toot de sweet in order to finance things. I don't know what it will be. I have got this typewriter for a month and expect to do something along the Beloved Literary Line in that time—and it helps oil the works to write to you.

Ha, Watson, also I have another great interest in life which I cultivated in Paris: music, good music,—I mean listening to it, not playing a flute or singing a wicked tenor. The family is already being made the more or less unhappy victim of my research for the records of songs I learned to love over there away from Jazz. I never quite got into the spirit of the thing here, despite or because of Billy Graves recommendations, but in Paris I became an opera hound and a concert spaniel. While the world goes along trolling Dardanella and The Sky Blues and Shanghai Mary Sings Dixie Like Mother Macree in Far Off Brazil I hum snatches from famous things. The Dream from Manon, the Musetta Waltz from Boheme, He Will Come Again from Madame Butterfly are a few of 'em, but boy, oh, they can never take the place of Sing Me to Sleep Rose in the Bud and Slumber Boat of the Eva O' Long Ago. You used to sing the Sing Me To Sleep ballad accompanied by the well known uke sometimes on 14th Avenue, bringing the old Eve right into the room with us, but as far away as she sometimes still seems. . . .

Some of the things in literary lines I am working on are: a book for next year's Scarlet Maskeraders,—possibly—; an original sort of Washington Square thing called "The Fourth Mrs. Bluebeard"—the other wife who gypped the Homme de barbe bleu, you know, but who was never written about—she beat him by modern feminine craft. "The Call" which is powerful in my mind, but which will no doubt fail,—a Henry James sort of thing with another special trick of mine as the basis, namely a gift I have at long but awfully vivid intervals of receiving mental telepathy messages from friends or family in trouble. Don't believe I ever told you that trick. It has really worked but five times in my life, one of which I will never tell but which is the most beautiful and complicated of all—and which, damn it, is the basis for my story, so I guess I'll have to do it under a nom de plume. Oddly enough, two of the five instances happened here since I returned, and of them had nothing to do with trouble at all, it was just a freak working. My mother has had the same thing several times. Then I am working on a comedy about a French wife with a new twist—(ps-s-t the story has the twist) an article along the line of "France and America, Last and First Impressions," which no American magazine would print, probably, since my status is about 67 to 33 favor France. And there are minor poems and things. . . .

One way or another, Thurber was tidying up his life. The soul-wrenching quandary of Eva and Minnette, which had plagued him for so long, was suddenly resolved; Minnette went off to Chicago, and Eva, through Thurber's masterful use of Jamesian casuistry, dropped several notches from The One and Only to just another disappointingly homey Ohio girl. (Robert Thurber thought at the time that his brother actually wanted to marry Eva but she spurned him. However, he said that "Jamie never really confided in me about those personal things. He only confided in Elliott Nugent.") Minnette married someone else in Chicago, and Thurber never saw her again, thus silencing forever the feared tongues of the "riff-raff" (a dismal Jamesian excuse, if there ever was one). As for Eva Prout—the girl who probably set an all-time record for abject adoration by one boy–man—she gave up all hope for a renascent theatrical career and took a job as a waitress in a small Ohio town. On one of Thurber's later trips to Columbus, he found out where she was working and stopped by the restaurant to visit with her. "It was a very stilted meeting," Helen Thurber, who was along, recalled. "They had nothing to say to each other. I believe Eva ended up working in a music store in Florida." Still, his searing idolization of Eva stayed with Thurber for a long time. In one of his rare straight short stories, "Menaces in May," written in 1928, he modelled the old-sweetheart-married-to-a-dullard character after his one-time One, Eva Prout. And he always had a weakness for ladies of the stage.

His romantic problems tempered for the moment, Thurber settled down to his rented typewriter and tried to write. He had gravitated towards the small theatrical clique at O.S.U., particularly his old outfit, The Strollers, and a new group called the Scarlet Mask Club, which put on hairy-leg revues in the Hasty Pudding tradition. Two of Thurber's college friends were authors of the first Scarlet Mask production, *Taint So*, in the spring of 1920—Ralph McCombs and Thomas Meek. "I was *the* founder," McCombs said, "but then I went to New York, and Thurber took over. The following year, he helped write *Oh My, Omar!* I would come back to Columbus from time to time and sit in at rehearsals on the campus—our performances were in a rented theatre downtown—and I'd help out. As a lyricist and book writer, Jim was talented, but I wouldn't have said he would ever make it in real show business."

Thurber's plans for musical books on the fourth Mrs. Bluebeard and a Jamesian mental-telepathy idea were junked in favor of *Oh My, Omar!*, which was produced in early 1921. There was no reason to be struck by the talent displayed in *Oh My, Omar!*—an opus having something to do with Omar Khayyam reappearing in the Jazz Age amid an olio of flapper and Oriental numbers. The other four Scarlet Mask productions Thurber had a hand in showed just slight improvement.

More important than his theatrical dabbling uptown at the O.S.U. campus was the pressure of making a living. Thurber was, after all, in his mid-twenties and was still living with his parents. Whatever he had saved from his code-clerk salary had gone into the family coffers and quickly out again. In the summer of 1920, he found a stopgap position as a clerk in the Ohio Department of Agriculture. Once again, he was able to earn money only as a clerk. Even more discouraging was his extra assignment as a ticket-taker at State Fair side shows. While he flirted with amateur theatre and considered the possibility of reentering Ohio State in the fall, he applied for openings in the more practical vocation of newspaper work. In August, he was hired as an apprentice reporter by the Columbus *Dispatch*—a daily owned by the Wolfe family, an aptly named clan which also owned a great deal of the rest of Columbus—for twenty-five dollars a week.

As a cub general-assignment legman, Thurber had severely mixed feelings about his work. He was getting paid for using words, not just shuffling papers, and that was to the good; but there was excruciating tedium in the restrictions of hard-news writing and assignments, especially for a young writer whose head was bursting with Jamesian allusions and prose flights. The harsh enforcer of these restrictions was the *Dispatch*'s city editor, Norman "Gus" Kuehner, an untutored ox of a former police reporter who could easily have been Hecht and MacArthur's model for *The Front Page*. Kuehner was the sort of city editor who ate cub reporters for breakfast, particularly one-eyed, gangling, easily distracted, educated cubs. Thurber was terrified of "the drunken s.o.b." (as Ralph McCombs, who later worked on the rival *Ohio State Journal*, called Kuehner) and also in awe of him. Decades afterwards, Thurber devoted a whole chapter in *The Thurber Album*, entitled

"Newspaperman—Head and Shoulders," to Kuehner and claimed he actually found some warmth and kindness in the man, besides the hard editorial talent. He told of the fear the city editor still evoked in him:

. . . In one of my own recurring dreams, I am pounding away at a story I can't handle, because my notes are illegible and the type bars make no marks at all on the gray copy paper. The hands of the clock on the east wall of the city room, facing the reporters' desks, are frozen at a quarter after one, fifteen minutes past deadline, and there is a large, amorphous figure just over my right shoulder, standing there gloomily, saying nothing—the ghost of Norman Kuehner . . .

Given the new-boy treatment by Kuehner during his first few weeks on the job—totally ignored or overworked or taunted with the epithet "Phi Beta Kappa" (based on Thurber's academic mien, not his academic achievement)—the awkward cub finally made the grade with his city editor by garnering a photograph of a drowned boy, after the best police reporter on the staff had failed. Instead of wheedling or stealing a snapshot from the dead boy's family (in the hallowed journalistic practice), Thurber used his good brain and legally obtained a picture from the boy's high-school yearbook, which was available to the public. Kuehner was undemonstrably impressed and he promoted Thurber to political reporter on the City Hall beat. He also stopped calling him "Phi Beta Kappa" and started calling him "Author." He had heard of Thurber's writing ambitions.

In "Memoirs of a Drudge," an exaggerated 1942 answer to the labelling of Thurber's newspaper work as "drudgery" (by Walter Blair in his book *Horse Sense in American Humor*), Thurber described his City Hall sinecure with the tough nostalgia of most ex-reporters:

. . . [the] city editor seldom knew where I was and got so that he didn't care. He had a glimpse of me every day at 9 A.M., arriving at the office, and promptly at ten he saw me leave it, a sheaf of folded copy paper in my pocket and a look of enterprise in my eye. I was on my way to Marzetti's, a comfortable restaurant just down the street, where a group of us newspapermen met every morning. We would sit around for an hour, drinking coffee, telling stories, drawing pictures on the tablecloth, and giving imitations of the more eminent Ohio political figures of the day, many of whom fanned their soup with their hats but had enough good, old-fashioned horse sense to realize that a proposal to shift the clocks of the state from Central to Eastern standard time was directly contrary to the will of the Lord God Almighty and that the supporters of the project would burn in hell.

After this relaxing and often stimulating interlude I would stroll out to the Carnegie Library and read the New York *World* in the periodical room. It so happened that the city offices, which I was assigned to cover, were housed at that time in the library building, the old City Hall having burned down the first night I ever attended a council meeting in it. After I had put the *World* back on its rack, only a little fragment of forenoon remained in which to gather the news, but I somehow managed the aggravating chore.

Nor were the city offices dull and colorless places. Secretary Killam of the Civil Service Commission had a tuba, on which I learned to play a few notes, an exciting and satisfying experience, as anyone who has brought forth a blast from a tuba knows. The lady dance-hall inspector was full of stories of the goings on in the more dubious clubs about town, in one of which, she reported, the boys and girls contrived to two-step without moving their feet. And the Mayor's office was frequently besieged by diverting and passionate taxpayers: an elderly gentleman who could get KDKA on the steel rims of his spectacles, a woman who was warned of the approach of earthquakes by a sharp twinge in her left side, and a lady to whom it had been revealed in a vision that the new O'Shaughnessy storage dam had not been constructed of concrete but of Cream of Wheat . . .

It all sounds pleasant enough, the way Thurber described it more than twenty years later, but he privately admitted that he was bored silly by the City Hall beat. He had seen too much of politics and politicians as a boy, and he was weary of the whole business, except as a source of funny anecdotal material. Still, the City Hall fire was a big Columbus story, and Thurber got the scoop on it. He was covering a City Council meeting, when a fireman poked his head in the door and shouted, "Hey, you guys, get out of here! The building's on fire!" Thurber persuaded the *Dispatch* to put out an extra built around his lucid eye-witness story, written from memory without notes. He received a five-dollar-a-week raise for his efforts and a lot of kidding from Kuehner, who discovered that Author had only managed to save from the flames somebody's overcoat, a watch, and some old blueprints, all easily replaceable items. Kuehner, insistently, wanted to know why Author didn't bother to rescue any used carbon paper or thumbtacks, while he was about it.

Thurber's relationship with Kuehner nevertheless improved after the fire scoop. They were at odds over Thurber's news-writing style, but Kuehner developed a certain respect for his sense of accuracy and vocabulary. Ruth Young White, an advice-to-the-lovelorn writer on the *Dispatch* in the early 1920's as well as a former East High School and O.S.U. classmate, remembered a "running battle" between the two of them. "Norman Kuehner knew that Thurber was different and a good writer," she said, "but he just thought that he ought to write less flamboyantly for the news stories. We all knew that Thurber was better than we were. He really developed as a friendly person, I think, on the *Dispatch.*"(2) Thurber may have been bored with his prosaic duties, but his pride in good reporting for the newspaper—in fact, for all journals —stuck with him throughout his career. In 1951, he wrote Harold Ross (the other strong editor in his life and spookily similar to Kuehner in many ways) about that old newsman's pride of his. "For three years," Thurber boasted, "I was the tough Gus Kuehner's top boy."(3)

Gus Kuehner's top boy got his next big journalistic break also as a result of being a City Hall reporter. He and two other City Hall men from the *Journal* and the *Citizen* were invited to the first open-air meeting and cross-burning by the Ku Klux Klan ever held in Columbus, a city mightily moved by D. W. Griffith's *The Birth of a Nation.* The three were blindfolded, put in a Packard limousine, and driven circuitously through the city to the secret meeting grounds. (They all knew exactly where they were driving at any given moment by the pattern of sounds the car made over familiar roads.) It was an exciting and illuminating evening for Thurber, his first real brush with native Fascism, and it would have made a superb story for him to publish. However, an editor higher than Kuehner cut Thurber's vivid two columns on the event down to an emasculated paragraph, with the explanation that the discreet thing would be to see how the people of Columbus felt about the Klan before honestly reporting its activities. Thurber was furious, especially when the *Journal* printed a full, unstinting account of the meeting the next day. The *Journal* was, of course, edited by Robert O. Ryder, the paragraphing master, "who never in his life waited to see which way anyone was going to jump before he made up his own mind."(4) Thurber dearly wanted to be working for Ryder from that moment on.

But he stuck doggedly, if unhappily, to the *Dispatch* because he was receiving more interesting assignments. He interviewed his boyhood friend, Donald Ogden Stewart, who was visiting Columbus after making something of a splash as a humorist with his book, *A Parody Outline of History*—a splash, by the way, that dampened an envious Jim Thurber. (They buttressed their old friendship, however, with some Prohibition hooch and attendant singing during the interview.) He also covered the opening of the new James Theatre and the Ohio Stadium, and he paragraphed a bit on the *Dispatch* editorial page. He was even sent to New York in 1921 to review plays and write feature stories on such figures as Al Jolson, Zoë Akins, and the Nugents, *père et fils,* who were making it big back East.* "BROWSING ABOUT BROADWAY: DIS-PATCH STAFF MAN WRITES IMPRESSIONS OF 'DULCY,' 'THE HERO' AND THE DRAMATIZED 'MAIN STREET' " ran a Sunday *Dispatch* headline. Another read: "DOING WHITE WAY WITH OLD MISTER BAEDEKER HIM-SELF." Clearly, Thurber, too, was making it, but only within the city limits of Columbus, Ohio.

Although he was still living with his parents (the expedient thing to do on a salary of thirty dollars a week), Thurber had several homes away from home, where he could relax and discuss something more profound than Hank Gowdy's batting average or the latest proverb contest. They were the Scarlet Mask Club and The Strollers on the O.S.U. campus, the Phi Psi house (though the joy of the brothers' company was beginning to pall, since Thurber was by then the old man of the fraternity), Mar-zetti's and its professional badinage, and a bohemian salon—a photogra-pher's studio near the *Dispatch* offices where the more aesthetic writ-ers of Columbus, usually frustrated newspapermen, did their serious drinking and talking. It was in the salon that Thurber met John Augus-tine McNulty.

. . . McNulty was a widely experienced newspaperman at twenty-five, when he arrived in Columbus from the East, to work for the *Ohio State Journal* at sixty dollars a week, higher pay than any reporter in town had been getting. I have forgotten, if I ever knew, what whim or compulsion had sent him into the Middle West. It was probably an impulse peculiar to his volatile spirit, such as that which sent him one day, years later, to New Iberia, Louisiana, to visit the tabasco factory there. In Columbus he lingered for a dozen years. Before the first of these had passed he knew more people in the city than I did, although I had been born and brought up there . . .(5)

That was how Thurber, discreet as he could be, described McNulty's arrival in Columbus in 1921 (from the vantage point of 1957, in an appreciation of the deceased author of *The World of John McNulty*). Actually, according to McNulty's second wife, Faith McNulty Martin,† John McNulty loved to tell the story on himself of how he met Thurber in Columbus. After he recovered from wounds received in World War

---

*While in New York, Thurber not only interviewed Nugent but stood by him and his bride, Norma, as best man at a quick pre-matinée marriage ceremony. Nugent was in the play *Dulcy* and wowed Thurber by not missing a performance for a mere nuptial event.

†Thurber introduced McNulty to a Columbus girl named Donia, who became the first Mrs. McNulty.

I, the son of an Irish storekeeper from Lawrence, Massachusetts, worked for the Associated Press and several newspapers in New York. He rapidly gained a reputation as a crackerjack reporter, an unorthodox wit, a temperamental employee, and an intemperate drinker. Even with a brutal hangover, McNulty could write faster and better than most clear-brained newspapermen, but, still, he exhausted within a couple of years all the employment opportunities in the Big Apple. He was fired from the A.P. for picking up a typewriter and heaving it across the city room, and he was dismissed from one of the papers for refusing to write, for the ninetieth time, a heartwarming story about a barking dog saving a family of ten in a burning house. He was out of work and broke in 1921, when some of his more devoted saloon friends thought it would be a good idea if he cleared his head out of town for a while. They telegraphed the *Ohio State Journal* that an esteemed New York reporter was willing to spend a brief period in Columbus, and the *Journal* took the bait. McNulty's pals bought him a train ticket, had his suit pressed, and supplied him with a pack of Sweet Caporals, but they gave him no money, in order to insure his timely arrival in Columbus. He lit his last Sweet Cap as he sauntered into the *Journal* city room, trying to look like a pro New York newspaperman. He was hired, and soon thereafter he met Thurber at the salon. McNulty was fond of telling, years later, how Thurber was awed by this shining specimen of cosmopolitanism. "Jimmy thought I was a big guy," Faith McNulty remembered her husband saying, "just because I'd been in New York. He never stopped to think that if I was so great in New York, what the hell was I doing out in Columbus, Ohio!"

But McNulty turned out to be much more to Thurber than just a romantic version of the big-time, hard-drinking newspaperman with a larky view of life. He had that practically nonexistent quality, an original, literate sense of humor—something that immediately endeared him to Thurber as a soul mate and drinking companion. One form of McNulty's wit that especially attracted Thurber was his impromptu use of the wild generalization with the mote of truth to it: "Only people with Vincent for a middle name write about leprechauns" . . . "Girls named Dolores become hairdressers" . . . "All watch repairers are named Schneider" . . . "All ranchers' cats are named Pete."(6) Another McNulty favorite was the pointed, well-acted practical joke and/or hoax, which, after all, was in the Thurber family tradition. For instance, he would arrange to have Thurber approach him on a crowded street, with Thurber pretending to be a Ku Klux Klan recruiter and muttering maniacally all the while. They also delighted together in inventing words that filled great gaps in the English language—like "passevante," which they coined to mean the little sidestep and skip one performs when entering a revolving door that has revolved a bit too far.

McNulty was the proverbial ray of sunshine for Thurber in overcast Columbus. He made the town possible for him, and, as Helen Thurber said, "It was a great day for Jamie when McNulty became his friend." McNulty, too, was a lover of words and writing and people and fun, and they both hungrily shared these loves. They drank and whored and cavorted and argued about Columbus together. It was all a barrel of laughs for a while. Thurber had found a strong replacement for his distant confidant, Elliott Nugent.

Within the tight little Columbus intellectual community, Thurber made yet another lasting and profound friendship, with Herman Miller. Miller had known Thurber slightly when they were both undergraduates at Ohio State, but it wasn't until 1921 that they became firm friends, mainly through the auspices of The Strollers. He was a moody, unconventional English instructor and playwright–actor *manqué* at O.S.U., whose alcohol-inspired wisecracks won him something of a reputation around town—good with a few faculty members and Thurber, bad with all the other faculty members and the rest of Columbus. (A close friend of Thurber and an acquaintance of Miller, F. R. Ted Gardiner, said, "I never knew what Jim saw in Miller. He was usually such a rude, unpleasant intellectual.") It was their intellectual communion, particularly in the works of Henry James, that made them close, so close, in fact, that Thurber later took the rare step of dedicating two of his books to Miller and often referred to him as "my oldest and in so many ways my closest friend."(7) Besides their common intellectual and literary ground, they both appreciated good liquor, spontaneous wit, and the finely performed anecdote. "Herman always told his stories standing up, just like Jamie did," Helen Thurber recalled. "They both were perfectionists. When we visited Columbus after we were married, we always had to see Herman and his wife, Dorothy—especially for dinner, which Herman loved to cook. I was fond of Herman but I also found him tiresome when he was drunk. Jamie thought he had more potential as a playwright than I did. He helped him out with money—Jamie helped *everybody* out with money—and even considered making a play of *The Ambassadors* with him. It didn't work out."

Thurber was the senior triple-threat man of The Strollers. He wrote, directed, and acted in their productions. *Psychomania,* a one-act spoof of the Freud craze of the day (a satirical subject that was to occupy Thurber, in one form or another, for decades), was his only known original contribution to the student acting group's repertoire. Unfortunately (or perhaps fortunately), there is no known manuscript of *Psychomania* in existence, nor did anybody remember much about it except Herman Miller, who wrote in the Columbus *Citizen*, on December 1, 1940, that at the single performance of the play (during Christmas, 1922), one of the cast members froze. Thurber and Miller, working in relays, sandwiched in the stricken actor's lines with their own, which, of course, ruined the performance but cemented their friendship. "That friendship," Miller went on, "nurtured by a love of the same books, of nightlong talks, and of Roquefort cheese with a bottle of milk, has persisted these many years."

So out of Thurber's involvement with Columbus's mini-bohemia came two deep friendships. Out of the same tiny world came Althea Adams.

CHAPTER 7

The First Mrs. Thurber

Althea Adams was, in 1922, twenty-one years old and a striking, bright student at Ohio State University. She had not been raised in Ohio. Her father was an Army doctor, stationed for the most part in Hawaii and California, where she had spent her childhood; when he died, her mother, Mrs. Maude G. Adams, brought Althea to Columbus to live with an uncle who was the dean of the O.S.U. Law School. Mrs. Adams took a job as a home-economics instructor at the university, and Althea matriculated in 1918, the year Thurber left college. From her first appearance on campus, she was a center of attention. Five-feet-nine-inches tall, large-boned, dark-haired, with a handsome, unconventional face, Althea was rushed by every available sorority and almost every available male. (Some of the boys, however, liked to joke about her height and heft.) She chose Kappa Kappa Gamma, to which Minnette Fritts belonged, and, also like Minnette Fritts, she tended to play the field of young men. Enormously popular and active in dramatics, she (and, again, Minnette Fritts) was listed by the Ohio State yearbook, the *Makio,* as one of 1918's nine "Rosebuds" of "The Rosebush"—the result of an election by the student body honoring those young O.S.U. women whose attitude "helped make the Ohio of today" and whose "brightness, fairness and willingness to help others . . ." and "womanliness" were outstanding. In 1921, she was chosen as one of eight "Magic Mirror" girls, a signal recognition for feminine beauty and poise, and she was further rewarded with a tinted, full-page photograph in the *Makio.*

James G. Thurber, now keenly aware of the more practical aspects of female companionship, noticed the photograph in the yearbook and decided that he was going to marry Althea Adams. He sought her out at The Stroller rehearsals and at the literary salon in the photographer's studio, where she was brought around one day. On May 20, 1922—to the utter amazement of just about everybody in town—they were married in an Episcopal ceremony at the fashionable Trinity Church in downtown Columbus.

Ralph McCombs, a salon regular once he had returned to Columbus, was one of their acquaintances most astounded by their swift courtship and marriage. He saw it plainly as a case of a boy from the wrong side of the tracks marrying up. "She seemed to me to be the most unattainable woman," McCombs said. "She was aloof, attractive, ambitious, worldly, and very social—all the things Jim wasn't, particularly. About all that I could see they had in common was a lack of money. And their height, of course." Thomas Meek, another friend and a collaborator with Thurber in Scarlet Mask productions, said, "As I remember it, Jim had a project going to conquer Althea, which was quite a project since she was an Amazonian woman, both physically and mentally. I considered it remarkable that he finally captured her. A lot of us sat around thunderstruck, trying to figure out how he did it. They both had a passion for dogs. That was one thing, maybe."

Robert Thurber took a rather different view of the match. "Althea was the one who grabbed Jamie," he said. "She was the domineering type, bossy and pushy, always wanting her own way. She hooked him, sure as anything. Why? I guess she saw something in him that was different from the others. She saw his possibilities. Her mother, the teacher, was a nice woman, but her father was supposed to be a strict Army man. I think she got her disposition from him. Why Jamie married her, I'll never know. She was pretty, all right, but not in a feminine way, and she was intelligent, but no great brain. I didn't care for her much."

Nor she for him—nor for the whole Thurber family, as it turned out. Thurber, with characteristic secretiveness in his personal affairs, didn't tell the people he was living with of Althea Adams's existence until a month before the wedding, and then it was to announce their engagement. "The first time I ever spoke to her," Robert said, "was just before they were married. She telephoned our house and demanded to know where Jamie was. He wasn't home, and I told her so. She just hung up. No thank-you's, nothing. We could never make any criticism of Althea to Jamie. He just wouldn't listen to it." Robert was more or less chronically ill, and Althea told him bluntly that he was just a hypochondriac. She considered Thurber's other brother, William, who was embarking on an expedition into disastrous commercial schemes, as a laughable failure, not unlike his father. But it was Thurber's mother who drew the most contempt from Althea, and vice versa, for they were too much alike for comfort—domineering, aggressive, essential females. They disliked each other from the start. An amalgam of the two of them became, in a very real sense, what was later known to the world as the Thurber Woman. A friend close to both of them said that "Althea, especially, was that forbidding woman in the famous Thurber cartoon who stared menacingly at her little husband and told him, 'I'm getting tired of you throwing your weight around.' "

What most attracted Thurber to Althea was apparent in a prenuptial letter to Elliott Nugent, a tantalizingly happy newlywed and an immense success in his latest play, *Kempy:*

April 4, 1922

Dear Old Neglectee:

. . . I have neglected all my best correspondents and they are not many and of them you stand first, old love. Your vague notion that I might be peeved or something got a color of conviction from my horrible silence, but append this to your notes on Thurber, as I Knew Him: he was a man of singular affection and of love and faith, whose friend could do no wrong or say no evil, who loved and asked to be loved by a few and cared not much what was else. Here let him lie, then, having lived a lovely life. Requiescat in Roses.

Excuses for such neglect as mine cant be made. But I have unaccountable doldrums of the fancy and the will to write. Maybe there's something a tiny bit Freudian in it. I know damn well that's rot, but one must mention Freud. Work, much work which has left me worn at night and in idle hours has been the chief reason. I give you my pledge of much letters hereinafter and with a final genuflection craving your pardon for an unpardonable action, rest my case. May memories of me at my writingest plead sweetly in my behalf.

. . . I should love to have us four meet. Perhaps it would occasion a droll reflection mothered by recollection of a time when four met in May, but I promise you, no irony, no skepticism. Althea has heard more of you than of any other living American she has not met,—and of the charming Elliottess much also. Recently Strollers were given a dinner in the Barn, Columbus' newest and most unique restaurant, to which Althea and I came as the only invitees of the alumni of the gang. Such is our popularity, as who should say. A picture of the group was taken showing me very handsome with the somewhat prettier lady at my side. I wish for the two of you to see the pose and will send a print as soon as I get one made.

Pardon this diversion, but at a banquet given by members of the three Columbus newspapers, Althea was accounted by most the most strikingly beautiful lady in the 60 or more present, which I set down to let you know the Thurber is a nice judge of many things. Thurber, in other words, is the berries, says Thurber. Which is the very latest campus expression. Not only beautiful is she but ravishingly intelligent with characteristics so much like mine in many directions you would of course find her fetching. But this night she was more beautiful than new snow with the light of stars upon it, or than cool flowers in the soft of dawning,—ah, one raves. a new sheet, Watson.

So pretty was she that my managing editor, a man of few words and of less commendation, wended to my desk the next morning to tell me I should be proud indeed, whereupon a nice girl reporter seated near and hearing, observed the Lady Althea was easily the prettiest girl in the room. Watson, this must be the same sheet.

How goes the old married life, youngsters? Papa would crave words relating the beauty of it all, the magic and the wizardry of two lives bound in a single plait. Ah, speak not that it has its bad hours. I firmly believe each moment must be enchantment. Watson, the disillusioner, quick.

She and I are set to kick off the single coils and face a ministerial barrage of nice sounding phrases in October. Money has not flowed in fast enough to warrant a setting nearer of the date yet. But prospects look good. Two weeks ago I got the Columbus correspondence for the justly great Christian Science Monitor of your whilom city. It means a lot in possible prestige and not a little in money since they pay the wonderful rate of 37 and one half cents the inch, or about 8 to 10 dollars a column, and since they use much academic, literary and educational stuff I plot many articles of length. Also, I am set to handle occasional telegraph stories for the Cleveland News Leader, and I have a press agent job for a concert operator who brings Farrar, Rachmaninoff and others to this God forsaken place to cudgel what passes for the artistic sense of the benighted heathen. That will mean 300 rocks for little effort over a period of two or three moons. I am, as usual, also, planning writing free-lance stories whenever I get set to it. Many droll stories, rich in the salt of American existence and bright in the coloring of our little scene crowd the chancel rail of the mind asking for holy water and once I set my writing mitre on straight and dip my fingers I shall throw it. Look for me in the Century or the Smart Set or the Housemaid's Annual,. I am toying with a story of university and Columbus life introducing a mooncalf of a sort, the thing to be a neat, if possible, parody, but written with every evidence of intense sincerity. Such an one as critics years to come will seek to find the true motive in and the actual purpose, a rather hard task since perhaps it will develop neither.

Last night Althea and I went to Newark* in the cute little Ford coupe the lady of my choice has recently obtained. Her mother is head of the university domestic science school for teachers and supervisors, with a nice income, for two at least, and she decided a Ford should be the starter. They need one.

We visited Curly and his wife, Curly the Davis you know. He married Beatrice Sherwood, a Kappa and Althea's special chum. We had quite a nice evening, or rather night, with little sleep, playing cards till late and afterwards engaging in a spontaneously invented pastime in which one twirls the lids of milk bottles, the paper stoppers, as I believe they are technically called, at a receptacle, the object being to see who could toss in the greatest number, as you might have guessed if you followed me clearly to the receptacle. Curly is working in his father's dairy, which accounts for the stoppers. We had used

---

*A town east of Columbus.

them previously for poker chips. Extraordinary things, milk stoppers, having · undreamed of utilities. We must have tossed seven thousand of them at the receptacle, a waste basket plumped down at an angle on the davenport, and I believe I was leading Curly by about 456 when we quit. It meant early arising to shoot back to Cols in time for work and in fact we didnt make it, the weather being rainy and the way treacherous going. I got to work half an hour late and ran plump into "Man Loses life In Storm, Leaving Widow and Nine Children." It was my task to worm from a heavy minded and wide breasted widow, her eyes rimmed with the redness of much crying, the thin story of their lives, and to line up all nine youngsters in various states of excitement and happiness, for it was all like a circus to them, that the photographer might shoot a flash at them. The raising of the flash above his head, precipitated a riot and it took a new half hour to drape them about the family horsechair sofa again. Its a hard, but interesting life, working for the zest of pathos craving readers.

I shall a tale unfold to you ere long of a plan of mine to return to Europe which I am keeping under the headdress in this burg so that it wont go off prematurely and be ruined. It looks like a million dollars on paper. Briefly, it involves a lad here whose friendship I made a year ago, a wonderful camera man with movie outfit or graflex, and a remarkable nose for news. With his doing the mobile and static end of the pictorial work and me the cut lines and the leaders can you not see a chance to build up a service from the other side which should knock the movie weekly's and the educational films' eyes out? With it I intend to build up a series of letters across too, if all works out. We plan to turn the thing over in mind for a year and then, all being thumbs up, to go across. I know of a thousand opportunities for pictures and stories which have never been touched. This chap's name is Hal Cooley, a truly likable and faithful soul, clever, chocked with a fine sense, full of intelligence and with a go-gettem spirit not to be beaten. He has worked a camera on special assignments for Underwood and Underwood and for the Fox Film Weekly, also he turned a crank at the Selznick Long Island studio for a year. I met him last year when he contrived a local movie here of which I told you and showed you press notices when in New York. Financially it failed, as it must here, but he put out some highly creditable work, as professional as might be. I think with his luck and mine we could occasionally scoop the world over there, thus getting me an undying fame as a sidelight to my undying mediocrity, perhaps, as a writer of note. But toward that latter end I must always yearn and strive and, gloom aside, must someday attain. Every now and then the spark of conviction flares in me and if I weren't so damnably lazy mentally of late I would be hacking away at it now. I really must get to it. You really must urge me with many dear lies and highly festooned implications of merit swung in a sling.

As to any news from this center of population, I must cudgel the old brains. Let me see . . . what has happened you would care to hear in the cases of persons you cared to know?

Ludwig Lewisohn, whom perhaps you knew better than I, has issued a new book called Up Stream, an autobiographical thing in which he takes up Columbus, under a name not that, and the university and subjects the whole scene to a searching north light, revealing with deft satire, much bitter pinking with swords and not a little hurtful truth, the ways of people and things as he saw them here. It is a smashing indictment of what he pleases to call the mental and intellectual vacuity of the region. I have read only quotations in reviews and news stories so far, but suggest we both get the book and chuckle as we see his Menckenian lunges leap past us at everybody else whoever went to school here . . .

My Scarlet Mask play "Many Moons" as I called it went over very well, being called by Billy Graves and others the best yet. It netted me $350. I agree. I was not without a light moment or two when the lines went easily.

I guess that's all.

Forgive, but dont forget. Write right away.

With my very best love to you and the lovely and well-remembered Norma, I promise once again never to do it again. Shrive me this once and make your own delinquency the penalty of a second offense. Then indeed would the lights descend.

Hell,—all is happiness.

Yours for ever and what they call aye,

Jim

Thurber could scarcely contain his swollen pride in having won such a highly desirable and desired young Rosebud of Columbus. He knew she wasn't Mme. de Vionnet nor did he pretend to call her The One and Only (he was getting a trifle old for that sort of talk, anyway), but he insisted for many years thereafter that she was "one of the most beautiful girls in the country."(1) There was no question that she represented a decided improvement over Minnette Fritts, Eva Prout, and the demimondaines of Paris and Columbus. His conquest was more than a half-blind, spindly, basically lethargic man could hope for. He wore her like a badge. And yet, as Thurber would sometimes admit in the future when the subject of Althea came up over too many drinks, "She always scared me."

But through the bluster of conquest there was a trace of reticence. While both of them were pretty hot stuff for Columbus, Thurber was, after all, writing to Elliott Nugent, no less than a Broadway lion. His criticism of Columbus, via Ludwig Lewisohn, was more outspoken and less naïve than ever before, but it was still tempered by remnants of Joe College talk—Kappa girls and Strollers and old-chum gossip—almost as a strengthening of the only viable connection left between the small-city newspaperman/would-be humorist and the theatrical celebrity.

Thurber's allusion to his "undying mediocrity" was really a clumsy way of justifying his nonsuccess. Yet, he was making some extra cash as a stringer for the *Christian Science Monitor** and the Cleveland *News Leader,* as a press agent for a concert series, and as an author of Scarlet Mask Club shows. (His scheme for starting a news service in Europe with cameraman Hal Cooley was empty bravado, mostly for Nugent's sake.)

Althea and Thurber decided not to wait until October "to kick off the single coils," since there was about as much money in their common till in the spring as there was likely to be in the fall. So, after breaking the news to his family in time for them to rent the proper clothes, Althea and James were married in a short, antiseptic Episcopal rite on May 20, 1922. Ed Morris, the high-school friend who broke Thurber's heart when he pledged Chi Phi, was the best man. Robert did not attend the wedding.

Thurber wrote Nugent, who was unable to come to Columbus, two days before the wedding, advising:

. . . Althea and I leave here Saturday aft. [the day of the wedding] for Washington to remain thru Wednesday, then running up to NY for a day or two. I will contrive to have a few minutes with you, famous though you be. Please leave word with all sub-assistant secretaries that J. G. Thurber, a friend of your lowly, only by comparison, days, is to be allowed the freedom of all your town houses, your five cars, your Long Island estates and your personal theaters,— the Nugent Theater, the Elliott, the J.C. and the Ruth Roof, also the Grace Garden. Expect then, on Thursday or Friday, a word with me and Mrs. James G. Thurber.

With the honeymooners in Althea's little Ford coupe was, inexplicably, another couple—a wheeler-dealer friend named Red Morrison and Morrison's wife. Both the motor trip and the honeymoon were less than satisfactory. For one thing, Althea didn't want Thurber to drive. He had inherited from both sides of his family a comical ineptitude with machines of all sorts, and his single eye didn't bolster her confidence any. Althea, on the other hand, was a natural driver and, of course, very much a woman; the emasculatory tension hung in the air and turned out to be a source of numerous pieces Thurber wrote later on. They had only a week or so for their trip and a lot of miles to cover. It wasn't much fun.

------

*The *Monitor* consistently gave him the by-line "Miss Jane Thurber," despite his strenuous efforts to have this corrected.(2)

Then, too, there was that old spoiler of honeymoons and other rites —sex. Althea was, by most accounts, oversexed, or, at least, sexually active. Thurber was ambivalent. There were moments when he could match Althea's appetites and moments when it was all too much for him. Sex was certainly more important to him in 1922 than he had indicated it was in his confessional letters to Nugent in 1920, but he still suffered from a Victorian hangover and acute pedestalism. Dropping into brothels with McNulty was fun; serious marital attentions were another matter. In general, Thurber's sexual performance varied from poor to fair. With Althea, it hovered just north of poor. As a result, Althea had a crucial psychological advantage over her husband from the start. He once told his friend Ted Gardiner that "sleeping with Althea is like sleeping with the Statue of Liberty." He wasn't referring to any lithoid coldness. He might as well have said it was like sleeping with a Thurber Woman.

By the time they reached New York City and the Nugents, the honeymoon was, if not over, waning. Althea was not in the best of humor. The Nugents did not take to her. They felt she wasn't the right woman for Thurber or for his career. Their disappointment in his new wife was not lost on Thurber; he hardly mentioned his bride in his letters to Nugent from then on.

Back in the modest flat they had taken near the O.S.U. campus, the newlyweds fell into a narrow routine. Althea quite naturally emerged as the family manager and practical wife. "She was very tough on poor Jim," said Ralph McCombs. "Every morning when he went off to work at the *Dispatch* she gave him just enough money for carfare and lunch. She watched over him like a mother hen." This hold over Thurber did not further endear Althea to the Thurber family, particularly Mame. Indeed, her son's relationship with his wife was a mirror image of her own with Charles. She could see herself too clearly. Thurber spent little time with his family, even though they were living just a few miles from each other. Althea's strictures cut down severely on her husband's social life. The old fellowship with McNulty, Miller, and the others dimmed. Most of their social and professional interest was wrapped up in the Scarlet Mask Club productions.

One of those shows, *Many Moons*, which Thurber mentioned in his April 4, 1922, letter to Nugent, was the first with a book written entirely by James G. Thurber '19. (Thurber happily forgot, in later years, his work for Scarlet Mask, but he remembered the title of his first big production well enough; in 1943, he published his first fairy tale and called it *Many Moons*.) The show did receive good notices, as Thurber said in his letter, but, even for the frivolous times, it was nothing to be proud of. Its slim situation had to do with a politically troubled country called Polonia and a strange doctrine called Bolshevism, with a dramatis personae including such names as Maxixe Maxmilian Moderato Mazurka, Mrs. Van de Vere Leigh, Plotzki, Kwinine, and Ima Dora Jarr. The only lyrics Thurber wrote all by himself were for the Act I finale, entitled, appropriately, "Many Moons":

> *We will sail soon far across the sea*
> *To a foreign land so merrily*
> *We will rule in joy and gladness*
> *And so happy we all will be*
>
> *We think we know just the proper way to make the country bright*
> * and gay*
> *We'll give the Bolsheviks the razzmataz*
> *And this is what we'll say*
>
> > (CHORUS)
> > *There are many old moons in this world it's true*
> > *There's a moon of cheese and a moon of blue*
> > *There's a moon with a man who smiles so bright*
> > *And a moon full of moonshine ev'ry night*
> > *But we wear the moon of a sad little place*
> > *That beams sadly down on a poor little race*
> > *It will take many moons to change tears to tunes*
> > *But we'll light up a smile on its face.*

And even more bracing was the "Philosophical Finale" (words and music by W. W. Havens '23), which maintained, in part, that "Happiness is not restricted to a certain class/ Joy is meant for ev'ry lad and lass."

Thurber eschewed politics for the central theme of his next (1922–23) Scarlet Mask show, *A Twin Fix,* coauthored with Hayward M. Anderson '22. Little is remembered about that production, but in the 1923–24 entertainment, *The Cat and the Riddle*—a spoof of *The Cat and the Canary* species of mystery drama—Thurber, the sole author of the book, returned to a vaguely political theme. There were characters named James L. Barton, Mayor of Unionville, Pa.; Billy Curtis, his City Attorney; Rockford Huntington Esselstyn Chimes; Matthew, a Colored Gentleman; and Red McGann, a crook. The program credits listed Thurber not only as the librettist but also as the coach of the principals and one of eight lyricists. *The Cat and the Riddle* was a cut above the work he had previously done since it smacked of parody, a form

Thurber was becoming attached to. Herman Miller was moved to write, in an *Ohio State Lantern* review of the musical on February 5, 1924: "It is a good book lifted above the level of parody into Thurberlesque by such pixie-pranks of the imagination as the amazing lantern scene, which reads like a page from 'Alice in Wonderland.' "

The following year, Thurber was the author of two more Scarlet Mask efforts, *Nightingale* (which wasn't produced) and *Tell Me Not*. The latter was set close to the heart: "The living room of Dr. Beamish's home in a fashionable suburb of a university city," where Dr. Beamish, "an old-fashioned professor," has his life thrown into disarray by the untimely arrival of Countess Spezzorini, "a fin de siècle lady." It was the plot germ of *The Male Animal*. Again, Thurber was coach, lyricist, and author, and Althea found work in the all-male company as a costume designer and a scenery and lighting assistant. *Tell Me Not* was also a proving ground for another favorite Thurberian situation of later years —satire of Freud and psychoanalysis. His lyrics were beginning to show some glimmer of professionalism (in the rhymed-cliché school of lyrics that has since become a fine craft), especially in a number called "Kelley," about a scientific sleuth:

> *If a fellow killed his sister*
> *When dear old Dad was young*
> *A jury of his equals*
> *Had him sent out and hung.*
> *But the use of such rough tactics*
> *Is abolished in the land*
> *And we let 'em go if they can show*
> *A low pineal gland.*

The title song, too, showed a touch of promise:

> *Tell me not, how when you were a girl dear, living lacked*
> *This hurly burly whirl dear*
> *Eighteen forty life was just as sporty*
> *But like you dear girls were just as true dear*
> *Tell me not*
> *The girls now raise the devil,*
> *Tell me not, for they are on the level*
> *Tell me not that life's an affectation*
> *Tell me not for life's a recreation*
> *And you know a little syncopation*
> *Helps to put the joy in life.*

> *Tell me not, about the modern throng dear, tell me not*
> *That modern days are wrong dear*
> *Lad and lassie are a lot more classy*
> *Than your grandma for she was declassé*
> *Tell me not*
> *In any mournful numbers,*
> *Night was made for any quiet slumbers*
> *Silk pajamas may appear as smarty,*
> *Yet you bet the life of any party*
> *Tell me not that life is wrong my hearty*
> *Life is what you make it to be.*

Whatever slight promise showed through was too little and too late for a then almost thirty-year-old man in Columbus, Ohio. Thurber wisely held few illusions about his early theatrical talents. In 1956, he composed a curriculum vitae for a *Newsweek* cover story and mentioned the Scarlet Mask shows. "They weren't very good," he said. "Also directed the principals, not very well."(3) But he earned about three hundred dollars a show, which was the equivalent of about two months' *Dispatch* salary. The tours the company went on during the Christmas season (to such culture-starved towns as Chillicothe, Ohio, Huntington, West Virginia, and Ashland, Kentucky) got him out of Columbus for a while and away from Althea's tight grip. Occasionally, Thurber would step in at a moment's notice for a performer who couldn't hold his hooch, which further delighted him. (The touring Scarlet Mask Club apparently had quite a time of it. The troupe met its demise in 1937 when a girl was discovered in its railway car in compromising circumstances.) The shows gave Thurber a sense of a more exotic world than the parochial one he was trapped in with an increasingly restive wife.

September [1922]

Dear Old Nugie:

Your letter, which was waiting in my box for me when I got back to the office from a very drab round of city offices this morning, was like the whispered promise of a shot of Chambertin 1904. It revived me. Columbus is a rutty place, whatever you say, and it takes a jolt to shake up the ambition in me. Such jolts you provide in those rare occasions when you cease doffing a constant hat to your public and curry your Corona. . . .

If the weather has been as bad in NY as here recently it would serve to melt the plot considerably. But better days are in store with October in the offing, —the finest month of them all. Too bad you cant be here to whiff the football air and to see the Stadium dedicated. It is nearly completed now, a wonderful structure, set down in the pastoral back eighty of the OSU like a modernized Greek temple or a Roman coliseum born of mirage. Michigan plays here on Oct. 21, dedication day, just before your own play goes around right end for a touchdown.

On football, I wonder if you have heard of the truly sad condition of Chic Harley. He has been in a bad way since last winter and is variously reported as hopeless, his case being diagnosed as dementia precox by a number of examiners, although the Harley mind, unless known of old, might bother any medical man. At any rate he has dropped out of life, and is now in a Dayton sanitarium. There is food for deep reflection in his case. Perhaps the most striking figure this town has ever known in point of popularity, and now, at 25 or so, it is all ended. I used often to wonder what would ever come of him after football days were over. It seemed to me that his last game must mark the end of him, but little did I think it would be such a pitiable end. Some middle western Henry James might "do" Chic in a really great story. The only immortal piece written about him so far is my own epic poem in three eight-line plunges, called "When Chic Harley Got Away" and having as its refrain "Like the glory of the going when Chic Harley got away . . ." to grace a two column box in the state edition which is to be made notable as I told you by the Outline of Nugent History. . . .

I am at this moment in my career contemplating an attempt to get Daisy Krier's place on the Ohio S.J., as I am informed she will be married next month, though this rumor has not been verified and I am, for other reasons, too, not announcing my intentions of quitting the Dispatch to hurl the Journal into nationwide fame as a sheet noted for its brilliant dramatic critiques of the picture shows and the occasional dramas that pierce this far. A Bill of Divorcement plays the Hartman next week while The O'Brien Girl opened the season this week.

Now as to my own plans other than this I have an idea for a play which I think I will tryout on Strollers next Spring if I get it written. It will be an honest but probably unsuccessful attempt to enunciate Columbus, to pull the curtain upon the average middle class family which makes up this university city,—a town by the way as typical of America outside of New York as any other city in the United States. It has often appeared to me that the cities of this size have been lost sight of in the dramatization of the small town folks and foibles. It seems to me there is a rich mine of stuff here. It is of this stuff that the second novel I mentioned would be made,—a chronicling of people in this thoroughly Middle Western town, largely autobiographical as we are told all good novels are and written from a University-Paris-Newspaper chronology of events, impressions and developments. It would be quite melancholy since the longer you live the more you see that life is a melancholy thing, dont you think. Nothing to get morose about, for there are many pleasures and lots of fun, if one has a sense of humor, to keep one going, but what a welter of futility, commonness, unenlightenment, frailty and insignificance life is made by the average person. Out of living here I get only an increasing conviction that America has no cultural or intellectual or even intelligent future. The signs of it are everywhere. It is all stocks and bonds, automobiles, real estate, super movies, business deals, pettinesses and other junk, with one person out of 10,000 who seems inspired by any outside light at all. When you think about it it is amazing. Columbus is reading avidly Ludwig Lewisohn's "Upstream" which I believe I told you to get. It is I found on reading it a few weeks ago after waiting weeks to get it from a library, one of the most remarkable documents ever written in this country. If only for the beauty of the man's literary style, it is worth the reading. But to an Ohio Stater the book is indispensable for its pictures of people in the university and in Columbus. He has caught the city and the university with cruel truthfulness, exaggerated here and there by the marks of animus and bitterness, but in the main marvellously right. You will find in it Doc Thompson, rather terribly maligned in spots, Jim Light, in passing, the Sun Dial, the Sanscullotte, the co-ed, the men students, the class room, the faculty and the faculty's wives. Dont miss it. It is a book worth buying and I most urgently advise you to get it.

I dont get as much time for reading as I would like to, for it would take a long time each day to read the things one ought to keep up, on. But I do manage to skip through all the more important periodicals and to read, after a fashion, the more important books.

I really expected to write a much better letter than this when I began, having in mind such worthy things as an analysis of happiness, an appreciation of Ernest Dowson, a more concrete exposition of American cultural deficiences, and an examination of modern literary tendencies among the young writers of this country, but I shall allow you to go to sleep without a furrowed brow till another time.

Meanwhile, every so often, favor my recluse state with such another letter as today's. I appreciate your crowded hours, but the continuation of this correspondence we owe to our country, or something, and one must make these sacrifices in the interest of a coming generation which is already jeopardized by a paucity of belles lettres. How would "Hells Belles Lettres" be for a book of essays?

My deep devotions towards you and Norma and the same from Althea.

Always,
Jim

The immortal "epic poem" about the gridiron hero Chic Harley ran in the *Dispatch* shortly after the above letter was sent. It read:

WHEN CHIC HARLEY GOT AWAY
By James G. Thurber

The years of football playing reach back a long, long way,
And the heroes are a hundred who have worn the red and gray;

You can name the brilliant players from the year the game began,
You can rave how this one punted and praise how that one ran;
You can say that someone's plunging was the best you ever saw—
You can claim the boys now playing stage a game without a flaw—
But admit there was no splendor in all the bright array
Like the glory of the going when Chic Harley got away.

You can tell the tale of Gibson, who ran for 80 yards,
Bowling Michiganders over like a row of paper cards;
You can sing the song of Barrington, whose deadly toe oft sent
The hurtling ball to victory when his men were all but spent.
There's a thousand other stories of the games of other years,
But one from out the thousand like a flash of light appears,
And there's nothing half so thrilling from the first year to today,
Like the glory of the going when Chic Harley got away.

Declaim accounts of smashing lines and plunging backs and then
Shout a little louder and declaim them once again,
"There never was another time like in the good old days
When they used to play a man's game with the mass formation plays."
You can laud the Powells and Dunlaps as the mountains in the line
That made the game of football something superman and fine,
But still there's nothing in it all, when you have had your say,
Like the glory of the going when Chic Harley got away.

Old grads can mention how they fought when Kenyon came to town,
And how they used to up and knock the bleeding foemen down,
And we'll admit the good old days were red and raw and rough
And the men that wore the moleskin surely had the oldtime stuff.
Or you can laud the recent days and name a field of stars
As scintillant as Jupiter and as militant as Mars—
But there'll never be another thing can light up all the day
Like the glory of the going when Chic Harley got away.

Thurber's discontent with the *Dispatch* was growing. His hope of replacing the drama and movie critic of the *Ohio State Journal,* the Ryder-edited paper he admired so, might have become a reality but for two things: Early in 1923 he won first prize in an essay contest sponsored by the Lazarus department store and he was offered a Sunday half-page by the *Dispatch* to fill pretty much as he saw fit.

The Lazarus essay contest, its theme a projection of what Columbus would be like in 1951 (Thurber's projection was quite accurate), provided a first prize of only one hundred dollars but a lot of prestige. Headlines in the local papers proclaimed Thurber the winner and an award ceremony was led by Mayor James J. Thomas, whose new secretary was none other than Charles L. Thurber, formerly a clerk in the Municipal Court. (Charles held that post until 1932, when he ran sixth in a field of ten for the elective office of representative to the Ohio General Assembly.) But it was the Sunday *Dispatch* half-page, called "Credos and Curios" by its much talked-about author, that made Columbus bearable during 1923.

All in all, Thurber wrote forty-two half-pages that year, for which he received no extra pay, although by the end of his tenure on the *Dispatch* he was making forty dollars a week. More than thirty years later, he reread some photostats of the columns with, as he put it, "alarm, disbelief, and some small pleasure here and there. . . . It was practice and spadework by a man of 28 who sometimes sounds 19, praises 'clean love' and such books as 'Faint Perfume' and 'If Winter Comes' and practically any play or movie I saw, and attacks Cabell, Joyce, Hecht, and Sherwood Anderson. I was a great Willa Cather man." (4) That is as accurate an evaluation of the "Credos and Curios" columns as anybody is likely to make.

The half-page department was an imitative mix of paragraphs, jokes, definitions, private allusions, book reviews, verses, puns, observations, personal reminiscence, humor pieces, newsbreaks, and drawings (the last category by a staff artist named Ray Evans; Thurber had neither the urge nor the encouragement to draw then). It owed a great deal to Franklin P. Adams, Robert O. Ryder, Mark Twain, Finley Peter Dunne, and George Ade. As literature, humor, or opinion, the half-pages were, in the main, unimpressive, yet they plainly revealed the gnawing contradictions at work in Thurber's busy mind. Also, they provided space for the genesis of so much of his later writing, which developed into that original body of work known simply as Thurber.

The contradictions—most of which nagged him all his life—fairly leap from the half-pages in bewildering inconsistency. In some pieces, Thurber was the staunch defender of Ohio, football, Columbus, and what he termed the "uncomplicated" American Way; in others, he rather bravely damned his hometown and its values. For instance, in his column of September 23, 1923, he drenched with praise Columbus's leading celebrities (Mary Katherine Campbell, Hank Gowdy, Chic Harley, and Captain Eddie Rickenbacker) and further down the page wrote, "The Pollyannas are stupid, the worst possible quality in a human being. . . . We like a man who yells and swears and kicks the dog when all is lost." Or he would reflect the conservative, common-sense humor of the Middle West in a regular section called "Dad Dialogs"

(" 'We used to enforce the good old rule about children should be seen and not heard,' said Dad, propping his slippered feet upon the footstool and searching in his pocket for pipe and pouch. 'But in this day and age the only children who are seen and not heard are Jackie Coogan and Wesley Barry.' "), and then he would turn around and gleefully quote from that master of mordant wit, his comrade John McNulty ("John McNulty has taken the lead in the furious clothes buying duel we are waging, by buying what he calls a 'missing-man's' suit,—that is, a dark gray mixture which, according to Mac, all men, missing out of New York, are wearing when last seen"). And he rarely lost an opportunity to elevate H. L. Mencken to Parnassus. It was a tricky high-wire act he performed.

Perhaps most contrary were his attitudes towards literature. He led a crusade against the realistic novels of the day ("The most significant thing about Zona Gale's 'Faint Perfume' is its note of idealistic love . . . it is flung like a fresh rose among the sordid sex stuff that prevails in present day novels, the novels of Hecht and Lawrence and Joyce and Anderson"), and, with equal fervor, he attacked the Ohio State faculty and student body for not supporting its current daring literary magazine, the *Candle*. Throughout the columns, as throughout his life, he galloped off in all directions, especially when it came to literature. He never really made up his mind which writer was his favorite—not even Henry James, about whom he said, at the end of his life, ". . . the more I reread Henry James, the more I realize he didn't have a great deal to say except in skill and in the relationships of sensibilities."(5)

Other individual contradictions spilled out of the columnist Thurber like jellybeans from a child's hand: the prude vs. the ribald; the Pullman-porter hater vs. the Ku Klux Klan hater; the occultist vs. the practicalist; the regular guy vs. the sensitive man; the hick vs. the sophisticate; the woman detractor vs. the woman idolizer. The "Credos and Curios" department was, in a way, a cheap psychoanalysis for Thurber. All the frustrations, doubts, and internal quarrels of twenty-eight troubled and bleak years had a chance to vent themselves.

Equally important was his use of the columns as a proving ground for various humor styles and ideas, many of which were recognizable in future pieces. He threw away nothing, including the name of his department; "Credos and Curios" turned up as the title of the last collection he was planning, published posthumously in 1962. An arch, quasi-analytical lecture on spooning and petting was certainly the precursor of the satirical subject matter he and E. B. White used in *Is Sex Necessary?* six years later. He experimented with short pieces on his family's eccentricities as comic material; for example, one bit describes how "our brother," upset at the barking of the family Airedale at breakfast one morning, hit the animal in the eye with half an orange from thirty-five feet—a situation full of the flavor of *My Life and Hard Times.* In a longer piece called "The Menace of Mystery," Thurber suggested new versions of Shakespeare's plays that would leave in doubt till the very end who really were the murderers, in the manner of the current mystery dramas like *The Bat;* this was the substance of one of his most famous pieces, "The Macbeth Murder Mystery," in which a Thurberian lady, a detective-story fan, theorizes that the nice Macbeths had nothing to do with the horrid bloodshed. There were several rough attempts at the short-piece form (which read now as if a talented college sophomore were imitating James Thurber), and many of them blossomed into his familiar word-game and reminiscence pieces of later years. He aired his pet hates—among them the song "Yes! We Have No Bananas," literary symbolism, and James Joyce—and lauded his friends —McNulty, Nugent, Herman Miller, Donald Ogden Stewart, and Joel Sayre—just as he did for decades thereafter. And, perhaps most significantly, he polished his style of parody, a form he was more and more at ease in, with an endless Arthur Conan Doyle burlesque called "The Cases of Blue Ploermell."

Two other bits in "Credos and Curios" are significant. In a piece about waiting to see an eye doctor, he referred to his own partial blindness, a subject he had been previously loath to discuss even with his closest friends and relatives. This may have been a sign of some kind of realistic acceptance of his lot. And in his penultimate column, he criticized one of his heroes, Franklin P. Adams, for reprinting in "The Conning Tower" a jokey All-American football team roster (Tube of Colgate, Bust of Lafayette, etc.) from *Life* (the extinct humor magazine, not the extinct picture magazine), when almost the exact same list was published two years earlier in the *Dispatch.* Thurber was one of the authors of the *Dispatch* list, and he was exceedingly proud of it.

"Credos and Curios" lasted until December 9, 1923, when an item printed in the other half of the page offended some prominent people in Urbana, Ohio. Robert Wolfe, the paper's publisher, caved in under the Urbana complaints and decided to drop the entire feature page, including Thurber's blameless work. (It may have been, too, that Wolfe was just looking for an excuse to drop his erratic columnist.) Thurber was deeply bitter—about Ohio pettiness, Wolfe's unfairness, and the evaporation of his local celebrity as a man of letters. He never really lost that bitterness.

CHAPTER 8

Partly Cloudy

Immediately after the cancellation of "Credos and Curios," Thurber went on tour with his latest Scarlet Mask Club show, *The Cat and the Riddle*, during the Christmas holidays. The out-of-town reviews were excellent ("Plenty of fun and numerous comical situations kept the audience in the best of humor during the mirthful production."—*Ashland Times-Gazette*) and the tour itself took Thurber's mind off the shock of losing his column. There was also the show's run in Columbus, in early February, 1924, to think about and there was the next season's *Tell Me Not* to plan. But after the excitement of the February opening and three-day run in Columbus of *The Cat and the Riddle*, Thurber and Althea fell into an umber funk. He was suddenly just another political reporter on a feckless newspaper again, hanging around the press room at City Hall, where even his father had more influence than he did. It was a thoroughly inauspicious condition for a young couple, already in some marital trouble. Some change was needed.

Althea was particularly eager to get out of their "rutty place." She was becoming bored with their circle of friends, the salon and the Scarlet Mask Club and the newspaper cronies; she wanted a new circle, somewhere well to the east of Ohio, where urbane writers and artists lived. She put increasing pressure on her husband to pack up and leave Columbus for New York, and test his talents, full-time, in the open literary marketplace. "Althea thought—and it was very bright of her—that something in Jamie would be her ticket out of Columbus," Helen Thurber said. "It is possible she believed this all along and set a trap for him as the likeliest ticket out of town. Of course, you can never discount love as a motive, but Jamie in that period needed somebody strong to steer him, and Althea was strong, like her father, the Army officer. Jamie ended up marrying Captain Converse in drag. Still, I think he would have left Columbus sooner or later, even without Althea. Probably much later."

In any case, it was clear that Elliott Nugent was at least partially wrong about Althea. She was the right woman for Thurber after all, in the sense that she provided him with the necessary push to leave Columbus. He was disgusted enough with his lot there to want to leave, but he needed somebody to prod him a little. The editors of the *Dispatch*, particularly Gus Kuehner, despised New York, and they scared their more ambitious reporters by telling them horror stories of the East and assuring them that they would not be rehired if they came crawling back broke and defeated. This tactic had its effect on Thurber (though not on Althea); however, it was inadvertently the *Dispatch* that made it possible for the Thurbers to quit town. During the previous year, Thurber had been sent to New York by his paper for another one of his play-reviewing junkets, and while he was in the East, he visited the Nugents at their place in Connecticut. He met a friend of Nugent there who owned a cottage in the Adirondack hamlet of Jay, New York. The friend offered to let Thurber use the house, called "Corner Bright," over the summer of 1924 as a secluded spot where he could concentrate on his writing. It wasn't exactly Greenwich Village, but it was something. At the nadir of despair in the winter of 1924, Thurber and Althea took this generous patron up on his offer. They had some money saved and a couple of potential sources of income lined up, one of which was yet another assignment to review some more plays for the *Dispatch*.*
The other chance for income on this free-lance adventure was the frail possibility of turning his unproduced 1923 Scarlet Mask libretto, *Nightingale*, into a Broadway musical comedy, in collaboration with a composer named William Haid (O.S.U. '24) and a professional song huckster named Frank Bannister, creator of such numbers as "Say It with a Ukelele" and "Bringing Home the Bacon." What happened with that tenuous project was explained by Thurber in a 1954 letter:

... I never used to make carbons, and the libretto of a musical comedy I wrote in 1923 was left on a subway train by a young musicker named Haid, one of fifty guys who wrote nice music for Scarlet Mask and who knew absolutely nothing else at all, including his ass from a hole in the ground, or how to button his own pants. That libretto was last heard of between Chambers Street and the Brook-

---

*He reviewed no less than ten plays—including *Cyrano de Bergerac*, *The Beggar on Horseback*, and *Fata Morgana*—in a *Dispatch* piece headlined "MR. THURBER GOES TO THE PLAY" and mysteriously datelined "Jay, New York, May 24." There are no plays in Jay, New York, outside of the annual Christmas pageant at the elementary school.

lyn Museum stop. It has been read by thousands of subway riders. Guy named George Choos had some idea of producing it and a guy named Bannister was going to supervise the music. He telephoned WJZ while I was in his office and asked if he could come over at three and he took his tie off and they gave him a mike and a piano player and he sang two, three songs. That was radio. One of the songs had been written by Haid and was called "Pretty Mary Ann." Bannister was New York and sophisticated and he knew that wouldn't do. He changed it to "Better Stay Away." . . .(1)

Actually, a typescript of Thurber's libretto is on file in the Library of Congress. By any reading, it was sheer luck on Thurber's part that it wasn't produced. But the umbilical cord was snipped, and in May, 1924, he and Althea found themselves free at last and howling in the wilderness.

Settled in at "Corner Bright" in Jay, Thurber stuck to a scrupulous regimen of work. He was at the typewriter most of every day, writing short stories and humorous essays on everything he thought would please the *Saturday Evening Post* editors. Althea was cooperative but mildly bored; there was, to say the least, no salon in the darkest Adirondacks. One story Thurber wrote was entitled "Josephine Has Her Day." It concerned a young writer, Dick Dickinson, and his wife, Ellen, who rent a summer cottage in an Adirondack town called Dale, where Dick plans to spend his time writing stories. Josephine, a runty bullterrier puppy they had purchased earlier in lieu of a Scotty, arrives in their house, but its sickliness disenchants its owners. They decide to give it away, the dog ultimately winding up in the household of a cruel and feared local bully. Dick, remorseful, tries to buy the mistreated puppy back. He fails, and, blinded with rage, he socks the apelike bully before the astounded natives in the Madden's general store (there really is a Madden's general store in Jay, New York). In an access of righteous power, Dick knocks the bully out, with thrown hammers and tin cans, and wins back the dog, along with the admiration of the natives.

"Josephine Has Her Day" turned out to be the first short story Thurber ever directly received money for (finally, after much travelling, from the Kansas City *Star* Sunday Magazine, which published it on March 14, 1926). It wasn't a great improvement over "The Third Bullet." Full of the same stilted Dink Stover dialogue, the same meticulous clichés, the same embarrassing autobiographical fantasies of strength and prowess, the same emphasis on violence as a means of holding the reader's attention, "Josephine Has Her Day" offers not the slightest clue that in a few years' time its author would be writing radiant pieces for something called the *New Yorker*. A small sample of the narrative style should demonstrate this point:

... With a quick, mad, desperate movement he hurled himself straight at the feet of the charging form. Not for nothing had he dived like that at football dummies in his school days, battering his body at the swinging stuffed moleskins as a member of the scrub team—the fighting scrubs ...

In 1955, Thurber, as a kind of self-needling joke, included "Josephine Has Her Day" in a collection called *Thurber's Dogs*. He had this to say about it in the book's Foreword:

... I have decided that the story has a right to a place in this museum of natural, and personal, history. For a time I considered tinkering with James Grover Thurber's noisy, uninevitable, and improbable climax, which consists of a fight in a grocery store, but I came to the conclusion that this would be wrong, and a kind of tampering with literary evidence. Since I have had thirty-two more writing years than Grover, I would end the story, if I had it to do over, with the wife's buying back Josephine for the fifty dollars she was going to spend on a Scotty. I have apparently always had a suppressed desire to take part in a brawl in a grocery ...

The Fight in the Grocery Store

During this Adirondack idyll, Thurber met with only one other bit of success—a drab paragraph on bullhead fishing, which Heywood Broun printed in his column "It Seems to Me" in the New York *World,* on August 14, 1924. The rest was all *Saturday Evening Post* and *American Mercury* rejection slips (only one of which was friendly), poison ivy, Althea's growing discontent, and worrisome eyesight trouble. He mentioned the last affliction in one of his most touching pieces, "The Admiral on the Wheel," in 1936:

. . . To go back to my daylight experiences with the naked eye, it was me, in case you have heard the story, who once killed fifteen white chickens with small stones. The poor beggars never had a chance. This happened many years ago when I was living at Jay, New York. I had a vegetable garden some seventy feet behind the house, and the lady of the house had asked me to keep an eye on it in my spare moments and to chase away any chickens from neighboring farms that came pecking around. One morning, getting up from my typewriter, I wandered out behind the house and saw that a flock of white chickens had invaded the garden. I had, to be sure, misplaced my glasses for the moment, but I could still see well enough to let the chickens have it with ammunition from a pile of stones that I kept handy for the purpose. Before I could be stopped, I had riddled all the tomato plants in the garden, over the tops of which the lady of the house had, the twilight before, placed newspapers and paper bags to ward off the effects of frost. It was one of the darker experiences of my dimmer hours . . .

So with practically nothing to show for their adventure in free-lancing, Thurber and Althea, penniless and discouraged, slunk back to Columbus as soon as the quick chilly fall hit the Adirondacks. It appeared for the nonce, anyway, that Althea had bought the wrong ticket out of Ohio.

The *Dispatch* editors were true to their word: If you quit, you didn't come back, no matter how you crawled. They rather relished seeing one of their old boys return a failure from the East, his tail between his legs. There were I-told-you-so's from almost everybody. Setting up a life together again in Columbus was not easy, but Thurber and Althea showed they were made of resilient stuff. The 1924–25 Scarlet Mask Club show, *Tell Me Not,* had to be finished, rehearsed, and performed over the Christmas holidays—that was good for about three hundred dollars and some ego-boosting—and Thurber also revived his credentials as an able free-lance press agent, this time for an amusement park, a movie house, the Elks Circus, the Cleveland Symphony Orchestra, and several famous music soloists in a concert series. "A Columbus clubwoman without journalistic sense was in charge of a committee on publicity," he wrote Frank Gibney of *Newsweek*, on October 31, 1956, recalling his press agentry. " 'How can we get a front page story in the paper about Pablo Casals?' she asked me. 'By persuading him to bathe in a window of the F. & R. Lazarus Co.,' I told her. No front page story." And in his spare time, he tenaciously kept at his short-story writing.

Oddly enough, by the spring of 1925, he was making more money than ever before, even though he was having no success selling his stories. He was almost at ease again with Columbus, but not so Althea. She was restless and importunate, deftly applying pressure on her husband to pack up and abandon Columbus—this time not for the Adirondacks or New York City, but for France, where all the writers and artists were going in the 1920's. At that juncture, Thurber seemed to be mainly after some sort of security, but for Althea it was still a question of a more scintillating life far from Ohio. Going to France (a country he had come to appreciate more than he had in 1918, since he had discarded most of his moral reservations about it) meant, however, cutting the umbilical for the second time in a year, a drastic piece of surgery. Still, France was seductive, and Althea's confidence in his ability to make good outside Columbus was fortifying. It was a measure of her strength and persuasiveness that he finally agreed to go. As Thurber later put it: "It is the women who love the insecurity before they are thirty. Althea forced me to give up my good paying jobs in Columbus and sail for France."(2) They saved enough money for two student-class tickets on the *Leviathan*, said their sad good-byes for the second May in a row, and on the seventh day of that promising month embarked for France, like thousands of other escaping young Americans in search of art, or something.

They landed in Normandy and rented a room in a cheerless farmhouse near Granville, where Thurber set about writing, of all things, a —the—novel. The farm was owned by a widowed virago, whom Thurber called Madame Goriault in a piece he wrote a decade later ("Remembrance of Things Past") about his Normandy sojourn:

. . . I recall the little farmhouse clearly. I saw it first in a slanting rain, as I walked past sheep meadows in which poppies were blooming. A garrulous, tall old man with a flowing white beard walked with me to the farm. He dealt in clocks and watches and real estate, and it was in his dim, ticking shop in the village of Cassis that I had heard of Madame Goriault's and the room on the second floor which she rented out when she could. I think he went along to be sure that he would get his commission for directing me there . . .

Madame Goriault herself was a French version of the Thurber Woman ("Madame was large and shapeless and possessed of an unforgettable toothiness. Her smile, under her considerable mustache, was quick and savage and frightening, like a flash of lightning lighting up a ruined woods").(3) She, and the American prototype in his own marital bed, were almost more than female-shy Thurber could take. (He got his revenge on the Frenchwoman, anyway, by throwing pieces of bread soaked in Calvados to her chickens, thus sousing them blind; he evidently had a thing about chickens during this period of his life.) His novel—an autobiographical story touching on easily identifiable Columbus characters—went no better than his relations with the womenfolk in the Norman farmhouse:

. . . It didn't work out because I got tired of the characters at the end of five thousand words, and bade them and novel-writing farewell forever . . . (4)

He and Althea both knew the novel, all five thousand words of it, was terrible, and Thurber ultimately threw it away—although since he never threw anything away mentally, bits and pieces of it probably surfaced in his later work.*At last, Normandy and the novel were too much for him. With practically no money left, he escaped to Paris, his wife in tow, and looked for a way of surviving.

Just as the logical livelihood in Columbus was journalism, so it was in Paris. The problem was that scores of other writers converged on that hapless city with exactly the same idea, and there were only two American English-language newspapers—the Paris edition of the New York *Herald* and the Paris edition of the Chicago *Tribune.* The *Herald,* far and away the more prestigious of the two, turned him down flat; as for the *Tribune:*

. . . In the middle Twenties, everybody was in Paris, from us unknown boys to Hemingway and Scott Fitzgerald. Most of us had very little money, and I learned that my chances of getting on the Tribune were small since there were at least twenty-five applications ahead of mine. I was taken to call on Darrah [Dave Darrah, the city editor] one night and found him editing a piece of copy. He said over his shoulder, "I'll put your name down, but there's a long list ahead of you," and then he added, "By the way, what are you—a poet, a painter, or

---

*Thurber claimed to the end that he never really wanted to write the expected long work of fiction and that he had no sense of frustration because he hadn't. He said he preferred writers who were "taker-outers" (F. Scott Fitzgerald, for instance) to "putter-inners" (like Thomas Wolfe).(5) Still, this vacuum in his work made for more frustration than he was able to admit publicly.

a novelist?" "I'm a newspaper man," I said, and he practically leaped out of his chair when he learned that I had spent four years as a reporter, and could write headlines. He told me to come to work the next night. In those days we all sat around a big table, eight or ten of us, and rewrote the French papers. The boy on my right, a slender, dark-haired youngster in his early twenties, was obviously just learning to smoke a pipe, and constantly used to study a small black and red French dictionary. I figured he was in Paris, like the rest of us, for six months or a year. His name was William L. Shirer. . . . (6)

The ace headline-writer and translator of French news stories received twelve dollars a week for his professional skills, and was thankful for each and every dollar. He didn't think much of the paper; in the first place, he disliked its Chicago parent ("The World's Greatest Newspaper") and, in the second, he felt the business manager tried to gyp him out of some of his salary. He would have much preferred working for the *Herald* and being a part of its more literary staff, but he settled for being on the fringe of the Paris scene. There were a lot of laughs even on the fringe:

. . . one of my tasks was handling the international financial situation. "What casting!" as Joe Sayre said the other day about this. I had to have Bill Shirer look up the word "moratorium" in his small French-English dictionary. We had thought it had something to do with death or memorials or both. . . . I knew less about finance than anybody in the world. I was also assigned to do a series of articles on Poland, including the condition and history of the zloty, this series being mandatory because Poland took advertising in the Tribune. I got my international finance stories by rewriting Le Figaro and one other so-called semi-official newspaper.

I had had three years as City Hall reporter on the Columbus Dispatch and was one of the few trained newspapermen on the Paris desk at the time. I knew how to write headlines, too, and almost always handled the two-column 14-point Cheltenham feature story headlines. Eugene Jolas pounded a typewriter so hard he usually used one up every three weeks—we all had French keyboards, and if you wrote fast enough and fell into the American keyboard style, everything turned out in commas and parentheses and other punctuation marks.

I used to write parody news features mainly for the enjoyment of the other slaves, and one of these accidentally got sent down the chute and was set up, two-column headline and all, by a linotyper who didn't understand English. Dave Darrah found it on the stone and darn near dropped dead, since it involved fifteen or twenty famous international figures in an involved mythical story of robbery, rape, extra-marital relations, Monte Carlo gambling, and running gun fights. Ragner later figured that the Tribune would have had to pay about eight billion dollars worth of libel if the story had appeared. Darrah threw it away, of course, but lectured me only mildly. Some of us still dream about that libel suit that was never filed.

Darrah was always hollering up the tube for short filler items of a sentence or two, and I got away with a dozen or more phonies which were printed. The only one I remember went like this, with a Washington date line: " 'A man who does not pray is not a praying man,' President Coolidge today told the annual convention of the Protestant Churches of America.". . . (7)

A moment around the big *Tribune* copy table that burst into Thurber legend was the time the city editor handed Thurber a cable dispatch reading "CHRISTY MATHEWSON DIED TODAY AT SARANAC." (The *Tribune* received only fifty cabled words a night from America, and snatches of the dispatches were doled out to Thurber, Shirer, and the other boys for rewriting off the tops of their heads.) The Ohio rewrite man with the fabulous memory summoned forth his vast baseball lore, nurtured by long evenings at home with father and brothers, and dashed off a full-length obituary on Mathewson, amazing the hell out of everybody. Another coup during his early days on the *Tribune* was writing extemporaneously about the crash of the dirigible *Shenandoah* in Ohio, given nothing but the bare fact of the disaster.

His life with Althea outside the office was more or less standard for an American in Paris in the Twenties. They lived in the obligatory Left Bank hovel, with Thurber finding no faults with France. Althea, who cherished change and travel, also found contentment.* Their acquaintances were *Tribune* journalists, mostly, down-at-the-heels Americans, and a few old French people like Madame Rocagel, a shopkeeper whom Thurber had known during his code-clerking days—all definitely a cut below the Lost Generation-Paris *Herald* crowd. Shirer was one of his best friends there, as he was in later years when they both settled in New England. But Thurber never met in those Paris months Hemingway, Dos Passos, Fitzgerald, or Gertrude Stein, although he knew Robert Coates who was close to those figures. Unlike them, he wasn't at all a studied expatriate. He could just get by in French, ordering a simple meal and translating news stories, and he still had more Ohio in him than he could smother. Probably the main reason that they were out of the in-crowd was an acute lack of francs. Althea was more upset by their peripheral circumstance than her husband was, but at least she

---

*It has been said of her that she never developed great loyalty towards people or places because she loved change so much. When she moved on to a new place, she tended to forget the old place and the people in it.

was not in Columbus. From the outset, they borrowed money from anyone they could, just to keep eating regularly. Thurber even wrote his family a post card alluding to his financial situation, perhaps hoping for some help—an abrupt switch that didn't pay off.

To satisfy his creditors and make a more comfortable life for himself and his hungry wife, Thurber, with admirable tenacity and discipline, began to spend his days (he worked on the paper at night) banging out free-lance articles, which he sent on to George Bye, a New York literary agent. Bye succeeded in placing eight pieces, principally with the Sunday magazine sections of the Kansas City *Star* (which had bought "Josephine Has Her Day"), the New York *World,* and the New York *Herald.* Most of them dealt with an American's bemused view of France, or French subjects of particular interest to Americans. For instance, " 'Tip, Tip, Hurray!' The Battle Cry of Greedom" (in the Kansas City *Star*) treated the insatiable French porters and cab drivers with the same scorn he levelled at the lavish, brash American tourists. (The anti-tourist sentiment was one of his favorite and more surly themes in later pieces.) He also sold an interview with a Frenchman Thurber had known in 1918, Léon Barthélémy, who was President Wilson's barber during the Peace Conference ("Wilson's Paris Barber Calls Him Greatest of the World-Famous," in the New York *World*); a biographical sketch of Myron T. Herrick, the publicity-crazy former Ambassador to France and erstwhile Ohio politician ("The Evolution of an Ambassador: How Myron T. Herrick Won His Laurels as the Foremost American Dignitary in Europe," in the *Star*); a piece for the *Herald* entitled "Balm for Those Who Didn't Go Abroad: If Compelled by Circumstances to Remain in the United States, This Confession May Reconcile You to Your Fate"; short features on the cruiser *Pittsburgh* and the fate of Joan of Arc's white armor (both in the *Herald*); and a frothy thing about railroad trains in France (which found a secluded home in the *Detroit Athletic Club News*).

But his literary triumph of that year was selling a piece to the catchall department "The Lion's Mouth" in *Harper's Magazine.* It was called "A Sock on the Jaw—French Style" and it concerned the marked difference between French and American street fights. In essence, it held that what France needed was the good old American sock on the jaw to settle its myriad arguments, not the favorite Gallic outdoor sport of community debate and gestured threats. The piece was funny, even lapsing into parody of a French newspaper editorial on the national consequences of one arguer actually hitting another. For the observant *Harper's* reader, it was a sign of the Thurber yet to be. The name James

G. Thurber was displayed in one of America's smartest magazines and the author was billed as a "new *Harper's* contributor." But besides that uplifting prestige, the payment for the piece came just in the nick of time:

... We owed a Left Bank hotel a couple of hundred francs when I got a check for $90 from Harper's Lion's Mouth. This made us violently rich and is the most financial fun I ever had ... (8)

In the late fall of 1925, Thurber was sent to Nice with his wife to help get out the slim Riviera edition of the *Tribune.* His pay was raised to fifteen dollars a week, but better still, Althea was appointed society editor, so together they almost had enough money to live on. Both Thurber and Althea fell in love with Nice—a naughty, heedless carnival city then—and consequently fell in love again with each other. They were never so happy before or after their Riviera idyll. It was a carefree, benign period, the only truly carefree, benign period of his life. When he revisited Nice with Helen Thurber in 1937, his memories of the earlier period were, Helen said, "suffused with joy," even though that joy was originally shared with a whole other wife.

A lot of this love and fun and happiness shines through in a reminiscence of his newspaper work, "Memoirs of a Drudge," which Thurber wrote sixteen years later:

... Seven or eight of us had been assigned to the task of getting out a little six-page newspaper, whose stories were set up in 10-point type, instead of the customary 8-point, to make life easier for everybody, including the readers. Most of our news came by wire from the Paris edition, and all we had to do was write headlines for it, a pleasurable occupation if you are not rushed. For the rest, we copied from the *Eclaireur de Nice et du Sud-Est*, a journal filled with droll and mystical stories, whose translation, far from being drudgery, was pure joy. Nice, in that indolent winter, was full of knaves and rascals, adventurers and imposters, *pochards* and *indiscrets*, whose ingenious exploits, sometimes in full masquerade costume, sometimes in the nude, were easy and pleasant to record.

We went to work after dinner and usually had the last chronicle of the diverting day written and ready for the linotypers well before midnight. It was then our custom to sit around for half an hour, making up items for the society editor's column. She was too pretty, we thought, to waste the soft southern days tracking down the arrival of prominent persons on the Azure Coast. So all she had to do was stop in at the Ruhl and the Negresco each day and pick up the list of guests who had just registered. The rest of us invented enough items to fill up the last half of her column, and a gay and romantic cavalcade, indeed, infested the littoral of our imagination. "Lieutenant General and Mrs. Pendle-ton Gray Winslow," we would write, "have arrived at their villa, Heart's Desire, on Cap d'Antibes; bringing with them their prize Burmese monkey, Thibault." Or "The Hon. Mr. Stephen H.L. Atterbury, Chargé-d'Affaires of the American Legation in Peru, and Mrs. Atterbury, the former Princess Ti Ling of Thibet, are motoring to Monte Carlo from Aix-en-Provence, where they have been visiting Mr. Atterbury's father, Rear Admiral A. Watson Atterbury, U.S.N., retired. Mr. Stephen Atterbury is the breeder of the famous Schnauzer-Pincher, Champion Adelbert von Weigengrosse of Tamerlane, said to be valued at $15,000." In this manner we turned out, in no time at all, and with the expenditure of very little mental energy, the most glittering column of social notes in the history of the American newspaper, either here or abroad.

As the hour of midnight struck twice, in accordance with the dreamy custom of town and church clocks in southern France, and our four or five hours of drudgery were ending, the late Frank Harris would often drop in at the *Tribune* office, and we would listen to stories of Oscar Wilde, Walt Whitman, Bernard Shaw, Emma Goldman, and Frank Harris. Thus ran the harsh and exacting tenor of those days of slavery.

It is true that the languorous somnolence of our life was occasionally broken up. This would happen about one night a week, around ten o'clock, when our French composing room went on strike. The printers and their foreman, a handsome, black-bearded giant of a man, whose rages resembled the mistral, wanted to set up headlines in their own easygoing way, using whatever size type was handiest and whatever space it would fit into most easily. That is the effortless hit-or-miss system which has made a crazy quilt of French newspaper headlines for two hundred years, and André and his men could not understand why we stubbornly refused to adopt so sane and simple a method. So now and then, when he couldn't stand our stupid and inviolable headline schedules any longer, André would roar into our little city room like a storm from the Alps. Behind him in the doorway stood his linotypers, with their hats and coats on. Since the Frenchmen could comprehend no English and spoke only *Niçois*, an argot entirely meaningless to us, our arguments were carried on in shouting and gesticulating and a great deal of waving of French and American newspapers in each other's faces. After a while all the combatants on both sides would adjourn to the bar next door, still yelling and gesturing, but after four or five rounds of beer we would fall to singing old Provençal songs and new American ones, and there would be a truce for another six or seven days, everybody going back to work, still singing. . . .

We had the long days of warm blue weather for our own, to climb the Corniche roads or wind up the mountain in a *char à banc* to the magical streams and million springtime flowers of St.-Martin-Vésubie. Sometimes we sat the day out on the terrace of a restaurant overlooking the Bay of Angels and gave the tireless Albert suggestions as to where he might find Henry James. Albert was a young Englishman whc did interviews for us with distinguished visitors to the

Riviera, and he had got the curious idea that the celebrated novelist was hiding away in a *pension* somewhere between St. Tropez and Mentone, rewriting "The Golden Bowl." We decided that Albert had got his tip about the whereabouts of the great dead man from some aging aunt who lived in the parlors and the gardens of the past. It was one way to spend an afternoon, sitting over our glasses of vermouth-cassis, bringing back to life the poor, sensitive creator of Peter Quint and Mme. de Vionnet, figuring him lost and wandering, ever so wonderfully, somewhere among the bougainvillaea and the passionflowers . . .

There were other moments of his nearly cloudless Riviera days that Thurber remembered just as lovingly. He was assigned to get a statement from Isadora Duncan just after a wire arrived at the *Tribune* office reporting that her ex-husband, the Russian Serge Yessenin, had killed himself in Moscow ("it sometimes seemed to me that this nasty business of interviewing bereaved women was what editors figured me to be cut out for . . ." Thurber once wrote).(9) It turned out that Miss Duncan hadn't heard the news yet, and her response of "No, no, no, no" shook Thurber more than the tragic news shook her. He remembered, too, how "indestructably healthy" Rudolph Valentino looked on the Riviera just before his death, and how Harry Sinclair, of Teapot Dome fame, refused to meet his gaze during an interview.(10) And the time a sudden mistral gust toppled fifty tons of brick parapet just behind Thurber and Althea as they walked down the Avenue Félix-Faure. For years afterwards, he delighted in telling stories of the con men, thieves, and rioters of La Grande Ville de Plaisir, where he was once very happy.

Some of his Riviera newspaper work he took rather seriously. A rare example of this was his coverage of the Helen Wills–Suzanne Lenglen tennis match of February, 1926, one of the great matches in tennis history and an absolute must for international society within a week's sail of the Carlton Tennis Club in Cannes. Thurber loved the game and pageantry of tennis (he could never play it well but he continued to write about it), and, often, he found the raw material of a morality play in the characters and action. This surely was the case with the Wills-Lenglen match, which Lenglen won 6–3, 8–6. Thurber viewed it, in his extensive front-page *Tribune* account of February 17, 1926, as the gutsy but feminine girl from California pitted against the polished and professional La Belle Suzanne, or the New World vs. the Old World, America vs. France, even Goodness vs. Evil. It was an odd regression for Thurber, drifting back to 1918 when he wrote Nugent that he would trade all the French ladies for one decent, uncomplicated American girl. He was an Ohio boy again, and his writing showed it:

. . . Wills, tired, game, defeated, but carrying a radiance all her own, left the court of honor with its cups and its flowers and its "bravos" to Suzanne Lenglen. Suzanne Lenglen was tired. Tired, pale and drawn. "She knew she was in a match," someone breathed, a little awe-struck. It was like seeing a goddess in pain. Even in her moment of glory she was, first of all, tired and worn. The youngster from America had had her on the run . . .(11)

Thurber got his morality-play characters a little mixed up, in his short reversion to chauvinism. Most tennis experts now agree that it was Lenglen who was the more feminine, edgy player and Wills who was the cool, aggressive pro, in spite of her years. "Your piece didn't show any knowledge of tennis at all," Thurber later quoted John Tunis, the sportswriter, as telling him, "but it was the best piece on the match because it showed a real knowledge of women."(12) Well, apparently it didn't succeed in knowledge of women, either.

The significance of the halcyon days on the Côte d'Azur was not in Thurber's dedication to reporting. (He would later say that he was just a mediocre, unaggressive reporter,(13) and he once wrote Wolcott Gibbs that working for newspapers like the *Tribune* or the *Ohio State Lantern* "was something like playing a cross-eyed left-handed woman tennis player. You never know where anything is coming from, and everything takes a queer bounce.")(14) The significance was in simply having some fun out of life. But even fun in the sun tends to pall.

In the spring of 1926, two afflictions reappeared: money and marriage. The good life in the south of France was expensive. At one point, Thurber sent a collect cable to Red Morrison, his old pal and honeymoon travelling companion, pleading for a loan of three hundred dollars.* He

---

*His fiscal relationship with Red Morrison was a stormy one. Thurber ultimately paid back all the money he owed him, only to have Morrison borrow larger sums from him in the 1930's and not honor the debts. Thurber's outrage was superb in an undated (probably late 1930's) letter to his loyal and good Columbus friend Ted Gardiner, who was also a victim of Morrison: ". . . Morrison has failed to pay anything on his loan since August or so. It's only 34 bucks a month. I get threats, phone calls, every day. Every day I phone bastard and he promises to kick in. If the son of a bitch lets the $400 mature in a lump on Christmas Eve, I will kill him. He's home sick now with bastarditis. Says it's all your fault (just as he told you it was all my fault). Seems that two Jew lawyers named Bastardsky and Sonavitch snatch food off his plate at the automat, steal his overshoes, climb down his chimney. I hope so. But I'll bet a dollar you're not getting any jack out of him. Well, he pays $80 a month rent, has Mary, their Bexley maid, etc. When I was down, Althea and I had no maid, paid $40 a month, asked Red to go on notes. If I had the $2400 he lent me in those days, I'd pay

even had to borrow a few hundred francs on his *Leviathan* return ticket.

The *Tribune*'s Riviera edition was in danger of folding (it did indeed fold shortly after Thurber's tenure), and to return to Paris would have meant, in all probability, that he would be just another underpaid journalist or failed novelist. He wasn't homesick at all and he was still having a pretty good time, but it became suddenly and abundantly clear that any substantial future he might hope for, financial and professional, was in New York.

Meanwhile, all was not well with his marriage. Althea was attracted to one of the other members of the *Tribune* staff, enough so that she showed no inclination to return to America just yet. She had, however, no objection to Thurber's returning alone and setting up some sort of life in New York City before she followed. He decided to do exactly that, having become a rather thick-skinned fellow in his second tour of France. "What are gaiety and vodka in the old sleigh," he told a friend later, "when that thing bumping your elbow is a wolf."(15) Borrowing enough to redeem his return steamship ticket, he bid an affectionate farewell to La Belle France in mid-May and sailed in steerage on the *Leviathan* for New York. Once again, unwittingly, someone—Althea—had been an instrument of severe change in his life. She was in the watershed gallery alongside his brother William, Elliott Nugent, and O.S.U. President William Oxley Thompson.

While on board ship, Thurber wrote a letter to his Columbus friend and newspaper colleague Joel Sayre, in which he mused about his literary career:

> . . . I write mostly soi-disant humor since I haven't brains enough to write more solid articles and wouldn't if I could. I often worry about my future since I am no doctor and at best but a mean scrivener, but out of all the things one does, from pipe fitting to testing seamless leather belting and from ceramics to statesmanship, I can do only one thing, even passably, and that is make words and space them between punctuation points . . .(16)

While he set down those stark, confessional words, it was just possible that a memory fluttered in a tiny niche of his mind about a news item he had read in the Paris *Herald* the previous November. It concerned

---

off his note. We got thru without borrowing from anybody after we got back from Paris . . . He not only made his money on paper, he *is* paper. I'll touch a match to him next time I see him. Or erase him. But to hell with him . . ."

a stir created in New York by a lightweight exposé of Park Avenue society written by Ellin Mackay, the daughter of a millionaire and later Mrs. Irving Berlin. Her article was entitled "Why We Go to Cabarets/ A Post-Debutante Explains," and it appeared in a hard-pressed new humor magazine, which desperately needed all the publicity it could get, called the *New Yorker*.

CHAPTER 9

Arriving

When Thurber disembarked from the *Leviathan*, in early June of 1926, he was wifeless and penniless once again. Actually, he had a wife in France and ten dollars in his pocket. He looked up a soft touch he knew (a young lady, this time) and borrowed enough money to keep his head above water for a few weeks. His relatively dry head was located much of the time thereafter in a cheap rented room on West Thirteenth Street, where he worked on new pieces and reworked old ones, and at local doughnut shops and anonymous cocktail parties, where he cadged canapés ("anchovies, in case you don't know, are not good for breakfast," he later said). (1) In due time, he presented himself at a literary agency, Brandt and Brandt, with a pile of unsold manuscripts and asked what could be done with them. An agent looked them over and suggested sending them to that struggling periodical called the *New Yorker*, which Thurber remembered from the item about Ellin Mackay in the Paris *Herald*. The new magazine sounded just right for him, but, as he wrote long afterwards, "My stories came back so fast I began to believe the *New Yorker* must have a rejection machine." (2) Indeed it did—a human rejection machine named John Chapin Mosher, who took a special pleasure in turning down unknown writers for the almost unknown magazine. But one of Thurber's stories, a piece about Alfred Goullet, the six-day bicycle racer with whom Thurber had shared a stateroom on his return from France in 1920, was held at the magazine longer than the others. A hopeful Thurber visited the dingy, cramped *New Yorker* office in the West Forties and asked to see Mosher, who appeared in the reception area "looking like a professor of English literature who has not approved of the writing of anybody since Sir Thomas Browne." Mosher explained that he had misplaced the manuscript about Alfred Goullet, but nevertheless was rejecting it, as usual. "You see," he told Thurber, "I regard Madison Square Garden as one of the blots on our culture."(3) Thurber was crushed; his work wasn't even good enough for a pitifully slim new magazine, let alone the giant journals of the day.

He should have been ready to throw in the towel at that point. By early July, his borrowed money was all gone and he was running out of soft touches. The year before, in Paris, he had met the vacationing city editor of the New York *Evening Post,* who offered Thurber a reporting job on that paper, if he ever needed one. Thurber was grateful, but, dipping into his reserve of self-confidence, he turned down the offer for the time being. He had begun a monumental work of parody—when finished, a thirty-thousand-word, four-in-one satire of the current best sellers *Microbe Hunters* by Paul de Kruif, *Nize Baby* by Milt Gross, *Gentlemen Prefer Blondes* by Anita Loos, and *Why We Behave Like Human Beings* by George Dorsey. Thurber's stunning title for this hodgepodge was *Why We Behave Like Microbe Hunters,* certainly one of the wilder ideas of his career.

His confidence was enhanced, too, by the appearance of Clare Victor Dwiggins, the creator of the comic strip "Reg'lar Fellers," whom Thurber had interviewed, borrowed five hundred dollars from, and become friendly with in Nice. (At one point, "Reg'lar Fellers" had two characters named "Jim" and "Althea.") Dwiggins liked Thurber and invited him to spend the summer at his country place in upstate New York, near Albany. Under the benevolent wing of the Dwiggins family and away from steaming New York, Thurber had a restful and productive summer. He finished all thirty thousand words of *Why We Behave Like Microbe Hunters*—an incredible length for a parody—and, at the end of August, Dwiggins even lent his odd friend a hundred dollars in order to get back to New York City and reestablish himself with Althea, who had returned from France, ready to take up the role of helpmeet again.

With the kind loan as a push for a new start, the reunited couple rented a basement apartment on Horatio Street, near the Ninth Avenue El. The breadwinner set about alternately trying to peddle his titanic parody to magazines and book publishers and to write new pieces. All the magazines, including the *New Yorker,* turned down the parody cold; as for the publishers, Thurber later wrote a friend:

. . . Twenty-seven years ago I came to New York with a parody of best sellers of the day, entitled "Why We Behave Like Microbe Hunters." Said one Brandt to the other Brandt, "We'll never place this, but take it home and read it, it's funny as hell." It was turned down by Farrar, without a word, Harper, with a lot of crap, and Henry Holt, over the protest of a great guy [Herschel Brickell], the only man in town to see a new humorist coming up. His sales department laughed him down and said, "Tell the man to write a novel." . . . The hell with it . . . (4)

(Thurber exacted his revenge not many years after this setback. Both Harper and the *New Yorker* unwittingly used parts of the parody, cleverly rewritten, in *Is Sex Necessary?* and *Let Your Mind Alone*. Again, he wasted nothing.)

With his confidence now fading, Thurber was about ready to pack it in and go back to Columbus, with or without Althea, and take up again a career of press agentry. However, two things happened in rapid succession: The job of general-assignment reporter on the *Evening Post* was offered once more, at forty dollars a week, and Franklin P. Adams accepted and devoted an entire "The Conning Tower" column, in the September 28, 1926, *World,* to one of the pieces the *New Yorker* had rejected. "The Conning Tower" acceptance was called "If the Tabloids Had Covered the Famous Sport 'Love-Death' Scandal of Hero and Leander," and it was signed "Jamie Machree" (for some arcane reason, Thurber wanted to be thought of as Scottish at that precarious moment in his life). It read as follows:

I.

LOVE PACT IS BARED
AS LEANDER DROWNS!
—*Daily Tab. Sept. 15*
SWIMMER MISSING IN
HELLESPONT CROSSING
—*Daily Glass, Sept. 15*

II.

HERO WRITES FOR TAB
"MY LOVE WITH LEAND"
—*Daily Tab, Sept. 16*
HINT PUBLICITY STUNT
IN HELLESPONT "DEATH"
—*Daily Glass, Sept. 16*

III.

HERO SEES FOUL PLAY
IN LOVE SWIM DEATH
—*Daily Tab, Sept. 17*
POLICE PROBE CHARGE
LEA HIDING IN GREECE
—*Daily Glass, Sept. 17*

IV.

"HE SWAM TO SEE MAMMA
EVERY NIGHT," PENS HERO
—*Daily Tab, Sept. 18*

TURK SWIMMER SAYS LEA
NEVER CROSSED HELLES
　　　　—*Daily Glass, Sept. 18*

V.

"LEA CROSSED IN 2 HOURS,"
WRITES HELLES DEATH GIRL
　　　　—*Daily Tab, Sept. 19*

LEA, NO SWIMMER, FELL FROM
BOAT, SAYS TURK CHAMPION
　　　　—*Daily Glass, Sept. 19*

VI.

"WHAT BOAT?" IS PITIFUL
CRY OF LEA'S LOVE GIRL
　　　　—*Daily Tab, Sept. 20*

ROWBOAT DRIFTS ASHORE!
LEA'S LOVE CRAFT, CLAIM
　　　　—*Daily Glass, Sept. 20*

VII.

HERO SAYS 'SPONT BOAT
FRAME-UP BY TURK RING
　　　　—*Daily Tab, Sept. 21*

POLICE FIND INITIAL "L"
ON HELL-LOVE BOAT, CLAIM
　　　　—*Daily Glass, Sept. 21*

VIII.

HERO WILL SWIM H——L TO
PROVE LOVER COULD CROSS
　　　　—*Daily Tab, Sept. 22*

TURK FLAYS GIRL'S LOVE
SWIM AS MERE HERO STUFF
　　　　—*Daily Glass, Sept. 22*

IX.

HERO CHALLENGES TURK
TO "HEL" PRIZE SWIM
　　　　—*Daily Tab, Sept. 23*

"SHE'LL BACK DOWN" IS
TURK CHAMP'S HEL-DEFI
　　　　—*Daily Glass, Sept. 23*

X.

STAGE SET FOR HEL-RACE
HERO IS WELL, CONFIDENT
—Daily Tab, Sept. 24

HERO, PALE, SHAKEN, AS
TURK SCOFFS AT RIVAL
—Daily Glass, Sept. 24

XI.

GREASE SHORTAGE BLOCKS
HEL-TRY; TURK PLOT SEEN
—Daily Tab, Sept. 25

HERO "FEARS COLD-WATER;"
'SPONT RACE IS HALTED
—Daily Glass, Sept. 25

XII.

HERO WINS HEL-SWIM!
—Daily Tab, Sept. 26

DRUGGED! CRIES TURK!
—Daily Glass, Sept. 26

XIII.

CROWDS ROAR WELCOME AS
HEL SWIM HERO ARRIVES
—Daily Tab, Sept. 27

TRAINED SHARKS WERE SET
TO HAMPER HIM, SAYS TURK
—Daily Glass, Sept. 27

XIV.

HERO'S MOVIE OFFERS ARE
WORTH MILLION, SAYS MGR.
—Daily Tab, Sept. 28

NEW WITNESS FOUND IN
SHARK DEATH CROSSING
—Daily Glass, Sept. 28

XV.

CRIPPLED GRANDMA SETS
NEW HEL DEATH SWIM MARK
—Daily Tab, Sept. 29

WOMAN, 87, EASILY BEATS
HERO'S "RECORD" MARK
—Daily Glass, Sept. 29

The Hero–Leander piece wasn't bad, easily as good or better than any casual* the *New Yorker* was printing at the time. Its publication brightened Thurber's spirits, even though his real name wasn't associated with it.

On Thurber's first day of work at the *Post*, the paper ominously lowered its price from five cents to three. However, his tenure there was happy and productive. He was back in the city room again, every bit the house character, just as he was on the *Dispatch* and the *Tribune*. He would have preferred to loll in the more relaxed milieu of the feature-story writer, but he was hired as a general-assignment reporter, and that was what he had to be. The *Post* was laden with first-rate feature writers then—Nunnally Johnson, Russel Crouse, and Laura Z. Hobson, to name a few—so Thurber was assigned to cover hard news, in his inimitable way. Once, he was sent to Brooklyn to report on a four-alarm fire, but he became helplessly lost in the subways, always ending up back at Chambers Street. Hours later, after surrendering to a taxi as his only feasible means of getting to Brooklyn, he passed a kiosk and saw the front page of the *Post*'s latest edition, which was filled with news of the fire. He redirected the cab to his apartment. Just as he had suffered the abuse of Gus Kuehner after the Columbus City Hall fire episode, Thurber had to listen to his newest editor rave, "A four-alarm fire, and this fellow just can't find it!"(5)

His reputation as the city-room cutup was secured after the editors demanded that all news-story leads be tightened up to as few words as possible. Thurber obeyed the order with the following lead on his next crime story:

Dead.
That was what the man was the police found in an areaway last night.(6)

---

*The term "casual" was used early on at the *New Yorker*. At first, it meant any short piece of fiction, particularly the seemingly offhand kind that magazine was most fond of. As the short stories became less informal and more serious, the term shifted its meaning to include pieces of humor, any kind of humor. For instance, the Hero–Leander piece was an idea-situation casual, in which a funny notion—Hero and Leander in a Twentieth Century situation—is carried to extremes. Other casual forms are the first-person reminiscence (especially when the reminiscence is more fiction than fact, as in Thurber's *My Life and Hard Times* pieces), the parody casual, the essay casual, and the nonsense casual. The trick of the form is to make the piece seem as if it came out whole, so to speak—effortlessly and spontaneously born fully clothed. Its actual process of creation, of course, is precisely the opposite; the casual is one of the most difficult and painstaking forms of writing known to humankind. In fact, it is often sheer hell to get one down on paper, let alone accepted for publication.

It was shortly after the lead-tightening incident that Thurber was put on the feature-story beat. He enjoyed the company of the other feature writers, especially Nunnally Johnson, who became his lifelong friend, and he performed his tasks with what might be called relaxed verve:

. . . I wrote only one story a day, usually consisting of fewer than a thousand words. Most of the reporters, when they went out on assignments, first had to get their foot in the door, but the portals of the fantastic and the unique are always left open. If an astonished botanist produced a black evening primrose, or thought he had produced one, I spent the morning prowling his gardens. When a lady in the West Seventies sent in word that she was getting messages from the late Walter Savage Landor in heaven, I was sent up to see what the importunate poet had on his mind. On the occasion of the arrival in town of Major Monroe of Jacksonville, Florida, who claimed to be a hundred and seventeen years old, I walked up Broadway with him while he roundly cursed the Northern dogs who jostled him, bewailing the while the passing of Bob Lee and Tom Jackson and Joe Johnston. I studied gypsies in Canarsie and generals in the Waldorf, listened to a man talk backward and watched a blindfolded boy play ping-pong . . . (7)

A couple of Thurber's features on the *Post* were scoops and won him a certain attention in journalistic circles. One was a rare and exclusive interview with Thomas Alva Edison, in West Orange, New Jersey, on the occasion of the inventor's seventy-ninth birthday. Edison had been angry at newspapers for years because many of them had ridiculed the written examinations he devised for prospective employees. He accepted Thurber's request for an interview because Thurber used the clever expedient of sending him written questions in advance. Throughout the interview, Edison kept repeating, "The radio will always distort the soprano voice."(8)

His other coup was a story about Harry Houdini's widow and the estimable Houdini library. (Thurber's interest in Houdini continued to grow; in his last years, he was determined to write a long treatment of Houdini and his magic, which never came to pass, however.) He explained the Houdini scoop in one of his infrequent letters to his family:

Gotham,
Feb. 6, 1927

Dear Father, Mother, Brother and Airedale:

You will be interested to know that I have just come into possession of seventy-five volumes of the late Harry Houdini's famous library. I was sent on an assignment to Sing Sing prison a few days ago and with my usual good luck on assignments got there the same hour that Mrs. Houdini did. She was taking

Houdini's set of old books on crime and penology to Warden Lewis E. Lawes, an old friend of the magician. On the way back to New York I found myself on the same train with Mrs. H and asked her for some more information about the books. She proved to be a very sweet and charming lady and certainly interesting to talk with. The warden, by the way, is a fine chap, strangely unlike a Sing Sing warden should be,—very quiet and gentle and courteous soul. Before I left Mrs. H, in the Grand Central, she asked me if I would like to come up and pick out some of the Houdini books for myself. I said YES. I went up twice to her house, the second time with Althea. Houdini left a library on dramatic and theatrical literature valued at $500,000. His library on magic, an extremely valuable collection, went to the Library of Congress, and his psychic books to the American Society for Psychical Research. The family and a few friends shared the rest, his miscellaneous books. I was certainly lucky to be one of the "friends".

She gave me a rare Latin book on magic, dated 1648, to start with. One of my prizes is a book presented to Houdini by Harry Kellar, the great magician, containing Houdini's signature and an inscription by Kellar. That book is doubtlessly valuable. There are also three first editions of James Russell Lowell's works, two volumes in German on German cities, with the bookplate of David Belasco on the inside front cover, one of them having a sentence in Belasco's writing on the fly leaf. Many of the volumes are more than a hundred years old and deal with all sorts of subjects. I think one collection of thirty-two paper backed song books is perhaps a very rare and valuable collection. They are American song books, some of them printed as early as 1845 and all together they contain probably all of the American songs from Yankee Doodle to The Sidewalks of New York. One of the song books is "The Harrison Log Cabin Song Book", published by A.H. Smythe Columbus, Ohio, in 1888 and edited by O.C. Hooper. Its full title is "The Harrison Log Cabin Song Book of 1840 revised for the Campaign of 1888 with Numerous New Songs to Patriotic Airs". Many of the songs deal with old Allen Thurman. Originally sold for about 25 cents, its cover is marked 75 cents,—the price Houdini paid for it some years ago due to its comparative rarity. . . .

A very rare book is one called "The Life and Death of John Wilkes Booth", published in Memphis. Houdini is said to have bought up almost every copy of this book to make it rare. I have the only copy outside his family. . . .

I have no doubt but that our collection will someday, if indeed not now, be worth upwards of a thousand dollars, maybe more.

Mrs. Houdini told us a lot of interesting yarns about him, his relations with Conan Doyle, their arguments about psychic phenomena, her friendship with Anna Eva Fay who wrote her recently, "I used to bring spirits to others but I have tried in vain for 18 years to get a message for myself." Remember Anna Eva Fay?

Mrs. Houdini believes all mediums fakes and none of them has yet come close to getting the message from Houdini that he arranged to send her. He tried for years to get a certain word from his mother but never did. He must have been a very interesting man, and they were unquestionably very happy.

It occurs to me that the papers might care to print a little story about the books and you might, if you want to, show the first part of this letter to the reporters that cover city hall. It doesn't make any differnece to me whether they use anything or not, but when I was a city hall reporter I would have considered it a nice little feature yarn, in view of the importance and interest in Houdini and his library. For your own confidental information she is selling the half million dollar dramatic library to the NY public library for $50,000,— or will if they accept,—and why shouldnt they? No one knows this yet and the deal hasnt gone through, so I'm keeping it quiet, in order to get a news beat when it does go through. I got a $5 bonus for the Sing Sing books story,—since it was a beat. Ive collected several such bonuses, including one on trench mouth being epidemic here. Funny thing I had a slight recurrence of the trouble the day after I wrote the story and I went to the specialist whom I had quoted and he treated me for nothing and gave me medicine to use. He knows Dr. Hayden, he said.

Tell Colonel Duffy that I have just completed a survey of the NY water situation from the atandpoint of metering the city, and will have three stories in the Post on the subject which I will send him. The editor in chief took my word for it that the city should be metered after I conducted my "survey" and the stories are written from that viewpoint. I found Columbus was 100 percent metered and that seemed a good argument. The NY water supply system being the greatest in the world is an interesting thing to study up and my city hall training in Columbus helped me to know how to go about the thing.

Greetings to the gang,

Jamie

PS. If the boys want to write a piece about the books, please ask them to omit any reference to the probable value of them. They are valuable, and thats enough. . . .

Gotham life with Althea was not all that exciting. They kept pretty much to themselves in their flat near the Ninth Avenue El, where most evenings were spent by Thurber writing short pieces. They were subsisting on forty dollars a week and had many debts. As the *New Yorker* grew thicker and more noteworthy, Thurber grew more determined than ever to sell something to the magazine. People—at least, New Yorkers—were talking about it, and the young magazine was printing more original, subtle humor and less of the old *Life* and *Judge* variety (*i.e.*, jokes, pieces, and cartoons predicated on the supposedly hilarious drunkenness of the Irishman, cheapness of the Jew, and laziness of the Negro). The magazine attracted him and seemed made to order for his talents, but all he had to show for this potential symbiosis was a discouraging collection of twenty rejection slips. It was "phenomenal that a thin, nervous type like me could stick it out that long," he once wrote a friend about those rejections.(9) However, it was Althea who insisted that he stick it out. She was sure he could make it as a writer, with the *New Yorker* or something more prestigious than the *Post;* it was merely a question of tenacity and ambition, both of which she, at least, had in abundant supply. Those qualities spilled over onto him. He later said, "If you come to New York you don't dare go back to Columbus, so you either die or become a success, I guess."(10)

At one point, Althea concluded that her husband was slaving over each piece too long. She told him to set an alarm clock to ring in forty-five minutes and force himself to have something finished by the time the bell went off. So he began writing about a little man, not unlike Charlie Thurber, who goes around and around in a department-store revolving door, as anxious citizens, the press, and the police look on. At last, the little man sets a world's record for revolving-door revolutions and is instantly rich and famous. "An American Romance," as Thurber titled it, was a good *New Yorker* idea-situation casual, heightening to dizzy absurdity the basic absurdity of the flagpole-sitting crazes of the day. It was short and funny, though neither shorter nor funnier than the Hero–Leander piece. Still, Althea's time-limit idea succeeded (it almost never worked again), and within forty-five minutes, Thurber had a rough draft of a casual. He polished it and sent it off to the *New Yorker.* It was immediately bought. They celebrated the check's arrival by buying a Scotch terrier, which they named Jeannie. There was no question of having a child yet, and they had always wanted a Scotty.

On the *Leviathan* going to Europe in 1925, Thurber and Althea had become friendly with a married couple named Illian. Mrs. Lillian Illian (a nominal combination designed to captivate Thurber) spoke often of her would-be writer brother, a production assistant in an advertising agency, whose name was Elwyn (which Thurber remembered as Elton) Brooks White, and whose nickname was Andy, because every young man named White who went to Cornell was automatically dubbed Andy, after Andrew White, Cornell's first president. In June of 1926, when Thurber had first visited the *New Yorker* office in search of his misplaced manuscript on the French six-day bicycle racer, he had learned that Elwyn/Elton Andy White had recently sold several pieces to the magazine. He asked if he could see him, but he was told that Mr. White was not in. Eight months later, in February, 1927, after Thurber had sold *his* first piece to the *New Yorker*, White and Thurber met at a party in the Greenwich Village apartment of a common friend, Russell Lord. Lord was a most appropriate person to bring Thurber and White together, since he had attended both Cornell and Ohio State, and also worked for the *New Yorker*. Thurber and White liked each other immediately. "The magazine was doing slightly better," White recalled, "and I knew Ross was looking for new talent on the small staff. Thurber was looking for another job, and so I arranged for him to meet Ross." Not long after that Russell Lord party, White introduced Thurber to Harold Ross, the mysterious founder and editor of the *New Yorker*, who hired him on the spot.*

The man who hired Thurber so impetuously was a study in flagrant paradox and a source of rapt curiosity for Thurber and everyone else who knew him. No one tried harder than Thurber himself to capture the essence of the man, in dozens of letters, conversations, impersonations, unfinished plays, and finally in his book *The Years with Ross*, and even Thurber was never entirely successful. It is just about impossible to describe credibly a rough-tongued, untutored son of turn-of-the-century Aspen, Colorado, who feared any unpleasantness; a sentimental old newspaperman who abhorred journalese; a compulsively literate editor who was literarily illiterate; a blushing choirboy in the presence of earthiness who attacked comely ladies in taxicabs; the creator of the most sophisticated, witty magazine in the English-speaking world who often missed the point of some of its most sophisticated, witty pieces and cartoons; a poetry-hater who printed good poetry; a genius who ran a complicated, temperamental artistic apparatus almost solely by intuition and challenged perfection with his intuition and inspiration. "There is only one word that fits him perfectly, and the word is Ross," Thurber ultimately conceded.(11)

It was undoubtedly Ross's superb intuition that made him grab Thurber as an employee at first sight, just as had grabbed White the year before and Wolcott Gibbs, Dorothy Parker, Robert Benchley, and

---

*Thurber had varying versions of his first encounter with White and Ross. In *The Years with Ross* he wrote: "That day in February, 1927, when I first saw Ross plain and talked to him, I had been brought to his office by White. Andy called me on the phone one day to say that his sister had mentioned meeting me on the *Leviathan* and that he was, like myself, a friend of Russell Lord. . . . I didn't meet White until five minutes before he took me in to see Ross, but Ross always believed that White and I had been friends for years." In his autobiographical letter to Frank Gibney, Thurber claimed that, after several sales to the magazine, Ross sent for him. Whatever the case, White said that the sister-on-the-*Leviathan* story was merely coincidental. The essential fact is that Thurber met White, then met Ross, and then was hired as a staff member of the *New Yorker*.

every other talented person of American letters. The trouble was that Ross grabbed Thurber as an editor, not a writer. During his first interview with Ross, Thurber told him he wanted to write. Ross snarled back at him, "Writers are a dime a dozen, Thurber. What I want is an editor."(12) He went on to explain that he didn't need just any old editor; he wanted someone to emerge as a kind of super efficiency expert—the "Jesus," as the post was called around the magazine—who would sit at a central desk and "make this place operate like a business office, keep track of things, find out where people are. I am, by God, going to keep sex out of this office—sex is an incident."(13) Thurber, with deep misgivings and no immediate affection for this odd man, accepted the unlikely challenge, one that several other ex-newspapermen, including James M. Cain, were to fail at:

... "Done and done, Thurber," said Ross. "I'll give you seventy dollars a week. If you write anything, goddam it, your salary will take care of it." Later that afternoon he phoned my apartment and said, "I've decided to make that ninety dollars a week, Thurber." When my first check came through it was for one hundred dollars. "I couldn't take advantage of a newspaperman," Ross explained . . .(14)

As Thurber remembered it, his life as a *New Yorker* editor was holy hell. He told Frank Gibney (and later echoed much the same recollection in *The Years with Ross*):

... I found out that I was managing editor three weeks later, when I asked my secretary why I had to sign the payroll each week, approve the items in Goings On ["Goings On About Town," a calendar of events in the front of the magazine], and confer with other editors on technical matters. I wrote pieces for the *New Yorker* at night for which I was not paid extra, until after they had printed about eight. . . . During my first four months on the magazine I worked seven days a week, often until 11 P.M. We edited the Sports Departments on Sunday night. Ross almost never went home. He would work any editor to death because of his own driving devotion to the magazine and to nothing else in those first few years. I lost ten pounds . . .

This ordeal was exaggerated, as indeed was the editorial position Thurber held. He was not made managing editor, since there never was a managing editor after Ralph Ingersoll's tenure from 1925 to 1930 (which, of course, impossibly coincided with Thurber's own supposed term as managing editor). The roster of editors in 1927 was very small: Ross, Ingersoll, Katharine S. Angell (later Mrs. E. B. White), Rea Irvin,

R. E. M. Whitaker, Carmine J. Peppe, and a few others who came and went. These editors, and an equally small number of staff writers, oc-. cupied a disorganized floor of a building at 25 West Forty-fifth Street (the office moved to 25 West Forty-third Street in the 1930's). Only two people had offices to themselves, Katharine Angell and Ross. Everyone else shared offices or simply had desks crowded into a limited floor area, city-room style. (The Spartan accommodations at the *New Yorker* prompted one of Dorothy Parker's better lines. Ross ran into her somewhere and asked her why she hadn't come to the office to write a piece during the week. "Somebody was using the pencil," she replied.) Only Ross had his own secretary, and if anybody was going to sign the payroll, it was Ingersoll or Ross himself. What Thurber was employed to be was specifically the Sunday editor—and a writer, when he had the time. He —and all the editors—often worked till the early-morning hours, sometimes seven days a week, because they were short-handed and were driven by Ross's incredible example in his desperate reach for perfection. If Thurber lost ten pounds (or, as he put it in *The Years with Ross:* "I was losing my weight, my grip, and possibly my mind"), so did every other editor. It was a crusade, not a magazine, and everybody involved had to lay down his life for it, as the leader did.

After a few grinding months as editor, finding less and less time for his writing, Thurber began to make deliberate mistakes and clown around, "hoping to be demoted to rewriting 'Talk of the Town,' with time of my own in which to write casuals."(15) He ignored some queries from Ross and fouled up on a sports article one Sunday night, which Ross surprisingly took in stride. As the office cutup, he rolled water-cooler bottles about the floor (causing Ross to instruct an assistant, "Go and find out what the hell is happening—but don't tell me"); he ripped an offending pay-telephone booth off the wall and stretched out inside it as if it were a coffin; and he drew on a corner wall an innocently walking man about to confront, around the corner, a large woman wielding a club.

Finally, Ross agreed to give his new man a two-week vacation, something a worried Althea had been demanding. Thurber, Althea, and Jeannie, their Scotty, returned to Columbus in something approaching triumph. He saw his family and old friends again, and was living proof to the Columbus newspaper crowd that a local boy could make good in the East. As they were about to go back to New York, the Scotty somehow got lost, and Thurber overstayed his vacation by two days to search for her, with the aid of the police department and newspaper ads. The dog was found and Thurber returned to New York to face a furious Ross.

"He and I were, respectively, growling bulldog and trembling poodle in 1927," Thurber later said, adding:

> . . . When I got back Ross called me into his office about 9 P.M. and snarled, "You overstayed your vacation to look for a dog. I consider that the act of a sis." I saw red and many other colors, including some new ones. "Get up out of that chair," I told him. "That's a word you've got to prove" . . . He hated physical violence and yelling. "Why don't you get one of your friends to help you?" I asked him. "I don't think you're a match for me." "Who do you suggest?" he asked. "Alexander Woollcott," I said. Ross began to laugh and laugh for five minutes. Then we went out and had drinks at Tony's, our first extra-office get-together. From then on he and I were great friends. He was one of the closest and most important persons in my life . . . (16)

Not long after that ripening of friendship—or, perhaps, more of a loose father–son relationship, though the editor was only two years older than Thurber—Ross made his decision, helped a bit by lobbying from Dorothy Parker and other staff writers. He told Thurber, "I thought you were an editor, goddam it, but I guess you're a writer, so write. Maybe you have something to say."(17)

Thurber started to write in earnest. In his first few months at the *New Yorker*, while he was mostly performing the duties of an editor, he had published the casual "An American Romance" (about the little man breaking the revolving-door record) and four other pieces, all signed "James Grover Thurber" or "J.G.T." They had a similar ironic edge to them: "News of the Day" concerned an Irish mother bursting with pride over the public attention given her murderer son (there was still a touch of the *Life–Judge* humor left in the *New Yorker*); "More Authors Cover the Snyder Trial" was a parody of Gertrude Stein and James Joyce (his old literary prejudices), as they would report that famous murder case (ghastly crimes fascinated Thurber then and continued to fascinate him for years); "The Youngsters as Critics" involved current books as reviewed by children; and "Tidbits" was a slice-of-life conversation piece about embarrassed grown males buying exotically named candy bars. All of them showed humor and promise in their conception, but none of them displayed very good writing skill. Thurber obviously felt comfortable in the casual form, but he wasn't exactly sure how best to execute it.

Some light verse was also printed, with similar ironic twists. Actually, two of the poems, "Street Song" and "Villanelle of Horatio Street,

Manhattan," were the first writings of Thurber the *New Yorker* published, in its February 26, 1927, issue; "An American Romance" was the
first piece accepted, but it was printed a week after the poems. "Street
Song" is interesting, not for its poetic talent but as a glimpse into its
author's mood during his days on the *Post:*

> In Paris town the carts go down
>   Rain-gray byways to the Seine,
> And many little brazen bells
>   Jingle in each horse's mane,
>   Jingle in the rain.
>
> In New York town but once I found
>   Such a gray and rainy street,
> And then I heard a teamster shout:
>   "Pick up your God damn feet!
>   "Pick up your feet!"

Almost from the first days of Thurber's *New Yorker* career, he was
assigned a tiny office "just big enough for two men and two typewriters."(18) The other man at the other typewriter was E. B. White.
"We got along fine together," White said, "and from the first we loved
each other's stuff. But Thurber was often broody because he was troubled by Althea and his marriage. He could be a broody man, even then.
Still, it was fun and good work."

White had come to the *New Yorker* via Cornell, a Seattle newspaper,
Alaska, and, finally, a New York advertising agency. Shortly after the
magazine was founded, in February of 1925, White sent in pieces, and
Ross and Katharine Angell, the literary editor, were impressed by the
young man who wrote as if he had invented the casual form, which, in
many ways, he had. He sold his first piece to the magazine in April, 1925,
and, after much persuasion, he agreed to work full time in the fall of
1926. He lent distinction to the tasks Ross assigned him, writing "Talk
of the Town" pieces, developing the more editorial Notes and Comment section into a model of persuasive language, making up cartoon
captions and newsbreak taglines (the latter activity still lovingly performed by him on a regular basis),* writing verse, and, of course, casuals
—all done in a manner and tone that made Ross's dream of sophis-

---

*Thurber once contributed a standing newsbreak category—the "How's That Again?
Department"—but he admitted that he was baffled by the task of writing taglines.

ticated literary perfection come true before his unbelieving eyes. Besides Ross, White was the unexpendable man on the magazine. He has always been incapable of writing a bad sentence in English. His simple, crystalline prose rang in the air at 25 West Forty-fifth Street and, increasingly, throughout the nation. It could not help but sound in his office mate's good ears.

To his last day on earth, Thurber was unstinting in his acknowledgment of White's influence on his writing style. White, by a kind of gentle osmosis, taught him to set down the clean, intelligent declarative sentence, which had generally eluded him up to their office-sharing:

... Until I learned discipline in writing from studying Andy White's stuff, I was a careless, nervous, headlong writer, trailing the phrases and rhythms of Henry James, Hergesheimer, Henley, and my favorite English teacher at Ohio State, Joe Taylor. . . . I think I got most of my "clean love" dedication or complex or whatever from Joe Taylor's praise of beauty in life and the heroine of James's "The Ambassadors," Madame de Vionnet. . . . The precision and clarity of White's writing helped me a lot, slowed me down from the dogtrot of newspaper tempo and made me realize a writer turns on his mind, not a faucet . . . (19)

At the beginning of their friendship, Thurber worried that White could be too strong an influence, but his relief at getting away from journalese-*cum*-Henry James calmed that worry (although some of his later "Talk of the Town" work is indistinguishable from his mentor's). After Thurber was so happily demoted to a writer, he and White together put out practically the entire "Talk" department, with White usually writing Notes and Comment and Thurber doing original pieces and rewriting the work of other "Talk" reporters (such as Charles H. Cooke, the first Our Man Stanley). He wrote and rewrote "Talk" off and on for a total of eight years—so well that Robert Coates, Thurber's Paris friend and a *New Yorker* writer in 1927 through Thurber's recommendation, once said that " 'Talk' was just made for him, as he was made for it, and it is no more than simple fact to say he 'made' the department."(20) As with most things, it wasn't that easy to convince Ross:

... Ross had been sure I couldn't do it because I would never get away from journalese. He was sure nobody could do anything and it took months to convince him. He made me rewrite a Talk piece about Billy Seeman, buddy of Jimmy Walker, six times. "Now you got it," he said. "Write it the way you would talk to a dinner companion." He meant the way *he* would talk to one, offhand, casual. . . . I wrote about a million words for Talk in my time . . .(21)

Slowly, through the rest of 1927, the White effect began to show up in all Thurber's work. His casuals got funnier, sharper, less forced, and, as they were increasingly set in the first person, more original. His parodies and especially his nonsense casuals took on the familiar sheen of Robert Benchley's pieces, which started running in the *New Yorker* in January, 1926. Thurber often acknowledged his debt to Benchley, too: ". . . one of the greatest fears of the humorous writer is that he has spent three weeks writing something done faster and better by Benchley in 1919."(22) But the gracious and benevolent older-brother* influence of White (who was actually five years younger than Thurber) was most telling.

Like White and several of the others, Thurber was getting known around town as an original talent. At the age of thirty-three, he had arrived as an almost whole man: He had a real career, a real father (Ross), a real brother (White), and more influential instruments of change than he could handle. All he needed was a real wife.

---

*William, his true older brother, was also in New York in 1927, working for the Waterman Pen Company. Thurber avoided him as much as he could. In June, Charles Thurber came east to visit his two older sons, leaving the youngest, Robert, still trying to get back on his feet in Columbus.

CHAPTER **10**

Menaces

At the beginning of 1928, Thurber, Althea, and their Scotty moved to more commodious digs at 65 West Eleventh Street, on the fringe of Greenwich Village where the 1928 action was. The action consisted, in great part, of overindulgence in bad Prohibition booze, left-wing causes, and some dedicated sleeping around, which Ross referred to as "S-L-E-E-P-I-N-G." ("He was the only man I've ever known who spelled out euphemisms in front of adults," Thurber once said.) (1) Whether it was the pressure of work or the looser circle of friends or the hooch, Thurber and Althea had increasingly thorny sexual problems. There were times when Thurber was simply not able or willing to meet Althea's demands. To add to the marital tension, Thurber was developing a reputation not only as a humorist but as a social wit, while Althea seemed to many of their friends to be growing more morose and humorless. Mrs. Malcolm Cowley, who knew both of them well during that period, described Althea as "having no sense of fantasy," and Mrs. Richard Connell, another friend from the Greenwich Village days and the wife of the short-story writer, concurred. "Althea was strangely reticent," Mrs. Connell said, "especially when Jim and my husband would fall into their bouts of elfin humor. She wanted to talk about property, luxury, dogs, and the more elevated artistic world."* As a result, there were daily spats, confrontations, abrupt leave-takings, and both civilized and uncivilized indiscretions. At one point, Althea went off to Europe and stayed there for two months. Thurber was again an unhindered but lonely bachelor. His brother Robert was well enough to come to New York and visit him (especially since Althea wasn't around), but after Robert returned to

---

*On occasion, however, Althea could get off a mot worthy of her old Columbus form, which so attracted Thurber to her in the early 1920's. Once, they were with a friend and his new Turkish wife, who unluckily was the target of an unexpected vomiter. The husband was horrified, shouting that it was an abominable thing for a Moslem girl to be vomited upon. "American girls aren't crazy about it, either," Althea told him.

Columbus, Thurber was bedevilled. He disclosed his feelings in a rare outpouring to his favorite brother, written sometime in March of 1928:

Dear Robert:

You must think I am a coo-coo, as the French say, not to have written you, but several things have had me down: first the hemorrhoids, known to the Sioux tribes as Flame-in-the-Bowels (which would be my tribal name, if I am ever made President like Coolidge) and then a slight attack of dysentery, crick, naushy, spring sickness and a recurrence of the old Black Plague. This added to the fact that I have to get out a little work to hold my position kept me floundering, but I seem to be okay now. I sent off your slippers, terribly late, because the maid had placed them on top of the highboy, or old Chippendale garmentoire, where she wanted to see if I could find them without being told, a sort of game she plays because she lives in Jersey and gets such little fun. For days this went on, me missing her when she came here, so that she couldnt even help by saying "cold" or "warm" when I searched. Finally I found them and mailed them from the drugstore postoffice down the street, Bigelows, which you probably remember. Thus I have your stamps which I will send back so that you will be reminded to write. If you dont want them, send them back and we will keep them going back and forth for ever so long until finally we get a piece in the papers about it: THURBERS KEEP TWO-CENT STAMPS GOING FOR TEN MONTHS.

Columbus Boy and Former Columbus Boy Believed
To have Set New World's Record Exchanging
Little Bunch of Stamps
—
LOTS OF FUN, SAY BROTHERS, WHEN INTERVIEWED.

. . . I certainly felt badly about Muggs [the recently deceased family Airedale Thurber didn't like], on account of you and the rest, and the old dog himself. I know what it would mean to me if Jeannie passed out and we've only had her little over a year. When I lost her in Columbus I was nearly nuts. That's the hell of having a dog. I still feel bad about Rex and often dream of him. They cant live long, and ten years is a long time for a dog. Why cant we have alligators as pets, which live to be 1500 years old, or crows which live to be ninety? Seems strange that God would pick such cumbersome and morose animals and birds to live that long and give a dog the bad break of a handful of moments, as the years go. Still, our family has been lucky about deaths and we got to buck up against them because the years are going on and people die and what the hell, a person simply must build up a philosophy that will endure it all. I have, because my imagination is forever running on ahead of the present and I know that the blows are set to come and a person has got to set himself to meet them. It wont save anyone from grief but it will set up a reserve power finally to meet grief and stand it. It's a strange life, and so far I dont seem to see where anyone has figured it out, but sometimes it seems to me that time goes by like a flash of rain and that's all we amount to in this world. Some of the rain is clear and pretty and some is muddy and bounces off of rainspouts and down into the mud and our family seems sometimes to have been selected to play the part of the rain drops that do most of the bouncing, but my idea is that in the end we seep into the ground somewhere and help a hyacinth to grow or something like that, or maybe seep farther than that and spatter on some hot gentleman or lady in Hades. There ought to be some point to it all and I live in the hopes that the adventure of death is something equal to the adventure of life which is pretty colorful and interesting even if hard. It would seem strange to me if God made such a complicated world and such complicated people and then had no more to offer than blankness at the end, so I live in the curiosity and the hope and the excitement of what there may be afterwards and thus I have got myself to believe that those who pass on perhaps pass on to something as interesting, but lovelier and more happy, than this life. I may be wrong but I have persuaded myself that I'm not and so I dont have the terror of things that some do. None of it helps blunt the edge of grief, though, and no one will ever discover a way of doing that, but as time goes on what once was grief becomes easier to bear if you believe that it all isnt plain useless and silly. At any rate a hell of a lot of people have gone on and I have heard no complaints from them, that's one thing. I have always expected to find Rex in the company of some such guy as, say, Frank Luke, or Raoul Lufbery and maybe Muggs will have Christy Mathewson with whom to scamper across the porphyry and chrysophase fields. Jeannie will be excellent company for someone like that too and I expect any day to find that she has wandered off and got lost upstate or been killed—not, however, by another dog, I have decided after reading that story in Collier's which tells of that Scotty killing a Doberman Pinscher, which is a huge, terrible black dog. The Scotty, this story tells, fights from off his back,—lays down and then when the dog leaps on him, uppercuts him and gets a hold on his throat. A Scotty has a mouth like a shark and jaws like iron and their grip is rated greater than a bull terrier's. When Jeannie was four months old we used to swing her off the ground with a rope or a strap and she would hold on for minutes at a time. The Scotty is a wonderful dog. Jeannie is going to have pups this spring and if you want one, just say the word. Maybe I'll ship one out any way and you'll have to keep her as it seems that the Scotty is not very well known in the Middle West (from the clipping you sent) and most people that dont know a Scotty dont realize what a grand dog it is, and wouldn't have one. They are tremendously expensive some of them but yours will be FOB nothing, New York. They are not only brave and intelligent but dignified and playful at the same time, easy to teach and easy to house-break, tremendously loyal and affectionate and noted for their fine dispositions. . . . One day our dog, left here to her own devices too long—both of us were gone from eleven in the morning until eight at night—got fed up on having nothing to do and dragged down, or out, or up, everything we had, practically. The house looked like twenty-seven burglars had organized and gone through it hunting for money. Hats, coats, pans, rugs, spools, needles, cigarettes, clocks, overcoats, suitcases, pillows, pillowslips, bedspreads, letters, bills, manuscripts, books, magazines, lamps, dish cloths, curtains and ties were strewn from one end of the house to the other. Many things were chewed but a lot were not. She had specialized on the cigarettes the match boxes and the bag that held Althea's sewing things, especially chewing the spools of silk thread. Only one book was gnawed and that was one we had borrowed from a lady and it was autographed by the author —the one book of our six or eight hundred that she should not have got hold of. Althea corrects her but when I come home alone and find the dog has got things out I always say, "For God's sake, dog, let's hurry and straighten up here or there'll be hell to pay." She is wise enough to know that I will not beat her (which I should). When Althea and I come in together and she has been chewing, she crawls under the bed. Althea says in a firm contralto voice, "Come here, Jeannie". Jeannie bats her tail once. Finally, she comes out for punishment and gets it. She seldom yelps, no matter how hard you spank her, but she yelps if you step on her. When I come home alone and she has been up to something she doesnt crawl under the bed but takes to running up and down the apartment like a race horse, thus interfering with me putting the spools, coats, hats, bedclothes and matches back where she got them. This is to show her pleasure at getting away with murder. She knows she will get licked for raising hell but she does it because she is willing to stand the gaff— you can tell that by the way she comes out for it. She used to sleep on the bed and we spanked her, so that when she heard us coming she would get down and crawl under the bed, and then come out slowly looking sleepy and surprised. But she neglected to pat the pillows and smooth out the bedspread where she had been laying. This is a trick she has never learned but if I come in on her someday patting the pillows into shape I'll call the police, or a minister.

Althea will not be home before the 15th of April I think. She is scheduled to sail on the 8th. It is too bad you had to leave here just as it got fine weather. Today was like June. I didnt wear a coat and have the window open now (I never get a cold and didn't have one this last week—just the old Black Plague). I wish you could get back and stay till Althea comes, because it gets pretty lonely here. I dont like to stay alone at nights, even in an apartment house and on such nights as I see a mystery play or read a mystery story, I leave the light on in the bathroom.

My God, I almost forgot to explain the ten dollars enclosed and the check, which tear up. I wrote a story for Talk of the Town, on the O.Henry region, which appears in next week's issue and I put through a check for $20 for you, and had it made out to me. I explained that the story was yours (we always pay for tips and the dope, and then write the story ourself which is what makes my job pretty complicated, as few people can write the stuff just the peculiar way we want it, or short enough, or whatnot, so if we get a good story we either rewrite it, or send it back and pay for the idea. Someone just turned in one about a toy railroad a mile and a half long some guy built here, a musician, but the story was not right, so we paid the woman for the idea and White went up and looked at the railroad and will write the story). Thus the O. Henry idea was absolutely yours as we never would have thought of it if you hadn't brought on the book. Too bad that you couldnt have gone with me to the rest of the places because, just a few feet from the house at 55 Irving Place, I found the "Old Munich", the place where he wrote "The Halberdier of the Little Rhein-schloss". At first I was disappointed when I came on the Third Avenue entrance which I recognized from the picture in the Mentor, for the place was vacated and the room bare and dusty. Then I found there was an entrance around on the other street—Seventeenth street—and inside was the fine old beer hall just as it was, rafters, white-clothed tables, a big fire place and steins and tankards all around. The son of the manager was there and he had been there when O. Henry was and showed us (I went with Charme Seeds) the table O. Henry ate at, right before the fireplace, and mentioned that his favorite drink was Scotch (which you couldnt get down here). (That is you can get it here, but *you* couldnt get it *down*.) It was very interesting and if we had had any luck we would have stumbled on it the day we were there. So I wrote a piece about it, which I will send you when it comes out next Wednesday. I wish you could in some way get more idea checks from us, but naturally it isnt every day that such a yarn comes up. I had to hold the story to about 800 words, because our space is limited.

The other day Charles Speaks came home with a dice game, two dice with golf terms written on them, by which you play golf. One dice has "In the Cup" on one side and you have to throw that before you make a hole, or, that is, sink a putt, so the number of times you throw before you get that tells how many strokes you take. That reminded me of our old dice game, baseball, which you invented and which I elaborated for myself. Last year I had an idea of market-ing the thing and played several games and carefully preserved them on paper. I still think the thing could be put over and go big and I am going to find out who are the people to see. The way I have it now, it is almost an exact duplicate of a baseball game and the scores are exactly right. . . .

I wish I could think of some way to put this over: and maybe I can, in which case, if it looks good, you might come on and help out in getting the thing ready. There are probably things that should be in it, or things in it that should be out. . . .

This is getting to be a hell of a long letter and I'll probably have to send it in two envelopes. I wish you could get back here—maybe if you could scrape up the money, we could dope out some way for you to make expenses here, so it wouldnt really cost anything. There are hundreds of ways to make money in this burg.

Love to all,
Jamie

This malaise emerged publicly, soon after Althea's return, in Thurber's first straight short story for the *New Yorker*, "Menaces in May" (published on May 26, 1928). The story impressed Katharine Angell so much that she thought for a while that Thurber's serious writing could be as promising as his humor. "Menaces in May," unabashedly autobiographical, concerns a lonely protagonist running into his old hometown girl friend (modelled on The One, Eva Prout) and her dreary husband on a rainy street in New York. The protagonist, once a withdrawn teacher's pet, wonders what his life might have been like with this searing old flame, as the phonograph in the couple's hotel room plays a sentimental Jazz Age accompaniment. He leaves the couple at last and thinks of his cultivated wife, Lydia, who "has been away a long time." Outside, in the dark and the rain, he is confronted with the menaces of the city—lurching drunks, banging ashcans, raunchy violence, sick wanderers—and he cravenly gives too many coins to an offensive panhandler. He wishes he could face menace and death like Lord Jim or Cyrano de Bergerac, but something robs him of this show of manhood. Finally secure in his locked apartment, he looks through some photographs of Lydia:

. . . Here is Lydia in April sunlight, when she was eighteen. Lydia in college, Lydia feeding the silly gulls at Nice, Lydia in a snow of lavender crocuses at Saint Martin Vesubie—that had been in May—two, Lord, three years ago. Lydia on a hillside across from Saint Paul du Var that Sunday when they listened to the ancient bells of the town over the valley. What a finely wrought thing they had made of life . . .

At the end of the story, he reasons that it is Lydia's fault he is not Lord Jim or Cyrano, that he cannot snap his fingers at "an alien and nameless terror." His unhappiness, his fears are the fault of his lovely, Jamesian wife, not the frumpy, ordinary old sweetheart.

Other young married couples in similar straits might have tried to patch things up by having children; in Thurber and Althea's case, they decided to let Jeannie have a litter of Scotties. The blessed event began at 6 A.M. in the Thurbers' shoe closet. The last puppy was born three hours later on the corner of Fifth Avenue and Eleventh Street, where

Thurber had taken Jeannie for a revivifying walk. Thurber stuffed the final arrival in his coat pocket and hurried home. "It's seven Scotch terrier pups at Jim (Newyorker) Thurber's," wrote Walter Winchell in his New York *Graphic* column, and the hot news was picked up back home in the Columbus papers. For a while, the puppies took up a lot of the Thurbers' time and temporarily brought them a little closer together; but, like children born into difficult marriages, the pups didn't really cure anything. The squabbling continued.

There were many new and interesting people to be met and cultivated in those days, and several of them were influential forces in Thurber's life, though not of the proportions of Nugent, Althea, White, and Ross. One of these was John "Jap" (so named from an early case of yellow jaundice) Gude, a radio executive who later became Thurber's theatrical agent and the most doggedly loyal friend a man could have. "Jim from the first was a moody, charming, good drinker," Gude said. "He was a nice guy with wide-ranging interests, who loved to argue about sports and practically anything. But there was constant bickering with Althea—a very good-looking, determined, and, I think, calculating woman. She was ambitious for herself and Jim, and this was to the good because it got him moving and writing. But Jim still had a trace of that Ohio puritanism in him. He put certain women on pedestals, and not many of them in the Village belonged there. As he got better known and printed more pieces in the *New Yorker*, he wanted to be surrounded all the time by friends—like me and my wife and Bob Coates and Andy White and Morris Markey and the rest of the *New Yorker* group—but Althea wanted to be surrounded by a more glamorous set of writers and artists, the sort that lived in Westport, Connecticut. She didn't like most of the *New Yorker* people, and vice versa. Also, Althea had the bad habit of doing everything as well as a man could, which infuriated Jim. There was friction between them almost all the time and no real affection. One was always walking out on the other after some blow-up."

Besides "Menaces in May," Thurber wrote several other devastating pieces based on his own marriage. He and Althea *were* Mr. and Mrs. Monroe, in a series of eight stories published in the *New Yorker* during 1928 and 1929. Every Monroe story was founded on a real incident of their waspish life together. As Thurber wrote his Columbus friend Herman Miller: "The Monroe stories were transcripts, one or two of them varying less than an inch from the actual happenings." (2)

They are anecdotal, light pieces, sometimes funny, sometimes flawless opals of life, in the Dorothy Parker style of the laughable, sad truth about male–female relationships. John Monroe—a prototype of the ineffectual Walter Mitty, as well as an alloy of Thurber *père et fils*—is a bumbler with machinery, with nature, with sex, with officialdom, with society, and, of course, with his wife. Mrs. Monroe is everything that Althea was and Thurber wasn't; she is at peace with the mechanical and natural worlds and is brusque and efficient in all other matters. Only her slight size is at variance with Althea. John Monroe is in danger of being emasculated by his wife, or something, on almost every page: A bat paralyzes him, hot-water faucets panic him, moving men brutalize him, details frustrate him, a "flitting, clothes-closety" sound in the night terrifies him, the prospect of infidelity drives him to Henry James and the security of his own warm bed. Somehow, beneath John Monroe's dissolving manhood there is the feeling that one day he is going to explode and become a key figure in a trunk murder. He never does, of course. He remains a hopeless prisoner of womanhood and life's other menaces.

The Thurbers cooled their tempers in the country whenever they could. They had two distinct sets of country-loving friends, dividing their time between them, as a compromise. Althea favored the West-port circle of writers and artists—the elite salon she had always dreamed of belonging to, with such established figures as Hendrick van Loon, Howard Brubaker, Van Wyck Brooks, Guy Pene DuBois, and John Held, Jr. (Most of them used the Westport area as a weekend and summer place; it was still a country town then.) Thurber preferred a sort of communal farm rented by several friends from the *New Yorker* like Coates and White, near the Amawalk Reservoir in Westchester County, New York.

They were introduced into the Westport set by the Richard Connells, who met the Thurbers in Greenwich Village through Charme Seeds, of O.S.U. and Red Cross-girl-in-Paris fame. Louise Connell recalled 1928 Westport as a place of fun and games. "I remember Althea being there most often alone," she said, "but Jim would occasionally come up on weekends and play doubles on our tennis court. He could play all right if he was in a position that favored his good eye. Althea adored having passes made at her by the men, and the men obliged. You felt there was something wrong with you if nobody made a pass. It was the local sport —that and drinking bootleg gin and ginger ale at parties. How we survived I don't know. The alcohol was delivered to our door by a taxi driver and his girl friend. Her skirts concealed gallon cans of the stuff and small bottles of juniper juice. We made the so-called gin by mixing the alcohol with water and adding a few drops of juniper juice and then shaking it well. If you were confused about the mixture, the party could get pretty wild and eventually somnolent. I did that once. We danced to phonograph records and ate popcorn and pretzels and mouse cheese. It was a lot of fun, I guess.

"I liked Althea but I never felt close to her. She wasn't a warm person. Jim tended to ignore me. I got the impression then that he was a man's man—that is, he wasn't too interested in women he had no designs on or didn't worship from afar. Maybe he was afraid of women. A lot of people said that."

Thurber wasn't afraid of women at Amawalk, or at least one woman. It was in the little *New Yorker* community there that he met Ann Honeycutt, a transplanted Louisiana belle whom every close friend of Thurber has described as the great love of his life. Honey, as she was inevitably called, has also been described as "the girl friend of the *New Yorker.*" She was linked at one time or another not only with Thurber but with, among others, Wolcott Gibbs, John Lardner, and St. Clair McKelway, whose third wife she ultimately became. ("We were married for about fifteen minutes," she said, "but we shared an apartment for one year.") Honey was and is an attractive, acerbic blond writer, who, as E. B. White put it, "wanted to be one of the boys, a drinking pal, not just a sex object. Thurber treated her as such. He looked on in wonder as she held her own at any bar or party in town."

At Amawalk, there were also good times in the Westport manner— Prohibition drinking, phonograph dancing, and a lot of flirting. As Honey remembered it: "We all had strong independence and a high sense of original, witty fun. On weekends, when all the men came up, we drank and danced and laughed at each other's lines. I think we invented the frug, or something just like it. Althea spent most of one summer there, and Thurber turned up whenever he could. They rented the icehouse part of the farm. I was brought there for the first time by a boy friend, and I immediately noticed that Althea and Thurber were going their own ways, quite openly. I couldn't figure out why she had married him. Maybe it was to use him, a sort of marriage of convenience.

"I liked Jim a lot. I liked his mind, mostly. He was good company, and we had some good times together. For some reason, he wanted to fight with me, though. He would argue about anything, and it would suddenly turn into a fight. Once in a while, the fighting got rather violent. I didn't mind fighting with him, either. But he fought dirty. He'd hit below the belt, which made me hit back harder. I was a counterpuncher. He liked that. When he was drinking, he wasn't very sensitive or vulnerable—just a bully, with sudden rages. Once, at 21, he slapped me from across the table, so I threw a glass of Scotch right back at him. We were thrown out, but we finished the fight on the sidewalk. It was like that in those days. But he had a gentle hick Ohio side of him, too —there were so many contradictions in him—and, now that I think of it, I liked that side better. That was the part that showed his great humor, humor that came out of all the hurts of his childhood. He overcame the hurts by making characters out of the villains, that peculiar family of his and all those other Columbus people. He even treated the city of Columbus itself as a character, another crazy member of his family. I believe he was headed for a crack-up ever since he was a kid —farmed out to that Aunt Margery and all.

"With other women and me, he wanted to appear as the great lover —whether Althea was around or not—but it was a ridiculous role for him. He simply was not a roué type. He had a fantasy life about ladies, just as he had about Columbus and his family, but he wasn't half as successful with the ladies. I think he was afraid of women—felt inadequate with them, sexually and otherwise. I knew him from the eyebrows up. It wasn't really a physical relationship we had, except for the fighting."

Thurber's stormy affair with Ann Honeycutt was no quickie infatuation. She came in and out of his life with disrupting regularity until his last days. "He always carried a torch for her," said Jap Gude. "She was something special, perhaps unattainable, for him." Another friend who knew them well said that Honey was a tease, a Southern coquette, who enjoyed leading Thurber along. In any case, from Amawalk on, whenever he was lonely or depressed, which was often, he turned up in her apartment or met her at one of their bars, looking for some solace. The persistence of his infatuation with Honey was apparent in a letter he wrote to a common friend of theirs in 1956:

... They come in fascinating packages from Louisiana, and if they get close enough to kiss they may bite your ear off. She used to be a woman of sparkling personality only ... and then she developed this new character, complete with 1952 religion and philosophy. So many interesting things happened when I was riding shotgun on her that I declare I could write a book called "Honey, Honey, Break My Heart," but at 61 I am too old to write about women. Honey is a great friend and we all know that, and a wonderful girl to visit whether you want to live with her or not ... (3)

And to E. B. White—with whom he continually and sometimes jokingly corresponded about Ann Honeycutt—he wrote in 1952 that Honey had finally decided Thurber didn't like her: "She is right and I have figured out why. Our love never ripened into friendship." (4)

Thurber and Althea, separate or together, were in demand and had their weekends and vacations booked solid. Besides Westport and Amawalk, Thurber visited Katharine and Ernest Angell (the celebrated lawyer and Katharine's husband till 1929) at Sneden's Landing, New York, just north of the city, along the Hudson River. Thurber was very concerned about the breaking up of the Angells' marriage; he liked both of them and their children a good deal, but he worshipped E. B. White, who shortly after the Angells' divorce married Katharine, although White was not the reason for the divorce. "Jim was a comfort to me when I was going through the misery of the divorce," Katharine said. Althea was also close to Katharine—as close as she could be to any female acquaintance, especially one connected with the *New Yorker*. White, about that time, had bought an interest in a boys' camp in Ontario, and he invited Thurber to come up and visit him there. "It was on the lake near the camp that I almost deprived the United States of America of James Grover Thurber," White said. "I had to pick him up across the lake in a canoe. I also had to pick up a hundred-pound bell. Thurber was terrified of water. He couldn't swim, and in the canoe he had to sit between me and the bell. He talked constantly, as he always did when he was tense, and he began to move about. The canoe tipped and took on water, but we just made it to the shore. I still fear for what might have happened out there in the middle of a deep, cold lake."

As the separations from Althea became more frequent and of longer duration, Thurber was less guilty and gloomy about them. In November of 1928, he and Elliott Nugent made a triumphal bachelor jaunt to Columbus to visit family and friends and to see the Ohio State–Iowa football game. Thurber received more notice in the local press (thanks to John McNulty, who was working for the *Citizen* then) than did Nugent, and that certainly cheered him. Nugent didn't seem to mind; after all, Thurber was still known in Columbus as his protégé. They both thoroughly enjoyed being there (in Thurber's case, perhaps for the first time in his life), and Columbus's newest literary son wrote a little piece for the *Citizen* commemorating it all:

THE CORPORAL'S GUARD
by
James Thurber, son of Charles L. Thurber.

(NOTE—When this letter was written, Jamie was just 34 years old. The editor prints it here exactly as written, thereby conserving the naive charm of the 34-year-old prodigy in its entirety).

Dear Mamma:

Well I am now on the train for New York and I am glad. Columbus is nice because I always lived there but was too excited this last visit by the crowds so can not come back for a very long time. In New York there is only about 15,000 people at shows like in the Madisohn Square Garden for Horse Shows, Hoover, and other shows. This is a very big crowd for New York. So at the stadium where I went to see the Iowa-Iowa game I was certainly surprised to see so many people. I think they was certainly about 25,000 people there but a man next to me laugh when I says there are certainly about twenty five thousand people here. He says they are about forty-five thousand people here! So I realized there are about forty-five thousand people there and this is about thirty more thousand people than are at the Horse Shows or for Smith or six day bicycle races. Well I said, this is the biggest crowd in the world isn't it? I wonder where everybody is he says. There don't nobody come to the games anymore. So I pointed at everybody and he says this is what comes from rain and lack of interest in Iowa in Iowa. He says if it hadn't of rained there would have been quite a crowd but this is just a caporal's guard. So I am glad we will soon be back in NY where you can get around.

Yours truly,

JAMIE.(5)

It was during an extended separation from Althea, in 1928, that Thurber was working late at his *New Yorker* office one night. Katharine Angell was also working late, clearing up last-minute business before she left with her husband, Ernest, and her children, Roger and Nancy, on a midnight sailing for Europe. Just as she was about to leave for her apartment on East Ninety-third Street, Thurber rushed into her office. "Katherine, can I ride up to Ninety-third Street with you?" he asked her. "I can't see anything." She was shocked. "I didn't know what to do," she recalled. "I couldn't very well ask him in and take care of him because we were sailing in a few hours, and I knew Althea wasn't around and that he would have to go downtown to an empty apartment. All I could do was phone Ross and tell him, for heaven's sake, to get Jim to an oculist, which Ross finally did, I think. Jim did go with me to Ninety-third Street and then he kept the cab so he could go downtown in safety. I remember that I held his hand in the cab all the way uptown and I tried to tell him that probably the one eye was just tired. The sudden blindness was, of course, only temporary, but it gave him a frightening sense of impending doom."

The menaces were very real.

CHAPTER 11

"Jamie the Boy Artist" (1)

A compromise was struck in 1929, a convenient and expedient solution to the Thurbers' marital problems. They would give up their New York City apartment and rent a house in Silvermine, Connecticut, not far from Westport, where Althea would feel more at home and would be able to raise Scotties. Thurber, meanwhile, would spend most of his time in New York, working and living at various hotels, and would, when his guilt or loneliness became too much for him, stop by Silvermine for visits. The new routine worked fairly well. Jeannie and her puppies thrived in the country, and, as the kennelling grew more serious, the Scotties were joined by two Siamese cats (Thurber distrusted cats, all of which showed negative female characteristics, as far as he was concerned) and a black standard French poodle and her eleven offspring.

The poodle, Medve (Hungarian for "bear"), was an extraordinary dog, a natural mother, and a Thurberian eccentric. Her master wrote several loving pieces about her and talked about her constantly. Medve, like so many other living things close to Thurber, was a rich source of literary material. An intelligent show dog, she won Best of Breed in the Novice Class at the 1929 Westminster Show and took blue ribbons at other exhibitions. Her opposition wasn't that strong at Westminster (poodles weren't so popular then); she won first prize in her class after being displayed for only two minutes. Althea burst into tears at the announcement, with the poodle howling, too, "in the mistaken belief that their mingled tears were meant to express disapproval of the judge, the bedlam, and the whole distressing spectacle."(2) Medve didn't like show business, primarily because she always had to ride in an automobile to the show and cars made her wretchedly sick. She was compelled to wear a degrading red-rubber bib, sit on newspaper, and sometimes ride in the rumble seat, with Thurber appointed to hold an umbrella over her head when it rained. In "And So to Medve," he wrote: "She threw up [on the newspaper] like a lady, leaning far down, looking as apologetic as she looked sick." The dog shows were a new tack for

Thurber, something to take his mind off himself and provide a shared activity with Althea. They even gave him an outlet for cutting up a bit:

 . . . At one of the last dog shows in which she [Medve] was entered with two or three of her best male pups, she was reluctant to get up on the bench assigned to her and her family, and so I got up on it myself, on all fours, to entice her to follow. She was surprised and amused, but not interested, and this was also true of my wife, who kept walking past the bench, saying, out of the corner of her mouth, "Get off that bench, for the love of heaven!". . .(3)

But alone and at large in the city, Thurber was a less innocent cutup. Sporadically rebuffed by Ann Honeycutt, Thurber was hurt again, but not enough so that his attentions didn't wander elsewhere. One woman —who might be called his second greatest extramarital love—practically fell into his lap. Paula Trueman, an actress who looked at the time remarkably like Ann Honeycutt, was appearing in a revue called "Grand Street Follies." She was on the lookout for new talent to write a good extra sketch for her in the show, and having read some of Thurber's *New Yorker* casuals, she decided he was the man. She got in touch with him, he took her to lunch, and another long relationship began.

"He never did write the sketch for me," Paula Trueman said, "but we saw a lot of each other. Most nights, he would pick me up after the show and we'd go out together to a bar—that is, a little speakeasy like Tony's. There would always be friends of his there—Andy White or Bob Coates or Wolcott Gibbs or sometimes Ross, who sounded to me like a taxi driver. There was a lot of drinking, of course, but Jim didn't need to drink to be witty. I didn't drink at all. I was quiet and dreamy, off in another world—sort of loony, like his mother. Jim liked that, I guess —someone who just listened, or pretended to listen—because he talked all the time. He wasn't a very attentive boy friend, and I suppose I didn't pay too much attention to him, either. I don't remember him as particularly angry or argumentative. There was no physical violence with me, the way there was with Ann Honeycutt. He said what he thought, though. Sometimes, he was so unhappy, such a solitary person. When we first met, he told me about losing his eye. It was very brave of him, but it wasn't a terrible handicap for him then. He wasn't bitter about it and he didn't use it as an excuse or ask for pity.

"I am an actress but it was Jim who was stagestruck. I think he really envied me my profession. He just plain loved to perform. He said it was so easy to succeed: You just had to be slightly better than the others who have no brains or talent. He had plenty of both. At one point, he said he was going to leave Althea for good and he asked me to live with him. He even found an apartment, but later he said, 'Althea wants to come back to me,' and that was the end of a not very serious affair for a while. Another time, later, he was in my apartment, looking out the window, and he said, 'Let's get married.' I looked out the window, too, and I said, 'No, I don't think so.' I never regretted it. But there was nobody else like Jim. He was a complete individual, as a man and a writer."

1929 was not all play and no work, by any means. He wrote twenty-seven casuals for the *New Yorker*—five Monroe stories, several parody pieces of Fowler's *A Dictionary of Modern English Usage* (Ross's bible), other parodies of the contemporary literary and drama scene, satires of self-help psychology books (salvaged, in part, from *Why We Behave Like Microbe Hunters*), doggerel trifles, and a few "Talk of the Town" originals, as well as his rewritten "Talk" stories. And for *Magazine of Business*, he wrote two frolicsome pieces about American mercantile rites. The quality of his pieces was uneven; it ranged from memorably brilliant to easily dated and forgotten, with the reportage always solid. The parodies and the Monroe stories stand out. Despite his success and facility, Thurber was still learning his peculiar and dangerous trade.

Being pointed out around town as one of the stars of the *New Yorker* didn't get him his own office, however. He still shared a cubicle with White, and the way their relationship had grown, it was unlikely that either of them wanted a private office. It was probably one of the happiest and most relaxed professional friendships in history. Thurber was perfecting his writing of the simple sentence in the manner of White, without actually aping White. He was becoming very much Thurber. As White described it: "Somehow, there was always time for us to write our own things. We wrote short in those days and ran everything through the typewriter a couple of times because we tried to be perfectionists. Thurber was a good critic and a good reporter, but he was perhaps too emotional to be a great reporter. What made his casuals pure Thurber was his marvelous sense of the incongruous, the unexpected."

There was also time for Thurber to continue his cherished role as the office prankster. Wolcott Gibbs once said that when Ross refused to get Thurber a new typewriter (he was hard on typewriters), Thurber simply called up the Underwood company and asked for its most expensive machine to be delivered to his office, charged to the *New Yorker*. He let the word get around that this ploy worked, and soon everybody was doing it. Another time, he burst into the office of R. E. M. Whitaker, a general editor at the magazine who was in the habit of writing queries and emendations in red ink on galley proofs. Thurber pulled out a toy pistol, pointed it at Whitaker, and shouted, "Are you the son of a bitch that keeps putting notes in red ink on the proofs of my 'Talk' stories?" Whitaker fainted. He was never known to use red ink again.

One of Thurber's most complex practical jokes involved White, whose Buick sedan was stolen from a garage near his apartment. The car was used in a daring bank robbery in Ardsley, New York, and was later abandoned by the escaping bandits after a gun battle. Naturally, the police were interested in questioning White, especially after Ross, something of a kidder himself, had told two detectives who arrived one day at the office that "you're on the right track. White has been silent and brooding—he's definitely got something on his mind that's worry-ing the hell out of him." The detectives were shown into White's office (as Ross said expansively, "There's your man, officers"), where they noticed Thurber's highly suspicious graffiti on the walls—particularly White's memorandum of a feared dentist appointment, over which Thurber had scrawled "Der Tag." By insane coincidence, the dentist-appointment date and the bank-robbery date were the same. On the basis of this hard evidence, the detectives decided to question White a few more times, and during each grilling Thurber would telephone White and loudly imitate a thug's voice, being careful to use words like "loot" and "caper." At last, in spite of Thurber's worst intentions, the police gave up on White and returned his Buick, with a few bullet holes in it.

On the face of it, both Thurber and White were natural candidates for the Algonquin Round Table, that witful gallimaufry of which Ross was so fond. Not all the resident wits had taken Ross and his new magazine seriously at first, and most of them helped him in the begin-ning only left-handedly—which prompted Herman Mankiewicz, a full-time wit, to say, "The part-time help of wits is no better than the full-time help of half-wits."(4) One day, Ross took his two star writers to lunch at the Round Table, and both Thurber and White quickly decided they didn't like it one bit. They never returned. White, an extremely private, introspective man who preferred to lunch alone, said that the Round Table in the late 1920's was already dying out. "Thurber and I were much younger than most of the others," he re-called, "and everything they said seemed so rehearsed, as if they had been planning their lines all the previous week, which they often did, I understand. Alexander Woollcott was just an old poop then."

Thurber experienced a chemical loathing of Woollcott at first sight.

He had been working on a "Talk" piece about the forthcoming theatrical season, and Ross suggested that he visit Woollcott for more information. Woollcott greeted Thurber at his apartment door in his usual attire
of pajama bottoms and askew dressing gown and proceeded to attack
the editor of the *New Yorker,* an old friend with whom he once shared
a cooperative house, as a philistine and a ninny. As Thurber delicately
put it: "The legendary charm of Alexander Woollcott, the still talked-
about spell he cast, did not come over me."(5) Indeed, Thurber's bias
endured, as an April 9, 1958, letter to Groucho Marx, another old Woollcott pal, revealed:

. . . This here, now, total recall memory of mine has brung back, sharp as a
dagger, a photograph, torn in four pieces, that the late Morris Markey showed
me one day when I could still see photographs, so it had to be before 1941. I think
it had been taken by a news photographer in Los Angeles, and it showed Old
Vitriol and Violets, a man as fragile as nails and as sweet as death, seated in a
big chair and surrounded by the four Marx brothers, all standing. Trouble was,
les vêtements de Harpo étaient dérangés, deliberately, and in such impish
fashion that his what's-its-name was clearly visible. I thought it was funnier than
hell, and a terrible thing to do to Aleck, and I'm damned if that doesn't describe
almost everything that happened to him. . . . To me Woollcott was such a
pompous Grand Marshall of his own daily parade that all men wanted to put
banana peels in his path, and all the ladies he praised and insulted in the same
sentence wanted to pick him up when he fell . . .

And as for the heavy-handed practical jokes of the aging Round Table
crew, Thurber went on to Groucho:

. . . All those guys, including Ross, played pranks so elaborate and long they
became burdens. And all this time they had a fine example of how to do it, set
by you and your frères. For example, you did not have to build the house that
wasn't next door and put the painting in it. They did, and that was what was
the matter, in part, with the Round Table . . .

Still, Thurber liked and admired many of the Round Table habitués
—Dorothy Parker, Robert Benchley, George Kaufman, and, of course,
Harold Ross—and for the rest of his life he was a habitué of the Algonquin himself, but just of the hotel and its pleasant bar and restaurant,
not the shaky Round Table.

Thurber not only pencilled odd pictures and ominous phrases on
office walls, he doodled on tablecloths, envelopes, and on reams of copy

paper, as a kind of tic or nervous habit, like biting one's fingernails.* He had, of course, been doodling since he was six years old, in competition with his more steady-handed brother William. He drew in school text-books, for the *Sundial* at Ohio State when the other artists went off to war, and during his tenure on the Columbus *Dispatch* merely to kill time. Most of his childhood scrawls were approximations of dogs, spe-cifically the famous hunting hounds of the Duke of Westminster, a lithograph of which hung over the dining-room fireplace in Grandfa-ther Fisher's Bryden Road house. For some reason, the lithograph of six droopy-eared, Talmudic-eyed bloodhounds haunted Thurber, the child and adult. (He later explained that it was their "dignity and common sense, two qualities which people I draw are said not to possess.")(6) At the drop of a hat, he could rattle off the hounds' brave names—Calypso, Marcano, Sereno, Lentenor, Nicanor, Barbaro.

The canine drawings were perfected (if that is the word) during Thurber's *Dispatch* days. He had a Columbus friend, a frenetic real-estate agent, and whenever Thurber dropped in to see him, there were invariably two or three phones ringing at once and several memo pads being scribbled upon. To make a nuisance of himself, Thurber would draw one of the Westminster hounds on every page of the memo pads, so that his friend had to search all his pads through for a clean scrap of paper in order to jot down an important name or number. But the pads were small and Thurber couldn't fit an entire bloodhound onto the diminutive pages, once he had started with the large, sad head. He corrected for this lack of foresight by giving his dogs the stunted legs of a basset hound. "The hound I draw has a fairly accurate pendulous ear, but his dot of an eye is vastly oversimplified, he doesn't have enough transverse puckers, and he is all wrong in the occipital region. He may not be as keen as a genuine bloodhound, but his heart is just as gentle; he does not want to hurt anybody or anything; and he loves serenity and heavy dinners, and wishes they would go on forever, like the brook."(7) (Certain owners of well-fed golden retrievers swear by the Thurberishness of their dogs.) And so a new breed, the Thurber Dog, was born out of the mysterious imagination of a bored, prankish Midwesterner.

He was just as compulsive with a pencil in his hand at the *New Yorker* in 1929 as he was in Columbus in 1922. Whenever the writing muse had

---

*He did not, however, bite his fingernails. His fingernails were so long and strong, in fact, he could puncture a beer can with his thumb.

temporarily fled from Thurber, the doodling muse would magically appear. On walls, memo pads, and yellow copy paper he not only scrawled his truncated hounds in quick, light strokes, he scrawled peculiar representations of the human form and even human appurtenances, like overstuffed chairs and sofas. "The drawings were everywhere in our tiny office," White said, "on the floor and the desks and in the wastebaskets. They were funny doodles and they made me laugh. He had a great economy of line, like Clarence Day. Thurber could do two drawings in one minute, and they would both be very funny, even brilliant. Then, he would throw them both away and do two more. There must have been thousands of them around that office at one time or another."

White was no idle assessor of drawings; he wrote captions for *New Yorker* cartoons, including the celebrated lines for the 1928 Carl Rose masterpiece in which a mother coaxes her vegetable-eschewing child with "It's broccoli, dear," and the child answers, "I say it's spinach, and I say the hell with it." (It was a caption that gave "spinach" a whole new meaning.) On a spring day in 1929—a day that has since rooted itself in American aesthetic legend—White noticed and laughed at a thirteen-second sketch Thurber drew on yellow copy paper of a seal on a rock looking at two far-off specks and saying, "Hm, explorers." It was too funny for the wastebasket. White impetuously took the sketch, inked it in ("My hand was shaking," he later said), and sent the drawing on to the magazine's weekly art meeting, where all submitted art material was evaluated and polished by Ross and other editors. Nobody at the art meeting knew what to make of the unlikely, untutored lines, but because White had sent it along, it got special attention. Rea Irvin, the bewildered art editor, drew a realistic seal's head on the same piece of paper and sent it back to White, with the notation "This is the way a seal's whiskers go." White promptly resubmitted the drawing with an attached note reading, "This is the way a Thurber seal's whiskers go." The drawing bounced back again, without further word. Thurber later said: "Naturally enough, it was rejected by an art board whose members thought they were being spoofed, if not, indeed, actually chivvied. I got it back and promptly threw it away as I would throw away, for example, a notification from the Post Office that a package was being held there for me. That is, not exactly deliberately, but dreamily in the course of thinking about something else."(8)

For weeks thereafter, White inked in more Thurber drawings and submitted them, only to see them summarily rejected. At one point, Thurber decided to shade and crosshatch his drawings, as he had done

on the *Sundial*. White sagely warned him, "Don't do that. If you ever got good you'd be mediocre."(9) Ross's only comment to Thurber about this wayward turn in his career was "How the hell did you get the idea you could *draw?*"(10)

Thanks to White's encouragement, Thurber did get the idea that he could draw pictures that would affect people. He did not then, nor did he ever in the future, pretend that he was an artist in the full-blown sense of the word, but he discovered that he could elicit laughter and other mixed responses by his unsure pencil lines, even from an audience as hard to amuse as E. B. White.

About the time of this discovery, Thurber and White realized that they were both writing, independently, parodies of the same subject—the weighty, psychological sex books of the day. (The heavy writers, as White said, had got sex down and were breaking its arm.)(11) They decided, rather cleverly, not to compete against each other but to pool their output, not exactly collaborating but combining their individual efforts. The result, by the late summer of 1929, was the book *Is Sex Necessary?* And therein is another tale resting lightly in legend. White insisted that Thurber do the illustrations. Thurber obliged by dashing off a sheaf of pencil sketches in about an hour, and White, in several hours, inked some of them in ("The difference between genius and pluck," White later said).(12)

Harper & Brothers had recently published a book of verse by White, entitled *The Lady Is Cold*, and so that publisher was elected to receive their division of labors. The authors courageously walked into the Harper offices with the manuscript and the Thurber sketches. "Neither of us felt any assurance that it would be accepted for publication,"

White wrote. Eugene Saxton, the Harper editor, was unawed. "The American public was at that time not aware of James Thurber's art, and I'm sure Saxton had never seen a Thurber picture . . . Mr. Saxton looked at what we had spread out on the floor and simply said: 'These, I take it, are the rough sketches from which the drawings will be produced?' 'No,' I said, cheerfully, 'these are the drawings themselves.' "(13) Despite some embarrassment all around, Harper published the book in early November, just after the 1929 Crash. Thurber and White were so astonished by Harper's acceptance that they didn't object when the book was brought out with practically no advertising. It should have been a disaster along the proportions of the Great Depression itself, but the book was as unpredictable as its own humor and drawings. "It was well received," said White, "and it sold fifty thousand copies the first year, which was a big surprise and a delightful bonanza." White married the former Katharine Angell that same month. Thurber's wedding present was a series of drawings called "La Flamme and Mr. Prufrock."

Is Sex Necessary? or Why You Feel the Way You Do (to give its full title)—currently in its twenty-fifth printing—is really a compilation of six pieces by White and six pieces and several drawings by Thurber. The White pieces are the Foreword, Chapters II, IV, VI, VIII, Answers to Hard Questions (which was one of White's standard newsbreak headings), plus A Note on the Drawings in This Book; Thurber's contributions are the Preface, Chapters I, III, V, VII, and the Glossary. Dedicated to Daisy and Jeannie,* the book owed, and probably still owes, a good deal of its success to the fact that it had the word "sex" in its title. (A paperback Armed Services edition, printed up during World War II, perplexed many a G.I., who was seeking to slobber over the very thing the book was ferociously parodying.) It is a deft and funny parody, with an ancestry that goes back a long way, at least in Thurber's case. He had written a mock-scientific piece on petting for his "Credos and Curios" department in the *Dispatch*, on April 15, 1923, and, ever resourceful with unpublished material, he used whole chunks of his rejected *Why We Behave Like Microbe Hunters* here and there in *Is Sex Necessary?* Being a humorist and tending—then, at least—to see the problematical in comic terms, Thurber quite naturally ground some of the edge off his own sexual troubles by making fun of the psychological cures for them.

---

*Daisy and Jeannie (spelled "Jeanie" in the dedication) were two of Thurber's Scotties, daughter and mother, respectively. "We decided on this dedication," White said apologetically, "because they were the first two female names that came to mind. It was our first book."

Strangely, it helped him in a psychological sense; what he could laugh at didn't hurt so much. White's main motive for writing the parody was his dismay at the proliferation of "deep and lugubrious books on sex and marriage," particularly *The Doctor Looks at Love and Life*, by Dr. Joseph Collins, stripe.(14) Then, too, they were both very interested in making some extracurricular money.

The parody came down hard on poor Dr. Freud. In the Preface, Thurber wrote:

. . . When Man first came into being, he did not think that the female was extraordinary. He did not think that anything was extraordinary. The world was unattractive physically, and a little dull. There was no vegetation, and without vegetation there can be no fancy. Then trees came into existence. It was trees that first made Man begin to brood. In pondering their leafy intricacies he got his first crude concept of beauty. He used to tear great branches out of trees and take them home to his cave woman. "Here," he would say to her, "lie on these." The man then reclined in a corner of the cave and watched the woman's hair mingle with the leaves, and her eyes shine through them, until he fell asleep. His dreams were troubled. Woman came into his dreams as a tree, then a tree came into his dreams as a woman. He also got her eyes, shining through the leaves, all mixed up with the moon. Out of this curious and lamentable confusion grew the tendency in Man's mind to identify Woman with the phenomena of the burgeoning earth and the mysteries of the illimitable heavens. As time went on Man rather enjoyed cultivating this idea. It was something to think about. It wasn't much, but it was something. Thus was the subconscious born, with all its strange mixture of fact and symbol . . .

They made up funny names—for example, Lt. Col. H.R.L. Le Boutellier, C.I.E., and Walter L. Mouse (of Columbus, Ohio)—a comic maneuver they would both avoid like a tainted tin of sardines in later years, and, borrowing a favorite device from the master Benchley, they invented ponderous scientific terms: Übertragung Period, Diversion Subterfuge, Osculatory Justification, Schmalhausen Trouble, Recessive Knee, and Fuller's Retort. It is all nonsense and parody of the highest —which is to say, Benchley—order, and it holds up surprisingly well today. Its weaknesses are length, some repetitiveness, and a general slowing of pace around Chapter VII (by Thurber). It will live in American humorous literature as a tour de force by virtue of its originality, exuberance, and dazzling display of promise. As in all good parody, there are truths lurking in the madness, and it should be stated that the book is one of the few satires of sex and sex literature ever written that is not in the least bit dirty. Not once did the authors resort to an easy joke or pun at the expense of sex. Of course, one of them was, at the time, a recently converted puritan.

As for the *Is Sex Necessary?* drawings, they are among Thurber's most economical and funny. What he did with a slight one-en dash for an eye, a sweeping line for an arm in motion, a shaky, shallow curve for a woman's breast is an art lesson. The more careful drawings of men are unmistakable self-portraits.

The less careful pictures he made fun of, captioning one as the work of "Grace McFadden, aged 11, of Bucyrus, Ohio."

In A Note on the Drawings in This Book (White's explanation for the unwarned reader), the inherent strangeness of Thurber's art was beautifully set down:

. . . When one studies the drawings, it soon becomes apparent that a strong undercurrent of grief runs through them. In almost every instance the man in the picture is badly frightened, or even hurt. These "Thurber men" have come to be recognized as a distinct type in the world of art; they are frustrated, fugitive beings; at times they seem vaguely striving to get out of something without being seen (a room, a situation, a state of mind), at other times they are merely perplexed and too humble, or weak, to move. The *women*, you will notice, are quite different: temperamentally they are much better adjusted to their surroundings than are the men, and mentally they are much less capable of making themselves uncomfortable.

It would be foolish to attempt here a comprehensive appreciation of the fierce sweep, the economy, and the magnificent obscurity of Thurber's work, nor can I adequately indicate the stark qualities in the drawings that have earned for him the title of "the Ugly Artist." All I, all anybody, can do is to hint at the uncanny faithfulness with which he has caught—caught and thrown to the floor—the daily, indeed the almost momently, severity of life's mystery, as well as the charming doubtfulness of its purpose . . .

Those book buyers who could still muster a laugh after October 29, 1929, were laughing at and talking about *Is Sex Necessary?* The book was high up on the best-seller lists and both of the authors were heavily in demand at parties. Thurber attended every one he could. Two copies of the book even found their way into Sing Sing prison, and it was reported that the inmates liked it because it helped them laugh off sex, or, in their case, the lack of same. Back in Columbus, the newspapers were full of Thurber, and when the town's own literary lion showed up there in person, in February, 1930, to attend, of all things, the fiftieth-anniversary celebration of the O.S.U. Phi Kappa Psi chapter (he also addressed a journalism

class and a Sigma Delta Chi luncheon), the place went wild. Suddenly, he was good old Jim Thurber '19, and everybody remembered charming and flattering anecdotes about him. But Thurber was in a bad mood, for all the attention he was getting. A student reporter on the *Ohio State Lantern* wrote that he looked sad and

answered questions with either "I don't know" or "No."(15) His father, Charles, was in a rare outgoing mood, however. He posed for photographs with his famous son and he was quoted in a local journal as saying, "In my opinion it's a darn good book but that name sort of bothered me at first. I spent plenty of time dodging the young women every time I visited the public library. Imagine having to carry on a conversation with the girls on the question, 'Is Sex Necessary?' I slipped off into a corner at home and read the book and found out that it was all in fun and then I let Mrs. Thurber read it and every thing was lovely. We were just a little doubtful at first though."

And back at the *New Yorker*, Ross was confused. His two stars were famous for something they hadn't printed first in his magazine, and one of them—who scratched out curious pencil sketches in a matter of seconds—was also famous as an illustrator. It was one of those circumstances that made Ross mutter, according to Thurber, "How I pity me!" He walked into Thurber's office one day and asked him where the goddam seal drawing was. Thurber reminded him that it had been rejected and then dreamily thrown away. Ross asked him to do it over again. Thurber said he would, but he didn't get around to that task until December of 1931. When he tried to recapture the rock from which the seal viewed the explorer dots, it came out looking more like the headboard of a bed. So Thurber, with his typical capriciousness in artistic matters, turned the rock into a headboard and put his wrong-whiskered seal on top of it and a bed underneath, occupied by a virago and her disturbed mate. The new, inspired caption he added was: "All right, have it your way—you heard a seal bark!" Ross bought the cartoon and printed it on January 30, 1932. As everybody knows, it became one of the most celebrated and often-reprinted cartoons of the twentieth century. (Ross always denied he had rejected the original seal-and-explorers picture in the first place.) The highest praise for the drawing, from Thurber's point of view, was an ecstatic telegram from Benchley, who received the original in gratitude.

The first Thurber drawings to appear in the *New Yorker*, in 1930, were his odd creations illustrating a casual series called "Our Pet Department," an untamed parody of newspaper question-and-answer pet columns. The drawings dealt with animals out of the darkest reaches of the Thurber imagination, including the famous horse with antlers tied to its head:

Q. My husband paid a hundred and seventy-five dollars for this moose to a man in Dorset, Ontario, who said he had trapped it in the woods. Something is wrong with his antlers, for we have to keep twisting them back into place all the time. They're loose.

MRS. OLIPHANT BEATTY

A. You people are living in a fool's paradise. The animal is obviously a horse with a span of antlers strapped onto his head. If you really want a moose, dispose of the horse; if you want to keep the horse, take the antlers off. Their constant pressure on his ears isn't a good idea.

(As an indication of how lightly Thurber took his drawing talent, he allowed one of his girl friends to sketch in the horse's teeth. His smudged and crumpled pictures constantly had to be retrieved from wastebaskets and under desks. He gave them away like smiles. "I have yet to meet anybody I have ever known, even casually, who hasn't got at least one of my drawings," he wrote Herman Miller, in a 1940's letter. "It seems that at times I have drawn as many as thirty pictures for drunken ladies at drunken parties, drunken ladies whom I had never seen before but who now pop up here and there and remind me of our old intimacy." Those who received the pictures treasured them like

Picassos. Katharine Angell's son, Roger, was once given the original of a Thurber classic, and when it vanished, never to be returned, from the wall of his room at boarding school, he was grief-stricken.)

After the "Our Pet Department" illustrations, Thurber submitted, at Ross's urging, cartoons—or idea drawings, as they were sometimes called. Thurber's fame and confidence were such that White no longer was appointed to ink in the faint pencil lines and do the submitting. Of the dozens of ideas and sketches that poured from Thurber's fertile mind in any given day, a few would be turned in and accepted with a certain regularity. Soon, Thurber drew straight off in ink, although he preferred pencil because, with his poor eyesight, he didn't have to keep dipping a pen in a tiny bottle opening, often ending up with the ink spilling all over the place. (He was nothing if not clumsy.) When his first bona-fide cartoons were printed in 1931, he was bold and prankish enough to let himself into Ross's office late one night with a passkey he had copied and forge the editor's "R" on all the drawings Ross was still considering. The "R" meant that the drawings were approved and should start going through the publishing process, which they did, ultimately being printed. Nobody, including the victim of the felony, ever said anything to Thurber about this. Ross was at first bemused and then pridefully amused by the artistic primitive in his midst. When one of

"All Right, Have It Your Way—You Heard a Seal Bark!"

the more schooled cartoonists on the magazine complained, "Why do you reject drawings of mine and print stuff by that fifth-rate artist Thurber?" Ross corrected him. "Third rate," he said.(16)

With the publication by Harper of his second book in two years—*The Owl in the Attic*, a collection of the Monroe stories, an expanded Pet Department, and the Fowler parodies (all with drawings, new and old) —Thurber's reputation as a writer *and* artist was solidly established. The book, dedicated in spite of everything to Althea, did well for the threadbare era, both in America and England. And for those readers who were seeing Thurber drawings for the first time, an Introduction by E. B. White eased the shock and explained the phenomenon once again. The Introduction began as a kidding and gently insulting version of Thurber's "life," portraying him as a Conradian figure of the South Seas, who lost his left eye when he mistook stump powder for pancake flour during a turn in a ship's galley—"a circumstance that has since greatly influenced his character, because it carried with it the necessity always of sitting on the left side of a person." So it went, in the joshing, clubby tradition of American writers writing about other American writers (Mark Twain did the same sort of thing about Emerson and Whittier), until at the end of the piece, White said, with his sharpest insight:

... In his drawings one finds not only the simple themes of love and misunderstanding, but also the rarer and tenderer insupportabilities. He is the one artist that I have ever known, capable of expressing, in a single drawing, physical embarrassment during emotional strain. That is, it is always apparent to Thurber that at the very moment one's heart is caught in an embrace, one's foot may be caught in a piano stool.

Thurber has now served his apprenticeship in life. He has learned to write simple English sentences, he has gone through with the worming of puppies, and he has practically given up trying to find out anything about sex. What he will go on to, no one can say, not knowing the man. At least, safe in these pages, are the records of his sorrows.

His curious, sorrowful records did not escape the notice of some serious art critics, one of whom, the British artist Paul Nash, wrote in an English review after seeing Thurber's work in *Is Sex Necessary?* that the scrawls were done in the manner of Matisse. This comment was picked up, enlarged, and distorted until some American columnist wrote that Thurber was the only American draftsman Matisse truly admired. Thurber was embarrassed, especially since he doubted that Matisse knew him from, say, Addams. His doubts were proven correct in 1937, when he attended a one-man show of his drawings in London. One of the gallery owners thought it would be a good idea to telephone Matisse and try to arrange a meeting between him and Thurber. Matisse's secretary replied curtly that the old man had never heard of either Mr. Thurber or the *New Yorker.**

Paul Nash came to the United States in 1931 to be one of three foreign judges for the Carnegie Exhibition of paintings in Pittsburgh. He was told that a luncheon would be held for him at New York's distinguished Century Club, so that he might meet the cream of American artists. When asked what artists he particularly wanted at his table, Nash replied, "Milt Gross, Fania Marinoff, and James Thurber." (Fania Marinoff was an actress and the wife of Carl Van Vechten.) The three were duly invited by the astounded hosts, but only Thurber could make it. He lovingly described that luncheon and other matters in a May 4, 1951, letter to Anthony Bertram:

. . . I was living in Connecticut at the time, and some official in charge of the luncheon phoned me long distance, beseeching me not to fail to show up at the lunch. Even now I do not know much about art, American or otherwise, and then I knew very little, except the names of a few famous painters. At least twenty were on hand when I arrived at the Century Club, and I recognized the names of Jonas Lie, Burchfield, and four or five others. Paul was a little late, and when he did get there, we all lined up to greet him, like the front file of a platoon. He wandered slowly down the line, shaking hands, smiling, and obviously ignorant of most of the names that were mentioned. When he came to me, he embarrassed the hell out of me, stopping to talk, while the other men shifted uneasily and there was a lot of nervous coughing. He insisted that I sit on his right, and I began to get extremely restless and afraid. Across from us sat one of the most formidable figures I ever saw, an enormous man with flashing dark eyes and a great spade beard. Paul looked at him and said, "Do you know how I could get in touch with Milt Gross?" The gentleman, probably the director of a gallery or editor of a recondite art magazine, replied gruffly, "I am sure I wouldn't have the faintest idea." Paul stared at him. "He is one of your great artists," he said, and I kicked him under the table. They had only given us one drink of Scotch, and we decided to hook the bottle on the sideboard, and did. I needed more drinks to get through that amazing lunch. When we finally left, I said to him, "You didn't seem to realize that you were in the

---

*However, Thurber was vindicated after World War II. Albert E. Lewin informed him that in 1946, when Lewin was a soldier stationed in Europe, he visited Matisse in Vence and asked him who was America's outstanding artist. Matisse instantly answered, "Monsieur Toobay." Lewin was nonplussed. He had never heard of an artist called Toobay, so he asked Matisse to spell the name. Matisse spelled out T-H-U-R-B-E-R.

midst of the forefront of American art, and that none of those men ever heard of me or Milt Gross." He looked at me and said, "From what I know of their work, they are bringing up the rear of French Modernism."

I told him I had not met Gross, but would arrange a meeting, and the next day I took him to see the short, fat, jolly newspaper comic artist, who shared a studio, high up in the Chrysler Building, with H. T. Webster, cartoonist of the NEW YORK HERALD TRIBUNE. Gross had got out at least two of his hilarious "small novels," done in his fantastic slapdash cartoons, and Paul had one with him. Milt is a genial friendly man and he instantly began calling us Paul and Jim. "What is your wife's name, Paul?" he asked, and the delighted Nash told him it was Margaret. So Gross wrote in the book "To Paul and Margaret, with love." Nash did not know Webster's work, because it was not in his area of delight, being a straightforward, realistic daily cartoon of middle-class life in the home.

My wife and I arranged a cocktail party for Nash and asked several of THE NEW YORKER cartoonists he wanted to meet. Twenty minutes before Paul arrived at our hotel apartment, I had started to take a bath, turned on the hot water full force and filled the bathroom with steam. It was too hot there for me to turn off the water, and when Paul arrived—we had left the hall door open —the living room was dense with steam. The hotel engineer had to turn off the water for a while in the whole building. Paul, of course, loved this incident, and especially the fact that, when the fog had cleared, there was Otto Soglow sitting on a chair. Soglow is scarcely more than five feet tall, and was one of the men Nash admired for his "Little King" drawings and the rest. But Otto is a man of moods, and he said nothing but monosyllables until Paul rose to go and then suddenly burst into a flow of amusing talk. Again Nash was delighted and sat down for another hour . . .

In talking about the inability of comic artists to deal with death, he said that the common drawing of a man falling from a building and speaking to someone on the way down did not represent death, since the man was forever poised in the air, and it was Paul who said of my drawing "Touché!" that the man whose head had been cut off was not actually dead, because he could obviously put it back on again. This line has been widely quoted in America, usually without credit. . . .

Nash seemed to know everything about the United States, as he did about the British Isles, and he was eager to meet Harold Ross, the fabulous editor of THE NEW YORKER, especially after I told him that Ross knew nothing about art, or music and, as Alexander Woollcott once said, he had the utmost contempt for anything he didn't understand. I took Nash to his office and introduced him, and Ross began by saying, "Nash, there are only two phony arts, music and painting." Once more Nash was delighted. I know he must have been capable of anger and temper because he was a fine artist, but they never arose out of anything like that. His utter absorption in the unique and the unusual overcame all other emotions, and he thought Ross was one of the great sights of New York. . . .

Thurber and Nash became close friends and saw a lot of each other in England, until Nash's untimely death in 1946.

Another index of notice as an artist that suddenly and surprisingly enveloped Thurber in the early 1930's was an incident that took place during a class in painting Thurber was talked into attending. For the first time in his life, he put colors on canvas with brushes, and he was vastly pleased with his rough efforts, like a tot in a mud puddle. The instructor had not caught Thurber's name when they were introduced, and when he wandered over to the one-eyed student's easel, he saw a child's version of a man and a woman in black and bright yellow and red. "Good Lord, man, what are you trying to do?" the instructor said. Jap Gude, who was along, told him, "I guess you have to let Thurber do it his way." "Thurber?" said the instructor. "Good God, yes!" He hid behind the other students' canvases for the rest of the session. Thurber never went to a painting class again, however.(17)

Despite the serious acclaim from certain quarters and the not-so-serious acclaim from the rest of the world, Thurber himself didn't take his drawing very solemnly. As he wrote in the 1940's to Herman Miller: "Like the discovery of San Salvador and the discovery of pommes soufflé the discovery of my art was an accident." He never slaved over a drawing. He merely threw it away if he didn't like it, and, in less than a minute, drew another one. His sketches were rapid, unrestrained graphic abbreviations of what might have taken weeks to come out of his subconscious mind through the medium of the typewriter. They were quick bursts of the incongruous, and they made many people laugh, squirm, and sometimes cry. E. B. White thought then and still thinks that Thurber's drawings were "works of genius, greater than his writing." But after his total blindness, when he could no longer draw anything, Thurber told a thoroughly depressed Ross that "giving up drawing is only a little worse than giving up tossing cards in a hat. I once flipped in forty-one out of the whole deck, at twelve feet." Then he added, "If I couldn't write, I couldn't breathe."(18)

CHAPTER 12

Big Nights

By the time *The Owl in the Attic* was published, in February of 1931, Althea had given up kennelling, except for Medve and her six pups, and had moved back to the city. She and Thurber sublet an apartment. Poodles and all, they set up house together again as man and wife. With two books by James Thurber on his shelf and weekly sales of cartoons, casuals, or reportage to the *New Yorker*, there was enough money to live well, the Great Depression notwithstanding. They still rented a house in Silvermine (the Connell's unwinterized place called the French Farm, on whose walls near the telephone Thurber had scribbled a mural, later painted over by unappreciative lessees), but their presence was demanded in New York. For one thing, Thurber was asked to make radio appearances on something called Bill Schudt's "Going to Press," at 6:15 P.M. on the Columbia Network, reading his own pieces in his own flat monotone. For another thing, Thurber and Althea had constructed a reconciliation of sorts, a spackling of marital fissures, which culminated in the pregnancy of Mrs. Thurber. The reconciliation was, to all intents and purposes, of little more than a few weeks' duration. As a close friend of theirs said, "It was one of the few times he had slept with her in those years. A month or so later, he decided that he had enough of Althea and was going to move in with Paula Trueman. Althea turned on the tears and announced that she was pregnant, and Thurber was shaken enough to give in to her. Most of us thought she had planned to have a baby just to keep him. John Mosher, one of the few *New Yorker* people Althea could stand, told her, 'Stick with Thurber and you'll be wearing broadtail.' She did, for a while, and it was a good thing, too, otherwise Thurber would never have had a child."

Once hooked by impending fatherhood, Thurber settled down to a life of enforced relative calm. He stayed home most nights and plunged, sometimes sullenly, into his work, the casuals reflecting an increasingly abrasive view of marriage and other man–woman relationships. By the summer of 1931, with Althea gravid, he was even happy with his lot.

They were invited with the Connells to a week-long houseparty at the old Victorian manse of illustrator Frank Godwin and his wife, Sylvia, in Skaneateles, New York. Louise Connell remembered the Skaneateles houseparty as days and nights of rare wit, good liquor (smuggled over the Canadian border), and estival fun. "How I wish I had a recording of that table talk," she said. "Sometimes we sat at breakfast until lunch-time. I don't know how Sylvia managed to pacify the servants, but she never made us rise from a meal while we were engrossed in conversation. Nobody got really drunk—except the butler, who, once when he was supposed to be serving dinner, was found under a pine tree out cold —although we did drink a lot. When we were not at meals, there was swimming, walking in the woods, boating, and fishing. Jim discovered another sport that he enjoyed more. It was goosing earthworms. The Godwins provided us with an electric gadget for catching bait. You stuck its metal spike in the loamy soil, wet the ground well, and turned on the battery. Very soon at least one lively earthworm would scurry to the surface. This pastime so delighted Jim that he caught all the bait the rest of us needed for fishing. He just loved to goose earthworms."

Later in the summer, an expansive Thurber bought Althea a Colonial farmhouse on twenty rolling acres of Sandy Hook, Connecticut—"a gift of appeasement," as Jap Gude described it. Like Silvermine, it was near Westport, and it wasn't far from Yale University, whose more artistic graduate students and professors were yet another attractive set for Althea. They reestablished their kennels, reclaiming Jeannie and her brood from foster masters, and tried hard, in the comforting Connecti-cut countryside, to make some semblance of a happy home for them-selves and their forthcoming child. Thurber, in one of his reflective, confessional moods, wrote his friends Herman and Dorothy Miller, speaking for the first time as a man of real property:

Sept. 22, 1931

Dear Herman and Dorothy:

Sitting on my porch this warm night, with a small breeze and four dogs wandering across, I got to thinking for no reason that our correspondence has been terrible. Dorothy of course does beautifully, you badly, I worse. I never even properly, if at all, acknowledged the incredibly nice things she said, on paper and over the radio, about One Hour in the Attic. Perhaps I was reminded of her tonight because of another incredibly nice thing which happened to me. Or maybe it was the sight of the lovely wooden dog, which, while waiting for its real owner, has got a lot of exercise. It pulls beautifully on wooden floors, being a bit uncertain only on rugs, and I have enjoyed it. It was terrible missing you in New York. Nothing in the world is so disastrously unsatisfactory as telephoning: it must be a whole lot like the intercourse that goes on between cells in a crazy house.

Of course I've been leading a mixed-up and fretful life, with the heat, approaching fatherhood (although Althea is unquestionably the world's most patient and finest mother-expectant), office work, meditation upon the probability that I shall never write anything really as good as I should like to, and so on. You know: the thoughts of a man of thirty-six. Anyway, here I am now at my country estate, having a few weeks' vacation (Althea's mother is here, which is a kind of sanctuary) and sitting for hours at a typewriter thinking muddled thoughts and putting down absolutely no words that are interesting or novel. I did write the first chapter of a novel to be called Rain Before Seven, but I am afraid all of my novels would be complete in one chapter, from force of habit in writing short pieces and also from a natural incapability of what Billy Graves would call "larger flight"—which is a veritable Banshee wail, anyway. So I try to write and dont and then I read something, now and again dropping a pencil or rattling some papers so that Althea, reading in the next room and thinking the softly confused, half-ethereal, half-economical thoughts of approaching motherhood, will not know that my mind has become a blank and my creative talent, such as it was, gone. I have read Evelyn Waugh's two books, which are my favorite two books, Crime and Punishment, and the letters of Frances Newman and her first novel. Kind of a mixed lot. I dont suppose it has helped my thought processes any. Meanwhile, outside, there is the intermittent fall of apples from my apple trees, and the curiously unnerving raspberry which my neighbor's sheep hand me, and the sounds of my five female dogs, two of them in heat (I inadvertently let Jeannie loose one day and she didn't show up till next morning, with seven of the finest specimens of manhood among the shepherd dogs of this county following her, each trying to outdo the other in ardor of attention). I have twenty acres, and a house a hundred and twenty five years old, and a view over a valley to a Connecticut town that was flourishing when Washington was seducing the Mount Vernon chambermaids. I also have arranged a series of croquet wickets so that they make a golf course running completely around the house. Every few hours I get out and struggle trying to make the course under twenty-three which is my record so far. It is maddening to me, my wife, her mother, the cook, and the dogs. But nothing so completely holds me as competitive endeavor. Nothing except sleep and, I suppose, sitting in a speakeasy on a rainy evening with somebody else's wife. I really like that. I sometimes wonder at just what age I will get over my, until now, secret desire for and belief in fairly clandestine monkey-business. Of course I justify my numerous loyalties in a number of ways which, if I could only put them down as beautifully as I feel them, would make a wise and lovely piece of writing. Ah, well. That will be for a time when all the wheels are run down and the beauty of it all is not so fresh and vibrant as to make literary tinkering with it a kind of hollow and painful desecration. I suppose even I will one day reach a quiet place where I can view tranquilly and, please God, with more humor than I have ever been able to thus far, the sad, sweet, mixed-up pulsing of sex and beauty and drink and unfair kisses. Herman, you should have taken notes on me rather than on Mrs. Taylor, for we have had perhaps enough, or will have had when your novel is done, chronicles of persons with one idea in mind. There should be some fine novel of a not despicable but also not admirable person, whose pleasant habits and even noble dedications in one chapter are seen with their hair in their eyes and an utterly unexcused desire on their lips in the next—and so on, turn about. Which is all too unstudied, however, to make much sense. I could give you the notes, though, and the thing would unravel. Ask me some time. Any novel by and of me, however, would be so flagrantly historical as to be embarrassing. . . . Of course I could never do a novel seriously: it would slowly begin to kid itself, and God knows what it would turn out to be like.

But: it is as an artist, dear people, that real fame has come to me, I so regret that you, who enjoyed so very much my acute physical embarrassments that day when I was waiting for an old girl of mine to appear, can not be here—could not have been here last week—to see the funny goings on about my art. By the way, speaking of that awful day, it would be fine to do a novel with all the impressive periods of a Henry James "Beast in the Jungle" about a charming fellow, a sensitive gentleman, whose great good fortune it is to enjoy a number of lovely encounters with lovely ladies but who, at the most exquisite moments —those moments, rare and far apart and ineffable which mean everything in life—is suddenly assailed by a horrible necessity to pee, and not only to pee, but to pee again and again. I leave it to you. I think you could do it—God knows you have all the notes you need on that side of *my* life, anyway. I had thought of a final chapter, with a setting like our own—a university building. The sensitive gentleman, waiting there, with the dying of a pretty day, for the loveliest Encounter of All, has arrived in time so that he may run in and out of the Great Good Place as often as need be and thus be fully prepared to go through the meeting in comparative peace, when She arrives. A friend is with him who eventually, as the lady fails to arrive, has to go. The gentleman is now left alone and it gradually is proved to him that, instead of abating, his cursed necessity is increasing, so that when at last the porter locks up the men's room for the day, he is forced to leave by a side door just as he beholds the lady of his tallest dreams coming down the Long Walk. There is nothing in James more haunting than that ending . . .

Love,

Jim

The itchy thoughts about infidelity he expressed in his letter to the Millers became hard actions before another week was out. Althea and Thurber had moved back to New York to await their child's birth (a room was reserved in Doctors Hospital and Dr. Virgil "Duke" Damon,

Thurber's former fraternity brother, was scheduled to be the obstetrician), but no sooner had they settled in the city again than a major fight ensued and Thurber stormed out. He wasn't the first nor the last man on the verge of paternity to vent his fears and frustrations on a Madonnalike wife, but he picked a poor time to disappear. On the night of October 6, 1931, Althea checked into Doctors Hospital with labor pains, while her husband was out doing the town with Ann Honeycutt. Thurber's evening ended late in the Honeycutt apartment, where, in one of what Honey called his "sudden rages," he banged a vase of flowers off a piano and put his hand through a glass door. A little later, he turned up in Jap Gude's apartment on Waverly place, "dazed and a bloody mess," according to Gude. "My wife, who always had a way with Jim, calmed him down, bandaged up his hand, and put him to sleep on the living-room couch," Gude continued. "The next afternoon, when he woke up, he was presented with the news that Althea had given birth to a baby girl. He got to the hospital, somehow, and made up with her." (Althea, in describing the hospital reconciliation scene, was quoted years later in the *American Weekly* as saying: "He looked dreadfully, and as he walked around the bed I saw one of his hands was covered with blood, and then he said he had been in some sort of a—he had been out all night and had been in some sort of an altercation, and put his hand through a taxi window, and then the nurse came on duty and they took him out.")

Dr. Damon recalled that Thurber was still dazed when he came to visit his wife and see his newborn daughter, Rosemary. "He seemed to have other things on his mind, many other things to do," Damon said. "He looked at the child as if she were a puppy. He liked children, I guess, the way he liked dogs—sort of amazed at them. He didn't pay too much attention to Althea. He must have been embarrassed. Jim was probably a good father but not a good husband. I wasn't at all sure the marriage would last because of the baby. But all in all, he did the best he could, being Thurber."

Astonished and frightened at first by his infant daughter and the attendant responsibilities, the thirty-six-year-old father would, when family life was too much for him and he was in his cups, loudly insist that Rosemary wasn't the fruit of his particular loins. Ted Gardiner remembered him once screaming at Althea, "The baby's from that chinless wonder you met on the beach." Gardiner said that Thurber really believed this fiction for a while, perhaps as a way of excusing his initial lack of paternal devotion. The chinless wonder who sired Rosemary was, of course, James Grover Thurber—a fact plainly evident to anybody who knew Thurber and the child. Rosemary has an unmistakable Thurber stamp to her features: large, direct eyes, a short, gently curved nose, a narrow face, and a very small chin.

E. B. White thought that Thurber was too egotistical in the early 1930's to be an ideal father. "He was the most self-centered man I've ever known," White said, "but he did have love for Rosie. It showed through." Ann Honeycutt, whom Thurber continued to see off and on after the tumultuous eve of his child's birth, was surprised that Thurber wanted a baby in the first place. "He didn't behave like a father of a newborn baby," she said. "He said that he liked the idea of it, deep down, but then, he was always a good actor." As Thurber became more accustomed to the realities of fatherhood, he became more of a father. "I remember him striding across our field in Connecticut with the tiny girl in his arms," Louise Connell said. "He showed her to us with such pride and love. She was an enchanting little thing, and Jim, at that moment, seemed so happy."

His pride and love swelled to indulgence as Rosemary grew older. He bought her a cart and two ponies, Rowdy and Jingle, which they kept at the Sandy Hook farm, and he even let her play with impunity in his new car, which she liked more than the pony cart. Very little was too good for her, when daddy was around. Rosemary's earliest childhood memories are, naturally, limited, but she could recall the Sandy Hook house and the mother who dominated it. "I don't remember them together," she said, "but I remember them separately. Althea was both father and mother to me most of the time, but when my father was at home, he never disciplined me. It was a fairy-tale land with him around. He was patient and good and always gave in to me. I can see now that my mother had a rough time of it, being both parents in one. Maybe she was a little martyrish about it, too.

"I never really knew my father as a truly sighted person. I used to like to sneak up behind him, but he always heard me coming. My first memory of him is of a tall, thin man throwing a ball over the house, which really wowed me. Also, I remember him drawing inside my books, and I quickly filled in the drawings with crayons because I was shocked at someone scribbling in books. Now, I wish I had those books. I can remember going to visit him at the *New Yorker* offices and seeing Daise Terry, who sort of ran the place, and playing with tracing paper. Ross fascinated me. He was more like a football player than an editor. It was a strange early childhood."

Thurber's mixed feelings about his daughter's existence can be traced back to his determination (as expressed in his April 4, 1920, letter to

Elliott Nugent) "never to bring any children into this old vale to inherit the Thurber nervousness." Perhaps out of sheer guilt or shame, he deliberately kept Rosemary away as much as possible from her grandparents and uncles in Columbus. (Rosemary was the only grandchild Mame and Charles Thurber ever had.) "The couple of times we saw Rosemary as a baby," Robert Thurber said, "Jamie and Althea were always on edge, afraid we'd say the wrong thing, or whatever, to her. She was a stranger to us, never acted like part of the family. I think Jamie wanted it like that. He thought we'd ruin her in some way, I guess. Later, when she was grown up and we visited her in the East, she hardly talked to us and she was very cold. We had hurt feelings."

For her part, Rosemary didn't remember seeing her grandparents or uncles until she was a teen-ager. "My father and my grandmother were both so scared of each other then," she said. "They circled each other all the time. I wanted to be an actress, and Mame liked that idea because she once wanted to be an actress herself.* I don't remember my grandfather at all. Robert was like a little old lady, wiping off the silverware and all that, and William was actually a letdown after seeing my father's imitations of him. They were a different family from a different world."

At last, the fearful wonder of being a father couldn't be denied. To John McNulty, he once wrote:

... Rosemary used to glance in my direction with about the same interest she had in a window pane or a passing charwoman. It wasn't until she was two and realized she was stuck with me that she said, during a walk through autumn leaves, "I love you.". . . (1)

By the middle of 1932, the barking seal on the headboard was the most talked-about drawing of the year, and its creator had attracted a sizable following, sizable enough so that Harper & Brothers decided it was time to being out a collection of Thurber art called, aptly, *The Seal in the Bedroom and Other Predicaments*. Thurber rushed to complete enough new drawings to fill out the book for the November, 1932, publication—only forty-seven of the eighty-five drawings in the book were printed beforehand in the *New Yorker*—and it turned out that

---

*Rosemary later acted the part of her own grandmother in a disappointing play, based on *My Life and Hard Times*, entitled *Jabberwock*. Written by Jerome Lawrence and Robert Lee, *Jabberwock* had its world premiere at the dedication of the Thurber Theatre at Ohio State University, on November 18, 1972. It experienced the unhappy fate of most transformations into another medium of a near-perfect literary work.

there were more Thurber fans than Harper had thought. The book was an unqualified success, and Thurber was surprised as well as pleased. He still couldn't fully believe that anybody would pay good coin to see his facile work, especially in the middle of a depression.

In this first drawing collection, the patterns of his work were firmly set. The feckless, formless men, almost always bald and rubbery, are caught in various odd postures, from compromising situations with young ladies to equally compromising situations with large dogs. In the more fanciful predicaments, they have only the merest suggestion of clothing, or any other equipment, for that matter: the all-revealing dot for an eye, the basic flipper for a hand, the faint diagonal line across the fleshy nose for glasses (making the meekest Thurber male appear meeker yet). The women, of course, are a hairier race, enormous, butch, voracious, sometimes dumb. They never seem to comprehend either the Thurber men or the Thurber dogs. Thurber children are just smaller versions of Thurber adults.

There are menaces, human and inanimate, lurking everywhere, and what E. B. White called "the incongruous" always overlays the proceedings like a benediction from the devil. Madness in subject and temper is comically present in most of the drawings, along with a great deal of autobiography. One cartoon has two of his frumpishly gowned ladies, seated on one of his hilarious sofas, having a soul-baring confrontation. Above them, hanging uncertainly on the wall, is a version of the Westminster hounds portrait. The caption read: "I yielded, yes—but I never led your husband on, Mrs. Fisher!" Other tidbits of autobiography emerge in sections on tennis and drunken parties, displaying the author's intimate knowledge of both diversions. Two series called "The Bloodhound and the Bug" and "The Bloodhound and the Hare" dwell on the fundamental decency and common sense Thurber felt was in animals, particularly dogs, but not in their masters. Virtuosic draftsmanship sometimes appears in the captionless drawings (especially in a lovely scene of mounted huntsmen and their hounds), and a section called "The Race of Life" (which Doris Humphrey later made into a ballet) is one of the world's rare examples of a successful merger of pure nonsense with impure philosophy, the Marx Brothers and Lewis Carroll notwithstanding.

Dorothy Parker took over the E. B. White chore of introducing and explaining Thurber to the reading public, although at the rate of a book a year he needed little in the way of introduction and explanation. However, what she wrote was every bit as brilliant an analysis of the almost unanalyzable as White's. In part, she said:

... These are strange people that Mr. Thurber has turned loose upon us. They seem to fall into three classes—the playful, the defeated, and the ferocious. All of them have the outer semblance of unbaked cookies; the women are of a dowdiness so overwhelming that it becomes tremendous style. Once a heckler, who should have been immediately put out, complained that the Thurber women have no sex appeal. The artist was no more than reproachful. "They have for my men," he said. And certainly the Thurber men, those deplorably *désoigné* Thurber men, would ask no better.

There is about all these characters, even the angry ones, a touching quality. They expect so little of life; they remember the old discouragements and await the new. They are not shrewd people, nor even bright, and we must all be very patient with them. Lambs in a world of wolves, they are, and there is on them a protracted innocence. . . .

Of the birds and animals so bewilderingly woven into the lives of the Thurber people it is best to say but little. Those tender puppies, those faint-hearted hounds—I think they are hounds—that despondent penguin—one goes all weak with sentiment. No man could have drawn, much less thought of, those creatures unless he felt really right about animals . . .

As a corollary to Dorothy Parker's "unbaked cookies" observation, Richard Connell once remarked, "His pictures sell like hot cakes, and look like them, too." (2)

The novelty of fatherhood and permanent country living wore off after the éclat of *The Seal in the Bedroom*. Soon, Thurber and Althea fashioned another one of their arrangements: He would spend most of his time in the city, living in hotels, while she would have the Sandy Hook house, Rosemary, the dogs, her friends, and an occasional visit from her husband. The visits became more and more occasional. Althea was later quoted in the *American Weekly* as saying:

... Some of the time he was absent for a number of days at a time, and other times he was away for two or three days, and as time went on he got to coming home less and less, so that sometimes a week would go by before he would come home, and sometimes ten days. It got to be more and more frequent so that I wouldn't know where he was or when he was coming home . . .

And when he did turn up, she continued:

Oh, he just practically ignored us lots of times. Lots of times he wouldn't get up until four or five in the afternoon and spent most of the day in bed. It just seemed to me that he was resting from the way he had been going on in New York. His few times at home amounted to just practically that . . .

"Have You Fordotten Our Ittle Suicide Pact?"

"What Kind of a Woman Is It, I Ask You, That Goes Gallivating
Around in a Foreign Automobile?"

"Two Best Falls Out of Three—Okay, Mr. Montague?"

The Enormous Rabbit

Speakeasy

Four o'Clock in the Morning

Placement

"Here's a Study for You, Doctor—He Faints"

"Will You Be Good Enough to Dance This Outside?"

Once, Thurber packed Althea and Rosemary off on an extended Bahama vacation, but, for one reason or another, he neglected to send them any money during their last few weeks in Nassau. When it was time for them to take the steamer back to New York, the hotel held her baggage until the bill was paid, and the ship almost left without her, since she hadn't paid her return passage, either. At the last minute, Thurber sent the money for her passage and the hotel bill, but he somehow missed meeting her at the New York pier because of "a big night the night before." (3)

The big nights of that period were just about every night. His close friend Robert Coates remembered him then as a noctambule, reversing the working–sleeping habits of more conventional folk. He crawled from bar to party to bar, seeking companionship from old and new acquaintances, never quite getting his fill. Then, usually alone, he would return to his Algonquin Hotel room, with dawn not far off, and sometimes write letters or work on pieces till he collapsed with fatigue. His health, of course, suffered, and his personal habits, never exemplary, were worrisome. For instance, he neglected his laundry, simply throwing soiled clothes into a closet and buying new garments as he needed them. When the closet would hold no more dirty apparel—or an alarmed friend would discover the mess—he would change rooms or even hotels. He was forever without an overcoat in cold weather and light clothing in warm. He tended to wallow in his absent-minded dishabille, referring to himself, in print, as looking "like a slightly ill professor of botany who is also lost."(4) If the saloon life paled, Thurber would abruptly appear, unannounced, at a friend's apartment (usually at the Gudes) and expect to be taken in and given solace. But on weekends when he avoided Sandy Hook and his friends were away, he often found himself alone and desperately drinking.

He developed a notorious reputation for obstreperousness. Thomas Meek, his friend from Ohio State and Scarlet Mask Club days, was working in New York then and spent a lot of time with Thurber. "It was difficult being with Jim," Meek said. "He seemed to like misbehaving, being the bad boy. It was an antisocial strain in him. One time, Tony threw him out of his speakeasy for acting up, and another time, during dinner at Elliott Nugent's place, Jim started to smash the furniture, insulted everyone, and even got into some scuffling. He was perverse, like a small boy, taking the opposite point of view just to annoy and provoke you. It was sort of an intellectual exercise, I suppose, just to see what would happen. For instance, I am a Republican. Jim knew that full well, yet he launched a tirade against Republicans whenever I was around. At Costello's one night, he had too much to drink and called me a 'cold, calculating capitalist.' I resented it, but I was amazed when he phoned me the next day to apologize, which he rarely did then. But I respected Jim as a genius. What can you do with a genius?"

Even E. B. White's patience with Thurber was wearing thin. White said: "Wolcott Gibbs, during that sad time, once remarked about Jim that he was the nicest guy in the world up to five o'clock in the afternoon. Gibbs was right. Jim was good until his third drink and then sometimes he became a madman, tempestuous and foul-mouthed. I spent a lot of evenings with him but I didn't enjoy them. Jim had it in for women and he was obnoxious about it. He would lash out at the nearest woman, and one night the nearest woman was my wife, Katharine. I wanted to hit him, but I couldn't hit a one-eyed man. The best thing was to avoid him at night, which we often did. He was probably slightly insane. But there never was a kinder, nicer friend—when he was sober."

Sober or not, Thurber could be utterly charming, too, although in a compulsive, nonstop fashion. St. Clair McKelway recalled that he would often hold forth with his fantasy tales of Columbus, performing all the roles and deftly switching characters.(5) Most people were amused, at least at the first hearing, according to Malcolm Cowley. And Donald Ogden Stewart remembered a late night at Tony's when Stewart, Benchley, Dorothy Parker, and Thurber sat around singing old favorites till Thurber abruptly left to go home. He reappeared a few minutes later mumbling something about elephants walking west on the street outside Tony's, holding each other's tails. They all assumed Thurber was having an attack of delirium tremens, but a peek out the door showed a parade of Ringling Brothers pachyderms making their way to Madison Square Garden, where the circus was about to open.(6)

Other Tony's regulars were less enchanted by Thurber. Lillian Hellman described a night in the speakeasy when Thurber threw a glass of whiskey at her.* Dashiell Hammett, her boy friend and an old Pinkerton man, rose to her defense and pushed Thurber against the wall, but Thurber heaved another glass at Hammett, missing his target and hitting a waiter, who happened to be Tony's cousin. Tony decided he had had his fill of Thurber and called the police, an extreme action for a speakeasy proprietor. As Lillian Hellman put it, almost everyone

---

*There is something about Lillian Hellman that makes many men, and some women, want to throw whiskey at her. Thurber simply and inexcusably did what everybody else thought better of doing.

agreed with Tony about Thurber but nobody squealed when the police arrived, "and while I don't think Thurber liked me afterwards, I don't think he had liked me before. In any case, none of us ever mentioned it again."(7)

None of his friends of that period ever went so far as to call Thurber an alcoholic. Jap Gude, for instance, said that he was, in the main, "a good drinker." Dr. Virgil Damon said that "Jim could hold his liquor a lot better when I knew him in New York than he could at the Phi Psi house in Columbus." But Thurber, then and later, took his drinking seriously. He worked out an ethic about drinking, which varied very little throughout his adulthood. How one drank became the measure of the individual, in much the same way as it did in, say, the fraternity house or the Paris café. He once wrote Malcolm Cowley:

> . . . I do not believe that Fitzgerald was a worse drinker than most of us, but this is always mystical ground. Hemingway called Scott a rummy, O'Hara says that Eustace Tilley [the *New Yorker*'s monocled symbol] has no right to talk about Hemingway's drinking—obviously a crack at Gibbs and Sally Benson— as if O'Hara could not have held his own with Scott or anybody else, except Benchley and Sinclair Lewis in the days when he went to bed full of Scotch at three a.m. and got up at six a.m. for more Scotch. . . . I also give my own definitions of rummy, souse, drunk, sot, and the others. The drunk, for instance, is the stranger who annoys your party on the sidewalk as you are leaving 21; the rummy has several suits, but always wears the brown one; and the sot doesn't know where he is, or who you are, and doesn't care; and so on . . . (8)

As Thurber's drinking-man reputation grew, alongside of Fitzgerald, Hemingway, Benchley, O'Hara, and the rest, so did the mythology. Most stories were untrue and some were positively grotesque; for example, one story had it that Thurber, on his big nights, would carry a special set of glass eyes, graduated in rubricity, which he periodically replaced to keep up with his reddening good eye.

Whether because of or in spite of alcohol, Thurber was hectored by sex. He was still having potency difficulties, cruelly matched by his infatuations with one girl or another. He was attractive to many women, and every so often one of them would lure him into bed. An especially bitchy lady, a writer, lost little time in reporting to his friends that "Thurber wasn't good in the hay" (as one of those friends remembered her evaluation), and when Thurber learned of this public critique, it didn't do much to soften his ambivalence towards females. He didn't chase girls so much for sexual purposes as for social and romantic ones. From time to time, he gave up chasing girls entirely. "His attacks on women," Gude said, "probably came out of his lack of success with them. But for the rest of his life, most of his best friends were women." Thurber himself once said, "Women have always come to my rescue."(9) When he was at his loneliest and had nothing else to do and biology called, he would turn up as a customer at Polly Adler's famous house, where he was accorded the full privileges of a regular.*

His fiction of that tumultuous time was a clear reflection of his agonies, especially a short story called "One Is a Wanderer." Written with the same autobiographical aching of "Menaces in May" (the protagonist's forsaken wife is even named Lydia, as she was in "Menaces"), the story begins:

The walk up Fifth Avenue through the slush of the sidewalks and the dankness of the air had tired him. The dark was coming quickly down, the dark of a February Sunday evening, and that vaguely perturbed him. He didn't want to go "home," though, and get out of it. It would be gloomy and close in his hotel room, and his soiled shirts would be piled on the floor of the closet where he had been flinging them for weeks, where he had been flinging them for months, and his papers would be disarranged on the tops of the tables and on the desk, and his pipes would be lying around, the pipes he had smoked determinedly for a while only to give them up, as he always did, to go back to cigarettes . . .

The hero, Kirk, wanders about midtown, thinking of seeing his second movie that day, thinking of working in his deserted office, thinking of his lost wife and present girl friends. Two narrative streams converge: the song "Bye Bye, Blackbird" (which had a mystical significance for Thurber) and the rivulet of alcohol (which courses through almost all his pieces). Drinking several brandies back in the lobby of his hotel,

---

*Almost twenty years later, the chickens came home to roost, as Thurber explained in a letter to Wolcott Gibbs:

September 29, 1952

Dear Wolcott:

I got a letter today from Polly Adler, who lives and is probably in business, too, out in Burbank. She calls me Jim and "my old friend" and then says she has written a book that will be published by Rinehart & Co. in the spring. It is called "A House Is Not A Home." Maybe you know about this already.

I figure in a mild anecdote about some pictures on the wall of what seems to be the office of a woman prison psychologist. Here appears the fond expression "my old friend Jim Thurber." Polly enclosed a release for me to sign unless I objected to any part of the anecdote, and told me to send it to her lawyer, Gertrude Gottlieb in New York. I wrote Harriet Pilpel at Greenbaum, Wolff and Ernst right away, saying uh-uh, and explaining that my mother is a hundred years old and would drop dead, and that the eyebrows of my daughter, a senior at Penn, have risen high enough because of me . . .

an undisguised Algonquin, Kirk considers calling on his married friends, but decides that "two is company, four is a party, three is a crowd. One is a wanderer." He feels himself slipping into "one of those states when people don't like to have you around." He goes out to a favorite bar and drinks with vague acquaintances until three in the morning. In the cab taking him back to the hotel, the driver delivers a paean to home and family, and his passenger sadly agrees. At last, in his room, Kirk sings softly and crazily to himself: "Make my bed and light the light, for I'll be home late tonight . . ."

It is a stifled cry from a decaying man for solidity, family, home, love, and it is one of the most affecting pieces Thurber ever wrote.

One of the girls Thurber dated with some regularity during this dark estrangement from Althea was an intelligent, witty, rather strong-willed career woman named Helen Muriel Wismer. An established editor of pulp magazines in the 1930's, she was a daughter of the former Mary Watt, who was born in Scotland, and Ernest Wismer of Nebraska. A religious man of Canadian ancestry, Ernest Wismer decided to become an ordained Congregationalist minister when Helen was one year old. He moved his family to Bangor, Maine, where he attended divinity school. He then entered Yale University, and later won congregations in New Haven and Bristol, Connecticut, spending his summers in northern Vermont. Helen was educated in the Bristol public schools, where she showed literary promise (she was valedictorian of her high-school class), and then entered Mount Holyoke. At college, she became a friend of Jap Gude's future wife, also named Helen. She went to New York after her graduation from Mount Holyoke, found work, and was soon very much a part of the literary–artistic Village scene. Tall and fearsomely thin, with a face that is at once delicate and firm, she attracted several beaux, among them the artist Aristide Mian and Reynolds Benson, the husband of the New Yorker short-story writer Sally Benson. ("I was a good friend of Sally, too," Helen said. "That was how things were in the Village in those days.") She also knew a young lady named Ann Honeycutt, who lived near her on Charles Street. Obviously, it was just a matter of time before she would meet James Thurber.

Just after Is Sex Necessary? was published in late 1929, Ann Honeycutt threw a party with the semiserious intention of announcing her engagement to Wolcott Gibbs. Aristide Mian asked Helen Wismer to the party. "Whatever my life is or isn't is due to Ann Honeycutt," Helen said. "I remember that it was a very drunken evening. God knows what we were drinking—raw alcohol, gin drops, and grapefruit juice, probably. We all drank so much. We ended up in a basement speakeasy, and

Gibbs's head fell in the soup when the engagement was announced, so nobody paid much attention to it. What everybody did make a fuss over was James Thurber, who was on the *New Yorker* and had just published a successful book. He arrived at the party with two sorority-type girls from Columbus, not at all taking the engagement announcement at its face value. I was definitely interested in him right away. My first words to him were 'Is sex really necessary, Mr. Thurber?'—mostly so he'd notice me over those fawning Columbus girls. He did notice me—he laughed—but that wasn't surprising, considering the competition. Jamie got bored with too much adulation. Anyway, I liked him and I hoped he would call me for a date, but I knew he was seeing Ann Honeycutt and Paula Trueman and others, not to mention Althea."

But it was more than a year before Helen saw Thurber again for any appreciable time. It was at the Bensons' New Year's Eve party, and Thurber brought along, of all people, his wife. "Because it was New Year's Jamie must have been feeling guilty, so he invited Althea," Helen said. "She was bright, a good talker, but a little sullen. There was a lot of tension between them. Althea left early." From then on, Thurber and Helen dated off and on, the pace picking up after Thurber's arrangement with Althea, when he moved out of Sandy Hook. Helen truly liked him, was honored to be with him, and was willing to shape her own life to his, whether it meant staying up all night in a saloon or listening to Thurber declaim his works. "On our first big date together," she said, "Jamie recited to me and Gibbs all of *My Life and Hard Times*, which he was writing then. I was enthralled by it. How could someone not be attracted to a man who could do that? But I never intended to marry him, he had so many other girls. Once, I remember, he gave a party in his room at the Algonquin and invited all his girls at once, including me. That was Jamie being playful. Duke Damon was there and so was Gibbs, who took one look inside the room, shrugged his shoulder in that funny way of his, and ran. I didn't run."

Another of those big nights, in April of 1934, was an evening purposefully made notable by a sentimental piece he wrote in 1951 called " 'Scott in Thorns,' " in which he described how he accidentally met F. Scott Fitzgerald in Tony's at ten P.M. and spent the next nine memorable hours with him, drinking, wandering, and talking. Fitzgerald was a hero to Thurber—for his drinking capacity, his luster, his tragic grace, but most of all for his incredible and enviable talent. He was very much what Thurber might well have given his good eye to be, at least before April of 1934.

As Thurber reminisced in " 'Scott in Thorns,' " he persuaded Tony to introduce him to Fitzgerald and the two writers struck up a quick, boozy acquaintance. *Tender Is the Night* was about to be published and Zelda was having a show of her paintings in New York, though she herself was off in the midst of another breakdown. Fitzgerald was bursting with pride over *Tender Is the Night* (his "testament of faith," Thurber quoted him as saying) and Zelda's show, catalogues of which he passed out like cigarettes ("By midnight I must have had a dozen of these in my own pockets because he kept absently handing them to me," Thurber wrote). By three A.M. Fitzgerald asked his new friend, "Do you know any good girl we could call on?" Thurber preferred to keep it stag, but he obligingly called Ann Honeycutt and Helen Wismer, both of whom turned him down on grounds of the hour and his companion. His third try was Paula Trueman, who said O.K. but in half an hour. "The next few hours were spent in tranquil conversation about a great many things," Thurber wrote. "Most of the time I sat in another room, since it was he who wanted to talk to a good girl." He said that Fitzgerald did nothing messier than strew some more catalogues around Paula's apartment.*

The Fitzgerald evening ended with a long cab ride through Central Park, during which they each complained about their respective wives, ages, and daughters. Fitzgerald kept ordering the cab to stop every so often so Thurber could throw up, despite Thurber's protestations that he was perfectly all right. (Thurber never threw up from drink, except when he was sick from other causes, Helen Thurber claimed. "He had an iron pipe from his mouth straight down," she said.) To Thurber, the big Fitzgerald night was strangely uplifting: Another talented American writer had even more troubles than he did. "I have been a bad behavior boy myself, God knows, but . . . it was not fundamental," he later wrote Malcolm Cowley, apropos of " 'Scott in Thorns.' "(10)

The casuals about Thurber's fictive Columbus, which so enthralled Helen Wismer and others in recital, were printed in the *New Yorker*

---

*Paula Trueman's version was slightly different. "Jim called up, drunk," she said. "He wanted to bring somebody over, he told me, and he admitted finally it was Fitzgerald. I got dressed and over they came. They stayed for an hour and a half and had some more to drink. Fitzgerald wanted to spend the night but he didn't persist. They were both slurring drunks but also gentlemen. Fitzgerald wasn't so dashing; he was just a writer who had too much to drink. But he was worldly, just as Jim was naïve. I'm afraid Jim made up the part about leaving the ads for Zelda's show behind, for the good of his story."

Ann Honeycutt didn't recall any phone conversation that night from Thurber and Fitzgerald. The only time she remembered ever having met Fitzgerald with Thurber was in the Algonquin, just before Fitzgerald rushed to catch a train for California.

throughout 1933 and were published in book form, with drawings, by Harper in November of that year. The pieces were called, of course, *My Life and Hard Times*, the most celebrated work of his career. It is also his best work, best because it is unadulterated Thurber at the height of his unique literary and graphic invention. He equalled the prose and pictures of *My Life and Hard Times* in many later individual efforts, but never again was there a single series on one theme so immaculate. It is to Thurber's *oeuvre* what, say, *Duck Soup* is to Marx Brothers films; there are just as glistening moments in other Marx Brothers movies, but there was never such wondrously paced, sustained brilliance as *Duck Soup*.

Those closest to Thurber generally agreed that the writing of *My Life and Hard Times* was his way of exorcising the devils of his family and his Columbus childhood. It was another cheap psychoanalysis, more rewarding for the readers than for the author. What he did was take a seed of truth from his real past—for example, his father's bed actually falling in the middle of the night—and allowed it to root in his fecund creative imagination until it fully bloomed as that classic American Beauty, "The Night the Bed Fell." From the finest first line in all casualdom ("I suppose that the high-water mark of my youth in Columbus, Ohio, was the night the bed fell on my father") to the last (" 'I'm glad,' said mother, who always looked on the bright side of things, 'that your grandfather wasn't here' "), the reader is held in a state of giddy madness, rather like having the giggles at your best friend's funeral. It is quite a trick to bring off, and Thurber did it in all nine pieces. Not even Mark Twain could match that virtuosity.*

---

*From the publication of *My Life and Hard Times* on, Thurber was consistently compared, always favorably, with Mark Twain. Indeed, in an Introduction written for the Bantam paperback edition of that very book in 1961, John K. Hutchens made the literary parallel and added, "The man from Hannibal, Mo. and the man from Columbus, O. have much in common." But Thurber himself disliked the comparison for most of his life. He wrote Harvey Breit, of the New York *Times* Book Review, on November 25, 1949: "If there is any outstanding fact about me, it is the unbelievable one that I have never read Tom Sawyer or Huckleberry Finn. I have always intended to, and said in the preface to the Carnival [*The Thurber Carnival*] that I had even reread the books. This was to keep people from running me out of town." However, his long-term friend and distinguished English professor Kenneth MacLean thought that this strange boast was "a typical Thurber extravagance." In his last years, Thurber often compared himself to Twain in that nobody took either of them seriously enough, MacLean said. E. B. White, too, thought that Thurber must have read more Twain than he admitted. "He just didn't want any American humorist to be better than he was," White said, adding, on reflection, that he preferred Thurber to Twain. As it turned out, Thurber and Twain were the only two

Each of the *My Life and Hard Times* pieces follows the same quasi-autobiographical pattern: "The Car We Had to Push" and the hereditary Fisher–Thurber incompetence with machinery; "The Day the Dam Broke" and the real Columbus flood and mob panic of March, 1913; "The Night the Ghost Got In" and the allegedly haunted house the Thurbers lived in at 77 Jefferson Avenue; "More Alarms at Night" and more of the same eerie nocturnal doings on Jefferson Avenue; "A Sequence of Servants" and an early glimpse of Thurber's parade of eccentric maids; "The Dog That Bit People" and an early glimpse of Thurber's parade of eccentric dogs; "University Days" and his mercurial stretch at Ohio State; "Draft Board Nights" and his brush with the Selective Service System (even the seed of truth is manufactured here). The characters in all these wild adventures—whether cut from whole cloth or loosely patterned on real screwballs, such as one female relative who believed electricity was dripping all over the house from empty plugs and sockets—are delineated with love and grand humor (again, like Twain's people). Each piece is a writing lesson in first-person reminiscence and nonsense. There is not a weak or unnecessary word, and —a test of all great writing—one wants more at the end.

The critical reception of *My Life and Hard Times* was loud and clear. John Chamberlain wrote in the New York *Times* that he "hit the floor pretty hard." Ernest Hemingway was moved to send a dust-jacket blurb reading, "Even when Thurber was writing under the name of Alice B. Toklas, we knew he had it in him if he could only get it out," and Hemingway told Dorothy Parker that Thurber's was "the best writing coming out of America."(11) It was even rumored that T. S. Eliot was a helpless Thurber fan.

Ross was still confused, if impressed, by all the acclaim Thurber and his latest book were receiving. But even more confused was the Thurber family back in Columbus. The book was dedicated simply to Mary A. Thurber, and while most of the family names were changed, the seeds of truth stood out for the knowing folks down home. The dedicatee, for instance, was upset by her son's accurate anecdote that she put food out for the mice, along with the other household pets' rations. "People will think we're trash," she told him. Thurber later wrote about this to his family:

. . . "My Life and Hard Times" would have lost the incident of the mice if Mama had got her hands on it. Now nobody in the world believes that I didn't

American writers ever to be invited to join the *Punch* editors at their hallowed luncheon table.

make it up. It is also a fact of human nature that the disinterested reader is not impressed by facts as such and forgets them in a week. Tests have shown that the names of characters and even of the author are forgotten. As for length, it is a quality and a quantity that comes out after many rewritings and consultations with editors, five or six of whom read everything . . . (12)

Charles Thurber was also displeased, in spite of the attention the family was getting in Columbus. A friend met him on a Columbus street after the book's publication and congratulated him on his son's work. Charles expressed himself so vehemently on the subject that he "scared the squirrels over in the State House yard," according to the friend. (13) The Fishers were content to warm themselves in the indirect glow of Thurber's celebrity; for them, a Thurber had, thank God, finally made good.

As for Thurber himself, he wrote his own introduction to his book this time. It was called "Preface to a Life," and it was just as circuitously revealing as anything by E. B. White or Dorothy Parker:

Benvenuto Cellini said that a man should be at least forty years old before he undertakes so fine an enterprise as that of setting down the story of his life. He said also that an autobiographer should have accomplished something of excellence. Nowadays nobody who has a typewriter pays any attention to the old master's quaint rules. I myself have accomplished nothing of excellence except a remarkable and, to some of my friends, unaccountable expertness in hitting empty ginger ale bottles with small rocks at a distance of thirty paces. Moreover, I am not yet forty years old. But the grim date moves toward me apace; my legs are beginning to go, things blur before my eyes, and the faces of the rose-lipped maids I knew in my twenties are misty as dreams.

At forty my faculties may have closed up like flowers at evening, leaving me unable to write my memoirs with a fitting and discreet inaccuracy or, having written them, unable to carry them to the publisher's. A writer verging into the middle years lives in dread of losing his way to the publishing house and wandering down to the Bowery or the Battery, there to disappear like Ambrose Bierce. He has sometimes also the kindred dread of turning a sudden corner and meeting himself sauntering along in the opposite direction. I have known writers at this dangerous and tricky age to phone their homes from their offices, or their offices from their homes, ask for themselves in a low tone, and then, having fortunately discovered that they were "out," to collapse in hard-breathing relief. This is particularly true of writers of light pieces running from a thousand to two thousand words.

The notion that such persons are gay of heart and carefree is curiously untrue. They lead, as a matter of fact, an existence of jumpiness and apprehension. They sit on the edge of the chair of Literature. In the house of Life they have the feeling that they have never taken off their overcoats. Afraid of losing them-selves in the larger flight of the two-volume novel, or even the one-volume novel, they stick to short accounts of their misadventures because they never get so deep into them but that they feel they can get out. This type of writing is not a joyous form of self-expression but the manifestation of a twitchiness at once cosmic and mundane. Authors of such pieces have, nobody knows why, a genius for getting into minor difficulties: they walk into the wrong apartments, they drink furniture polish for stomach bitters, they drive their cars into the prize tulip beds of haughty neighbors, they playfully slap gangsters, mistaking them for old school friends. To call such persons "humorists," a loose-fitting and ugly word, is to miss the nature of their dilemma and the dilemma of their nature. The little wheels of their invention are set in motion by the damp hand of melancholy.

Such a writer moves about restlessly wherever he goes, ready to get the hell out at the drop of a piepan or the lift of a skirt. His gestures are the ludicrous reflexes of the maladjusted; his repose is the momentary inertia of the non-plussed. He pulls the blinds against the morning and creeps into smoky corners at night. He talks largely about small matters and smally about great affairs. His ears are shut to the ominous rumblings of the dynasties of the world moving toward a cloudier chaos than ever before, but he hears with an acute perception the startling sounds that rabbits make twisting in the bushes along a country road at night and a cold chill comes upon him when the comic supplement of a Sunday newspaper blows unexpectedly out of an areaway and envelopes his knees. He can sleep while the commonwealth crumbles but a strange sound in the pantry at three in the morning will strike terror into his stomach. He is not afraid, or much aware, of the menaces of empire but he keeps looking behind him as he walks along darkening streets out of the fear that he is being softly followed by little men padding along in single file, about a foot and a half high, large-eyed, and whiskered.

It is difficult for such a person to conform to what Ford Madox Ford in his book of recollections has called the sole reason for writing one's memoirs: namely, to paint a picture of one's time. Your short-piece writer's time is not Walter Lippmann's time, or Stuart Chase's time, or Professor Einstein's time. It is his own personal time, circumscribed by the short boundaries of his pain and his embarrassment, in which what happens to his digestion, the rear axle of his car, and the confused flow of his relationships with six or eight persons and two or three buildings is of greater importance than what goes on in the nation or in the universe. He knows vaguely that the nation is not much good any more; he has read that the crust of the earth is shrinking alarmingly and that the universe is growing steadily colder, but he does not believe that any of the three is in half as bad shape as he is.

Enormous strides are made in star-measurement, theoretical economics, and the manufacture of bombing planes, but he usually doesn't find out about them until he picks up an old copy of "Time" on a picnic grounds or in the summer house of a friend. He is aware that billions of dollars are stolen every year by bankers and politicians, and that thousands of people are out of work, but these conditions do not worry him a tenth as much as the conviction that he has wasted three months on a stupid psychoanalyst or the suspicion that a piece he has been working on for two long days was done much better and probably more quickly by Robert Benchley in 1924.

The "time" of such a writer, then, is hardly worth reading about if the reader wishes to find out what was going on in the world while the writer in question was alive and at what might be laughingly called "his best." All that the reader is going to find out is what happened to the writer. The compensation, I suppose, must lie in the comforting feeling that one has had, after all, a pretty sensible and peaceful life, by comparison. It is unfortunate, however, that even a well-ordered life can not lead anybody safely around the inevitable doom that waits in the skies. As F. Hopkinson Smith long ago pointed out, the claw of the sea-puss gets us all in the end.

J. T.

Sandy Hook,
Connecticut,
September 25, 1933.

If Thurber provoked his Republican friends, like Thomas Meek, for the sport of it, he provoked his left-wing colleagues for more profound reasons. It began flippantly enough with a light, needling first-person casual in the *New Yorker* of June 9, 1934, called "Notes for a Proletarian Novel," in which he pointed out how proletarian literati concerned themselves with everything but the ordinary workingman. Since Thurber had a lot of traffic with ordinary workingmen, during his odd jobs in Columbus, he was more qualified to speak about and for them than were the literati. Gradually, as the lines of battle were drawn between the regiments of "bourgeois" writers for the *New Yorker* and other slicks and the legions of bitter, doctrinaire proletarian writers, Thurber became downright bellicose. Armageddon was at a bash in the New York apartment of Malcolm Cowley, then an editor of the *New Republic,* to which Thurber was brought by Robert Coates.

"I decided to throw a huge party for everyone I knew at the time," Malcolm Cowley recalled. "And everyone came—Communists, Fascists, Republicans, Democrats, and so on. Thurber arrived, started drinking, and got into a loud argument with Mike Gold, one of the tougher proletarian writers there. Gold said that all the petit-bourgeois writers like Thurber were nothing but college punks who couldn't get it up any more. Well, this really hit home with Jim. He took exception and there was almost a brawl. Somebody broke it up, finally. Oh, it was a great party! I just wish I saw more of it."

But Thurber wasn't just twitting the Left, nor was his anger just from a personal insult. He was philosophically anticommunist. A short time later, he sent Cowley one of his remarkable wee-hours letters spelling it all out. The bulky credo was fifteen double-spaced typewritten pages long, and Cowley, thinking it was a manuscript, put it aside until manuscript-reading time. When he at last opened it, he read this testament:

Dear Malcolm:

I am writing this to you as a friend of mine and not as an editor. I have no notion and no desire to have it printed. The idea of writing it came to me tonight when I was sitting alone in the Algonquin lobby reading the current New Republic and, in particular, your article on Krutch's new book. I went over to a bar and had a drink or two and while standing there began to turn over in my mind a lot of things, which I suddenly decided to put down on paper and send to you. I have not very well planned out exactly what I want to say, or what I want to ask, but I do know this: I am essentially going to ask for information and for guidance, genuinely and sincerely, and such elements other than that that come in will be by the way. I don't know exactly where this is going to go or, in detail, exactly what it's going to be like.

In the past few years, certainly the past year, a great many things concerned with economics, communism, writing, proletarianism, life, happiness, love, and whatnot, have bothered me as much as they have bothered anybody. I am not so tied up in my own interests and in the peculiar field of my own thought and writing that I have not observed that Great Changes have taken place and are taking place. My essential weakness, in this regard, is that I am not, in certain subjects, well enough read to be able, conscientiously, to set myself up as a spokesman, a student, a protagonist, or even a sound and well-documented opponent of many of the great and important factors that now enter into national and international life from the standpoint of government politics and economics. I find myself, when such subjects come up, at a loss, but being me, not at so great a loss that I don't put my oar in and argue. I have argued, even fought, with certain literary people who espouse Marxism, Communism, etc. and I admit that they have usually, technically speaking, won the arguments, but they have never won me. If I have resorted to invective and silly talking, etc. and have been unable to point out exactly what I want and what I don't want, it seems to me that they have also been unable to point out exactly what they want and dont want.

I refer, I think, especially to my unhappy and, in some ways, deplorable set-to with Michael Gold some months ago at a party to which I wasn't even asked. Even Bob Coates, who took me there, was disgusted with me and as tolerant and generous as he has always been with me, in my cups and my moods, he told me, out in the street afterwards, that I had made a horse's ass of myself and he disappeared into that New York night he loves so well, leaving me to get home as best I could in a taxi, having only thirty or forty dollars on me. After every such scene I always wake up to remorse and regret and real anguish. It was originally never my nature to engage in such scenes and that, being a fact, is a curious thing, because it is not recognized or believed by even my best friends. Of the things I know about myself I know this best: I am always willing to face the real facts about what I am, think, and do, insofar as anyone can face and untangle and identify them. So many elements go into what a man is, thinks, and does that this is not always easy. There is no one of us who can be absolutely sure that his arguments last night came purely out of his dispassionate beliefs about politics or writing or whatever and were not, in some way, influenced by his emotional nature, something his wife said before the party, something that happened years ago and was grazed in his consciousness by a stray bullet that night, some subtle, hard to recognize beast in the jungle of his experience, his past, his desires, suppressed, thwarted, or (what is even more important) satisfied.

I suppose that I am peculiarly open to that weakness: the inability to think and argue straight, uninfluenced, coldly, about things, and yet I have, in my time, never met a single person, not even those who agree with me, who seems to me to think and argue without the handicaps and the conditioning and distortions of whatever personally, emotionally, temperamentally is the trouble with him as an individual, entirely set apart from any other individual, entirely set apart (whether he knows it or admits it or not) from any group, any body of thought, any plan, dedication, or anything else beyond himself.

I have been accused by several persons, as the result of arguments or diatribes on this or that, of being unintelligent. If that were true, it would end this letter. The unfortunate fact is that I am not unintelligent. I have my distortions, my special leanings, my highly specialized ambitions and feelings, my silly and curious desires and hopes, lusts and vagaries, but I am not unintelligent. I have acted unintelligently at times, as you yourself know, but then who hasn't?

A great many things have happened to me since the night of the Gold argument to worry me, to make me turn my thoughts to things which, that night, I roundly and egotistically and childishly and horse's assily dismissed. I should have been hit on the head and taken away (but of course Bob is too damn broad-minded and gentle and passive to do that: live and let die being his excellent plan). Nevertheless, in going back over the whole evening in my mind there is left to me a certain residue of memory which, after all these months and in all sobriety, I think I was sound about.

One of my arguments was that I dislike "literary communists". I did then and I still do. I regard Mike Gold as a literary communist. He and various others like him are enough to make me turn against the whole idea of communism, the worker, Russia, proletarianism. I think that what communism needs is communists, more communists and fewer writers. Maybe Communism has them, but where are they? I am bewildered now, in a genuine desire to know about communism and what it is and what it wants and where it stands, by the most tremendous whirlpool of literary writing that has befogged the horizon since all the boys jumped in and fought, with equal bewilderment and eloquence, about the New Humanism and, later, Technocracy. For their short hour each of those occupied the identical Big Spot that Communism and Proletarianism now occupies. No use to go back to Babbitt and More and Granville Hicks and Grattan and everybody else on those subjects now, for they are as dead as Lincoln, those subjects now. And yet if I did go back, to the files of the New Republic, the New Masses, the Saturday Review of Literature, I would find the same final, glib, thundering articles, the same warnings, threats, and ominous announcements and prophesies, wouldn't I, that I find now in the same journals about proletarianism?

Of course, it might be easy to prove that communism, the state of the world, the plight of the worker is much more important than Humanism and Technocracy ever were. All right, but—and this is one thing I am (in my small way) aroused about: is literary communism any more important than the other two things were? Humanism, essentially a moral and religious idea and ideal, was turned into a literary idea and ideal by writers; Technocracy, essentially an economic thing, was turned into a literary thing; isn't it true that proletarianism, essentially a governmental and political thing, is being turned—has been turned—into a sheer literary exercise? Communism may be fine, proletarianism —whatever outside of literature it is—may be fine, the plight of the worker may be fine, but haven't they been buried under such a deluge of writing by writers that their real and original purposes have been largely lost sight of? Who is one great American communist, able, important, persuasive, who is not essentially a writer, a literary critic? Are all such men completely inarticulate? Have they no ghost writers, who can put down, bluntly and accurately what these men think and would like to say? Or are there such and have I missed their message?

It seems to me that every article I pick up on the subject has been written by a man who is essentially a literary man. These men give their own ideas, I have never yet seen one of them quote, directly, a worker or a leader of workers. Of course, I have not read every article, I have missed hundreds, but, at random, I have read a great deal. I have read Gold himself on the subject of Ring Lardner and on the subject of Thornton Wilder. Am I to believe that before Communism can get anywhere all writers must cease to write anything that isn't proletarian? Is that, really and truly and soundly, the first essential, or are these literary men, merely for their own amusement, doing nothing at all about their real cause and simply showing off what they know about writing in America, bad or good?

In turning these ideas over in my mind I have come to one conclusion which interests me. I have studied the articles I have read on communism and proletarianism from the standpoint of sheer writing: of style, and composition, and so on. And I have discovered what anybody instantly would: the best writing, the best prose in America today, is the writing and the prose of literary critics. Leaving you out of it (and God knows you can write) there are Edmund Wilson and Ludwig Lewisohn and virtually all the other critics—Krutch, him-

self, even Granville Hicks. They all write like a streak: they are brilliant, eloquent, persuasive, excellent! There isn't a plain, blunt line in the whole business. There are hundreds and hundreds of lines in which the fact or the thought
or the immediate point—even the clarity, as far as argument goes—are sac-
rificed to style, lilt, effect, even, as God is my judge, musical sequences of words!
I wonder sometimes what the average worker, or leader of workers, would
think, if he could read, or have read to him, the great accumulation of beautiful,
sonorous, musical, eloquent wordage that has been put together in the past few
years on the subject of communism and proletarianism. It is, as writing, an
undying thing. It must go into anthologies down through the ages, anthologies
of the best essays, the best expository writing. Hundreds of years from now,
when the cause is lost and forgotten, the ring of the words must still be in the
ears of sensitive appreciators of literature.

Now what I started out to ask you was this. There must be in this country
hundreds of persons like me, intelligent, groping, not, in the field of economics
and politics, well read—because we have largely let the world go to pieces
around us, thinking it would all blow over like the Civil War and take its little
place in history. We know now it won't. We know that the structure, the fabric,
the destination, the purpose of everything has changed. We are caught with our
mental pants down. We dont know where to turn for the facts, for the drawn
lines of battle (fairly and dispassionately outlined) for the causes, paralleled by
some unbiased and unheated person (if there are any). It is our own fault that
we have thus been caught out of life, fishing in our little stream, nursing our
own baby, planning our vacations, making love to a girl, writing silly little pieces
about timid men afraid of the night that comes with sundown, oblivious of the
night that comes with revolution. But there we are! What books, what few
articles, what leaders' statements, what rules and by laws, what statements of
purpose are we to turn to out of all the million-word welter of fine writing?
Would you, or could you, set down such a list, being as fair to Krutch as to Gold?
Would Gold do it, would Krutch do it? It seems to me up to someone. Every
now and then I go and read a book which someone says must be read if one is
to Understand. One such book I read was "City Street" (I believe that's the
name—maybe "City Block") by Waldo Frank. Some critic said that it would be
impossible to 'understand' unless one had read that book. Tommyrot! Almost
every single incident in that book could have taken place in the White House,
or at 277 Park Avenue. I refer, for one concrete instance, to the woman who
lost her child and who smothers to death, in a passion of defeated motherhood,
the child of another woman. And that brings me to one of the things which
caused me to raise such a fuss when talking with Gold. It seems to me that the
literary communists have almost got to the point where they believe that
motherhood and passion and love and all that belong solely to the communists.
That you must be a communist to make even your private life important. It
seems to me that that is not only a foolish but a deadly tangent of thought, an
offshoot of their philosophy which should be sharply brought up, thought out,

and stopped. I remember that when Gold and I were arguing—and by the way he started it by saying to me (whom he didn't know then, even by name) that the New Yorker was edited by "College punks". Again the tendency to make of everybody except a communist a punk or something equally low. Of course I called him a non-college son-of-a-bitch, matching fighting words with fighting words. Instantly he took the sweet martyred attitude that all Bourgeois people want to fight, to use bad words, because, as he said, they are all inferiority complex people. Two other men who came up later both used, separately of each other, the words "inferiority complex". That struck me as odd and as significant and as revelatory. The instant desire to fling that accusation is certainly one of the simpler forms of psychological complex. However, I am off the track. What Gold emphasized was that if I understood Marxism I would do better and truer and more important stories and, yes, even pictures. For, it seems, I deal, in my stories and pictures, only with this strange amorphous indescribable group known as the Bourgeoisie. I thought I had an opening there and I plugged at it. It was my contention, admitting that I did not understand or know about Marxism, much, or Communism or the proletariat, it was my contention that my stories and my pictures were about relationships between men and women which are entirely apart from any consideration of economics, politics or anything of the sort. I asked him if he was married and he said yes. I asked him if he was happy and he dodged that. Later he came up to me, alone, and said that he hadn't answered that question because, as a matter of fact, he had not been happy with his wife for five years. I asked him if it were any different being unhappy with your wife when you were a communist. I asked if bedroom familiarities and intimacies, morning before-coffee irritabilities, evening grouchinesses were any different. He smiled his patronizing smile, as much as to say certainly, they were. That is the seed of a dangerous illusion, that is the little weed in the cranny that can, finally, break down a castle. It is there, for one place, that proletarianism, having been taken over by the writers and not the workers, goes off the track and causes people who still hold on to Capitalism, or still ignore the present world situation, or still blindly keep to themselves and their little private lives to become afraid of this great plan for a new world because they see in it, way down in the core, like a worm, a partly unconscious envy of, and hatred for, and incipient desire to destroy not only the economic regime of the capitalistic people but the personal culture and the individual destiny and happiness of those people. And in "those people" I include everyone whose state, whether it be financial, political, or cultural, is —by communistic standards—above the state of the communists. When mobs break in they dont only arrest Louis and Antoinette, they take a special joy in hacking to pieces fine paintings and in pissing on royal beds. This, I will admit, may sound a little hysterical and exaggerated, but it is so only to prove my point, or at least to show a feeling I have which I should like to have argued away.

If I keep mentioning Michael Gold it is now, believe me, not as a person with whom I was personally involved in a crazy argument but as a person whom I take to represent, in a great way, one large part of communism, the communism not only of the actual worker but of the literary man and the literary critic who, along with everything else, wants to change literature and culture. I don't see how anybody could fail to see, in his writings on Wilder and on Lardner and in his talk to me—a viewpoint which a dozen of his colleagues have endorsed —a desire to subject the individual to the political body, to the economic structure, to put the artist in a uniform so like the uniform of the subway conductor that nobody would be able to tell the difference. It is this desire to regiment and discipline art—the art of writing and the art of living—that some of us are afraid of, that some of us seem to see a greater menace in than the critics do. Who has stood up and opposed it, with the sharp, flat, challenging words it deserves? My God almighty, Max Eastman, in a flabby, soporific ten thousand words explaining that Art, really you know, has nothing whatever to do with purpose or with politics or with function or with utility! We dont need someone to say that that is true—we know it is true—we need someone to say, listen, you sons of bitches, hands off—keep your noses in your economic and political dishes or we'll knock them off! Max, again, is one of those writers of really excellent, well balanced, swinging periods,—he has the mot juste and the sentence juste and the paragraph juste. They all write, when they write such stuff, a whole lot like the Cabell whose lovely swinging periods they denounce. By the way, have you ever noticed that most criticisms of Cabell are written in Cabell's own critical style?

I have admitted that I am largely ignorant about Marx and about Communism—as an economic and governmental matter. I should like to know more about it. I have tried Marx. I have tried the dozens of explanations of Marx. I cant go it. Any more than I can go Racine or the Greek tragedies. I think I do know a little about literary proletarianism and I know that I dont like it and that I feel it should be as consistently attacked as it is consistently advocated and fought for. Poor old Mencken, who now, in his old age, just waves everything aside, is not the man for it. Too bad, for he has the bludgeons for it. It needs bludgeons. The whole thing should be, once in a while, brought out of this realm of decorous, nicely written exchanges of shots between critics of opposing thought.

Have you ever noticed: a man writes a book on a subject of great importance. It is reviewed by a brilliantly writing critic. Sometimes the critic barely mentions the book in hand; usually, at least, he doesn't get around to the book for three or four hundred words—being busy writing a little essay of his own, showing to begin with how much he knows about this and kindred subjects. Then comes a few quibbles about wrong dates, misspelled words, things left out that should be in, and finally, maybe, a word or two of praise for the really good points that the man makes (only isn't it too bad that the points are not the ones he should have made!) Then the author sits down and writes an answer which it takes him a whole night of rewriting to get down to six hundred cold calm words, explaining that the critic has missed his point entirely, that he hasn't understood a God damn thing, that the author did not say Pareto on page 217, he said Proust. This is printed in the magazine which printed the original criticism and it is followed by the critic's answer to the author's answer, in which the critic says that the author's answer shows that he is just as far off the subject as he was to begin with only more so. And the careful, struggling reader of the whole business, looking for a little light, puts the whole works down and goes out and gets cock-eyed at Tim's bar and asks Tim, an old Ballyhaunis man, what he thinks of things. "It's all balls," says Tim, and the reader goes home to bed, sure of only that one thing.

Somebody in the New Masses a month or two ago took the annual crack at the New Yorker. Overlooking the fact that the New Yorker is a business enterprise which would fail if we all began to write like the Masses, the writer descended to such silly and unimportant work as to seriously analyze and show up the fact that we writers here are not "living in this world" because we don't write about the worker. The Wilder-Lardner thing all over again. We all inhabit a Lost Atlantis, we drink our old-fashioneds to the last drop careless of the fact that the world is crumbling around us. In short, we don't attack communism but we don't go for it, head over heels. Therefore, the inference is, what we write—no matter how funny or well done or, in its way, right—should be stopped. If these men, who write such attacks, should ever get in control, do you think there wouldn't be a commissar of literature who would be appointed and commissioned to stop it, who would set us at work writing either poems in praise of the American Lenin or getting up time tables for work trains? If you do, you're missing a low, faint, distant rumbling.

Another thing: I read in the New Republic that unless the working class is saved, and not saved to be the tool and slave of the upper classes, all the other classes must fall. Well, they haven't yet but they might, maybe they even will. (And by the way, I dont think that either you or Krutch completely exhausted the possibilities of argument and prophesy in the ancient Roman decline and fall.) What I want to know is, just what constitutes saving the working classes? I read about the woes and the perils of the present system, of Roosevelt's plans and ideals and fumblings, I read all kinds of threats and prophesies of disaster, but I have not put my eye yet on a succinct statement of just what it is that the communists, or the socialists, in this country want? Where can I go to find out what they want? Where can I go to find a statement, or a plan, or a whatnot, which will describe for me exactly what is to be, or roughly what is to be, the status of the working class in the revolution, in the new world, just what the place of the present ruling classes, just what the place of anybody? If it all came about the way Gold wants it, and everything is hotsy-totsy, then would it be all right for a Lardner or a Wilder or a New Yorker writer to write what he wanted to write, or wouldn't it?

The Robert Forsythe, I think it was, who stooped to so trivial a task as denouncing us New Yorker writers seemed fond of the idea that we were writing about a Lost Atlantis. The Lost Atlantis of love and marriage and child-birth, of course, among other things—that is, love and marriage and child-birth among the Bourgeosie, which, in some miraculous way, must go out—has gone out—with the new regime of thought about the emergence, if not dominance, of the proletariat. Yet our own lives must always be the subject for our writings, come what may. Why dont they see that? As I said to Gold, you have your Cantwells, and your Halpers (My God, they now even have their Saroyan, and welcome to him!) Why not let the other alone? You can't live by bread alone, or by factories and foundries alone. Why is that such a difficult thing to see, I wonder—such a difficult thing to concede?

If you say that I have got the wind up simply about a small group—the Gold group—I would point out that dozens of literary communists, outside that group as well as in, have caught the new ideal: nothing but literature that takes in the social background. Read Hicks' amazing criticism of what was wrong with Emily Dickinson, with James, with Stephen Crane! It's incredible in this so-called enlightened age. If I were to name somebody besides yourself to say for me the things I have so roughly and impetuously and unstudiedly put down here I would take Cantwell, whose article on Henry James in the same New Republic my piece was in [a review of L. Frank Baum's Oz books] was a remarkably fine piece of fair writing and sound analysis. So far as I know—and I've read most everything on James—he is the first man to point out that James knew the people he wrote about were lost, trivial, nasty, that he didn't adore them or revere them. But then I suppose that outside of me, Cantwell is really the only person who ever read all of the James Prefaces, hard going for the first time but amazingly clear, interesting—as unified as any of his novels—when you read them altogether.

I have been working for weeks on a Saroyan parody—I get so mad I spoil it and have to let it dry. It seems to me significant that this man, who can not write and in admitting it really boasts that he can, should have caught whatever fancy it is that he has caught. Is he a proof and sign of the fact that if your writing deals with poor people out of work, etc. it is now bound to sell, no matter how bad it is? Was it the consistent pounding of the critics about proletarian writing that put him over? I wonder. Naturally I sympathize with Hemingway's attack on him in Esquire. I thought it was just the way he should have been attacked, drunkenly, sloppily. I thought Hemingway's saying aw, what you need is a smack in the puss was precisely the right note. Thank God there are only 70,000 Armenians left (which leaves a total of 490,000 rugs unsold). I couldn't even worry about those Armenians on Musa Dagh after reading Saroyan. Even when they shot Bagradian I didn't care.

Saroyan maunders along in his sentimental, folie de grandeur way (he writes a whole lot like Jack Johnson, the colored heavyweight would write if he could) about a man who shot himself in the stomach with a shotgun. He worries about that. The guy was out of work, sick, a victim of the system (he supposes; although we have no way of knowing that he hadn't just been divorced by his wife). So he drools along about that. And because it is about a worker, or a man out of work, it is important, it is fine. Why, exactly? Are the proletarian writers going to have the added advantage of writing sloppily and mushily just because whatever they have to say is so important it doesn't make any difference how they say it? I worry about things, too. I am so constituted that I cannot worry about an unknown man who shoots himself in the stomach in a house a few doors from mine. I tell you what I worry about, a thing that sticks in my mind the way that man's groans sticks in Saroyan's mind. I worry about the first time I ever saw my daughter look out of a window at night, a window in an old Connecticut farmhouse, and watch, with wide, wondering eyes, the first snow she ever saw, falling silently over the old orchard behind the house. That to me is as important as any of the things that happen to the people in "The 42nd Parallel" or "1919" (none of whose names I can remember). Must I explain this, to anyone except myself? Must I answer for it in a communist's literary court? Must I have been confined in Bellevue because I say I could write a novel about it and want to write a novel about it and will write a novel about it? And let 19 men be blown up in a Kentucky mine while I am working on the novel, and never mention that catastrophe, not even mention how one old lady, wife of a miner, krapped her bloomers at the news?

One of my favorite characters in another Lost Atlantis was a mythical figure named Tristram. He was born in a land called Lyonesse which sank into the sea. There is no trace of that land now, no proof of it. There is no trace and proof of the men he fought with (with usually no social purpose in mind), no sign left that ever a woman named Iseult lived. Yet he was wont to say, and every now and then I hear him saying it, "I come from Lyonesse and a gentleman am I." I like to think of that; I get a kind of solace out of repeating a line never said by a man who never lived from a land that never existed.

It must be almost dawn.

Yours,
Jim Thurber

I told you I didn't know where this was going to go or what it would be like.

This has all the demerits—& merits—of not having been redone at all.

J

As a result of Thurber's extraordinary missive, Cowley asked him to write a review for the *New Republic* of Granville Hicks's mammoth anthology, *Proletarian Literature in the United States.* Thurber agreed and slaved over the review, rewriting it many times. It was finally printed in the March 25, 1936, issue, under the heading "Voices of Revolution." (Strangely, Ross didn't assign Thurber any reviewing for the *New Yorker,* the logical outlet for his natural critical ability; perhaps Ross couldn't believe that his star was capable of yet another talent.)

The review of Hicks's anthology was well-considered and intelligent. Thurber called proletarian fiction "hysterical and overwrought," never really coming to life, except erratically in the case of Dos Passos. He said that he never really believed the writers were "there," that they were simply disseminating propaganda. He criticized their poor English (his *New Yorker* training), and rued their lack of humor. ("Some of the richest humor in the world is the humor of the American proletariat.") In contrast to proletarian propaganda, he praised the care and detachment of such reporters as Robert Coates and St. Clair McKelway. "Art," he said, "does not rush to the barricades." The review caused a predictable tempest, and Thurber was besieged at parties by all factions for his temperate stand. Not so temperate was another mere postcard of nine pages to Cowley, which accompanied the review's manuscript to the *New Republic* offices:

Dear Malcolm:

I have written, I suppose, at least fifty thousand words in my fifteen or twenty rewrites of this piece. I have spent at least fifty solid hours of work on the mere writing, perhaps twenty on the reading. It came out to be a thing I had to do, and to do right. Here is the right way I had to do it. I am sorry it is so long— but it's not as long as Arvin's "letter". He didn't have time to write a review, a shorter piece. I have been influenced by nothing except my own feelings, definitely my feelings as a writer, possibly my feelings as a bourgeois (a hell of a goddam loose word to apply to all Americans who are not proletarians. After all my grandfather had a stand on Central Market and my father never made more than $50 a week in his life).

One cannot poke into such a book, certainly one cannot actually exhaust the whole thing, without wanting to do six or seven pieces on the general subject. I would like to do, certainly, an essay on this recurrent, curious subject: the sexual practises and the spiritual content of the bourgeois fucker. Has anybody done it? Just what, after all, makes the proletarian unlecherous, fine, spiritual —I can understand what makes some of the bourgeoisie lecherous, humping, loveless fuckers, but just what is there in Marxist theory and in proletarian practise that makes the worker's love a fine and beautiful, almost James M. Barrie thing? God, do I wish I had the time and leisure and money to go into that subject and write it up! As it exists now, fucking and love, spiritual attachment to a woman and lechery, are merely muddy objects that bourgeois and proletarian writers and critics fling at each other, crying "yah, yah, dirty screwer!" as they do it. The same thing, you remember, came up [in] the old bitter Humanism fights—I myself heard Babbitt, in effect, say that Carl Van Doren screwed too much, and I heard Van Doren reply, in effect, that Babbitt couldn't screw at all. I couldnt, and can't, miss the fact that we American boys are still youngsters behind the barn, measuring cocks, seeing who can piss the farthest, etc. That all comes out, and so oddly, in this proletarian-bourgeois literary fight. It seems almost to be confined to the writer and the intellectual. I don't really believe that the factory owner and the worker bother much about it. Each lays his woman, gets his "hide"—to use an old proletarian expression (and isn't it true that most of the vulgar, derogatory terms for sexual love are proletarian, rather than bourgeois? "Piece of tail" came out of the circus. "Piece of ass" is, I believe, factory and foundry.) I would, really, like to have time to run this whole thing to earth—although just where I could expound it, I don't know. Certainly something must be done to divorce and dissociate fucking and even the highest form of spiritual embrace from the general artistic and literary discussion. It has begun to distort and mar virtually every piece of criticism written about anything today.

I remember, in this connection, a pertinent story I heard twenty years ago about a Lancastershire mine worker. He came home tired and went to bed and had intercourse with his wife. "Do you love me, Joe?" she asked, when it was over. "Ah, fuck love," he said, or words to that effect. "Well," she asked, after a while, "If you don't love me, why do you sleep with me?" "Ah," said he, "Why do I shit?" There's a lot of sadness, and some authority, in that story. Now when this particular worker learns about Marxism, does he change his feelings on the subject of a piece of tail? . . .

What is the essential matter with "Proletarian Literature in the United States"? I'll tell you. Here are, first of all, a bunch of writers. Nobody, reading this book as carefully as I have, can fail to see that these people are, for the most part, essentially writers. You feel that, as such, they would, first of all, like to have this be a Utopian world, as quickly as possible, in which it would be all right to write for the New Yorker. But it isn't such a world. Therefore, they go over to writing about the proletariat (about whose actions, reactions, idioms, and gestures they betray a constant pathetic ignorance) and because they *have* to do this rather than *want* to do it there arises bitterness, anger, and, of all things, this curious wail and plaint against the sex life of the bourgeois. John McNulty, an old newspaper friend of mine, discussing here the other night the farmer and the city man said "Hell, for one thing the farmer knows the city man has better women than he has!" For one thing, I'm afraid, the proletariat writer and critic —I mean only certain ones, like Freeman, believe the bourgeois has lovelier and more passionate women. I don't know Freeman, but I have met certain others and, as I flatly, if drunkenly, told Gold: there is no escaping the utterly silly but nevertheless important fact that most literary Communists are personally and physically unattractive. I know few as attractive as, let us say at random, Carl Van Doren (although I guess the Communists have grabbed him, or let him in with a growl, or something—but he's essentially, in his mode of life, a man who lives in the kind of personal leisure that J.P. Morgan describes), or take Joe Krutch—a more attractive man than Gold. I mean he could have first shot at Garbo if only Garbo and Gold and Krutch were alive today. Ah, Malcolm, maybe here we're beginning to get at something which explains that bitter sexual complex of Freeman and his pals. . . .

Now, I don't by any means go fully over to the side of the Freudians. They've missed a lot. But, just as you must, so do I know that dwelling on sex differences, hurling sudden sex challenges, is likely to be based not on intellctual opinion, not on ideology, not on dialectics, not on class feeling, but on plain personal intimate and private disturbances. It seems to me that something of that sort comes out of Freeman, and out of a lot of those boys. It is, of course, a thing that none of us can really get at. I happen to know a lot of bourgeois people, and especially a lot of bourgeois writers, but I don't know how I'd go about finding out whether their sex life and ideology is really this or that. I don't think Freeman, not having my advantage of acquaintance and friendship, could come as close as I could. Well, then, he bases it on books? On things like O'Hara's "Butterfield 8"? I believe he does. But what, then, are you going to do about Chad Newsome and Madame de Vionnet in Henry James's "The Ambassadors"? What about Gene Stratton Porter's "The Harvester"? What, even, about "My Antonia" (dismiss it, and all the rest, except "A Lost Lady"?). The field is so wide, the writers, the characters, the regions, the feelings are so diverse: and the nasty taunt of the Freemans is so narrow and tight! And on what persons, what characters, what writers, does Freeman really base his challenge that *all* the bourgeoisie are merely lechers and Narcissists? Just what is the difference, sexually, spiritually, between him and me, since we are both writers? Is it true that my Columbus background and my early teachings and his Greenpoint (or whatever) background and early teachings have done something irreparable to us? Or that, having grown up and seen literature and the class struggle from different viewpoints, something has happened to make a gap between his reaction and my reaction to any girl he might want to pick—and hers to us? Oh, come, it's all too silly and fuddled up! And yet nobody, from Isidore Schneider down, challenged his silly points. Does no Communist writer listen to any other? Don't they give advice, don't they ever come out with "horse's ass" and "god damn fool"? Well, they should. In mere unthinking solidarity, Malcolm, there is nothing but the grain of ruin: through sentimentality, through distortion, and through excited complaisance. You can't fight an intellectual cause, or a literary cause, with your cock. Behind every mind is a cock, certainly, but nobody can suddenly leave his literary peroration behind and begin waving a bigger cock, and proclaiming a finer sense of sex values, than the other fellow.

It is an odd thing but amorousness to me, and to most men I know, has always been something more, much more, than lechery. As you know, as Freeman, in his calm moments must know, the very nature of a writer, of what-ever class, causes him to put a probably exaggerated importance on the emotional and spiritual values of sex contact. It has nothing to do with the worker or the capitalist as such, but it has a lot to do with the artist as such. Therefore his whole argument falls down because he is talking about the worker and the capitalist, the proletarian and the bourgeois, in the terms of the artist—which are the terms he knows best. This effort of the critics on both sides to stretch what they know and feel of the writer to cover the case of the worker and the employer is pathetic. Will ever any first rate writer rise up out of the masses to tell the truth? What I want is a first rate critic from the masses, a lusty, healthy guy whose had his fling, his love, and finally goes in for critical writing. Then we'd learn something. But, sadly enough, what we would learn would only be what he has to say for himself, just as we learn from poor Freeman what he has to say for himself.

Now, I might seem to be protesting too much, unless one understood exactly what I'm protesting against, and why. I'm protesting, mainly, against being classed as a bourgeois who does not, cannot, know the feelings of the proletarian. That's one reason I undertook this book: I want to know, and feel at home, among these proletarian writers. I'm too proud to believe that I can't grasp their viewpoints, feel their struggles, know what it's all about. I wont be put down as a person and a writer who, as Forsythe says, writes in a vacuum and lives in a lost Atlantis. Of course I know I am not. By I wanted to get hold of the weapons and the arguments by which I could prove myself. I have done that, more or less, only to realize that nobody wants to accept you in friendly debate: they want to mark you off as a definitely lost person, who could never fairly understand them and their viewpoint, their ideology, their struggles. Well, I've been through as much worker trouble, as a boy of poor family and as a newspaper man, as anyone—probably as much as Freeman (I really don't hate him; it is really Gold whom I should like to understand and who I would like to have understand me). But what comes out of it all is a cheap and vulgar and meaningless bitterness revolving for the most part around the sexual practises of men! Men of the arts, as God is my judge. Therefore a personal and paltry thing. The whole anthology reeks of that. Those writers really want to be writers, making money, laying lovely women and handsome men; they don't really want to be out suffering with the worker (after all, they remember Waldo Frank and his broken head and that it wasn't the police or the strike-breakers who broke it).

Well, here I go on again. I am not really worried or broken, as the boys would like to think. I have probably more fun than most people. I don't think the revolution is here or anywhere near here. I believe the only menace is the growing menace of fascism. I also firmly believe that it is the clumsy and whining and arrogant attitude of the proletarian writers which is making that menace bigger and bigger every day. They won't compromise, they wont debate, they wont listen, they just annoy and disturb people. They have made a god-awful mess of Scotsboro but, like the little boy who owned the baseball bat, they won't get out of the game. Communism, and literary proletarianism, loses friends every day. Why, in God's name, can't they have one or two likeable, genial, humorous, natural human beings to espouse their cause? Why is it that people like Cantwell and you and Coates just cannot fully bring yourselves to going over completely? Well, I'll tell you: Bob, being a sound and sober thinker, is no more sure than I am that fascism in this country would be any worse, if as bad as, Communism. Cantwell, being an admirer of and student of Henry James, knows he could not burn James's works for all of the Communist principles in the world. You, being a wise and philosophical man, know that leftism often means a mean, tawdry, and stupid viewpoint; you know that there can be no sharp line drawn between the worker and the bourgeois in this country—that often the bourgeois is right and the worker wrong; you know that, in friends, in home, in family, in parties, you have had more real and genuine fun with the non-proletarian writer or the partly proletarian writer than you can ever have with the Freemans and the Golds. You know, whether you say so or not, that Cantwell and Coates and even myself, none of us so much anything class or political as we are writer appreciator and human being, are not only better company but sounder Americans than the ranting writers for whom you write a poem to go on the back cover.

Well, that's all this time.

> Love and kisses to you and
> the wife and the baby, and
> if they were only starving
> wouldn't that be realer
> and better?

P.S. Remember that only when you're out of a job does love mean anything. (Did you, though, happen to know that in weariness, fatigue, and sleeplessness sex becomes merely lust and that only in calmness, quiet, and, if possible, leisure and luxury, it blooms best?) (Well, tell Mr. Freeman).

Mike Gold's digging, durable sexual taunt and its consequences aside, Thurber was obviously vexed by the proletarian-literature business. His social instincts were liberal and strong, and he should have leaned towards the Left, as so many other liberal writers of the 1930's did; but his upbringing and training were pure bourgeois, with puritanical icing. So he found himself in yet another constipating contradiction, a corollary of the yokel-vs.-sophisticate contradiction Ann Honeycutt mentioned. In the end, he was proven correct about the proletarian-literature aesthetic, but there was little joy in the victory. As E. B. White said, "It was to his credit he didn't fall into the Left rut in the Thirties. I resisted it, too. Thurber had a real social conscience, though, but it was all mixed up with and confused by Ohio Republicanism. There was everything in James Grover Thurber."

Now fully accredited as an appraiser of literature, as well as an American humorist and comic artist, Thurber lovingly played his roles, issuing the first of a long series of proclamations on the state of humor. He told Max Eastman (who took on the thankless task of analyzing comedy in his 1936 book, *Enjoyment of Laughter*) that his humor was really about one thing: "beaten-down married people. The American woman is my theme and how she dominates the male, how he tries to go away but always comes back for more, being romantic and everlastingly nice and having an almost religious feeling about marriage." Certainly posturing for Eastman, he admitted a predilection for standard Fred Allen lines ("How much would you charge to haunt a house?") and colored-maid jokes ("HOUSEWIFE: 'Did you seed the grapefruit?'/ COLORED MAID: 'Yes, ma'am, I seed 'em' "). Alluding to the heart of *My Life and Hard Times*, he said, neatly reworking Wordsworth, "I think humor is the best that lies closest to the familiar, to that part of the familiar which is humiliating, distressing, even tragic. Humor is a kind of emotional chaos told about calmly and quietly in retrospect." He also stated, "You have to enjoy humorous writing while you're doing it . . . You can't be mad, or bitter, or irate. If you are it will be no good."(14) It was an observation that would prey on him throughout his last years.

What really set him off was a 1930's debate between Benchley and Donald Ogden Stewart on the subject "Shall There Be Humor About the Working Classes?" Stewart took the negative, and Thurber never quite forgave him for it. He was even more irate when the leftists waged a campaign to abolish racial or ethnic humor—colored maids were appearing regularly and brilliantly in several of his casuals—and when Dorothy Parker was quoted in the *New Masses* as saying that humor is a shield, not a weapon. "Humor has as big a fist as any other form, or maybe bigger," he wrote White.(15) The Marxist abhorrence of free, pointed humor, especially in the *New Yorker* manner of pricking the pompous and pretentious, was unthinkable to him, a valid reason in his view for a verbal duel. "Later on," E. B. White said, "I think he came to understand that humor is both a weapon and a shield, and sometimes neither." Recalling Will Rogers's gently joshing, regular-guy praise of the 1926 Mussolini (he disliked Rogers, before and after 1926), Thurber said in 1958, "Political satire can be dangerous as an unguided missile when it is unsound."(16)

During these years of immense personal, professional, and political strain, of dissipation and loneliness, Thurber managed to find the time and energy for some extracurricular activities and even a few duties. On March 30, 1933, his esteemed professor and erstwhile literary mentor, Joseph Russell Taylor, died suddenly in Columbus. Thurber had last seen the man a couple of years before in New York City, where Taylor had mistakenly turned up a week too soon for an academic meeting. Thurber was as amused and awed by Taylor's distracted erudition then as he was back in the Henry James sessions at Ohio State. When in 1933 he learned that Taylor had died, he agreed to go to Columbus and speak at a Saturday morning memorial service at the O.S.U. Faculty Club. James Pollard, a member of the faculty then, recalled that "Thurber was very nervous that morning. He stood behind a davenport and kept pressing against it and actually moving it on the floor towards the audience, and his hands fluttered while he spoke."(17) Nevertheless, he delivered, by all accounts, a moving tribute to the man who had influenced his tastes so, at a time when he had desperately needed some good influencing.

Also, the artist Thurber was asked to gather together some drawings for serious shows—a signal honor during the depression and one that surprised nobody more than the artist himself. In 1933, Smith College presented an exhibition of drawings by George Grosz and Thurber, and a year later the Valentine Gallery, on Fifty-seventh Street in New York, actually offered a one-man show of eighty scraggly Thurber pictures. The Valentine show was well-attended and provided a chance for art critics to have some fun. The New York *Herald Tribune* reviewer wrote, "The result is something that has never been seen before and probably never will hereafter." And *Time*, after snidely reporting the "arty" event itself, said that the pictures "are enormously funny, and like most lasting humor, are the products of an unhappy mind." People were slightly shocked to see that many Thurber specimens were lewd and blasphemous. Three of the drawings on display at the Valentine Gallery were obviously fast *New Yorker* rejections: an irreverent outrage called "The Thurber Madonna"; a scene of evil-eyed senior citizens ogling the Virgin titled "The Three Wise Men"; and "The Gates of Hell," which showed a girl hoisting her skirts before a legless war veteran, as tears marked the amputee's cheeks and busy pedestrians rushed by.*

The Valentine drawings were priced from thirty-five to one hundred dollars (most of them went for thirty-five), and Thurber's take from the show was an unexpected eighty-five dollars, not at all bad for 1934. He still took an oblique view of his art work. Since he continued to distribute his sketches like so many gumdrops, he hardly believed in their monetary worth, either. However, he was indignant, some years later,

---

*A little earlier, Thurber had sketched some illustrations for Robert Coates's 1933 book, *Yesterday's Burdens*, many of which were of yielding, large-nippled ladies and grotesque, large-lipped blacks. The book was published without the illustrations, which were discovered years afterward by Malcolm Cowley.

when he discovered that a noted American millionaire, an art patron and a fervent Thurber fan, bought up some drawings for ten dollars each, rather than pay the full gallery prices, and then gave them to wealthy friends. But even the self-deprecating Thurber had to be more than slightly honored in 1936 by the inclusion of one of his drawings in the Museum of Modern Art's Fantastic Art-Dada-Surrealism exhibition.

A less formal and infinitely more cherished exhibition of Thurber art was the permanent Costello collection. Tim Costello, the Ballyhaunis philosopher, speakeasy proprietor, and post-Prohibition publican Thurber and his friends were so fond of, decided in the bleak 1934–35 winter to redo the dingy plaster walls of his Third Avenue bar. Costello covered the walls with wallboard painted white, and the temptation of a clean canvas, as it were, was too much for the impromptu muralist Thurber. Soon, the walls were adorned with some of the finest Thurber work to date: rampant men, women (clothed and unclothed), dogs, rabbits, and the memorable football scene of a running back straight-arming a gowned lady tackler over the caption "Mt. Holyoke 14–Yale 0." The murals drew the customers Costello liked best and they kept his prize patron's thin, nervous hands busy. It is said that Thurber was so taken with the murals that he even worked on them one Sunday, when the bar was closed. At one point, a wall painter Costello hired, figuring that the scrawls were simply boozy graffiti, painted over some (Costello said, "I could have killed that man."),(18) but Thurber obligingly redrew them.

In 1949, Costello moved next door and he had all the wallboard carefully taken down and transported to the new place, along with his blackthorn stick and other necessary implements of his trade. The move won as much attention in the press as the Pietà's coming to America.*

Thurber also sketched on Tim's tablecloths as he drank, ate, and talked. One of these casual masterpieces was rescued from the waiters by a female admirer, who embroidered over the faint lines stained with

---

*By April of 1972, the once white wallboard at Tim's place had tarnished with the fumes of thousands of cigarettes and cooking grease into a bilious ochre, almost obliterating the lines of Thurber's drawings. A group of artists—many of them veterans of *Yank*, the World War II soldiers' magazine which was billeted in the 1940's on nearby East Forty-second Street—volunteered to restore the drawings by painting white around the fabled lines. Their prime motive was love for the familiar murals; another motive was a public-relations stunt for a ghastly movie based not loosely enough on certain Thurber material. The film was called *The War Between Men and Women* and all its prints should be burned unceremoniously at a used-car lot in Whittier, California.

steak juice and whiskey, and presented the laundered napery years later to Helen Thurber.

Another example of Thurber's extracurricular activity (and professional promiscuity) was an invitation he received in the spring of 1934 to broadcast his own fifteen-minute radio program every Thursday evening at 10:45 on the Columbia Network. Ann Honeycutt, then the assistant to a C.B.S. producer, and Jap Gude, the chief of publicity at C.B.S., cooked up the idea, with the grudging assent of Thurber. He was supposed to ramble on about anything he wanted to talk about—mainly, but not exclusively, tales of mysterious Ohio—and he was given this unusual license because of his successful audition. At the audition, Thurber stood before the microphone and said Hemingway had just announced that a male lion can run a hundred yards in eight seconds, which showed that Hemingway ran the same distance in at least 7.5 seconds. Thurber got the job, impressing everybody but himself. Chatty rambling to the contrary, he needed a good 2,500 words of script before he could go on the air. He quickly wearied of this extra chore, and Ross complained that he was siphoning off some good stuff to radio. As he often did when he was in a difficult situation, he played the fool (which his grandfather had punished him for doing three decades before). During one program, he pretended he had lost the script but continued to drone on while searching his pockets for some helpful scrap of paper. After the heart-stopping fifteen minutes of live radio were over, Thurber calmly explained to the ashen radio executives that he was only kidding, he had memorized the script. He also covered C.B.S. office walls with murals, repeating the prank as often as the graffiti were painted out. Just before air time on another night, he made believe he was drunk, causing all the executives present to blanch again. But a few weeks after that incident, Thurber, thoroughly bored, appeared at the studio certifiably drunk and insisted on broadcasting. The producer was enraged and replaced him with piano music. And that was the end of Thurber's solo radio career.

Besides offering a broader renown than magazines and books, radio brought Thurber face-to-face with one of his heroes, Fred Allen. Jap Gude arranged a lunch for the two of them. "Jim worshipped Fred and vice versa," Gude said, "and they both looked forward to meeting each other, especially since Jim was on radio, too. One of Jim's favorite impersonations was of Fred Allen, when he wasn't doing Ed Wynn or Jeeter Lester or all those Columbus people. Anyway, they greeted each other warmly at the restaurant and then they both froze. Even the drinks didn't loosen them up. It was a disaster. Each was afraid to talk because he thought he would bore the other by his stories, they had that much mutual admiration. After an hour of strained pass-the-salt-please conversation, they parted with a great deal of embarrassment. Later on, they exchanged letters but they never saw too much of each other again."

Meanwhile, back in Sandy Hook, Althea had had just about enough of their arrangement. In the late summer of 1934, she hired a Connecticut lawyer and announced her intention of legally separating from her husband. Thurber was at first shaken and then, quickly, understanding, even helpful. He had his attorney, Morris L. Ernst, of Greenbaum, Wolff & Ernst, draft a separation agreement which was both generous and gentle. Althea received custody of Rosemary (with "reasonable" visiting rights for Thurber and extended rights after she reached the age of twelve, the child keeping the name Thurber), all of the family life insurance to date, the Sandy Hook house and land, child support, alimony until remarriage, and Thurber's advance and first-year royalties for *My Life and Hard Times*.

In a heady mix of emotions over this turn of events, Thurber needed a change of scene to think things over. He drove out to Columbus with his friend Robert Coates. It was a larky, meandering bachelor fling, full of spontaneous detours and frivolous embellishments. As an example of how sportive was his mood, he stopped at a phone outside Columbus and called up his family, which was unaware he was coming to town. The result of the call was one of his more accomplished practical jokes. Summoning his best Jewish accent, Thurber asked for William, who he knew was in Columbus at that time. "This is Abe Schlotzheimer, man's tailor," said Thurber, and launched into an involved story of how he had measured and fitted William for an English broadcloth suit months ago but William hadn't come by to pick up the finished product. William was taken in and irately accused the caller of extortion. Thurber–Schlotzheimer threatened to take him to court unless he paid. Finally, William, in desperation, put his mother on the phone. Mame Thurber could smell a good con job a mile away, being a famous confidence woman herself. "If you're so smart," Mame said, "what does my son look like?" Thurber–Schlotzheimer paused for a moment before shouting, "A great mother! A great mother that don't know what her own son looks like!" She hung up, and she was still mad even after Thurber called her back and told her who the tailor really was.(19)

One of his first Columbus stops was at the house of his friend Ted Gardiner. While he was there, he heard by telephone that Althea had filed divorce papers in the Superior Court of Fairfield County, Connecticut, on grounds of "intolerable cruelty." Thurber was upset because he knew that Connecticut was a difficult divorce state and the grounds would have to be exaggerated to satisfy the court. The proceedings were certain to be messy. "We all went out and got drunk as goats," said Gardiner. "Jim, Coates, and I picked up Herman Miller and various other people along the way, and we went to the Rocky Fork Country Club. As I remember it, it was a very bad evening. Some coquettish girl at the club got drunk, and Jim, Coates, and Miller all tried to make her. They began to fight over her and, of course, none of them succeeded. Jim was in a bad way that night. He carried a small torch for Althea, I think, in spite of their troubles. Later on, he used to say, 'Nobody knows what to do about Althea or Nasser.'

"When he was mean drunk, like that night at the country club, he could give you a tongue-lashing for no good reason. He would suddenly say to me, 'You are the lowest of the low!'—and I didn't even know what he was angry about. He sometimes worried my wife, Julia, when he stayed all night drinking and swearing. Once, she just put him out of the house. But most of the time, he was the kindest, most considerate man. My daughters loved him. He wasted more comedy on us. He'd just sit there in our living room, his mind working away, and then he'd come up with some imitation or weird rhyme or backward limerick, as we called them.* I admired the quirks of his mind, even when I didn't especially admire him."

While Thurber and Coates were setting unwary Columbus on its ear during that visit of late 1934, another revered wallboard mural was born. Thurber wandered up into the attic of the Gardiner house one night and sketched in blue chalk on brown plasterboard some questionable drawings, with cryptic captions such as ". . . and keep them for pallbearers." He didn't mind if others added their own graffiti. Gardiner has long since sold that house, but the new owners, recognizing art when they find it in their attic, have taken a cue from Tim Costello and salvaged the faint murals.

---

*One his favorite backward limericks, later used in *The 13 Clocks*, was:

> A dehoy who was terribly hobble,
> Cast only stones that were cobble,
> And bats that were ding
> From a shot that was sling
> But never hit links that were bobble.

Divorce was not a fact of life to be taken lightly in Columbus, but the Thurber family, given only the flimsiest details, nevertheless raised no strong objection to the imminent parting of Thurber and Althea. As Robert said, "We never warmed up to her in the first place."

After returning to New York, Thurber found it impossible to get down to writing and drawing again. His officially sanctioned freedom was stifling him. He was drinking more and holding it less well, and the guilts, mainly about his three-year-old daughter, were piling one upon the other. He tried to reestablish himself, more earnestly this time, with Ann Honeycutt, but he failed tragically. (The previous summer had seen a disastrous tryst in a Martha's Vineyard cottage with Honey and another male friend of hers, a writer named Edward Angly.) He eked out a few so-so casuals—one of them a prophetic piece about Japanese militarism—and some of his most anti-female drawings, including the fabulous house whose rear section is a forbidding woman. He felt himself slipping on the perilous banana peel of Thurber "nervousness," and he sensed that people didn't like to have him around, as he so plaintively wrote in "One Is a Wanderer." At last, in March, 1935, with the divorce grounds of intolerable cruelty being concocted in various lawyers' offices, he gave himself up to Fritz Foord, who ran an upstate sanitarium popular with *New Yorker* personnel (so popular, in fact, that it was called by wags "the *New Yorker* retreat"), for some resolute drying-out. While he was there, he wrote Ann Honeycutt a last-stab letter, as touching and open a confession as any of his old outpourings to Elliott Nugent:

Dear Honey,

The grand thing about this place is the discipline. Not strict or rigorous, but gently firm—the hours, the meals (including a quiet tea time), the walks, the baths, the massages. It makes the rusty wheels of my mind begin to turn in rhythm again—old thoughts and plans and ideas fall into line; I can think, already, straight again. Before, it was just a jumble out of which came all kinds of detached, unconnected stories and pictures. From the Japanese Navy piece to the Wanderer piece—and what a symptomatic, tight, egocentric, constipated piece *that* was! (But good, technically). I wonder at it and at its acceptance by editors instead of its rejection by doctors.

I'm not completely whole yet—but it takes time. I'll always have to fight to hold what I get up here, but I believe I will, even in the welter of obligations (which first cracked me up). You see, I'm still thinking about myself a lot but that will wear away, too, to normal, which is high for me. I can't ever be a strong, silent type—a banker or a truck driver (any more than you could be a banker's moll.) But I'll get my feet on my own ground, which, in its way, is solid ground. Such men take some looking after, but not enough to spoil them. I have thought about your dilemma (did you know you had a dilemma?) Your dilemma is that in every way except intellectually you need a banker. As you have said, you need someone to look after *you* (some banker) being in no shape to look after anyone else (some writer). But there you are, caught between the two. Your emotional nature, however, follows your intellect (which is bad for the happiness of the banker) . . . I think that the theoretically dangerous imminence of marriage to me a month ago set you to thinking (and hiding away). You don't like doors closing or arms opening . . . This is the last time I will ever talk or write about us but after all I didn't answer your question and it keeps popping up in the idle hours.

The only test, for you and me . . . is one of time, and I mean time after I am divorced . . . I think that within six months after my decree you will be married. (There was just a knock at the door. It was my masseur, walking companion, and pal, Mr. Reiderson, a Norwegian of perhaps fifty, ruddy, gentle, and a swell guy; also, I found, an extremely well read man with a good mind. He walked me 2 miles the afternoon I arrived. I had stayed up all night Saturday so as not to miss the train—it's a long, restless trip, with a change of trains. He thought I was a good walker—"with the build and practise of it" as he said. I think he had genuine admiration when I said I hadn't been to bed. The next morning at 9.30 we did five miles in snow. He doesn't seem to think I need anything but a return to regular hours. Physically, I amaze myself. Most of the wrecks that come here have to be built up slowly to five miles and they end exhausted. I have gone right in to ping-pong & deck tennis, till he stopped me . . . I can't tell you of my present loathing & dread of New York. I feel as if I had escaped from Matteawan with its crazy inmates and dreadful nights. That isn't healthy, but it's presently good. In time I'll enjoy being in NY for a while at a time, but never more than a while. I'm not emotionally strong. I'm emotionally crazy, but that will be abated with mental and spiritual strength to help it. The mind rises and falls with emotional weather. Once I get them all to working together, I'll be fine . . . You have never really had the Jims. And I don't blame you for guarding against them.

A person who can be emotionally bad can also be emotionally strong. I've been through the worst case anybody has had. I don't believe I will ever get it again. After all, I'm forty. Emotion belongs to the youngsters, like measles and whooping cough. I will be satisfied with a plain, sane, ordinary life, no far reachings, no romantic illusions, no exaggerated protests. But, I do want the peace of mind and the calm foundation that, for me, can only come with someone with whom I can share my life. Life alone to me is a barren and selfish and pointless thing. The thought of it gags me. But that's me, not you. You are, in some ways—not all—the best aloner the world has ever known . . . In eight months you will be married. I don't know who to. The situation has nearly wrecked us, maybe it has. You were dreaming of bees four years ago, bees that I let loose (but in the dream you were also hunting a house—in Bermuda).

. . . It is still my secret conviction that you will marry within a month after I am divorced. After all, you can be mildly irrational yourself—you can do crazy things in a moment. But you better decide not to do anything till October, no matter how drunk or panicky you get.

After this, no more about you and . . .

Jim

Dried out, color in his cheeks, and strength in his legs, Thurber returned to the city with a new zest for life and some vague hope of winning Honey. "I saw a lot of him during that pre-divorce period," she said, "and we had some fun together. I even thought of marrying him a couple of times, he was such a good companion, really. But no, I chickened out. It wouldn't have worked." Honey was also seeing a lot of St. Clair McKelway, and, after a while, she announced that she was going to marry him. This news put Thurber's foot squarely on the banana peel again. Not only had he lost Honey but he had lost her to a man he at once disliked, greatly admired, and, above all, envied. It was McKelway he had singled out for his fine reporting, in the *New Republic* review of *Proletarian Literature in the United States*, and it was McKelway who had been writing excellent Profiles, casuals, and movie reviews since 1933 in the same magazine Thurber worked for. McKelway was also an urbane wit, a handsome charmer, and, most enviable of all, the kind of romantic Conradian figure Thurber always wanted to be but never would—the former editor of the *Bangkok Daily Mail*, an old Asia hand, and a swashbuckling reporter. Mean words passed between McKelway and Thurber after the Honeycutt–McKelway banns were posted, and Thurber was soon skidding back to the unhealthy state he was in before his treatment at Fritz Foord's sanitarium. In the final analysis, Althea had turned him down, Honey had turned him down, and Paula Trueman had turned him down. Of all the women he cared anything for, there remained only Helen Wismer.

"One spring morning, when Jim was in bad shape before the divorce," Jap Gude recalled, "he showed up at my apartment quite early. My wife and I both thought, Oh-oh, we're in for another siege of Thurber, but Jim was in a rare mood. Like a kid after his first big date, he told us that he had been out with Helen the night before and suddenly, while kissing her good-night, he realized she was the girl for him. 'There she was,' he said, 'under my nose all the time.' We were thrilled for both of them. Jim was right; Helen was the best possible woman for him in the whole world."

But first there was the messy matter of the divorce, due to be heard before Connecticut Superior Court Judge Ernest A. Inglis on May 24, 1935. The agreement on assignment of property and custody of Rosemary had long since been amicably settled by the lawyers. However, since the divorce was taking place in Connecticut, the grounds of intolerable cruelty had to be satisfactorily proven. Their marriage was hardly a serene, virtuous one, but even the seamy facts of the case were not considered quite strong enough. Althea, for instance, had to summon their mutual friend Louise Connell, who came east from Hollywood to testify for the plaintiff. "I was asked," Mrs. Connell said, "to say in court that Jim was a habitual drunkard, but I simply couldn't. Jim was a party drinker and liked to show off how well he could hold his liquor, but he wasn't a habitual drunkard. When a lawyer asked me if he was an alcoholic, I said no." However, when Althea took the stand, she claimed nonsupport (citing the time she and Rosemary were stranded in the Bahamas), extreme infidelity, desertion, lack of concern for their infant child, and violence (recounting an incident at a summer houseparty when he provoked a fight with another man by insulting the man's wife, but ended up throwing an unlit kerosene lamp in Althea's direction). These black deeds were enough for Judge Inglis. He granted the divorce.

The testimony was painfully magnified, which made it all the more juicy for the tabloids. As Thurber later said, "All the newspapers in New York City were friendly to us, knowing the situation, and in deference to another newspaperman. The Mirror, under Stanley Walker in one of his son-of-a-bitch moods, made a pretty terrible thing out of it."(20) Other scandal sheets across the country picked up the *Mirror* story— including the Columbus *Sunday Star*, which headlined its piece "WAS SEX NECESSARY TO JIM THURBER?" and had one of its staff members unflatteringly imitate the famous Thurber scrawls, showing Thurber in distasteful situations—and everyone involved was embarrassed by the journalistic mayhem, especially the Columbus Thurbers.

Shortly after the divorce became final, Althea wrote Thurber a friendly letter saying that she was sorry about the quotes in the yellow press and that not one of them was accurate, but she wasn't willing to go through the further scandal of suing. She also disclosed that on the very day she was writing the letter she was going to be married to Francis Comstock, an archeologist from New Haven, whom she had met the previous September. Thurber's financial responsibility for her, she added, was therefore over, "which I know will be a relief."

But before the scandal sheets appeared and before he received Althea's letter, Thurber's mood was shining. He was in love with Helen

Wismer. On May 25th, the day following the divorce trial, Thurber had a date to meet Helen in the Algonquin lobby, after she finished work. "My eyesight wasn't very good," Helen said, "but I wouldn't wear my glasses when I knew I was going to meet a man, I was that vain. Jamie loved to watch me go up to the wrong people and peer into their faces. He loved that. When we finally found each other in the Algonquin lobby that day and sat down to have a drink, he just turned towards me and said, 'Will you marry me?' I said, 'Wait a minute,' went to the ladies' room to recover, and when I came back, I said, 'Yes.' "

PART 3
Angst

CHAPTER 13

The Second Mrs. Thurber

In one of Thurber's earliest *New Yorker* casuals, an insecure first-person piece entitled "My Trip Abroad" and published on August 6, 1927, the narrator mentioned his wife "Helen." Whether this was just a funny coincidence or prescience (as Thurber liked to believe) is moot, but on June 25, 1935, a month after his divorce from Althea, Thurber married one Helen Muriel Wismer.

The rites were performed by Reverend Ernest Wismer, the bride's father and then the pastor of a Newport, Rhode Island, Congregationalist church. The setting was the Reverend's vacation cottage in Colebrook and/or Winsted, Connecticut (the town line cut through the front lawn, so two licenses were required because it was unclear up till the last minute whether the ceremony would be in the house or on the lawn, the house, or Colebrook, winning out—a typically Thurberish hitch). There were misgivings. "My parents were, naturally, very religious," Helen said, "and they were at first dismayed and then dubious about marrying off their daughter to a celebrity who was involved in public scandal. Also, it was the first time my father had ever performed a marriage ceremony for a divorced person. But as soon as they met Jamie, they adored him, and everything was fine.

"Just before the wedding day, Jamie and I were at 21, where we ran into Don Stewart. When we told him we were going to be married, he insisted on being best man and even giving us the wedding. We said no, Bob Coates was the best man and my father was giving us the wedding, but Don, ever the pixie, alerted the press. As soon as we arrived in Colebrook, an hour before the wedding, my mother nervously started to serve us Heublein Manhattans. We were already hung over from the night before at the Coateses. I had the worst hangover of my life. During the ceremony, the phone kept ringing—it was Don Stewart's press calling—and when somebody finally took the receiver off the hook, the telephone company put the howler on, so we had that for background music. We were all slightly hysterical and very hung over. When my father pronounced us man and wife, Jamie burst into tears.

My father said to me afterwards, 'What kind of a man is this?' I honestly didn't know what to answer. It was quite a wedding."

The wedding night was spent in a nearby Litchfield, Connecticut, inn, and the following day the newlyweds went to Coates's house in Sherman. There was more celebrating before they headed back to New York and a room at the Hotel Seymour, just down West Forty-fourth Street from the Algonquin ("The Algonquin had too many old memories for Jamie just then," Helen said). The reaction of their friends to their marriage was mixed. Ross, for instance, liked Helen immediately (the fact that she had edited magazines until she was married didn't hurt any), but he was afraid that if Thurber happily remarried, it would influence the abrasive nature of his fictional women, which had become his literary trademark. Ross even went so far as to ask Benchley to speak to Thurber about the dangers of a second marriage (Ross himself was married three times). Benchley, circuitously, did talk to Thurber about this, but after meeting Helen, he was sorry he had. So was Ross when he saw no noticeable truce in Thurber's intersexual wars.*

The Whites and the Thurbers' other close friends were happy for them. "We didn't see them very much," White said, "but we knew Helen was good for Jim. He needed a lot of straightening out and she helped him, but very gently and patiently. She even managed his money for him."

---

*A short story called "A Couple of Hamburgers" particularly encouraged Ross, since it was written not long after Thurber's marriage and reflected, if anything, growing tension between his men and women. "A Couple of Hamburgers," one of Thurber's few credible straight short stories, is about a bristling married couple so far past the point of no return to harmony that they spend their waking hours torturing each other in the most baroque ways possible. The husband is not at ease with machinery, especially automobiles, and the wife delights in pointing out strange engine noises sounding like "a lot of safety pins being jiggled around in a tumbler," an impending burned-out bearing. He delights in loudly singing songs like "Who's Afraid of the Big Bad Wolf?" and "Harrigan" and "Barney Google," which he knows she can't stand. They are discovered driving home from a long trip through the rain, and they are hungry. She is put off by all the "dog-wagons," as he irritatingly calls them, but at last he stops at a plausible diner and orders coffee and a couple of hamburgers with "lots of onions," knowing she hates onions. Although she is famished, she orders just a pack of cigarettes and decides to wait in the car. The coffee is terrible, but he tells her it was "damn fine" because "he knew she loved good coffee." They start off for home again on the wet road, he singing "Harrigan" at the top of his lungs and she contentedly hearing the now more insistent sound of jiggling safety pins in a tumbler. It is a striking, personally felt study of the extremes of meanness in a rapidly escalating marital war, and it was a theme Thurber used in many more stories and casuals, but never again so successfully.

Thurber's old girl friends, Ann Honeycutt and Paula Trueman, were less gracious at the time. Paula Trueman said, "I was frankly surprised at their marriage. They didn't seem to go together. Jim had spoken to me about her, but I didn't think he would marry her. In the end, though, she was a good wife for him, maybe the best there was." Ann Honeycutt felt that Thurber had married Helen on the rebound. "When I told him I was going to marry McKelway," she said, "he wanted to beat me to the altar by marrying first, just to show me. But I always liked Helen—after all, I knew her before Jim did—even though she later used to egg Thurber and me into fights when we were all together. Occasionally, we did have fights, like a couple of tired old vaudevillians."

As the second Mrs. Thurber, Helen found traces of the first Mrs. T. everywhere. Althea had been extravagant with Thurber's money, or lack of same; consequently, the name "Mrs. James Thurber" produced a dull ring in the credit departments of New York's better stores, as Helen soon discovered. "I couldn't open charge accounts under my married name," Helen said, "and I didn't realize just how broke Jamie was until I married him. Why, I even had to buy my own wedding ring at Saks—it was the only place open, as I recall. I tried to make some sense out of his finances, but it wasn't easy." What with the Sandy Hook property, the divorce, child maintenance, Althea's old accounts, ancient debts, checks to Columbus, new expenses of marriage, and Thurber's frivolous way with a dollar, his finances were a mess. As Thurber once said, "When I married Helen I had three pints of rye and no money, and owed $2,550."(1) Actually, he owed the *New Yorker* alone ten thousand dollars on the drawing account—a complicated fiscal arrangement in which money is loaned to a writer against what he will write for the magazine, with bonuses added for high productivity. Ross was edgy about lending Thurber more money "on the draw," as it is familiarly called, because with his divorce and remarriage, there weren't many pieces and drawings forthcoming. Checks were bouncing like baby boys.

Nevertheless, Thurber was determined to give Helen something of a honeymoon. He rented a primitive summer cottage near the Gudes' place in Menemsha, on Martha's Vineyard (it was the very same cottage Thurber had rented the summer before with Ann Honeycutt and Edward Angly), and they embarked in early July on the Fall River Line boat to the island for a month's stay. It was on board the steamer to Fall River that Thurber got the idea for the casual "The Departure of Emma Inch," a touching, wholly imaginary piece about a hired cook and her wheezing, aged Boston bull terrier, neither of whom could bear the severe transplantation to Martha's Vineyard. "When we arrived at the Menemsha cottage," Helen said, "we found sand all over the floor, no plumbing, and no electricity. We ate most of our meals at the Captain's Table, just a shack then, and we saw a lot of the Gudes. The check for the cottage rent soon bounced, and so did the check for the second-hand Ford we had to buy to get around the island. So Jamie sat down and in five hours he wrote 'The Departure of Emma Inch.' He was a very fast writer; all that crap he used to tell interviewers about rewriting dozens of times was only true in certain pieces he had trouble with. So he sent 'Emma Inch' right off to the *New Yorker*. Ross bought it and came through with some more money, and we were bailed out for a while. But it broke the ice and he began to work hard again." (As Thurber put it: "I had proved I could make money if I put my mind to it and quit sitting around thinking up new ways to kill Ann Honey-cutt.")(2)

One of the more amusing means of making money that 1935 summer was covering tennis matches for the *New Yorker*'s "The Tennis Courts" column, in the loose style of his 1926 reporting of the Wills–Lenglen encounter. Thurber liked to watch tennis more than ever, and he jumped at the chance to visit Newport, Rhode Island, for the Budge–Shields match, the Longwood Cricket Club for the doubles, and, three times, Forest Hills, during August and September. His columns show knowledge of the game, especially its mechanics, and a critical appreciation of tennis manners and the eccentricities of the players, with closest attention paid to the ladies. He reported tennis, in season, for three years—variously signing the columns Foot Fault, T.J.G., and G.T.J.—and he delighted in sneaking complex puns past Ross. ("I am tired of seeing the body of America's hopes brought back home on our Wood Shields," he wrote, referring to Davis Cup players Sidney Wood and Frank Shields. Ross had disallowed Franklin P. Adams's "the Red Budge of Courage," when Adams wrote the column before Thurber.) Helen enjoyed the game, too, since she had learned to play it well as a young girl in Vermont.

Between their junkets to the East's finest tennis grounds, they spent several weeks at the Wismers' cottage in Colebrook, where Thurber again confronted the typewriter and sketch pad. He was back in the fiscal good graces of the *New Yorker* once more, and he was making the most of it. A good deal of his Colebrook writing time went into letters to friends—as he tended to do whenever he was either very high or very low; it was his way of stimulating the writing juices—and one of these was the first of a series of epistolary essays to E. B. and Katharine White. When he wrote to the Whites, it was, Helen said, as "a student writing to his master. He put down things he thought would please Andy and Katharine." The Whites were at their North Brooklin, Maine, farm, where they spent an ever-increasing amount of time. They had invited the Thurbers to visit them there.

Dear Katharine and Andy:

I suppose that was the first successful call ever put through from Winsted 334-Ring 5 to Sedgwick 30-Ring 3. No wonder we got cut off. Not since they shot McKinley had there been such a to-do over the phones as when I tried to resume connections. I talked with four operators, Miss Tynan (there had been an old abandoned call in from her), Manhattan operator No. 73, and a chap named Floyd Bullsware, who was trying to reach Old Orchard about a plane or something. Seems like a nice fella. I was a little nervous about the call and am still afraid I shut Katharine off. I was lying on a chaise-longue in my Japanese lounging suit at the time and let pencil, paper, and map fall behind it, so since I wanted to talk with you, too, I got all snarled up, what with everything—and didn't even say hello to Nancy.

Your card had come in just before I called NY and so I asked for your phone number. (Ross kind of mauled up and chewed on that Whiteface Mt. comment I wrote, but the point of it came through, I guess). I was fond of the old Whiteface. [An Adirondack mountain near Jay, N.Y., where Thurber spent the summer of 1924.] Helen and I have been having a lot of fun. We had to buy a car in Martha's Vineyard because you simply couldn't get around to the beach and places without one—you were marooned. Jap had an old Packard he bought at a rummage sale but we could hardly keep calling on them. Before we got the car we had to walk to their house, half a mile away. I picked up a Ford V-8— a 1933 they told me, but it turned out to be a 1932—the year that ate up the oil like a baby eats mashed bananas. It had only gone 25,000 miles, though, and in the 2500 I have driven it the engine has held up swell. I have to get oil every 100 miles but I get 15 miles on a gallon of gas. The engine has a lot of pep and pick-up and is nice to operate. I drove it around the Vineyard for three weeks and got back into my old easy driving style, reminiscent of the days when I was the terror of the roads in Ohio and my mother wouldn't drive with me because I went around the wrong side of streetcars and shouted at the motormen. I find that I am just as natural born a driver as Morris Markey, Public Enemy of the Highways No. 1. We left the Vineyard on the last day of July on a boat at 6. A.M. —got up in pitch darkness, groped down some coffee, and were off. We got off at Wood's Hole and drove to Colebrook, which is 175 miles from there. That was my first long trip ever (it aint long to me now but it was then). I made it in six hours, and we had to drive through Providence and Hartford. Bob Coates had told me that Providence was the damndest city in the country to drive through, what with trick light signals, twisting streets, etc. I made it gracefully and calmly. Last week we drove over to Newport for the tennis there, and once again took Providence and Hartford in our stride, and came back that way, so I have no fears left. Didn't so much as collide with a bus full of schoolchildren.

I got my license in Danbury, and having a license made me feel easier in my mind. I am an Ohio boy driving a car with Massachusetts license plates and a Connecticut driver's license, up to Maine, but I may be able to explain that if I am asked to. It does sound evasive or something.

We have been living in the Wismer cottage at Colebrook, a nice place, since the first. I have got two casuals done—one that you saw and one that was really good about a husband who is afraid to drive the car and then gets so he isn't afraid. It's called "Smash Up"—which has a symbolical connotation.

I weighed 164 pounds the last time I was weighed—which is six or eight more than I weighed before I was married and four more than I ever weighed before. My lovely charming and noble wife has gained only one pound, but she is younger than I am. Did I tell you that I suggested calling our cottage at Martha's Vineyard "The Qualms" but Helen said she hadn't any and I said I hadn't either —and we haven't, either—so we just called it Break Inn, since once Mrs Max Eastman came and stole half a bottle of rye and a honeydew melon.

The first two months of our wedded life has been serene and fine. It took me just forty years, six months and sixteen days to arrive where I should have been when I started. The hazards and honeycutts along the way were rather disturbing for a time, but all that is a faint mist far behind me as I roar along at fifty miles an hour, passing the mckelways and shouting at them to get over. It will amuse you to know that when we arrived at Matty's Vineyard, the only cottage available was the one Honey and Ed Angly and I had occupied last year, in a perfectly stainless (at least as far as I am concerned) but confusing (to the neighbors) way. I told Helen when we looked at it the quaint and tortuous story of its previous occupancy; but she took it like a good sport with a laugh—she always referred to it as the Old Honeycutt Place . . . But she liked it and I did, too, and we had a nice time there, without any ghosts from the past to haunt us . . .

Except for these privates notes I am making, my past has long been decently and thoroughly buried. Ahead of us stretches Route No.1, clear and long and curving (I hate straight roads). There is the promise of elms and unexpected lakes and mountain coolness over the rise. You'll find us an agreeable couple. We hardly drink anything at all any more. The hold of 21 and Tony's has been broken, headlock though it was.

Jap had a hell of a time driving his Packard to the Vineyard. It is a sedan about five years old and it heated up on you so that hot water spurted out from the radiator cap and splattered the windshield. It took him 13 hours to drive to the island, because he couldn't go more than 30 an hour. That got him to the Vineyard after dark and it is a mass of narrow faint country lanes, intertwisting, dying out, wandering off into dumps and sumac growths, ending up at the far estates of Jews from Manhattan. He had a hell of a time finding his own house. Joe McElliott was with him but he was no help because he had passed out from whisky. In the back seat was the baby's play pen. Jap had to hold that up off Joe with one hand and drive with the other. "Turn the light out whenya leave a room," Joe would growl whenever he did come to, and then go back to sleep again.

Welllllll-l-l, ten feet from the back door of the Gude cottage is a stone wall, about three feet high, the top of it flush with the backyard up onto which you drive. Jap went right on over that wall. There he was, finally at his own house after hours of struggle and cursing and sweating and despair, and he crashed within fifteen feet of the cool sheets of his beddy-bye. Jap got out and surveyed the damage. The two front gasket-heads had been shorn off like butter, the pan-drain and baffle-board were crushed in like berry-boxes, the universal joint had been driven completely through the bearing-discs and into the crank-case shaft. The borings were torn loose, one differential wheel had been snapped off, and a connecting rod had bent up in such a way that it pressed on the klaxon button and kept up a continuous shrieking. "Go sleep now. Shutta door now," said Joe and made himself more comfortable, at a list of 33 degrees. Jap sat down on the ground and cried. He actually did. You cant blame him. And Jap is one of those calm men equipped with non-crying devices and tear-wipers.

I told him that it would have been worse had somebody emptied out the kerosene from the kitchen stove into a bucket and had the car caught fire and had he run into the kitchen, seized the bucket and, thinking it was water, doused it on the Packard. It did not cheer him up. His car was out of commission for ten days. They had to send to Detroit or someplace for gaskets, wheel-ratchets, and a new pan-drain. Some of the parts, such as the screw-bevel on the differential shafting—which had been wrenched loose—had to be specially made, since there are no parts like that in stock any more for the 1930 Packards.

But I dont know why I am telling you everything I know when I am going to see you. I'll only tell it all over again. I hope you forget how it came out, then you wont be bored.

Love to all,
Jim and Helen

After watching the doubles matches at the Longwood Cricket Club, in Chestnut Hill, Massachusetts, the Thurbers drove their 1932 Ford V-8 north to Maine and the Whites. At Ogunquit, Thurber had a whole new sad automobile tale to tell. The Ford's differential (certainly a Thurber–Mitty mechanical invention, like the "baffle-board") became unratchet-ted, and they had to wait three days for a replacement. At last, they made it to North Brooklin, humming along on a brand new differential. It was an idyllic, relaxing visit with the Whites, complete with a sail on Penobscot Bay. "The only odd thing was we discovered that Andy couldn't eat shellfish, not even Maine lobster," Helen said.

While their money problems weren't solved, their checks, at least, were inelastic. They finished out September in Colebrook and then, rather daringly, sublet a furnished two-hundred-dollar-a-month apartment at 8 Fifth Avenue, since, as Helen said, "Neither of us had any furniture to speak of."

At 8 Fifth Avenue, the Thurbers fell into a murderous schedule. It was "Matteawan with its crazy inmates and dreadful nights" all over again. "Jamie would work all night," Helen said, "and then he'd have breakfast and wander uptown to the office, mostly for laughs. After office hours, there would be drinks with his friends—usually at Costello's or Bleeck's—and he'd come home plastered. Very often, we'd go out again to parties, when we weren't entertaining in our apartment. Neither of us was getting any sleep, and it began to show."

At Bleeck's—officially known as the "Artists and Writers (formerly Club) Restaurant" and unofficially known to its clientele, mostly newspapermen who called themselves "the formerly Club," as "the drugstore" or "the mission"—the big attraction, besides the company, was the match game, which Thurber adored. The regulars—Thurber, Stanley Walker, John Lardner, John O'Hara, Richard Watts, Wolcott Gibbs, and Richard Maney—played the match game for drinks, and they were serious about it. The way it worked was two or more players put any number of ordinary matches, from zero to three, in their individual clenched fists. Each had a chance to guess the total number of matches clenched, and the one who guessed correctly first would drop out, assured of a free drink. The last remaining clencher had to buy the round. "There was a lot of form and tradition to the game," said Richard Watts, who was a drama critic on the *Herald Tribune* then. "You had to wait a while for your turn sometimes. Walker and a *Trib* man named Tex O'Reilly were the best. They rarely paid for their drinks. Walker once played a hundred straight games as a sort of test to see if there was an advantage in going first or last; he found a slight advantage in going first. Thurber was just a good player, not championship calibre. We all got drinks off of old Jim. Nobody, though, ever took advantage of his poor eyesight. Anybody who did would have been shot. Once, I remember, Russell Porter of the *Times* was needling Jim, just as Jim liked to needle the others when he had a few. Jim was provoked too far and he flew across the table at Porter. Nothing much happened, but it was a hell of a shock. Usually, though, Jim was friendly. O'Hara was the one everybody fought with. As Gibbs said, he was the master of the fancied slight. He wouldn't speak to people for years over some insult he imagined. I would say to his face that he was sensitive, which usually amused and calmed him. One time, I brought around a man I called 'the untaciturn Scot,' a Conradian steamer captain named William Blake Ballantine Paul I had met in China. Well, Thurber fell in love with him and his stories, and he promptly drew a dog for him. That was Jim then."

Thurber also drew ten mural panels for Bleeck's showing the intricacies and subtleties of the match game. The murals became as much a part of the place as the match game itself. Unfortunately, they disappeared from the walls when Bleeck's was sold in 1953.

For an urgently needed intermission in the Thurbers' reckless fall and winter of 1935–36, they ventured to Columbus so the family and friends out there could have a close look at the new wife. (They were to take a similar pilgrimage to Ohio just about every year thereafter, generally around the Thanksgiving–Christmas season.) The new wife was an enormous success with the home folks. She cheered knowledgably at the Ohio State–Notre Dame football game and she made a lasting, warm impression on everybody from Herman Miller to Robert Thurber. "She couldn't have been a better wife for Jamie," Robert said. "We could see that right away. She was a manager. She took care of him and even made him dress right. My parents loved her, especially as compared to Althea." And Ted Gardiner remembered how, when Thurber would pick out a tune on the Gardiner piano with one finger, "Helen would sit watching and listening as though he were Chopin. She was perfect."

Helen herself was diverted at seeing in the flesh the prototypes of *My Life and Hard Times.* They more than lived up to her expectations, based on her husband's writings, anecdotes, and impersonations. "The father never really seemed to be present," she said. "He would sleep on a cot in Robert's bookstore—Jamie financed two bookstores at different times for Robert—rather than be around the family at home. He never belonged in that family. He never really belonged anywhere, I guess. Mame was so very evident all the time, and the brothers were always screaming at each other. The only serene relationship was between Jamie and his father."

In November of 1935, *The Middle-Aged Man on the Flying Trapeze* was published by Harper. Dedicated to Bob and Elsa Coates, it is a discriminating collection of the best casuals and short stories Thurber had written to date, not including the pieces collected in his earlier books. A sprinkling of first-rate captionless drawings, germane to every story, filled out the book, which went into four editions by the end of the year, bringing in some cash. The reviews were uniformly excellent.

If there is a central theme in such a disparate batch of parodies, short stories, reminiscences, and sundry casuals, it is the one that became identified with Thurber in general—the constant, sometimes bitter skirmishing between the sexes. Since almost all the pieces were written during his marital combat with Althea, the theme is patently autobiographical. Naturally, Thurber sided with the male characters, who, in their total or near-emasculation by the females, are early specimens of the Walter Mitty genus: Mr. Brush finally outdoes his wife in inventing girlish wild poker games ("Everything Is Wild"); Mr. Pendly dreams of fixing a car his mechanically adept wife wants to buy by merely tightening a "winch gasket" ("Mr. Pendly and the Poindexter"); Mr. Bently insanely shrieks an Indian war whoop at his genealogy-obsessed mate ("The Indian Sign"); Mr. Bidwell drives to divorce his hopelessly conventional wife by holding his breath and multiplying numbers in his head ("The Private Life of Mr. Bidwell"); Mr. Deshler is driven to the madhouse, where he still isn't safe from his interrupting, correcting wife ("The Curb in the Sky"); Mr. Preble is thwarted in murdering Mrs. Preble by her nagging help ("Mr. Preble Gets Rid of His Wife"); Mr. Bruhl goes through a remarkable metamorphosis from drab husband to snarling gangster ("The Remarkable Case of Mr. Bruhl"); a dreary, beaten husband makes a meager stab at varying his marital routine ("The Evening's at Seven"); and Mr. Trinway deftly avoids a bad automobile accident and gets no praise from his wife ("Smashup").

There were other hints in the book of things to come. More or less veracious Ohio reminiscences provided some of the ground work for *The Thurber Album*, and "The State of Bontana" began a long string of word-game casuals. The best all-around piece is "The Black Magic of Barney Haller," the chilling saga of a foreign hired man who says things like, "Dis morning bime by, I go hunt grotches in de voods" and "We go to the garrick now and become warbs," causing the narrator to counter with some equally cryptic Lewis Carroll. It is a model of Thurber's sharp ear for language and the fun he had with it. The most famous piece in the collection is the often-reprinted "If Grant Had Been Drinking at Appomattox"—really a parody of the *Scribner's Magazine* series of the "If Napoleon Had Escaped to America" genre—in which a pickled General Grant hands his sword to Robert E. Lee. Certainly the most disturbing piece, for Thurber's friends and readers, was "A Box to Hide In," the tale of a miserably lonely man on the brink of insanity searching for a womblike box to call his home ("It circumscribes your worries and the range of your anguish. You don't see people, either," the man explains to a grocer.) The story ends:

. . . I haven't found one yet, but I still have this overpowering urge to hide in a box. Maybe it will go away, maybe I'll be all right. Maybe it will get worse. It's hard to say.

Thurber wrote to Herman and Dorothy Miller about what he thought of his thickest, most ambitious, and most revealing work to date:

. . . Thanks for your sweet words about the middle-aged man hurtling through the air towards his wife's unoutstretched hands. You say why didn't I choose "One is a Wanderer"—but I did, and I guess you maybe meant "Menaces in May"? If so, I read that over and after the years it seemed a little sugary and fuzzy. I do like "A Box to Hide In" myself, but I couldn't resist drawing that dog sniffing around the box. Mrs. Parker once said I should keep my writing and my pictures separate and I guess I should, only I have so much fun drawing pictures. I'm glad you liked "The Evening's at Seven" because I like it myself and so far you are the only person who has mentioned it. I've got some nice reviews particularly from Soskin in the American who came out with the truth: namely, that the book is better than "Of Time and the River", "The Green Hills of Africa", and "It Can't Happen Here". Those lads have got a long way to go, but they have promise. It's kind of funny to see the favorites that some reviewers pick. Me, I've always been strangely fond of "The Black Magic of Barney Haller". What does that prove? . . .(4)

For all the distractions of city life and his sleepless schedule, Thurber was getting a lot of good work done. In early 1936, he began to write (really rewrite, since some of the *New Yorker's* best reporters, like Eugene Kinkead, were doing the research) a number of short, retrospective Profiles called "Where Are They Now?" His nonfiction craft rose to a new high in these excellent pieces, which lent themselves to his human approach. The first "Where Are They Now?" was entitled "Boy from Boston" and concerned John Joseph Killion, alias Jake Kilrain, the bare-knuckler who went seventy-five rounds against John L. Sullivan in Richburg, Mississippi, and in 1936 was a foreman at the Quincy, Massachusetts, shipyards. From this piece on, Thurber showed an intuitive feeling for the has-been living out his life as best he could; there was also a painless history lesson in the bargain. He was just as reticent about signing his real name to this nonfiction as he was with the tennis columns (Foot Fault, G.T.J., T.J.G.). He used the pseudonym of Jared L. Manley for all the articles. The name occurred to him as a result of the first piece on the old boxer—"Jared L." from the initials of John L. Sullivan and "Manley" from the manly art of self-defense— and again it was Winchell who bared the truth of authorship to a breathless public.

He wrote almost two dozen "Where Are They Now?" pieces over the next two years, and some of the most moving ones showed Thurber's lifelong fascination with juicy crime stories: William Sulzer, an impeached governor of New York; the surviving figures in the Rosenthal–Becker case; and "Crazy Willie" Stevens, the quasi-genius and acquitted defendant in the notorious Hall–Mills murder. Former child geniuses also drew his interest. He wrote about Wilber Huston, a scientific boy-wonder, Edward Rochie Hardy, a Columbia prodigy, and William James Sidis, who astounded the Harvard mathematicians when he was only eleven. The Sidis story got the *New Yorker* into a lot of trouble. Lawyers for Sidis sued the magazine for breach of the right of privacy, and the landmark case ultimately reached the United States Supreme Court, which refused to review a lower court's ruling in favor of the *New Yorker*. Thus, an erstwhile public figure was still legally considered to be a public figure and could be written about accordingly, even if the results were unpleasant. The remaining "Where Are They Now?" articles covered a broad range of subjects, many of them reportorial gems: Strickland Gillilan, who wrote "Finnigin"; Gertrude Ederle, who swam the English Channel; Andrew Summers Rowan, who carried the message to Garcia; Virginia O'Hanlon, who was the "Yes, Virginia, There Is a Santa Claus" girl; Edward Streeter, who wrote the "Dere Mable" letters; and Irving Conn, who created one of Thurber's all-time pet musical hates, "Yes! We Have No Bananas." The articles still stand as lustrous mirrors of their times.

By March of 1936, the murderous New York schedule caught up with the Thurbers, and they decided that they should "go away somewhere to get organized," as Helen put it. They selected Bermuda, where Thurber had once visited several years before; they liked it so much they stayed till May—sleeping and eating well, working on "Where Are They Now?" and other pieces, playing tennis, sailing, and generally having a lot of fun. At first, they lived at Waterville, a guesthouse owned by Ada Trimingham, who welcomed vacationing *New Yorker* writers, but the most lasting consequence of their restful Bermuda stay was the relationship they formed with Ronald and Jane Williams. Ronald Williams was the editor of the *Bermudian* magazine (which Thurber occasionally wrote for gratis) and the tenant of Felicity Hall, the mansion where Hervey Allen composed *Anthony Adverse*. His wife, Jane, was what one friend of Thurber called "a perfect lady, probably the only woman Thurber was never nasty with." The Thurbers loved them both, and after a few weeks, they moved into Felicity Hall, which was a historical landmark and was frequented at odd times by sightseers.

Thurber took a grim joy in working at Hervey Allen's desk and telling curious visitors that he was writing *Anthony Adverse* backwards. The whole sense of relaxed discovery and sheer fun came through in a letter to the Whites:

Dear Katharine and Andy:

It was fine to get the little woman's letter today which certainly contained a lot of news in two pages. It came in on the Lafayette this—Saturday—afternoon and we read it just before dinner. I wouldn't have been able to read it earlier because last night we started with Manhattans at our little cottage and then went dancing at the Bermudiana with Ronald and Jane Williams, two lovely youngsters I met when I visited the Sayres here. He edits the Bermudian magazine. Jane is one of the world's prettiest girls (Helen says I kept telling Jane last night she was *the* world's most beautiful girl). We sat up all night and drank Scotch—the first time we have misbehaved really. Then today we had tea as our first meal at a nice place on the water front called the Little Green Door. Nothing in my life has ever tasted finer than the strawberries and cream and tea and toast. I shall remember it all my life—we were virtually starved, having missed breakfast and lunch at Waterville . . .

Helen has put on five pounds (she weighed almost nothing when we came here), and she looks better than ever I saw her. So do I. We are both tanned. Mrs. T (dear Ada) you will be sorry to know has been ill for ten days, was in bed a week, from neuritis or something that gives her a bad pain in her back. She had to have a hypo today, and there were 3 doctors in. She is much better tonight and we went in to see her and I read her your message of love, which pleased her. She thinks a great deal of you and Andy. And of John Mosher and Benchley and Gertrude Benchley (one of her favorites is Gertrude Benchley). She really loves people and keeps track of everybody who comes here (even after they go). There has been the usual run of fascists at the house, lawyers, insurance men, etc., but all pleasant enough, if not stimulating. People from St. Louis and Philadelphia. You know. Ronnie Williams, by the way, has one great desire and that is to meet Andy. He thinks Andy's comment is the most consistently fine column of writing in the civilized world (which it is). Andy would like him greatly. He went to sea when he was 16 sailed before the mast, became an officer, was at it six years. He is, like Andy, a great lover of sailing boats, and an expert. He's English, but nice English. The Williamses—he's 28 and she 23 —are the sought after people down here. They usuaslly have a writer in their home, which is tough, but they like it. Sinclair Lewis is one of their great admirers and we all went to dinner with him one night. Your dinner with him, my sweets, was nothing. Nothing. I'll tell you about it later. We decided, though, that he would be quite a swell guy sober. Maybe because he can, and did, recite most of the Owl in the Attic. The only drunken writer I ever met who said nothing about his own work and praised that of another writer present. He was poured onto the boat that took him home. He did one swell thing: he brought down here the 83 year old mother of his secretary, paid her way for two weeks in fine style. She was a wonderful old lady who had never been out of Rutland, Vt. before. Lewis went into a church with her, and knelt down when she did (and he brags about being the world's leading atheist). He was extremely fine with her and I liked him for it.

I wore my mess jacket last night and looked cute, my friends. I bought it a year ago and never wore it. My hair is turning as gray as an Ohio woman's past. Andy once said I looked like a third-rate British novelist in a dressing-gown when my hair was long. I don't know what he would think I looked like in my mess jacket. It didn't hike up in the back or anything, though. I weigh 165 now.

Of course, we both want to stay down two weeks or so longer. It has done so much for both of us, especially Helen. Except for last night's break-over, we have got up every day at 8 and eaten 3 great meals and gone to bed at 10.30! This is the first time Helen has ever eaten anything in her life. It has turned us around fine and I hope we keep it up. Two more weeks and Helen will be a big fatty, which would be fine. Ada's meals are still far and away the best on the island . . .

We have avoided Seabrook and Stong, my hearties, and Hergesheimer. Steegmuller was a minor problem at Ada's because she didn't know he was Jewish when she took them in and while she does not care, she knows her fascist guests often do. The second night they were there they had two friends, named Goldblatt or Finkleblat, for dinner. Everything worked out all right. I like Steegy, as we did not call him. One woman, an admirer of my works, told us how she also enjoyed the Morris Markey reporter piece on the mountain girl. My life is like that, my beauties. Whereas I usually get from one to seven letters about every casual, I did not get a single letter about that piece. Maybe Markey did. I did get a nice note from of all people Dorothy Canfield Fisher, complimenting me on my "keen and penetrating" review of Proletarian Literature in the New Republic. She said she would have liked to be the author of it. She is an Ohio State woman, her father having been once president of the university. I got $35 for the proletarian review and spent weeks on it, but I enjoyed doing something different for a change.

Mrs. T has two copies of Rackety Rax at her house and all of Benchley (which I have re-read in toto). There is no doubt that Benchley is our No. 1 humorist. He has simply said everything. I think his "Pluck and Luck" published in 1924 or thereabouts, is the best collection of humorous pieces in the country, my colleagues. I thought his crack back at Pierre Loving was swell in the theatre department. I wonder if he knows that Loving's real name is Abe Finklestein? Or something a whole lot like Abe Finkelstein. We'll run him out of the country when the fascists get control.

We like our little cottage on the hill among the cedars very much. Hope Williams had it last year, if you collect bits of information like that. Ada lets us have it for $8 a day each, altho it's $10 for every one else. Except you and Andy.

We were asked not to tell other people (except youse guys) about the special rate.

I have found it nice to work here. I also found out that it is better to work in the day time than at night. Don't you think I have kept up pretty well in my work for a man in the Isle of Rest and Enchantment? I am absolutely sure that Gibbs got ahead of me with a piece on Wake Up and Live, but I had to write it . . .

Ada has a tennis court, on which we played ten sets in two days, me cursing every second stroke, . . . I got 5 games in the ten sets by some miscues . . .

I saw after writing my tennis piece that the Herald Trib writer also said Murray would be among the best ten in the world in a few years. I didn't go that far, but I could have. He is the best looking youngster in tennis. Helen has thrown out Frank Shields and gone over to Bob Murray. He has a lock of gray hair on the top of his head.

Helen says I have used too many "my pals" etc. in this letter, so you can cut them out. She is always right.

I must tell you a lovely story about the Governor of Bermuda, Sir T. Astley Cubitt—whose incumbency here just ended after 5 years. I ran into him first with Ronnie in the bar of the Yacht Club, an exclusive place in Hamilton. I was delighted with him because he is the perfect type of English military man. He is six feet four with great moustaches and beetling brows (you know, beetling brows—they say Waterloo was won on the beetling brows of Eton), straight as a ram-rod (how do you like my freshly turned similes?) looking a little like Kitchener and a little like Pershing. No dogs are allowed in the Yacht club, except his two dogs, which look like him and act like him. They were lying on the bar floor, great big animals, like a cross among shepard, boxer, and setter. Ronnie bumped into one of the dogs and we were both sure it said, "I beg your pardon, sir!" Well, the Gov was standing at the bar talking to three men and it went something like this: "Douglas Haig sat on my right and Pershing on my left. Here and there at other tables sat my brigadiers." Etc. The perfect voice for it, too. It was lovely. Well, the story about the old general is that his wife once asked him to carry down from upstairs a priceless Ming vase (probably a Chung vase, but Ming is all I know). The old fellow limps slightly, from a war wound, and half way down the steps, in the presence of his horrified wife, he slipped and came down feet first, but miraculously held the vase safely in his arms. Bumpity, bumpity, bang! down he came, twelve or fourteen steps, finally landing at his wife's feet, the vase clutched to his great chest, unharmed. "*Mercy*, Astley!" cried his wife, "You might have *broken* that *vase!*" Astley got to his feet, unaided, drew himself up to his full height and, without a word, *wham-bang!* he dashed the vase to the floor at his feet, bursting it into ten hundred million pieces. Isn't that beautiful? Now, we can't use it because Ronnie runs a kind of Talk column in his magazine and he told me he was going to use it and I promised I wouldn't use it. I still think that we could run it just after he does, since so few people read the Bermudian—and we could give credit to it or to him. Having seen T. Astley, the story is gorgeous to me, but I could build it up so it would go.

To revert to tennis a second, it is hard for me to realize I just can't walk up to the service line and serve like Stoefen. I have the height and the reach for it. My measurements are almost identical with Vines's . . . However, I am much better every time I play. Helen is really very good, although she hasn't played for ten years. She used to win cups and things. She trimmed the panties off papa, too. Once in a while I got in a fine forehand drive down the line. But in making a backhand I look and act like a woman up under whose skirts a bee has climbed. I will get over this. I must get over it.

I got the proofs of the Where stories, two of them, and will send them back with this, first boat. I suppose they better send the rest to me, and I will make what changes I can. We wont be here later than May 1, if that long. I want to thank you for getting some action on those pieces. I was pretty gahdam low about it all when we came here, because I thought nothing would ever be done and I said to Helen that I hoped Kilrain and Ederle would have a suicide pact and ball up the whole dam works. I know it will be a big hit (the series, not the pact). I signed the piece on Kilrain Jared L. Manley for no sane reason. There ought to be another name. I don't want mine used because as I have said I don't feel I have a right, or would want, to take full credit for pieces on which Kinkead and others have done so much work. Please see to it that Kinkead knows how fine I thought his reporting and writing of the last four pieces I got was. It was one of the best jobs ever done around there, and I want him and Ross to know that I appreciate it. He deserves a great deal of praise for the intelligent and thorough way he went about those pieces.

You need have no fear that I will not keep the pieces going. I think I have showed I will. I enjoy doing them, especially now that I know they are going to be printed. Ross says he is going to pay Talk rewrite rates on them, and I suppose that is all right but I have spent on each of those stories from four to ten times as much work as I ever put in on a Talk piece. I just had to. The thing is a very special job, and requires a very special way of doing. Maybe, in view of this, I should get $10 a piece extra, or something. It is not really Talk rewrite. The leads on each piece required a special kind of slant and one hell of a lot of work. I did the Ederle lead at least twelve times before I was satisfied with it.

Did Andy, the old Pribiloff islander, read that piece on seals in the SatEvePost for March 7? You must get that, Andy. I haven't enjoyed an article in years more than the story of the love life of the seals, and the two pictures in the article are priceless—one showing a male seal actually kissing a new female he has added to his harem while two of his older wives toss their heads in shame and disgust, and the other showing a bull seal raising hell, on an eminence, with all his wives and children, who surround him. He's had just about as much babbling and chatter as he can stand.

Give my best regards to everybody, and kiss Ross. He is, as my mother said, a mighty splendid man and, as his mother said, I hope some day he will become connected with the Saturday Evening Post. He deserves a future and I think he will go far.

Special love to you both, from both of us,

Jim & Helen

I got a cheap Brownie Kodak & we've taken a 100 pictures of which here a few. I'm proud of the time exposures, all taken after 5 pm on a cloudy day— 12 to 20 secs exposure.

Sunday:

I got to 4 games—all with Helen—today, but she was not to be denied, as the sports writers say, and ran out the set and the next 9 games. She was way off form.(6)

Apart from Fascists, unexpected Jewish tourists (Thurber maintained a modicum of fashionable anti-Semitism until World War II made it unfashionable), and tennis losses, the only other hitch Thurber ran into was an infected insect sting on his leg. A gruff doctor told him of a case in which an amputation resulted from a bee sting, and this medical news inspired Thurber to a bit of verse:

BERMUDA, I LOVE YOU

Hark, my child to a tale of disaster,
Of yards of gauze and casts of plaster,
Of festering lips and shattered feet
Of hearts that suddenly ceased to beat.
Harry O. Jones was a bike-riding fool,
And what was the liquid in that little pool
That turned his socks red
And moistened his head?
Listen, my child, it was not milk or mud,
It was not Scotch or rye; it was red, it was blood.
Maribel Smith scratched her hand with a stick,
She didn't bleed much and she didn't feel sick.
There was just a small cut on one of her paws
But in forty-eight hours she could not move her jaws;
In five or six days they were lighting the candles,
And they bought her a box with bright silver handles.
Or consider the case of Herbert A. Dewer,
Healthy at noon and by nighttime manure.
Herb would have said you were certainly silly
Had you told him that *he* would be soil for a lily;

Or list to the tale of Harrison Bundy,
Here on Tuesday, gone on Monday;
And over the grave of Beth Henderson sigh;
She died from the bite of a common house fly.
And here close beside the murmurous sea
Lies a tall nervous writer stung by a bee.
Oh, Bermuda is lovely, Bermuda is bright,
But beware of its claws and beware of its bite,
Remember H. Dewer, remember H. Bundy,
Remember Sic Transit Gloria Mundi.

The infection subsided, and so did the idyll of the Bermoothes, among the natives so hungry for mainland wit. The Thurbers returned to New York in the late spring, having made an important decision: New York City was not good for them all the time, so they would give up their sublet at 8 Fifth Avenue, Thurber would free-lance, keeping a contractual arrangement with the *New Yorker,* and they would live in the country. They went back to the Wismers' cottage in Colebrook and made it their home base while they travelled about visiting relatives and friends, covering tennis matches, and hunting for houses in northern Connecticut. "Once we had realized we would live more sensibly and get more work done out of the city," Helen said, "we decided on Connecticut, especially the hilly, green Litchfield area. Jamie never really had that deep a feeling for flowers and animals, as such. He used them as literary material, in the same way he used people. He was a gentle man, though. When he caught a mouse once, he had to let it go because he couldn't bring himself to kill anything. But what he loved about the Connecticut countryside was the greenness. The landscape couldn't be green enough for him. He could *feel* the greenness, he told me."

Some of this literary using of nature delightfully emerged in a summer of 1936 letter to White from Colebrook:

Dear Andy:

Aint heard from you yit but 'pears like you're busy in yer garden. The corms are gittin our thrips already, but none of the thisbies has yit bin torn from the zatches. The gelks are in the pokeberries agin, though, and grandma has lurbs in her hust. Look out for drebs . . .

Their summer travels brought them to upstate New York (where they visited with Frank Sullivan in Saratoga, and Thurber showed Helen the Adirondacks he had known with Althea), Vermont (where they visited with Helen's sister, and Helen showed Thurber the scenes of her child-hood), Canada, New Hampshire, Maine, Massachusetts (Martha's Vine-yard again, but in a boarding house), Rhode Island, and back to Con-necticut. All this was covered by automobile, Thurber driving. There were amazingly few problems on the road, although Thurber was dis-turbed by the accidents he saw along the way. He was working hard, too, on his tennis columns and a spate of casuals dealing, not surpris-ingly, with country life. In the middle of the summer, he received a vague offer from M.G.M. for one of that studio's famously seductive thousand-dollar-a-week contracts. It would have solved all his money problems, but after the first feeler he heard no more about it. "I don't care much," he wrote White.(7) However, since Sayre, Kaufman, Stew-art, and several others were raking it in out in Hollywood, he may have been posturing for White's sake.

In the late summer, they drove to Sandy Hook to see Althea and five-year-old Rosemary. "Jamie also wanted to get back his complete set of Henry James from Althea, which he did," Helen said. "It was the second time I had seen Althea, and we all got along just fine. She blamed Ann Honeycutt, not me, for their marriage breaking up. She didn't like Honey at all, but then again, neither did Jamie, really." The retrieval of the Henry James set prompted an elegant observation on the master, in an October, 1936, letter to Herman Miller:

. . . Speaking of Henry, I went down to my first wife's home and got the set of H.J. she once gave me for Christmas and I have been reading some of the 17 volumes I never had read (all I had read was the other 17). I had never, God bless my soul, read The Spoils of Poynton. What a nicely glowing point of honor he put upon two people for giving up Love for a principle! It seems so far away in this day when we give up principles for Love—and somehow the Love they gave up seems, God help us all, rather more worth the having, and the princi-ples not so much. He would have been most unhappy now, I'm sure, in an age when the male sometimes doesnt even take off his hat or the woman her overcoat. (In bed, of course, I mean). There's an essay in it, my friends. Apropos of the present fun that pops up out of his faint far adorations, look at this from The American:

> She came in at last, after so long an interval that he wondered if she had been hesitating. She smiled at him, as usual, without constraint, and her great mild eyes, while she held out her hand, seemed to shine at him perhaps straighter than before. She then remarkably observed, without a tremor in her voice, that she was glad to see him and that she hoped he was well.

Their candles burnt at one end and they will last the night . . .

The Thurbers also found time to go to Boston and see Noel Coward's one-act plays, *Tonight at Eight-Thirty*, about which Thurber wrote an illustrated article for *Stage* magazine. Coward and Thurber hit it off spectacularly, their Boston meeting not at all like Thurber's luncheon with Fred Allen in New York. Thurber wrote Herman Miller: "We had dinner with Coward, just the three of us, a lovely time, a swell fellow. I loved his plays, too, and he dashed them off all this summer."(8) When the plays came to New York, Ross and Thurber gave a party for Coward at Ross's apartment. The British jack-of-all-trades was in many ways what Thurber wanted to be professionally, especially since he had been smitten by theatre, but the element of competition wasn't strong enough to affect their relationship then. A chill developed between them after Coward took offense at something the *New Yorker* had printed about him, although Thurber had nothing to do with it.

Another literary lion the Thurbers befriended about that time was Carl Sandburg, whom they met during a 1936 Thanksgiving visit to Columbus. Sandburg (the "singing poet," as he was billed) was in Columbus to give a concert, and at a reception thrown at a local matron's house, Thurber and the singing poet carried on in a manner designed to shake the wattles of the good burghers. Shocking the Ohio bourgeoisie only added to their fun in singing, reciting stories, and drinking together. Thurber commemorated the evening with some drawings, which Helen called "pale reflections of what really went on that night."(9)

Sandburg heartily approved of Thurber's views on proletarian literature and of his talents in general. Years later, he wrote Thurber and reminisced about "that dandy all-night session in Columbus, Ohio." He saluted him as "old-fashioned black-walnut Quaker mixed with modern-chromium philosophical anarchist and you can't organize it," adding that Thurber was "a clown and an architect and amid all your shenanigans a man of great faith."(10) The solid-American admiration was mutual. Thurber cherished the poet's parting words that dandy night in Columbus—"Lots of life!"—and he wished him a "bucketful of life" himself.(11) Sandburg, like Coward, was obviously another "swell fellow" to Thurber, but, unlike Coward, he was no real competition.

Before the Thanksgiving trip to Columbus, the Thurbers, still resolutely avoiding New York City, rented a house in the historic old Connecticut town of Litchfield, surrounded by the scenery they liked best. "We have three bedrooms," he wrote Herman Miller, "three baths, three everything. Acres of elms and maples. Across the road is the house

in which Henry Ward and Harriet Beecher were born. Down the road is the birthplace of Ethan Allen. Around the corner is a house built by a Colonel Talmage of Washington's staff. In it the colonel's great grand-daughter lives, now 96. It is all the most beautiful place . . . I've joined the men's forum and am known."(12) He was entranced by the smell of history and rurality about the place, but it was a life that needed some getting used to as winter neared, especially for the old king of the big-city big nights. "We had no schedule," Helen said. "We learned to live without one. Jamie was no morning worker. He got up when he was hungry. He hated breakfast in bed or reading in bed because it re-minded him of hospitals. He worked in the afternoon, and if a piece was going well, he would work straight through. I'd have to stop him so he'd eat. If it wasn't going well, he'd listen to a ball game or a soap opera on the radio. He loved the radio. He also walked a lot. We avoided the more boring local people—I remember having to have dinner with a dreadful retired diplomat who lived nearby—but we saw a good deal of our friends in the area, like the Coateses and Cowleys, and other friends would come up to visit. When we desperately missed the city or theatre, we'd get in the Ford and drive to town and stay at the Grosvenor on a day-to-day basis. Jamie still connected the Algonquin with unhappiness. If it was a lonely, quiet life sometimes, it was also good for us."

In the dead of winter, Thurber's father arrived by train for a visit. Charles's tenure as secretary to the mayor of Columbus had ended in 1931 when the mayor left office. Then, after his unsuccessful run for the Ohio General Assembly, he more or less retired, earning pin money by sporadically winning prizes in newspaper contests and helping out Rob-ert at his insolvent bookstore. Thurber took over most of the family support from 1932 on, when Mame's Fisher Company stock ran low. "His father had prostate trouble," Helen recalled, "and on the ride up to Litchfield from New York, we had to stop every few minutes. He annoyed me to hell in Litchfield, doing things like eating bits of bread before meals and then saying he wasn't hungry for the dinners I'd slave to prepare. Jamie was working hard, so his father left him pretty much alone. He became friendly with all the local cops and firemen, as I remember. He was proud of his son."

Throughout the Litchfield winter, Thurber kept up a brisk correspon-dence with White, sending him items of interest and raw material for newsbreaks. They discussed in their letters such subjects as the origin of vanilla, the clothing of Indians, rare old magazines (which Robert sent to people he admired, like White), other authors' work, and, of course, each other's writing. The White correspondence helped Thurber feel he was still in touch with the less secluded world and it plainly evoked his new placid life:

... I've joined the Men's Forum in Litchfield ... and probably will open my trap again during one of the discussions following the talk. This first time it was "Morals in a Changing World". Pretty funny. Sinclair Lewis wrote the whole meeting.

Lovely as a larch here. Take a gander at this snap of the house, showing only a bit of the grounds; and my art study from a turn of the stairs looking onto the lawn. Got to have you up here ere long. Bob and Elsa are coming this weekend and the Connells soon, but that's all we have lined up and we're to be here a long time . . .(13)

And later in the season, this appreciation of literary eccentricity:

Dear Andy:

Try to get aholt of a book called "Abinger Harvest" by E.M. Forster, Harcourt Brace, published a year ago. It's a book of essays by this English writer, and a nice essay he writes, too. The best piece on Sinclair Lewis I've read, and by a guy who was never in the United States. Especially I like the piece on one Howard Overing Sturgis, an English writer, American born, who lived between 1855 and 1920 and wrote three novels. Mainly he wrote to please his friends. Writes Forster, in all seriousness: "Sturgis was a domestic author, of the type of Cowper—he wrote to please his friends, and deterred by his failure to do so he gave up the practice of literature and devoted himself instead to embroidery, of which he had always been fond." It's a way out, all right.

Then, further on: "I once went to Sturgis' house myself—years ago—I don't remember much. A novel of my own had just been published, and Howard Sturgis' urbanity about it rather disconcerted me. He praised very neatly, and conscious of their own crudity the young are not always reassured by neatness. He was neat in everything. . . . My host led me up to the fireplace, to show me a finished specimen of his embroidery. Unluckily there were two fabrics near the fireplace, and my eye hesitated for an instant between them. There was a demi-semi-quaver of a pause. Then graciously did he indicate which his embroidery was, and then did I see that the rival fabric was a cloth kettle-holder, which could only have been mistaken for embroidery by a lout. Simultaneously I received the impression that my novels contained me rather than I them. He was very kind and courteous, but we did not meet again."

In later years, when somebody confuses my books with the books of Chic Sale or Thorne Smith, I will not be perturbed, but let them mistake a kettle-holder for one of my embroideries and there will be a scene. It's a rather comfortable life to look forward to.

I'm fond of this man Sturgis, the embroidery king. The piece goes on: "As to his character, kindness and malice, tenderness and courage appear to have blended, as they occasionally do with the highly cultivated . . . He was at the mercy of life, yet never afraid of it, and almost his last words were 'I am enjoying dying very much.' "

There are dozens of other pieces in the book, on all kinds of people and subjects, all very fine. I just this second came across this in his piece on Mickey Mouse:

"But is Mickey a mouse? Well, I am hard put to it at moments certainly, and have had to do some thinking back. Certainly one would not recognize him in a trap."

The guy is full of swell lines.

I like this, also about Mickey Mouse: "He is energetic without being elevating, and although assuredly he is one of the world's great lovers he must be placed at some distance from Charlie Chaplin or Sir Philip Sidney." And, in discussing Mickey and Minnie Mouse as a pair, he says: "It seems likely that they have married one another, since it is unlikely that they have married anyone else, since there is nobody else for them to marry."

Well, that's all for the nonce.

Jim

15 minutes later: poem enclosed for which I got the idea by pondering that word "nonce".

What Thurber was working at so hard in Litchfield was a series of devastating humorous exposés of the current flood of inspirational books. The *New Yorker* was printing the pieces as fast as he wrote them, and the series, together with the best of his most recent casuals and stories, was brought out as a book by Harper in late 1937 under the title *Let Your Mind Alone! and Other More or Less Inspirational Pieces*. It was dedicated to Helen.

The genesis of *Let Your Mind Alone!* was his unpublished olio parody, *Why We Behave Like Microbe Hunters* (bits of which also found their way into print in *Is Sex Necessary?*) and some strong reviews of inspirational popular-psychology books he did for the *Saturday Review*. Perhaps even more basic was his horse-sense loathing of the panacea psychologists and their simplistic nonsense. Nonsense satire is particularly effective when the subject attacked is patently nonsense of a more notorious stripe. "I've had to read the most incredible crap—dozens of books like 'How to Worry Successfully'—but filled with such a walking into my spider trap as you wouldn't believe," Thurber wrote Herman Miller.(14) The other books he assailed, besides David Seabury's *How to Worry Successfully*, were Dorothea Brande's *Wake Up and Live!*, Sadie Myers Shellow's *How to Develop Your Personality*, Dr. James L. Mursell's *Streamline Your Mind,* Dr. Louis E. Bisch's *Be Glad You're Neurotic,* and the giant of them all, Dale Carnegie's *How to Win Friends and Influence People.* The mind-numbing drudgery of slogging through this dismal swamp of mental enlightenment was worth it in the end; the pieces are the finest and funniest digressive satire Thurber ever wrote. They gave him a rich opportunity to dwell on some of his favorite new themes: the superiority of undisciplined Marx Brothers logic over the so-called streamlined mind; the supreme joy of a good practical joke; the eccentricities of Midwesterners; the perils of machinery; the excesses of Freud; and the innate sanity of dogs. It was all done with charm and wit of the highest sort.

Of the casuals and stories—the *Other More or Less Inspirational Pieces*—one stands out, although they all are representative of Thurber's best. It is "Nine Needles," one of the most glorious casuals ever written. "Nine Needles" is the type of piece that Thurber and White could do better than anyone, including Mark Twain. It is essentially an essay on the American medicine chest and its latent booby traps. The slight line of the piece finds a hung-over Thurber alone in a friend's strange bathroom one morning (a not unusual circumstance for Thurber). He cuts his ear shaving, and, while searching in the medicine chest for a styptic pencil, a packet of nine needles falls into the filled basin. His search for the needles snowballs into chaos, culminating with the entire contents of the cabinet smashed on the bathroom floor. It is man's helplessness and hopelessness in coping with a world he never really meant to make, the butt of the sad joke always being man himself. The seemingly trivial, thin idea that holds "Nine Needles" and so many other *New Yorker* casuals together has disturbed many critics through the years. But there is nothing to be apologetic about in writing such pieces. When it is done well, it is the gentle work of genius and it can move hillocks that heavier, bolder pieces cannot budge.

Since 1935, Thurber had been reexperiencing periodic problems with his eyesight; that is, the sight of his good right eye. The first worrisome sign of trouble was on that 1928 night, when he complained to Katharine Angell that he couldn't see well enough to go home from the office. After his marriage to Helen, his ocular troubles appeared more frequently. In August of 1935, he wrote Herman Miller this vivid, if jocular, account of one such incident:

. . . Helen Thurber and I have just returned from dinner at the Elm Tree Inn in Farmington, some twenty miles from our little cot. It was such a trip as few have survived. I lost eight pounds. You see, I can't see at night and this upset all the motorists in the state tonight, for I am blinded by headlights in addition to not being able to see, anyway. It took us two hours to come back, weaving and stumbling, stopping now and then, stopping always for every car that approached, stopping other times just to rest and bow my head on my arms and ask God to witness that this should not be.

Farmington's Inn was built in 1638 and is reputed to be the oldest inn in these United States. I tonight am the oldest man. You know my sight of old, perhaps. I once tried to feed a nut to a faucet, you know, thinking it was a squirrel, and surely I told you about the time I ruined my first wife's tomato plants by riddling the white paper sacks she had put over them to keep off the frost. I thought they were chickens pecking up the garden and I let them have it with a barrage of stones. (The faucet was in the statehouse grounds). A further peril of the night road is that flecks of dust and streaks of bug blood on the windshield look to me often like old admirals in uniform, or crippled apple women, or the front end of barges, and I whirl out of their way, thus going into ditches and fields and up on front lawns, endangering the life of authentic admirals and apple women who may be out on the road for a breath of air before retiring.

This was the worst driving experience I have had in five or six years. When I was in the O S U and drove the family Reo to dances I once drove into a tulip bed and once again, taking a girl to Franklin Park, I ran into a clump of trees, and once reached the edge of Goodale Park lake, thinking it was asphalt.

Five or six years ago, when I was visiting my former wife at Silvermine, she had left the car for me at South Norwalk and I was to drive to her house in it, some five miles away. Dinner was to be ready for me twenty minutes after I got into the car, but night fell swiftly and there I was again. Although I had been driven over that road 75 or 100 times, I had not driven it myself, and I got off onto a long steep narrow road which seemed to be paved with old typewriters. After a half hour of climbing, during which I passed only two farm boys with lanterns, the road petered out in a high woods. From far away came the mournful woof of a farm hound. That was all. There I was, surrounded by soughing trees, where no car had ever been before. I dont know how I got out. I backed up for miles, jerking on the hand brake every time we seemed to be falling. I was two hours late for dinner.

In every other way I am fine. I am very happy, when not driving at night. And my wife is very happy too, when not being driven by me at night. We are an ideal couple and have not had a harsh word in the seven weeks of our married life. Even when I grope along, honking and weaving and stopping and being honked at by long lines of cars behind me, she is patient and gentle and kind. Of course, she knows that in the daytime, I am a fearless and skilled driver, who can hold his own with anyone. It is only after nightfall that this change comes upon me. I have a curious desire to cry while driving at night, but so far have conquered that, save for a slight consistent whimpering that I keep up—a sound which, I am sure, is not calculated to put Helen at her ease.

Looking back on my hazardous adventures of this evening I can see that

At the Algonquin on November 29, 1938, to celebrate the success of Frank Case's book, *Tales of a Wayward Inn.* Seated, left to right: Fritz Foord, Wolcott Gibbs, Case, and Dorothy Parker. Standing, left to right: Alan Campbell, St. Clair McKelway, Russell Maloney, and Thurber.

Off to Bermuda again.

E. B. White.

Harold Ross.

Thurber with brothers and mother at the opening of "The Male Animal" film in Columbus.

Drawing with the aid of the Zeiss loop, 1944.

Match game, posed for *Life*. Left to right: Richard Watts, Robert Montgomery, Thurber, and Ann Honeycutt. Mrs. Elliott Nugent is on the mantel.

Degree conferral at Kenyon.

Left: "The great good place."

Rosemary before her wedding.

At the Algonquin, 1950's.

Coauthors at the 1952 revival of
"The Male Animal." Thurber's
thyroid condition is evident.

Tim Costello and customer.

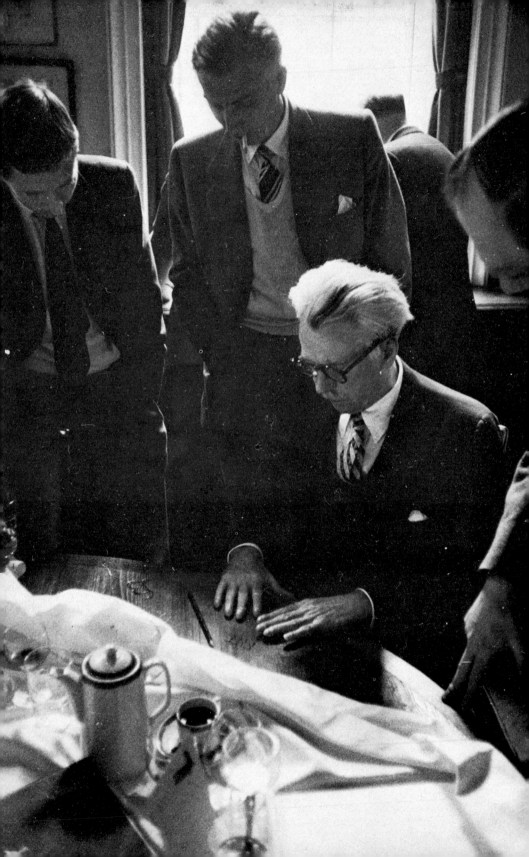

At Cornwall.

Left: At the *Punch* table, 1958.

Denney Hall dedication speech.

Right: New Broadway star and wife, Fall, 1960.

Above: After the Broadway opening of "A Thurber Carnival," February, 1960.
Left to right: Paul Ford, Peggy Cass, the author, and Tom Ewell.

With Rose Algrant in Cornwall.

Drawing in the air.

Thurber and Poodle.

whereas I was anguished and sick at heart, Helen must have felt even worse for there were moments when, with several cars coming toward me, and two or three honking behind me, and a curved road ahead I would take my foot off of everything and wail, "Where the hell *am* I?" That, I suppose, would strike a fear to a women's heart equalled by almost nothing else. We have decided that I will not drive any more at night. Helen can drive but she has been out of practise for some years. However, she is going to get back into it again. She can see. She doesn't care to read, in the Winsted Evening Citizen, some such story as this:

"Police are striving to unravel the tangle of seven cars and a truck which suddenly took place last night at 9 o'clock where Route 44 is crossed by Harmer's Lane and a wood road leading to the old Beckert estate. Although nobody seems to know exactly what happened, the automobile that the accident seemed to center about was a 1932 Ford V-8 operated by one James Thurberg. Thurberg, who was coming into Winsted at 8 miles an hour, mistook the lights of the Harry Freeman's hot-dog stand, at the corner of Hermer's lane and Route 44 for the headlight of a train. As he told the story later he swerved out to avoid the oncoming hotdog stand only to see an aged admiral in full dress uniform riding toward him, out of the old wood road, on a tricycle, which had no headlights. In trying to go in between the hotdog stand and the tricycle, Thurberg somehow or other managed to get his car crosswise of all three roads, resulting in the cracking up of six other cars and the truck. Police have so far found no trace of the aged admiral and his tricycle. The hotdog stand came to a stop fifteen feet from Thurberg's car." . . .

The lovely image of the admiral in full-dress uniform riding a tricycle was the seed of one of his most personal pieces, "The Admiral on the Wheel," included in *Let Your Mind Alone!* In early 1936 when he wrote the casual, he had roughly two-fifths vision in his good eye without glasses, and in the piece he used this distressing fact as a fanciful lens to show the reader the visual wonders a nearly blind man sees: ". . . I saw a cat roll across a street in a small striped barrel, I saw bridges rise lazily into the air, like balloons . . ." and, of course, he saw the admiral, who "might have been starlight behind a tree or a billboard advertising Moxie."

This circumstance was less poetic for Thurber's ophthalmologist, the highly respected eye surgeon Dr. Gordon Bruce, who from 1935 on was the Thurbers' good friend as well as physician. (Dr. Bruce was recommended by Thurber's other medical acquaintance and fraternity brother, Dr. Virgil Damon, who had delivered Rosemary; the two doctors developed a playful competition for their famous patient's attentions.) "When I first examined Jim in 1935," Dr. Bruce recalled, "he had a growing cataract in his good eye. The sympathetic ophthalmia, which had inflamed the eye after the other was shot out by his brother, had subsided over the years and, all things considered, his eyesight then was O.K. But by 1937, the cataract had grown some more and the lens was clouded. He was seeing things that weren't there, and it was obvious that he was going blind. Sooner or later, I knew I would have to operate or he would be totally blind. He knew this, too, and he faced up to it pretty well. He was gloomy and ornery about the prospect—Wolcott Gibbs used to call him 'the harassed rodent'—so I didn't make too much of a big deal about the operation, although I knew there would be only a fifty–fifty chance of his being able to see well enough to draw. Jim told me he wanted to show his wife Europe, and so we put off the operation for a while."

There were other motives for a trip to Europe: a one-man show of Thurber drawings was planned for the spring of 1937 at the Storran Gallery in London; neither of the Thurbers had ever been to England before; a change of scenery and a real honeymoon were available; and Thurber felt confident enough in his free-lancing to perform it any-where, even in Europe. One way he could keep in touch with things American was by dedicated correspondence with friends back home. His letters, therefore, are an extraordinary and complete journal of his travels.

They gave up the Litchfield house in May, loaded themselves and their trusty Ford on board the *Ile de France* on May 14th, and landed in Le Havre about a week later. They intended to spend about a year away from home, a kind of working sabbatical at the decade mark of his *New Yorker* endeavors. As in any sabbatical, it was a good chance to clear the mind.

As he had done with the first Mrs. Thurber, he started by touring Normandy. It was "ten days of swell weather and 500 miles of beautiful country"(15) this time out, however, and they finished their tour in the Seine town of Caudebec-en-Caux, where Thurber had visited in 1919.

By the beginning of June, they had motored to Paris, and again circumstances were brighter than in earlier Parisian stays. They were very much at the center of things in the cafés, spending a great deal of time with Hemingway, Lillian Hellman, Vincent Sheean, Janet Flanner (the *New Yorker*'s Genêt), Dorothy Parker, and Aristide Mian, who had married an American girl named Mary. (The Mians soon became French counterparts to the Bermuda Williamses in the Thurbers' roster of friends.) The talk was mainly of the Spanish Civil War. Thurber, for all his social conscience and antifascism, was nevertheless at odds with most of the other American writers in Paris, who tended towards active involvement in the war on the Loyalist side. He still felt then that the business of writers was writing. His view was expressed in a letter to White, sounding as if he were trying to convince himself:

. . . It is the easiest thing in the world nowadays to become so socially conscious, so Spanish war stricken, that all sense of balance and values goes out of a person. Not long ago in Paris Lillian Hellman told me that she would give up writing if she could ameliorate the condition of the world, or of only a few people in it. Hemingway is probably on that same path, and a drove of writers are following along, screaming and sweating and looking pretty strange and futile. This is one of the greatest menaces there is: people with intelligence deciding that the point is to become grimly gray and intense and unhappy and tiresome because the world and many of its people are in a bad way. It's a form of egotism, a supreme form. I've toyed with it myself and understand it a little. It's as dangerous as toying with a drug. How can these bastards hope to get hold of what's the matter with the world and do anything about it when they haven't the slightest idea that something just as bad and unnatural has happened to them? A frenzy has come upon writers and, although I can understand and sympathize with a lot of it, too much of it is going to be just too bad . . .(16)

The cynosure of one night's hot argument at the Deux Magots was young James Lardner, a son of Ring, who had been a reporter on the New York *Herald Tribune.* Lardner was agonizing over going to Spain to fight, and Thurber was about the only person present who tried to talk him out of it. "Jamie told him to go as a reporter, if he must," Helen said, "but not as a soldier. Hemingway and others tried just as hard to convince him to go as a soldier. James Lardner went to Spain and was killed. He was so young. But even after we heard of his death, Jamie couldn't get involved in the Spanish war, although his name was used in various committees and groups."

As Thurber said about the James Lardner incident decades after: "I was one of the last to plead with him in Paris not to go to Spain, but he just gave me the old Lardner smile. Hemingway and Jimmy Sheean were pulling against me."(17)

Life was less argumentative and political in England, the Thurbers' next stop after three weeks of Paris. What with the publicity for his one-man show and the recent British publication by Hamish Hamilton of *The Middle-Aged Man on the Flying Trapeze,* Thurber was welcomed by the English as an old friend. He made some instant close friendships with various Londoners, not the least of which was with Hamish Hamilton, who published just about every Thurber book ever written, a rare consistency in Thurber–publisher relations. His books sold well in England (the eccentricities of his characters were pure British), and some reviewers were beginning to take him seriously as a man of letters. Thurber returned the compliment by giving interviews freely and writing some short bits for British newspapers. He even appeared on something called television, drawing men, dogs, and women with crayon on large sheets of paper; he said it all came out "clear as a bell."(18) It was reciprocal love at first sight, but, according to Helen, his heart was still in France, his first big love, at that time. France meant romance to him, although the French never took to his work the way the British did.

The show at the Storran Gallery was a "tremendous success, much greater than all my US shows put together. They sold 30 pictures, many of them for 18 guineas each! I was only counting on making a hundred dollars or so out of it but have already got a check for 130 pounds, with another of the same size to come!"(19) The art critics took his drawings as seriously as some literary critics took his writing. Many spoke of the surrealistic and psychological aspects of his work, which certainly amused that old Freud-baiter Thurber. Two of the drawings were stolen from the gallery, further establishing his worth in the eyes of an admiring public. He made enough money to take a flat and stay on till August.

He made even more money by covering the Davis Cup matches at Wimbledon for the *New Yorker,* in four pieces all signed Foot Fault. ("It cost the New Yorker 3 pounds a ticket for us—on account everything is sold out in January and speculators even ask as much as 5 and 10 pounds a ticket for the last few days."(20) He wrote in the *New Yorker* tennis columns about viewing the Budge–Parker match on an eight-by-ten-inch television screen twelve miles away from Wimbledon at Alexandra Palace. It was "like watching a photograph in an album come to life." The later Budge–von Cramm match he called "the greatest in the history of the world," and he easily compared Budge to Lindbergh, which may have been an indication of what a high time he was having.

The Thurbers had dinner with Charles Laughton and his wife, and met H.G. Wells, David Garnett, Alexander Korda (who asked Thurber to write dialogue for one of his movies, which Thurber declined), and they saw a lot of Paul Nash and, for that matter, *tout* London. It was, as he told the Williamses, "lots of fun" and "a wonderful time."(21)

One of the most enduring friendships to come out of the London high life was with John Duncan Miller, an architect in 1937 and later a writer, journalist, and banker. They met at the inaugural party for a short-lived, *New Yorker*-ish magazine called *Night and Day* (after Cole Porter), for which Thurber did a series of drawings, "The Patient." Miller recalled that "Janet Flanner introduced us. She had a tough way with Thurber that he admired—then, at any rate. She would put him in his place. I hit it off with Helen and Jim from the first. I remember he was worried about his reception by the English, but he was fortunate in that we were all adoring American writers in the Thirties and he was one of them we adored most. Compared to what I had heard about him, he was on his best behavior. He drank a lot, true, but he wasn't too quarrelsome, although he did monopolize the conversation. He sometimes provoked people by taking the opposite point of view, as an intellectual exercise. He was gloriously inconsistent on all subjects, mainly to provoke, I suspect. An utterly charming man—witty, refreshing, generous. His one consistency was his loyalty to his best friends. But all else about him was contradictory, especially that Ohio quality, which the British, by the way, ate up."

In mid-August, the Thurbers took a breather and drove in the Ford to Scotland via Wales. On their way to Skye, they stopped at the edge of Loch Ness, where the legend of the monster tweaked Thurber's imagination more than most legends. (In 1957, he wrote a rambling report on the Loch Ness monster for *Holiday*, entitled "There's Something Out There!") He sent to his family in Columbus a postcard with a picture of a bloodhound on it, writing on the other side:"This is more like my dog than any I've seen."(22) It was in Glasgow that a hoist attendant at their hotel stole from their room Thurber's passport and some empty billfolds. Thurber later got everything back, including a pair of eyeglasses belonging to a man in Camden, New Jersey, which perplexed the efficient Glasgow police no end, to Thurber's amusement.

They returned to London in September and made plans to revisit the Continent, even Austria and Italy. Thurber was fond of telling people that he wanted to spend the next six months in a foreign, quiet place, brooding over whether he was basically an artist or a writer. But Helen said that such dramatic statements were the sort Thurber occasionally liked to make in order to impress. "He never thought of himself as fundamentally an artist," she said, "only as a writer. Besides, he knew his eyesight was failing." Whatever the reason, they took their Ford by boat to Holland, where they drove leisurely and happily through the countryside visiting little galleries and museums. Soon, they were back in Paris, both of them with roaring colds. That situation and the murmurs of a larger war didn't help his mood any:

Dear Andy:

You may be a writer in farmer's clothing but you are still a writer . . . In the October Atlantic Wilson Follett deplores the annihilation of the sentence in one place, while Gertrude Stein drops bombs on the sentence in another place. Every man must make his choice: you are either for Stein or for Follett. This is not a time for writers to escape to their sailboats and their farms. What we need is writers who deal with the individual plight and who at the same time do not believe in Lippmann. It came to me today, walking in the rain to get Helen a glass of orange juice, that the world exists only in my consciousness (whether as a reality or as an illusion the evening papers do not say, but my guess is reality). The only possible way the world could be destroyed, it came to me, was through the destruction of my consciousness. This proves the superiority of the individual to any and all forms of collectivism. I could enlarge on that only I have what the French call 'rheumatism of the brain'—that is, the common cold.

David Garnett has come out with the quiet announcement that I am the most original writer living, but I have no clean handkerchiefs and the linge is not due till tomorrow. I started to make a list of all the writers living but the names blurred on me. Of course, if you are no longer a living writer you don't belong in the list, which ought to cheer you up. Garnett goes on to say that in one miserable place I sound like Mark Twain talking from the grave, which ought to cheer you up, too. (This is where I say that I don't believe in scientists). He thinks I ought to give up ideas and institutions, which I have long suspected, as after a great deal of study of them I feel that I do not know anything at all about them. This leaves me with only the dog and the wood duck and my own short-sighted blundering into other people's apartments and tulip beds, to deal with. Which is just as well. Garnett points out that Twain ended up by telling everybody there is nothing at all in art and music, in the aesthetic in general, and I guess he feels I will end up by telling everybody there is nothing in science, whether natural, organic, inorganic, or Freudian. It's high time I shut my trap and was reminded of the time my father got locked in the men's room on his wedding night. Well, his warning came just in time (Garnett's) for I have been on the verge of saying there was nothing in collectivism or in Lippmann's denunciation of it, either, and one more step from there and you are in Twain's grave. Garnett does not know that Ted Shane put Twain's mantle on Nunnally Johnson's shoulders. And then called on the Johnsons and wouldnt leave for three days. The Garnetts' toilets will not flush; Elliott Nugent directs Madeleine Carroll through dark glasses, and you hide away in Maine . . . Here's McNulty [whom Thurber brought to the *New Yorker* in 1937] pacing the floor and imitating Rosoff, Ann Honeycutt writing a book on dogs, Johnny Parker cutting great pieces of chaos out of the Third Avenue night, and my brother William losing one of his testicles at 43.

Helen has been in bed in our red room (everything in the room is red) for three days and I have established a remarkable relationship with a waiter at the Cafe de Flore on the corner. This cafe is one of the few places in France which makes orange juice the way Helen wants it: pressed out of fresh oranges, strained, served with ice. Last night I went there to explain in my unusual French that I wanted a glass of orange juice to take to my sick wife in the hotel Crystal just around the corner. The waiter wanted to sell me orange juice that comes in a bottle, but I said I had to have it in a glass. So everybody in the cafe got in on it and finally the patronne of the cafe said all right, if I paid a deposit of three francs on the glass. So I did that. Then next time I borrowed a glass from the hotel and, taking the cafe's glass back, explained that now they could keep their glass and give me the three francs and put the fresh orange juice in this, my own glass. Helen said I would never be able to work that, and she was right. There was a discussion in French, English, American, and gestures, about this, and although I got my idea over it was flatly rejected. All the waiters got in on it, as well as the patronne, the gerant, the patron, his sister, a dishwasher, and two Frenchmen who were sitting in a corner. It was decided that the orange juice should again be put in the cafe glass which I had brought back and that the hotel glass should be returned to me, which it was. I have made several trips since then, taking the cafe glass back and having it filled up again. I'm going to try to work in the hotel glass again in a few days when things quiet down and although I dont expect to get away with it, it is all very good practise in speaking French and in understanding the French people. Donald Moffat would have known right away that the business of substituting my own glass for the cafe glass wouldn't work. It is things like this, small, intense, unimportant, crucial, that make life in France a rich experience. There's no use in you or anyone else trying to get at the fundamental reason why I couldn't work in that hotel glass. These things are, au fond, beyond the comprehension of our simple and direct Western minds.

I havent had a common cold since House and Wilson were friends but one threw me here: at 42 one's sentinels are asleep and the outer walls begin to crumble. You dont need any Trojan horse, you just walk in through the chinks in the wall. Everybody we know is cracking up. The loss of my brother's testicle will probably affect our trip, as my mother is frantic. I gather there is some talk of cancer, and I am pretty frantic, too. Life seems to close in. It's the personal and intimate that really affect one's life. All this concern about political forms is nonsense. I have arranged it so that when the bombs start to fall Helen will lean out the window and say, 'Cut that out! My husband is trying to write a letter!" It is the attitude to cultivate. When the mobs form under my window, I shall simply say to Helen, "Throw 'em a book." Burning the book will keep them busy till I finish the letter. No government in the world is as big as a man's liver. Hitler is bellicose but he is also costive and I think it is the latter condition that will bring him to book and to bed. Individual physical idiosyncrasy is behind everything; the state of the nations is simply a symptom. It is comforting to know that when the bombs begin to fall, all I have to do is try to work in that hotel glass again to get my own mind and the whole neighborhood's off of the bombing.

I may do a piece on the hotel glass, which may well make Garnett believe that not only Twain but Whitman is speaking from his grave.

You are not the writer who should think that he is not a writer. Let Cabell do that. Why doesnt Cabell decide he is not a writer? Why does Hervey Allen go on thinking he is a writer? What makes De Voto put down so many words? H G Wells has got the idea he is three or four writers. Meanwhile the bacteria are working quietly away. The sheep tick in England has just about got sheep and man, too, where he wants it. And forty thousand of them don't have to drill with spades all at once, either. The sheep tick knows what he is doing. Up in Warsaw, owls attacked an old woman who was just walking along. Owls know what they are doing, too.

We may be back home soon; I dont know. We wanted to spend the winter in Southern France, or Corse, or somewhere. But I cant desert my family. My daughter will be six tomorrow, and I must see her soon. Elsa says she looks like me now, poor child, but then its possible for a girl to look like Ross or Sayre and still be lovely. This is one of God's great dispensations. This letter has not held together in any way, and does not form a logical statement of anything, or even make a pretty pattern, like a stone tossed in a brook. Ah, well.

as ever, JIM

love from us both to you-all(23)

His odd mood extended to his already profound prejudice against Americans in Europe, particularly those in his beloved France. In October, he published a short piece in the *New Yorker*, called "The City of Light," about abysmally dreary and unhappy Midwesterners in Paris. It showed off his good ear for Midwesterners-in-Paris dialogue, as did the following untitled, hitherto unpublished poem:

What was it happened to France la Doulce?
The Americans know, my friend; drink up, quit talking, and listen:
Listen to the tapping of a thousand typewriters,
listen to the moving of a thousand tongues;
The Americans know, and they will make you know, they will get you told;
They are still talking, they are still tapping: listen:
Listen to the lady on your right at dinner: for two weeks every year
for ten years she spent two weeks in Paris buying dresses from
    Francevramant and Mainbocher.
Listen to her, she knows, she'll make you know, she'll get you told.
Listen to the tapping of the thousand typewriters, listen to the lady on your
    left.
Her great grandmother was born in Alsace, in a town, she thinks, near
    Strasbourg,
so she knows, she will make you know, she will get you told.
Listen to the man who drove his own car from Paris to Juan les Pins and
    back in 1937,

he knows, he will make you know, he will get you told.
What was it happened to France la Doulce?

Are you deaf, my friend, don't you get around, don't you hear
    the Americans talking?
don't you listen to the tapping of a thousand typewriters?

Hark to the man who owns a Juan Gris:
"Listen, will you listen to me? I was in Paris in '34,
two other times I was there before.
Listen, my friends, listen to me."
(Hark to the man who owns a Juan Gris).

What was it happened to France la Doulce?

Stop in at the bars, stop in at the clubs,
Talk to Mr. and Mrs. George Stubbs.
"Well, we stopped at the cafe in Dijon and George said to me
    and I said to George,
and you couldn't help seeing, you just felt they were,
and she says to me and I says to her—"

What was it happened to France la Doulce?

Listen, my children, and you shall hear
of Mrs. Bert Robertson's wonderful year.
She kept her eyes open, she knew what was up,
The things that she saw made her sick as a pup.
(Oh it wasn't the Chambertin mixed with the rye;
the coffee is lousy, they can't make a pie).

He also drew some pictures, evoking a lot of the same sentiment.
    Seeking some warmth, they left Paris in early November and drove south to the Riviera. Thoughts of returning home were dispelled as they doffed their winter coats and met head-on the stunning French countryside, with its lush history, food, and wine. A *Guide Michelin* handy, they ate and drank their way through Dijon, Valence, the vineyards of Burgundy, Aix-en-Provence, Marseilles, Toulon, and finally Nice—the scene of old triumphs and joys. His mood picking up the farther south they drove, Thurber wrote ecstatic letters to Nugent, White, and McNulty about their heedless, epicurean life. From Nice, he told McNulty that nobody could "do justice to this blue, purple, warm, snowy melange of sea, mountains and valleys. God, what a place to

drive a car in! You're always a mile high looking down at the sea, or on a valley floor looking up at a town a mile above you . . ."

> We're going to Italy a week from today, then back here to find a place for the winter where we can have a villa on the sea and I can write a play . . .
>
> Did I tell you that Helen, who was treated by a Harley Street doctor in London for a badly cut bridge of the nose, due to a fall in a bedroom, scaring me to death, was stretched out on an operating table in a doctor's office in Nice when we'd only been here two days? Well, one night she went out to the ladies' room just across from our bedroom door and there was this tinkle of glass. I ran out and here was Helen holding her left wrist which had a gash in it as deep as a well and as wide as a church door. She had knocked the glass out of the can door in some manner and cut herself to the bone. I screamed, "That this should happen to me!" (I always go into the subjunctive when Helen gets hurt) but she was calm and brave. Seven stitches had to be taken and this made me a little sick but Helen was fine. She just lay there and let a French doctor sew her up like a torn mattress. It's okay now, but what's funny is that whenever we set out in the car Helen is a little uneasy—after all we have been in some dangerous spots, such as Devil's Elbow, Scotland, in a rain storm and, just today, on the outside rim of a curving 16 foot roadway half a mile above a sheer drop, with no retaining wall—look (24)

Despite the dangers, Thurber was driving well, as long as there was good light. They made the Italian border without incident, but there the world abruptly changed. "Il Duce was everywhere," Helen recalled, "and so was all the bureaucratic red tape of Fascism, which made Jamie furious. For some reason, they put our names down on our visa cards as 'J. Thurber' and 'H. Muriel,' which meant, I suppose, that we were living in sin throughout Italy. People were afraid to talk, and Jamie hated that. He wasn't at all awed by the trains running on time."

Thurber never had much affection for Italians in general (he rarely

lost a chance to make fun of their accent in casuals), and with the advent
of Mussolini and Fascism, he looked upon them with the same regard
as that of a Presbyterian minister blundering into Polly Adler's domi-
cile. In Paris, he had argued with a Paris *Herald Tribune* editor over
that newspaper's acceptance of pro-Mussolini advertisements. Nevertheless, they made Rome in one piece and enjoyed themselves sightseeing in the usual places. He spent his forty-third birthday there and
found the "lovely city" easier to drive in than Paris or London. (25) Soon
enough, an incident with the government soured any further pleasure
in Italy. He had printed up some Christmas cards in Paris—featuring a
Thurber drawing of a little girl lighting candles, an oddly decorated
tree, and a rabbit—and they were supposed to be sent on to him in
Rome for further mailing. The cards were held up at the border by the
Italian authorities, who suspected the drawing of being some sort of
anticlerical propaganda.

More Italian difficulties, and other important questions, were aired in
another essay to White:

. . . We came down from Rome today over the old Hannibal route, a route
I've always wanted to follow—like the Custer route in our West and the Andrews route in Markey's South. Janet is handling the Alps part of the Hannibal
route—over by the little St. Bernard pass where the Gauls rolled rocks as big
as freight cars down on Hannie and his 37 elephants and 9000 horses and 50,000
foot soldiers. It has always been a sad thing to me that after crossing the
Pyrenees and the Alps with those goddam elephants, he lost all but one in his
first battle—on the flats. He reminded me of Rex, my old bull terrier, who, as
a pup, worked for three days trying to get a telephone pole in through our
kitchen door, only to have it taken away from him, with some effort, by eight
linemen who had been wondering where it was.

From Rome down here it is only 140 miles and I made 131 of it like a breeze.
At lunch in Formia I was bragging about how the car had held up. The battery,
to be sure, ran down in Durham, England—on that remarkable occasion when
a garage truck hauled me 2 miles whilst I wore my ankle out pushing the clutch
out and letting it snap in, without having the thing in gear. The garage man just
stared at me—not in anger but in profound wonder at a man so far from home
who behaved like that . . . Most of my 3,000 miles have been without mechanical
incident, though—and thank God, because over here it is nothing to be as far
as 30 miles from a gas or service station. Often for hours you see nobody but
peasants on muleback who speak a bad local dialect backwards.

In Rome I had the gas tank filled to the top—the gauge showed it and the
guy that filled it said he could just get in the last litre, it was so full. Well, bowling
along ten miles out of Naples I was non-plussed to observe that the gauge
showed very little gas—a full tank should have taken me twice as far as I had

come and then some. I figured the gauge had tricked me the way it did in the Lake Country one day when we ran out of gas while the gauge showed half-full. Well, she gave suddenly that "phaaf" sound when I pressed the accelerator—"phaaf—guh—phaa"—you know. And stopped. The luck of the Thurbers was with me—half a mile back was a gas station.

On the way back to it I thought as I walked along how bad off I was—stuck in Italy without knowing anything about Italian or anything about cars. Doubly stuck. But I had my little book with me—"Manual of Conversation for Motorists" given me by the A.A.A. in N.Y. I found "I have run out of gas": "Non ho più benzina." This I said to a garage man who without a word went and found a man who spoke English. A boy on a bicycle carried 10 litres of gas to the car which was by this time surrounded by men afoot, on mules, on carts. They were very amiable; the air was full of suggestions in Italian. The engine wouldn't turn over. One man spoke a bastard English. He got me excitedly out of the car to look at a fender bump 2 years old, he said we gotta wipe off the bougies with a bandana (bougies is French for spark plugs). I was against wiping off the bougies with a bandana. So they pushed the car—backwards *and* forwards. Nothing doing. It started suddenly on the starter but wouldn't pick up beyond 30 miles an hour most of the way in. Naples is 3 times as hard to drive in as Rome —which is the easiest town in the world to drive in—easier than N. Brooklin, Me. It got us to the hotel, though, past Vesuvius smouldering in the dark and past the lighted Rex in the harbor.

I know nothing about a motor (my mother knows less than nothing in that she believes you can run one without gasoline but that it is bad for it if you do). The trouble, though, I diagnose as both a clogging and a leakage in the tuyau d'alimentation, of Benzinaflussrohr—as the Germans say—alimentatore to the Italians—gas feed line to you, White. This is merely my whimsical guess. For all I know it may be a faulty kontaktschraube or trouble in la scattola di velocita, but I know nothing is wrong with the cinghia del ventilatore (fan belt). These, too, are okay: das hinterachogehause, der geschwindigkeitsmesser, l'amortiz-zatore, and le gicleur . . .

We'll be here for Christmas—brought our presents with us, each in his own hiding place, together with all the tissue paper, ribbon, stickers, cards, etc. Like Englishmen dressing for dinner in the desert, we will bravely carry out a Connecticut Christmas in the midst of these palms and olives and oranges . . .

Europe may cease to exist as it now is before many years—I give it four . . . In four years I too will have ceased to exist as I now am. I'll be as old as Benchley (it's cheering to know Benchley is four years older than me—he's so happy. He sing, he shout, he drink, he gay. Well, me too! . . .

Have you noticed that unconscious snobbishness about playwrights? A novelist, Comment-writer, casual writer, historian, or poet can do his work and at the same time get a lot else done, but playwrights think they must shut themselves away from the world and stop the business of living completely while writing a play. They go—often in pairs—to ruined farmhouses, abandoned islands, West

Indies beaches, mountain cabins, yawls at sea. There seems to be some odd compulsion to make it all pretty hard to bear, you will notice. It turns up in the autobiographies of playwrights. One will say, "That was the year that Cyril and I rigged up a tent on an old flat car on a siding at Higgins' Beach and wrote 'The Moon Is Up.' " Or, "In January Bert Lagoon and I rented a slaughter house in Canarsie and with 3 pencils, a bag of booze, and a ream of paper went out there to write 'Love's Joke.' "

I think there is defense mechanism in it somewhere, for outside of a few touches which you can get Abbott or Connelly to do for you on the stage of the Hudson Theatre or in a room in the Algonquin, plays are easier to write I believe than anything since Livy's history of Rome. This is because to write a play you do not have to be a writer. Hence play *wright*—like wheelwright. It's that confusion in words that has caused people to believe a playwright is a writer. Plays do not have to have sentences in them—just scraps of phrases . . . Here I am travelling all over Europe, monkeying with a car in foreign strands, writing casuals, Talk, reporters, Onward & Upwards, drawing pictures, and keeping up a correspondence with *fourteen families* steadily—from 3 to 5 letters to each family so far—and about a dozen other letters a month in addition. Take it in my stride, too. I reckon I've written 75,000 words to friends and family—but I have gained 3 pounds and never miss my morning exercise or my after-dinner romp with the dog . . .

Well, Happy New Year!
Jim (26)

Like every American motoring through Europe, he was tediously concerned about automobiles, but with Thurber, automotive machinery and its care and feeding became more of an obsession. To play it safe, they put themselves and the Ford on a steamer back to France from Naples. It was a terrifying experience for both of them, watching the car loaded onto the steamer with peppy Italian inefficiency. They were convinced they would never see the car again—or France, for that matter. But both the Thurbers and the car turned up in France, just slightly the worse for wear. They headed for Cap d'Antibes down the coast from Nice, where the Villa Tamisier awaited them at forty dollars a month, complete with a large, genial cook named Maria, her slight Russian husband, Olympy Sementzoff, and a spectacular view of the Mediterranean.

With actual or near war not far off, the Thurbers found a blissful sanctuary at the Villa Tamisier. The South of France enchanted him and its natives could do no serious wrong. A more political man probably would have been embarrassed by the serene life he led in the Midi, while just over the border in Spain people and doctrines were being blown to bits. In Thurber's case, there was at first just a touch of almost apologetic *Weltschmerz*, which, naturally, came out in another far-ranging essay to White:

Dear Andy:

I agree, as usual, with all your sound conclusions about things except the one about not being able to escape from beaten states, and like periods, by merely taking a boat and watching somebody balance a 20-gallon water jar on her head. That is, it seems to me, the only way to escape from such things. Grimly holding on, getting tangled in lampshades, getting so close to one's child and his school that you feel neither one nor the other can go on without you, can not possibly resolve anything. We Americans have a way of becoming an integral part of everything; we can't muse a little pace like Lancelot and say she has a lovely face: we are a part of the face, we drift down to Camelot on the goddam barge, clothed in white samite and looking a little silly. I felt I could not leave New York and my trips to Cambridge and my nervous overnight post looking toward Columbus where hell of one kind or another pops every few minutes, or did. But my daughter and I have established a new and strong tie; we engage in a fine and remarkable correspondence, notable for her ability to say everything that is necessary in two sentences without punctuation and my own surprising ability to write that hardest of all things, a letter to a girl six years old. My family seems to have taken on new courage and strength now that I am away; my mother's letters, while no funnier, are more cheerful, William is coming along all right, Robert has never been better, my father is doing all right. And nine months have gone by, all quite easily. I had worried a lot about being away a year, came close to abandoning the idea as being impossible, and then saw that because of, as well as in spite of my fussing about it, I'd have to go. You got to get away where you can see yourself and everybody else. I really believe you got to do that . . .

Of course, I havent got my child with me, and when I do have I'll be tied down by school, too. And on looking back on my own childish school years and realizing how really awful and useless they were, how much more a child gets out of his life outside the school and how almost nothing inside it, it seems a great pity that school has to tie down both child and parents, to say nothing of a lot of teachers who ought to be raising families of their own. Like every other system now in vogue, it is top-heavy, over-elaborated, and fine-sounding, and it does not work very well. The school system is slowly stagnating and the parents are sinking into the marsh. The simple way out would be to let the brighter children, from 6 to 15, run things, but nothing will ever be done about that. The basic trouble, of course, is the astounding fact that the offspring of man have not developed the ability to become self-sustaining until their parents are practically worn down and in the grave. The guinea pig is on his own the second he is born—even has his eyes open, leaps from the womb to the nearest carrot or lettuce leaf. Dogs are raising families of their own before the first anniversary of their birth; and so it goes among all the known species of animal except man, whose young are practically no good at all until they have wobbled around the house for almost a quarter of a century! This is perhaps the most fantastic fact about human life, and I imagine the other animals never get over their astonishment at it. Have you never caught your dog giving you that straight, long puzzled look—friendly, of course, pitying, too, but puzzled? What the goddam hell, he seems to say? A man marries the nearest eligible female, or the one next to her, gets a job within walking distance of his home, raises children that will be underfoot until his arteries begin to harden, and devotes his life to the opening of envelopes containing pieces of paper with numbers written on them. That is the second most fantastic fact about human life. Our everyday lives become, right after college, as unworkable as a Ford in a vat of molasses, but nobody is giving this frightful problem any thought. Everybody is monkeying with the superstructure of economics, politics, distribution, etc. which stick up out of the vat also covered with molasses. I know damn well, of course, that nobody will ever get the supersturcture cleaned off, let alone the Ford out of the vat. A world in which there are millions of people, hundreds of millions, can have no possible chance of working. If you get more than six people together in a room, it wont work. More than twenty is a loud, idiotic shambles. Nobody has really got anywhere in the study of that either: I can tell by simply reading the titles of books bordering on the subject, and the names of their authors. But there is a whole wide field of psychology, sociology, and philosophy that lies practically virgin in the fact that a person alone is a different entity from a person in groups of three, eleven, forty, four thousand, sixty thousand, and so on up. Wars could not possibly be fought in a series of single combats. Whenever that has been tried, as in the case of the Arthurian knights and the aviators during the war the practise degenerated into something not far removed from love and kisses. They did not hate, they did not really want to kill; the knights of old embraced and bound up each other's wounds, the winning aviators risked their lives to drop wreaths on the spot where they brought their man down. All the studies I know about dealing with mass psychology in its relation to individual psychology, and vice versa, grow out of that academic stuffiness that invariably falls upon the men who devote themselves to such things, and it either has the stodginess of a ship's manifest or the cloudiness of a piece by the late William Bolitho. The thing demands imagination, uncluttered up by book learning, it demands a certain amount of that high courage known as humor, and it demands knowing personally people like McNulty, Tim, Miss Terry, the grocer's boy, the people around Camp Otter, Maria Sementzoff, hundreds of children around the age of six and eight, and very few, if any, professors. But all these things are in the hands of stuffed shirts, bloat-faces, blue-noses, highbrows, dustdrys, and others of the same ilk and kidney; the same ilk and kidney. And Roosevelt, with his smile. Of course, it is well established that the disease which brought him down, sent him up. All infantile cases, research shows, become mentally sharpened up, emotionally elated, like mazda light bulbs that have been burned out, shaken around, and burn with a new high intensity. They can't last long, and they dont mean anything, but they make quite a show. As an old manic depressive (i.e., normal man) whose high periods of elation fall like the angel Joel White imitates, I know there's nothing to laugh about. That is, consistently. Never has there been so much to laugh at off and on. Those of us who are able to do that must keep on doing it, no matter who or what goes to hell, if only because Joe Freeman and his gang says we shouldn't . . .

Today I bought De Kruif's book called "Why Keep Them Alive?" and you really have to read it. After spending many years writing about the wonderful cures for ravaging diseases discovered by brave solitary geniuses he suddenly discovered a year or so ago that people are still dying like flies, with medicines, food, clothing on all sides of them. I share his indignation—which rises to such a pitch that he writes like a drunken man—but he has apparently gone over completely to working, worrying, and shouting about the hell that life has become. He has got to the point of thinking he oughtn't to eat nice things or drink good wine with so much suffering going on. I haven't finished the book but he seems to me headed to break his heart and brain against the System that allows little children to die and some guys to wallow in limousines. It's wonderful how so many people are just discovering that life and its arrangements are tough and seem to believe that never before has anybody thought of doing anything about it. Every American wants to get his oar in; we are becoming a nation of Hugh Johnsons; we will finally end up with everybody cursing and screaming and saying he's got the answer and listen you bastards and I say no! and on and on, and papa Roosevelt smiling and announcing the cure and Dorothy Thompson coming out with carefully rewritten pieces saying that everything he believes is exactly contrary to the real right answer, and some guy on the Baltimore Sun saying they are both wrong and hundreds of people not reading what any of them are saying, being too busy writing letters to the editor explaining what's the matter. There is so much cozy egotism and show-offery mixed up in it, it's hard to get at the sincere truth of what anyone believes; but you can't miss the sincerity of old de Kruif, who is mad as a son of a bitch. It took him, as he admits, a long time to discover that although tannic acid will cure burned children, a lot of em don't get it, and that although it is silly for a child to die of diphtheria now, lots of them do, and that though children are starving for want of wheat in Pennsylvania they are using wheat for fuel in Nebraska, and so on and on. "It was now clear to me that the whole human show wasn't decent," he says. This was clear to my old pal Cato the Elder exactly 2,050 years ago and to certain wise guys in Babylon a thousand years before that. But everybody has to go suddenly nuts about it now.

Well, it is all a long way beyond me. I believe that it is also a long way beyond anybody living, and that Stalin and H.G. Wells and Malcolm Cowley dont know any more about it than Rosemary and are simply befogging all the issues with a lot of persuasive crap. I think that maybe if women and children were in charge we would get somewhere. It is almost impossible to have any faith at all in the adult male in these days; he continues to boggle everything as he always has boggled it. But because he is doing this I see no reason to go to pieces personally. I see every reason not to. I dont think the barricades is an answer, nor giving up appreciation of and interest in such fine, pleasant, and funny things as may still be around. A couple of Englishmen have written books recently saying that the better minds, the finer souls, the nobler spirits, should kind of go into a monastery, form a group on the old pattern of the monks, and see if that wouldn't help. Everybody wants to do something strange, and is. It remains for a few people to stand and watch them and report what it all looks like and sounds like. Among such persons there isnt anybody better qualified for the job than you. If you will quit sending pieces to the Saturday Evening Post. I have pondered all day about you sending the Memoirs of a Master there. What was the matter with that excellent weekly called the New Yorker? It is important that things like the Memoirs of a Master be printed and continue to be printed. You got to get out of the habit of "retiring" pieces that come back from Joe Bryan—incidentally a quite handsome and nice fella with whom I have played the match game in Bleeck's and who was, wasn't he, on the bowling team you bowled on last year with Morris Ernst? You shouldnt submit your mind to Joe Bryan and the rest of those guys on the Post, for the God's sake. I wish you would explain to me what all this Post business is, anyway. That's not your audience. Harpers, Scribners, the Forum, maybe, if you must get outside the New Yorker, but not the Post. The piece you did for them last year was the best piece they ever had and the best written they ever had, and probably thousands of readers wrote in to complain about that. Of course, it is my carefully arrived at and calmly studied opinion that the New Yorker is the best magazine in the world. I think that, of such intelligent people as there are, most of them read the New Yorker. More than read anything else. There is, on the other hand, I imagine, nobody of any importance at all in the United States of America who reads the Saturday Evening Post.

Of course, it does no good to reason with you in these matters, but still I keep on trying. I not only feel, but know as a fact, that anyone who can write the way you do has to keep on writing. I don't mean any crap about the Urge or anything like that. I mean it is a point of moral necessity. It seems to be easy for you to rationalize, deprecate, and dismiss this, but I dont think it will really work. Like tucking sex in the back of your mind and saying well, that's *that*. (Writing, as Zaner has pointed out, may *be* Sex, or Sex, Writing, which makes everything a cycle similar to that of killing pigs to provide fertilizer to raise cotton to plough under—one of the things that has got de Kruif down, as you will see if you read his book). Let's see—where were we? Oh, yes: you got to keep on writing. I doubt very much that your 'year off' has been any less productive than mine —except that I got away where I could look at myself and people. The Memoirs of a Master, sight unseen, is unquestionably better than my pieces on Nice, Macbeth, Cato and Col.Johnstone, and the Michelin Guide. My output in nine months would discourage you if you were me. The thing is to keep your hand in. Nobody can write anything who doesnt. You say maybe you should write a piece called "What's So Funny?" and then add but you're sure you wont. It is that fecal matter, as my brother Robert says, which you must get out of your writing bowels. I want you to write that piece called "What's So Funny?" if only for Jamie, the boy artist.

Enough of this goddam lecturing or whatever it is.

The case of a swell guy like Don Marquis is enough to depress anybody. It makes you think of God as somebody like Max Baer. There must be some kind of strange law about disasters piling up on certain people. Take my brother Robert. He not only had goitre, but pleurisy, t.b., eye trouble, soft teeth, permanent rheum, and a dozen other things, including duodenal ulcer which he seems to have been born with; also he broke his right arm in two places, his left in three, sprung out the spool pins of one ankle, fell out of a bus on his head as a child, was run over by a milk wagon, and so on. I got shot in the eye at six years old and they called it a day. And even then it was the luckiest shot in the eye that medical science, optical branch, has probably ever known. Ten million men out of ten million and two would have lost the sight of both eyes as a result of what I stepped into. Oculists love my eye, since it is the only one they ever saw in which an unstoppable infection, having passed the sixth stage, stopped just so short of utter blindness that the naked eye cant figure out what mine sees with. Marquis goes blind playing pool, and for a strange reason. I see for an even stranger reason. This does not improve my argument about anything; but I often wonder what I would be like now if I had gone blind at the age of seven. I see myself as kind of fat, for some reason, and wandering about the grounds of a large asylum, plucking at leaves and chortling.

It was funny to get your letter and one from the Coates in the same mail, you talking about giving up your town house and life and moving to the country, they talking about selling their country place and moving to the city; both of you uncertain as to whether you can, or ought to. You two families ought to get together and compare notes. We are all against their selling their country place. They have got to the city after too long a time at a stretch in the country and have fallen under the city's spell—a pretty strong one at first—but in a year or so they would be exactly where you are, only they wouldnt have a home they own to go to. I think you should firmly argue them out of selling the country place. I am going to scream against it. The New York life will get them sooner or later, probably sooner, as it gets everybody. I dont mean "city life", I mean New York City life, two different things. There is nothing else in all the countries of the world like New York City life. It does more to people, it socks them harder, than life in Paris, London, or Rome, say, possibly could. Just why this is I have been very interested in pondering over here. I know it is a fact, but I am not sure just why it is. Perhaps Gibbs gets close to it in the comment of January 8th when he speaks, rather more easily and naturally than bitterly, of "our horrible bunch." He means, of course, their horrible life. And God knows it sometimes is. People have to run away from it, broken or screaming, at the loveliest times of year, on fete days, just before parties, on Christmas Eve. It has been interesting to see the perfect picture drawn in a few sentences in each letter we get, of New York life. "There has been a steady traffic to Foord's and back among the Gibbs, McKelway and unstrung group." If I got out my letters from everybody else and put all such sentences together it would be an amazingly vivid and accurate picture of that city and its life. It rather scares me. I know I never want to live in it again for long at a time, just run down for a visit now and then. God knows it got me. I was the leader of those it got. This seems remarkable to me, now, from here. I can see that tall, wild-eyed son of a bitch, with hair in his eyes, and a glass in his hand, screaming and vilifying, and it's hard for me to recognize him. I know that I will never let him get on the loose again. I also know that a steady life in New York would do it. Oddly enough, I dont think this is due to weakness, any more than having your leg carried away by a shell is due to weakness. A city made of steel and cement, with very few trees, and such trees as there are, paltry and vulgar, sad and almost sordid, a city in which it is possible to live for weeks and move around for miles without seeing green grass and blue sky and never to hear crickets or frogs or silence can have the same unavoidable effect as a shell from a gun. The men who studied the effect on the minds of soldiers of living in devastated areas, such as those around Verdun, came to the conclusion that it did horrible things to them and that this cannot be avoided in places where there is no green and blue, no birds and no animals and no insects. New York is nothing but a peaceable Verdun, with music and the theatre—the only things that keep people as sane as they are. Liquor, of course, tends to keep people away from music and the theatre. Bleeck's, when you analyze it, is very much like a front line dug-out —the noise, the dogged courage of the men holding on till zero hour, the fits of hysteria, the sitting around in sullen gloom. The women are like the shattered trees of Verdun or the shells whistling overhead. A Place like Bleeck's would be impossible, I think, in Paris, Rome, London, Vienna. To see Villa Borghese, Berkeley Square, the Bois du Boulogne, is to realize that Central Park with its grim mall, its brave trees, its iron and cement closing in on all sides, is merely an extension of Bleeck's offering no liquor. A person can admire New York and so on, and all that, but I feel it is absolutely impossible to love the place. One more or less holds on there. It is an achievement to have lived there, not a pleasure to do so. It has to be seen now and again, visited, lived in for short periods, but I swear that all the laws of nature and of the constitution of man make it imperative not to live there. Not, at least, in our horrible bunch. Something, I suppose, could be done about the dreary, fatiguing, and maniac parties, although it is a little late. They could be given up completely for a while. Why is it that people go on the wagon instead of giving up all intercourse? It may be the intercourse rather than the liquor, although I think it is both. The cocktail parties at which it is obviously impossible to have any fun at all look very strange and wonderful from here. I keep telling people about them; nobody believes me. They no longer sound real to me as I tell them: everybody slugged or sick at a quarter to seven, holding on without dinner until 10.45, going home to sleep in a draught with one's hat on and a cold corner hamburger sandwich in one hand, rousing up at twelve to vomit and call somebody up and say you're sorry and to hear him shout at his wife to shut up, it's just Bert calling back. I say nobody believes it, and I am beginning to doubt it myself. And then back to bed, without quite getting your pants off, and the bell rings and it's Harry and Ella, he sick all over his Christmas scarf, she wanting to go on to Harlem. And wonderful stories of how Louise let everything burn or get cold so she and Jack didnt get any dinner at all, and how they left Merton asleep under the piano, and the whole crowd went over to Spitty's on Third Avenue for steaks but didnt eat them when they were brought. And Mike finally got Bill told off about his wife and she screamed that she loved Mike and Bill just sat down and cried, only on the overturned chair, so Mike stayed on and Greta made scrambled eggs for all three of them.

This thing is running on and on. I got to get to bed. I'm sorry as hell you are going to miss the sweet life that revolves around the little villa. It's terribly nice, my boy, with the rosemary in bloom and the fragrance of the mimosa trees coming in your room like rain when you open the windows, and sunsets such as nobody ever saw before, and Maria's chats about the political situation and life in general just before she leaves us for the night, after serving the coffee, and a great peace and quiet all over everything (and bottles of scotch and rye and brandy untouched upstairs for weeks, awaiting the arrival of Miss Flanner and our bi-monthly party). We would like like hell to buy this villa which is for sale—for about $5000—it rents in the summer, when we wouldnt be here, for enough to pay back the purchase price in ten years.

Well, let me hear from you.

love to you all, from us both,
Jim

P.S. I finished all the foregoing off last night after midnight and here it is 3 o'clock of a fine summer, or maybe spring, afternoon. I can see, in this new light, that your problem about the city house is not so easy. What's the matter with renewing the lease and kind of living there half the time, Maine the other half? Or anyway, your three months in Maine. (make it four). Eight months in New York, with visits to the Thurbers in Connecticut is bearable, and anyway you like New York and except for walking into cars you dont let it get you so much. I also think you should go back to comment, without letting it depress or kill you, because it was the best column in the country and something to find satisfaction in doing—with periods off now and then. I also think the magazine will rot from the base up if you never do any more newsbreak lines . . .

I was asking Helen today how she liked having had nine months without winter and in the ensuing conversation she mentioned your fine paragraph about Maine. We both decided it made real American winters seem the best. But Helen also said, "Andy makes an idyll of it, but your feet get cold." If there were no women there wouldn't be any such brief, penetrating comments as that.

Well, keep bundled up,

Jim (27)

Besides visits from occasional guests on the order of Janet Flanner, there were some well-spaced but memorable parties, the most memorable being tea at Maxine Elliott's villa. The Duke of Windsor was there with his new bride, and so was Winston Churchill, enjoying one of his last moments of peace before all hell broke loose. Churchill was Miss Elliott's house guest, and he was playing mah-jongg upstairs when the Thurbers arrived. Told by Vincent Sheean that James Thurber was downstairs, he had difficulty placing the name. Finally, it rang a bell. "Oh, that insane and depraved American artist," he said. Thurber learned of the epithet even before he was introduced to Churchill, and when the great man asked for a drink, Thurber vengefully made him a Scotch and soda with practically no soda. Churchill drank it straight down and promptly went back upstairs to bed. "While he was upstairs," Thurber later wrote a friend, "I was shown a few of his watercolors— one of them a view of the Mediterranean that made it look as uninspiring as an Indiana lake . . . I remarked, 'The trouble with Mr. Churchill as an artist is that he is not insane and depraved enough, I guess.' " (28)

But mostly it was hard work at the Villa Tamisier. Several drawings and as many casuals were dispatched to the *New Yorker*, seven of the latter being nothing less than love letters to France. The seven, plus a rejected eighth, were included in the collection *My World—And Welcome to It*, published in 1942, with this explanation, in a Foreword, for writing so placidly about a nation on the skirts of war:

The stories that follow were written in Europe, most of them in France, in 1937 and 1938, so far away, so long ago. Since France, whenever I was there, made my heart a lighted place, these small, random essays are neither searching nor troubled. Everyone in those ending years of an epoch must have had some sense of the dreadful shadow ahead, there were so many signs and intimations. I left the examination and report of all this to those better equipped for such a task, and set out to drive the long, straight, quiet roads of France, and to walk the old familiar streets of favorite towns. These are merely pieces of the color and pattern of the surface which is to me the loveliest in the world. Anything written about France out of lightness of heart must seem now a little melancholy and incongruous. My hope in reprinting these stories is that they may start up some bright, cherished memory of the France which so many of us will always love, the France which we know will rise again.

The French he wrote about emerged from the pages not unlike his Ohioans—more interesting and earthy, perhaps, but with similar eccentricities and confusions. He found French politics almost as beguiling as the shenanigans inside the Columbus City Hall, in a piece called "You Know How the French Are." The colossal misconceptions of an alien life were treated warmly in "La Fleur des Guides Français" and "There's No Place Like Home." (The meat of these two casuals was offered for tasting in letters to White.) He reminisced about his past in France in "An Afternoon in Paris" and "La Grande Ville de Plaisir," and he expounded on European driving habits in "After Cato, What?" and "A Ride with Olympy." Olympy was the Russian gardener–chauffeur who came with the house, along with his wife, Maria, the cook. He had the same problems with the French language and automobiles Thurber did, so they were natural soul mates (a good man, Thurber seemed to be saying, should *not* be a good driver). Maria, while colorful, is not quite as much fun as other Thurber servants, black or white. (Yet, it was Maria who, as American troops liberated Antibes from the Germans, ran into the street asking each soldier if he knew a "Monsieur Thurber.")

The eighth billet-doux to France, which Thurber didn't sell to the *New Yorker*, is called "Journey to the Pyrenees" and is about exactly that. It is also about composure in the face of disaster—the trance of trivia that clutched Europe just before World War II. It is a kind of negative piece of war correspondence. The Thurbers wanted to visit Austria after they gave up the Villa Tamisier in April, but the Anschluss took care of that plan. They had heard so much about Spain and the refugees crossing over the mountains into France that they decided instead to see that situation for themselves. They got as far as Luchon and discovered that the refugee stream had been stopped and the border closed. Nobody seemed to care very much about anything in Luchon, so they headed north to Paris, via Grenoble. In Paris, it was as if they had never left; the talk was all of Spain. Thurber wrote Katharine White:

. . . We've been in a lot of Spain-politics-war-arguments and talks, since getting to Paris. People, including me, never seem to understand exactly where I stand on all this. Sheean wanted to take me to Spain with him and on 2 scotches I said fine, but on Maturer Reflection—which is as mixed up in my case as the Heat of Argument—I decided I would only get in Spain's way. I am somewhat convinced that Spain-politics-war, etc. is not Precisely My Field. Either writing about it or blundering around in it . . . (29)

So in place of another stab at Spain, Thurber showed Helen some of the World War I battle sites he had visited in 1919. Paris, he wrote Katharine White, was no city for writing casuals in—"though it's a mighty sweet city in May" (30) and before long, they were back in London.

They settled into a service flat near Piccadilly, waited on hand and foot by one McCulloch, the building's factotum, and they enjoyed themselves immensely. "Whores frequent this part of Mayfair," Thurber wrote McNulty, on June 1, 1938, "and often six or eight are prowling up and down before the house. At 3 or 4 in the morning they play together, toss, catch, pig-in-a-poke, kitten-for-a-corner, you-chase-me, etc. also in front of the house. Their approach: 'Would you like to talk with me?' "

Thurber was still the freshest adored American writer in London and he was in demand. Plans were under way for Hamish Hamilton to bring out an exclusively British edition of his drawings and writings, *Cream of Thurber*, skimmed from all his books to date. There was quite a bit of selecting to do. (The book was published in June, 1939, and helped keep Albion's spirits up during the Blitz.) At one point that summer, Ross arrived at the Dorchester, and *tout* London wanted to meet him. Thurber, as a recognized friend and associate of Ross, was even more in demand. One of the people he introduced to Ross was his new British friend John Duncan Miller, who later told Thurber, "During the first half hour, I felt that Ross was the last man in the world who could edit the *New Yorker*. I left there realizing that nobody else in the world could." (31)

The Thurbers took a week out for another trip to Scotland, this time to see some of Helen's relatives, and then, in late August, they returned to Paris to await the sailing of the *Champlain* from Le Havre on the 25th. Ross turned up there, too, and each showed the other the Paris he knew. Ross's Paris consisted of the old *Stars and Stripes* building, where he had served as editor during World War I, and a drab bistro, where Ross had difficulty ordering a beer. He wasn't at all interested in Thurber's Paris, and he felt comfortable only at the Ritz, among English-speaking waiters.

"We had pretty much had Europe by then," Helen said. "Jamie wanted to go home. War was in the air, and Mame wrote that the family was anxious for us to leave before it broke out. Despite Jamie's little run-in with Churchill on the Riviera, he was all for him and England —and, of course, France. He felt Americans couldn't even consider letting them down. His politics may have been tepid then, but he was never an isolationist. Why, he didn't even like Lindbergh *before* the war."

They arrived in New York on September 1, 1938, as negotiations began in Munich to give the Sudetenland to Germany and exactly one year before Hitler invaded Poland. It was nice to be home.

CHAPTER 14

As Unmistakable as a Kangaroo

They stayed at the Grosvenor on a day-by-day arrangement, making quick excursions to Connecticut to look for a suitable place to rent, still determined to avoid the perilous New York City rut. In Woodbury, Connecticut, a 225-year-old "poem of a house" (1) was available, the property of a balmy Columbus widow, who named the house "Joywalls" because she held, "joy came right out of the walls of the place." (2) (So did cold drafts, Helen Thurber recalled.) They rented the house till June and began to pick up the loose threads of their life in America, after more than a year away. First, there was Thurber's seven-year-old daughter to see and become reacquainted with—a meeting delayed by the September, 1938, hurricane, which struck New England so hard. Father and daughter were happily reacquainted at ravaged Sandy Hook ("I have always had a feeling that nobody close to me is going to be ended by a flood or earthquake," Thurber once said. "This is a silly feeling but there it is. Fly-paper is something else.") (3) Then, there were all the friends and colleagues in New York to catch up with again, but those meetings were not so happy. Thurber felt somehow detached, out of it, especially where the *New Yorker* was concerned. He wrote White:

... I feel pretty far away from the arms, the councils, and the understanding of the New Yorker. It's not the place I worked for years ago, when you and I removed Art Samuels' rugs and lamps in order to draw pictures and write lines for Is Sex Necessary. This is perhaps because I am an older man, with my youth definitely behind me and fifty around the corner. There is an air of college halls about the place; people bow to you; there is a faint precise ticking sound; an atmosphere of austere incoherence dwells there. (They sent me a caption, approved by the art conference, to put on a drawing. I did a drawing and put the caption on it. They advised me that they liked the drawing but they didn't like the caption. My anger is exhausted; I just get tired).

Except for dear and wonderful Miss Terry, I feel that I am looked upon as an outsider, possibly a hasbeen . . . With my name no longer on the list of editorial folk and no room of my own to go to, this is only natural . . . The aging humorist I suppose is bound to be a sad figure. They go in for the fleeting smile down there and the neatly pressed pants and I have the notion that they shake their heads politely over what I think is funny. Of course, I withdrew from the actual halls but I never considered myself as withdrawing from the magazine. If only one person had asked me what I thought of one idea in the dozen times I was around the place I would have felt less like a waiter in the Beta house . . . I didn't like New York and was glad to get out of it . . . (4)

A few weeks after settling in at the Woodbury house, he again complained to White about the New York life—and a few other things:

Dear Andy:

I just had a roast of lamb cooked expertly (not dangerously) by Margaret, our new cullud maid, who looks a strong fifty but is sixty-eight and has seven children and fifteen grandchildren. We found her on a dirt road near Hotchkissville which is just exactly 1.9 miles from our house. We got back from New York a few hours ago, worn and a little depressed, the way I have never been otherwise than, in getting back from New York. I cant take it calmly or slowly or happily down yonder. We slipped into town this time—four days ago—without letting anyone know, so as to get to bed and be ready for the dentist, oculist, and rectologist. But I came down from my room for some cigarettes and there in the lobby were Gibbs, McKelway, Alan and Dorothy Campbell; so it goes. The next night there were Charme and Mary Rennels and John Mosher and Bob Coates and all the others named above, to say nothing of Lois Long, her husband, Ursula Parrott, Howard Baldwin, and not Spaulding but that other man from above-stairs. You find yourself drinking. This is a practise I no longer care very much about but fall into, the way a man whittles or eats salted almonds or reads Life.

It is nice to be back under the 200-year-old maples and the apple trees. Cows from up the road get into the yard when I leave the gate open and their owner comes for them around one a.m. on a motorcycle. One morning (he having said the hell with it) I heard a cow eating apples under my bedroom window. It was 7 o'clock. After she had eaten 27, by actual count, I got up and chased her home in my nightgown. I figured she must have eaten a couple of hundred during the night; she is up and around, though, giving cider and apple jack, I suppose.

I sold the newyorker an onward and upward on which I spent a week of days and nights: a report on Punch for 1889–91, 1879–81, and 1863–65. The house here holds all the bound volumes from the first one (1841) to 1891. I found myself having to use 14 different source books before I was finished, checking up on Phil May and Du Maurier and when Alice in Wonderland was first published etc. (It was published in 1865). The library here is wonderful and has every history, anthology, book of quotations etc you ever heard of and some fifty nobody ever heard of. I could find everything I had to look up. It was interesting to read that Du Maurier who drew a dozen pictures a week for Punch for 20 years or more was "a satirist of modern fashionable life" and then to turn to that quaint embarrassingly bad, for the most part, satire. I dont know whether Cruikshank, who illustrated Dickens, ever drew for Punch or not, but I think not; anyway, in reading a sketch on him I learned that in his old age he claimed to have written Oliver Twist. My mother's uncle Milt claimed in his old age that he had written "Dixie". So it goes. God knows what you and I will lay claim to in another thirty-five years. I somehow hope I wont get the idea that I am Donald Culross Peattie [a contemporary author of nature books].

My bottom doctor, Robin Hood, told me he had had a man in his office who was "almost exsanguinated". My favorite expression now for bleeding to death. Fellow had just let his rectum go for twenty years, taking a little iron and liver compound from time to time . . . Asses to ashes, I said to him, dust to dust . . . My dentist says I will have my teeth for "quite a while". My ophthalmologist says I wont need reading glasses for "a time". My rectologist says, well—.

Margaret, our cook, is rounding nicely into a casual. She says one of her sons works into the incinerating plant where they burn the refuge; has had the job since the Armitage. I'm going to have to combine her with another lady of the vicinity who pointed out a flock of fletchers on her lawn and who also told me of a young man who had passed his civil service eliminations. As far as real estate values goes she says there is great disparagement. You begin to feel insane after an hour or so of this. Margaret lost only one child, "a beautiful girl of 24"— Margaret is very black and so is one living beautiful girl of hers we saw. I asked what had carried the other girl off and Margaret said, "Tuberculosis. She got it from her teeth. Went all through her symptom." I'm hedged about by mis-named terrors. Much worse than old familiar terrors you can put your finger on . . .

I am thinking of getting around to that play—the one that gave you an idea for a poem eight years ago or so . . .

I was by no means satisfied with my piece for the Sat Review but was caught between all the mill-stones you get caught between writing a piece about a friend for the Sat Review.* I dont really know them very well, you see. Your quality of thought is tempered by the magazine you sit down to write for, I think. The time of year, the year of life shape the contours, too. Bob said it was "ornate." The Thursday before or the following Friday I would have been better. Everybody liked the piece, all right, but I am planning for my next book a piece called E.B.W.: Second State, which will be better. Little apt sentences come to you in the night, paragraphs reshape themselves, ideas take off their dancing shoes and sit down so you can see what they are. Meanwhile the piece has been locked in the forms and there you lie remaking the living room of the story, putting in a rock garden, selecting new bedroom wallpaper, and on and

---

*An appreciation of E. B. White Thurber was asked to write for the *Saturday Review*. It was published on october 15, 1938.

on. One would talk in a different way to Sayre, for example, than to Henry S. Canby, meeting him in a club car. With Canby you would exchange legends and snuff boxes . . .

Did I tell you about seeing Rosemary? I helped move in here one Saturday, then drove to Sandy Hook and helped Althea move, then took a walk in the woods with Rosemary and helped her move fallen trees out of the path, a thing which it seems had to be done. I share her conscientious compulsions in these matters, which sets me off for her from all the other adults in the world, I guess. She has the most calm and poise of any child of seven I ever saw. But there's a lot of sparkle, too. I was overwhelmed by her. She came running out of the house and threw her arms around me, and I saw she wasn't a baby any longer. Always it used to be that I had to win her over, with skill and patience. She played me two pieces on the piano and read to me. She is inclined to think that Hitler will not be satisfied with what he has got. She pressed the bags out of the knees of my spirit and combed my spiritual hair.

I keep reading that France has become a third-rate power (The Nation says so, too). Just which are the second-rate ones? Denmark? Holland? Or is Britain second-rate and only Germany first? France third, and Denmark and Holland fourth?

We all loved both your pieces in Harpers (J.Mosher is virtually incoherent with praise). Helen is very fond of the hens who can sit around singing and whoring. The Sat Review is right when it says you are among the great living essayists.

I expect to get down to some casuals pretty soon. Right away, in fact. The Columbus trip comes next week and that will take two weeks out. Forum, by the way, asked me for some pieces, adding "Say one every two months. We dont have a department in mind." They thought maybe I was getting envious of you, or something, I guess. Also they apparently have about half the money they had the year they wanted one piece a month.

I am glad you are getting out a book of casuals. I have already been through The Fox twice. It is swell.

I keep planning a book on Columbus: the story of her murders, football, flood, etc., a kind of Profile done in Reporters at Large or something. None of her history, just her high lights, her passions, and her gestures. There is Dr. James E.Snook, who lived in sin with a woman under the name of Dr.John E.Snook, and then murdered her; there's the mamma in the furnace; there's Hank Gowdy's homecoming; there's the calm, factual story of the day the dam broke; there's Chic Harley.

Ross undertook to edit a sentence of mine, which needed editing because I had mentioned two different Washingtons without realizing it. It read, originally:

"Montana, the Dakotas, and Washington were admitted to the Union and Washington breathed more easily when Sitting Bull was shot dead."

Ross tried: Montana, the Dakotas, and the state of Washington were admitted to the Union and Washington D.C. breathed more easily etc.

I told him it would have to be: Montana, the Dakotas, and the *territory* of Washington, etc.

Finally, I showed him how to change the second Washington to "the government," and everything was all right, but it was fun when we got to the point of a parentheses explaining that a state is a territory until *after* it is admitted, etc. I said you can't "admit a guest" to your house if he just happens to drop by, because he isn't a guest until he is in the house. The question of whether he was a guest before he was admitted if he had received an invitation came up, ending in a sentence like this . . . (5)

The trip to Columbus Thurber mentioned served as both the annual visit and to see if something couldn't be done about Charles Thurber's health. His prostatitis had grown worse over the past year and a kidney infection had set in, but Charles absolutely refused to permit an operation (there was still a Christian Science movement in the family), and in the ensuing months his kidneys began to fail. Later, in 1939, Thurber got word that his father was in a Columbus hospital and was sinking fast from uremic poisoning. He waited until the last minute to go to his bedside, because it was felt Charles would be frightened by his son's presence. In the early spring, Charles Thurber passed on to a greater reward. The Christian Science dalliance notwithstanding, there was a long, crowded wake and funeral with all the Methodist trappings. Robert was most affected by the death (he had always been the closest of the three sons to the parents), while Thurber was sadly relieved that the poor man's lifetime of suffering was over. After the eulogies faded, Charles Thurber went out as he came in—a good, honest man, easily forgotten. His second born, James, was left as the unquestioned sole support of the family.

Thurber's own health was becoming more problematical, too. He could joke with White about his proctologist (with the marvelous name of Robin Hood), but he was experiencing some real hemorrhoidal discomfort in that uncomfortable region. There was certainly nothing to joke about ophthalmologically. It was clear to Dr. Gordon Bruce that Thurber's eyesight had worsened since he had left for Europe. The fifty–fifty cataract operation was more necessary than ever, but Dr. Bruce didn't press the point because he realized that his patient was so involved in various projects. He continued to allow Thurber to drive a car, since the cataract process is a slow one. But it was while driving his new Ford from Woodbury to Waterbury, Connecticut, to take Helen to the hairdresser's (Helen is a very regular hairdresser patron; Jap Gude remembered Thurber once saying, "When I'm on my deathbed, Helen will be at the hairdresser's") that Thurber had another of those frightening ocular incidents. "Jamie suddenly had to stop the car and get out," Helen said. "His vision had gone dangerously blurry. I knew then that he was in for trouble, because it was daylight and he could usually see well enough to drive in daylight. The blurring finally stopped and his sight returned, but he didn't drive very much after that."

The blurred-vision incident on the road to Waterbury was particularly frightening because, since moving to Woodbury, Thurber had embarked on what was plainly going to be the most productive year of his life. Exciting projects were fighting for attention inside his head. There was the idea for a play, which he had mentioned to White. He was completing illustrations for a book called *How to Raise a Dog in the City and in the Suburbs,* by James R. Kinney and, of all people, Ann Honeycutt. (Ann Honeycutt had sent Thurber her manuscript while he was in Europe; he liked it and agreed to do the illustrations. The book is still in print.) He also contracted to illustrate *In a Word,* a collection of unusual word derivations by Margaret S. Ernst, the wife of his lawyer, and to do some drawings for *Men Can Take It,* a frippery about male fashion by Elizabeth Hawes. The Ernst book, on one of Thurber's favorite subjects, inspired some of his best and most varied art work to date. It was a frolic for him, and his joy in words for their own sake comes through in the lovely drawings. The Hawes book merely elicited familiar Thurber. Perhaps, the rush to draw original illustrations for three books in one year was a reaction to the bad news he suspected was forthcoming from Dr. Bruce, sooner or later.

An engrossing project for Thurber during this period of racing-against-the-clock productivity was the writing of fables, a light literary form he had long admired. He tried his hand at the form, with middling success, back in 1932, with a *New Yorker* piece called "The Bright Emperor"—about a nasty little girl who kills a king with gifts, the moral being Never trust a nasty female bearing gifts. Now, in 1938, in his second marriage, with war looming, with deception, poverty, and sin on all sides, the fable seemed a likely, simple, and pithy way of saying what must be said, without being pontifical. As he later explained, "Every writer is fascinated by the fable form; it's short, concise, and can say a great deal about human life."(6)

The fables and accompanying illustrations appeared in the *New Yorker* all through 1939 and into 1940. There were thinly disguised Hitlers and Mussolinis, refugees, Altheas, Charlie Thurbers, and, of course, the author himself in the fables' animal and human characters.

And he still had a marksman's eye for nasty little girls. In an updated version of "Little Red Riding Hood," Thurber had the lass whip out an automatic and shoot the wolf dead (Moral: It is not so easy to fool little girls nowadays as it used to be). The most famous and the most satisfying fable, literarily and morally, is "The Unicorn in the Garden." It is quintessential Thurber, with all the classic ingredients: an unbelieving, shrewish wife, an imaginative, open husband, and the wonderful white-and-gold unicorn the husband discovers in his garden eating roses. The husband tells his wife of this thrilling discovery, and she loses no time in calling the police and a psychiatrist, in that order. They, in one of Thurber's traditional switches, take *her* away to the "booby-hatch" (a word the husband loathes), when she tells them of her husband's mad fantasy of the unicorn eating roses in their garden. The husband lives happily ever after, and the moral is Don't count your boobies until they are hatched. The ultimate victory of the imaginative male over the dull female was a theme Thurber had used many times before and would use many times again. It seemed to gratify him in a special way, as well as his readers.

With all the pleasure and talk the fables stimulated, and as he continued to use the form through the 1950's, Thurber placed himself as the last in a line of the great fabulists Aesop, Phaedrus, and La Fontaine. In later years, he took the form, and its history and effect, too seriously, losing the freshness, fantasy, and impact of his earlier fables, which, besides selling well in the 1940 book *Fables for Our Time and Famous Poems Illustrated*, turned up as readings, a ballet, revue sketches, and, in the case of "Unicorn," as an animated movie. While the pointed freshness lasted, the fables were remarkable.

About the same time Thurber wrote his first set of fables for the *New Yorker*, he came up with another wild and amusing, if less pertinent, idea called "Famous Poems Illustrated." What he did was take nine romantic-heroic standards—the sort every schoolchild has to memorize and, in adulthood, often attempts to recite from memory at late parties* —and draw his outrageous, demented creatures, sometimes in modern dress and attitudes, to fit the text literally. The results are nothing short of hilarious, and, if anything, the poems are strangely enriched.

Thurber had a sad young man marching through the snow of an Alpine village actually bearing a banner marked "EXCELSIOR!", while bemused citizens—in that frozen way Thurber always drew wonder— look on. Lochinvar is a kind of New York City dandy on a horse. The Housman narrator is a Costello's debaucher. Barbara Frietchie is a determined, slightly mad Columbus matron, while Stonewall Jackson is straight off a pedestal in an Ohio town square. Thurber's Leigh Hunt lions are every bit as ferocious as his seals, dogs, and rabbits. The fun made of the poems is satire springing from deep affection. They were the fondly remembered lessons of a Victorian American youth, and their basic worth was appreciated by Thurber. Ross was especially fond of these drawings and wanted Thurber to illustrate more poems of the same ilk. ("There are forty million," he once told Thurber.) (7) Thurber later tried to do Poe's "The Raven," but was discouraged when his raven looked more like a cornfield crow. (The unpublished "Raven" drawings were discovered by Helen and were included in her posthumous collection of her husband's work, *Thurber and Company* (1966).)

Besides this burst of breezy, original writing and drawing during the Woodbury sojourn, there was his old stand-by, the casual. In keeping with his other work, the casuals he was writing were better than ever

---

*"Excelsior" by Henry Wadsworth Longfellow, "The Sands o' Dee" by Charles Kingsley, "Lochinvar" by Sir Walter Scott, "Locksley Hall" by Alfred, Lord Tennyson, "Oh When I Was . . ." by A. E. Housman, "Curfew Must Not Ring Tonight" by Rose Hartwick Thorpe, "Barbara Frietchie" by John Greenleaf Whittier, "The Glove and the Lions" by Leigh Hunt, and "Ben Bolt" by Thomas Dunn English.

and destined to be his best known. Margaret, the new "cullud" maid whose transfigurations of language Thurber so gleefully related to White, did in fact "round nicely into a casual"—the estimable classic called "What Do You Mean It *Was* Brillig?" Margaret (Della in the casual) was a black, female version of Barney Haller, another of Thurber's great servants of the English word. She really did say, "They are here with the reeves," propelling Thurber to one of his many dictionaries:

> . . . I found out that there are four kinds of reeves. "Are they here with strings of onions?" I asked. Della said they were not. "Are they here with enclosures or pens for cattle, poultry, or pigs; sheepfolds?" Della said no sir. "Are they here with administrative officers?" From a little nearer the door Della said no again. "Then they've got to be here," I said, "with some females of the common European sandpiper." . . . "They are here with the reeves for the windas," said Della with brave stubbornness. Then, of course, I understood what they were there with: they were there with the Christmas wreaths for the windows. "Oh, *those* reeves!" I said . . . (8)

And so it went with Margaret/Della, the unwitting rival of Lewis Carroll. "She lived with us in Woodbury," Helen said, "and most of the time she was the only other person Jamie and I saw, he was working so hard. Her language was entertaining and she was a good cook, especially with pastry, but, my God, she was dumb! At Christmas, she put a dollar bill in an envelope and hung it on the tree for us. That was our present. It was pretty lonely out there at times, with Jamie working over the furnace register upstairs and Margaret and me downstairs."

For all her stereotypical colored-maid obtuseness (it would be next to impossible to get away with such condescension in a casual, no matter how funny, nowadays), Margaret/Della was wisely prophetic. Thurber quoted her as telling him, "You work too much with your brain" and that his mind worked so fast his body couldn't keep up with it. As it turned out, she was absolutely right.

The zenith of the Woodbury winter, and perhaps all his winters, was the writing and publication of "The Secret Life of Walter Mitty." The creation of Mitty was not afflatus—what Thurber conceived of as something that "takes place above the right ear during sleep and the writer is often astonished later when he sees it coming out of his typewriter" (9)—but rather as a supreme distillation of Thurber people and Thurber themes, reaching all the way back to his Douglas School class prophecy: the emasculated, daydreaming little man, a would-be Conradian figure hiding in a three-button suit; the emasculating, practical wife, a virago hiding inside a shrew; the love–fear of modern machinery; the attraction of fantasy as a release from reality; and, as always, the fascination for words. Here it all was, put together cleanly, brilliantly, definitively.

The setting for "Mitty" was fitting and familiar for that Woodbury winter—a man driving his wife to Waterbury, Connecticut, where she has an appointment with the hairdresser—but there the autobiographical similarity ends. ("Of course, I'm not anything like that Mrs. Mitty," Helen Thurber said.) Some friends of the Thurber family saw a good deal of Charles Thurber in Walter Mitty, while others saw brother William as a prototype. (Thurber cherished the story of once seeing William standing in front of a mirror at home in Columbus "arresting" his rich Fisher relatives for cheating on their store's weights and measures. "I'm going to take you in," he said sternly to his own image.) Thurber explained his concept of the perfectly named character in a letter to an inquiring librarian:

The original of Walter Mitty is every other man I have ever known. When the story was printed in the New Yorker 22 years ago six men from around the country, including a Des Moines dentist, wrote and asked me how I had got to know them so well. No writer can ever put his finger on the exact inspiration of any character in fiction that is worthwhile, in my estimation. Even those commonly supposed to be taken from real characters rarely show much similarity in the end . . . (10)

The actual writing of "Mitty" went fairly easily, once the basic situation of the henpecked protagonist thrust into dramatic reveries was established in Thurber's mind. He polished it into one of the shiniest pieces ever written, but after its astounding success, he tended to exaggerate the amount of work he put into it. He told Alistair Cooke that the "4000 words" of the Mitty story took him eight weeks to complete, "working day and night," with fifteen rewrites. (11) The story is only 2,500 words long.

Whatever the case of its technical creation, "Mitty" was an almost immediate smashing success from its first appearance in the *New Yorker* of March 18, 1939. Everyone who read it, especially the men, caught a bit of the universality, the instant identification with the boy–man lotus-eater who thought nothing of going forty kilometers through hell with just his Webley-Vickers automatic, who disdained a handkerchief before the firing squad—a Lord Jim, "inscrutable to the last." Identification, after all, is what insures a story's popular greatness, and "Mitty" has more than its share. Who hasn't discovered himself in a Mitty reverie from time to time? And besides, the story is just plain funny. High praise came rushing in from all quarters, and continued to for years as the story went through a stunning series of reprints, from the *Reader's Digest* to college textbooks. It prompted Ross, the casual's most ardent fan and movie-sale promoter, to write Thurber: "In your way you are just about the all-time master of them all, by Jesus, and you have come a long way since the old N.Y. Evening Post days." (12)

Of course, the very name Mitty and the leitmotif sound effect "ta-pocketa-pocketa" slipped quietly into the English language. During World War II, there were Mitty clubs in both the Pacific and Atlantic theatres of operation, bombers were named for the story's characters, and "ta-pocketa-pocketa" was used as a password in the front lines. Fighter pilots seemed to be especially prone to Mitty identification. They would introduce themselves over the radio as "Walter Mitty" or "Ta-pocketa," tales of which pleased Thurber enormously. They made him feel, somehow, that he was actively contributing to the war effort, which, in a way, he was. Now, more than ever, Mitty (which appears in the dictionary as an English localism for a stormy petrel) is a function of everyday speech. The British medical journal *Lancet* has labelled daydreaming on a grand scale as the "Walter Mitty Syndrome," and Nixon's subordinates, apropos of the Watergate affair, were once described by Stewart Alsop as suffering from a "Walter Mitty complex." (13) It is not unusual to hear a television sportscaster say, "If you want to play Walter Mitty for a moment, put yourself in the place of that guy" —as one said during a Rams–Raiders exhibition game on N.B.C., August 19, 1972.

Besides the numerous and profitable reprints, "Mitty" has been pummelled and worried into a Samuel Goldwyn vehicle for Danny Kaye, an opera by Ohio composer Charles Hamm, a blessedly short-lived Off Broadway musical (numbers entitled "Marriage Is for Old Folks" and "Hello, I Love You, Goodbye" give some indication of its merit), a tired sketch in Thurber's own revue, *A Thurber Carnival*, and, most aesthetically satisfying, a radio adaptation in 1944 starring Robert Benchley, who felt at ease in the role and performed it beautifully. Moss Hart at one time wanted to make a play of it, but Thurber was anxious for Rodgers and Hammerstein to create a musical around it. Neither of these projects came to pass—probably for the best, because no other medium could improve upon the literary flawlessness of the original. Financially, few, if any, other writers have realized as much money per word from one story.

A measure of any triumphant work is the plagiarism claim. Sure enough, Charles Yale Harrison, the author of a novel called *Meet Me on the Barricades*, directed the attention of Thurber and his lawyer to the alleged similarity between his book and "Mitty." Harrison conceded that Thurber might have been inspired unintentionally by his novel, but Thurber was indignant. He pointed out that he had been in Europe when Harrison's book was issued, had read neither the book nor its reviews, and had been writing daydreamer stories for years (as indeed did Benchley). Nevertheless, the Harrison claim—"a time-consuming nuisance," in the words of Thurber's lawyer—dragged on and proved to be rather expensive in legal fees. Thurber ultimately refused to submit the case to arbitration before a panel of writers, and the matter was dropped shortly thereafter. By 1947, when the plagiarism claim was brought up, anybody who hadn't heard of James Thurber and/or Walter Mitty either couldn't read or didn't go to the movies or simply wasn't listening to conversations at parties.

On top of everything else during the hectic 1938–39 winter, Thurber got an idea for a play—a form of writing he liked to talk about, scoff at, even tinker with, but never studiously work at. As Helen remembered it, the idea came to him while he was, for some reason, standing on the garage roof in Woodbury. The general situation of the play—tentatively entitled *Homecoming Game* by Thurber—was predictable, given the directions Thurber's mind followed: He planned a "pure comic triangle," set in a Midwestern college town, not unlike Columbus, and dealing with "two men, one typifying mind and thought, the other body and action. It was the ivory tower against the gridiron, insecurity against fame, the spirit lamp against the football . . . Thought and sense and liberality seem to be losing." (14) The two opposing male types would strive throughout the play to win over the comely wife of the intellectual type. If the play were to concern Columbus, Ohio State, and a comic love triangle, the obvious collaborator for Thurber was Elliott Nugent, then a prosperous and esteemed Hollywood actor and director. They rarely saw each other any more (Nugent seldom came east) and they corresponded irregularly. Thurber, in 1939, felt more than Nugent's equal, of course, and he no longer was envious of him. However, he still owed him about ten thousand dollars in old debts, to say nothing of priceless gratitude for past services rendered. He wrote Nugent a brief outline of the idea, proposing that they work on it together, since Thurber had little sense of dramatic structure. Nugent wrote back and said that the idea didn't appeal to him particularly and, besides, he was too busy to work on a play. Thurber, however, kept pressing him with urgent letters, but it wasn't until Nugent saw a chance to add a bit of social significance to the lightweight plot (social significance was "obligatory by 1939," Nugent said in his autobiography, *Events Leading Up to the Comedy*) that he became truly interested. Thurber wasn't as "jumpy" (15) about social significance then as Nugent was, but he was pleased that Nugent was at last willing to try a collaboration with him. In May of 1939, the Thurbers gave up their rented Joywalls and made plans to travel to California. The Thurber–Nugent college pledge to work together on a project someday was about to come true.

The Thurbers went by boat to California, so they could take their new Ford along. "We were told we needed a car out there," Helen said, "but it was a mistake to go on a boat. We travelled by way of Havana, the Canal Zone, and then up the Pacific coast to Los Angeles. It was the hottest I've even been in my life, and neither of us could stand great heat. All that glaring tropical sun aggravated Jamie's cataract. He insisted on playing Ping-Pong on the open deck, and he reached the finals in a tournament but lost to a pretty girl. He blamed the unstable deck, but the truth was it was another blindness attack, like on the road to Waterbury. By the time we arrived at the Nugents' house in Bel-Air, he couldn't see well enough to read a newspaper."

His vision continued to blur and, for two weeks, he was able only to talk to Nugent about the play. He sent an anguished telegram and then a slightly panicky letter to Dr. Bruce about the developing menace:

June 9, [1939]

Dear Dr. Bruce:

I guess you better give me the name of a good man out here who can get me some reading lenses. The old eye is the same as ever for distance but I'll be goddam if I can read—except—and this is funny—under a big umbrella outdoors in a bright sun; under those conditions I see to read even newspaper type exactly as well without my glasses as with my *distance* ones. (Not reading ones —or anyway, almost the same). If I use my right lens as a magnifying glass and pull it away, I can see as clearly for a fifth of a second as I did in 1896. I can also do a lot of other tricks, but I am getting crosser and snappier and sadder every minute straining and struggling to type and to read and to draw (the latter is the easiest). I'd rather atrophy those muscles in two years than by god go through life like a blindfolded man looking for a black sock on a black carpet. If I use the old distance lenses and only have stronger ones for reading, wouldn't that even up on the atrophy problem? Couldn't I go without glasses when not reading, or something? Life is no good to me at all unless I can read, type, and draw. I would sell out for 13 cents. Seems to me the eye began to dim slightly on the third day at sea—anyway I had been able to read for two days and then it got slightly harder . . .

Dr. Bruce sent him the name of a good eye doctor in Los Angeles and soon Thurber could see well enough to type and read with comparative ease. But his temper didn't improve much. He was plainly uncomfortable in the relentless California sun, and both he and Helen "longed for the cool, green shade of Connecticut and the smoky gloom of Bleeck's," as Nugent put it. (16) ("They send the air in by cans from the desert," Helen remembered her husband saying on bad days in California.) He would abruptly fly into a tantrum, creating "waves of argument and invective," and then retreat to contriteness the next day, saying, "Was I bad last night?" (17) Still, in spite of everything, the collaboration began to produce some tangible results.

It was an odd collaboration because they never actually wrote anything together. After a few weeks, the Thurbers moved out of the Nugents' house and took a bungalow in Beverly Hills. There, during the day, while Nugent was busy with his movie commitments, Thurber would write dialogue. At night, they would get together (if Nugent's active social life permitted) and hammer what Thurber had written into shape. Thurber's progress was too slow for Nugent, so Nugent wrote Act II by himself, and before long they were rewriting each other's stuff. They made of equal weight to the brain-vs.-brawn theme the question of academic freedom: Whether or not Tommy Turner, the intellectual English professor, would be allowed to read the celebrated Bartolomeo Vanzetti letter to his composition class (a seemingly ridiculous predicament in any institution but a Midwestern state university). This injection of social significance was, of course, Nugent's idea, but it was Thurber's notion to express it through the device of the Vanzetti letter. Thurber was more interested in the literary quality of the letter than the sociopolitical one; he was always respectful of his friends' involvement in the Sacco-Vanzetti cause, but he was never a dedicated partisan in the affair. As Helen said, "Jamie was really rather conservative, but when his friends were affected by the force of politics, he became interested because of his involvement with his friends. Politics was personal with him." (It was ironic that Nugent was the instigator of the academic-freedom theme; during the late 1940's and early 1950's he was one of the more right-wing Hollywood figures.) They also changed the name of the play—wisely—from *Homecoming Game* to *The Male Animal.*

By the end of the 1939 summer, *The Male Animal* had settled into the rough shape by which the world would later come to know it as a small classic of the American theatre. Like a tipsy midget at a teamsters' outing, its academic-freedom theme bravely, absurdly, asserts itself in an otherwise conventional Broadway romantic comedy, not far

removed from the Jean Kerr school of theatrics. It even has the traditional dumb-colored-maid-on-the-telephone exposition scene in the
first act—Cleota out of Della. One hardly cares a hoot about the one-
dimensional, pasteboard characters—Tommy Turner, the drab quasi-
intellectual; his pert, sensible wife, Ellen; Joe Ferguson, the ex-Chic
Harley type with a qualified brain; Ed Keller, the blustering, reaction-
ary university trustee; Dean Frederick Damon (modelled unabashedly
after Dean Joseph Denney of O.S.U.), the clear spirit of academe; and,
of course, the stunted state university itself, perhaps the most interesting character in the whole thing. There is the obligatory drunk scene
(especially obligatory in any Thurber work), the inevitable domestic-
fight scene, and the necessary revelation scene. The conflict of the play
was one of the many conflicts within Thurber himself (and, perhaps,
Nugent): old-fashioned liberalism, constitutionalism, individualism vs.
old-fashioned conservatism, chauvinism, herdism—in short, the princi-
pled Middle West vs. the parochial Middle West. But what lasting value
The Male Animal had in its conception, or has in its present-day reviv-
als, is in that feisty midget of academic freedom.

During the four months of his Hollywood stay, Thurber did not avoid
completely the fabled Tinseltown. He was known and admired by a
surprisingly large segment of the Hollywood colony (the ones who could
read), especially after the local papers did long feature stories on the
strange visitor from the East. However, there were notable exceptions.
When Jack Warner was introduced to Thurber one night, he asked him,
"Are you any relation to Edna?," and Charlie Chaplin abundantly
praised Thurber for a piece written by E. B. White. Thurber had previously met Dave Chasen through Harold Ross and spent many a long
evening at Chasen's restaurant, in the company of a circle of cronies—
Nugent, Nunnally Johnson, Humphrey Bogart (an old drinking pal from
21), James Cagney, George Murphy, Spencer Tracy, Robert Montgomery (a close friend and later a producing partner of Nugent, who failed
to enchant Thurber), and Ronald Reagan. Once, at Chasen's, Thurber
took it into his head to sketch appropriate murals on the men's-room
walls, but an officious busboy wiped the walls clean, and was fired by
Chasen for his puritan pains. Thurber's traffic with the Hollywood Left
was light. "One night we followed Melvyn Douglas to a fund-raising
party off in the hills for the Joint Anti-Fascist Refugee Committee,"
Helen recalled. "Jamie was driving but he couldn't see Douglas's car
ahead. It was the worst ride of my life. There were too many parties."

Thurber had always liked movies but he had an aversion to the place
where they were made and the people who made them. "He really

hated Hollywood," Helen said, "and he wasn't seduced at all by the money and the life out there. He didn't mind sitting around Chasen's with his cronies, but the fast, phony social pace and all that constant movie talk irritated him. He didn't like movies *that* much. He tried to convince Elliott to leave Hollywood by damning the whole place, but he didn't get anywhere. Also, we didn't have much money while we were out there and so we couldn't live it up in that Hollywood style. I was snubbed by the hatcheck girls because I didn't own a mink or decent clothes. I told Jamie that I'd never come back to Hollywood until I had a mink."

The central symbol for Hollywood in Thurber's mind, as it was in the minds of so many writers who loathed the place, was the Jewish producer. Several years later, he wrote John McNulty (who had become a high-salaried writer for Paramount):*

... We are all glad Paramount is looking after your physical being and hope they treat your spirit and mind as well. Dotty Parker once put an ad in a trade journal there (which you'll too) reading
WITH PARAMOUNT
THANK GOD
I visited the studios with Nugent several times. The place seemed clean and quiet and there was a Jewish producer who spoke French—no other studio can make that statement . . . (18)

Thurber's distaste for the eternal Hollywood symbol came out in a short story, "The Man Who Hated Moonbaum," which concerns a pretentious, gross producer who invites a literary visitor (named Tallman) to his colossal home for a late nightcap of hundred-year-old brandy. The diminutive, cigar-chomping movie man is a composite of the standard

---

*McNulty's temporary departure from the *New Yorker* for Hollywood gold prompted one of Ross's most quoted lines. When McNulty told Ross he was leaving the magazine, Ross said, "Well, good luck, McNulty, goddam it." Out in Hollywood, McNulty, still the fastest writer in the East or West, was given an assignment his first day on the job at the Paramount writers' building—to work up a rough treatment of a particular movie idea. That same afternoon, McNulty was seen by a veteran Hollywood hack walking down the corridor carrying a sheaf of paper. "What have you got there, McNulty?" the writer asked him. McNulty told him it was a treatment he had just written for a movie and he was on his way to turn it in to the appropriate producer. The old hack paled and, calling his colleagues out of their offices for help, he pinned McNulty against the wall. "Look," he told him, "you don't turn in a finished treatment the first day. A treatment takes *months* to finish. We get paid by the week here, remember?" Shoving him back into his office, they threatened to lock him up if he ever did that again.

Hollywood moguls, typified by Jack Warner, but the character's banalities were actually patterned after the professional Irishman Leo McCarey. Helen was along when McCarey invited Thurber to his mansion to talk literary and drink ancient brandy. The story was almost exact reportage. "His wife," Helen said, "even refused to come down when she was rung for, just as in the story."

When *The Male Animal* was deemed ready for a tryout production in the late summer of 1939, Thurber had just about run out of patience and money. His tiffs with Nugent over the play were more frequent, and he felt he should return to New York and make some quick income at what he knew how to do best—writing casuals and drawing cartoons. Nugent, meanwhile, contracted with Arthur J. Beckhard to produce and direct some limited tryouts that October in San Diego, Santa Barbara, and Los Angeles. By the time the rehearsals began (with Nugent reluctantly taking over the Tommy Turner role, when Myron McCormick dropped out), Thurber and Helen had put their Ford and themselves on a train for New York. They had had enough of the Far West for a while.

A lot of Thurber's malaise was due to the beginning of World War II. Germany had invaded Poland and troops were marching in several directions. When he arrived in New York, he shunted aside the old unpleasant West Forty-fourth Street memories and took a suite at the Algonquin. There, "depressed and shaken by the war," according to his wife, he sat down at the writing desk in his room after dinner one night and started to draw some pictures in pencil. Inspiration must have been screaming into his right ear, for within a few hours he had an entire book sketched out in drawings and text: *The Last Flower*, a parable in pictures about World War XII, the world's near-total devastation, the disappearance of love and art, the nurturing of the last flower on earth, the new flourishing of civilization and art and love and soldiers, World War XIII, and the world's total devastation save for one man, one woman, and one flower. Like its conception, *The Last Flower* is simple, brief, optimistic, and (if there is such a possibility) divinely inspired. It is also the most affecting work Thurber ever wrote or drew.

Perhaps what makes the book so moving and telling is the use of gentle humor in a tale of doomsday. His smashed works of art are somehow delightful; his disillusioned dogs deserting their masters make one smile; his plague of rabbits descending on the former lords of the earth is insanely funny; his generals and "liberators" are superb satire; and his people, of course, are pure Thurber. It is on the surface a children's book, but its humor, sophistication, and message are very adult indeed. (Children tend to be at once frightened and encouraged by it.) Thurber's prescience, by six years, of atomic destruction is eerie, but, above all, there is touching hope in the little book.

Right after that apocalyptic, poetic evening in his Algonquin room, Thurber polished the text, inked in the drawings, dedicated the book to his daughter ("For Rosemary in the wistful hope that her world will be better than mine"), and showed the finished draft to several close friends. They were unanimously ecstatic. Braced by the reaction, Thurber phoned up Harper and told his editor, Gene Saxton, that he had a very different kind of Thurber book for immediate publication. (He didn't submit the book to the *New Yorker* first because he feared that the flux of pictures would put Ross off and cause an unnecessary delay in the book's printing.) Harper, after seeing the draft of the book, agreed to publish it as soon as possible, replacing on its list *Fables for Our Time*, which was scheduled for that November. *The Last Flower* was rushed into production, and in a week's time there were proofs available, although the Harper office staff members grabbed up every loose set for their own pleasure. With the tidy advance in his bank, Thurber took a train back to California, where *The Male Animal* was about to open in San Diego.

In one sense, he should have stayed in New York to oversee the book's production. Because of the rush to get *The Last Flower* into the bookstores in time for Christmas, Harper committed some errors in manufacture and promotion, which gave Thurber an acute case of the furies —or "the Thurbs," as Helen called them. He wrote the Whites:

. . . I am about five pounds lighter than when I saw you, on account of the play and Harpers.

In addition to reversing cuts and leaving blank spaces in The Last Flower, Harpers has got out ads which sound as if they might have been written by some of the old ladies Mary Petty draws. I am sure they would stir Mrs William Tecumseh Sherman, or the late Mrs William McKinley.

They lead off at the top in black type with "The Book That Captured a Hundred Over Night" leaving you to guess what that means. I guessed it meant maybe people they had sent advance copies to (including Mrs Roosevelt, I see by Saxton's list—I once wrote a bitter parody of My Day when it wasn't as good as it is now). Then Harpers got into some kind of jam with LIFE which wanted to run a page of the drawings this week. It came out a double page spread, using 26 pictures, or practically the whole book, certainly the whole story, only probably cut to the bone and ruined—the cuts will be terribly reduced. I was not told about this till it was too late. Saxton demanded money for me, they offered $250, he asked $500, and today they called him back and bullied him into $350—only I will get into action on that. I am always buttoning Harpers pants and seeing that they have lunch money and a clean handkerchief before they start out in the morning. Then they get lost in Central Park and I have to go out and find them. You cant turn your back on that ancient firm. Gene also wanted me to put the $500 LIFE money into a fund—with $500 of their own money for ads! I had a long talk with him today and said My God no. It's too bad that nice gentlemen like Harpers have to be so bad at publishing books or rather promoting them. They couldnt sell a bottle of pop to a man dying of thirst. S&S would plug this book with thousands of dollars and probably sell a hundred thousand. I feel that if it sells 20,000 that will pleasantly delight the boys down there. They have no guts and they have no courage—about as much gambling instinct and real blood as a clay pigeon.

You got to choose between gentlemen who know the nice places to eat and the guys who sell your books. I havent much cared till now, but this book I want to see sell. (The Times Book Review ran an unsigned review under Children's Books—along with Patty, the Pacifist Penguin, etc.)

This light isnt good, so if I hit wrong keys, I wont be able to fix the words . . .

(By the way, the hundred who were captured over night turned out to be secretaries, editors, Lee Hartman, printers, Rushmore, Mrs. Rushmore, phone operators, engravers, Saxton, etc. Well, your guess was as good as mine. I pointed out to dear Gene that when you run a big boast about a hundred copies on the same page with boasts by other publishers running into the 27th edition and 234,000th copy, it's like saying "Fifty People Jam Carnegie Hall to Hear Gluck.")

They've got me signed up for the Fables, but after that I think that the clause in the contract where it says "on terms to be mutually agreed upon" will be the stumbling block . . .(19)

Thurber did split with Harper after it issued *Fables for Our Time* in 1940, and he did not make peace with that company again, for an original book, until 1957, going with Harcourt, Brace and the awesome Simon and Schuster in the interim. Some of Thurber's finest moments of outrage were reserved for publishers, yet he counted many book editors, including Gene Saxton, among his close friends.

Production and promotion errors notwithstanding, *The Last Flower* did extremely well, going into nine hardcover editions. Except for the slightly absurd, and absurdly slight, *Times* review, it received a good deal of attention, not the least of which was from W. H. Auden in the *Nation* (January 13, 1940). Auden compared Thurber to Edward Lear, stating that their common "icon" was the "average nonpolitical man of an industrialized society." He complained that *The Last Flower* was "at once too pessimistic and not pessimistic enough," but added that "it would be as impertinent as it is unnecessary for me to praise Mr. Thurber's work; everyone knows and loves it." Helen has said that *The Last Flower* was Thurber's own favorite book in his latter years. It was always E. B. White's favorite.

Thurber arrived in San Diego in time for opening night, on October 16, 1939. It was the usual show-biz story of out-of-town chaos. Nugent had taken over the Tommy Turner role and was also co-director, as well as co-author. His father, the venerable trouper J. C. Nugent, stepped in as the Red-baiting trustee, Ed Keller, at the last minute, and while Thurber appreciated his theatrical facility, he didn't want him permanently in the part. (He ultimately won that tiny battle.) Mary Astor was Ellen Turner and Leon Ames was Whirling Joe Ferguson, the ex-football hero and former beau of Ellen. Despite its roughness, the play filled the San Diego theatre for two nights and pleased the audience and critics. Thurber loved the idea of theatre but he was by no means enchanted with its disciplines. He worked hard with Nugent, cutting and rewriting during the following week's run in Santa Barbara and, finally, in Los Angeles. There were twelve tryout performances in all and a lot of problems.

On opening night in Los Angeles, all literate Hollywood showed up, the word having gotten around that there was a fresh wind blowing from the East. Thurber later wrote the Whites:

... It was wildly received in San Diego, Santa Barbara and Los Angeles, even when it was full of dull spots and bad writing and some gags that creep in when your back is turned. The theatre would drive you nuts in a week, White. I did some fancy screaming myself ... Jed Harris liked our play very much and so did the Spewaks, Bart Cormack, Norman Krasna, King Vidor, Myrna Loy, Walt Disney, Harold Lloyd, Groucho Marx. Connelly took it apart for us in a long speech but, as Charlie McArthur said to me the other night, "Marc is an instantaneous orator." He used the word "therapy" (Connelly did) several times as he lectured to us out there and I began to feel easier. Even easier than when he mentioned Brahms fifth. (I think he only did four symphonies, anyway). He said we had the United States in the palm of our hand but also had a mandolin there, too, or something. God knows you get all kinds of viewpoints. Everybody wants to change this or that or put in business or suggest lines. When I got out there the play had lines in it and business suggested by secretaries, cousins, mothers, bat boys, doormen, and little old women in shawls ... (20)

Groucho, Thurber felt, gave the soundest criticism of all. He told Thurber that *The Male Animal* was too funny, that plays came to New York with a thousand laughs and folded in a week. He advised the authors to scrape off some of the easy gags and reveal the seriousness underneath, which they did. Jed Harris, on the other hand, advised them to put the gags back in. Marc Connelly said he would direct the play in New York if it would be made even more political. And so it went. At last, Thurber blew his stack, after deciding that the play was more Nugent's than his. He accused Nugent of "incredible naïveté" (according to Nugent's autobiography), and Nugent stalked out. They made up, but the play closed in Los Angeles after a week and its future was very much in doubt. Thurber returned to New York to greet the publication of *The Last Flower*.

Back in New York, Thurber, considerably cooled-off, still had hopes for *The Male Animal*. This seemingly unfounded optimism caused his old Bleeck's drinking pal and theatrical press agent Richard Maney to taunt him a bit by suggesting that the estimable Herman Shumlin would be a likely producer. Thurber thought it was a wonderful idea, and an astonished Maney set up a meeting. First, though, Nugent came east, and he and Thurber rewrote the play completely. When they thought it was in presentable enough shape for a tough professional like Shumlin, Nugent read the play aloud to him. Thurber described the event to the Whites:

. . . Elliott and I have spent ten days rewriting the play and last night read it—Elliott did—to Herman Shumlin. Took three hours. He had never had a play read to him before, but since Elliott had acted in it and it had been produced, he wanted to hear it. Warned us he would just listen and then take the script home and go over it by himself. But at the end of the reading and a short discussion of changes he wanted made, he said he would do the play. This is pretty near a record, I think. Selling a play in three hours to the producer who has the biggest record for successes in town and who can have his pick of the play crop. He gave us our first advance royalty check today. Sort of offsets the clumsy Harpers crowd . . .

We both liked Shumlin a lot. He is a quiet, solid gentleman, very polite but straightforward, not a bully and bastard like Jed Harris. I was prepared, if he didn't like certain parts, to say no, but he liked the important things and objected only to the last part of the third act, which I hadn't liked anyway. It got trite and hurried, and seemed heavily plotted, and fixed things up too patly. I can do it and get it right. He counts on opening the play here New Year's week, even that is rushing it a lot. We'd have to play Xmas week in a tryout city. I am confident that we have a swell play now, and that it will be a big hit. I think as big as Life with Father . . . Life with Father is much better I think than when you saw it. Plays have a way of improving 75 percent after they leave their Skowhegans . . .

You got to come down for the opening. We are going to the Sayres in Philadelphia for Thanksgiving, just for the day, as I cant lose more than one day now.

Let me hear from you. We are now in two lovely rooms, each with a bath, very quiet and comfortable, at the Grosvenor, 35 Fifth Avenue. I could throw a rock in any direction from my room and hit some old misery of mine . . .

I go on Information Please next Tuesday night.

This is James Thurber saying—goooood nite!

James Thurber
the Boy Artist(21)

Cheered by Shumlin's decision not only to produce but to direct *The Male Animal*, Nugent (and Robert Montgomery) invested heavily in the play. Thurber was just as optimistic about it as before but he had little folding money to back up his faith, so he stood pat with his royalty share. Cast changes were made (Ruth Matteson took over the Ellen Turner role, Matt Briggs replaced the elder Nugent, and a pretty young thing named Gene Tierney played the part of the ingénue) and rehearsals began almost immediately. Both Thurber and Nugent were a trifle sensitive about the obvious proximity of their play's milieu to Columbus–O.S.U. They would tell visiting firemen from Columbus that it could be about any Midwestern campus town, but the visiting firemen didn't believe them for a minute. The college songs and references weren't even thinly disguised.

With its university theme, Shumlin selected Princeton as the first tryout town. Everyone but Thurber was worried during the dress rehearsal there, and afterwards, Thurber joined the others in drinking up everything in sight. But Princeton loved it, and with new hope the company moved on to Baltimore for a successful two-week run. In Baltimore, they rewrote every night till 3 A.M.—they didn't have a real first- or second-act curtain until Thursday of the first week there*—but still there was time for a gala party given by Ogden Nash and for Thurber to meet with his old idol H.L. Mencken.

Thurber had corresponded lightly with Mencken since the previous spring, when Mencken had asked him the exact date of a quotation from *Punch* that Thurber had used in his piece attacking that magazine's snottiness towards America. The quotation was: "If the pure well of English is to remain undefiled no Yankee should be allowed hence-

---

*The authors' college classmate Ralph McCombs turned up to see the play in Baltimore. He remembered Thurber as "terribly nervous and temperamental," with Nugent as "the steadying factor."

forth to throw mud into it. It is a form of verbal expectoration that is most profane, most detestable." They were clearly soul mates in their concern for language—especially the American language—and they had a great deal to talk about in Baltimore, as they had at later meetings in the company of Ross. Ross was as much a wonder to Mencken (who wrote often and well for the *New Yorker*) as he was to Thurber. Years afterwards, Thurber told the man who had once been in trouble for "subversive tendencies":

... I am anticipating the gruelling probe of my own iniquities, in a forthcoming issue of what I openly call The New Worker, as it will soon be known to one and all. It is a matter of common knowledge that Ross has long planned to overthrow the Government and only two considerations now restrain him: his finicky complaint that revolutions cannot be successfully soundproofed, and his strange absorption in a program to eliminate the comma entirely. With this in mind, he has engaged in some agile and unfortunate wrassling matches with the prose style of my colleagues and myself. We have recently got him down, broken his pelvis, and made him desist. He instantly turned his attention to a daring attempt to rid the language of the word "which." It is with proper pain and the honesty you have always observed in my devotion to the cause that I inform you I have been known to refer to Ross's present plan as a which hunt . . . (22)

(Mencken replied that he hoped Thurber would be jailed in the North, since Southern hoosegows were extremely uncomfortable. He also hoped that Thurber would drop by Baltimore again so that he could show off the "ruins of a once great medieval city.")(23)

Throughout their spotty correspondence are items of curiosa, which each knew would amuse the other. Thurber sent on to Mencken a clipping about a Rev. Jesse W. Routte, the Negro pastor of the Holy Trinity Lutheran Church in Jamaica, Queens, who wore a turban to Mobile, Alabama, and was treated like a visiting foreign dignitary. In the same letter, he told of hearing, on a Fundamentalist radio program, that Christ was the senior partner of a shoe-store proprietor in Paterson, New Jersey. ("I hope that He somehow finds time to watch over you and keep you.")(24) The best item was a personal calling card, which had come into Thurber's possession, reading:

ANNA HEYBERGER
DOCTEUR DE L'UNIVERSITÉ DE PARIS
LAURÉATE DE L'INSTITUT DE FRANCE, PARIS, 1930
PROFESSEUR AU COLLÈGE COE
CEDAR RAPIDS, IOWA

To which Thurber added, "In case you have ever doubted the class and tone of the persons with whom I engage in correspondence, I submit the enclosed card.

Yours,
James Thurber
de l'université Ohio
à Columbus State"(25)

All in all, the frenetic out-of-town show-biz experience had been rewarding for Thurber. But throughout, he maintained a literary aloofness which kept him safely above the Broadway rabble and tumult around him. This keen objectivity for the theatrical experience came out in a gratuitous and brilliant letter to Wolcott Gibbs, who, in 1950, was about to suffer the same pains himself with his play called *Season in the Sun*, about a magazine editor suspiciously like Harold Ross:

. . . As a man who has crossed the Gobi desert, I feel the Christian desire to point out some familiar terrors that you will have to endure. One of them is comic promotion lines about using your big toe on the typewriter shift. These get worse. If you have Maney you avoid a lot of this, but Maney is likely to phone your wife, the way he phoned Helen from Princeton, and growl, "Stay where you are. Only one funny scene". He had watched dress rehearsal with six other guys wearing hats and overcoats and smoking cigars. One of the actors fumbled every line and kept saying "Balls", so that fifteen speeches ended with this word. It was the night before opening and we had to cut twenty lines from the first act; sitting up too late; drinking too much; eating too little. There was the usual last-hour panic. Shumlin wanted to put spectacles on the villain to make him comic and Nugent wanted to put his father into the part. Someone had quietly re-written the charm out of the dancing scene and it had lines like, "What do you say we shake a leg"?

At a party after the opening in Princeton, Dean Gauss insisted on meeting Ivan Simpson, who played the dean of English and who Gauss felt sure was a kindred intellectual spirit. At these parties you always meet an old girl, married to a man twice your size who uses expressions like "Shuteye" and "Long time no see". Drinks are likely to be blue or come in tinted glasses.

You can't expect to have your second act curtain until the night before you hit Broadway. You are certain that two actors are going to get tonsilitis and you are likely to demand a run-through at quarter to seven. Meredith's (Buzz) girls are pretty sure to put lines in your play and so is the producer's secretary and a middle-aged woman in brown you never identify. Some of these lines are good and they stay in.

During rehearsal you discover that your prettiest lines do not cross the footlights, because they are too pretty, or an actor can't say them, or an actress doesn't know what they mean. There comes the horrible realization that phrases like "Yes you were." or "No I won't" are better and more effective than the ones you slaved over; especially the ones that survived the eleventh re-write. On the thirteenth day of rehearsal, the play suddenly makes no sense to you and does not seem to be written in English. You wonder why you wrote it and have a wild intention to ask the producer to postpone it a year. In this state you are likely to fall into the orchestra pit or find yourself taking an actress to Jackson Heights in a cab. She will praise Benchley and Perelman and ask you if you believe there are people in real life like those in Tobacco Road. You will only have a twenty-dollar bill and she will pay the cab. Your wife will wonder until she dies why you had to take the girl home and why you don't know more about the play if you attended every rehearsal.

At least a thousand more people will ask you where you got the guts to do it and your agent will arrange a pattern of rest for you and a quota of drinks.

On the opening night in New York you will decide not to see the show, but you will; standing in the rear, expecting door-knobs to come loose, lights not to light, entrances not to be made, and actors to put in new lines. You will remember W. H. Davies' "What is life then, if we cannot stand and stare like sheep and cows?" None of these things will happen, but you will go out for a drink when the scene comes up that never was done right in rehearsal or out of town. —It will be done perfectly. Some actress will tell you, at the bar, that she always gets diarrhea on opening night because all actresses do. You will then decide to watch the second act back stage and guys you haven't seen before will call you "Mack" and "Buddy" and push you around. Watch out that you don't pick up an important prop from the prop table and forget what you did with it. Don't walk through any door, or you will find yourself on stage. At least one actor will have a comic drunken uncle, also an actor, at liberty, who will wander on stage and say, "Do you people want any pressing done?". Doors of dressing rooms should be left ajar, since actresses can close them in such a way that it takes a carpenter to get them open.

At the beginning of the third act you will be appalled by the fact that everyone is whispering and that the crosses have been slowed down. You will then be sure that they are doing the first act over again. This is because of third-act ear drum, which makes everything sound dim and causes important lines to sound like "Did you find the foursome in the two green bags?". It is now time to go to the bar again where you will find a large man in a tuxedo, who walked out on the play. He will tell you that he hasn't sat all the way through a show since "The Lion and the Mouse". You will get back to the theatre in time to see Dick Watts running for his typewriter. He will say something to you that sounds like "Organ recital; vested fever". You will not be able to mingle with the people coming out; the best thing is to go bravely back stage; but at this point you are on your own. Whatever happens, avoid Marc Connelly. He told Nugent that we had given Brahms Fifth to a man with a mandolin. Fortunately for us, there isn't any Brahms Fifth. This is the only real comfort I can give you. Best of luck and God bless you.

Jim(26)

The Male Animal opened at the Cort Theatre (where, coincidentally, Gibbs's *Season in the Sun* opened) on Tuesday evening, January 9, 1940. As Thurber later wrote Gibbs, he watched disbelievingly from the back row, but he wasn't surprised when, after the final curtain, there was a great clamor and shouts of "Author! Author!" He took his bows, made a curtain speech, and loved every second of it. At several parties afterwards, he showed supreme confidence in their winning good reviews and the Pulitzer Prize. At least he was right about the reviews, which found the play to be well above the usual Broadway romantic-comedy fare. It was, the critics agreed, a palatable way for the theatregoer to take his dose of social conscience. "There is more than meets the funny bone in this scrawled lampoon on the civilized male at bay," Brooks Atkinson of the *Times* said the next morning, in one of his less memorable lines. The critics compared it favorably with *The Man Who Came to Dinner* and *Life with Father*, the other comedy smashes of that sterling season. Richard Watts, reviewing the work of his Bleeck's drinking friend, to his relief liked the play, which was made even more attractive for him "because I fell instantly and hopelessly in love with Gene Tierney," as he put it. *The Male Animal* was a commercial and artistic hit.

"Jamie was always a great 21 guy," Helen said. "He had lived the 21–Tony's life before, God knows, so all that wasn't new to him. But then, after the success of the play, New York City was all his, and he ate it up. He was asked for autographs—although not too much, since he didn't have a visual fame, really—and he drank, well, only a little more than usual. But how he loved the attention and gregariousness at 21!"

Thurber was rich and famous all over again. He could pay off his debts with the royalties and subsidiary rights, and he was suddenly in a position to do pretty much what he pleased with his life. 1940 was consequently a slow year for him at the *New Yorker*, and Ross was miffed. (Ross was also proud of his golden boy; on opening night he telephoned his grudging congratulations, after reading the rave reviews.) Whatever creative time Thurber could spare from "21-ing," as Helen called it, was spent doing such things as drawing scenes from *The Male Animal* for *Life* and illustrating the ads and window cards to help Richard Maney's promotion.

"Jamie handed out tickets to all of Ohio, it seemed," Helen said. "I was in charge of dispensing house seats, and that damn phone never stopped ringing. I never had time to eat. My weight dropped to 102 pounds and I got a case of anemia. I had to go to the hospital." Besides the scary setback of Helen's illness, there was another even more frightening eyesight incident. Thurber was examined by Dr. Bruce, who set a firm date for a cataract-extraction operation in June. For Helen's recuperation and to fortify themselves for the coming ordeal, they went to Bermuda for the remainder of the winter and the spring—with two weeks out to stand a deathwatch over Helen's father in Newport, Rhode Island. From Bermuda, he wrote Herman Miller, who had just given up his teaching job to become a full-time writer:

... What happened was that Helen and I both went to pieces physically at once, nervously, and mentally, too, I guess. I have been until just a few days ago a shadow of my former self, a shell, a relic, and an old pooh-pooh. From about the time of your first letter I began to lose grip, what with rewriting the damn play, staying up too late arguing and fussing, smoking too early in the day and too often, and drinking too much. The tryouts in Princeton and Baltimore took a lot out of us and the New York opening more. We should have ducked right then but we tarried and had to submit to interviews and god knows what else every day for weeks; I also had to do most of the publicity drawings and stories. We didn't get a moment of rest or quiet and nobody heard from us at all. Every day I counted on being able to write, but I just wasn't. I figure we both lost about ten pounds—I was described in interviews as "emaciated", "painfully thin", "peaked", "moribund" and "washed up." Helen's collapse was fast and bad: she was taken to the hospital where she stayed two weeks with a blood count so low they were scared to death of leucoemia or leuchoemia or whatever it is. She only had six red corpuscles left and four white ones. They jabbed her full of liver extract and she gradually came up out of the vale. Meanwhile I was down in bed in the hotel, running a fever, seeing mice with boxing gloves on, and the like.

They finally bundled us on a ship for Bermuda and we are just now beginning to get some color in the cheeks and some flesh on the bones. And the strength and the spirit to be able to write a letter. We have rented through May a lovely old house down here on a turquoise bay with birds and flowers all about. The weather has just got fine and the light bright enough for me to see by—for my eyes took a header with the rest of me and for a while all I could see was the larger Neon signs and 45-point type. That also kept me from quill and typewriter ...

Our house is really called "Les Revenants," which my limited French tells me means ghosts. If you know of a more soothing translation, please let us know ...

The only ideas I have had down here haven't been much. I'm going to do a book of animal drawings for young and old, with text describing them: the bandicoot, the platypus, the coatimundi, Bosman's potto, the aardvark, and half a hundred others. The kind of easy and soothing idea that a broken-down playwright gets. The only book I've read has been "Bernadette of Lourdes", the amazing and well-written story of the little girl who saw the visions, done by a woman psychologist with no monkey business or shenanigans. It struck me there was a play in that. I wish you would read it.

Our play got good notices and happened to click fast—it's like tossing a coin, I guess.

What ideas have you got for plays? It seems to me that you are probably a natural born playwright. Maybe we could get together on something.

There are some naturals in "Bernadette", such as when the unfriendly priests and local officials try to argue her out of her "Lady", or scare her into denials —none of which worked for they were talking with a little girl who thought she saw the Virgin and who therefore, for all her purposes, did see her. "What language did she speak to you in?" snapped a priest. "In the patois of the region," said the girl. "Hah," he said, "the Virgin doesnt understand that language," To which Bernadette said, "How do you know she doesn't?" Score: 15-love.

Then one day Bernadette came to them and said her lady had asked for a shrine and a procession, and did that have them beside themselves with fear, doubt and uncertainty: was this a lot of goddam nonsense for which the little girl should be quietly put away somewhere, or had the Lady picked out Lourdes as a place in which she wanted a shrine and a procession? Put her away, said some. How are you going to do that, said others, when there will be four thousand people from miles around at the grotto tomorrow at dawn waiting for her to come down there? It was a beautiful and lovely and exciting mix-up, the story of the little French girl who saw the Virgin. You cant put a saint in jail. Why not? If she's a real saint, she'll get out. Um, hm, and what will you say to the Prefect then. Finally the Emperor of France got in on it.

The thing would have to be done with great care and tenderness and more understanding of what priests say to curés and curés say to monseigneurs than I have—but I do know what prefects say to mayors and what mayors say to little girls . . .

One reason I had wanted to write you was to tell you that my book called "Fables For Our Time and Famous Poems Illustrated" which was to have come out last fall but was put by until spring in favor of The Last Flower, has been dedicated as follows: For Herman and Dorothy. That dedication page was set up months ago. You'll get the first copy when it comes off the presses . . .

If you need any money for cheese and crackers until the checks begin coming in, there is no one you know who would more happily, or could more easily, thanks to Broadway, send it. *Dont forget that.*

Jim(27)

CHAPTER 15

"They're going to put you away if you don't quit acting like this." (1)

Even with the pleasant weather and company in Bermuda, life piled up for the Thurbers again. The lingering death of Helen's father was a trial; then the news about the same time that Mame Thurber had skin cancer and would have to go through an operation that summer; and, most depressing of all, Dr. Bruce's disclosure that Thurber's cataract would require not just one but two operations, in June and October. "Everything hit us at once," Thurber said.(2)

His eyesight in Bermuda improved enough so that he could read from time to time, but he didn't con himself. He wrote a progress report to Dr. Bruce from Bermuda in the spring of 1940:

Dear Dr. Bruce:

I wonder whether you know about Hints on the Care of the Eye for Young Ladies as outlined by De Quincey a hundred years ago. "The depth and subtlety of the eyes varies exceedingly with the state of the stomach, and, if young ladies were aware of the magical transformations which can be wrought in the depth and sweetness of the eye by a few weeks' exercise, I fancy we should see their habits in this point altered greatly for the better." That's all he had to say.

I dont know about depth and sweetness, but what I allude to laughingly as the "power" of my eye seems to be about what it was when I saw you. I probably see as well as the water buffalo, reputedly the blindest of all large jungle animals. It is interesting to note that the water buffalo can lick a tiger in spite of his opacities and indifferent, if not, indeed, detached retina.

My opacities, or spaniel hair, as I like to call them give me lots more annoyance than my buffalo sight. Since I cant see very far beyond them, I sometimes just sit and look at them. I am familiar with all the new shifts they make and could draw an accurate map of the whole dirty brown constellation. (If I actually did, the Bermudians might think it was a map of the islands and put me in the military jail).

I was thinking the other day that you might be interested in the charts of my

eye kept by the late Dr. C.F. Clarke, of Columbus and now in the office of his
son (or nephew) a younger Dr. Clarke. I think there are about forty feet of
readings, findings, and soundings. I could not have been more than 10 when he
first examined me and I went to him off and on for fifteen or twenty years, I
think. I thought this might be of some help about the time of appearance of the
opacities. I remember how Dr. Clarke, who was supposed to be a good eye man
(as good eye men in Ohio go), was all during the years I saw him astonished that
I could see as well as I could, and would call in other eye men and show me
off to them, whereupon they would all exclaim, as if they had been watching
a contortionist. He said there was a "veil" or something through which I saw.
That may have been something else again. There are more things in my eye
than were dreamed of in Horatio's day, anyway, or maybe Hamlet had opacities
and thought they were ghosts. This would also explain Macbeth's looking at
nothing at all in the banquet scene and shouting "Take any other form than
that!" I think I know how he felt, if it was opacities he saw and not Banquo.

We get back June 6th and I'll get in touch with you right away . . .

They did return in early June and they rented a 1775 red-brick house
on the village green in Sharon, Connecticut, a red-brick's throw from
the imposing Buckley family estate. Sharon was selected because it was
near Lime Rock, where Helen's widowed mother lived, and it seemed
like a suitably green and serene town for a preoperative patient to calm
his jitters in. They had taken a favorite Bermuda maid and a butler–
chauffeur back to Sharon with them. Life eased a bit. Then, all too soon,
it was time for his first operation. Thurber checked into the Institute of
Ophthalmology at Columbia Presbyterian Medical Center in mid-June
for a week's stay, just before his mother's six-week stint in the same
hospital for her skin-cancer operation.

The cataract extraction was performed by Dr. Bruce and was considered a success. There was a remission, but later in the summer his sight
began to fog again. In the familiar territory of the Sharon house, he was
able to navigate easily, but during a visit to the Gudes on Martha's
Vineyard, he stumbled and barked his shins a lot. For the first time, he
was afraid to walk alone. He was generally cheerful, however, with the
horrors of another operation in October and the world's political collapse getting to him only occasionally. He wrote the Williamses:

. . . I have not had a very good summer in my mind, it being full of dark
gibbering figures dressed in black bombazine with lamb's blood on it, whilst in
the background scamper the gray wet bodies of dozens of little cheeping wail-
wice and grunting chudhubs and small round mailbacked creeblies whose
scales come off in your hand and stick to you like wet onion skin . . .

It is almost time for me to go back to Hospy-wospy for more monkey business. I can't see any better but I don't see much worse and can write on the type-writer with ease, having just finished and sold a 7500 word story to the Sat Eve Post, a baseball story, which won't be printed until next year because I got it in too late. Ross wrote me when he found this out that for two months he has been going around in his stocking feet shushing everybody and talking sadly about how I couldn't see anything smaller than the sign made of flowers and reading ELYRIA to guide the airmen flying over that Ohio town. Now, he says, I find you are writing serials for the Saturday Evening Post . . .

Of course I get into some trouble on account of not seeing too good. "Do you raise them?" I said to a lady on a bus. "Raise what?" she says. "Those chickens like the one you have in your lap," I said. She pulled the emergency cord and brought the bus to a halt and got off at the corner of Mobray and Pineberry Street in Jersey City. What she had on her lap was a white handbag. I may be put away any day now by the authorities . . . (3)

The baseball story for the *Saturday Evening Post* (the magazine he ridiculed a couple of years before) was just about the only decent work Thurber published between June, 1940, and August, 1941. Ross had good reason to complain, since all he was receiving from Thurber was some spot drawings, mostly of dogs. (Thurber usually drew his dogs to fill gaps in composition.) The *Post* story is called "You Could Look It Up," one of Thurber's funniest nonfirst-person pieces. It concerns a fictional midget, given the lovely name of Pearl du Monville, who is hired as a surprise pinch hitter by a slumping baseball team—with, of course, the intention of his drawing a base-on-balls every time he is at bat. It was written as a salute to Ring Lardner, complete with Lardnerian malapro-pisms. (Life boldly aped art when Bill Veeck, then the owner of the lamentable St. Louis Browns, signed on the three-foot-seven Eddie Gaedel in 1951, Veeck being a Thurber fan from way back. Veeck's Gaedel walked during his one time at bat, while Thurber's du Monville was thrown out at first with the bases loaded when he tried to belt the ball, against all instructions to the contrary.) "You Could Look It Up" was a favorite of Grantland Rice, Red Smith, and Harold Ross.

Meanwhile, in August *The Male Animal* closed on Broadway and reopened in Chicago to a milder reception. It continued its run on the road till the following spring. (There was some talk of Thurber playing Nugent's Tommy Turner role on the last night of the Broadway run, but his eyesight didn't permit it.) Money was not a major worry, thanks to the movie sale of the play. But unable or uninspired to draw cartoons or write casuals for the *New Yorker*, Thurber started to doubt his talents between operations. Ross complained but he also understood that

Thurber was going through a difficult period and needed time to get back on the writing track. When the old *New Yorker* hand Ralph Inger-soll took over the crusading newspaper *PM*, he invited Thurber to write and do spot drawings for a twice-weekly column, "If You Ask Me," about anything Thurber wanted to say, at a hundred dollars a column. Thurber needed this unexacting, confidence-boosting literary freedom more than the money. He accepted the offer and received Ross's grouchy blessing.

The *PM* columns, knocked out from September, 1940, to July, 1941, were notable mainly as therapy for a writer and artist who feared he was no longer fully able to write and draw. Relaxed sometimes to the point of drowsiness, the pieces allowed Thurber to get in some small lumps—against Will Rogers's 1926 encomium to Mussolini, women who don't answer letters, radio ball-game interruptions, long-winded writ-ers like Thomas Wolfe, famous Nazis, and tennis-reporting errors. They are reminiscent of his Columbus *Dispatch* "Credos and Curios" col-umns, but with considerably more polish and professionalism, of course. A few of them even found their way into later Thurber collections, but most were thin imitations of "Talk of the Town" pieces. Still, the news-paper's readers could consider themselves lucky to have this serendip in the bright pages. And, as it turned out, Thurber could consider himself lucky to have this literary therapy available to him in what was to be the most crucial year of his life so far.

They had to give up the Sharon house in October, the month set for the second operation, but they took another house in nearby Salisbury as a likely recuperation spot during the winter. The second operation was technically for secondary glaucoma and for iritis, which dated back to the sympathetic ophthalmia of his childhood accident. Before Thurber checked into the Institute, his surgeon's problems were com-pounded by some strange requests from the patient's mother, Mame. She wrote Dr. Bruce on October 10th:

Dear Dr. Bruce:

I am writing you in regard to my son James—in whom we are all interested —and naturally being his mother I am [a] little worried about his condition— as only having the one eye. I want you to know we all have *implicit* confidence in you and know he could not be in better hands and I feel everything will come out O.K.

Now please do not think me *foolish* or *childish* if I tell you I am interested in Astrology—and we all know it is a Science—and does work out in most cases. The time set—Oct. 22nd for the operation so happens to be a "perfect time" according to Astrology—I believe his wife wrote me—early in P.M.

Now if it could be after 1:30—Eastern Standard Time—would be *ideal*—but if anytime before this hour—*according* to his Planets would not give such good results—so if you could change it—(if you had in mind before 1:30) to a little later hour if convenient to you—if only to please the *mother*—I'd thank you very much indeed—if it does not interfere with your plans. The time he was and had his other operation was also a very good time for him as I told his wife—I know it would be O.K. and it was, but remember it was done also by an *expert* oculist which means everything too.

When I was in hospital in N.Y. last June—my operation day and time was set by my Astrologer and I came out fine in every way—and at my age—74—and only weighing 85 lbs. it didn't look very encouraging—but with an *expert* surgeon—which I had also and Planets in right position—I came out of it and am very well indeed—and I surprised every one with my rapid recovery.

James knows I am interested in Astrology—but he wouldn't wish me to interfere with your plans—if exact time is set—I mean the hour—I am sure you understand with the *best* oculist in N.Y. and correct time it will be bound to come out all right.

I am enclosing stamp but it isn't necessary for you to take the time to answer as I know how valuable your time is but will know what ever you do will be satisfactory to me.

Most sincerely,
and with Best Wishes

Mary A. Thurber

(Mrs. Chas)

Then, two days later, she sent this afterthought to Dr. Bruce, suggesting, movingly, a guilt going back almost forty years:

Dear Dr. Bruce:

I was just thinking—as I understand *wonderful* things are being done at the Eye Institute.

In case Jim's operation wouldn't be a success or should get worse afterwards —wouldn't it be possible to graft an eye so that he could be able to see? I mean, this is only *in case* it would not come out as you expect it to—we are all very hopeful and I feel in my heart he will be O.K. but I just meant—it could be done —but with the time set and your skill and confidence of Jim and all the rest of us in you he is bound to come out with flying colors—I know I am perfectly willing and would gladly give him one of my eyes—I have really very good eyes —my age and all—I only wear glasses for very fine print is all. I write all my letters without glasses—my father and mother were past 80 when they died and neither one ever wore glasses only reading fine print as I do—so Jim has a good inheritance you see—well—just know I feel "all will be well"—but as you know —I do feel a little concerned—he is such a darling boy and has accomplished so much and needs his eye to continue his work, and I feel God will give him even better sight than before.

Excuse me for taking up so much of your time.

Sincerely yours,

Mary A. Thurber(4)

Dr. Bruce, "like a damn fool," as he put it, went along with Mame's astrological request, scheduling the operation for after 1:30 P.M. on October 22nd. He told Thurber about his mother's plea and Thurber "laughed his head off." A no-nonsense man of science, Dr. Bruce said that Mame, whom he had previously met, was "as nutty as a fruitcake," and added, "Jim's father was an oddball, too. It makes you wonder about genetics. Jim was the only Thurber who ever amounted to anything." The possibility of an eye transplant, which Mame proposed, was out of the question, Dr. Bruce explained, since "the wire of his telephone was deteriorating, and putting in a new mouthpiece wouldn't help." The surgeon had grown increasingly fond of Thurber; the operations were almost as emotional for him as for his patient. "My knife didn't shake, though," he said. "But I felt sad because I knew there was less and less chance of success. I loved the guy like a brother."

Dr. Bruce's skill and Mame's astrology were not enough. The secondary glaucoma and iritis recurred. Thurber suffered a good deal of pain and clouded vision after surgery, and he had to remain in the hospital thirty-one days. At one point, he was bothered by two black spots that kept looming through the clouds. "They look like eightballs," he told Dr. Bruce. "You would be behind *two* eightballs," the doctor said.(5) The thirty-one days were too much for Thurber; he grew to despise the very idea of the hospital, any hospital. Helen felt at the time that Dr. Bruce wasn't telling them the whole truth about Thurber's prognosis, and she was probably correct. Thurber adored relating how doctors found it miraculous that he could see at all after his childhood accident, since he had "lost all apparatus for sight." This was not true. "Jim had a sharper visual imagination than others," Dr. Bruce explained. "Many other blind writers had the same thing. He claimed he could see with his eyes closed. This wasn't hallucination, but the result of phosphenes. His line about being a living miracle was the result of my encouraging him by saying, 'Keep up the good work and you'll be a miracle man.' People hang on to more than they have. He read into what I said and made more of it than there was. Once, when he told me in the hospital that he saw a bird very clearly, I didn't discourage him. It was a handle of hope."

Thurber became so restive in the hospital ("His bed was shaking most of the time," said Dr. Bruce) that a psychiatrist was called in, and, when that didn't calm the patient, a Catholic priest turned up. Thurber liked the priest, not for any spiritual solace he offered but because the priest enjoyed talking sports with him. Finally, Thurber was discharged and was taken to a suite in the Hotel Grosvenor, where day-and-night nurses and Helen took turns administering eye drops and eye-bathing solutions. Over Christmas, they felt he was well enough to go to the house in Salisbury, but within a few days the iritis flared up again and he had to be rushed back to the Ophthalmological Institute. The Salisbury house was abandoned as a hopeless project, and the Thurbers sublet an apartment on Washington Square West. One of their nurses didn't help matters any by contracting measles, leaving Helen as the chief eye-bather and cheerer-upper. When he felt a little better, Thurber and Joel Sayre worked together on an idea for a movie of *My Life and Hard Times*, but nothing much came of it. And Ross broached ways for Thurber to see better mechanically, but nothing much came of them, either. "Jamie was most unhappy at not being able to work," Helen said, "but his spirit was still holding up, somehow."

His spirit, however, plummeted over the next six months. It reflected the fragility of a blind man's temper, when he can no longer put his complete trust in human beings, animals, and devices, when he is at everything's mercy and constantly menaced. An unbelievable three more operations were performed, with, like the other two, just local anesthesia: two discissions, or cross incisions of the scar tissue over the lens to allow light to pass, and, finally, in May of 1941, a glaucoma procedure, in which fluid was drained from the eyeball in order to relieve pressure on the optic nerve and retina. It was the glaucoma that ultimately produced blindness, for after the last operation, Thurber was indeed legally blind. He had gone under the knife five times in one year, had suffered extraordinary pain and depression, and, after all that, he was blind.

Through it all, Thurber had displayed singular guts and grit, despite his plummeting spirit. As Helen wrote the Williamses in Bermuda (just before Ronnie Williams left for war duty with the Royal Navy): "I cannot think of anyone else, at least among our little group in New York, who could have gone through it and come out sane. But of course his brand of sanity was always different from anyone else's, and that probably helped."(6) Thurber, in the same letter, said: "They dragged old Jamie through all the corridors of hell, where I left most of my weight and two thirds of my nerves, but things have quieted down now, and after one more operation in the fall, I should be able to see again, normally." The proposed sixth operation in the fall—the last and most panacean—was offered as perhaps the largest handle of hope by Dr. Bruce, although he doubted whether it would be of any use, or even take place. Meanwhile, he advised the Thurbers to get away for the summer and relax as best they could. They rented a big house in Chilmark, on Martha's Vineyard, not far from the Gudes.

Ensconced at the Chilmark house with Helen and the two Bermuda servants, Thurber began to write again. He had to adopt new mechanics for his craft; he set words down in soft pencil on yellow copy paper (about twenty scraggly words to the page), without really being able to read what he had written, and Helen would copy the draft on a typewriter. Revisions were done in his head, thanks to his remarkable memory. It was the most expedient method for a blind writer with a blessed memory, but an unsatisfactory substitute for the meticulous methods Thurber used before. Far stranger was what he wrote, not how he wrote.

Besides his few remaining *PM* columns (getting darker by the week), he started work on three *New Yorker* short stories and, of all things, a children's book. The first story, "The Whip-Poor-Will," seethes with despairing madness ("It came somewhere out of a grim fear in the back of my mind," he later said in an interview).(7) It is about a man named Kinstrey who, while summering on an island like Martha's Vineyard, hallucinates to the chilling accompaniment of a whip-poor-will, in the manner of Poe's "nevermore" raven. As Kinstrey's "nerves get the best" of him, despite his wife's encouragement to use (pun firmly intended by Thurber) his "will power," he goes careering off the deep end. The very words "whip," "poor," and "will" unhinge him, as does the black maid's information that where she comes from a whip-poor-will singing near the house means imminent death. With his injured mind jangling with "whip-poor-will" and attendant puns, still half in hallucination, he kills his wife, two servants, and himself with a long carving knife, first asking one of the servants, "Who do you do first?"

The story was snapped up by the *New Yorker* and a pleased, if alarmed, Ross. When it was published in early August, other alarmed friends wrote Helen and asked, only half-jokingly, "Are you all right?" A few were truly worried about both of them, to say nothing of the servants. "When I look back on it," Helen said, "the knife seemed a symbol for all the cutting Jamie had gone through that year. He thought he was being castrated with all that cutting."

He also worked on "A Friend to Alexander" and "The Cane in the Corridor," both as unorthodox as "The Whip-Poor-Will." The first story

is really a companion piece to "The Whip-Poor-Will," only the protagonist, Andrews, hallucinates an intimate relationship with Aaron Burr
and Alexander Hamilton, taking the latter's side in their celebrated
duel. Andrews comes to feel he must dispatch Burr before he can harm
Hamilton, and practices with a pistol, terrifying everybody. Again, off
the deep end, Andrews dies of a mysterious heart attack, his fingers
frozen around an imaginary pistol. "The Cane in the Corridor," an
intricate, mean, unThurberish story with some superbly turned dialogue, involves an attempt by the hero, who had recently been hospitalized, to seek cruel revenge against a friend who hadn't visited him.
Alcohol flows through the piece like the Monongahela, supplying the
fuel for the ultimate triumph of vengeance. It is unThurberish in its
inherent meanness, but it is also highly autobiographical in that it
sprung, fully clothed and venemous, from Wolcott Gibbs's squeamish
failure to visit Thurber after any of his eye operations. In that dark and
grim period of convalescence from "the corridors of hell," the worst,
the angriest, the maddest in him came pouring forth.

Perhaps Thurber in his calmer moments sensed this, even as he
scrawled his unseen words on yellow copy paper, for as the summer
wore on he began to write a simple fairy tale for children, called *Many
Moons.* He mentioned it in a determinedly holographic letter to the
Whites:

Dear Andy & Katharine:

I keep expecting to write to you any day, or to hear from you. It is easier for
you all because you dont have to scribble away in the dark, like this. My new
glasses . . . bring everything three feet nearer than it was and even enable me
to see the pencil more and the faint black track it leaves. (I cant see the words).

Your publishers sent up formal release papers to be signed for the pieces of
mine you selected for the book. [*A Sub-treasury of American Humor,* edited
by the Whites and published in 1941.] I approve of the choice . . .

I have just finished the first draft of a fairy tale—its about 1500 words long and
I thought might make a Christmas book, with colorful illus. by some colorful
artist . . . (8)

". . . with colorful illus. by some colorful artist . . ." That signalled the
end, to all intents and purposes, of his drawing. The draftsman of *The
Last Flower* had pretty much concluded that, handles of hope aside, an
enormous part of his life and career was coming to a rapid close. There
would be precious few Thurber men, women, and dogs drawn any
more.

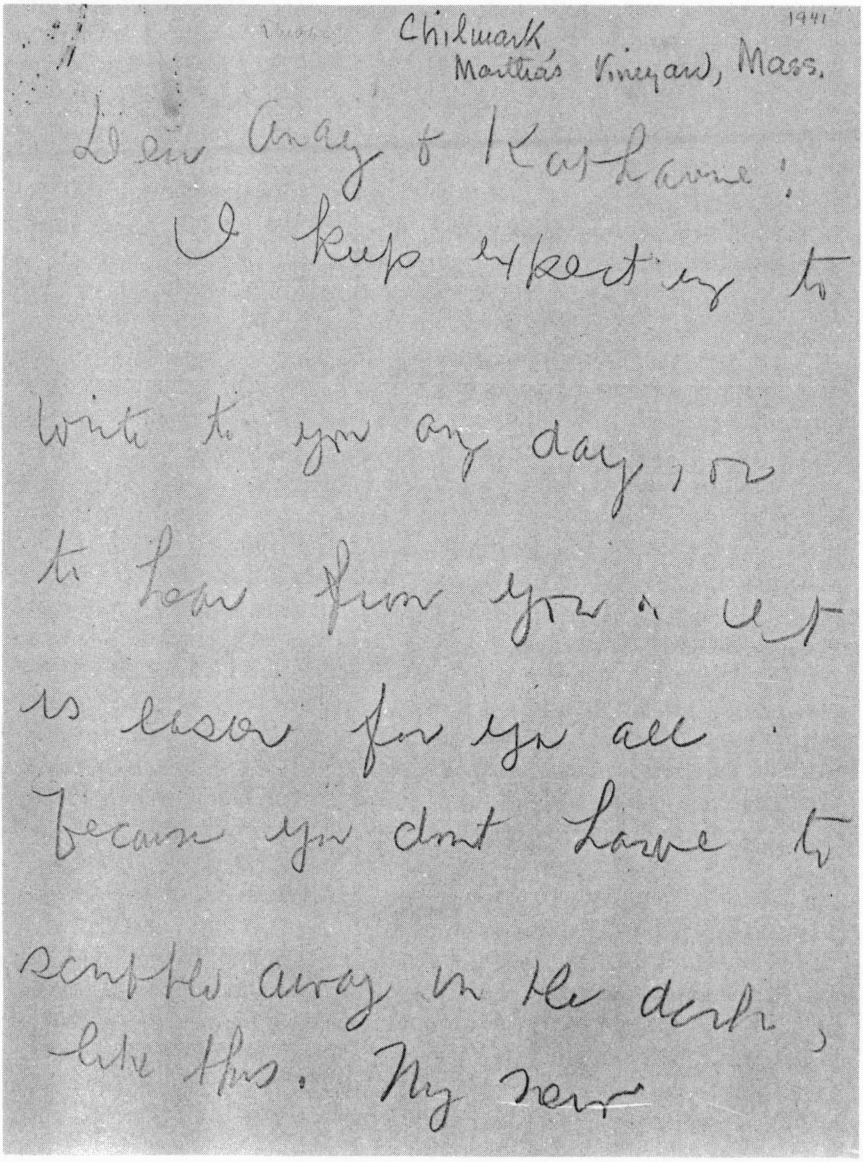

Chilmark,
Martha's Vineyard, Mass.

Dear Craig & Katharine:

I keep expecting to

write to you any day, or

to hear from you, & yet

is easier for you all

because you dont have to

scribble away in the dark,

like this. My new

The writing of the "horror stories," as Helen called them, and the sudden switch to a child's fairy tale were clarion signs of impending trouble. Sure enough, about midsummer, all hell broke loose. There was another flare-up of iritis. Fortunately, Dr. Arnold Knapp, a noted oculist and colleague of Dr. Bruce, was vacationing in Edgartown, at the other end of Martha's Vineyard. He blamed the flare-up on too much sun glare and treated the iritis, but the discomfort of yet another eye inflammation was too much for Thurber. "He was suddenly nervous all the time," Helen recalled. "There were lots of parties and Jamie was drinking—but cheerlessly, without singing or chatting with the others. After drinking, he threw up, which made me positive he was seriously sick. I was puzzled by it all and worn out myself, almost as worn out as he was. He also had what I suppose was a castration complex from all the surgery. He felt he could never make love to anybody again—just as he believed he couldn't really draw or write any more—and the result was he wanted to make love to me all the time. It was just so sad. He would wake me up, shaking, and I would give him a drink to calm him down and then talk to him. He liked to hear me talking to him; it made him feel more secure, as if he was with a group of people."

His burst of work on the fairy tale was a kind of escape therapy for him. The idea of writing something just for children had apparently been in his mind for many years, and it picked this tragic time to emerge. He worked tirelessly at it, then pronounced it finished one hot afternoon, and promptly flew to pieces. "He told me he wanted to move in with the Gudes," Helen said, "that he couldn't be alone in the house with me and that he had to be surrounded by lots of people. I didn't know what else to do, so I went along with it. The Gudes were marvelously understanding. They gave us their guest room and put up with some awful behavior. Jamie would sit in the Gudes' living room, with the clatter of kids and guests going on around him, and stare straight ahead, like a schizo, looking inside himself and finding nothing there. The Gude children didn't pay much attention to him, thank goodness, and everyone in that house was stalwart and fine through it all. Finally, a doctor was called in—a woman named Ruth Fox, who lived nearby and specialized in alcoholism treatment. She gave Jamie massive shots of vitamin B-1 and made him promise to cut down on his drinking. She came every evening before his bedtime, when he couldn't sleep for the d.t.'s. She continued the B-1 shots after we returned to New York, which caused a black streak in his hair in front. People thought I got up every morning and dyed Jamie's hair. After Dr. Fox, Jamie slowly began to pull out of his tailspin, as he called it. But it was hell while it lasted."

It was hell for the Gudes, too, but they were remarkably devoted friends. Jap Gude, who, in 1941, was still a producer for C.B.S. in New York, recalled that he was telephoned by his wife from Martha's Vineyard. She told him that Thurber was hallucinating and having a nervous breakdown, and that he and Helen had moved into the Gude house. Gude rushed to the Vineyard to help out. "I found Jim propped up in bed, shaking and drenched with perspiration," Gude said. "He told me he didn't want to be alone with his wife, for some reason. I held his hand and said we would all be there to help him. I guess he knew his sight was going for good and he simply couldn't face it. But his biggest worry then was being committed. He grabbed my arm so tightly he bruised it and said, 'Promise me you won't let them put me away.' I promised, but I wasn't so sure. Jim was also terrified by some erectionless ejaculations he had been having. He was a mess, all right. Finally, my wife suggested calling in Dr. Fox. She slowly brought him around and told Helen that Jim should be under a psychiatrist's care. He continued to see Dr. Fox when he was back in New York. He also saw a lady psychiatrist Joel Sayre recommended. Sayre and the Coateses were on the Vineyard pitching in, too, and Althea dropped off Rosemary for a visit after Jim and Helen returned to their rented house."

Thurber's partial recovery in late August was a glorious victory for him, physically and mentally. He was able to handwrite Dr. Bruce, who was about to become a U.S. Navy doctor serving with the Marines, this rather healthy letter:

Dear Gordon,

Four weeks ago today I went into a tailspin, crashed, and burst into flames. This is to let you know that I am rapidly getting into shape again. B–1 injections, haliver oil and luminol have helped tremendously. It seems that the nerve exhaustion Russell detected just wasn't being helped enough by Vita-Caps. I have to have more help than that, for I had been hanging on by my fingernails for a hell of a long time. Even through the worst days, I began to gain weight, which I had not done. The Lord, who keeps doing all He can for me, sent in Dr. Ruth Fox, who is a gal with a fine background in neurology, and she pulled me out of it with great skill and understanding.

The things that inhabit the woods I fell into are not nice. I never want to crash there again if I can help it. Helen, my Scotch wife, has been like three nurses rolled into one, and has stood up under it all like the Black Watch.

I paid little attention to the eye during the battle of Chilmark, and strained it in the sun, as Helen told you, I think. Well, we found that uncle Arnold Knapp was up here, so we crashed in on him, knowing you would approve. He was very kind and helpful, suggested scapalomine and compresses, once a day. The eye began to whiten and is almost all white now. I saw him three times. He even made two little jokes, too. We said little about the nerves, as all he would say to that was humph-humph.

We are to call Knapp tomorrow to report, and I doubt if we will have to see him again.

I began writing a play in the midst of all the hell. They call me Iron Man Thurber.

We will be here until the 15th, and then to N.Y. for the winter.

We both hope you and your family had a good vacation. You have one coming to you.

Look out for bows and arrows.

As ever,
Jim(9)

(Dr. Bruce might well have humph-humphed, too. He later remarked that the five eye operations didn't necessarily make him fear for Thurber's sanity. "Others have taken much worse operations without having nervous breakdowns," he said.)

It was for the Whites that Thurber reserved his brightest, almost childish optimism. A late-summer holographic letter to them read:

Dear Andy & Katharine:

It was swell to get your fine letters. I have been in a tailspin and power dive combined which was awful, but I am pulling out of it with the help of Dr. Ruth Fox, Helen, the Gudes and the Coateses and Sayre, who was here for a few days. I simply cracked wide open and it has been frightful, almost insupportable, but now I'm fighting back. I have had to have hypos of B–1 and luminol, etc, and they are building me up. I think I may have to have help from a psychiatrist, for I got into a complex or two, the kind that frequently results from such things as I have been through . . .

The Coateses are with us now and that helps a lot.

I like the selections of mine you are using in your book, and am very proud to be so lavishly represented. You certainly took on a lot when you started on that venture.

I have a swell idea for a play which I want to get at. I need someone to help me on it, though. I want to do most of the actual writing, but talking it out with someone is important to me, especially now. I may get a girl in to dictate to, and wish I had Margaret Thurlow. She was up here for a day or two. I think the idea has more stuff than The Male Animal and will be funnier.

I wish I could sit around and tell the idea to you. It is a little hard to do it in pencil in a semidarkness . . .

I wrote a fairy tale just before I cracked up, and when it is copied, I want you to see it. I thought it might make a Christmas book, and would like your opinion. The whip-poor-will story was quite an achievement technically, since I wrote it longhand, on some eighty pieces of yellow paper, and since I had to use a new form of composition, doing all the rewriting in my head, before putting the final lines down. We—Helen and I—did a little cutting out later, but no rewriting. I was glad you liked it. Ross wrote me probably his longest known letter about it—some 800 words. He has been very good to me. The new word rate for casuals was partly my work, and the letter told all about that.

We would, of course, love to have a Minnie puppy, and it breaks our hearts that we wouldnt be just right for a dachshund just now. It has long been our dream to have six or eight variegated dogs when we buy our house in the country—a dachshund, a poodle, a water spaniel, etc. There is a wonderful black male poodle up here, name of Hugo . . .

I hope you can read this, but I dont see how the hell you can . . . God knows I have been down in the bowels of terror, but I have climbed out of it with what Dr. Fox thinks is remarkable speed.

I wont go on any further, because this will be task enough for you, the way it is. It's my first finished work of any kind in two weeks. It gives me lift and confidence to get back at my writing table. Helen will go over this and translate the most horribly garbled words. We love to hear from you, about your life and Minnie's and all, so write again before too long.

Love as always,
Jim.

There is nothing pathological about me, babies, just nerves. I used to think nervous breakdowns were not so terrible. I know now how wrong I was.

During his recuperation from the breakdown, an extraordinary meeting took place at a Vineyard beach party. As a consequence of it, a solid twenty-year friendship began. The meeting was between Thurber and Mark Van Doren, the irreplaceable poet, critic, and teacher. "I met this nearly blind man Thurber," Van Doren recalled, a year before his death, "and I was almost speechless. I could hardly say a word about eyes or sight or health. Also, he was a celebrity, and I don't like to pump celebrities. But he was soft and mild then, full of veneration for me as a professor. He had a thin wall of respect for English professors, a weakness for the species. I remember how soft his hands were—long, slender fingers like insect antennae when he reached for an ashtray, which he did just about all the time. We talked a little and he asked to see me again the next day.

"The following afternoon, we met and I led him to some chairs on the lawn of the house I was staying at. We talked some more about things, and then suddenly he began to cry. To see tears coming from those dead eyes was one of the most touching moments of my life. He was crying, he said, because he had always made fun of people and never praised them as I did. He asked me if I thought that blindness was a punishment for the writing he had done—being trivial and destructive and showing the weaknesses of others, instead of their goodness and strength. That made me uncomfortable, but I knew he was going through an emotional upheaval. Here was a man I admired as a wholly original writer and humorist—a truly unique person—and he was in despair because of his work. I told him that as a satirist he must be on the attack so he can point out the lack of goodness and intelligence in the world. It was such a simple answer, really, but it cheered him up. After a while, I had to bring myself up short and remember that he was blind. I was touched by Thurber then and I was always touched by him afterwards, even when he was in his fury."

As Helen Thurber put it, "Jamie poured out his heart to Mark, and Mark helped him get back on his feet that awful summer as much as anybody."

When the Thurbers finally abandoned Martha's Vineyard in the middle of September, they left behind—along with all the horrors and torments—the draft of the amiable fairy tale *Many Moons*. Thurber had quite simply forgot about it. A lot had happened to him since the afternoon he had declared it completed. The following spring, it was found in the Gudes' house by the caretaker. When it was published by Harcourt, Brace in September of 1943 (with colorful illustrations by colorful Louis Slobodkin), it was an immediate success and it is still selling well at Christmas and other times of the year. It won the American Library Association prize for best juvenile picture book, was made into a Burr Tillstrom television puppet show, and has been adapted for dramatization. An edition in braille was brought out by the American Printing House for the Blind.

The road to mental recovery took, by Thurber's own admission, five years to travel. Helen decided that it would be better for her husband's health to stay in New York City for a while. "He still had to see people," she said, "every night. He couldn't be alone, and I was a wraith with exhaustion." They checked into the Algonquin and set to the formidable task of healing Thurber.

The first step was to continue the Dr. Fox counselling and vitamin treatments. The second was to get Thurber to a good psychiatrist. A friend of the Sayres, Dr. Marian Kenworthy,* was on holiday in West-

---

*It is interesting that two of the few doctors Thurber wholly trusted were women. "My reputation as a woman-hating writer is largely myth and misconception," Thurber once

chester County, and Thurber was driven up to see her for a preliminary interview. He went in alone to talk to Dr. Kenworthy and drank a good deal of her whiskey during the interview, while Helen and the Sayres sat out on the lawn sipping beer. After three hours of this, Thurber emerged, happy and drunk, with the doctor. "Your husband no more needs psychiatric treatment than my dog does," Dr. Kenworthy told Helen. "Can I see your dog?" Helen replied. (The dog, apparently, was in good shape.) Dr. Kenworthy also advised that anybody would have cracked under the pain and strain of five eye operations (contrary to Dr. Bruce's opinion on the matter), and she said it was normal for Thurber to react neurotically. Thurber was, of course, uplifted by this diagnosis, since his greatest fear was still insanity and commitment, a fear harking back to his young manhood and his family history of "Thurber nervousness." So much for psychiatric treatment.

The third step was for Thurber to get back to work, and find a *modus operandi* for doing so. Dr. Bruce was off in the Navy, so the possibility of a sixth eye operation departed with him. It wouldn't have helped, anyway; his eye was too far gone. Aside from his blindness and erratic mental state, there was nothing to prevent Thurber from writing well again. He especially wanted to write more for the *New Yorker.* They sublet an apartment on East Fifty-fourth Street and Thurber started to sort out his career. It was obvious that he would have to learn to write by dictation. Ross sent over a *New Yorker* secretary, and, perversely, the first project they worked on together was a review of F. Scott Fitzgerald's *The Last Tycoon* for the *New Republic.* The book was read to him and a short essay on Fitzgerald was laboriously dictated, with mental revisions. The result was crisp and adoring. ("Writers who rewrite and rewrite until they reach the perfection they are after consider anything less than that perfection nothing at all," he said of Fitzgerald, and, obliquely, of himself.)(11) Not so adoring was a following review for the *New Republic* of John Steinbeck's *The Moon Is Down,* in which Thurber criticized Steinbeck for not making the Germans and their war bloody enough. The review caused a tiny tempest in a medium-sized teapot, as readers wrote in arguing about how bloody warfare and the Germans really were. At least, he was writing again. But what of the *New Yorker?* On October 20, 1941, he icily wrote Ross:

---

said. "Psychiatrists, however, always male, have offered to take me on for nothing after looking at a lot of my drawings. Women psychiatrists try to find out what is the matter with you, but the male ones love to show off their implementation and try out their nomenclature on you."(10)

Dear Mr. Ross:

After you suggested the other day that I try to do some captions for a sheaf of [Mary] Petty drawings which seems to have stacked up almost as high as the photostatic copies of rough sketches around the office, I got to thinking that it wouldn't be a bad idea to let me spend, say, two afternoons a week in the office not only trying to write captions to pictures, but also having a look at the captions to pictures which have been bought. Since I haven't sent in an idea drawing of my own for a year and a half, my beloved art meeting could hardly say that my criticisms were based on a sheaf of my drawings having just been rejected.

You already have filed away for your autobiography some 50 or 100 blasphemous notes from me on what is the matter with the magazine. Most of these were written, I suppose, just after I got 3 or 4 of my best drawings back. Now we are on a new basis, since I am a blind, gray-haired playwright who still has a great affection for the magazine and is still capable of indignation. It seems to me that something is the matter when the first 3 drawings in the magazine turn out the way they did in the issue of October 18. The parachutist, the man with the little fire extinguisher, and the man painting the sign ("Did he want this on white or rye?") should not have followed one right after the other. These are all definite gag ideas and belong to the rather labored formula type. Most of the great New Yorker captions have not had to depend on some character holding something: a parachute, a fire extinguisher, a cat-o'-nine-tails, or a tomahawk in the scalp. Just to quote a few of the great ones—"I'm the one that should be lying down somewhere," "Yeh, and who made 'em the best years?", "I want to report a winking man," "You're so good to me and I'm so tired of it all," "With you I have known peace, Lida, and now you say you're going crazy"—most of the great ones, I repeat, did not have to depend on somebody holding, wrapped up in, or pinned down by, any implement, invention, or piece of apparatus. The really great New Yorker drawings have had to do with people sitting in chairs, lying on the beach, or walking along the street. The easy answer the art meeting always gives to the dearth of ideas like the ones I am trying to describe is that they are hard to get or that nobody sends them in any more. It seems to me that the principal reason for this is that the artists take their cue from the type of drawing which they see constantly published in the magazine. Years ago I wrote a story for The New Yorker in which a woman who tried to put together a cream separator suddenly snarled at those who were looking at her and said, "Why doesn't somebody take this god damned thing away from me?" I want to help to take the cream separators, parachutes, fire extinguishers, paint brushes and tomahawks away from four-fifths of the characters that appear in The New Yorker idea drawings.

There are other things, too. It must have been 6 years ago that you told me drawings about psychoanalysts were terribly out of date. The next week I turned in one in which the analyst says, "A moment ago, Mrs. Ridgway, you said that everybody you looked at seemed to be a rabbit. Now just what did you mean by that?"* You are still basically right. Drawings involving analysts have to have something fresh and different in them, such as the one I have just so modestly mentioned. But you can't publish a drawing about an analyst and a woman with the caption, "Your only trouble is, Mrs. Markham, that you're so horribly normal." This is one of the oldest, tritest, and most often repeated lines in the world. If you will look up a story of mine called "Mr. Higgins' Break-down," published more than ten years ago, you will find that the first sentence is as follows (I quote from memory): "Gorham P. Higgins, Jr., was so normal that it took the analyst a long time to find out what was the matter with him." Just after that story appeared, the editor of Redbook sent for me and said he wanted me to write something for him because he had been so enchanted by that line. At that time, I have the vanity to believe, it was not old. But the years roll on, Mr. Ross, and turn into decades. So what you probably need is an old blind man sitting in one corner of Mr. Gibb's office and snarling about certain captions which you are too old to remember helped make certain issues of The New Yorker way back before the depression.

Another fault of the art meeting, it seems to me, is your tendency to measure everything with rulers, stop watches, and calendars. I told Andy White the caption I sent in for Mary Petty and he laughed more wholeheartedly than he has since his teeth began to go and arthritis took him in the back of the neck. I understand that the art conference decided Mr. Swope was not old enough to be known to the old lady in the suggested drawing. She certainly would know old Jacob Swope's boy, Herbie, just as a woman of your mother's generation would know about Mrs. Ross's boy Harold. Furthermore, there are at least a dozen variations of that caption which I could have suggested.

If you ever write a comedy for the theatre you will discover that the best laughs invariably follow some simple and natural line which the characters involved would normally say. Thus, one of the best laughs in The Male Animal followed the simple statement, "Yes, you are." To show you what I mean, let's take the specific example of the drawing which appeared in the issue of October 18th in which the salesman says to the lady at the door, "Couldn't we go inside and sit down? I have a rather long sales talk." This is such an extravagant distortion of reality, it is so far removed from what any salesman would ever say, that to be successful it has to be fantastic. But since the situation is not fantastic, it ends up simply as a bad gag. All salesmen that get into drawings in The New Yorker ring the changes on cocksureness, ingenuity, or ignorance. When I was a little boy, in my early 20's, in Columbus, my mother opened the door one afternoon to a tall, sad salesman with a sample case, who said, "I don't suppose you want to buy any of my vanilla. Nobody ever does." There is such a thing as a tired, sad, defeated salesman, but even if there weren't we could use one. I can hear this salesman in the October 18th issue saying, "I just want

---

*This caption was printed as: "You said a moment ago that everybody you look at seems to be a rabbit. Now just what do you mean by that, Mrs. Sprague?"

to say to begin with, madam, that I have been through a great deal today." Or, "I simply must talk for a few minutes to some understanding married woman, madam. It's not about my products." I'm just batting these rough ideas out to give you an idea of how a situation and its caption can be explored, as Marc Connelly puts it. In an hour's time I could get 2 or 3 perfect captions for this particular drawing. The best laugh you get in the theatre comes from the women and as the result of hitting a universal and familiar note. The closer you come to what a human being might say, the funnier your caption is going to be. A woman laughs at a line about salesmen because it reminds her of what that funny little Fuller Brush man said to her sister Ella. No salesman ever said to any housewife what you have him saying in the cartoon I am talking about. That is a gag man's idea.

I'll talk this all over with you any time you say. I can't go on any kind of salary basis on account of the State Income Tax, but I am willing to be paid by the caption. You must feel free to reject my ideas if you don't think they are right. I just want somebody to listen to them.

Love,
Thurber

This both plaintive and quarrelsome call for a new connection with the *New Yorker*—which had been taking on the quality of a cherished but nagging mistress for Thurber—was probably a healthy sign. He wanted to get back to some regular magazine work, and while he could no longer report or draw pictures in the old sense, he naturally leaned towards writing cartoon ideas and captions. A week after the letter to Ross, he submitted, as a kind of test, as many captions as he could think up in half an hour. He sent the resulting nine to Ross in a clump, daring Ross and the Art Department to do something with them. Meanwhile, the magazine continued to run his old unpublished drawings and use some of his new cartoon and spot ideas. As for the few original drawings he managed to execute, others in the Art Department would clean up and ink in the scratchy lines. Far more importantly, he started to work on old-style casuals again. It was yet another new beginning.

The Japanese attack on Pearl Harbor, the day before Thurber's forty-seventh birthday, had no greater effect on him than on other Americans. He knew it was only a matter of time before America was in the war. His sentiments were so pro-British and -French (and anti-German, -Italian, and -Japanese) that he wanted the mess over with as soon as possible, with as few casualties on the Allied side as possible. Dr. Bruce was in the thick of it with the Marines, Ronnie Williams was seeing combat with the Royal Navy (Jane Williams was living with her family in upstate New York), the *New Yorker* was being thinned out by the draft and direct commissions, and old friends and colleagues were going off to serve every day. At the beginning of the war, Thurber was so involved with himself and his private world that he wasn't overly depressed by the mayhem. The war, however, prevented trips to his beloved Bermuda and the Williamses.

Relapses occurred with some frequency during the dark winter of 1941–42. Over Christmas, there was a bad one, and Thurber decided to revisit Fritz Foord's sanitarium and take Ann Honeycutt along. Helen was actually pleased at this arrangement, since "it would get Jamie out of the house over the holidays and give me a little rest." Thurber called for his car and black chauffeur, stopped by Ann Honeycutt's apartment to pick up his travelling companion and three bottles of whiskey, and headed north to Foord's. He was not allowed to check in; the reason given was that he was blind and the sanitarium couldn't cope with a blind patient. In the Christmas tradition, a local inn turned them away because he and Honey were under the influence, but Thurber went to the police station and demanded that they and the driver be permitted to register at the inn. Thurber somehow won his point. However, the next day the nonplussed chauffeur drove them home, to a less than warm welcome from Helen.

Throughout that winter of occasional relapses, his sexual attentions wandered, as he still tried to prove his potency to himself and the world. He had an affair with a *New Yorker* secretary, but his blindness made for tactical problems. He had to rely on one of the magazine's office boys to lead him about; as his run of bad luck would have it, the office boy assigned to him was eighteen-year-old Truman Capote. "I worked as a boy in the Art Department then," Capote recalled, "and one of my jobs was to take Thurber to his girl friend's apartment. She was as ugly as sin, so it served him right. I would have to wait for him at the apartment till he was finished, and then I'd dress him. He could undress by himself but he couldn't dress by himself, couldn't even cross the street by himself. Now since Helen Thurber would dress him in the morning, she knew how he looked. Well, one time I put his socks on wrong side out, and when he got home, I gather Helen asked him a lot of questions. The next day, Thurber was furious at me—he said I did it on purpose. But I was still assigned to lead him to the girl's apartment—back and forth, back and forth. Also, he was a terrible drinker. He breathed fire when he was drunk. Very jealous man, too, of other people's fame."

In March, there was a necessary time-out from all these activities for a personal and business chore. Columbus, Ohio, had been chosen—after heavy pressure by the Columbus Variety Club—to be the site of the world premiere of the Warner Brothers film version of *The Male Animal*, starring Henry Fonda, Olivia de Havilland, and Jack Carson. (The movie was about the same as the play, but the basic anticommunism of Tommy Turner had been enhanced by some stronger dialogue.) Thurber and Helen were integral to the gala opening festivities, and they arrived to a hero's welcome at Union Station. The mayor was there and so was Mame Thurber and Robert Thurber and some Hollywood people and one Lillian Kodiak, who was selected in a promotional stunt as "Miss Average Girl." A crowded agenda was scheduled for the Thurbers during their short stay: a reunion dinner for a hundred people at the Phi Kappa Psi house, to which "Miss Average Girl" was escorted by O.S.U.'s own "Mr. Male Animal"; a Male Animal Ball, featuring Cab Calloway broadcasting over the Blue Network; an Ohio State Faculty Club luncheon; an appearance before the entire student body, with Thurber slated to address the assembly on the theme "Our War Effort Needs the Rah-Rah Spirit" (he didn't do it); tea at the O.S.U. president's house; visits to the Gardiners and the *Dispatch* offices; and, finally, the premiere itself, at which sorority girls served as hostesses, fifty soldiers from Fort Hayes were honored guests, and a girl chosen as "Female of the Species" was presented. It was an enervating few days in Columbus, and neither Helen nor her husband was heartbroken when the time came to leave for New York. Columbus, for its part, was proud but saddened over the condition of its illustrious son. The movie was a smash.

Thurber's efforts that winter at casual writing took him back to the reminiscence form, a psychological retreat and regrouping of forces. He wrote and published in the *New Yorker* a piece about an old fussy grammarian English teacher ("Here Lies Miss Groby") and an eccentric-relatives piece about his pioneer ancestors ("A Good Man," later expanded as "Adam's Anvil"). They were recognizable, watered-down Thurber, but at least they were something. In the spring of 1942, a change of geography was recommended by Dr. Fox, who thought the country would be better for his health and productivity. So the Thurbers rented a small white house in the center of Cornwall, Connecticut, for the summer. The village seemed so right for them that they decided to keep the house indefinitely.

Cornwall was and is a lovely place of grand trees and wide fields and rounded Berkshire hills, but what pleased the Thurbers most was the people of the area. Mark Van Doren and his wife, Dorothy, would alone have made the move to Cornwall worthwhile. And the Thurbers' next-door neighbors, during the summer, were Kenneth MacLean, a professor of English at Yale, and his wife, Sara, to whom they were especially close. The painter Armin Landeck became a good friend. The most important new relationship they struck up was with Rose Algrant, a French teacher (of Franco-Turkish ancestry) in a local private school, who for almost twenty years continued to have a peculiarly calming and stimulating effect on Thurber. Cornwall was an ideal sanctuary for the Thurbers during the war, since they couldn't travel, anyway. While the writing came hard ("I still don't see well enough to read or to get about alone"),(12) he was making peace with himself.

"The Catbird Seat," a story that Thurber worked on that first Cornwall summer, was the surest sign that he was recovering his old stuff. It is one of his best and most famous pieces. Sired by an uncollected 1934 casual called "Thirteen Keys" (about a meek, dreary clerk falling into misadventure), out of "The Unicorn in the Garden"—with "The Secret Life of Walter Mitty" in obstetrical attendance—"The Catbird Seat" is the remarkable tale of unremarkable Erwin Martin, the loyal, dull head of the filing department at a company called F & S, who decides after two years of being browbeaten by Mrs. Ulgine Barrows, the emasculating special assistant to the company president, to rub her out. In Thurber's first version of the story, he had the little man actually kill Mrs. Barrows and get away with it, but he realized it wasn't right. Mr. Martin, he once explained, could no more murder someone than Thurber himself could.(13) After much reworking, the twist that makes the story came to him: Martin would behave outrageously in front of Mrs. Barrows; she would report him to the boss; the boss would think she was mad for even imagining such behavior from Martin and dismiss her (just as the wife in "The Unicorn in the Garden" fable was committed for saying her husband saw a unicorn). The piece is *echt* Thurber, and with its well-deserved reception by the *New Yorker* and a grateful public, his confidence was restored.

The Cornwall summer was made even more bountiful by his assembling, with Helen, his best pieces over the previous five years for a new collection to be published in October, 1942, entitled *My World—And Welcome to It.* Dedicated to Norma and Elliott Nugent, the book flourished in a nation mainly concerned with matters of life and death—and also experiencing a paper shortage. It was obligatory reading for any Thurber fan, since it contained "The Secret Life of Walter Mitty," "What Do You Mean It *Was* Brillig?" and "You Could Look It Up." Part Two of the book consisted of those pieces written in Europe during 1937 and 1938, so there was a rather timely and poignant quality to Thurber's memories of ante-bellum France. Again, Thurber was heartened by the book's success and the fact that blitzed England had permitted Hamish Hamilton to bring out a British edition in December. (There was also a special Armed Services edition in 1943.) He was doing his part, even though he wrote Ronnie Williams, on August 18, 1942, that he was good in the war effort only for "listening for submarines."

Thurber and Helen intended to stay in Cornwall right through the winter, but in January of 1943, the fuel oil necessary for heating their drafty house was unavailable because of rationing. And, feeling more buoyant, he was itchy for the city again. They had been travelling back and forth by train between Cornwall and New York, and the difficult trips were getting to them. In coldest January, they left Cornwall temporarily and moved to an East Fifty-seventh Street apartment they managed to find after bribing the super and landlord with cash and canned goods. Thurber fell all too easily into the manic city life again.

They saw a good deal of their English friend John Duncan Miller in New York. Miller had been assigned to the British Army Staff in the United States. Whenever he was in New York, he did the pub rounds with the Thurbers. "I was amazed then at the difference between the London Thurber and the New York Thurber in his own bars and among his own friends," Miller said. "He, of course, drank a lot in both places, but in New York, barely able to see even shadows, he was so perverse, so quarrelsome. I never had a fight with him because, I suppose, I was never with him long enough, but I witnessed too many incidents. Time meant nothing to him. He was up till dawn most nights. Being blind, it was always the same hour in his sight. Once, when I was visiting him at his apartment, Althea suddenly appeared. She had missed the train to Amherst, where she lived with her professor husband, and she needed something to do, I guess. We all went out to dinner together. Helen and Althea both quickly got smashed. Thurber was absolutely delighted at this spectacle of both his wives in the same difficult situation. I shall never forget how he laughed. He was such a visual man that blindness for him was a frightening frustration. Yet, it gave him a wonderful excuse to monopolize the conversation, even more than before."

In the 1943 spring, Thurber heard about the Zeiss loop, a sort of magnifying helmet worn by precision workers in defense plants. He obtained one and found that with the loop's help he could draw fairly detailed pictures in bright light on 24" × 16" paper. His doctor allowed him to do two drawings a day, five minutes for each drawing, since the loop was an added strain on his negligible sight. He was quoted as saying, "There must be an amiable God who had it in mind for me to do these drawings and is not opposed to them."(14) To Herman Miller, he wrote that with the Zeiss loop he looked "like a welder from

Mars."(15) Defensively, he continued to deprecate his art work and artists in general. "I never took an art lesson," he said, not entirely accurately, "and I'm glad that I didn't. God, but artists are dumb."(16) But his drawing output nevertheless increased.

As for his writing, he spent more and more of his time working on a play, the same dramatic idea he had mentioned in his letter to the Whites after the throes of his breakdown. As it turned out, he spent whole chunks of his remaining writing years toying with the idea, never quite getting it into producible shape. Entitled at first *Make My Bed* (again, the "Bye Bye, Blackbird" effect), the play was ostensibly about Ross and the *New Yorker,* which was why Thurber tried to involve E. B. White in the project, first as somebody to talk the play out with and later as a collaborator. White discouraged him on both accounts in 1942, but it was still to White that Thurber wrote, on May 15, 1943, about his play:

... I have finished Act I of a play for this fall. It takes place in the room at the New Yorker occupied by Terry [Daise Terry, an administrative queenpin of the magazine and friend of Thurber], who figures largely in it. So does Ross. So does a guy named Jeff Crane, who could be you. Everybody comes out well. Nothing to worry about. Helen and I are pretty excited about the first act, which is very funny. The second act will be funnier. Almost everything that ever happened is in it.

The second act ends with Ross (Walter Bruce) holding in his arms a Scotty with a red ribbon on its neck, as pneumatic drills roar off stage, and saying "God, how I pity me."

I have been working it out in my mind for a year . . .

White did not share Thurber's enthusiasm for the idea nor the humor of the play's subject matter. But Thurber kept at it. *Variety* announced the play as a November, 1943, production, but the rough script was in no shape for Broadway. For the next seventeen years there were at least seventeen versions of *Make My Bed.* The character emphasis shifted from Ross to Wolcott Gibbs to William, Robert, and Mame Thurber to a stereotypical congressman, the plot never really focussing on one subject. Those who read various versions through the years felt that, while the Ross character stole every scene, he was never truly clarified as a person. Thurber came to feel this, too, and it was part of the reason he wrote *The Years with Ross* in the 1950's—to clarify the character in his own mind for the play. He knew he was weak at dramatic construction; nevertheless, he worked the play to death. "He fussed with it so long," Helen said, "it became a tiresome project for him and everybody else."

The summer of 1943 was also taken up with assembling drawings for

Thurber's first collection in more than ten years, to be published by Harcourt, Brace in November. Thurber's original title for the collection was *The More I See of People,* but he wisely dropped that oily handle, "since it sounded too much like a retired lady librarian's sketches about her three spaniels."(17) Instead, he decided on the much more Thurberian *Men, Women and Dogs.* He asked White to write an introduction and/or accept the book's dedication:

. . . I would like to dedicate the book of drawings to you, who picked them up off the floor & stuffed them down a few throats. You would probably be too shy to have both the dedication & the introduction. You can have either or both . . .

You've done an awful lot of words on me and maybe you'd like to retire. I get to brooding about such things. Anyway, let me know . . . (18)

White accepted the dedication, which reads:

TO ANDY WHITE

who picked up the first of these restless scrawls from the floor fifteen years ago and bravely set about the considerable task of getting them published, this book is gratefully and affectionately dedicated.

The Preface was written, once again, by Dorothy Parker, who made a good deal of being asked to introduce two Thurber books of drawings. With the same rapt disbelief she evinced in her Introduction to *The Seal in the Bedroom,* she found Thurber's men more innocent and willing to please, and Thurber's ladies "increasingly awful."(19) Her amused analyses of the most famous drawings were again pithy and perfect.

And there were famous drawings galore to choose from; indeed, *Men, Women and Dogs* is the ultimate in Thurber art. They are all there: the doctor as rabbit before Mrs. Sprague; the startled severed head of the defeated swordsman; the butler named Parkins 'aving a bit of a time below stairs; the pitiful souvenirs of Dr. Millmoss at the feet of that strange beast; the Columbus-style house that is half forbidding woman; the hounds in hot pursuit; the "Well, if I called the wrong number, why did you answer the phone?" female logician; the kangaroo in court; and —probably the most alarming and inexplicable of all Thurber's works —the first Mrs. Harris on the bookcase.*

---

*Thurber was badgered into attempting an explanation of this drawing. He said the bookcase was originally a staircase, with a woman waiting at the top, but because of his

Men, Women and Dogs, rather hefty for a wartime book of drawings, was filled out with four series called "The Hound and the Hat" (man and dog vs. woman), "The Masculine Approach" (man vs. woman), "First Aid" (woman vs. medicine), and the celebrated "The War Between Men and Women" (woman vs. man). The last, of course, was to Thurber's art work what "The Secret Life of Walter Mitty" was to his writing. It must be seen, not described. As a distillation of Thurber's artistic career, the book is essential reading for anyone concerned with humor as something more important than the output of a stand-up television comic. It sold accordingly, going into a second printing immediately after a first of 27,500 copies. Sometimes the drawings are merely serviceable compliments to great captions and sometimes the reverse is true; but more often than not, both drawings and captions rise to invent their own art, the supreme originality of James Thurber.

Having two successful books published in a single season *(Many Moons* was brought out just before *Men, Women and Dogs)* gave Thurber a justified feeling of accomplishment, but it also gave him a roaring case of what Helen called "the Thurbs." She said that "Jamie was at his meanest—the meanest man in town—after he finished with a book." Instead of being at the top, he was at the bottom again, scratching and climbing.

After the 1943 Cornwall summer, they returned to East Fifty-seventh Street, where Thurber embarked on a whole new project—helping along the literary career of his friend Mary Shipman Mian, the wife of Aristide. Mary Mian had been writing some stories about her life in prewar central France, near the Creuse, her husband's native region. Thurber touted the stories to Ross, the Whites, fiction editor Gus Lobrano, and anybody else at the *New Yorker* who would listen. At last, the magazine began to buy the stories, and in 1946 they came out as a book, *My Country-in-Law,* with an introduction by Thurber. (He also wrote prefaces, in 1945, for Joel Sayre's *Persian Gulf Command: Some Marvels on the Road to Kazvin* and Mary Petty's *This Petty Pace: A Book of Drawings.)* Despite the Thurbs, he was at his most generous,

---

poor draftsmanship it turned into a bookcase.(20) No one was more suspicious than Ross about this drawing. When Thurber submitted the thing to the *New Yorker,* he was phoned by Ross, who wanted to know if the woman on the bookcase was alive or stuffed. Thurber replied that she was definitely alive since no taxidermist could stuff a woman, and, what's more, he wasn't responsible for the behavior of the people he drew. "Thurber's crazy," Ross would tell others, and he wasn't far off the mark, either.(21) The lady-on-the-bookcase cartoon was drawn between Thurber's divorce and remarriage, when his mental condition wasn't much more stable than it was in the summer of 1941.

"You said a moment ago that everybody you look at seems to be a rabbit. Now just what do you mean by that, Mrs. Sprague?"

"Touché!"

"It's Parkins, sir; we're 'aving a bit of a time below stairs."

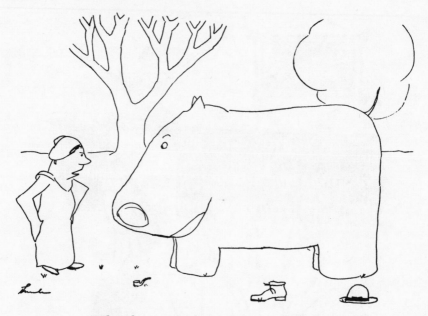

"What have you done with Dr. Millmoss?"

"Well, if I called the wrong number, why did you answer the phone?"

"Perhaps _this_ will refresh your memory."

"That's my first wife up there, and this is the _present_ Mrs. Harris."

dispensing favors and money to family and friends alike.

As he grew older, he seemed to be on the watch for literary discoveries, enjoying the mentor role. One of the finest discoveries any almost-fifty-year-old man of letters could hope for turned up in his mailbox in mid-November from Chicago. He received an advance copy of an article, from the December, 1943, issue of *Poetry* magazine, called "James Thurber: The Comic Prufrock." It was by *Poetry*'s young editor, Peter De Vries. Thurber was instantly taken with the piece, in which De Vries held that Thurber had more in common with modern poets than with modern humorists (especially in such word-manipulating casuals as "The Black Magic of Barney Haller") and that the middle-aged man on the flying trapeze was really J. Alfred Prufrock in comic clothing. Thurber was struck not only by the editor's flattering analysis but by a critic taking him seriously, the bugbear of his middle age.

Poetry was in its customary state of near-bankruptcy, and De Vries saw in Thurber's appreciation of the article, in a warm return letter,* a way for the magazine to make some money through a benefit lecture. Thurber accepted De Vries's invitation to speak at the Chicago Arts Club on April 8, 1944, although he confessed a "tendency to shake all over when I face a group of people."(23)

His nervousness increased as the lecture date approached. In an April 4, 1944, letter to De Vries, he complained of a "sharp pain in my stomach" from fussing over the coming ordeal. He suggested that he merely deliver a short preface to a long question period, with questions no more profound than "What is Dorothy Parker really like?" To insure that Thurber would be asked easy questions, a devious scheme was worked out in Chicago's Ambassador East Hotel on the night before the lecture: De Vries would make up questions based on Thurber's eloquent and casual remarks dropped in their relaxed hotel-room conversation, and he would read them to Thurber at the lecture as if they had come from the audience.

"In his hotel room," De Vries recalled, "I was Mr. Interlocutor to Thurber's Mr. Monologuist. I realized his offhand lines were great, full of warmth and anecdotes about every subject under the sun. Our little stratagem seemed to make the event less painful for him, and cooking it up, we had a pleasant evening together with our wives."

The next morning at the Arts Club in the Wrigley Building, De Vries introduced Thurber with some eloquence of his own. He said:

Even romantics now sense the connection between talent and trouble, and that all Art is, so far from being divine afflatus, some form or other of the artist's scratching where he itches. We have evolved a large medical jargon to express nothing more than old Emerson knew when he symbolized the creative misfit in terms of the wounded oyster, who "mends his shell with pearl." A more exact generation will only read "irritated" for "wounded." Thurber was profitably irked by something long before he lost the light of day; long, perhaps, before

---

*In the same letter, Thurber regretted not having met T.S. Eliot during his years in Europe. He was honored by Eliot's second-hand praise of *My Life and Hard Times* and Thurber, whom he called his "favourite humourist." In 1951, Eliot was quoted in *Time* as saying: "It is a form of humor which is also a way of saying something serious. There is criticism of life at the bottom of it. It is serious and even somber. Unlike so much of humor, it is not merely a criticism of manners—that is, of the superficial aspects of society at a given moment—but something more profound. His writings and also his illustrations are capable of surviving the immediate environment and time out of which they spring. To some extent, they will be a document of the age they belong to."(22) Thurber felt that this was the best estimate of his work ever. Despite his protestations, he was being taken very seriously by very serious people.

he saw it. Thurber is worse than unhappy—he is uncomfortable. His agitations can be imagined from the fact that even in repose he quivers like a tuning fork. But whatever his wound, and whether he has all the while been talking about it or merely guarding it more deeply from us, there is no doubt that he has mended it with pearl.

Thurber later told De Vries that after hearing that winning and incisive introduction, he knew that De Vries belonged on the *New Yorker*. Perhaps he also knew he must go some to equal his introducer, but whatever the case, after the first phony question was read by De Vries, Thurber was off and running handily, charming his audience with a nonstop monologue on such disparate subjects as Bermuda's Felicity Hall and the mechanics of his drawing. De Vries had no further use for the other bogus questions; he later said that it was "as fine a formal lecture as the audience had ever heard."(24) Another Thurber contradiction had shown itself, De Vries felt: apprehension and mastery of any given situation. "The bundle of nerves was a tower of strength."(25) His formal-lecture debut demonstrated that he might have been competition for Mark Twain in another field.

Because he immediately liked De Vries and admired his writing and wit, Thurber decided, in effect, to make him his protégé. When he returned to New York, he touted De Vries as he had Mary Mian and showed some of his pieces to Ross. Ross promised to read the pieces—although he doubted that they would be any good—but thirty minutes later he called Thurber and said, "Jesus Christ! It *is* good!" He wanted De Vries on the magazine. Thurber was thrilled with the quick success of his protégé, but he warned De Vries of the dangers of becoming a Ross *Wunderkind*. He feared that "Ross would decide that you are God, Donald Nelson, and Barney Baruch all in one"—which was, more or less, how Thurber started out at the *New Yorker*.(26) He suggested that even though Ross would want to hire De Vries full-time, a part-time job might be better. As De Vries's "sponsor and protector"(27) Thurber brought the young writer to New York and introduced him to Ross over lunch at the Algonquin. Sure enough, as Thurber had warned, Ross asked "DeVree" (as he consistently called him), "Could you do the Race Track department?" "No," answered De Vries, "but I can imitate a wounded gorilla."(28) Ross realized he'd been had, but he hired De Vries anyway as a part-time art-idea man and a contract writer. The rest is literary history, which Thurber was immensely proud to have had a large role in making.

"I thought from the first that Thurber was brilliant and princely," De

Vries said. "I never did agree with Gibbs's remark about Jim being a wonderful guy only till five o'clock. Whenever I saw him after five, he was usually on his best behavior. He never lit into me, although he was a little nasty once to my wife, Katinka, but it was nothing personal. I just told him to cut it out. He was that way with all women, except maybe Jane Williams. Once in a while he'd come out with a quick, surprising change-of-pace in the middle of a monologue. For instance, he'd suddenly launch a savage attack on E.A. Robinson, for no special reason."

Their relationship, always warm and close, grew through the years of increasing fame for both of them. It was fuelled by their mutual love of word games and puns. Once, De Vries and Berton Roueché proposed a logomachy to Thurber wherein single words must be found containing all five vowels in each of them—like "sequoia." Thurber accepted the challenge with uncurbed passion. He wrote De Vries:

> . . . SEQUOIA & its friends: discourage, precaution, precarious, auditioned, unintentional, aeronautics, mountaineer, automobile, manoeuvering . . .
> Damn Roueché & you for bringing this up!

Thurber went on to offer five-vowel names:

> . . . Louise Macy & Benjamin Clough . . .
> I am going nuts. Nuts! do you hear? NUTS. ha ha ha ha ha ha. Permutation, emulation, unconscionable . . . (29)

As for his own work, Thurber tried his hand at another fairy tale, this time about a Fascist, hypochondriacal giant named Hunder and a kindly, diminutive toymaker named Quillow who does the giant in. (The toymaker, except for his five-foot height, was a dead ringer for Thurber himself, complete with a shock of white hair.) *The Great Quillow* was a timely and pertinent allegory dealing with one of Thurber's favorite themes—brawn against brain, the bully against the gentle man —and any child could see Adolph Hitler in Hunder. For so slight a tale, it is chock full of anagrams, private allusions, and personal tenets, and it holds true to the quality for which Thurber once lauded L. Frank Baum's early Oz books—being "fairy tales with a difference" and containing nightmare and heartache along with whimsy and fantasy.(30) Like *Many Moons, The Great Quillow* made its first appearance (October, 1944) in book form. It was also illustrated in color by another artist (Doris Lee). It still sells briskly and, like *Many Moons*, often turns up in other media, finding its place in the classic children's story category.

But withal, sickness wouldn't leave him alone. At the end of the 1944 summer, Helen and he travelled to an estate eighteen miles from Geneva, New York, where Jane Williams was spending the war years with her family, while her husband was off on corvette duty. The occasion was the christening of Thurber's three-year-old goddaughter, Dinah Jane Williams. He sat up drinking too late one night in a drafty room, and the next day he came down with a virulent case of lobar pneumonia. Helen nursed him through two weeks of high fever—so high, in fact, that he soon ran out of pajama changes and all the men in the house had to contribute theirs—until, finally, some rare, primitive antibiotics, supplied by Navy doctors from the nearby Sampson Naval Training Station across Seneca Lake (one doctor fell in the water while disembarking from his boat), brought the fever down. Thurber described the event rather good-naturedly to the Whites:

. . . The Navy doctors at Sampson N.T.S. who knocked out my 105° fever in 2 days with sulpha say it is the first time on record a godfather failed to rally after a baptism.

I had no cold, sore throat, or chest discomfort—just a green apple belly ache. Always be examined for pneumonia first. Many people have their pubic hair shaved and are made ready for an appendectomy before it is found that they have pneumonia . . . Sulpha is no longer very toxic, and only one person in a thousand pees pink as a result. I peed amber through it all. You just take a lot of bicarbonate with the sulpha. I had one 42-minute chill which outdid the earthquake, knocking plates off the plate rail downstairs.

Pneumonia is no longer a menace, just a nuisance. Rosemary carried an unresolved pneumonia like mine for 8 months before it was found.

There is always a high fever, however. I was up in five days, and am better than ever. Good thing for a man.

Penicillin is not toxic at all, has no effect on pee. There will soon be enough of it for all, and we will live to be 130, they say. In this way we will one day have 13 living ex-presidents. White will live to celebrate the 200th anniversary of the Monroe Doctrine—think of it . . .

The only thing to worry about is the Mok-Mok—a weapon which will be invented for the next war. Four Mok-Moks will destroy the U.S. Look out for KM10 also and the horrible ZU58.

To be bumped off in Maine by something that lands in Michigan is not pleasant.

Zeeeeek!

BLONG!! . . .

The Zo-Zo 40 is absolutely silent in flight, but has a range of only 2500 miles.

See you soon

J. G16 Thurber(31)

However prophetic Thurber was about advanced weaponry, he was wrong about his own health. After he returned to New York, he suffered a relapse, worse than the original siege. Coming back from a movie at the Sutton near his East Fifty-seventh Street apartment, he suddenly had trouble walking. He was rushed to Doctors Hospital, where he spent three weeks recovering from the same virulent type of pneumonia. "We didn't think he'd make it," Helen said.

But he did. Then, in November, while vacationing at the Homestead in Hot Springs, Virginia (a Bermuda substitute during the war), his appendix ruptured and general peritonitis set in. The nearest place for an emergency operation was the small Chesapeake and Ohio Railroad Hospital thirty miles away in Clifton Forge, Virginia, a bleak railroad town. Thurber was sped there from the Homestead in the only available vehicle—a hearse—which grimly amused him through the pain and fright. At the hospital, it was discovered that the surgeon was off hunting quail and only an anesthetist was handy to pump out his stomach. While they waited for the surgeon to arrive, Thurber almost died. The emergency appendectomy was performed without a minute to spare, and Thurber began another long and difficult recuperation from near-death—his third in three months. He was obviously a very strong man.

Meanwhile, the Associated Press had dispatched a story about the incident and Walter Winchell had Thurber already rapping on pearly gates (Thurber listened to that disarming news on his radio, which certainly hastened his recovery). Ross sent urgently needed money, and dozens of telegrams and letters poured in from concerned friends. Helen, meanwhile, spent her time answering the mail and commuting from the Homestead to Clifton Forge on a slow C. & O. freight. She wrote a friend: "After my last trip, when one man got in with whooping cough and another locked himself in the men's can and had the screaming D.T.'s (and it wasn't Harvey he was in there with, either), I gave up and hired a guy to drive me over and back each day. The hell with expense—my sanity is worth saving."(32)

Thurber regained his strength on, at first, a diet of glucose and blood plasma. After two weeks at the railroad hospital, he returned to the Homestead and more substantial fare. Then, a few days after his fiftieth birthday, he was back in New York. His doctors insisted that he take it very easy for several weeks; since he was a bit dizzy and weak in the legs, he amiably complied. His sense of humor withstood the latest crisis as staunchly as his body (a sure sign of recovery, too, from his nervous breakdown). The ruptured appendix was discovered by the surgeon to be well behind his cecum; when Thurber was told of this, he quickly dubbed it "my hide and cecum appendix." And to his friends and well-wishers, he was remarkably chatty about his latest flirtation with extinction:

Dear Sayres and McNultys:

This is my first letter after coming home and I owe it jointly to the two families of pals who kept the letters coming and cheered me up most. So send this on to the McNultys, my dears. I got enough strength for a letter a day. I am feeling great outside of the weakness which decreases fast. Went down to lunch today. I weigh 143 stripped, a loss of about 8 or 9 lbs. I just found out about the ruptured appendix last night and took it with a slight shiver. I imagine old Jake Fisher's appendix busted about 1858 and he just took a stronger physic than usual, and gave it no mind.

I was glad this didn't happen in France a few years ago, say at the small town of Sans Chirurgien sur Mal, or Pas de Docteur en Rien. The C & O is a great hospital with a fine surgeon, John Morehead Garfield, and a great staff, including the best stomach tube manipulator in the country. Two great nurses—Nettie Jane and Bertha Garfield—a good colored cook.

I had a swell time. It was my remarkable wife who took it on the chin, waiting all night in a dreary hotel for the news of general peritonitis.

When I got onto the operating table I told the docs I was in fine shape. When they whisked off the hospital shirt, they must have wondered what it's like when I'm in bad shape. I was picked for a "break-down" of the incision and 2 weeks more in bed, but the chief said my recuperation was "remarkable." He ought to see Mamma and Robert and the Uncle Jake who lost 9/10 of his insides and sold pamphlets about it for 35 years.

I told Dr. Emmett that my great-grandfather could lift a horse, and he said, "The effects of the hypos will wear off in a few days now."

Best line read to me by a nurse: "He is a past Commander of the American Lesion."

. . . One orderly named Daniel would take a swipe at my bottom from the floor grunting "Dah!" each time and nearly killed me. Sounded like Dick Peterson cutting at a high curve ball. Nettie Jane had to change me twice like a baby, orderlies being busy. Now I can take anything. On the fifth night, starting at 2 a.m. I filled five bed pans because of the peritonitis, and when the orderly was called, I heard a Keystone comic shuffling along the corridor, breathing slow and hard. This ancient negro, who, I learned, takes a week to cut a small lawn, said his name was Garfield. Since the others are Lee, Jefferson, and Washington, I asked him if he wasn't a spy. "Yes, suh!" he said. Full name—Garfield Jett, no kin to the propulsion of the same name.

Next day I asked my day orderly, Charley, how come this Garfield. "My name is Garfield, too," said Charley, coolly. The thing began to take on the aspects of "Angel Street" and I suspected one of you guys was behind it. Full name—Charles Garfield Thompson—no kin to Jett. He was born in 1881, the year

Garfield was shot. Now when you know that my eye was removed at the Garfield Hospital in Washington, you can see how I lay there and brooded. I just call everybody Garfield now and find it restful, Garfield, my boy.

Some reporter called my nurse one morning and said, "Phone me the moment he dies. Don't monkey around the bed—get on the phone!" She hung up on him . . .

Yours for toujours,
Jim

P.S. I listened to Hildegard's program one night. Guest star: John Garfield.(33)

His convalescence in New York went well. "Jamie somehow pulled through the worst illnesses," Helen said. "With it all, he developed a fascination for medicine, and later on, homeopathic medicine—a leftover from his family and old Mrs. Albright. Once, he researched homeopathic drugs with a Litchfield pharmacist, and together they spent the whole day going over old cures. Jamie came to swear by wheat-germ oil and vitamins, but he was never a hypochondriac. When he got sick, he really got sick. But he was tough."

Miraculously, Thurber survived till his fiftieth year, against all reasonable odds. And he still was optimistic. He wrote Herman Miller the day after his birthday: "Since the Lord wouldn't let me go blind, either, I figure he has something in mind for me to do . . . I have just begun to write. These are the best years. I spit on the grave of my awful forties."(34) And in his Preface to *The Thurber Carnival*, his next and most successful book, he said: "Thurber goes on as he always has, walking now a little more slowly, answering fewer letters, jumping at slighter sounds." But, he insisted, the best years were still ahead.

CHAPTER **16**

King of Cornwall

He wasn't terribly far off the mark.
The next few years were comparatively good ones—for a blind man
with a proclivity to mental and physical upheavals. He was well-off
financially; his ego was maintained with care; the horrors of his illnesses
and the nervous breakdown were dimming; the war was just about over
and friends were returning in more or less one piece; and he was
working and publishing.

1945 began with *The Thurber Carnival*, the fattest and most exemplary Thurber anthology ever. Issued by his old publishing *bête noire*,
Harper, and dedicated to his favorite *bête noire*, Harold Ross ("with
increasing admiration, wonder and affection"), the book contains filling
helpings of *My World—And Welcome to It, Let Your Mind Alone, The
Middle-Aged Man on the Flying Trapeze, Fables for Our Time and
Famous Poems Illustrated, The Owl in the Attic, The Seal in the Bedroom, Men, Women and Dogs*, the complete *My Life and Hard Times*,
and six previously uncollected pieces, among them "The Catbird Seat"
and "The Cane in the Corridor."

Never before had Thurber been so widely and even extravagantly
reviewed. William Rose Benét said in the February 3, 1945, *Saturday
Review* (which also printed a likeness of Thurber on the cover) that
"here is one of the absolutely essential books of our time." Malcolm
Cowley reviewed the book for the March 12, 1945, *New Republic* and
said that Thurber "writes so naturally and conversationally that it is
hard to realize how much work goes into his stories," adding he hoped
Thurber would write longer works someday. The February 19, 1945,
number of *Life* called him "the most disturbingly funny humorist in the
United States." A New York *Times* Book Review critic said, on February
4, 1945, "We can no longer be content simply to laugh at what he
produces; we must make a determined effort to understand him as man
and artist." *PM* coaxed E.B. White into reviewing the book, and White
wrote of his friend's love and compassion for his characters. One critic,
Francis Hackett, in a 1947 volume called *On Judging Books in General*

The Hopeless Quandary

and in Particular, made such a determined effort to understand
Thurber as man and artist that he analyzed *The Thurber Carnival* into
the autopsy room, splitting every hair, and a few bones, in sight. He
contrived to spoil the real joy of Thurber, which is simply a God-given
ability to be funny and trenchant in a totally original way. Hackett also
took a nasty swipe at the *New Yorker* and its staff of writers (a practice
that has grown popular among certain critics, especially those who are
regularly rejected by that magazine), damning the magazine as a mu-
tual-admiration society.

Fifty thousand copies were printed up by Harper for the first edition,
and the Book-of-the-Month Club chose *The Thurber Carnival* as its
February, 1945, selection, ordering a further printing of 375,000 copies.
For the first time, really, Thurber's writing and drawing reached out to
a mass reading audience. He was quoted as saying: "If a humorist sells

20,000 copies, he's compared with Artemus Ward. When you sell 30,000, it's Edward Lear. Get to 60 or 70 and you're called another Lewis Carroll. But at 200 to 300,000—boy, you've just gotta be Mark Twain."(1) Actually, he sold about half a million copies and was on the best-seller lists for most of the year.* Even that confirmed foe of publishers James Thurber couldn't complain. He had money to buy a house, a long-sought mink for Helen, a Cadillac, and he could boast of a bargained-down Federal tax bill of fifty-five thousand dollars. "We didn't really change our style," Helen said. "We just could do more things."

As the inventor and primary victim of the post-publication Thurbs, Thurber cured himself by getting right back to work, like a kid with a skinned knee remounting his bicycle. He wrote very few casuals, as such; instead, he wrote a couple of pieces about himself for Sunday newspaper magazine sections (being suddenly as interesting to average readers as his characters were) and drew two series for the New Yorker, with the help of the Zeiss loop and other aids. They were called "Our New Natural History" (later collected as "A New Natural History") and "The Olden Time." The former series was, to everyone's happy surprise, about the best Thurber had ever drawn. For one thing, the idea was exceedingly witty and imaginative: Thurberian flora and fauna captioned as in a standard biology textbook but with nomenclature of apt puns and clichés. It was a kind of charming parlor game gone mad.

The most rabid fan of this series, which ran in the magazine till the middle of 1946, was Ross. He suggested several possibilities to Thurber —for instance, the Blue Funk and the Lazy Susan—when the artist's inspiration and infinitesimal vision at last flagged and Thurber could draw no more of his wild creatures. "I've come to the end of this series," he wrote Ross, "unless you want a man being generous to a fault—that is, handing a small rodent a nut. And I know you won't want a female grouch nursing a grudge."(2) Ross probably would have loved them, if only Thurber could have obliged.

"The Olden Time" series, a Thurber's-eye view of the Middle Ages, was only pleasing, without "Our New Natural History"'s flush of invention.

That same year, he began work on what, in a sense, was a lifetime's project—an appreciation through respectful parody of Henry James's assorted works, especially The Beast in the Jungle. As the intricate,

---

*The Thurber Carnival still sells, in paperback and a Modern Library edition. And there is a lively trade in secondhand hardcover copies. It is unquestionably the definitive Thurber collection.

difficult piece progressed, it turned into more of an emulative pastiche than a parody, a sort of loving salute to the master, as "You Could Look It Up" was a deep bow to Ring Lardner. He later said it was really a story as James would have written it.(3) Its stimulus was, of course, Thurber's early love affair with James, through the matchmaker Professor Joseph Russell Taylor. Its origin was a 1933 casual he wrote for the *New Yorker* entitled "Recollections of Henry James," a hokey memoir of a meeting with the master. Thurber borrowed freely from this piece for his pastiche, which was called "The Beast in the Dingle" and was printed in Cyril Connolly's British magazine *Horizon* in September, 1948, just after it appeared in another Thurber collection, *The Beast in Me.*

Thurber slaved, off and on, for three years over the pastiche. In 1946, he wrote his comrade in Jamesiana, Herman Miller:

. . . I am enclosing for your, I hope, fond, I have the vanity to believe, inspection, the third or fourth draft of my pastiche, or whatever it is, on Henry James. I spent four months on it two winters ago, but found on going back to it that it needs trimming and changes, particularly in the last section in which there are far too many poetic quotations and allusions of the kind our poor dear friend would most surely not have indulged in.

Edmund Wilson was all for shipping it off to the Atlantic Monthly but I still want to perform a few minor operations. I think that in the main it stands up, but I would like your feelings in the matter. During the four months I worked on it day and night, I was a nuisance around the house because I was unable to get out of the Jamesian phraseology in talking to Helen, and cook, or our guests.

I am planning an extended letter to you, chiefly concerned with the wonderful time we had at your house, and secondly, with a few thoughts on THE AMBASSADORS and whether or not it would stand up in dramatization. I have read it four or five times but not since about 1933, and it will be interesting to set down the scenes and episodes that I remember after so long an absence from the company of our poor, sensitive gentleman and his circle. It is quite possible, of course, that when I make this analysis what will stand out sharply and clearly for both of us is the impossibility, not to say the inadvisability, of attempting to transfer to so harsh a medium the last final distillation of what is, need I say, in its original form, the perfect, God save us all, statement of the precious dilemma . . . (4)

He was obviously in a fever of Jamesian imitation and still "a nuisance around the house," but by March of 1946, he had dropped the idea of a play based on *The Ambassadors*, although he was still tinkering with the pastiche. ("I may be working on it when I die, in which case my executors can retitle it 'The Sense of the Ivory Tower.' ")(5) Finally, he declared the piece finished and showed it to Ross first, as he had to do under the terms of his first-refusal contract with the *New Yorker*. Ross refused it first, saying, "I only understood fifteen per cent of the allusions."(6) Artsy-craftsy literary pieces were not for him or his magazine. However, he did buy and print another of Thurber's Henry James (*cum* Willa Cather) bits of nostalgia, entitled "A Call of Mrs. Forrester (After Rereading, in My Middle Years, Willa Cather's 'A Lost Lady' and Henry James's 'The Ambassadors')." Ross told him, "It's about a man and two women, and it comes over."(7)

Cyril Connolly was thrilled with the pastiche, which he had specifically asked Thurber to allow him to print in a special American number of *Horizon*. He compared it favorably with Max Beerbohm's famous parody "Mote in the Middle Distance," but said that Thurber's James parody had got down to the nitty-gritty—James's eschewal of the "normal animal facts."(8) Thurber was gladdened by this praise for perhaps the most toilsome and unrewarding piece he had ever completed. He answered Connolly:

> . . . Your fine letter cheered me up. Since I had been so close to the James piece for so many years it was hard for me to make judgments on it toward the end. It has been highly praised and also lightly damned in reviews of the book over here . . .
>
> I was delighted by the check which was larger than I had expected. Did I tell you the story of the Hollywood agent who flew east four years ago to offer me $3500 a week to write for Warner Bros? I told him I couldn't do it because I was engaged on a small pastiche of Henry James. He was bewildered but impressed. "How much will you get for that?" he asked. I thought it over. "Depending on what review I sell it to, anywhere from forty to ninety dollars." He backed away from me as if I were insane, and happily dropped out of my life . . . (9)

The most significant aspect of the pastiche for Thurber was at last getting the Henry James reverence out of his system. He was considerably more objective about James thereafter. He later wrote an inquiring reader that "the influence I had to fight off in writing was that of Henry James, and the influence that helped me most was that of E. B. White."(10)

While recovering from his ruptured appendix and peritonitis, Thurber had told Herman Miller:

... My new fantasy, or whatever, which runs to 15,000 words is called "The White Deer" and is a new version of the old fairy tale of the deer which, chased by a king and his three sons, is transformed into a princess. Suppose, I said, that it was a real deer which had saved a wizard's life and was given the power of assuming the form of a princess? Most fun I have ever had. I even go in for verse now and then, such as,

When all is dark within the house,
Who knows the monster from the mouse? . . . (11)

As his couplet implies, *The White Deer* is symbolically about blindness and other autobiographical matters. The King's stalwart, artistic son Jorn—easily identifiable as Thurber as seen by Thurber—wins the beautiful deer-princess by brave trust and love, over the other two more ordinary sons. Jorn must, among other labors, conquer the dreaded Mok-Mok, whose invention as a hideous weapon was mentioned in a letter to the Whites. Thurber's new fairy tale—"my best and longest"(12)—was conceived as a trade book for the general market, like *The Last Flower*, so that it would reach adults as well as children. He spent a total of eight months writing it, revising it mentally at least eighteen times by one count and twenty-five by another (he still tended to exaggerate his revisions). He said that he wrote the book for himself, "with no attempt to simplify plot or language" for the children's sake, since he believed that children neither needed nor wanted such simplification. "I hated to stop work on it," he said, it was so enjoyable.(13)

Besides being autobiographical, philosophical, and magical, *The White Deer* is a thicket of puns, spoonerisms, anagrams, iambic couplets, backward spellings, and private allusions. King Clode, a lovable, blustery ruler who thinks he is the eternal victim, is patently Harold Ross reaching for perfection. Clode even speaks the line Thurber most liked to quote Ross as bellowing: "Nobody ever tells me anything." When the palace astronomer advises the King that a huge pink comet has just missed striking the earth, Clode replies, "They aim these things at me! Everything is aimed at me." Thurber played with words in this medieval fantasy for the sheer fun of it, most of the fun reaching the reader by a kind of joyful osmosis. This is particularly true of the backward spellings: Artanis, the tarcomed and the Nacilbuper, Nagrom Yaf. Yollo was a name Thurber created on a ouija board with the Sayres' daughter Nora (the book is dedicated to the three Sayres). An illustration showing carvings on the Mok-Mok's sandalwood sides bears such in-initials as EBW, JG, MVD, and HWR. (Thurber did forty-six drawings for the book and Don Freeman drew three color illustrations.) The whirlwind of wordplay in this forest of medieval legend, Lewis Carroll, and L. Frank Baum gave Thurber immense pleasure. "Jamie liked *The White Deer* best of all his fairy tales, although I didn't," Helen said. "The playing with words and the private jokes made him happy, for some reason. Ross, by the way, didn't read the book, so he never knew of his role as King Clode. The private jokes were for Jamie's benefit, not so much for the knowing few."

Reviewers took *The White Deer* more seriously, perhaps, than Thurber himself did. No less a critic than Edmund Wilson reviewed it for the *New Yorker* (which could, somewhat nervously, permit a review, since it had nothing directly to do with the book, although its editor was a principal character). Wilson felt that fairy tales were a phase in Thurber's development from conventional humorist to comic artist, that they had freed him from bad literary habits. He went on to say that the first part of the book was one of the best things Thurber had ever written, but the end was cluttered with rhyme "not always skillfully managed." While Wilson believed that Thurber often was distracted by conceits and verbal tricks, the book had "the essence of poetry, and it ought to be read in preference to almost any best-selling novel."(14) What more could an author of a fairy tale—albeit an adult fairy tale— hope for? A serious review by Edmund Wilson; three large printings in rapid succession of his second best-selling book in one year; fan letters from scores of intrigued readers. Yet, Thurber was angry, particularly at Wilson. Wilson missed the point, he told anyone who would listen. Even years later, he wrote to his British publisher, Hamish Hamilton:

... I see by your catalogue that you list "The White Deer" under "for younger children." Among these younger children we must therefore count Edmund Wilson, W.H. Auden and Elizabeth Bowen. I wrote only two books for young children, "Many Moons" and "The Great Quillow." "The White Deer" was reviewed by Wilson in The New Yorker, who liked the first third of it. Later he told me, in surprise, that Auden liked all of it and thought his review was wrong. "Well I wonder what's the matter with him!" I exclaimed. There may be children in England who understand the symbolism of the three labors, but we don't have any over here although one little girl did figure out what the Forest of Artanis means . . . (15)

With the royalties pouring in during 1945, the first order of business was to pay a whopping tax bill. The second was to buy the house of his dreams, a permanent home. He described the dream house in his Preface to *The Thurber Carnival:*

. . . In the past ten years he has moved restlessly from one Connecticut town to another, hunting for the Great Good Place, which he conceives to be an old Colonial house, surrounded by elms and maples, equipped with all modern conveniences, and overlooking a valley. There he plans to spend his days reading "Huckleberry Finn," raising poodles, laying down a wine cellar, playing *boules,* and talking to the little group of friends which he has managed somehow to take with him into his crotchety middle age.

It was a perfect description of the house he finally bought in West Cornwall, and—except for reading *Huckleberry Finn* (which he had said he never did read) and playing *boules*—the rest of the passage was also accurate.

While the Thurbers had been renting the small house in the village of Cornwall, they had kept up a constant hunt for the Great Good Place. Through the Connecticut towns of Kent, Bridgewater, Roxbury, Sharon, Litchfield, and other parts of Cornwall they searched, until happily (since they liked Cornwall and its citizens best) they found just what they were looking for little more than a mile from their rented house. The stately, white fourteen-room Colonial, set among acres of fine trees and broad fields with a valley view, is situated between the Mohawk State Forest and a rare grove of towering cathedral pines. Its owner had been killed in the war, and his wife wanted to sell. "We grabbed it," Helen said, "and although Jamie never really saw much of it, he felt its beauty and its space. He loved the thought of the cathedral pines. He could sense their height and grandeur by their smell.* Of all the towns and cities he had lived in for half a century, Cornwall was the place where he was most at ease. It was, for the rest of his life, his "beautiful house" and his "beautiful trees," even if he had no eyes to see them.

Just as dearly held was "the little group of friends which he has managed somehow to take with him into his crotchety middle age." From almost his first appearance in Cornwall, Thurber became the cynosure of a tight circle of artists, writers, and teachers who made the town their summer or full-time home. "He was part of the Cornwall family and everyone's private family," the painter Armin Landeck said.

---

*The cathedral pines were as cherished as his house, especially when fire became a traumatic hazard for him later in his blindness. Once, Helen remembered, in their Algonquin room, Thurber awoke in the middle of the night screaming, "Fire! The cathedral pines are on fire and it's spreading to the house!" The "fire" turned out to be a red neon sign outside the hotel-room window, whose filtered glow had registered dimly in his minute vision.

"He was close to us all and fought with us all, just like a family member would. We put up with him, even at his worst, because we loved him." The 1940's were rich and happy years for him in the "one big open house of Cornwall," as Professor Kenneth MacLean put it.

No Cornwall house was more open than the Thurbers' new place. Most evenings for the dozen or so members of the circle were at the white house on the hill. There was a great deal of drinking, intellectual byplay, word games, politics, and too much gossip, local and literary. For Marc Simont, a pixyish artist of Spanish ancestry who had come to Cornwall about the same time Thurber did, everything revolved around Thurber. "He carried on monologues, without asking questions," said Simont. "He talked of strange people I didn't know, like McNulty, Ross, and White. But that was all right with me. I hadn't read much of his writing then, but I admired his drawings. As the junior member of the circle, I was at his feet. It was a one-way thing; he talked, I listened. Sometimes, he would do a sudden spontaneous bit—like delivering a sermon, in the style of a Methodist minister, on the Ohio State–Notre Dame game. He could be brilliant and funny, holding court like a king over us all."

For Mark Van Doren, too, the evenings at the Thurbers' were long, awash with alcohol, and always memorable. "They were great fun and sometimes infuriating, full of games, stories, singing, and, once in a while, fighting. I often think of him sitting in his favorite living-room chair, Helen leaning over to pour brandy into his glass, and Jim bounding up to go to the john—he drank so much, you see—and all the dogs and people in his path scattering as he reached for the doorway, which he used as a guide to the hall bathroom door. He invariably hit the same things en route; his shins were always bruised and so were those funny, pointed knees of his. Very Midwestern knees he had. Sometimes, we would go upstairs to the room where he worked, just the two of us, and go through his O.E.D. together. He was proud of that handsome set . . . 'set'—that word has one of the longest entries in the O.E.D., fifty-four columns of nouns, verbs, adjectives, I think. That was what fascinated Thurber. I would read him the 'set' definitions for hours on end. He depended on words for entertainment. Jim constantly had words dancing before him, when others danced with words only in bed at night, if then. He told me once about a trick he played on a nurse during one of his hospital stays. He asked her what seven-letter word had three U's in it. She thought and then she said, 'I don't know, but it must be unusual.' He never tired of telling that story, although some of us may have been tired of hearing it. He was an extraordinary man, though, with so many quick-changes: gentle and fierce, fascinating and boring, sophisticated and boorish, kind and cruel, broad-minded and parochial. You can't explain Thurber."

For Mark's wife, Dorothy, the best times at the Thurbers' were not the crowded, drunken evenings but when just she and her husband dropped over to see Helen and Jim. "We'd have a beer or two," she recalled, "and some late, late talk. He was the kindest, sweetest man then. That's what I remember, what I want to remember." And for Kenneth MacLean—who, like Marc Simont, was a good listener to the compulsive talker—the most endearing moments with Thurber were not at the parties. "I would drop in to visit sometimes at noon," he said, "and we'd sit and chat—or rather, I'd sit and he'd chat. The evenings were too confused. Our real sense of life together was at noon. He was most relaxed then. Our relationship sprouted from a New England–Ohio connection, I think. Sometimes, he would talk to me about Yale. It was the college he wanted to go to. 'Yale was really my college,' he would say. He had such youth of mind; he seemed always so young to me. It's hard to believe he's not here."

The second home for the Thurbers (and consequently the rest of the Cornwall Round Table) was the genial, child- and flower- and book- and art- and animal-filled house of Rose Algrant, the gently weathered Franco-Turkish teacher, whose charming way with the English language and life in general instantly drew Thurber to her. Helen and Rose were the two women Thurber loved and needed most in the Cornwall years, and, fortunately for everyone, they got along pretty much like happy sisters. "I arrived in Cornwall in 1940 with my son," Rose said, "and soon I am divorced. I would see this blind man led around the village by his wife. Then, I meet him at a party and then I ask him to my house. I never read him, but slowly I started. I don't know what to make of him, but I got acquainted. He never really saw my face. He said once he could see a bright yellow dress, but never my face."

To the Algrant house would come, with increasing frequency, the Thurbers, the Van Dorens, the Simonts, the MacLeans, the Lewis Gannetts, the William Shirers, and various others of the circle, including the teen-aged children. By accepted tradition, the big Thanksgiving and Christmas parties were at Rose's, the New Year's Eve party was at the Thurbers'. "Always Thurber had to be in his special chair in my living room, or at the head of the table," Rose said. "He knew his way around my house like his own. When he would rant and rave, my German shepherd would jump on him and I have to lock the dog in the kitchen. Then, sometimes, Thurber would disappear to visit the children in their rooms. He was full of love and kindness, but when drunk, sometimes a cruel man. We had drinks before dinner, which I cooked. A plain meal —roast chicken, salad, wine. Thurber would try out his ideas and do imitations around the table. Helen would match *repartée* with him. Carl Sandburg came once and there was much competition with guitars and songs. I didn't like. Others would challenge Thurber's beliefs, but I never challenge. He called me stupid, but I never challenge. Then, after dinner, much drinking till four A.M. Thurber only trust me to drive him home on icy roads. And he always called the next day to apologize for him to the others.

"We love each other without the sex. Thurber flirted with women as a pose. But he was so dependent on Helen. She dressed him beautifully, so handsome. Most women were scared of Thurber, and some were flirts. I was never afraid of him, even if he called me stupid—and I am. He would cut women, if there was a deep subject. Terrible to watch. For me, he was so dynamic, such a mind. He made me laugh. My English made him laugh. His big joke with me was 'We will go to Cleveland, Ohio, together, baby. I will show you beautiful Cleveland, and we will live in the same room.' I once meet Thurber's Ohio mother. She is a nuts. I like her, but she warned Thurber to stay away from foreigners, don't trust them. But *comparativement* to Ohio, she is a nuts."

For Rose's son, Rollie, who began, as a sixteen-year-old in 1945, to chauffeur and read to Thurber for seventy cents an hour, life with the Cornish King wasn't always so pleasant. "I worked on weekends and during summer vacations from Andover and Harvard," he said. "Thurber liked the way I read, and he listened well, rarely asking me to repeat. I remember reading Benchley and Fitzgerald, and I was surprised at how much Thurber could remember from those books. In the daytime, he could be very nice and interested in things you were interested in, like sports and teen-age problems. But at night. . . . He was on the attack, whether it was a friend or a newcomer. Always went straight for the most vulnerable spot, right in the kidneys. Inside of ten minutes, he knew where to hit. For instance, he once attacked Mark Van Doren for being a weak man, a minor man of letters. Mark was crushed. When Thurber met my first wife, he immediately reduced her to tears, as he did to so many other women. But he apologized—God, how he apologized! For years after, he was still apologizing. I've come to believe that he actually disliked most people in Cornwall, even his best friends there. Marc Simont was no competition, so he tolerated him, and some others were like servants to him. He strangely got along well with the strong women—my mother, Helen, Dorothy Van Doren. Perhaps he picked fights out of jealousy, not argument. The parties almost always ended badly. He had his chair, his throne, and he didn't like anybody else touching it. The evenings at my mother's often ended with her driving a drunk, raving Thurber home at three or four A.M. I used to go up to bed early because I knew how it would end. He picked on me once and I just went up to bed. Then he followed me up the stairs, but I told him I'm not taking that shit from anybody. He apologized, of course, and left me alone afterwards.

"My mother was also no competition for him, and she is strong-willed, which he liked in women. They would have small talk and gossip together, rarely discussing weighty things. He never resented that she didn't fully understand his writing, and he loved her accent and English mistakes. She is maybe the only person who didn't have a fight with him. Her house was a place for Thurber and Helen to relax in—comfortable, warm, with no servant problems, which they were always having themselves. Thurber was soft and tender to Rose, and vice versa. They never had an affair; it would have been almost incestuous. Helen was very much her own person, sharp and witty and sometimes abrasive, even when up against Thurber's position on something. And she and Rose had their occasional squabbles. They weren't always like sisters.

"Thurber's nastiness, I suppose, was because of his blindness. He wanted to see the same things as everybody else. He was not a good blind man, and he never really got used to it. He liked to believe he could see more than he actually could. When I drove for him, he would like to start the car. I would sit behind the wheel patiently while he pushed and twisted the cigarette lighter or the wiper switch, thinking they were the ignition. I guess I was no different from many other people in Cornwall who humored him only because he was blind and famous."

As the Cornwall years passed, Thurber's reputation for misbehavior, when in his cups, inflated. Once, for no apparent reason, he launched a personal diatribe against Mark's brother, the writer, editor, and critic Carl Van Doren, whom Thurber had never met. When one of Mark's sons spoke up in defense of his uncle, Thurber lambasted the son, too. "As I look back on the incident," Mark said, "I think Jim attacked Carl and my son because he was jealous; he wanted to be my *best* friend, my big brother, and if he couldn't, he wanted to hurt me indirectly. Later, he met Carl in Cornwall and was unctuously polite and friendly towards him. 'What's this all about?' Carl asked me. 'Why is he acting like this?' I told him and he understood. This snarling of Jim's was in proportion to how much he drank. It came out at the end of the evening, usually, and stopped the next day. I think it was his rage at everyone who could see—because he was *not* a malevolent man, God knows. Some called it artistic temperament and forgave him; others just hated him secretly. Sometimes his tantrums would be funny. There was a rich right-winger in Cornwall who once said in Jim's presence, 'Some of my best friends are Jews.' Well, Jim picked up a chair and smashed it. I think he hated the cliché as much as the sentiment. Maybe more."

Van Doren was moved to write a poem about Thurber's bursts of fury:

ANGER IS, ANGER WAS

The tumult in this shouting man
Gives way at once to dove's words.
Anger is, anger was,
But half between is holy ghost
Descending out of time gone.

The memory of this hunted man
Is barking wolves, is fool's gold.
But here a wing, and there a wing,
And all within is sleeping peace.
He walks again the good world.

Then, in the annals of Thurber's Cornwall reign, there is the story of the private-school headmaster, an athletic man's man, who adored Thurber and wanted to be his close friend. Thurber, however, loathed the man's man and goaded him at every opportunity. One particularly boozy evening, the headmaster could take it no longer and hit Thurber in the face. Some of the witnesses suspected that Thurber had planned to provoke the man to violence just so he would be damned as a coward who had struck a blind man, which was exactly what happened. That slap in the face cost the man his local respect, and to many it was a hint of the extremes Thurber would exercise to win a small victory.

The king's misbehavior extended to dalliance with Cornish ladies. He flirted with women and they flirted with him. Indeed, some women flung themselves at him, finding his handicaps utterly devastating. Others merely mistook the fumbling of a blind man as a pass, and responded according to their needs. Thurber liked the complications of trysts more than the trysts themselves. Most of his affairs were more of the spirit than the body. However, there were a few Cornwall liaisons that became rather serious, although Thurber would never have dreamed of leaving Helen for any other woman. Helen was what he called "my seeing-eye wife," who overlooked his indiscretions and failings in order to keep their marriage going and protect her husband. One night, she was confronted by a local wellborn beauty, with whom Thurber had been having a desultory affair. The home-wrecker told Helen, "I can have Jamie any time I feel like it." Helen stared her down and replied, "What will you do with him? He's blind, clumsy, and he needs constant help."* The romance cooled noticeably after that.

His liaisons, real or imagined, with Cornwall women got Thurber into one notable imbroglio towards the end of the war. Somebody had entered the Cornwall house of Harriet Higginson and bludgeoned her viciously on the head, so viciously that she required five brain operations and was long confined to a nursing home. Since robbery did not seem to be a motive, the Connecticut State Police—and all of Cornwall—assumed it was the work of a sexual attacker. Several warmly inscribed books and pictures by Thurber were found in the Higginson house, and the police learned that the Thurbers were among the first to discover the battered woman. Both Helen and Thurber were interrogated by a State Police captain, who, it became clear, suspected Thurber of having affairs with women left husbandless by the war. The captain noticed how Thurber, though blind, deftly smoked his cigarettes and always knew where the ashtray was. "I've seen blind men and men who could see," he told Thurber, "but until now I've never seen both." At another point in the interrogation, the captain wanted to know how a blind man could be an artist. "What kind of artist are you?" he asked, and Thurber replied, "I refuse to answer that question on the ground that it might incriminate me."(16) Thurber was at last stricken from the list of possible suspects when the captain questioned him about a certain Cornwall man. Thurber admitted he didn't like him because the man was anti-Semitic. The captain dismissed Thurber, with

---

*Helen's dedication to the care of her difficult husband was common knowledge to anybody who knew them. Thurber in his later years had to relieve himself often. In public places, Helen would lead him as far as the men's-room door and, in her words, "hope for the best or that some kind stranger would help." Once, she led him to what was, unknown to her, a labyrinthine men's room, and soon from within she heard Thurber cry, "Get me out of here, somebody!" She still didn't dare enter, but "a wonderful man" came to their rescue and set Thurber straight just in time.

Helen is also obsessively efficient and tidy. "I was always a neat person," she said, "but when Jamie went blind he had to have everything in the same place all the time or he would scream with frustration. So I got in the habit of utter neatness and I never lost it."

apologies for taking up his time. The captain, it turned out, was Jewish.

The local citizens were unpleasantly wary of each other for some months after the crime, until a male baby-sitter was picked up for a similar assault in a nearby Massachusetts town. The case was never officially closed, but the burden of guilt was taken off Cornwall, and faces and friendships brightened. As for Thurber, he was both amused and fascinated by his own vague involvement in the bloody mystery. He had long been a devotee of juicy crime stories (especially, the Hall–Mills murder case and O.S.U.'s own Snook–Hix scandal, both of which he wrote about), but being a suspect himself was a little too exciting. He was intrigued by gossip about the Higginson case for years; he also showed profound grief for poor Harriet Higginson.

Once Thurber's presence in Cornwall was established, Rosemary spent her summers with him there. During the other months, she lived and went to school in Amherst, Massachusetts, where Althea and her third husband, a history professor, resided. It was over these summer visits that Thurber and his daughter, a bright and pretty teen-ager, got to know each other and developed a sturdy relationship. "There was no generation gap in Cornwall," Rosemary said. "The adults were our contemporaries and we all went to the same parties together. I was close to Helen, but I can't say she was a second mother to me. She is at a loss with kids. I was also very close to Rose Algrant and her son, Rollie, and John Zabriskie, who was like another son to Rose. Also the Van Doren boys. It was quite a group, really. There were so many parties. Everybody got smashed. On the morning-after, when I told my father what he had said or done the night before, he would be all Jello or say, 'Don't tell me that!' I only saw him blow up a few times. I think he tried to keep under control when I was around. We'd know in the morning if it was going to be one of *those* days. He would pace about after a bad night, and the apologies would come much later. The best thing to do then was just stay clear of him.

"A typical working day for him began there at about nine-thirty, when he'd come down for breakfast. He'd pet and talk to our black standard poodle, called 'Poodle,' who worshipped him and always seemed to know when to get out of his way. Sometimes, my father wasn't really there; his mind was working, playing with words, even during meals. Then the secretary would come and he would dictate and chat with her. He would still be talking out loud even after she left, preparing, I guess, the next day's work. He had no luck with tape recorders, when they came out. He'd just sing into them—'Bye Bye, Blackbird' or 'Who.' He was simply no good with mechanical things. A milkshake before lunch was a big treat, and, if he wasn't working in the afternoon, he'd listen to a ball game, always rooting against the Yankees. 'The goddam Yankees!' he'd shout. 'Even the pigeons are on their side.' He had no Ohio loyalty for the Indians or the Reds; he was just against the Yankees. Then, drinks before dinner, wine or beer with dinner, and the radio news—Elmer Davis or Edward P. Morgan. If there was no party, we'd read to him or he'd listen some more to the radio. He didn't go to bed late on those nights. Reading aloud to him —the mail, newspapers, books—was fun. Once, when I was quite young, I started to read a rough John O'Hara letter out loud. My father screamed, 'Helen!' and they grabbed it away from me. There were advantages for the lack of a supposedly normal family life. I was a little afraid in Cornwall that I was popular because my father was famous, but I got over that. Nobody in Cornwall really had a normal family situation, anyhow."

Thurber dearly wanted his only child to be a writer. He was impressed by the writing she showed him ("My stories," Rosemary said, "were very sad, never funny, and always had a difficult mother character"). When she was a student at the Northampton School for Girls in the late 1940's, Thurber sent a revealing series of letters to the school's headmistress, Miss Sarah B. Whitaker. The letters were revealing of a loving, concerned parent and of a man fearful of the wayward course of education. As Rosemary veered farther away from a writing career and closer to one in acting, Thurber betrayed some worry. It wasn't so much that he was against her being an actress (after all, his own mother was denied such a choice, and Thurber himself relished the stage, whether it was in somebody's living room or on Broadway); rather, he wanted to insure her basic intellectual development.* To this end, he submitted to her, via the Northampton letters, a list of twenty personally important works of fiction, as a stimulus for Rosemary's, and any other student's, mind. The list included books by James, Cather, Hergesheimer, Fitzgerald, Hemingway, Lardner, White, Waugh, Wilder, and two new favorite female writers—Rebecca West and Elizabeth Bowen.

---

*An amateur production of The Male Animal was presented by the younger members of the Cornwall circle in the summer of 1948. Marc Simont played Dean Damon, Charles Van Doren was Tommy Turner, and Rosemary modestly took the role of Cleota, the colored maid. Thurber attended one performance and hailed it as the best he had seen outside the Cort Theatre. "Rosie was a triumph as Cleota and was picked as one of the two best by an old gal who played with Sothern and Marlowe," he wrote the coauthor, Nugent.(17)

He was in for some later disappointment from Rosemary, professionally speaking. After she was graduated from the Northampton School, she attended Skidmore College for one year and then became a drama major at the University of Pennsylvania. She showed promise as an actress there, but in the middle of her senior year, she married another student, Frederick Sauers, and her acting career withered, except for occasional community-theatre projects and the like. The pleasure he would have gleaned from Rosemary as a professional writer he received indirectly from Nora Sayre, the daughter of Joel and Gertrude, one of the dedicatees of *The White Deer*, and a kind of second daughter for Thurber. "He wanted Rosemary and me to be good friends," Nora Sayre said. "He'd buy us matinée tickets to dreadful plays and constantly try to get us together, so we'd be like sisters. But we two girls just didn't hit it off. I was sorry about that. Rosemary was so much more formal than I was. And later, when I announced that I wanted to be a writer, he encouraged me—especially at the *New Yorker*—and said he wished Rosemary would do the same. He was so sweet. And I was so cozy with Helen, too, although she had troubles with my father. Helen and Jim were like proxy parents."

When Dr. Bruce returned from combat with the Marines (highly decorated and partially deaf), he examined Thurber and found him hopelessly blind. The doctor didn't tell him so, exactly; he left a few hope handles sticking up for easy grasping, but he knew the blindness was irreversible. So did Thurber, in a way. He wrote Dr. Bruce, from his New York City apartment, on January 9, 1946:

... I never have counted on any further monkeying with what is left of my eye, so you can rest in the tranquil knowledge that I am perfectly satisfied to let well enough alone. It is going to be harder to get an instrument in my eye again than to find you for the next war.

Your suggestion about pooling our resources is a good one, except that my right ear has an idiosyncrasy that might give you trouble every five years. I hope that your ears have somehow turned the corner and that you will eventually be able to hear what people are whispering about you.

I'll be seeing you one of these days.

Yours,
Jim
The blind humorist
Ha, ha
T.

Yet, he would tell interviewers of one-eighth vision in his eye and refer to himself as "nearly blind." He retained some optimism and humor about it all. When Rosemary would lead him somewhere, he'd loudly call himself "the blinky." "Don't tease the blinky," he'd warn her. (He loved to tease Rosemary, however. Once when they were walking through Grand Central Terminal, he suddenly embraced her and shouted, "Hi, Momma!" and then rambled on about how their family had lived in Grand Central for generations.) "For a long time he could make out yellow," Rosemary said. "When I wore a yellow dress, he'd surprise me by knowing what color it was. And he'd also surprise us by drawing an angular version of his dog, without any mechanical aid. We'd put in the eye dot. Sometimes, he'd draw the dog in the air with his finger."

A few of the mechanical aids, like the Zeiss loop and special lights, were helpful but others were often useless. "People were forever sending us new kinds of phosphorescent paper and drawing instruments," Helen said. A special illuminated drawing board was manufactured for him, at Ross's suggestion. *Life*, on February 19, 1945, printed a photograph of a Zeiss-looped Thurber executing a commissioned drawing on a large piece of yellow paper with black chalk. It took him, *Life* said, exactly six and a quarter minutes. (The drawing was bland Thurber, though.) As for using a seeing-eye dog—a natural solution for a blind man who loved dogs—Thurber never considered it. "He liked a seeing-eye wife better," Dr. Bruce said. "And he resisted braille, too. It would have meant the end of the road to him."

For a man who took a certain resigned view of his own inherent clumsiness (he had mastered the trick, he once wrote, of "walking into himself"),(18) blindness only exaggerated his awkwardness. The sometimes slapstick consequences of Thurber's stumbling about amused Ross, who found the black humor in it a way of accepting the tragic fact. At a large party Ross threw for Rebecca West to meet his writers and cartoonists, there was suddenly a terrific crash as somebody knocked over a table loaded with glasses and bottles. Ross turned in his chair and simply said, "Thurber?"

Writing solely by dictation, Thurber experimented with different techniques until he found the method that suited him best. At first, he distrusted dictation because he felt his sentences were running long, but as he became more adept at mental revision, the sentences tightened up. Also, he found that he wasn't distracted any more by the things that distracted sighted writers—"flying birds or the breeze or a pretty girl walking by."(19) It wasn't until the appearance in 1948 of a woman with the name of Elfride Von Kuegelgen (called "Fritzi" by one and all) that Thurber was totally at ease with dictation. Fritzi (an American citizen caught in Germany during the war, who managed to survive and later captivate Thurber with her stories) took over the job of Thurber's Cornwall secretary from a friend of hers who quit. She worked for Thurber off and on till he died.

"In the beginning, I read to him and took dictation three afternoons a week," Fritzi said, "and I did the typing at home in the evenings. He decided he worked better with me in the afternoons than in the morning. Although he was almost completely blind, he sometimes tried to write in longhand, but then I spent too much time deciphering it. The dictation was painfully slow at first, he was so inhibited. I almost fell asleep. As he got better, I took a correspondence course in speed-writing and worked every afternoon. That story he loved to tell—where I supposedly said, 'Hey, slow up, I'm using my speed-writing!'—isn't really true. Once in a while, there would be only a single revision of a letter or a piece; other times, I would read something back to him, so he could revise, as much as twenty or thirty times. But the first draft was always set in his mind. When I read him books, he would amaze me by saying something like, 'Go back to around page thirty-five.' We usually started writing a piece from the beginning, page one.

"His mind never stopped working. But when he didn't feel like writing, we would just sit and talk. Every so often, he would get moody and reach over and throw the manuscript into the wastebasket. Only once, we had a big argument. It was about Germany. He kicked over the card table, and I walked out. All in all, he was a nice man to work for. Moody, though. He could be funny or dead-serious from minute to minute. All his life, he remained an Ohio boy at heart, with a universal wisdom."

Helen remembered that she would often see her husband alone in his working room just scribbling away meaninglessly on pieces of yellow copy paper. "He needed to perform the physical act of writing," she said.

What with the new Cornwall house, the experimentation in writing procedures, the war's atomic climax, and other confusions, 1946 was not a good year for literary productivity. In fact, he published only one piece the entire year, his smallest output since bleak 1924. The piece was called "What the Animals Were Up To." It was printed in *Life* and later included in a book for returning servicemen, entitled *While You Were Gone: A Report on Wartime Life in the United States.* Thurber's contribution dealt with the notorious World War II story of Blaze, the bull mastiff belonging to the actress Faye Emerson and her husband

Lieutenant Colonel Elliott Roosevelt. The dog was the innocent source of a cause célèbre when, with highest priority, it bumped a sailor on emergency leave off a military plane. Roosevelt dogs were forever raising eyebrows among the Roosevelt detractors, and Thurber's piece did a lot to put the Blaze scandal in perspective.

Thurber himself held mixed feelings about the Roosevelts, but America's entry into the war made him a believer. Through his lawyer, Morris Ernst, he had given President Roosevelt a drawing he did for Margaret Ernst's book, *In a Word,* showing ancient Roman political candidates smoking cigars. Roosevelt had just announced that he was running for a third term and appreciated the apt gift. Thurber became involved in a rather elaborate practical joke which had been dreamed up by the highly placed Thurber fan not long before he died. During a light moment at the Quebec Conference, Roosevelt, apparently a great kidder, told Mrs. Winston Churchill that the Brussels sprout was the favorite American vegetable and that the English were missing something by not knowing the thirty-four interesting ways to cook it. Mrs. Churchill was unconvinced, so Roosevelt instructed a friend to print up privately a pamphlet entitled *Thirty-four Ways to Cook Brussels Sprouts,* including mythical recipes and a cover design drawn by Thurber. The President specifically requested that the Thurber drawing show a long table holding a large glass bowl filled with human-faced Brussels sprouts, and lines of hungry, fork-wielding Americans descending on the table. Thurber was put off by the cannibalistic note in the requested picture (especially since it was going to be seen by the severe Thurber critic Churchill), but he agreed to try a design of just Brussels sprouts with faces. It wasn't easy. He spent days attempting to recall what the loathesome legume looked like, but he couldn't visualize one, and he couldn't even feel one because they were out of season. He asked Armin Landeck's professional help. Landeck told him, "Think of a miniature squeezed baseball, seam and all." It worked, and Thurber completed the drawing, throwing in one of his dogs reaching for a sprout, for good measure and to fill out the composition. Only the Roosevelt and Churchill families received copies of the pamphlet; Thurber never did get a copy and was justifiably peeved, although he was sent a warm thank-you note by Mrs. Kermit Roosevelt. Presumably, the drawing did nothing to change Churchill's earlier estimation of Thurber's talent, although the private sprout joke was reportedly a success, even after Roosevelt's death.

With a purported, and probably not exaggerated, 170,000 drawings committed to paper up to 1947, Thurber threw in the towel. The towel-throwing was performed with more personal pain than he admitted publicly. It was exacting simply too much physical and mental strain for him to scratch out his pictures any longer. His last original for the *New Yorker*—a spot of two men boxing—was printed on November 1, 1947. (The very last original drawing he was able to eke out anywhere was an accurate self-portrait with four rampant dogs, executed in white crayon on black paper, for his own July 9, 1951, *Time* cover story.) Ross, shaken by this turn of events, proposed that old cuts of Thurber drawings be reversed and elements in each be rearranged (a dog here, a piece of furniture there) to create whole new cartoons with new captions, thought up by Thurber. A young cartoonist named Frank Modell was one of the staff artists given the rearrangement chore by Ross. This slightly shady practice, along with straight reprints of old Thurber spots, began in 1948 and continued well into the 1950's, until the ruse was discovered by some observant readers and the London *News Chronicle*.

Thurber's fondness for denigrating his drawing and quoting other disparagers grew as the impossibility of continuing to draw became more apparent. When the director of the Columbus Museum of Fine Arts referred to Thurber as "Columbus's first artist," Thurber called that fact yet another poor reflection on the hapless city.(20) In interview after interview, he put his drawings down. "Drawing to me was a little bit more than tossing cards in a hat," he told Henry Brandon. "I don't think any drawing ever took me more than three minutes."(21) And he got a perverse kick out of telling the anecdote of his answer to a woman who wrote him that her baby son could draw as well as he, sending a sample of the tot's art to prove it. Thurber wrote her back: "Your son can certainly draw as well as I can. The only trouble is he hasn't been through as much."(22) But to his fellow-artist and friend, Marc Simont, Thurber's attitude towards his art work brought out another deep contradiction in the man. "He was split on how he wanted the drawings taken, seriously or jokingly," Simont said. "He really liked praise for his pictures, especially from another artist, and he would casually mention that he was compared to Dufy and Matisse by some critics. He never asked me, but I didn't go along with those comparisons, although I am thrilled to own some of Thurber's drawings. They give me great pleasure. He was a magnificent *literary* artist; his drawings usually alluded to something literary, like Lear's or Beerbohm's. But Thurber's was a child's technique—of a basically simple existence made complicated by life. The Thurber old man was like any other Thurber man, except he had a beard pasted on. His women and dogs were that way because that was the only way he could draw them. His drawings were pictorial handwriting, his own hieroglyphics."

There were other reasons for low productivity and a touch of sourness creeping back into his life in the mid-1940's. His brothers' respective futures and upkeep, like raising Arabian horses, were fraught with expensive problems, and his mother's health, in her eightieth year, was worrisome. Thurber and Helen travelled to Columbus in January of 1946 to honor the octogenarian Mame with a mammoth birthday party for fifty-five relatives and friends at the Deshler-Wallick Hotel (about which Helen had once written Robert Thurber that from the top of the Mark in San Francisco you see one of the most beautiful harbors in the world, whereas from the top of the Deshler-Wallick all you see is Columbus). The party was a success, with the spry matron a bubbling guest of honor. However, Helen and her husband arrived back in New York exhausted.

The irritations kept coming. Thurber found himself embroiled in what was known as "The *Sundial* Affair." The Ohio State humor magazine, which Thurber had once edited, was, in the rheumy eyes of the university's administration, becoming offensive (*i.e.*, dirty), as so many other collegiate humor magazines became after the war. The administration decided to suspend publication for a year and thereafter change the magazine's name to *Scarlet Fever*. Thurber, Nugent, Gardner Rea, and other *Sundial* ex-editors were indignant—especially Thurber, after he received a letter from the Secretary of the Ohio State University Association, John Fullen, blaming the smut on "an unhealthy gang of Cleveland Jews [who] got control and, brother, when they get dirty they don't fool around."(23) Thurber devoted days of good writing time rocketing off letters to O.S.U. officials, Rea, Nugent, and anybody else he could think of who would be interested in the censorship scandal. To Nugent, he wrote: "Some action seems necessary if 'The Male Animal' is not just a play."(24) To Rea, he said, apropos of Rosemary's possible academic future at Ohio State: ". . . I would cut off my daughter's hair if she suggested going out there."(25)

Growing more infuriated with each exchange of letters, he threatened to make a national issue out of the name-change and censorship brouhaha, but before he made good his threat, he had suddenly won his battle. In the spring of 1946, the O.S.U. administration reinstated the name *Sundial, Scarlet Fever* died as if shot full of penicillin, and a well-scrubbed version of freedom of the press survived at Ohio State. It was a good fight, but it took a lot out of him.

So, too, did other incidents, both public and personal. The habitually jittery New York *Herald Tribune* published an editorial at the end of 1947 concurring with the postwar witch-hunters that employees should be required to sign statements of loyalty and political belief. Many writers, most notably E. B. White, sent letters to the editor condemning the notion as unconstitutional, and the *Tribune* heatedly replied in another editorial. Thurber, at the Homestead again, leapt into the fray with the same spirit he had summoned for The *Sundial* Affair.* First, he wrote White:

Dear Andy:

I am enclosing a copy of a letter I just wrote. Helen read me your letter and the editorial reply last night and I stayed awake for hours getting madder and madder.

Of course The Tribune would like to take a sock at you because you can write and it can't . . .

The blow is also aimed at The New Yorker through you and the battle and the investigation are on. Do you remember when, in far less terrible times than these, Postmaster Walker, who had tried to close down *Esquire,* was reported to be itching to get at The New Yorker?

Keep your chin up and your powder dry and your eye on The Herald Tribune . . .

Thurber's enclosed letter to the *Herald Tribune* read:

Your editorial of December 2 entitled "The Party of One" and written in reply to E. B. White's letter in the same issue, could be used as a preface to a book on how to set up a totalitarian state under the bright banner of the security of the nation and the responsibilities of individuals to the Constitution. This is the familiar way in which all such states have been established.

Your editorial clearly suggests Chapter I for the handbook I have mentioned: How to Discredit Liberals as Dangerous Elements Who Imperil the Safety of

---

*Thurber was a staunch defender of E. B. White in other matters, too. When he was asked by Whit Burnett, the editor of the Story Press, to contribute one of his pieces to an impossibly conceived and titled anthology, *The World's Best,* Thurber sent Burnett a string of petulant letters stating that "there is surely nothing I have done under 3,000 words that belongs even in the collection of Connecticut's best" and that the omission of E.B. White ("one of the great living prose writers") would make Thurber feel pretty silly to be in such a book.(27) Nevertheless, Thurber allowed Burnett to use "More Alarms at Night" in the silly collection.

Earlier, he had turned down election to the National Institute of Arts and Letters because White was not also named. White was embarrassed by his stand. "It made no sense to me," he said. "I think Jim was more interested in an intellectual fight than in my being a member."

Thurber could also be a little catty about White. He once heard Mark Van Doren say that White was not a true poet. This judgment titillated Thurber; he told Van Doren, "I have something official on White now."

the Nation and the True Meaning of Its Constitution, and Who Stand in the Way of the New Freedom and the Greater Security.

But why should I instruct your editorial writer? He seems to have a natural gift and a peculiar facility for writing the handbook.

James Thurber
Hot Springs, Va.
Dec. 3, 1947(26)

A good part of Thurber's unease was due to an extended and celebrated confrontation with no less a personage than Samuel Goldwyn. With Ross's help, Thurber had been dickering all through the war years with several producers over the movie sale of "The Secret Life of Walter Mitty." The casual was well established as an American classic, and American classics had to be made into movies, for some reason. Finally, Thurber agreed to sell the film rights to Goldwyn for fifteen thousand dollars in 1944. Two days after the contract was signed, both Nunnally Johnson and Twentieth Century Fox offered thirty thousand. ("Tough, but usual, titty," Thurber wrote John McNulty.)(28) Johnson wanted it for Jack Benny, Fox wanted it for George Jessel, and Goldwyn wanted it for Danny Kaye—and that's where the trouble began.

As a vehicle for Danny Kaye, "Mitty" would no longer be "Mitty." Rather, it would be, as Thurber later said, "The Public Life of Danny Kaye."(29) The Mitty creator's first direct involvement with Goldwyn was in November of 1945, when the producer brought to New York a completed script, bespoke for Danny Kaye by a trio of Hollywood scriptwriters and Goldwyn himself. Thurber came face-to-face with a barely recognizable Walter Mitty, redolent with Kaye routines, Sylvia Fine's "git-gat-gittle" songs (as Thurber dubbed them), and such senseless changes as making Mitty's wife into Mitty's mother. Living up to his reputation, Goldwyn told Thurber that the last hundred pages of the script were too "blood and thirsty"—to which Thurber replied, after he had read the entire script, that he was "horror and struck."(30) Nevertheless, Thurber set about trying to remove some of the Goldwyn blood and thirst from the monstrous offspring, with the aid of one of the Hollywood scriptwriters, Ken Englund. It was arduous, frustrating, fruitless work; there was no fighting the incredible taste of Sam Goldwyn. The movie was, of course, made without most of Thurber's suggested changes.

In the meantime, other disgruntled Mitty purists were muttering darkly. A Walter Mitty Association, led by Frank Sullivan, sent threatening letters, and Thurber was forced to apologize in advance, through the *Times*'s drama section, for the looming profanation. The movie was released, with appropriate fanfare, in August of 1947, and Thurber vs. Goldwyn became more of a public debate than ever. Thurber was quoted as saying: "If they'd spent one-tenth the money, it would be ten times as good."(31) *Life*, on August 18, 1947, ran two letters from the prime combatants. Goldwyn's letter (so smooth and free of malapropism that few readers seriously believed Goldwyn had actually written it) praised the original story—"which added great luster to the little magazine in which it was first published"—and, with equal patronization, went on to give a Hollywood-sunglass view of Thurber's participation in the movie. Thurber's letter was one of his better forensic efforts. He explained in accurate and funny detail, with appropriate documentation, his whole ghastly role in the affair, ending the letter with: "Sorry, Walter, sorry for everything." He added a neat P.S.: "This letter was written by Jamie Thurber, aged 52, without help of his parents or teacher. 'The little magazine,' so much bigger than Goldwyn, Inc., except in physical size, needs no other defense than the revealing slur itself."

The Great Goldwyn–Thurber Debate was complicated by another business deal. Goldwyn had also acquired the rights to "The Catbird Seat" (which its author once said was "probably my best short story"),(32) with the stipulation that Thurber would write a fifteen-thousand-word movie treatment of the story by a certain date for ten thousand dollars against a total of fifty thousand, if his completed script was acceptable to Goldwyn. In March of 1946, Thurber told the Herman Millers that "I am about to dive into the preposterous adventure of a movie treatment for Goldwyn—a Baudelairean experience among the dark flowers. It will take only 2 months, anyway."(33) It took more than two months, and Thurber was still unsatisfied with the product. Somehow, through "Hollywood razzle-dazzle,"(34) the treatment turned up in Goldwyn's office ahead of the deadline. Goldwyn sent the ten thousand, which Thurber promptly returned, asking for his script and the rights back. He got both, tore up the script, and resold the rights to another film company. In 1959, a British outfit produced "The Catbird Seat"; it was the only worthy film of a Thurber work ever made. It was called *The Battle of the Sexes* and starred Peter Sellers, Constance Cummings, and Robert Morley. Reset in Scotland, the movie, though decidedly British–Scottish in tone, was still Thurber. Its wit and appeal showed that the English movie-makers had an appreciation for his material that their American counterparts could never muster—a national lesson that was not lost on Thurber, who liked what he heard when he attended a screening.

*   *   *

Money begets more money, or, at the very least, a desire for more money. Some friends of the Thurbers felt that Helen had put high ideas of high finance in her husband's head, a conclusion probably based on her bringing order from chaos when she took over Thurber's fiscal affairs after their marriage. Indeed, both of them appreciated luxuries, attentive servants, handsome furnishings, unrestricted vacations. Their medical bills alone were astronomical, to say nothing of support monies for the rest of the Thurber family. In a written agreement, signed in March, 1941, Thurber was to pay five thousand dollars a year to Helen for work as his "agent" in his "business affairs." By 1945, the fee was raised to $7,500 a year, and, as a Christmas present, he gave her *The Last Flower* original drawings, with a note advising that if she sold them, they "will keep you going." It was all cheap for the services above and beyond the call of duty Thurber got in return from his seeing-eye wife.

Whatever the cause, Thurber's sudden concern and quest for more money after his postwar bonanza took some strange forms. In 1947, he wrote Hawley Truax, then the treasurer of the *New Yorker*, and complained about some niggling payments he believed the magazine still owed him for his expenses at Wimbledon in 1938 and for six 1927 casuals that, he claimed, he was never fully compensated for at the going word rate. He was sincerely angry and even threatening about these minor alleged bookkeeping discrepancies. (Meanwhile, the *New Yorker* helped defray the expenses for his secretaries whenever he was writing something specifically for that magazine.)

His legal fees grew along with his financial dealings, so much so that he was moved to write this letter to one of his lawyers, Alexander Lindey, of Greenbaum, Wolff & Ernst, on April 4, 1949:

... Up to 1934 my budget for barristers had consisted of $500 which I paid on the occasion of my divorce from the Kappa Rosebud I married in 1921,* when I was getting $35 a week. With the approach of the arthritic period of life, with its Book-of-the-Month symptoms and its tendency to sell stories to the movies, I suddenly attained that primary mark of the successful casual writer: my annual legal fees assumed the proportions of those of a small business firm hiring fifteen people, nine men and six women. People began to make ballets, print dresses, fired enamel tea trays, beer coasters, recordings, and oratorios out of the small things I had written and drawn. Writers began to accuse me of plagiarism, invasion of privacy,

---

*He married Althea in 1922.

libel, and unAmerican activities. This is known as success in America.

Nor was the federal government idle during this period. There came the day, a few years ago, when one of your colleagues phoned me to announce "I have got your tax for this year down to $64,000." The idea that anything could be got down to a point that high distorted my thinking for several years, and when a movie producer wired me an offer of $300 a week, I wired back "Ross has met the decrease." It was some weeks before I could be persuaded that I did not deserve a cut in my word rate. Meanwhile, the government decided to give Helen half my income for the purposes of taxation, but as soon as Congress finds out I am married my full earnings will rightfully be returned to me. In the midst of all this, Chester Bowles, whom I elected, figures that I should pay a state tax of approximately $1400, and he points out that this will relieve me from the payment of New York State taxes to which I am not liable . . .

The print dresses, fired enamel tea trays, and beer coasters Thurber referred to in the letter to his lawyer were not all that exaggerated, for part of his treasure hunt was in the murky mines of advertising, commercial enterprises, and endorsements. There were in fact textile prints and coasters using old Thurber drawings as motifs. There were even ads for Aqua Velva after-shave lotion, Bug-a-boo insecticide, and the Franklin Simon department store ("Christmas in the James Thurber fashion. And that's all frolic, fantasy, nothing but fun.") He endorsed, for magazine layouts, *Webster's New World Dictionary of the American Language*, but turned down several other less cerebral endorsements, including Bostonian shoes and Old Angus Scotch.

His funniest and most aggravating commercial entanglement concerned an R.C.A. Victor brochure of commentaries on famous recording artists by equally famous contemporary authors. Thurber was asked to write not more than sixty words about Serge Koussevitzky, for the honorarium of some free Koussevitzky albums and $150. Thurber accepted the invitation, although he told an executive at J. Walter Thompson Company, which was handling the arrangements, "Nobody can write fifty or sixty words about anybody . . . but it amuses me to be able to tell Ross that I can get two dollars a word."(35) (In 1932, Thurber had rewritten a "Talk" piece on Koussevitzky, so he knew something about the conductor, even if serious music wasn't exactly a Thurber forte.) He wrote his little appreciation (typically using himself as the starting point), but the folks over at J. Walter Thompson wanted something a bit different. Two strained rewrites later, Thurber sent in his finished one-paragraph draft and the following letter:

. . . Enclosed is the Koussevitzky item, written by me, for the last time, too, and in the precise form in which it must be used. You say that the client liked the other two, but the hash of it destroys them both. Furthermore, I never permit anybody to write stuff for me and the job you sent me is awful beyond description. The client and your copy chief can both go to hell with my compliments if they prefer that to this piece. Any further work on it will cost you more money . . .

I shouldn't have got mixed up in this crap and I will be glad to raise hell personally if your butchers and Mr. Piffle at R.C.A. mangles what I have written again . . .(36)

The client and J. Walter Thompson accepted the piece (finally entitled "Old Thunder and Lilacs") and sped to Thurber a check for $150. What Koussevitzky never knew didn't hurt him.

When some of Thurber's fans began to send him complaints about his commercial ventures—particularly, the Aqua Velva ad—Thurber answered them with embarrassment. He weakly explained that he needed money in the 1940's.

One of the strangest writing projects Thurber ever embarked on started in 1947. It was a five-part "Onward and Upward with the Arts" series for the *New Yorker* on radio soap operas, called "Soapland." It was a product of Thurber's necessary attachment to the radio as a prime source of contact with the outside world, his desire to do some more research reportage again in the *New Yorker* manner, and an ever-growing emphasis in his writing on the aural. The few casuals he wrote in 1947 were almost all concerned with, as might be expected of a blind author, what he heard and thought, rather than what he saw. "Am Not I Your Rosalind?," for instance, is a rendering of a bitchy, boozy meeting between two competitive couples, in which a tape recorder plays a major part. "The Waters of the Moon" makes merciless fun of literary badinage and blather. "Thix" is a light comparison of children's radio serials and the old nickel novels of his youth. "The Ordeal of Mr. Matthews" is a boring ordeal of sheer sermonizing on the elusive subject of wit. And "Here Come the Tigers" is a shining, mad exercise in mental anagramming. There was, too, a link between Thurber's affection for Henry James and soap operas, for, as he once pointed out, James is soap opera on a grand scale.(37)

The five "Soapland" articles—dealing with, by turns, the soapers' origins, their content, their creators, their actors, and their listeners—were meant by Thurber to be more informative than funny. He wanted to show the inside and outside of a distinctly American cultural phenomenon, particularly as it pertained to his own view of the American Woman vs. the American Man. The soap-opera male was really the Thurber male with a resonant voice—weak, confused, dominated, and even emasculated by a variation of the Thurber female, who was Amazonian, a pillar of strength in constant crisis, and an indispensable pain in the ass. Being Thurber, he couldn't help but be humorous about all this:

. . . All men in Soapland must be able to drop whatever they are doing and hurry to this living room or that at the plaint or command of a feminine voice on the phone. Bill Davidson's one-chair barbershop has not had a dozen customers in a dozen years, since the exigencies of his life keep him out of the shop most of every day . . . "The Story of Mary Marlin," just to be different, had a President of the United States, but, just to be the same, he was made heavily dependent on the intuitive political vision of his aged mother, who, in 1943, remained alive to baffle the doctors and preserve, by guiding her son's policies, the security of the Republic . . .

And there was this observation of time in radio serials:

. . . Compared to the swift flow of time in the real world, it is a glacier movement. It took one male character in a soap opera three days to get an answer to the simple question "Where have you been?" . . .(38)

The question of whether the articles were to be basically factual or funny brought Thurber into some testy conflict with Ross and the fact editor assigned to the series, William Shawn, later Ross's successor.* Thurber wrote Shawn, on March 11, 1948:

. . . If the idea of length becomes predominant and you and Ross have the idea that this is a series of funny pieces then obviously any cuts you made without my knowledge would be on behalf of funnying-up the pieces by cutting out the necessary facts which make this a survey and give it an importance worthy of my time and your space. The humor in this series is coincidental.
I am willing and eager to consider fairly and respectfully all suggested cuts and changes and omissions you may want to make, but this series is not subject to any editing whatever without my knowledge and consent . . .
I am sure this will all work out simply and amicably and I was probably mainly upset by Ross's comment on length without a word about content, coming at the same time that my last casual was treated in typescript and proof as if it had been the work of an unknown beginner. Every now and then a professorial and

---

*The soap-opera pieces were the only ones by Thurber that Shawn directly edited. He recalled that it "wasn't a happy experience." Thurber was in an agitated state over Ross's queries, most of which dealt with the need for greater detail. Shawn felt the soap-opera idea was dated even then.

academic purism shows up in the proof reading and this is a menace unmixed, since it operates towards that dreadful "New Yorker style" which we deny and try to avoid. When I write "I had never been there before" the professors suggest "I never had been there before." I had this out with my teachers before the professors were born . . .

Once, when Shawn and Ross were trying to explain to him a fault in a "Soapland" piece, Ross lost his patience and blurted, "If you could see, you would know what we mean," which in turn propelled Thurber into a tantrum of invective.(39) A high hurdle Thurber had encountered in the year-long project was absorbing and collating all the hard research done for him by others. On March 24, 1948, he again wrote Shawn:

. . . The fact of the matter is that it was too much for a blind man to take on and this is why the Congress has just allowed me and the rest of us that $600 deduction. (Seriously, though, they are probably talking about the stone blind and my blindness is only plastic.)

Since there are a thousand items of source material for this series and I can't see them I have to keep as many in mind as possible and then have others read to me. Since no one could keep all these facts, figures, names and incidents in his mind I have had to dictate the last 4,000 words of this piece. After eight years of practice this is not too difficult . . .

In spite of my flare-up I am willing and eager to listen to all suggestions on these pieces but all rewriting must be done by me . . . None of the meticulous morphology of this monumental masterpiece was the result of accident or carelessness. It has been deliberately put together at the cost of blood, sweat and tears . . .

Flare-ups to the contrary, Thurber admired Shawn as an editor, although he didn't have the same warm relationship with him he had with Ross. Shawn, a retiring man and far more intellectual than Ross, wasn't exactly Thurber's type. When the "Soapland" articles were published in the spring and summer of 1948, they were very well received —and it was Thurber's "coincidental" humorous writing that was as memorable as his factual "survey" writing. The series is both a profound and witty analysis of a significant part of Americana, and it demonstrated that Thurber could still be a first-rate reporter and observer, in spite of everything.

In September of 1948, a new Thurber collection was brought out by Harcourt, Brace, entitled *The Beast in Me and Other Animals*. Dedicated to "Ronnie and Janey Williams/ In memory of the serene hours at Felicity Hall," the book is heavy with the pieces Thurber had written since his blindness. The resulting impression of the anthology is one of overconcentration on the aural and word-game pieces, dejection, and sameness. Besides the casuals, the book includes some thitherto-uncollected cartoons and series (with "A New Natural History" standing out), the "Soapland" articles, and, for good measure, some old "Talk of the Town" visit pieces, written between 1928 and 1936, and seeming fresher and brighter than some of his later casuals. The book didn't do anywhere near as well as his other collections; in fact, it was a dud compared to the skyrocketry of *The Thurber Carnival*. Perhaps, Thurber sensed this would be the case when he set down the Foreword to *The Beast in Me*. He wrote:

> A writer verging on his middle fifties, when he should be engaged on some work dignified by length and of a solemnity suitable to our darkening age, is a little surprised to find himself coming out with still another collection of short pieces and small drawings. He toys for a while with the idea of a prefatory note pointing out that all this is a necessary and natural rehearsal for the larger project that awaits the increase of his patience and the lengthening of his view. Then, in re-examining his material for evidence to sustain this brave theory, he finds little to support his argument and a great deal to contradict it . . .

He still felt somewhat guilty about not having written The Big Book, The Great Novel, or whatever, but in spite of this lacuna in his literary output and the apathy attending the publication of *The Beast in Me*, the continuing praise for the "Soapland" pieces gave him just the confidence boost he needed to overcome the Thurbs and other problems. Soon, he began to write with a vengeance. Casuals of all sorts came gushing out of him, as if released by a magic word.

CHAPTER 17

"What a writer needs is handicaps." (1)

At the enviable rate of a casual a month, Thurber wrote as well as he ever had for the *New Yorker*, during late 1948 and 1949. There was a lot of the old Thurber and less of the new in the spate of pieces. For instance, in "File and Forget" the snowballing-madness technique of some of his funniest casuals returned through the device of correspondence between one "J. Thurber" and the hopelessly inefficient Charteriss Publishing Company, which refuses to recognize his rightful name, address, or desires. J. Thurber, a Charteriss author, is plagued by unasked-for and unwanted orders of thirty-six copies of *Grandma Was a Nudist* and thirty-six copies of his own book, called, for the casual's purposes, *Thurber's Ark*. J. Thurber threatens to burn all seventy-two volumes in the middle of Route 7, and does exactly that, as chaos waltzes about him.

In "The White Rabbit Caper" Thurber reverted to straight parody of Dashiell Hammett radio detective programs, leaving no cliché of the genre unmocked. "What a Lovely Generalization!," a Benchleyish lecture on verbal habits of Americans, and "A Friend of the Earth," a happy annihilation of the unlikable country character everybody pretends to like, were also welcome signs of the old master at his good works.

One short story printed in 1949, "Teacher's Pet," was especially revealing. The writing itself showed no new turn of style or content; it is a switch-ending, autobiographical third-person short story about a onetime teacher's pet who, in adulthood, faces with mixed feelings a neighbor's boy of the same stripe. The protagonist's rage is directed at the weakling victim as much as at the mush-brained bully. Thurber was a classic teacher's pet as a child—the delicate half-blind boy with the brilliant mind, the favorite of every Miss Groby in Columbus—and he was often picked on by witless teases. Later in life, he at once appreciated and abominated the plight of similar lads; in 1949, he still considered himself basically a cosset, and that both disgusted and comforted him. (The man's man in Cornwall he had provoked into shameful violence provided a way, perhaps, of exorcising the stigma; indeed, the man's man was the model for the bully's bully father in "Teacher's Pet.") Thurber once told Peter De Vries that he was a teacher's pet in his relations with Ross. He said that he was fed up with playing that role. Shortly after he confessed this to De Vries, about the time of the "Soapland" series, there was a marked change in his attitude towards the *New Yorker* and its editor.

The Thurbers vacationed in Bermuda again, spending most of their time there with the Williamses (which he called his "family" or "children"). They had tried Nassau in 1949, but Helen didn't enjoy it because it was too doggedly social for her.* Ronnie Williams was once again the editor of the *Bermudian*, and since Thurber was living for such long stretches on the island, Williams persuaded him to write some casual essays for the magazine. Thurber agreed, mainly as a gesture of friendship and as a chance to try out some ideas without Ross's hovering presence. (Ross was upset that Thurber was wasting good material on a relatively unknown journal, just as he was when Thurber had written his own short-lived radio program.) He wrote more than two dozen short pieces between 1949 and 1954, most of them under the heading "Letter From the States," all without fee. Some of Thurber's *Bermudian* pieces were good enough to be collected later, but most were run-of-the-mill short essays, more outspoken than, but no real competition for, the *New Yorker*.

As 1949 passed, things started to go sour again. On cue from the devil, a procession of setbacks and calamities occurred, seemingly designed to throw Thurber for new losses. His various theatrical projects, bobbing about in title, subject matter, and essence, were not going well at all.

---

*In a letter to Ann Honeycutt, sent just after he returned from Nassau, Thurber said: *... We got a lot of sun and liquor in Nassau, and met a lot of nice people who served good drinks. At the Marquands' I heard two different groups of people discussing you. They included Dos Passos, Sarah Murphy, and my wife. I could tell that Helen was beginning to feel her rum when I heard her assuring somebody that you are the only old girl of mine for whom she gives a good Goddamn. This praise of her most dangerous rival is either neurotic or a darned nasty trick. The Marquands asked us for six, but we didn't eat until nine, after at least seventeen cocktails. I remember giving an owlish analysis of American novelists, complete with fuzzy and mythical quotations from their work. The most fun was a luncheon on an island nearby with three former American ambassadors, for whom I recited a long sentence in green code. At the end James Gerard, aged eighty-one, said, "Golux." This was a green code word meaning "Period." Mrs. Norman Armour, the wife of one of the diplomats, is a Russian lady whom you would love and who kept saying to me, "Don't fuss"—Helen was down in bed and couldn't come that day, and she had to look after me. I was more troublesome than Argentina ...(2)*

He considered junking the whole business of playwriting. And then, in April, Herman Miller died, after a lingering illness. The blow from the loss of this intellectual comrade on Thurber was devastating. He wrote a tender condolence letter to Miller's widow, Dorothy:

Dearest Dorothy,

It is hard to write down the day after Herman Miller's death, for it marks the end of my oldest friend, and in so many ways my closest. No matter how long it had been since we saw each other, an old communion was easily and instantly reestablished. There was no other man who knew me so well, and I took pride and comfort in his sensitive understanding. He remembered everything, over thirty-five years, and brought it out with his special humorous soundness. There was more depth and pattern to our friendship than to any other, and I have nothing that can take its place. It was more pleasure to have his laughter and appreciation than anyone else's, because he was the one who completely understood all the references, sources and meanings. I have known nobody else in whom sensibility and intelligence were so perfectly joined.

I tried to make as much of a study of him as he did of me, and since I knew his gentleness as few did, it was a private joy of mine to watch him raise his shield against the dull and ordinary persons whom he kept on the outside. Not many got through to an appreciation of his aristocratic mind, his fine judgment of people and books, and his love of the wonderful, from the comic to the beautiful. For those he loved there was no code or key, though. It was all free and open, generous and devoted. One of the nicest things about him was that genuine shyness which at first couldn't believe that the ones he loved, loved him. His happiness was all the greater when he found out. There was never a moment when he wasn't important to me.

April 22nd

I couldn't write any more yesterday, and since then I've been thinking about Herman's good old Henry James awareness, and his fascinated analyses of Joe and Esther Taylor, Billy Graves, Althea-and-me, and others. Helen delighted him like a Christmas gift, because he saw she was made to order for me—and a tough order that is. I keep remembering all our fine days together, the suppers at your home, the party at the Whites in New York, the old chalice in Brooklyn, the time I kept going to the bathroom in the chemistry building, waiting for Minnette, and Herman's magnificent laughter when she rode up in a car and he saw she was going to have to sit on my restless lap all the way to Broad and High. I got more pleasure and satisfaction out of Herman's laughter than any one else's. It was wonderful when his sides actually began to ache and his eyes to stream. I will always remember it.

When I think of Herman, I think of you both, in a thousand ways. There was no other life for him than with you, and you were his complete happiness. You were wonderful for each other, and there is nobody like you. We wish that for Dorothy Miller we could be of some real help. We want you to come to visit us when we get back. I am involved in a play with a Bermuda setting, so we won't be back until the first of June, but maybe that will be a good time for you. We will be very quiet, and it's a peaceful house and countryside. We want you to come, and hope that you will. I know it will be good for you.

The last time I saw Herman, he told me he was not afraid, but I hope and pray it was not bad. Please tell us what you can, but don't write until you feel up to it. I know you will bear up somehow, and I know you will find serenity in the perfect memory you have of your years together. Few people have had so much.

It is a deep sorrow that I couldn't have seen Herman again, and couldn't have been there with you. I didn't see him often enough, or write to him enough, and I so wanted him to meet Rosemary. But I have long and loving memories of Herman Miller, and I will always have them.

We send you our deepest love, Dorothy. We mourn with you, and we will think of you constantly. God bless you.

Always,

Jim(3)

Back in Cornwall for the 1949 summer, plugging away again at his plays and nursing his depression, Thurber received some more bad news. In July, Rosemary was in an automobile accident near Gloucester, Massachusetts, which resulted in a broken pelvic bone and a hospital stay of several weeks. The shock for Thurber was greater than for Rosemary, who recovered in time to enter Skidmore in the fall. To muddle matters even further, the young man who was driving the car antagonized Thurber by affecting a blasé attitude towards the accident. The vengeful father wrote the Whites:

... I want to get to the man some way, legally or otherwise. It is well known that many accidents are caused by the male ego using gasoline for sex. She had never seen the man before—just one of those horrible people who get into a group ... We live in jeopardy and accidents are increasing in spite of all efforts, to which the maniac pays no attention. The thing has knocked us very hard, but we are pulling out of it . . .(4)

Long after Rosemary had recovered, Thurber was still angry at the young man. He decided to press his legal case against him in the Massachusetts courts, but he also wanted to spare Rosemary the pain of a trial. At last, in 1951, he settled out of court for $1,050 and expenses.

His fears for his daughter in an increasingly dangerous world emerged some months after the accident in a letter to John O'Hara:

. . . A year ago I sat around in the Algonquin lobby with Charley MacArthur and Jap Gude, talking about our daughters. Charley was apprehensive about all kinds of things happening to Mary. At the end I told him nothing would happen to our daughters, and in a year his was dead and mine was nearly killed in a car wreck. Jap's daughter Liz, a lovely girl of sixteen, was the only one to come through the year all right . . .(5)

Just about the time of Rosemary's accident, Elliott Nugent, in Thurber's phrase, "went off his rocker."(6) Nugent was suffering from severe manic-depressive symptoms, some of which sent him into spasms of misbehavior which made Thurber's seem like those of a cutup at a vestry supper. Nugent's mental illness (from which he never fully recovered) scared Thurber. Besides worrying over the condition of his old friend, mentor, and collaborator, he sensed, in some of Nugent's irrational actions, a disconcerting reminder of his own conduct during troubled periods. After all, he had only recently tangled with mental illness himself. He researched the manic-depressive syndrome with diligence and talked to doctors about it; when he learned that total cures were almost nonexistent, it scared him all the more. He wrote several letters to his and Nugent's common friends, showing concern for their understanding and their aid in coping with the problem. It was something else for Thurber to fret about, and fret about it he did for the rest of his days.

Before long, it was Helen's turn for the troubles. She had developed several benign uterine fibroids, and a partial hysterectomy was performed in February of 1950. Also, a large ovarian cyst was removed. It was a painful and frightening experience for Helen, but probably more frightening for Thurber, suddenly left seeing-eye wifeless and in the care of friends and *New Yorker* office boys. As he described it to the Williamses:

. . . I had the worst time the day of the operation because she didn't talk normally for five hours and said some strange but modest things, including the common assertion "I am going to die" but she remembers none of this and is in wonderful shape . . .(7)

With her customary resilience, Helen was soon out of the hospital and recuperating in their favorite oasis, Bermuda, with her relieved husband and Fritzi Von Kuegelgen, who accompanied the Thurbers for both business and pleasure. It was a good thing that Fritzi had come along, because during the four months she and the Thurbers were in Bermuda, they all wrote a book. It was another fairy tale for adults and children, called *The 13 Clocks*. Actually, Thurber had intended to work on a weightier project in Bermuda, but he found the going too weighty for such temperate climes. As Helen put it, "He needed relaxation, the way drawing had been relaxation for him when he was stuck on his writing." Also, Bermuda, in Thurber's words, was "the perfect place to write a fairy tale." He wrote "a clock a week" there.(8)

The idea for the fantasy—at least, for some of the characters' names —had sprung from the euphonious green-code vernacular of his Paris cryptography days. Just about a year earlier, he had been reciting green-code sentences to ancient American diplomats in Nassau (as he had remarked in his March 24, 1949, letter to Ann Honeycutt), and one of them had answered with the cipher for "period"—"golux." Golux, as an aural writer of Thurber's calibre immediately sensed, was a terrific name for a bumbling fairy-tale wizard. With that as a starting point, and usurping the name of the Williamses' four-year-old daughter Sara Linda for his fairy-tale princess, he let the thing practically write itself. He had to be torn away from the manuscript, finally, by his new publisher, Simon and Schuster, he delighted so in tinkering with its word mechanisms. "He started it one day and just breezed through," said Fritzi, who both took dictation and typed up some pencil scrawls, as well as reading his drafts aloud to him countless times. "It went faster than anything else we had done. His memory made it possible; he would compose whole sections of it in his mind all morning, till I showed up at noon." And Helen, as usual, kept him braced with good criticism and encouragement.

The story is embarrassingly like *The White Deer*. Brimming with private jokes and allusions, *The 13 Clocks* also has a Rossian figure who, naturally, is the evil Duke, the uncle of Princess Saralinda. Like King Clode in *The White Deer*, the Duke says, "Nobody ever tells me anything." One of his stooges in a fit of rebellion shouts at the Duke, "You are the most aggressive villain in the world. I always meant to tell you that." There's a bit of Thurber, too, in the wicked Duke, since the villain had lost one eye when he was a youngster, was often tripping over things, and feared unseen creatures. Again, Herculean labors have to be performed by a disguised Prince for the hand of the Princess, but a new element, a concern with time (the dead Then against the living Now), pervades the story. The Duke has coldly murdered time and stopped the thirteen clocks of the castle. Verse, puns, backward limericks, odd-sounding words, hidden rhymes, Lewis Carroll inventiveness, L. Frank Baum fantasy all come together once again in a blend of unmistakable Thurber.

It is significant, at that delicate point in the author's life, that the theme of the story is humor. One labor for the Prince is to deliver to the Duke a thousand precious jewels. A woman named Hagga is said to weep jewels, but only laughter makes her weep any more. The Golux tries backward limericks (of the sort Thurber made up with his Columbus friend Ted Gardiner), but limericks bring forth only semiprecious stones and costume jewelry. The Prince's anecdotal tales just elicit pearls. But sudden, inexplicable nonsense laughter from Hagga ("It might have been the hooting of an owl . . . the crawling of a snail") showers them with precious stones. (Jewels of laughter, however, turn into tears in a fortnight; jewels of sorrow "last beyond all measure, but may the jewels of laughter give you little pleasure.") The moral of the fairy tale is the human need for love and humor. As the Prince and Princess ride off together to happier lands, the Golux tells them: "Keep warm. Ride close together. Remember laughter. You'll need it even in the blessed isles of Ever After."

Several readers read a lot of metaphysical meanings into the tiny book. Thurber answered their inquiries as follows:

> . . . I appreciate the interest of you and your wife in "The Thirteen Clocks" and am glad to try to clear up your wonder about its philosophy. I believe that narrative comes first in a fairy tale and I have found out that if you start out with a set philosophy in mind the story is likely to become stilted or even pretentious. All I did was to write a fairy tale whose plot, incidents, and characters interested me, as did the writing. I have no doubt that philosophy is inherent in such an approach and anyone is welcome to read what they want into the book. I didn't deliberately put it there, but I'm sure you are right. On a major scale, T. S. Eliot has said that there is probably more in "The Cocktail Party" than he realizes, or words to that effect . . .(9)

Even before the manuscript was finished, Thurber selected his Cornwall friend Marc Simont to do the illustrations. It was a happy choice. "He sent me the manuscript from Bermuda," Simont recalled, "and told me that everything was arranged with the publisher for me to do the drawings. It was the first I had ever heard of the book. I read and reread the manuscript so many times I felt I wrote it myself, after a while. Thurber was fantastic to work with. He asked me to describe to him each drawing in its color and form, but he didn't bug me. When I drew the Golux's 'indescribable hat,' I couldn't describe it. He said, 'O.K., good.' Still, I had nightmares of Thurber suddenly regaining his sight, seeing my pictures, and saying, 'I made a horrible mistake!' "

The book—dedicated to Jap and Helen Gude, "who have broken

more than one spell cast upon the author by a witch or wizard"—was published in November of 1950 (with the first name of the illustrator misspelled as "Mark"). It eventually went into nine printings. Having decided to go with Simon and Schuster, Thurber developed a close relationship with Jack Goodman, his editor there. At first he was pleased by the fabled Essandess promotion (large prepublication ads in *Publishers Weekly* and the like), but soon enough, in what was becoming a Thurber vs. publisher tradition, he took umbrage at reprint rights, further advertising, and royalty payments. When an accounting error of $1,500 was discovered, Thurber flew off the handle, even though the error was quickly corrected. Several letters of apology were exchanged between Goodman and his best-selling author before all was calm again.

The 13 Clocks was a natural for production in other media. Some movie interest was shown, and in 1954 a television musical version of the story was broadcast to rapturous reviews. It also played on a summer-circuit twin bill with Leonard Bernstein's short opera "Trouble in Tahiti."

After the fairy tale's publication and a restorative stay in Virginia, Thurber returned to that weightier work in progress, which he had put aside in Bermuda for the relaxation of *The 13 Clocks*. This project was a series of pieces about his ancestors, immediate family, and influential persons of his youth, set down in a style somewhere between *My Life and Hard Times* fantasy–truth and straight researched biography. The pieces were printed in the *New Yorker* throughout 1951 and 1952 under the heading "Photograph Album" and were brought out by Simon and Schuster in the spring of 1952 as *The Thurber Album*, dedicated to the late Herman Miller (who was the only non-relative to receive two Thurber book dedications). The end product was a kind of autobiography—the subject as seen through his relations with others—and it was the most formidable sustained work Thurber had written alone to date.

Why, at that stage of his life, did Thurber decide to add to his reams of autobiographical reminiscence with more of the same? The answer in a word was McCarthy. It was for Thurber a way of rediscovering a fundamental American truth (and rediscovering his own values, consequently) in a nation rapidly being eroded by the Republican junior senator from Wisconsin, Joseph Raymond McCarthy. Some years later, he said:

... Well, *The Thurber Album* was written at a time when in America there was a feeling of fear and suspicion. It's quite different from *My Life and Hard Times*, which was written earlier and is a funnier and better book. The *Album* was kind of an escape—going back to the Middle West of the last century and the beginning of this, when there wasn't this fear and hysteria. I wanted to write the story of some solid American characters, more or less as an example of how Americans started out and what they should go back to—to sanity and soundness and away from the jumpiness. It's hard to write humor in the mental weather we've had, and that's likely to take you into reminiscence. Your heart isn't in it to write anything funny . . .(10)

The old America of his youth became attractive new geography for his restless mental state. It was a means of assuaging some of his growing bitterness, his outrage—towards his infirmities, his years, his country, his world—and perhaps arriving at some conclusive summing-up of himself. His deep rancor at the cruel sport of witch-hunting came from vicarious involvement, mostly. *The Male Animal* was thought by only a few Red-scare operatives to be subversive; he had earlier lent his name to the League of American Writers, the Connecticut Progressive Citizens Committee, and the Joint Anti-Fascist Refugee Committee (a pro-Loyalist group during the Spanish Civil War) mainly because Ernest Hemingway and others had asked him to; at informal gatherings he was outspoken against Fascists of all kidneys, but so were millions of other intelligent people; and, as he once happily admitted, the seven-year-old daughter of Maxim Litvinov, the wartime Russian Ambassador to the United States, had sent him a drawing she had made and Thurber returned the compliment ("Don't know whether the F.B.I. knows this or not," he wrote Frank Gibney).(11)

But never was he hounded personally, nor was he denied a job, nor was he kept off television and radio through the bad offices of *Red Channels,* nor was he ever subpoenaed to testify before an investigating committee. "We were told," Helen said, "that his name would occasionally come up, but a congressman once said that Jamie was never interrogated because 'our wives and children wouldn't allow it.' Jamie loved that. But even though he wasn't political enough to be active in a left-wing organization, he often said he wouldn't be scared off of one he did believe in. During the McCarthy period, he became a real liberal, I suppose—unlike Elliott Nugent—but politics to him still remained just another literary device. He never suffered directly from McCarthy."

Indeed, Thurber was the militant anticommunist, antiproletarian-literature activist of the 1930's, as his lengthy letters to Malcolm Cowley attested. When *The Thurber Album* was published, he described the book to Harvey Breit of the New York *Times* Book Review as "about

Taft country but it's by an Eisenhower man."(12) (He switched to Stevenson before the 1952 election, however.) One of the lingering, most nettlesome contradictions in that most contradictory man was his liberal artistic temperament opposing his generally conservative Ohio view of life. Much of this showed through in a letter to E. B. White, written during the Korean War:

. . . I listen to all the news broadcasts in the crisis and what I cannot understand is the attitude assumed by most of them about Chinese intervention. It is either disingenuous, or plain ignorant, or a propaganda line to act bewildered about it, it seems to me. We were licking their side and so they fought back to lick us, precisely as we would do if Russia or China were on the point of conquering Mexico. MacArthur was flaunting to the world his easy defeat of Communism and it would have been a military and political loss of face to the Reds if we had celebrated a victorious Christmas victory. We had to go in there and we have to stay, but I hate to see the issue constantly distorted.

I was glad to see that Professor Rudin of Yale told the Junior League girls something about the nature of Communism, since we keep trying to set it up as a kind of one-man Nazism which an indignant free world must overthrow once and forever. Hitler did not have one third of Italy and one fourth of France and he could never have won over 500,000,000 Chinese. Communism is a powerful revolutionary world force, not inspired by a maniac twenty years ago, but strong enough to have lasted a hundred years, to have won the allegiance, at one time, of many of the most distinguished intellectuals from G.B. Shaw on down, including dozens of men you and I know. I was interested when James T. Farrell went on the air two years ago to support Lehman, but I wonder how many persons detected that he attacked "Stalinism" instead of Communism. There is a difference between justifiable indignation over open and notorious assault and considered opposition to a world force opposed to capitalistic democracy, and I am beginning to worry about the turn our propaganda has taken. I am an old vehement anti-communist who has argued and fought against it, even in the heart of their country, but I can't let myself be deluded by misrepresentations of the problem. We have to win and I hope you are listening to the new Elmer Davis-Pentagon program that began, I think, last night. It was heartening to know that we still have tough soldiers and the toughest training in our history. There should be more clarifications like this one, so that people will not reach the state we did a few nights ago when bewildered senators and congressmen, on the air, showed a complete lack of a grasp of the situation, our present state of readiness, and in rather frightened tones blamed the democratic administration and said we must turn to prayer. I am willing to pay the highest possible taxes cheerfully and I have great confidence in the boys from Arkansas, Ohio and the other states, if we do not keep confusing them by an almost childish failure to understand what is going on in the world . . .(13)

In truth, what got to Thurber most about the dark McCarthy era was the bullying tactics used against writers, many of them his good friends. He was outraged by the injustice of it all. Writers, to him, were a race apart; by definition of their trade, they must be acquainted with everything, left or right, high or low, in order to gain the experience and knowledge necessary to ply that trade. The open season on writers, he felt, was scaring and depressing everybody, guilty or innocent of Communist connection. "A writer is a man who devotes his entire life to writing and who has an intense respect for the English language, which almost all politicians abuse," Thurber wrote in a piece called "Dark Suspicions," for the *Times* drama section of July 27, 1952. Richard Nixon, he went on to say, is *not* a writer, in spite of a *Who's Who* listing of a 1936 Nixonian opus entitled "Changing Rules of Liability in Automobile Accident Litigation." A writer is somebody special, and should be left alone.

Thurber was almost envious of writers named on blacklists, as this letter to the novelist and former Ohioan Dorothy Canfield Fisher, who helped him in his *Album* research on old O.S.U. figures, implied:

Dear Mrs. Fisher:

I was infuriated to read your name in one of those damnable helter-skelter lists of eminent persons accused of connections with Communist fronts. It also contained the name of Mark Van Doren, a friend and neighbor of mine, who is not and never has been a Communist or a pro-Communist. As Helen completed the list she said with relief, "Well you didn't get listed." I suppose that, in due time, I will be listed along with every other writer that the crazy Congressmen—and there are lots of them—can think of or be told about. I felt that you would be tremendously upset and I wanted to be among the first to assure you that no sound person will give it a second thought.

I happened to join the League of American Authors when I was in southern France in 1938, the same month that Hemingway joined up, neither one of us being aware that it was a periphery organization. God knows what other items against me are in the files of the F.B.I., but any agent worthy of the name could establish the innocence of most of us in a few hours research. I am planning to write a piece on the subject, protesting vehemently against the increasing tendency in the United States to damn everybody who has any name at all, thoughtlessly, maliciously, and for personal advertisement. Some Congressmen and editors have discovered that the easiest way to publicity is to say something against a writer or artist or actor and this has become extremely dangerous in a country that condemns people by allegation, association, and just plain rumor. There must be some way to prevent the continuance of this kind of thing. As one of my friends pointed out, George Bernard Shaw would probably have served nine months in jail if he had been an American. America has never had the feeling for its writers and artists that is traditional in England and in France and there ought to be some standard way of striking back at infamous charges which are protected by immunity . . . If and when I am listed as an old Bolshevik, I will at least join the distinguished company of some of the patriotic Americans whom I love and admire . . .(14)

Informing by writers on other writers for personal gain also irritated Thurber. "Squealing hit Jamie very hard," Helen said. "He hated the opportunism of informing and thought it was very un-American. He admired the ones who kept their mouths shut, like Ring Lardner Jr. and Lillian Hellman." Thurber also had a pragmatic view of the informing situation: Since no literary person after Thomas Paine ever had any real authority in America, there was no need to fear writers; thus, there was no national-security necessity for writers naming names.(15)

Just as he had always believed that humor was a weapon totalitarianism could not withstand (it was the endemic lack of humor among Marxists that put him off them so in the 1930's), he now believed that humor would ultimately defeat McCarthyism. As the Army–McCarthy Hearings demonstrated a few years later, he was absolutely correct. With uncanny prophecy, he wrote in 1952:

. . . Fortunately, this is the country of the horselaugh, the raspberry, and the Bronx cheer . . . When a democracy begins to laugh at boogie men, it is no longer in danger of destroying itself, and it may even encourage the revival of its theatre, the primary evidence of a nation's culture . . .(16)

Ross didn't quite share Thurber's opinion of humor as a not-so-secret weapon against McCarthyism, even when the *New Yorker* itself was being called the *New Worker* and many of its writers were stigmatized. While Ross never cared what the political attitudes of his employees were, he didn't want "social-conscious stuff" intruding into his magazine. He wanted to protect the magazine, really, from mindless attack. Consequently, humor decreased in the pages of the *New Yorker* during the McCarthy days (there was little else to be satiric about), and Thurber had to tread lightly with his *Album* pieces when they dealt with the issue of freedom of thought. But with the research help of Dorothy Canfield Fisher, Ohio State professor James Pollard (to whom he paid three hundred dollars for "collaboration"), and anybody else he could round up in Columbus, Thurber ground out the *Album* pieces.

The result was a sometimes labored, sometimes rewarding, always well-written exercise in idealized personal nostalgia. Even the best-focussed *Album* snapshots came off as too tinted to be true. It was an America as it should have been but probably wasn't. The Thurber ancestors and immediate family were especially romanticized. They were all there in neat niches: step-great-grandfather Judge Stacy Taylor, cousin Dr. Beall, Aunt Mary Van York, great-grandfather Jacob Fisher, Jacob's grandfather Adam Fisher, grandfather William Fisher, grandmother Kate Fisher, father Charles Thurber, and mother Mame. Then, with even less substance, there was the mixed bag of influential characters of Thurber's youth: the interracial Blind Asylum baseball team, singular Margery Albright, the decent, eccentric craftsman and skeptic Julius Ziegfeld, the big three of the Ohio State faculty—Professors Taylor, Graves, and Denney, *Dispatch* city editor Norman "Gus" Kuehner, the just-folks *Dispatch* cartoonist Billy Ireland, and the man who introduced Thurber to written humor, *Ohio State Journal* editor and paragrapher Robert O. Ryder. A harmless, meatless, pleasant lot they all were in Thurber's *Album*, but the pieces about them turned out to be a can of worms.

First, there was trouble with the *New Yorker*. Ross was ill during much of the writing and editing of the pieces and he was away from his office for increasingly long periods. Thurber was working primarily with Gus Lobrano, a fiction editor whom Thurber admired a great deal, but with his new drive to become the *New Yorker*'s class pest rather than its teacher's pet, he was making things uncomfortable for Lobrano. He complained, for example, that his *Album* series was consistently being interrupted by "important pieces," such as Profiles of Truman and Duveen. ("The Truman piece was mentioned, as you all knew it would be, in news stories and editorials, and I am afraid I cannot offer you such publicity with my own stuff," he wrote Lobrano. "Who is doing the series of six pieces on Stalin?")(17) When some editors objected to too much of the self-conscious first person in one of the *Album* pieces, Thurber said that if they didn't want it he would sell it "someplace else . . . because it is definitely a picture of a man seen through my eyes and I's." He also requested that parts Lobrano didn't think were right not be shown to Katharine White. Thurber, in one of his sudden antagonisms, had decided that she was the root cause of his problems with the magazine.(18) And he argued with Lobrano about the *New Yorker*'s fear of warmth in a story:

. . . I have my series well planned, as to characters, viewpoint, and feeling, and its quality must not be diluted by the strange development of unemotionality among all the editors except you. We are sometimes more cold than detached, and more bloodless than sophisticated. We hate the word, but practice the act. When Gibbs, a genuine and authentic cold man, wrote of Dave Lardner's death [a *New Yorker* war correspondent killed in action during World War II] "We have rarely written a paragraph with more regret," I insisted that "regret" be changed to "sorrow," telling Ross for God's sake not to let the magazine deteriorate into that vein . . .

Thurber requested that Joseph Mitchell or A. J. Liebling be allowed to read his remaining *Album* pieces in manuscript, since, as old newspapermen, they would understand the need for warmth in them, adding:

P.S. You might try it on McNulty, too. He and I are the only two writers you have who are not afraid of warmth. The New Yorker can use some.(19)

He quarrelled, too, with queries from the magazine's checking department ("Nobody knows 'The Ambassadors' better than I do and I am going to be on 'Invitation to Learning' when it is discussed this fall. Marie de Vionnet was a countess, but we think of her mainly as Madame de Vionnet . . ."),(20) and when the checkers let through a misspelling of the first name of Ohio State's revered back Chic Harley (as "Chick"), Thurber exploded. It was an error no Ohio State man could ever live down.

But his troubles with the *New Yorker* were trivial compared to what went on with his family back in Columbus. Early in the publication of the *Album* series, Thurber received a few intimations of unease about the family image, as presented in the writing. Also, the emphasis on liberal American values didn't sit too well back in unwavering conservative Columbus. Thurber asked Lobrano to send proofs of his piece on Aunt Margery Albright to his mother for her reaction, although he knew this was against usual *New Yorker* policy. Mame's reaction was positive but edgy, and soon she and Robert—sharing quarters together in a Columbus residential hotel—wanted to see proofs of all the pieces. Thurber told Lobrano, at one point, to sweeten Robert's disposition by a scheme in which Robert would be paid fifty dollars by the magazine for research on Robert O. Ryder, the money being deducted from Thurber's account. He also asked that Lobrano pass on to Robert and Mame some compliments about the pieces, particularly "Gentleman from Indiana," the idealization of Thurber's father. But the placatory plan didn't work. After "Gentleman from Indiana" was printed, over the family's objection, in June of 1951, Robert loosed a diatribe at his brother by telephone and letter. Thurber described the unpleasantness to the Whites:

. . . I called my family in Columbus Saturday and my brother Robert answered the phone and began to bawl hell out of me for the piece on my father. He was so nasty that I hung up on him. It turned out that a letter from him was at the Algonquin desk and we got it and read it. It is a savage and relentless attack on almost everything I said and he seems to have persuaded my mother to react in the same way, except not violently. He says the piece should have been called "Hoosier Halfwit," claims I must have had a deep resentment of my father, and categorically denounces almost every paragraph. He said the piece should not have "seen the light of day." "I thought you would refer to his wonderful penmanship," is one sentence. Gus and I are worried about what they will think of the piece on my mother and Gus has sent a proof together with a letter of praise. I wrote Robert a sharp letter after waiting two days and another note quoting six or eight people who liked it. Joel Sayre has finished the cover story about me for TIME and inserted a sentence saying I had written a fine, affectionate piece about my father. I will put in a paragraph for the book, just to please the family, but it is a rather shocking situation . . .(21)

The family fight didn't stop there. Thurber sent almost daily letters and telegrams for a while, filing, in effect, an epistolary brief defending his position. He sent one letter with quotes from Nugent, Ann Honeycutt, Tim Costello, and other assorted friends praising "Gentleman from Indiana" as a "fine, honest story about a fine man," and so forth. He debated Robert's objection about not emphasizing their father's strong points of word-contest competition and penmanship ("the art of the donkey," Thurber called it).(22) As for Robert's howl about Thurber's ridicule of Ohio Republican politics, he was told:

. . . I was a newspaper reporter in Columbus for four years, covered the State House and City Hall, and developed my own convictions about Ohio politics. I am a writer who puts down his own convictions, changing them to fit nobody else's opinion and omitting nothing under pressure if I think it is right. Your judgement of the two Roosevelts is your own and you obviously feel deeply enough about it to use obscenity in a letter Helen had to read aloud . . .(23)

The incredible idea that Helen's sensibilities could be offended by any obscenity Robert dreamed up was the only light moment in the barrage of letters. He continued to fire quotes from the Whites and others about the "affectionate" piece, and insisted to the point of tedium that his father was portrayed as a rare honest, if unsung, politician among scoundrels. The publication of the laudatory *Time* cover story helped quiet the situation—although Sayre and the researchers got some anecdotes about Mame's eccentric behavior wrong—and so did a comprehensive genealogy of the Thurber clan sent along propitiously by one Charles H. Thurber of Grand Rapids, Michigan. The genealogy interested Mame and Robert, although it suggested that Thurber's apparent paternal grandfather was a milkman. ("We can make it dairy farmer," Thurber wrote the sensitive folks back home.) (24) He gave up, finally, on communicating with Robert, who refused to speak to his famous brother any more, but frequent letters to "Dear Mama" throughout the summer of 1951 concentrated on the common-interest point of genealogical research. The mother–son relationship improved somewhat when "Lavender With a Difference," the *Album* portrait of Mame, was printed in late July. No mother could have wanted a more fulsome love letter from her son.

Thurber was less sweet about the sticky situation in another letter to the Whites:

Dear Andy and Katharine:

Your wonderful and generous letters helped me and the situation a lot and I sent excerpts from them to my brother. Nothing much can be done about him, I'm afraid, since he has become a unique hermit in the past forty years, out of touch with everybody and everything, except his mother. He has no sense of English or of writing, actually thought "Daguerrotype of a Lady" was purely funny, and never reads any books. The life of a specialist in first editions and those made valuable by errata and failure is distorting. To him Sinclair Lewis's "Our Mr. Wrenn" is the most important Lewis book, because of errors in the first run-off. The early failures of established writers are worth more than their successes. Failure, mistakes, and scarcity make up a strange criterion of value. He never reads any of his prize items.

I suppose you have seen the Sayre piece in TIME, which was mainly lighted for us by the quotation from Andy. Nothing in it disturbed me, except his bungling of the anecdotes about my mother, and the strange, sad, proof in the writing of the ordeal Joe was going through at the time. You can see a dozen forces pulling at him, the need to get the damn thing done, the writing of some parts with gloves on, the heroic attempt to write TIME's style. I have told him it is wonderful and he is vastly pleased. Nobody was disappointed in what he said, but I was bewildered by sentences like "Thurber is an affectionate father and gets along with his daughter splendidly," for that is a sentence that could be improved in a dozen ways and still keep the precise thought . . .

Joe actually played down my unkemptness, but fortunately played up Elliott, which won't hurt his troubled ego. The only playing up, however, would be obvious to fraternity men, who don't take a man in because he wrote a theme. I had brought and laid at the feet of Phi Kappa Psi the two editorships, or I would never have got in. But I deliberately said the sequence was right. I think Elliott is in his depression phase now and, as he told me, "In the manic state you're on top of the world. The depression is hell." I'm glad Althea survived so well, since she has had the jumps lately . . .

I loved, and was loved by, two wonderful men named Carson Blair and George Packer, who had charge of the humorous monthly and passed it on to me when it could have gone to a man in their own fraternity. They did this three days after I rejected their effort to pledge me to their fraternity. This is the real kind of story that can't get into TIME, but should. There was also a girl I knew before Elliott, and it must have been love, because last week she sent me a lock of her hair. She is now fifty-five and a grandmother. This is not for TIME, because her husband might get sore. I guess nobody should write about his friends because we know far too much and far too little.

Thanks again and love and kisses from us all. Rosie is at the Falmouth Theatre and getting along all right, I think . . .(25)

His anger was clearly aimed at Robert, who stubbornly decided on a course of estrangement from his brother, even while his mother mellowed and they happily cashed the regular subsistence checks from Cornwall. All this created a tempest of emotions in Thurber, who at once felt guilty for using his family as literary props and irate at the ridiculous parochialism of his family and Columbus. When his mother was hospitalized for a circulatory condition, he sent more and larger checks.

"Jamie couldn't stand being estranged," Helen said, "especially after his checks to Columbus weren't acknowledged for eight months. He was hurt by the *Album* affair, even though he wasn't really that close to his family. The main trouble was with Robert, who felt his father didn't get his proper due. Most people thought his father came off far better than he deserved. William wasn't as angry. He liked the attention, I guess, and he wasn't as close as Robert was to their father. He was also more appreciative of Jamie's money, although he had a small pension from the Ohio Bureau of Weights and Measures, where he once worked."

Robert's version of the affair was that Thurber turned against the people closest to him. "Jamie was irritable, not friendly or sociable," he said. "It was in 1951 I first noticed his hot temper. He talked poorly to me and mother over the telephone, and unless we agreed with him on everything, he would fly off the handle. I didn't know what to say or not to say to him. I took issue with things he wrote and said about my father. I couldn't understand why William Fisher—who wasn't ever nice to Jamie—was glorified in the book and my father wasn't. I still think it should be the other way around. Maybe our grandfather was a more interesting character, although I thought the world of my father. Other people have told me since that there was nothing offensive in *The Thurber Album* stories, so it could be I just imagined the whole thing."

The Thurber Album was published by Simon and Schuster in April of 1952, with several emendations, deletions, and additions—designed, for the most part, to comfort Robert and Mame—and it was a best seller, though nothing like *The Thurber Carnival.* But Thurber, recuperating in Bermuda from a difficult year, told White at publication time that "I am going to write about imaginary people from now on since real ones take too much out of me."(26) Just before Christmas of 1951, he and Robert made up. "Jamie telephoned him," Helen recalled, "and told Robert let's pretend that nothing happened. Nothing *did* happen, really. We sent the usual Christmas presents. But the relationship with the family was never quite the same again. Jamie refused to go to Columbus to visit them for years. He just didn't want to face the old arguments and the pro-McCarthy people out there." His letter salutations began to include Robert again, and more sports news was discussed in the letters' contents.

The weirdest reaction to *The Thurber Album*—Robert Thurber notwithstanding—was a review in the right-wing journal the *Freeman,* by William Schlamm. Schlamm wrote that the book was actually the nostalgia of an "incorrigible conservative," as, he felt, all good humorists really are since professional reformers cannot laugh. The reviewer went on to miss the entire point of the book by stating that the characters of *The Thurber Album* would have sided with McCarthy, being wholesome American types. Why, then, Schlamm asked, was Thurber siding with the liberals and unfairly picking on poor Senator McCarthy? "Please, Mr. Thurber, come home—to Bob Ryder, to Huck Finn, to Columbus, Ohio!" the review ended.(27)

The subject of all this mossback casuistry was at first amused and then bitter. He wrote Carey McWilliams of the *Nation:*

. . . As for Schlamm's theory about homesickness and humor, his buttons are twisted. I have done only two out of nineteen books that could be called nostalgic, but some of the outland reviews of "The Thurber Album" point out that I have softened and changed, and one guy in Texas detects a note of farewell in the book. If I quit at 57 my wife and daughter and other dependents would get sore. Fact is, during the three years I was writing the book I wrote twenty-five other pieces, which will appear in a book next spring. This is a great country to pin a guy down on no evidence. I'd much rather write a piece about

"The Cocktail Party" or Sam Spade on the radio, or the sloppy way publishing houses are run than delve into the Columbus past. I had to soften the book a little, because of the people involved, especially my mother and brothers who wanted everything tinted like photographs taken at Buckeye Lake. The emotional debris was terrific, since Columbus is the heart of evasion and fatty degeneration of criticism. Said my mother: "It wouldn't go down very well with the young man of today if you reported that your grandfather sent a substitute to the Civil War." Said a man named Opha Moore out there years ago: "The story of Chic Harley does not point a good moral." (Chic had become a mental case in his senior year.) Said the city attorney of "Jurgen", after thinking a moment: "Why do writers write books that offend people?" There was so much rubble of this sort that the light I threw on the good people got stronger and stronger. "There is an alley between every street in Columbus," wrote one of the town's distinguished columnists, and all you have to do is jog to the right and see the whole scene from the alley. My unfond memories would fill a bucket. Just wanted to clear up this little point . . .(28)

So much for Columbus.

CHAPTER 18

The Aging Humorist

Life, as it had so often done before, contrived to jostle Thurber towards a coverless manhole. Already heavy with family feuding, post-publication blues, and a bad case of *Zeitgeist*, he had to face an entirely new dismal chain of events within the next year or so. There was Harold Ross, desperately ill, it turned out, with lung cancer, not just stomach ulcers as most thought. Ross spent more and more time away from the *New Yorker* at the Lahey Clinic in Boston, leaving the magazine in the editorial hands of William Shawn and Gus Lobrano. By the spring of 1951, the malignancy had been confirmed and Ross knew the prognosis was not good. He was separated from his third wife and was living, when not in the Lahey Clinic, at the Algonquin, as were the Thurbers, when they were not in Cornwall or Bermuda. The three were together a lot, eating and talking in the Algonquin dining room, and for the first time, really, the Thurbers and Ross became truly close. Before, in Helen's words, Ross had been more of "a professional friend," but in 1951, sick and lonely, he needed some warmth and companionship. The Thurbers rose to the occasion. Although Ross probably never told Thurber he had cancer, Thurber surmised as much when Ross's sense of taste disappeared. At one point, he told Thurber that he could taste only sardines. Early in December, Ross went to Boston, accompanied by his old friend Hawley Truax (at that time a vice president of the magazine), to have the malignancy removed. On December 6, 1951, Ross died on the operating table. Louis Forster, a devoted assistant to Ross (as he is now to Shawn), called the Thurbers at the Algonquin that night and told them the awful news. Helen answered the phone; she was able to say only, "No, no." The rest of the evening was a mixture of tears and alcohol at Costello's, as friends of Ross sought each other out to commiserate. "His death in surgery was so sudden and shocking," Helen said. "Jamie and I guessed that he probably wouldn't beat the cancer, but we thought he had more time."

For the Whites, Ross's death was even more shattering, since they had been closest of all to Ross. White was elected to write the *New Yorker*'s obituary for its founder and editor, while Thurber stood by in case his help was needed. (It wasn't.) The obituary was one of the most beautiful pieces of writing that ever appeared anywhere. Shawn, as Ross had requested, was made editor, and, with Lobrano and James Geraghty, the art editor, carried the magazine through the difficult transition phase into, if anything, an even stronger publication. But for a long time, the unique force and presence of Harold Ross was sorely missed in New York and at the *New Yorker*.

The effect of Ross's passing on Thurber was expressed most tellingly in a letter to Ronnie Williams:

. . . The New Yorker may be financially rich, but it has become terribly poor with the death of Ross. This was a shocking blow to all of us, and I find it hard to throw off. We had seen him several times recently and were greatly worried. He has known since about May that it was cancer, but he believed that it was being cured by new deep radium treatment. We are not sure, but apparently the doctors were not aware that it was deep and extensive until the operation. The part they were clearing up turned out to be small. He died without coming out of the anaesthetic. We were telephoned at 10:30 that night. Gibbs practically collapsed, but Andy wrote the obituary while I stood by that long and awful day. Five hundred people turned up at his funeral at which a reverend who didn't know him intoned stuff that Ross would have hated and rolled his "r's." As White said, there were wakes in a hundred bars that night.

Everybody keeps asking if the magazine will go on, and it will. Lobrano and Shawn have been getting it out alone most of this year, and they have been doing the buying of pieces longer than that. He suffered no great pain, but was bothered and kept awake by constant coughing. He lived alone at the Algonquin where we saw him a lot. On his last birthday we gave him a scarf and called on him, and I had dinner with him that week. When I called him and said "Happy birthday," he said "Thanks, old fellow" and then, "Goddam it, when Forster phoned me and said it was my birthday, I knew you would be calling up." He had worried for years about his friends dying in their fifties, especially Woollcott, Benchley, Broun, and MacNamara.

The day after he died, I showed Andy a drawing of mine showing my dog lying at the end of a grave and staring at the headstone. He was all for using it as the illustration for the obituary, but the conservative boys turned it down. Now Andy and I have made a pledge to use it for the obituary of whichever one of us dies first. I will either write his, or he will write mine. I'm going to do a piece about Ross, but it will take time. He was the principal figure in my career, and I don't know what I would have amounted to without his magazine, in which ninety percent of my stuff has appeared. He was also a great part of my life, and I realize how much I loved him and depended on him. There was

no appreciation quite the same as his, because it was all tied up with him and his life. What White and I did was a part of the guy, and we realize how much of our work was done with him in mind. For the first time I have become deeply aware of the chill sweeping across the cold and starry space. I felt it when Herman Miller died, but I saw him only once every few years, and Ross was a part of my daily life for almost exactly a quarter of a century. It is always hard to believe that extremely vital people can die. He represented life to me the way only a few others do. These include you and Janey. Take care of yourselves, and, as Ross said a thousand times, God bless you.(1)

As Ross wasted away and the family feud reached its climax, a whole new ogre breathed hot on Thurber's neck. In September of 1951, a frightened Ohio State University administration instituted a gag rule for campus speakers, after a faintly socialistic Columbia University professor had addressed an O.S.U. group. The gag rule demanded that any speaker would have to receive permission from the university president, with both the speaker and his speech coming under close scrutiny for possible subversive ideas. The ruling caught the attention of the McCarthy-wary national press, and once again there was the burning issue of academic freedom at Ohio State. Some of the braver O.S.U. faculty members and many other academicians (and potential campus speakers) from all over the country were aroused about the spectacle of lecturers having to pass inspection by a right-wing board of trustees at a state university. Naturally, Thurber, still heady from successful battle with the O.S.U. administration over the *Sundial* affair, was in the thick of things. He wrote Lester Getzloe, of the university's journalism department:

. . . That terrible institution, in its most recent horror, has reached the front pages of all decent newspapers in the country. I wish the entire faculty and student body would resign. Things will get worse instead of better . . . I believe that no decent speaker will appear ever again on the campus . . .

Nugent and I write a successful, and even famous, play about Ohio State, and our trustee, Edward K. Keller, is recreated in the actual body of the chairman of the board. This is mighty goddam discouraging. Anyway, we got you out there, and a few others, and it is a good thing to have some spies who are on the right side, even if they are in the wrong university . . .(2)

And to his *The Thurber Album* collaborator-in-research, Professor James Pollard, he said:

. . . It is my personal belief that a communist speaker could not possibly sway an Ohio State audience and that in refusing to let communists talk, the university deprives itself of a wonderful chance to heckle and confound such speakers. If we cannot be strong enough Americans to withstand such arguments, if we are in such danger of being politically debauched, then all we really have in the Western Conference is the greatest football area in the world . . .(3)

With all the gracelessness it was now nationally famous for, the Ohio State board of trustees decided just a couple of months after the gag-rule controversy to confer a Doctor of Letters honorary degree on James Grover Thurber—and in a pointedly second-rate manner. The trustees planned to award the degree at the coming December convocation, a definite slight for so renowned an alumnus, and they hinted that it could be conferred in absentia.*

---

*Thurber had already received two honorary degrees, both at June convocations and in person. His first was at Kenyon College, in Gambier, Ohio, in 1950. It was a memorably unconventional occasion for him and Helen, the latter describing the event to the Williamses as follows:

Dear Ronnie and Janey:

Well, it was worse than I thought it would be. In the first place the ceremonies began at six A.M. yesterday, because old President Whitney (1888–1912) always slept from eight in the morning until noon. We had to get up in the dark and Jamie hadn't got to sleep till two A.M. because of a bee in the room. It turned out that the caps and gowns out here are scarlet, and there was a ceremony called the Vine Walk, a serpentine procession covering a mile and a half and including a trip to the bell tower, six flights up, where each honoree rang the bell. You can imagine the state he was in when they reached the platform. Then came the citation with everybody standing and he was credited with "The Scene in the Bedroom," "Junior Miss," "The E.B. White Deer," "Many Moods," and "The Great Quiver." He was about to sit down when the president announced that there would be the usual ten minutes standing silence in honor of the late Dr. Whitney. During this each candidate had to hold a full champagne glass. Jamie had to use both hands and a gust of wind blew his gown out in back, so that he looked like a 1907 sports roadster about to take off. I don't know what happened then, because I ran . . .(4)

*   *   *

Thurber was insulted and indignant. He reasoned that the demeaning "honor" was the result of both his outspoken opposition to the gag rule and a footnote in the *Time* cover story, in which the suggestion was made that O.S.U. had never granted Thurber an honorary degree because it was upset by *The Male Animal*. Also, the letter from Ohio State President Howard L. Bevis proposing the degree was "curt and perfunctory."(6)

Ohio State's most celebrated literary son waited a week before replying to President Bevis. His original reply was long and contentious, but "Andy White wisely argued me out of it."(7) He finally sent the following letter:

December 6, 1951

President Howard L. Bevis
The Ohio State University
Columbus, Ohio

Dear President Bevis:

In reply to your letter of November 28th, it is with extreme regret, and after serious consideration, that I find myself unable to accept at this time Ohio State University's offer of the honorary degree of Doctor of Letters. I have faith that Ohio State will restore freedom of speech and freedom of research, but until it does I do not want to seem to approve of its recent action. The acceptance of an honorary degree right now would certainly be construed as such approval, or as indifference to the situation.

I regret that I could not answer your letter more promptly, but it has taken me long hours of thought to arrive at my final decision. I want to thank you for your letter and the committee, the council and the trustees for their offer, and to assure all of you that there is, in my attitude, no personal feeling against any individual, whatever. In conclusion, I wish to express to you my warm personal regards.

Respectfully yours,
James Thurber

Now it was Ohio State's turn to be mad. It had been rejected by an illustrious alumnus, and that sort of thing simply didn't happen in Columbus, Ohio, U.S.A. It was the first and only time an honorary degree had been refused at O.S.U. Several trustees, including Ohio's

---

And in June of the following year, he received a tonier Doctor of Humane Letters degree from Williams College, in Williamstown, Massachusetts, the institution's president calling him the "foremost humorist of our day and nation" who "has brought to a troubled America the priceless gift of laughter."(5)

conservative Senator John W. Bricker, blew their tops in a secret meeting, where it was determined that any mention of the matter be stricken from all records. Years later, Bricker was questioned about the rumored incident and said, "Jim was a peculiar fellow. . . . About that degree business, I don't know now if he refused it or not. I can tell you this. We trustees never passed on it."(8)

Ultimately, Ohio State eased up on the gag rule, as the pressure of McCarthyism abated throughout the land. But, as Thurber put it, the university merely "agreed to let freedom of speech and research get up on one knee, and to take the blindfold off one eye."(9) The whole gag-rule and degree mess took a lot out of Ohio State, but it took a great deal more out of Thurber, coinciding as it did with the death of Ross and the senseless anger of his family.

McCarthyism continued to spook Thurber, however. A couple of years later, in far-off Laguna Beach, California—where the natives are slightly to the right of Prince Klemens Wenzel Nepomuk Lothar von Metternich—a community-players group put on a production of *The Male Animal*. A reviewer for the Laguna Beach *South Coast News*, signing in as "Playgoer," attacked the play and its authors for holding "sincere Americanism up to ridicule," glorifying Bartolomeo Vanzetti, and other sins. Ordinarily, Thurber would never have heard about the political panning, but a California friend sent him a clipping of the review and Thurber was inspired to write a piece about it, as a guest columnist in Walter Kerr's space in the New York *Herald Tribune*. With broad sarcasm he said that he had at last been unmasked as a subversive for "my effort to prevent the building of college football stadia, my special pleading on behalf of extramarital relations and my attack on the competence of Republican Presidents, which shows up in the line, 'Hoover can't write as well as Vanzetti.' Many people who laughed at that line later thought it over seriously and joined the party, either the Democratic, or the Communist, or the one going on at '21' after the play. I couldn't be expected to subvert everybody." But the editors of the *South Coast News* weren't amused. They later quoted in capital letters a line from his piece that read, "The plan to undermine the security of the United States in three acts was entirely my own," and made the most of it. Humor, even broad humor, was not doing well in Orange County, California.

It was doing fairly well in New York, however. In the spring of 1952, the City Center cunningly revived *The Male Animal*—with all its obvious parallels to McCarthyism—for a limited run of two weeks. Elliott Nugent was to play his old role of Tommy Turner and Robert Preston was Joe Ferguson. Thurber, vacationing in Bermuda, left most of the arrangements to Nugent, but he did exert pressure to update the play to fit the peculiar times. However, the play was, wisely, produced in essentially its 1940 version, and the message was, if anything, stronger. So were its reviews and box-office receipts. New York had apparently been waiting for a comedy concerned, even obliquely, with McCarthyism. The critics pointed out its timeliness, and Brooks Atkinson called it "the funniest play of the season."(10) After its two-week run at the City Center, it moved to the Music Box for a healthy stand, and then it went on a national tour. Thurber and Nugent shared ten per cent of the gross, which amounted to an unexpected and delightful bonanza.

But Thurber, experiencing a persistent "neuritis headache" in Bermuda, didn't return to New York for the opening. He sailed for home in June and saw *The Male Animal* the night of his arrival. He thought it was better than the original production in every way; Nugent was funnier, he felt, and Preston brought a new level of comedy to the ex-football player role. He was cheered by the phenomenon of its revival success, but he was depressed all over again by America's troubles. He wrote a piece for the Sunday *Times*, ostensibly about the difference between the 1940 and 1952 productions. He found the 1952 audiences more tense and unhappy, with Broadway "looking moribund and demoralized . . . because of the Congressional probes of playwrights, among other writers, which began five years ago and seem likely to go on forever."(11)

There was, however, a far more personal reason for his acute depression. During his long stay in Bermuda, he not only had a constant headache but was generally florid, restless, and irritable. He also had very little tolerance for alcohol (a sure sign of sickness) and no concentration for work. He fought with everybody, especially Ronnie Williams (so vehemently that he wouldn't let Williams see him off on the boat), and had fits of uncontrollable anger. His British friend John Duncan Miller visited Thurber there and found him to be, intermittently, "a storming, raging, vituperative madman. If ever I was to have a real falling-out with Jim, that was the time. I couldn't bear to be with him during his spells."

For Helen, the spells were even harder to take. "Jamie went on the wagon down there and gave up smoking cigarettes, too, thinking it would help him," she said. "It only made things worse. He missed booze, and when he tried a pipe, he couldn't keep it lit. He needed the feel of a cigarette. During one of his violent attacks, we had an argument. I got so mad at him. He completely lost control and began to tear my clothes off. I just cried and then walked out on him. But, of course, I came right back."

Thurber blamed his spells on a "neuritis headache," brought on by the emotional crises of the past year or so. A Bermuda doctor he consulted couldn't find anything physically wrong with him, concluding that the symptoms indicated pregnancy, although the doctor had ascertained that Thurber was not a woman. Later, more learned medical men in New York diagnosed the illness as a toxic-thyroid condition. Thurber had long had what he called an "Ohio thyroid," an ailment common in the Great Lakes goiter belt. A thyroidectomy was once performed on his brother Robert, with the result that Robert had been lethargic and sickly ever since. Thurber was terrified of the same fate for himself, to say nothing of operations in general, so a thyroidectomy was out of the question. The New York doctors experimented with different drugs, but it was two years before an equilibrium was achieved. Meanwhile, Thurber and everyone he touched suffered.

For example, when he was in Bermuda he wrote Hamish Hamilton that he would agree to changes in various local and purely American references for the British edition of *The Thurber Album*. When Hamilton wrote back suggesting just such changes, Thurber answered with a vitriolic letter, complaining about "tampering with my books . . . It may be that this is not a book for you, or for England, and you can get out from under if you want to. It is definitely American, in fact it is as American as a Bloody Mary or a Purple Jesus."(12) The unpleasantness with Hamilton continued until July of 1952, when Thurber's medication calmed him down somewhat. He wrote Hamilton then:

> . . . I will be glad to sign the contract for the Album on the terms you mention in your letter. The book has done about 25,000 here, but I don't know how it will travel, as I have said. You must dismiss from your mind completely everything in connection with the Situation of a few months ago. Jack Goodman, getting a far less unreasonable letter, said over the long distance phone that he kissed nobody's ass and we made up and get along fine. You must not expect fairness or reason from us Americans, and you must not be hurt so easily. I beg you for the third time also to remember that I was seriously ill. Even so, I was a thousand times more kindly than Pope, Coleridge, Johnson, Evelyn Waugh, or H. G. Wells. I had lost twenty-five pounds and was probably plus 40 in metabolism. I'm taking medicine and it is somewhat better, but I'm an old shaken man who can't smoke and whose irritabilities will no doubt increase with the years. Love and kisses to you all . . .(13)

Other manifestations of toxic thyroid kept popping up. That fall, when Laura Z. Hobson, writing as a guest columnist for the *Saturday Review*, mentioned that Helen Thurber would compose a piece for a magazine series on the subject "The Man I Married" (as Mary Hemingway had done), Thurber became incensed. Firing off a letter to the editor, he admitted that he was "going through a thyroid thing" but went on to say, "I would never have married a woman who would write about me while I'm alive or when I'm dead. I am repelled by husband-evaluators . . . If I lived in Cuba, I probably wouldn't give a damn."(14)

And later, when Edward R. Murrow sent Thurber a printed copy of the C.B.S. broadcast series "This I Believe," Thurber answered him with his toxic-thyroid testiness:

. . . I've learned the hard news that belief, like many of the other pretty virtues, is largely a matter of sound body and high spirits, or anyway well-being . . . Individual belief represents, I suppose, what might be called the fragmentation of religion, or every man for himself. Of the American woman I have recently been saying: "She would rather believe than know" . . . The rewards of oblivion are not to be totally condemned and at least this propect never comes near the cackling marges of loose rockers. I remember hearing Mrs. Roosevelt on "This I Believe," and it was so old and familiar and meaningless that it surprised me in a woman of her intelligence. She made belief sound like Sunday dinner before the first World War . . .(15)

The treatment for his unsettling condition was long and frustrating. Just about the only writing he was able to complete during the remainder of 1952 and 1953 was petulant, exaggerated letters to friends, most of them about his medical problems and politics. For instance, this one to the Williamses:

. . . Next Wednesday I am going to see a thyroid man at Medical Center, since I have been much worse the past eight weeks . . . Six weeks ago I was only plus 3, but the damage had been done. It may take a couple of years to get back the sense of well-being, health, and any trace of energy whatever. The prospect bores me unutterably, and it is hard to make a brave effort in this terrible world. I often wondered what Chloe was like when the man beat his way to her through the smoke and flame and the dismal swamp land. Do you suppose she had taken to saying "Anyways" and to chewing Juicy Fruit gum? My mouth always tastes like a motorman's glove. I have to sit down to shave and I can do no writing except letters. I have been sleeping fifteen hours and getting up at noon, but in the last few days there has been a gleam of hope. I almost feel alive, can get up at ten, and now and then have a trace of appetite. For three months I had been choking everything down, including coffee. This descent into the sewers of the City of Negation has not even been interesting, and I have been struggling to write a piece, without much success, and would rather have a tooth pulled . . . I should have gone to Dr. Parsons at Medical Center long ago, since I went there in 1933, but I have been finally driven to it by the conflicting advice of my New York and Cornwall doctors. I was supposed to have had another metabolism two weeks ago, but the doctor is much too busy trying to save the ancient human wrecks that overpopulate every community. I hate the medical profession with its ethics, and its ignorance, and its sulkiness. I have never known a doctor who knew anything.

I see you have nobly tried to keep my name alive among the Bermudians who never heard of it, and I wish I could promise to resume my pieces in January, but I see no hope of this for another year perhaps. After I have had some competent attention maybe the view will be brighter. Right now I'm an old torn dollar umbrella stuck in a trash bin and it is beginning to rain.

Rosie is coming up here Saturday to register. She was twenty-one last week. Joe's daughter won't be able to cast her first national vote until she is twenty-four. We had dinner with the Sayres a few weeks ago. Gertrude is working for the Stevenson Committee. All my friends are for Stevenson, of course, but I'm afraid the ignorant, the mindless, the discontented, the frightened, the gullible, and the soap opera audience and its husbands may elect the amateur writer and statesman. It has been a terrifying campaign and the general morale and morality of the world has reached a low point indeed. It was bad enough when we found out that the general would do or say anything to get elected, but it was worse when we discovered that he would stop saying or doing something if McCarthy suggested it or Taft.

I think Stevenson would be the best President since Lincoln, and I cannot believe we would give up that kind of man forever on behalf of a man whose stature was largely mythical and who dwindles every day in the light of reality.

Love and kisses from Helen and me . . .

P.S. I used to be deeply interested in myself, but now I can't understand what I saw in me.(16)

Or this professional patient's report to another patient, Frank Sullivan:

Dear old Frank:

I didn't actually reach admissions, although I had thought I would have to stay all night for a basal. It turns out that this test is inaccurate and undependable and perhaps even touched by fantasy—"You get funny numbers," Dr. Parsons told me, "like 18." It seems that high blood pressure, for example, will make a normal metabolism rate seem high—the body, you see, doesn't know its veins from a gland in the neck. I swallowed a couple of lily cups full of radioactive iodine, which looks and tastes exactly like water, and the next day I came back and lay down under a geiger counter. They allow you as high as 45% in this new measurement, and are urgently concerned only if you reach 75. I did 56, which is a funny number, but not so terrible. I will take four pills a day for fourteen to eighteen months, and then see if I can get along without them. Fifty percent of people do, which is what I call the American Odds: fifty-fifty, heads and tails, six of one and half a dozen of the other, you go your way and I'll go mine, and so on. Moitié-Moitié, too, or one lark to one horse. I'm supposed to begin to feel better in a few weeks, and I think I already do after a few days.

We weren't so worried about you, and still aren't, having heard that you passed all tests with high honors and are now simply trying to think up a test you can't beat. You and I will outlive everybody, or at least you will, and I have a mighty good chance of lasting another twenty years unless I'm shot down like a rat in some alley by a plainclothesman. "Got him right through the Stevenson button," this fellow will say. I've got a couple of anonymous letters from one or two of the less cultured Eisenhower followers. One wants to know how much I got paid for my vote, and the other, signed Mac Vigilante, says I'm a conceited and silly Trojan horse pro-Communist . . .(17)

So he wasn't working, wasn't drinking, only occasionally smoking, and barely surviving. It was hell all over again, in some ways worse than the eye operations and nervous breakdown of a decade earlier. And there were still more troubles to come. Life piled up almost unbearably.

Some problems were of his own devising, an apparent symptom of a toxic-thyroid condition. Besides alienating friends, old and new, he was trying his level best to alienate the *New Yorker* editorial staff. The teacher had gone and died on the teacher's pet, and the pet was furious. One particular incident set him off like a fizgig. When Thurber was a reporter for the New York *Post*, back in 1926, he had met Harry Houdini's widow, who befriended him and shared some of the magician's extensive library with him. Ever since, he had gathered data on Houdini, aiming at some sort of writing on the man and his tricks—at first planned as a series for "Talk of the Town" and then, at Ross's suggestion, a longer piece tentatively titled "That Was Houdini. Or Was It?" It was a good idea for Thurber, not only because he had always been absorbed by psychic phenomena (via his mother) but because Charles Thurber had served on an ad hoc committee in Columbus that supervised the construction of an "escape-proof" box Houdini had escaped from out there in 1920.

For one reason or another, Thurber let the idea lapse, and turned over his material on Houdini to Ross, just before the editor died. Ross gave Thurber's data to Richard Rovere, an intellectual recruit from journals of opinion. After Ross died, Rovere, not overly enthusiastic about the subject, consulted Thurber for ideas on the proposed Houdini piece. He was interested in Houdini as an exploder of spiritualism, a concept that irritated Thurber since it took the focus away from the man and his odd craft. Hardly disguising his dislike of Rovere and the turn the *New Yorker* seemed to him to be taking, Thurber wrote to White:

> . . . I haven't heard anything about the Rovere pieces, since he is busy blowing up criticism like a tire, but if he hasn't started to work, I'm going to take the pieces away from him. This I'd do in the name of Harold Ross, who created a great magazine by staying away from the Roveres in the early days and almost up to the end . . . They are carrying on his magazine all right, I think, even though everybody I meet seems to suggest that it should now be called "Momentum." I try to explain, making it shorter each time . . .(18)

Both Rovere and Thurber ultimately dropped the Houdini project, but Thurber rarely let up on what he imagined was happening to his old magazine, subverted from within by creeping intellectualism and un-Rossian tastes. He poured out his feelings to one of his few intimates left on the staff, Peter De Vries:

Dear Pete:

I've been brooding about the kind of change that seems to have darkened the magazine's funny cartoons recently. There is much too much stuff about the man and woman on the raft and the two beachcombers. The first should have ended twelve years ago when the man said, "You look good enough to eat," and I thought I had ended the other one in the Ohio State Sun-Dial in 1917 with:

> 1st Beachcomber: "What did you come here to forget?"
> 2nd   : "I've forgotten."

I'm beginning to worry a little about Shawn's sense of humor and I hope you will tell me it is simply a case of an old magazine passing through the tail of a comet. I cannot believe the old magazine has begun to cackle, and I don't want to believe that Irvin is back. I wish to Christ Ross were. He would never have allowed these two stereotypes in the same issue. There is a definite carelessness at The New Yorker, for the fear that comes out of true respect is gone . . .

The best thing the New Yorker has ever done in comic art is the probable or recognizable caption dealing with the actual relationships of people in our middle-class society. All of us have had a fling at fantasy and formula, but they should never predominate. I had hoped to do a few drawings based on captions I have dug out of hell in the past two years, but I think the strain would be too much for me now. Maybe Darrow, who drew the picture for my "When you say you hate your species do you mean everybody?" could do this one about a long married middle-aged couple. The wife is saying, "You're always talking about how dark the future of Man is—well, what do you think I got to look forward to?" This is two years old in my head. I can't do anything now since my humor sounds like that of an assistant embalmer. I hope to God we never get back to the two men on the face of the enormous clock.

The psychiatrists say that there is always as much relief as grief at the passing of any great or beloved figure, and that the relief comes first. Maybe this explains the loose ratchets at the New Yorker, and I have no doubt, and every hope, that time will tighten them . . .

P.S. How about this? There is a double page spread of cows moving from left to right, and then another double page, and then another single page, all moving from left to right. The right half of the third spread shows the leader of the cows, a defeated biblical king who is presenting the cattle to a victorious biblical king, as reparations after a long war. The defeated king is saying: "Oh, I thought you said payment in kine."(19)

As Thurber's cartoon ideas (he had been trying to pawn off the cow gag on the magazine for years) amply illustrated, he was in a state of almost paranoid confusion about the *New Yorker* and its staff. That unhappy state would last, with a few blessed moments of relief, for his remaining years.

What with the rheumy world sneezing in his face, his bad bout of *Zeitgeist* grew into a terminal case of *Weltschmerz*. He was falling into an unattractive new role—that of the sour, dour Pontifex Maximus, the elder curmudgeon. It was a terrible role for a writer, particularly a humorist, and his work, already plagued by thyroid spells and blocks, suffered even more. When he did manage to set something down on paper, it was usually cynical and distinctly unfunny, which drew him into a vicious circle as far as the *New Yorker* was concerned. The more gloomy and bitter his pieces, the more likely that magazine was to reject them, which, of course, made him all the more gloomy and bitter. He could generally sell the rejects, but it wasn't at all the same as having his work printed in the magazine he had helped to invent. For Thurber, despite his loud protestations to the contrary, publishing elsewhere was like being cleanup batter for the scrubs.

In 1953, he was approached again, this time by Raymond Gram Swing, about recording a "This I Believe" radio program for C.B.S. He answered the request with what had become characteristic dejection:

Dear Mr. Swing:

I guess I've dodged that program because I believe that the imponderable is also the ineffable, and that something goes out of it when it is expressed in the well-known offhand conversational undiscipline of radio. I mentioned in a letter to Ed that Mrs. Roosevelt made her faith sound like a jolly Sunday noon dinner before the First World War. This was all very well, for those who are looking for icing or escape, but faith seems to me a sterner thing than that. I'm not so sure it's a time of affirmation, it may be only a time of self-delusion in which people want to be told that the house is not on fire, that the bombs won't go off after all, and that everything is going to be just dandy. I am also troubled by the fact that my belief changes from time to time and might even change during a brief broadcast. This would not reassure anybody. I also feel that networks have done more harm than any other business except advertising agencies in the recent years of suspicion and accusation and suppression. Furthermore, I'm not very good at this sort of thing and just don't seem to be able to know where to start. All the foregoing may be simply a defense that I don't understand very well myself. Maybe I am afraid to face myself on the air on this subject. Anyway, I have a Sound Mirror, which works, and if I had a tape I might be able to put something on it some day.

Mrs. Thurber and I are among your great admirers and were two of your most devoted listeners in the dark years when your voice was a great comfort, and she joins me in sending you best wishes for a good life and whatever comes after that.(20)

And in a letter to John McNulty, a shriller note of hopelessness sounded:

. . . I fear that where my fancy flowered and my wild invention grew, there is now a small and arid space. The fresh phrases are wilted and there is rust on my metaphor mixer. The imagery is trampled down, the rhetoric has gone to seed, and the proud English construction, which I called Narrow Range, leans to every wind. A single stalk of fancy stands, but see where even now the heavy foot of age is raised above it! One of these days I'll tear out that patch of weedy set-in-my-ways and plant a stand of inspiration, if I can find the seeds. That's honor bright and climbing integrity, there among the hardy growth of crack-up and fatigue. The stitch-in-time and second breath are doing only fairly well. I must divert the stream of consciousness before it sweeps away the pattern of the paths. One side, Mac, here comes the old man with the scythe.

I was thinking the other day, John, that one day a machine so swift will hit a structure so large that the awful law of Force will break in pieces greater than the whole. Look out. I figure that one can be hit so hard by something so fast, that one will not only cease to exist, but cease to have existed . . .

Stay under 1000 miles per hour.

Love,
Jim(21)

There were a few patches of light in the murk. His daughter, Rose-mary, a senior drama major at the University of Pennsylvania, announced that she was going to marry Frederick Sauers, a student at Penn's Wharton School of Finance, between semesters in February, 1953. The two had fallen in love when they were both in a college theatrical production. Thurber met Fred and liked him immediately, but he was against early marriages; he expected Rosemary to have more of a career before wife- and motherhood—and, according to a family friend, he secretly expected Rosemary to marry a somewhat more imposing fellow than Fred, the son of a Chicago park superintendent and landscape architect. However, he more or less resigned himself to Rosemary's decision. When the first hints of matrimony were in the air, he wrote Rosemary:

Dear Rosikins:

I'm enclosing a birthday check from Helen and me with our love and best wishes for a happy coming of age next Tuesday. Have fun from now on, because in seven tiny years you will be twenty-eight and then in twelve more you'll be forty and it will be all over. I meant to say you would be all over the place at forty because at that age women set their clocks back an hour, play three sets of tennis instead of two every morning, and are convinced that maturity is better than youth, which never did anything for them but trap them with a husband. The husband contracted in youth is always remembered, even when his picture is turned to the wall, so pick one out with great care and have him tested by doctors, psychiatrists, and old experienced wives. As a matter of fact, I have found out little about marriage after thirty years of it, but I think this may be true: a second wife may get into her husband's things and read letters from the first one, but a second husband is likely to read aloud to his second the letters he got from the first. Women are nicer than men.

A woman's greatest problem is this: how to make use of her uterus without losing the use of her brain cells. Since God and nature made woman the creative sex and remind her of it every twenty-eight days, it is natural that talent should be a subsidiary thing in her case. A man has to keep his talent alive even if it kills him, but a woman can let hers die like a rose in a book. It often dies in the shade of a man, but she has her children to compensate for this up until the time the oldest boy backs away from a filling station with a gun in one hand and the day's receipts in the other, and the prettiest of the twin girls runs away with a gambler from Memphis. I am glad to tell you that there is no record of homosexuality in my family as far back as "The Thurber Album" extends, or of insanity before the age of 78, or of any of the major diseases except egotism.

If you are married, never let your husband keep his service revolver in the bedroom, because recent news events have proved that if he doesn't shoot you on your way back from the bathroom in the dark, you will shoot him in his sleep because he has begun to get on your nerves and you're pretty sure the babies don't like him. The place for a service revolver is in the nursery, because every child knows how to use one and this will keep papa in his place.

Helen is sending you a few little presents, and by the time you get this you'll have got five books from me, picked at wild random as you will see. I think you are ready for "Vile Bodies" now, but if you're not you never will be . . . I know you're old enough for Ring Lardner and I know you will like him. Since you are an actress and theatre person, I thought you would be interested in "God and My Father" because when the play "Life With Father" was tried out in Skowhegan there was something the matter with it and the authors finally found what it was. They had been using the Clarence Day stories from the New Yorker and had overlooked the two wonderful God stories because they had appeared in Harper's. I read the first one when you were seven days old. They put in the story of the christening and the play's success was assured, I believe the expression goes. As for "The Constant Nymph," it was one of the great romantic best sellers of the early Twenties. When your mother and I got on the Leviathan on May 7, 1925 to sail for France, there was a copy of this book on every deck chair, and when we opened our bon voyage packages, we had a copy of it from Elliott and Norma. I loved the book and wonder if I still would. The Sanger circus is obviously inspired by Bok's family life. I don't know what became of the author except that she wrote another fairly successful book. She is probably in Heaven with the angels.

I don't need to explain "Tallulah" and even if I did, I couldn't. I don't know if I appear in the book, but I certainly should since I am one of her darlings and she often says so.

We're looking forward to seeing you and Fred in October.

When you graduate there will be more and better presents, and so you'd better graduate. I've already bought you a pearl-handled sub-machine gun that once belonged to Al Capone's mother, and I'm trying to locate her bullet proof Lincoln town car. Helen and I send you love and kisses unlimited and our finest collection of high hopes and best wishes.

As always,
The Old Man

P.S. I'll sign this letter some other year.(22)

Thurber also complained loudly and articulately about youthful marriages under the shadow of the atomic bomb, another war, Fred's unpromising and compulsory military future, and pre- and postmarital finances. The Ritz-Carlton in Philadelphia was settled on as a compromise location for the wedding, and an extensive, expensive invitation list was drawn up. Thurber wrote White:

. . . What scalds us fathers of the brides is that the fathers of the sons seem to put it all on us, beginning with the wedding reception, at which we buy all the liquor and they don't even set up one round. This spoils the sons-of-bitches, and they take it easy from there on in . . . Love does a lot, of course, so does youth, and they will come out of it fine, and Fred will have a job by 1956, but I don't know whether I will survive that long or not . . .(23)

(Actually, the bridegroom's parents, unable to attend the wedding because of Mrs. Sauers's convalescence from illness, threw a supper with a proxy host at the Barclay Hotel for the wedding party.)

The ceremony and reception went off without untoward incident. About one hundred guests came and drank up only five-hundred-dollars worth of champagne and liquor, which surprised Thurber, who claimed he drank seven bottles of champagne all by himself. ("Rosemary looked beautiful, I didn't fall down.")(24) Althea was there, and so were the Whites, the Van Dorens, the Armin Landecks, Rose Algrant, and others of the Cornwall circle. Everybody had a good time. It was a rare and savory moment of happiness for Thurber in those days.

After they were graduated from Penn, Fred was drafted and Rosemary became an Army wife for a couple of years, which both disappointed and amused her father. An executive job with General Motors followed, and the Sauers settled down to life in a Chicago suburb. Even with three children and prematurely gray hair, Rosemary still plays "middle-aged ingénues" in community-theatre productions, and recently she has been trying some more ambitious theatrical work, including readings and lectures about her father. "After I lived out in Illinois for a while," Rosemary said, "I came east to Cornwall to visit. I made the mistake of speaking with my newly acquired Midwestern accent in front of my father, calling a stream a 'crick' and gasoline 'reglar' or 'spreme.' I thought he'd explode. He shouted, 'Don't you ever speak with that damn accent again!' He wanted to protect me from the Midwestern evils of speech and thought."

Another collection of pieces, *Thurber Country*, was brought out by Simon and Schuster shortly after the wedding, and it was dedicated to "Rosie and Fred." *Thurber Country* won such high praise as David McCord's line, in the *Saturday Review*, that Thurber "is the greatest and most original humorist this country has produced to date."(25) The reviews and the sales provided another happy moment or two, but the collection itself was not one of his best. It was laden with his dyspeptic point of view and inferior pieces reprinted from the *Bermudian, Holiday*, and *Cosmopolitan*. Even the reprinted *New Yorker* casuals weren't up to par, with one sensational exception—the famous piece on the tantalizing word game Superghosts, brilliantly titled "Do You Want to Make Something Out of It? (Or, If You Put an 'O' on 'understo,' You'll Ruin My 'Thunderstorm')."

Superghosts is the super version of plain old Ghosts. In Superghosts, words are started in the middle and spread in both directions; for instance, "cklu" becomes the basis of "lacklustre" or "nehe" the middle of "swineherd." It was The Game played long and loud into the evenings in Bermuda and Cornwall. But what turns the casual from just a clever word-game piece into one of the maddest and most satisfying of its genre ever written—as well as a superb parody of no less a tome than *Webster's Dictionary*—is Thurber's invention of "bedwords," or insomniac Superghosts constructions that ring in the night after the game is supposedly over. Given, for instance, "sgra," Thurber quickly finds the bona fide "disgrace," "cross-grained," and "misgraff"—and then wanders off into nocturnal creations such as: *"kissgranny.* 1. A man who seeks the company of older women, especially older women with money; a designing fellow, a fortune hunter. 2. An overaffectionate old woman, a hugmoppet, a bunnytalker." Or *"blessgravy.* A minister or cleric; the head of a family; one who says grace. Not to be confused with *praise-gravy,* one who extols a woman's cooking, especially the cooking of a friend's wife; a gay fellow, a flirt, a seducer. *Colloq.,* a breakvow, a shrugholy." After this piece was published, every logomachist in the country, it seemed, wrote Thurber with his own "sgra" bedwords (*e.g.,* "prissgrammar" and "pressgrappler"). For his devoted readers, it was a magnificent touch of the old Thurber.

Another cheering event occurred not long after Rosemary's wedding. Yale University—the college Thurber really wanted to go to—granted him an honorary Doctor of Letters degree at its June, 1953, commencement. Despite his increasingly brittle attitude, he was sincerely honored by his selection (especially since E. B. White had been given a Yale Litt. D. a few years before). He told his Cornwall neighbor and former Yale professor Kenneth MacLean just before the conferral:

. . . By the time you get this I will have been hooded, and I hope I will have survived. We will go to the President's dinner Sunday night, following a small tea at the DeVanes. Helen talked to Mrs. DeVane, who said it was awkward to ask guests without telling them the name of the guest of honor. It also seems carrying secrecy a bit far on behalf of tradition. I don't know who the other candidates are since I'm not supposed to know. There are usually an elderly priest, a liberal banker, a patriotic merchant with $13,000,000, and a politically safe writer. You can't tap a writer until he's sixty and no longer able to drink, because the younger ones are emotionally unstable and are likely to prove exasperating. It's wonderful to have a blind writer who can no longer ogle the prettier wives at the teas and dinners. They don't know, however, that I can cross a dimly lighted room blindfolded and touch the prettiest bosom in the room with my index finger, nine times out of ten. This postman always rings twice, too. All these intimate revelations are, of course, strictly confidential . . .(26)

Thurber ended up having a wonderful time at Yale, treated with deference becoming a statesman and indeed prompting a greater ovation from the large commencement audience than Senator J. William Fulbright received.* He was in a trance of glory throughout the ceremony. During the academic procession, he was asked if he would keep an elderly degree recipient company while the others marched, a genteel way of saying it would be less hair-raising if Thurber didn't grope his way along in the procession. ("I could have made it easily," Thurber told Jack Goodman, "since this is my last good year. Colleges wait to give a man a degree until he can no longer drink and carouse and his eyes, legs, and prostate have begun to go.")(27) Yale kept up its interest in Thurber, asking for and receiving some of his papers for the Beinecke Rare Book and Manuscript Library. Although most of the Thurber papers have gone to his alma mater of record, a large share of them are with his alma mater of choice.

Another honorary-degree incident that spring proved to be less heartening. In mid-May, Thurber was sent a letter signed by one P. Leslie Woodbine, President of the Board of Trustees of Eureka College, in Eureka, Illinois, informing him that he had been chosen to be a recipient of an honorary Doctor of Letters degree on June 7th. Thurber wrote back that he was being conferred with a degree "at another college, here in the East," but would be happy to accept the honor in absentia.(28) He then proudly wrote the Williamses about the two degree offers in one academic season. The Woodbine letter was a hoax, although there really is a Eureka College in Illinois, a Disciples of Christ institution.

The son of Columbus's most esteemed female practical joker, the *New Yorker*'s finest office prankster, the perpetrator of the glorious E. B. White-police caper, the Jewish-tailor-on-the-telephone mimic, and the notorious destitute-colored-maid imitator* was wholly taken in but

---

*A 1953 Yale graduate said that the only inspiring moment at his commencement exercises, apart from being handed his own degree, was seeing Thurber receive his. "He was one writer we all knew and loved," the Yale man said. "That plus his blindness brought the house down."

*The destitute-colored-maid ploy went something like this: He would telephone some kind-hearted woman he knew at her apartment and say, "Dis heah's Edith Rummum. Ah used wuck fo yo frens was nex doah yo place a Sou Norwuck." The kind-hearted lady would ask what she could do for Edith, and Edith would answer that she needs work—

wasn't at all good-natured about the ruse, once he had discovered the truth. When the actual head of Eureka College (Burrus Dickinson, by name) exposed the hoax with profuse apologies, Thurber replied:

Dear Mr. Dickinson:

I don't really know the etiquette that should be followed in such a predicament as mine, but I feel that I owe you and Eureka College my sincere apologies. In my college days we played pranks too, but not on aging blind humorists. We selected stuffed shirts. If I had been able to read the letter head I received and to examine the typing and the signature, I don't think I would have been taken in. I was on the point of having my secretary reply signing her name Virginia Creeper, but I do not regard honor or honors as a fitting subject for kidding around. As for the name of the mythical president, it is surely not an unlikely one for the Middle West. An authentic honor was recently extended to me in a letter from an Ohio woman authentically named Mrs. Depew Head. I am a friend of a distinguished Ohioan named H. Morton Bodfish, and I'm a mild authority on a celebrated Bermudian gentleman named H. Outerbridge Horsey. As for my falling for a degree offered on such short notice, I can only report that I was offered one on the identical short notice by a Middle Western State university three years ago. Incidentally, I turned that one down. I am certainly glad that I did not reject the mythical one.

I am afraid I do not regard this hoax as a sign of "appreciation" by a student. If writers my age depended on appreciation from the modern college student, we would probably languish of some kind of malnutrition. I have several times pointed out in recent years that humor is dying in America, a terrifying thing, but not a surprising one in view of the condition of the world, the plight of our species, and the fearful state of the American mind and spirit. I hate to see humor replaced by vulgarity and cruelty, but I'm afraid that's what we're in for.

At least this whole business has given me a chance to find out about Eureka College. I understand that General Omar Bradley is a member of the denomination of the Disciples of Christ and I can't help wondering how in the world he was given that most hedonistic of names, Omar.

You can't blame me for hoping that your prankster student gets thrown out of college. I'm sorry that you have been bothered by all this, and if my apologies should be extended to any other individuals at Eureka, I trust that you will extend them for me.

Sincerely yours,
JAMES THURBER(30)

The "Ohio woman authentically named Mrs. Depew Head" Thurber mentioned in his letter to the authentically named Eureka prexy was

---

"Ah laundas." They would arrange to meet in the apartment-house lobby, and there would be Thurber, all smiles.(29)

an officer of the Martha Kinney Cooper Ohioana Library Association, which wanted to present Thurber with a special Ohio Sesquicentennial Career Medal for enriching Ohio and the nation. Thurber couldn't attend the October 24, 1953, ceremonies in Columbus, but he accepted the honor, even though it was offered by what seemed to be his least favorite state in the Union. It was a way of signing a truce with the folks back home. He even selected brother Robert to accept the medal for him. However, he conceded nothing politically. He wrote an acceptance speech—read by George Smallsreed, an old *Dispatch* reporter friend and then that paper's editor—which was an eloquent plea for humor as an instrument against totalitarian evils. "The only rules comedy can tolerate are those of taste, and the only limitations those of libel," Thurber wrote. All in all, it was a ringing denunciation of McCarthyism, right in McCarthy's own backyard—and it worked. Most of the audience was thoroughly taken with the speech, especially the statement that laughter was the undoing of dangerous men; it was a point not lost on people already snickering at the raving junior senator from Wisconsin. But even on the attack, Thurber threw Ohio some tasty scraps to nibble on. He mentioned "Ohio's unforgettable Bob Ryder" and quoted O.S.U. Professor Joseph Russell Taylor. ("If a thing cannot endure laughter, it is not a good thing.") And he ended the speech with the line: "The clocks that strike in my dreams are often the clocks of Columbus"—not adding that many of those dreams were nightmares.

The Ohioana speech won wider notice than Thurber or Ohio ever intended. It was reprinted in the *Library Journal* and was issued as a pamphlet, *Thurber on Humor,* by the World Publishing Company in 1954. Thurber included a shorter version of it, under the title "The Duchess and the Bugs," in his last collection, *Lanterns and Lances.* White was particularly fond of the essay, and that still meant more than anything to Thurber.

The reason he couldn't attend the Ohioana ceremonies was a traumatic one. It was another instance of bad Thurber luck, but fortunately one with a happy ending. Helen had been working overtime reading proofs of *Thurber Country* in August of 1953, when suddenly she told her husband, "There's a kind of shadow in front of my left eye, a crescent-shaped shadow." The symptom was known to Thurber, who rushed her from Cornwall to the Columbia-Presbyterian Medical Center Institute of Ophthalmology when the condition persisted. Frightened and once again seeing-eye wifeless, he took an adjoining room at the Institute and set about trying to locate Dr. Bruce, who was on vacation at an isolated ranch in the Colorado mountains. Thurber's fortunes being what they were then, there was a Colorado telephone strike and Dr. Bruce couldn't be reached. In desperation, he turned for help to the Associated Press, whose Denver bureau found Dr. Bruce in Parshall, Colorado. The doctor, with the aid of A.T.&T. lines, got in touch with Thurber and advised him to allow Dr. Graham Clark, a distinguished eye surgeon, to perform the necessary detached-retina operations. The hunt for Dr. Bruce attracted the journalistic attention of the A.P., and newspapers all over the country ran features on the Thurbers' plight.

Reassured, they went ahead with the operations, which were successful. Thurber held interviews in his adjoining room, mostly talking about blindness as a challenge. Helen spent a month at the hospital and two more weeks at the Algonquin (where Thurber had finally settled in) before returning to Cornwall. After a few months, she was reading the mail and newspapers to him once again, which made him nervous, since he feared not only for his wife's eyes but his, too, as it were. Yet, he was oddly buoyed by the experience. "I feel better than I ever have in my life," he wrote the Whites. "This goes for Helen, too. Apparently what we need is an ordeal every now and then."(31) As usual, when caught up in a medical situation, he grew manic about medical lore in particular and life in general. Again, he wrote the Whites:

Dear Andy and Katharine:

We're back in the country and Helen's retina is still sticking well, but she will have double vision for several months while the damaged retina tries to catch up with the good one. I thought you would be cheered to know how tough the eye is. It's almost impossible to infect it from the outside. It stands three drops of atropine, one of which, if placed on the tongue, would made a person spit cotton for weeks. You can get a foreign object out of the eye by pulling a hair from your head, making a circle of it, and dragging it across the eyeball. 80% of detached retinas are completely and permanently restored. The old-fashioned way of getting something out of the eye was by means of the human tongue, somebody else's tongue, like your wife's. No infection from this fascinating kind of kiss. If you ever wake up and your eye is completely scarlet, it is just a broken vein and will right itself in a few hours. Almost 100% of cataracts are successfully removed and original vision restored. There is no such thing as eye strain from reading in a bad light, just nerve and muscular strain. The eye snaps back to normal even after ten hours of reading in the dusk. These are just a few cheerful notes. They usually space retina operations three weeks apart, but Helen had hers in twelve days. She is a tough Scotchwoman and amazed doctors and nurses by her repose through it all. Dr. Clark said, "I could put a full glass of water on this girl's forehead and expect to find it there in the morning." . . .

He went on to reminisce about various old girls of his and his friends, discussing their peculiarities.

... Most of the girls I love have touchy retinas or bad gall bladders now, and I'm working on a sad ballad entitled "I Would Carry You Back to Old Vagina If It Weren't for My Incision." Ah well, we had our moments and now we have our memories . . .(32)

And to George Smallsreed, he wrote:

... Nearly a dozen men, all of them strangers to us, offered to give one of their eyes to Helen, with unbelievable courage and generosity. They all wanted to do it secretly and, although the human eye is worth a million dollars, each of these men would have done it for nothing. This kind of thing has increased our love and admiration of the human race. As it happens, and almost nobody seems to know this, the only part of the human eye that can be transplanted is the cornea and for this purpose the corneas of stillborn babies are almost invariably used. The human eye is exactly the same size at birth as in maturity, which makes this possible. Furthermore, as I told all these men, no reputable surgeon would remove a sound eye even if it could be done, since the effect on the other eye could not be predicted. There is, of course, no data on this so-called prophylactic operation. Operations on any sound organ for any purpose are frowned upon by the medical profession, which is only sound common sense, as well as professional ethics . . .(33)

Thurber was moved by these offers of eye donations, inspired, no doubt, by all the publicity given Helen's operation. While some of the potential donors were plainly unhinged, others were so taken by Thurber and his work that they sincerely wanted to carry out a supreme act of generosity.

As 1953 dragged on, Thurber turned in towards his family. With Helen her old self, Rosemary married, and relations with the Columbus branch improving, he reached out for those nearest and dearest. There were warm, loving letters to Fred and Rosemary. His letters to his mother and brothers were suddenly full of old sure-fire jokes ("Have you ever heard 'The Sweetheart of Sigmund Klein'?"),(34) sports and Ohio gossip, and great concern for Mame's health (so much so that he never told her the whole truth about Helen's eye operations). When, earlier, the rent at Mame's residential hotel was raised fifty per cent, Thurber sent a stern letter to the hotel's general manager, stating that the increase deprived aged persons of residential rights. He even asked George Smallsreed if, as the *Dispatch* editor, he could put some pressure on the local politicians to lower the rent. Finally, he moved Mame (and Robert) to another, less expensive hotel. It wasn't so much a question of money as renewed interest in his family.

He even went so far as to revive his Christmas-in-Columbus habit, travelling to Ohio with Helen for a few days over the 1953 holidays. It was his first visit there—and with his mother and brothers; they didn't come to Rosemary's wedding—since the onset of McCarthyism in 1950. All was forgiven as he sat by the bed of his mother at her hotel, Mame sporting a new permanent wave for the occasion. But apart from giving his mother some cheer, it was a gloomy few days. He figured out that "of the two hundred lively people I used to know there, all but six have died or moved away or been put away. My mother's mens is still sano, but her corpus is frail."(35) Lester Getzloe, one of his few remaining friends on the Ohio State faculty, and George Smallsreed were both visited in the hospital, and Thurber became a sort of instant clearing house for friends and strangers with eye ailments. Everybody wanted advice and help.

Two Decembers later, Mame Thurber, just three weeks short of ninety, died of a stroke. All her occultism and religions couldn't prevent the inevitable. While she gamely tried to stretch for ninety, Thurber and Helen spent an entire month in Columbus, most of it at Mame's bedside as she sank deeper into coma, not recognizing Thurber. She was buried beside her husband in the rambling Fisher plot at Columbus's Green Lawn Cemetery, and Thurber, more relieved than bereaved, returned to the East. But family problems continued to dog him. He had made a solemn promise to his mother to look after his brothers, especially Robert who was crushed by Mame's death. William was managing to get by (with his flamboyant schemes, his pension, and a lot of help from his brother), but Robert was wasting away with mourning and loneliness. At one point, Robert decided to leave Columbus and its memories for either Florida or Cincinnati. Thurber strongly advised against Cincinnati, and wrote William about it:

. . . I didn't intend to be rough on Robert and I know he cannot work, but I was afraid he was sinking into hopelessness. Probably he does go to the library and read the papers and have other activities. Inactivity to me is death or worse; he never writes about his routine and I was alarmed when he said he "Rested more and wrote less". He did some good research for me on the Ryder stuff in 1952, and I had some hope of something else like that. An hour a week or every two weeks, but I take it back.

I promised Mamma to look after him while I lived, and it seemed to me that Cincinnati in the winter would be out of the refrigerator into the snow . . . I suggest that you go with him to Cincinnati some Sunday and look over the situation and find a place. I want to send him an extra $25.00 each month and am sending it to him for November. His diet must be built up, and I wish he could see a good doctor in Cincinnati. I know he is utterly miserable, and it is miraculous that he can go on. I will be glad to send him to Florida, but he seems not strong enough, and you should both talk to your travel expert about it. The dangers and rackets there are famous for the traveler. Try to explain the situation to him and say I did not intend to hurt his feelings and that we must not get in another period of drawn-out difficulty. I'll write again soon. Love to you both.(36)

Robert ultimately chose to stay among the familiar faces and things of Columbus, where he still lives today, alone in a tidy apartment near the city's center. William died, after a long illness, in 1973.

In between the Christmas, 1953, visit to Columbus and Mame's death, the Thurbers did something they had not done in eighteen years—they went to Europe, sailing on the *Liberté* for France. In the spring of 1955, Paris for them was much as it had always been: a special delight and a good excuse for having some unrestrained fun with French friends and visiting Americans, like Elliott Nugent and his wife. Without the pall of war about the city, it was all charm and vitality again.

Then, it was on to London, which was rivalling Paris for Thurber's affections. There were so many people to see—old friends Donald Ogden Stewart (a political expatriate from America), former *Time* editor T. S. Matthews, Matthew's wife Martha Gelhorn (whom the Thurbers had first met when she was Hemingway's wife), and visiting Americans like Richard Watts, the Whites, and the Van Dorens—and even more new friends on the order of Emlyn Williams, D. W. Brogan, and a pride of aging British writers, whose endurance intrigued the sixty-year-old Thurber:

... There seems to be something about England that keeps its writers alive to a ripe old age, and we are thinking of settling down here. One of my English friends is going to take me to meet Walter de la Mare, who is eighty-four, but I won't be able to meet Max Beerbohm, eighty-six, since he is in Italy. Maugham is past his middle seventies and lives in Southern France. Eden Philpotts is now writing for television at the age of ninety-two, and today's Times notes that H.M. Tomlinson celebrated his eighty-second birthday yesterday, quietly at home. In America, as you know, most male writers fail to reach the age of sixty, or, if they do, they have nothing more to say, but occasionally say it anyway.

At one party I met J.B. Priestley again just after he had done his weekly television show consisting of half-a-dozen skits which he not only writes, but also appears in as actor. He was sixty years old last September and is still going strong . . . .(37)

Certainly the most noteworthy encounter, however brief, was tea with T. S. Eliot. Eliot was an early and devoted Thurber fan (Thurber was a late and lukewarm Eliot fan) who communicated with Thurber before he ever met him. He would send odd bits from British newspapers—for example, an item headlined "TWO BITTEN BY APE," in which a chimpanzee escaped from a London zoo, boarded a bus, and bit a woman on the leg and a man on the wrist before surrendering to the proper authorities—adding that he thought it was "a Thurber Item" and that London, as well as Columbus, was "Thurber Land."(38) Apart from his laudatory statement about Thurber and his work for the *Time* cover story in 1951, Eliot liked to join with W. H. Auden and Edmund Wilson in such Thurberiana as the following, related by a proud author to Malcolm Cowley:

. . . "Do you know the difference," Auden asked Wilson, "between the wall maps in GHQ men and GHQ women in 'The War Between Men and Women?' " Wilson spluttered that of course he didn't. "There is no Florida on the map in GHQ women," said Auden, severely and accusingly. What observers these English are, to be sure. Their best newspaper men see more than any of ours, and they do not arrange things in order of price and value . . .(39)

Not much is known of the Eliot–Thurber tea, except that Eliot complained about American television and autograph hunters, one of whom made him sign a bus ticket. In England—that "grownup country," as Thurber once called it(40)—there were no such complaints from Thurber. He was honored and feted like a Kuwaiti arms purchaser, and he was surrounded by interviewers. "The newspapers just loved him in England," Helen said. He gave at least a dozen afternoons to different British interviewers, including "the brilliant and amusing young critic of the Sunday Times, Kenneth Tynan," and he was on television with the editor of *Punch*, who "seemed much more nervous than I was."(41) He also did some work. Long engrossed by the legend of the Loch Ness monster, he planned on writing about it for the *New Yorker*. (The monster piece, "There's Something Out There!," appeared in the September, 1957, *Holiday*.) Thurber arranged to have the Inverness police archives thrown open to him during a visit to Scotland and he hired Nora Sayre, who was living in London then, as a researcher for the article. "His interest in the Loch Ness monster was mostly humorous," Nora recalled, "and as I gathered all that material for him, I thought this simply isn't going to be funny enough. But he was too easy to work for and he paid me well. He would ask only little favors, like buttering his bread."

In mid-August, he and Helen returned to Paris and to some more night life. He also took time out for one of the *Paris Review* recorded interviews, conducted by Max Steele and George Plimpton, which was later included in *Writers at Work*, edited by Malcolm Cowley. The rather feathery and pretentious interview was described by Thurber a couple of years later, in a January 18, 1957, letter to Cowley, as something "done when I was on physical and mental vacation and I think [it] has no real value . . . The transcribed interview seems to me a little like 'cold mutton,' as Oscar Wilde described his first experience of sexual intercourse with a woman. As I indicated in my letter to Plimpton, jabber is taking over, and careful writing is disappearing . . ."

The Thurbers were worried when they heard about the destructive floods in Connecticut during the 1955 summer, but their Cornwall house, on a hill, sustained just a wet cellar, although damage was heavy nearby. The poodle, Poodle, was safe in its kennel, missing only its home cooking, according to Rose Algrant. So they stayed on in France till October and then sailed for home. All in all, it was a rewarding and deserved mental and physical vacation.

They returned to America just in time for Simon and Schuster's publication of *Thurber's Dogs*, a concocted collection of pieces and drawings, some going back to 1926, having anything remotely to do with man's best friend. The book was an obvious commercial attempt by the publisher to cash in on the now world-famous breed of Thurber *Canis familiaris*. The fame and love attached to the Thurber hybrid was such that the June, 1946, *Metropolitan Museum of Art Bulletin* carried an article entitled "Mr. Thurber's Chinese Dog," by Alan Priest, the museum's Curator of Far Eastern Art. Priest told of the discovery of a Chinese seventeenth-century jade dog carving in a remarkably similar posture to Thurber's animal. And Robert Benchley's son, Nathaniel, once sent a letter to Thurber asking him if he ever had an affair with a basset hound, since every basset he had come across was named either Mr. Thurber, Thurber, Jim, James, or Jamie.(42) The breed's progenitor used his latest book as a forum for expatiating on dog's basic superiority to man. His brief was, as usual, thought-provoking, but the book wasn't a success, commercial or literary. Perhaps everyone had read the pieces before. It was dedicated to Sara Thurber Sauers, his first of three grandchildren, born on March 31, 1955.

Even before the Europe trip, he had begun to write casuals for the *New Yorker* again, and the New Yorker had accepted some. They weren't *echt* Thurber, by any means, but rather carping pieces about misused words and morality, with titles such as "The Psychosemanticist Will See You Now, Mr. Thurber" and "The Moribundant Life, or, Grow Old Along with Whom?" Besides some more work along the same lines, he returned tenaciously to his plays and other large, hopeless projects. His play about Ross and/or a troubled congressman was still going nowhere in all directions. Long synoptic letters went out to Nugent and Herman Shumlin, and while various announcements of its forthcoming production were printed, there was never any production. His other dramatic idea about the Williamses and Bermuda, entitled *The Welcoming Arms*, was now concerned with "the man of action against the man of sensibility and thought,"(43) hardly a fresh notion for the coauthor of *The Male Animal*. At another point, he decided on an amalgam of the two play ideas, using the original Ross play title, *Make My Bed*. With blindness a constant hindrance and a sense of dramatic structure not a Thurber strong point, there was only more confusion.

There was confusion, too, in a lengthy work of political satire he had started called "The Spoodle," which, with severe revisions, turned into "The Sleeping Man," which turned into "The Grawk," which turned into "The Nightinghoul." None of the titles graced a finished work, although snatches found their way into other published pieces. It was all very frustrating for a man who promised himself and the world a truly major opus.

But then, during the month-long deathwatch over his mother in Columbus at the end of 1955, the idea hit him of writing fables again, but more timely, pertinent, frankly political ones. In the gloomy circumstances of Columbus, the fables came pouring out of him, at the rate of one or two a day. "I wish everything were as much fun," he later told S. J. Perelman.(44) The new fables weren't "major," but they at least satisfied his driving need for political satire. They weren't all that much fun, either. Written by a man who had gone through two world wars, ghastly mental and physical afflictions, the atomic age, and McCarthyism, the latter-day fables were, in the main, dead serious, with humor showing through only in the inherent lightness of the form and in the use of puns (a toad's jewel is called a "toadpaz") and Joycean–Thurberian portmanteaux ("MORAL: Oh, why should the shattermyth have to be a crumplehope and a dampenglee?"). Dark and cynical, the new fables attacked, by turns, pure optimism, mankind, bureaucracy, impetuous youth, passion, the F.B.I., Communism, cats, the D.A.R., hypochondriacs, radicalism, witch-hunting, womanhood, Southern justice, intellectualism, teleology, war, informing, greed, and—most brilliantly —the lyrics of "Tea for Two." The political fables had the keenest cutting edge and pleased Thurber the most.

Gratified that Thurber was writing well, if darkly, again, the *New Yorker* bought the new fables as quickly as he wrote them. This symbiotic relationship restored Thurber's faith in the magazine, which had become his cruel mistress, and the magazine's faith in Thurber. For a while he was on top of the world. Then, in early 1956, Gus Lobrano, his fiction editor at the *New Yorker*, fell ill and died. "Lobrano's death had more effect on Jamie's relations with the *New Yorker* than even Ross's death," Helen said. "Jamie was spoiled as the fair-haired boy, but Lobrano usually knew how to handle him, to make him see the point of rewriting. William Maxwell, who took over as his editor, simply rewrote Jamie's stuff himself or rejected him cold. Jamie hated the arbitrary bossiness of the magazine, especially after Lobrano, and he felt they didn't like his writing any more."

The *New Yorker* rejected ten out of forty-seven of his new fables, but what infuriated Thurber was that he believed the ten were turned down for political or prissy reasons, not for their literary quality. In truth—as the saying goes in magazine circles—some pieces were not as good as other pieces. For the most part, the fables the *New Yorker* rejected were not as good as the ones it accepted.* Thurber's letters to Maxwell on the subject of rewrites and rejections were ill-tempered and often insulting, especially towards female short-story writers and the magazine's directorate:

... I can't help but feel in the air a certain developing "corporation" attitude up there, a kind of chairman-of-the-board censorship. I hope I am wrong about this . . .(45)

Other letters full of invective went out to just about everybody he knew on the magazine's staff. To R. E. M. Whitaker, he railed against the length of the *New Yorker*'s fact and fiction.(46) To Gibbs, he complained about the curt manner with which the editors informed him of purchases or rejections, not like Ross's "Jesus Christ, that was a swell piece."(47) To White, he sent two rewritten fables as a kind of resubmission. White, explaining first that editors have a freedom to be wrong, felt that the two fables in question didn't "explode" for him the way the others had . . . to which Thurber responded:

Dear Andy:

This exploding of fables, or their just lying there, goes back more than twenty-five hundred years. For me it goes back to when you were about three, and most kids dreaded Aesop or found him clammy. The best of the dead American fable writers was William March, and he wrote one called "The Last Fable of Aesop", contending the guy was killed for telling too many fables, without fuses. Once, with one that had a fuse sputtering, the old Greek quieted a multitude that was in no mood to be quieted. La Fontaine, known as *the* fable writer, has some that

---

*Shawn later denied that any of the fables were rejected for political reasons. The rejected fables, he said, were "weaker than the others," adding that the *New Yorker*'s attitude towards McCarthyism was much the same as Thurber's.

sparkle, some that go off, and a few that just lie there. Almost every source book refers to his "Two Pigeons", thus making it one of the most famous fables in history, but its celebrated charm eludes me, like that of "South Wind", "Death in Venice", "Of Human Bondage", and many others. On the other hand, "Wild Oranges", which has always delighted me, is very bad according to Helen and others, although they do not go so far as my daughter did when she described Emerson's work as "that nature crap". She got an A for a somewhat famous attack on your idol Thoreau, whose guts she always hated, and still does.

I was trying to make those two fables ring, because 70 per cent of the others are about death. I am the deathiest of the fable writers.

Shawn once told me that you never read manuscripts, as if he never heard of THE NEW YORKER of you and me, or of your saving "Menaces in May" and hence my further serious pieces, and your standing out alone for the drawings, week after week, against an art meeting of four opponents. This is the reason I turn to you for advice every decade or so—you also saw the flaw in "Many Moons". I readily forgive the others for rejecting the drawings, but not for pleading with me to turn in again the ones they had rejected, after the success of our book. There are certain things to which we cannot apply the word "freedom" and the belief that all caprice, carelessness, ignorance, or anything else deserves the holy protection of American liberty is one of the weaknesses of our way of life. An editor has a right to his own taste, but not to a capricious, or facetious disregard for another's. Free speech, to take up another phase of freedom, should not protect or defend loose talk, even though everybody from Winchell and Junior Lewis on up gets away with it . . .(48)

When the book of new fables, *Further Fables for Our Time,* was brought out by Simon and Schuster in the fall of 1956 (including the ten the *New Yorker* turned down), Thurber was expansive about the collection. He wrote to Elmer Davis, the liberal radio commentator whom he doted on and to whom he dedicated *Further Fables for Our Time:* "I am now becoming convinced it is my best book and this makes me happier than ever that I picked it for you."(49) The book sold briskly but received mixed reviews. One of the better notices, by Malcolm Cowley in the December 13, 1956, *Reporter,* evoked this response from Thurber:

. . . Lewis Gannett read your review aloud to us and others one night, and then Helen read it again to me. I can see what care you put in it, as you always do, and I greatly appreciate serious and well-written consideration in this period of hastily and badly written everything. A composite of American and English reviews of the Fables would sound like the jibbering of a manic depressive at his worst in both phases at once. For example: "The tired writing of a tired man" and "He writes with the verve of a young man."

No American has yet taken on humor the way it should be done critically— I mean there's been no comprehensive study. It might reveal why six of the following writers of comedy in America have written plays and why none of them has written a novel: Benchley, Sullivan, Gibbs, White, Kober, Parker, Perelman, Connolly, Thurber. I have two books coming out this year and I hope to get a play on next season. I've never had the vaguest desire to write a great love and hate or war and peace novel, but I do ponder and sometimes attempt pieces of the wonderful length of "The Aspern Papers" or "My Mortal Enemy." . . .(50)

An extraordinary number of requests came in for reprint rights of the fables in school textbooks, and, to Thurber's joy, he won the five-thousand-dollar American Library Association's Liberty and Justice Award for the 1956 book in the field of imaginative literature that did the most for the principles of liberty and justice. He was beaming over the award's citation and couldn't help flaunting it before the *New Yorker*.

The two books Thurber told Cowley he had coming out in 1957 were *The Wonderful O* and *Alarms and Diversions*. The latter (dedicated to Helen) was another thick retrospective collection of drawings and pieces plus several of his more recent polemical essays. As an indicative anthology, it can't compare with *The Thurber Carnival*, although it is a good complement to it. But it was the former book, the extended fable–fairy tale *The Wonderful O* (dedicated to Ted Gardiner and his family), that created the excitement in 1957. The story is even simpler than his other fairy tales: A pirate named Black, sailing the O-less bad ship *Aeiu*, arrives at the peaceful island of Ooroo in search of jewels. Black hates the letter O and all things with O in them (his mother ended her days stuck in a porthole is the reason; Black hates l*o*ve but loves his m*o*ther); he banishes all O words and things, when he finds no jewels in Ooroo. "What was the letter of the law is now the law of the letter," says Black's sidekick, Littlejack. The rest of the tale is a parable of McCarthyism and censorship, as well as an occasionally tedious word game. Thurber became something of a WASP cabalist in his mystical attention to O words; indeed, the moral of the book is the importance of never losing hope, love, valor, and freedom.

All in all, it is an amusing and charming superfable, and Thurber had a good, compulsive time writing it. Fritzi Von Kuegelgen, whose daughter Andrea was the namesake of the story's heroine, remembered that throughout the dictating, Thurber was obsessed with O words, so much so that she was often alarmed. "Still, he had fun," she said. And Marc Simont, who did the fine illustrations, recalled that Thurber talked to him about the book much more than he did about *The Thirteen Clocks*. "He wanted to write something lasting about McCarthyism," Simont said.

As with ten of the latter fables, *The Wonderful O* was the source of renewed rancor between Thurber and the *New Yorker.* Another Thurber–Maxwell controversy brought about a near-complete break with the magazine. The *New Yorker* agreed to buy the story but the editors felt it should be condensed by Maxwell. Thurber laid down certain ground rules for any cutting in a letter to Maxwell, adding a tiny parody of the magazine's notes at the end of its book column: " 'The Heart of Darkness,' by Joseph Conrad, was first printed in this magazine in a shorter version under the title 'The Aorta of Darkness.' "(51) It was a friendly warning, but Thurber almost blew his aorta when the condensation was read to him, since Maxwell had cut out his favorite parts about freedom. He talked it over with Katharine White, who suggested that he and Helen do the cutting. Thurber then wrote Maxwell:

. . . We shall cut it just as much as I feel can be done and The New Yorker can then take it or leave it with no hard feelings either way . . . I feel that The New Yorker is as much embarrassed by as it is interested in this book. But you can't make a dog out of a cat, as someone said of Henry James . . .(52)

By mutual consent, the *New Yorker* left it, when Thurber at last didn't have the stomach to cut it down to suit the editors' requirements. But there were hard feelings. While Thurber's ire was directed mainly at Maxwell, he damned the whole magazine for the better part of a bitter year. He rarely stopped by the offices or sent in casuals. As E. B. White put it, "The *New Yorker* was on the spot with the Thurber of those years. He was a pillar of the magazine and everyone was scared to death of him. Shawn didn't want scenes. Yet, they had to reject some of his pieces. They accepted a few of his very last casuals out of kindness. When Roger* took over from Maxwell as his editor, it was even worse. Jim was so fearful of rejections. He was never realistic about them."

A gauge of his temperament during this latest quarrel with the *New Yorker* was his selection of pieces to go in *Alarms and Diversions.* He decided to pick pieces representing the new, serious Thurber. "Jamie suddenly thought his earlier pieces were juvenile and typical old *New Yorker* stuff," Helen said. "He was even contemptuous of them. Once, when some older things of his were done on television, he said, 'Why in hell do those pieces? They're so inconsequential. I forgot I wrote one of them.' And he often said, 'You can't keep writing "Ten Rules for a

---

*Roger Angell, Katharine White's son and a fiction editor. Thurber knew him since Angell's childhood and consequently he couldn't tolerate the idea of being rejected or rewritten by someone he still thought of as a kid.

Happy Marriage" forever.' "

You could if it was original and funny, like most of the early Thurber. It was the curse of the aging humorist.

Although a rough equilibrium had been reached in his toxic-thyroid condition, his mood noticeably blackened and his actions were sometimes irrational. He was past sixty, and thoughts of death and disease were never far from him, especially since good friends and colleagues were falling ill or dying in frightening spurts. Just five months after Lobrano died, McNulty passed away. Thurber had spent little time with him towards the end (when McNulty was in one of his down periods, he avoided old friends and secluded himself with his second wife, Faith), but the effect on Thurber of McNulty's death was enormous. John McNulty—who in Columbus was Thurber's comrade and hero and later in New York became Thurber's protégé (even to the extreme where Thurber once warned Ross to "let McNulty's stuff alone")(53)— was one of the few people who could make Thurber forget himself and laugh, even after one of their boozy tiffs. The shocked friend wrote the McNulty obituary in the *New Yorker* ("Nobody who knew McNulty as man or writer could ever have confused him for a moment with anybody else. . . . His death darkened the skies for literally countless friends and acquaintances, for he seemed to know everybody . . ."), but even this simple, heartfelt act caused a Thurberian tempest. He grumbled about editorial tinkering with the obituary (Thurber wanted it to read "man and writer" and "darkened the day") and proceeded to lecture Shawn on English usage and rhetoric.(54) (After a recent rereading of the obituary, Shawn said that he preferred Thurber's original phrasing.)

Then, Gertrude Sayre, Joel's wife, sank into a desperate state of mental illness. As Nora put it, "Other friends just called but the Thurbers came on the first train. They were wonderful and knew just what to say to comfort us. Jim felt, I think, some kind of identification. He helped save my own mental balance then." And Jack Goodman, Thurber's Simon and Schuster editor and one of the few persons he liked in the publishing world, abruptly died at the age of forty-eight, in August of 1957. That death climaxed "a black summer," in Helen's words. Helen herself was experiencing opacities in her vision and uncomfortable side effects from the necessary medication, and her husband had a series of fierce allergy attacks. Within a year, Wolcott Gibbs would die. It was all more than a blind, aging humorist could take. He was primed to explode again.

CHAPTER **19**

"Why doesn't somebody take this goddam thing away from me!" (1)

It was the ever more familiar pattern of Thurber's unrelenting bitterness leading to seizures of irrationality. In the late 1950's, the world for him was diffused-gray, cold, and unpromising. His way of thinking and writing turned around. "For me, it was seeing the other side of the coin most of the time," Helen said. "He was, I suppose, paranoid, feuding with the people he loved most. He was in terrible despair and he would reverse himself all the time. After a fight with a friend, he would completely change his mind about the fight and the friend the next day. He was restless, and yet he hated travelling. When we'd drive into New York from Cornwall, he'd suddenly want to get out of the car, say, around Brewster. There was no explaining it. 'It's a long hike to New York City,' I'd tell him, and then he'd sit the rest of the way in silence. It is very hard to understand somebody—even your own husband—when he's sick in the brain."

Thurber's rancor towards the *New Yorker* increased and, to everyone's horror, became more public—no longer the product of just late-evening bar talk or personal letters. He offered himself to interviewers as if he were on a crusade to change the world through invective, most of it directed against his old magazine, which grew into a kind of symbol for him of America's weaknesses. To Henry Brandon, a British journalist compiling interviews with distinguished persons in various walks of life for a book called *As We Are*, he went on about his usual pet subjects of American womanhood, the decline of humor, McCarthyism, the superiority of dogs, solecisms, and Henry James, reciting his tried and tired opinions and anecdotes on each topic as if he had memorized them for an elocution class. It was for the *New Yorker* that he reserved his harshest language, paying the magazine back, as it were, for rejecting him. He called it "grim and long . . . a great big business" and said it was in a "tulle and taffeta rut" because of its emphasis on what he felt was the female, escapist reminiscence piece.(2)

He was drinking again, drinking more and holding it less well. His stumbling, brash, even riotous behavior around town was thickening to legend as grandiose as in the big nights of the Twenties and Thirties. For instance, at an Algonquin party celebrating the 1957 opening of Peter De Vries's play *The Tunnel of Love*, Thurber, in the words of another guest, was "a horror." "It was Peter's night," the other guest said, "but all Thurber did was drunkenly talk about himself, the did-I-tell-you-about-the-time sort of thing. Nobody could get a word in—even Peter—and the evening was ruined for me and a lot of other people there. Also, he kept setting fire to himself and the rest of us with his cigarettes and matches. We were suddenly firemen. He didn't seem to care about anyone or anything. I had always heard that he was a charming, witty man, but on the evidence of that night, he was a horror."

Sometimes, Thurber could be wryly charming, in spite of it all. Once, back in their Algonquin suite after a loud and long evening, Helen complained to a friend who had seen them home about her husband's condition and how difficult life was with him. Her friend answered that it was the price of being the wife of a great man. Thurber, supposedly asleep in an adjoining room, shouted, " 'at's tellin' her!" But for most people, even devoted friends, his charm had become gossamer indeed. "Jim got to be one hell of a bore," Ann Honeycutt said. "He was pompous and unbelievably humorless when he decided that he was a man of letters. He couldn't take success. It was tragic: a humorist who lost his humor. The life of pretense was a terrific strain on him. His family and friends didn't interest him that much, and he couldn't write well any more. All he seemed to care about was his own importance. He was so nasty and repetitious in his stories—and he never was before because he had so many stories—that a lot of his friends and myself tried to avoid him whenever we could. We'd peek in at Costello's to see if Jim was there. If he was, we'd flee."

Nora Sayre recalled once seeing him having brunch at the Algonquin during this period. He was miserably hung over and defeated, as she had never seen him before. At one point, he inadvertently stuck his finger in an egg yolk and then said to her, "You can't believe what's happening to me."

In his calmer, more rational moments, he knew what was happening to him, yet he felt he could get away with it—"stay out of the nuthouse," as he once put it(3)—because of his eminent position. He probably knew, too, that his logomachy was becoming logomania, not just word exercises for fun and casual material but a form of madness. In his opaque sight, he saw words dancing all the time, as Mark Van Doren said. Sometimes they danced the tarantella. But there wasn't much he would do about it. He refused to see a psychiatrist.

His condition was further complicated by an element of mysticism that crept into his thoughts and actions. While he had long borne a legacy of occultism and homeopathic medicine from his mother and his surrogate mother, Aunt Margery Albright, he had tended to laugh it off or use it sheerly for literary purposes, as he had his fascination with Houdini. Now, in his mid-sixties, he tended to take it rather gravely, to the alarm of those around him. Dr. Gordon Bruce was one of the first to notice the change in Thurber's attitude. "Years before, when Aldous Huxley claimed improvement in eyesight by staring at Mexican jumping beans," Dr. Bruce said, "Jim was once asked what caused blindness. He answered, 'Watching Mexican jumping beans.' That was Thurber then, but in his last years he wanted to believe in something—a miracle cure for blindness, maybe—even if it was obvious quackery. When you're older and sicker, you believe in things more, I guess. His mental powers were deteriorating and his wonderful sense of humor was fading. Some of the things he believed in, bizarre as they were, represented vague hope. Helen was worried about it, but I felt that anything that kept him interested was good, so I humored him along. Handles of hope again. Jim even insisted on willing what he thought was his miraculous right eye to the Eye Institute. He had this macabre satisfaction in feeling he might help science. I knew his eye was too damaged to be of much use, but, again, I didn't discourage him."*

Thurber had once waged a campaign against eye quackery. When odd people sent letters advising him to squeeze lemon in his eye or bathe it in virgin's urine or place hot flatirons against his temples or "think dark," he would either make public fun of them or blow his stack. He heaped equal scorn and ridicule on suggestions of a course of tubercle-endotoxoid injections, the Bates eye-exercise method, diet panaceas, and so forth, working for such organizations as the National Council to Combat Blindness and appearing on television and radio shows in order to air the truth about real help for the sightless. But in the late 1950's, his letters to Dr. Bruce showed an unsubtle change of

---

*The eye was given to the Institute after Thurber's death, and, as Dr. Bruce surmised, it wasn't of much scientific value. Still, slides of the eye were carefully examined by doctors.

view. He claimed that one morning "while washing my hands I suddenly became aware that I could vaguely make them out and I didn't think it was really imaginary. Up to that moment all I have been able to see was the flick of an electric light bulb going on, or a flash of a photographer's bulb . . ."(4) He listened diligently to Dr. Carlton Fredericks, the radio nutritionist, and asked Dr. Bruce about the validity of Fredericks's diet and exercise recommendations, adding, "I also have in mind a piece called 'The Ghost and the Miracle,' the miracle being my own eye. More than one great eye man has told me that for years I saw without the apparatus of vision, and it annoys me that intellectual laymen dismiss this as nonsense, the way they dismiss the ghost I heard in 1915 in a haunted house in Columbus . . . ."(5) And in a later letter, he mentioned God or E.S.P. as the reason for his eye "miracle." He went on to say: "The intellectual is often a man who seeks to delimit the phenomena of the human mind and body, because he is afraid of the word 'miracle,' and loves to define the experiences of others and to pontificate in areas he knows nothing about."(6)

The spookier aspects of the occult came directly from his mother, who had "always had a lot of fun monkeying around with the inexact sciences," as Thurber delicately phrased it in *The Thurber Album*. Throughout his youth and young manhood, mother and son had a game they played together in which they would experiment in reading each other's mind and sensing danger through E.S.P. It was a sometimes serious game. Most of the family believed that there was a special Thurber "talent" in such matters. Perhaps that was why they were so collectively attracted to Aunt Margery Albright, the witch of Columbus. "All Jamie's favorite ghost stories were true," Robert Thurber said. "I can't explain them, but they really did happen. My mother was forever giving readings on astrology and things, and Jamie loved to make out he had E.S.P. Of course, he was a kidder, all right. I think I'm psychic myself in a lot of ways. I know about people before they tell it. I know what's coming. I wouldn't be surprised if there was truth to a family talent. Only my father always had his mind on other things—contests and politics."

Through these mystical last years, Thurber retained his long-term agnosticism, although Helen noticed an increasing interest in religious miracles. But it was his involvement with mysticism that, as Helen said, was "too intense to be normal." Thurber showed this wayward intensity in a May 25, 1959, letter to Edmund Wilson, who had recently written a psychological analysis of *The Turn of the Screw:*

Dear Edmund:

I have sold The New Yorker an essay called "The Wings of Henry James," mainly about "The Wings of the Dove," the history of the novel itself and of its dramatizations, but also dealing with James and the theatre and a few other aspects of the old boy. Today I cut out of the proof a couple of too hasty paragraphs about "The Turn of the Screw," which I want to deal with separetely at a later date. I am rereading your "The Ambiguity of Henry James" and I want to reread Edna Kenton. Where does her analysis exist now? In a book, or in magazine files, or both?

This will all be only a section of a long planned extensive essay on ghosts, taking in the present legend that Houdini's house in West 113th Street is haunted by that old ghost hater and ghost breaker, an ironical fate for Harry, indeed. . . . There are other phases of the essay, too, including an apparition of a young woman that appeared and reappeared in the West Fifties, to the dismay of a married couple living alone there (a three-story brownstone). Long time friends of mine, now in their seventies, they had been as anti-ghost as Houdini, or indeed, as I once was. In his play "The Potting Shed" Graham Greene has a character say, "No one who has ever experienced a ghost can be argued out of believing he did." After laughing off my own ghost in my story "The Night The Ghost Got In," I now share with Greene the conviction that it was a supernatural phenomenon—Edel uses the expression "the unexplainable." I firmly believe James himself must have had some similar experience, so I see depths in "The Turn of the Screw" that do not occur to me as shallow or unimportant. (Incidentally, Edel carefully tracked down the true medical history of the accident Henry James called "hideous" and it supports my old conviction that he did not lose his masculine works and that they were not even involved. Carl Van Doren was one of those who said James had been emasculated by the explosion.) As I said to Edel, James would have applied the word "hideous" or "horrible" to the discovery of a hangnail at a dinner party. The old boy's desire to make what might be called a multiplicity of montages out of his characters and their experiences added, it seems to me, layer upon layer to the ghosts and children and governess, so that meaning and motivation become as complicated as life itself, anyway the life of the mind. I believe he stepped artistically beyond the literary tenet which insists that the novelist should at all times know what his characters are up to. Didn't T. S. Eliot say of "The Cocktail Party" that he kept finding things in it that he didn't know were there? . . .

Hill and Wang recently published a compilation of ghost stories of New York State, which must bring the literature on the subject direct and marginal to as many volumes as those on war. I figure that only a tiny percentage deals with the subject gravely or even seriously, for one admits he experienced a ghost with as much reluctance as he might admit having once been homosexual. Then, too, there are the vast numbers of crackpots who are taken about as seriously as Conan Doyle and his photographs of ectoplasm. I heard him lecture in the Twenties and was fascinated, if by no means as moved as the editor of the SCIENTIFIC AMERICAN, who went off the deep end about the whole business. As a result, the ghost has become either a figure of comedy or a dramatic device, or a symbol in poetry, and the result of *that* has been a remarkable indifference to sound exploration of death and after death. Doctors do tell me that a recent medico-surgical report reluctantly admits that the composition and configuration of the human brain give no clue whatever to how it could be the apparatus of mind and imagination. It is not so simple to understand as the horseless buggy, the talking radio set, and the human retina.

I am calling my long essay "The Ghost and the Miracle." The miracle fascinates and amuses me as much as the ghost, if only because it has thrown and annoyed some of the world's greatest ophthalmologists. Said my own great Dr. Gordon M. Bruce, after a careful examination of my right eye in 1938, "For 35 years or so you have been able to see without what we know to be the apparatus of vision. You can call it God or E.S.P." And they do hate E.S.P., the medicos, and think of God, most of them anyway, as just another vitamin. When I asked him if he wanted me to leave my eye to the hospital he said, "Want you to? We can hardly keep our hands off it now." According to him, there have been 30,000 recorded cases like mine, and only three of us did not go stone blind. The condition is this: removal of one eye so late that the most dangerous and destructive of all eye inflammations, sympathetic ophthalmia, had spread to and destroyed the other eye. Old Dr. Arnold Knapp, now dead, used to stop Bruce in the halls and say, "Remarkable," and this always meant my right eye. It was a word he rarely used. He believed that Aldous Huxley was psychologically dim of vision because his ailment, keratitis punctata, almost never obscures vision to a dangerous point and, if it does, can usually be cleared up by some such business as the Bates Exercise Method, that is to say, by an apparatus of psychology. Although Johns Hopkins will not admit it, it conducted a two-year study of the Bates Method, and found it without value even in the case of myopia, but we would all have our pants sued off if we said this.

In addition to all this, it was a commonplace with me as early as the age of six, to perform what seemed to others, to my astonishment, unbelievable feats of mental telepathy. I could usually baffle people when performing these feats with my mother, and I have no friend who does not believe that we had some kind of prearranged code. Yet the day that I, at the age of seven, ran three blocks to our house because I knew my younger brother was in peril, my mother, standing on the front porch, was unaware of it. I ran weeping up the stairs, past the room in which I had left him asleep and into a room into which he had been moved without my knowledge. He was lying on a flaming bed, but we got him off without a single burn, thanks to the speed with which I returned home from playing with some kids. It seems to me all this should be made a matter of calm and careful record, even if it upsets some people who think I am sane and will then think I am insane. I have not for a moment been swept off my mental or rational feet by any of it, any more than I have been by my possession of total recall, discovered not by me, but by Professor Weiss of Ohio State's Department of Psychology in 1913, after a series of class tests. He told me one day, "Like every one of the few persons I have known who have your gift, you seem to be less aware and proud of it than you are irritated because everybody else doesn't have it."

There are more things in heaven and earth, etc., and why is an open mind so often left open in order that serious considerations of the unexplainable can get out easily? . . .

P.S. You mention a standard old myth, or truth, about ghosts, namely that they are almost always seen or heard by a single person. This helps to bring comedy to ghost stories, if the author doesn't look out, and made James's task difficult, indeed. I do a recitation, in modern American, of the banquet scene from "Macbeth," showing that what you have there is about two inches from the hilarious. Says Lady Macbeth, to a lighted banquet room full of guys who have long known her husband, "Don't pay any attention to him, fellows, he has been this way since he was a kid."

Shakespeare's great perceptive line, to us Ghostians, is, "There is no speculation in his eyes." That was because, as Shakespeare must have known, the apparition is oblivious of the presence of living persons. It was the dramatist, of course, who made the apparition purposeful. My running ghost was heard by my older brother, too, and he ran to beat hell and locked himself in his room, not having said a word after my, "There's somebody down there" was followed by the steps coming up the stair two at a time. I should add that a man who had lived in that house in Columbus shot himself in an upstairs bedroom, having last been figured to be alive as he paced the dining room floor. We never heard it again, although I tried the words at the same hour, slept downstairs, or stayed awake, and so on. The neighborhood, once a snooty residential district, has now been taken over by the Negro population of Columbus, and I can only believe that the old specter hasn't walked or run for years. In my dreams I invariably rationalize that ghost, having dreamed most recently that I discovered an electrical device under the floor and under the stairs. Such a device was once used by Houdini to baffle old Conan Doyle.

Have you seen the new paperback edition of Dunne's "An Experiment with Time?"

To many around him, Thurber seemed like a drowning man reaching for waterlogged flotsam.

But there was also more buoyant stuff to cling to—for a while, at any rate. Thurber had it in mind to write something about, or around, Harold Ross for more than a decade. His various plays on that elusive subject hadn't worked out, so in 1954 he considered doing a series of magazine pieces about the editor, trying, as it were, to explain the unexplainable. At that time, he proposed to concentrate on anecdotes about the paradoxical man; such as, Ross asking, during a discussion of Willa Cather, "Did he write *The Private Life of Helen of Troy*?" As Thurber summarized Ross in a September 3, 1954, letter to Fred Allen: "He was one of those rare guys who, when they can't do it at all, can do it better than anyone else."

Several magazine editors, especially Charles Morton of the *Atlantic*, had been after Thurber to publish the anticipated pieces about Ross. Thurber thought that getting the essence of Ross down on paper would help him grasp the Rossian character for his unfinished play. He notified the Whites of his intention, because there had been a plan after Ross's death for six *New Yorker* people, including White and Thurber, to put down their feelings about the man for a book. The plan never worked out, however. Neither did Thurber's 1954 series on Ross. But Morton of the *Atlantic* was insistent. After one particularly importunate letter from Morton, Thurber answered:

> . . . You have been circling around me like the Indians around Custer. I have not finished 20,000 words about Ross, but merely roughed them out. I rewrite everything from ten to twenty-five times. I don't know that I want it published in any magazine. Many have been after it, including HARPER'S and ESQUIRE. I turned down ESQUIRE flat. I am finishing my second book of this year and am then finishing a play. I appreciate your interest in Ross and in my piece, but think you're pretty funny pussyfooting and tip-toeing around little old me as if I were Count Keyserling, or someone . . .(7)

Finally, though, he was worn down by Morton, and in the spring of 1957 he started earnest work on the Ross series for the *Atlantic*. "Jamie began to write mainly to shut Charlie Morton up," Helen said. Also, it was a way of reestablishing himself before the world as a *New Yorker* founding father, and maybe it would help him solidify his Ross play, after all.

The *New Yorker* did all it could to help Thurber with his project, even though the Ross pieces were for the *Atlantic* and it was less than enthusiastic about the idea. He was allowed access to the Ross files and he was given the cooperation of the magazine's library and checking department, as well as an office and a secretary. (As the secretary took dictation from Thurber one day, she said, according to Thurber, "Are you sure you're not making this up?")(8) He also asked for and received help on his research from, to name just a few, the Marx Brothers, Wolcott Gibbs, Hawley Truax, Philip Wylie, Gene Tunney, Alistair

Cooke, Frank Sullivan, S. J. Perelman, Jane Grant, Clifton Fadiman, Russel Crouse, A.J. Liebling, St. Clair McKelway, Robert Coates, Joseph Mitchell, and, of course, E. B. and Katharine White. To White, he wrote:

Dear Andy:

I'm writing several pieces for the Atlantic called "Ross," a project I've been working at for some years. Like you, I loved Ross and bore him great respect, and my pieces will all be mainly about Ross and me. A few other people I love keep coming into it, including you, and I find I need a little help from E.B.W. . . .

The New Yorker doesn't have to worry about this project, because it rises out of love and devotion, but the righter I get it the crazier it sounds. Nothing he did was more idiotic than his dogged attempt to make an executive editor out of me, and nothing more wonderful than the way he finally took me in for what I was . . .

P.S. It's a job of selection and memory. Ross once said to me of Thorne Smith: "He sits out there in a goddam candle-lit room rewriting Profiles on foolscap with a quill pen." I think you will like this phrase about Ross—wide-eyed and world-weary.(9)

Both of the Whites, and just about everybody else he asked, gave their unstinting help through letters full of impressions and anecdotes. Nevertheless, Thurber wrote most of the book relying on his own memory. He once told Helen, "Thank God I don't need them. It's all in my head." (He told an interviewer that he spent three thousand hours on the Ross book, what with research and rewriting.)(10) At last, on August 6, 1957, he wrote Morton:

Dear Charley:

The Years with Ross
That title came to me last night while talking with my guardian angel, and Helen and I think it is right. My story takes in more than mere working with Ross. I am working on him now and hard. I'm glad you liked the first piece. They get better.

Cordially,
JAMES THURBER

The first part of *The Years with Ross* was printed in the November, 1957, number of the *Atlantic* and an additional installment was published every consecutive month thereafter until August of 1958. It was clearly going to be a book, and Atlantic Little, Brown wanted to publish

it. For the book, Thurber added considerably to the ten *Atlantic* installments and contemplated two epilogues: one, called End Papers, a collection of short pieces by friends of Ross (commissioned by Thurber),
and the other, A Note in Conclusion, an astringent review of the
changes in the *New Yorker* since Ross's passing. Neither epilogue was
used in the book (brought out in May of 1959), nor was the original
dedication ("To Alva Johnston/ Who kept urging me to write this book,
it is dedicated with the love and admiration all of us had for one of the
nicest guys and best reporters in the world").* The official dedication
was "To Frank Sullivan/Master of humor, newspaperman, good companion, friend to Ross, this book is dedicated with the love and admiration I share with everybody who knows him." Neither dedicatee was an
especially close friend of Thurber, nor, for that matter, was the book's
subject.

The 310-page volume, to Thurber's surprise, turned out to be the
"major" work he had been promising himself and his public. It was the
longest opus on one theme he was ever to write without a collaborator.
In keeping with his ego and his preference for first-person reminiscence, *The Years with Ross* threatens throughout to become *The Years
with Thurber.* As biography it is unsatisfying; as literary history it is
sketchy; as human portraiture it is, in the opinion of many of Ross's
friends, inaccurate and inconclusive. Only as informal, anecdotal reminiscence does it hold up as worthy of Thurber, and it was a final irony
that his major work was, once again, informal, anecdotal reminiscence.

For all its drawbacks, the book was a hit with the reading public. A
best seller for several months, it received generally good reviews, went
into seven printings, was a Book-of-the-Month-Club selection, and had
two paperback editions, as well as, of course, a Hamish Hamilton British
edition. The pro reactions far outweighed the antis, with the glaring
exception of most of the *New Yorker* editorial staff.† Of all the staff
writers, only Gibbs (who read much of the manuscript before he died
in 1958), McKelway, Sullivan, Wilson, and De Vries (who found it "affectionate") had kind words for the book. Former *New Yorker* men, like

---

*Alva Johnston, one of the early *New Yorker* fact writers specializing in the Profile, had
died in 1950.

†Shawn's feeling about the book was that Thurber did not emphasize Ross's immense
energy and talent in creating and running the complex mechanism of the *New Yorker*,
overestimating his own role as much as he underestimated Ross's. Thurber dwelled on
the clownishness of Ross, Shawn said, although his anecdotes and ear for Ross's speech
were accurate. Shawn never acknowledged receipt of Thurber's book with a note.

Ralph Ingersoll and Stanley Walker, enjoyed it, although they had emendations to make. (Ingersoll felt that Thurber was, if anything, too easy on Ross. "He understated that incredible man," Ingersoll said. "I can top any Ross story anyone can tell.") George Kaufman wrote Thurber that one of the *Atlantic* installments was the best piece he had ever read about anybody, anywhere, at any time.(11) And Groucho read *The Years with Ross* twice and told Thurber he'd probably read it a third time—"a great job on a very peculiar man."(12)

Among the antis was Ann Honeycutt, who found the book to be a glorification of its author rather than its subject. "Thurber made himself out to be the great star of the *New Yorker*," she said, "but White and Gibbs did more for the magazine." No criticism against the *Atlantic* pieces or the book hurt Thurber as much as the Whites' disapproval and pique. The first sign of their distress came after an *Atlantic* installment dealing with Ross's method of payment to authors was published in the spring of 1958. Katharine White wrote Thurber that he was "all wet,"(13) and Thurber responded that "you are a little damp yourselves." From there, the conflict escalated. White sent Thurber a long letter explaining that the early chapters were fine but the parts concerning sex and money caused White to "fade out." White added that he wanted to love the entire book but simply couldn't.(14) Thurber answered:

Dear Andy:

Some of your letter is you, and perfect, and some of it isn't you at all, but you have been through more with a non-real me than I have ever been with the other you. I do not lose great friendships for reasons of weather, mundane or mental. The great ones I hold onto are yours, Jap Gude's, Nugent's (and, boy, have we been through something), Sayre's, and Ted Gardiner's, who phoned me the other night from Silvermine, where he had arrived with wife, children, and grandchildren, twelve people in all. Ted, like the late Herman Miller, was a chief support of mine in Columbus during the Years With Althea there. I think that what friends have done for me and what I believe I have done for them form something one can take with him, when he leaves sex and money behind. I never argue with men about sex and money, only with women. What I have finally had to say, in anything I ever wrote, has been honorable and never truly questioned by anybody I love, or who knows me. Incidentally, we once asked together "Is Sex Necessary?" and if we had known we wouldn't have asked, as I once said of Alexander Werth and his book "Whither France?" . . .

In what amounted to my twelfth or thirteenth rewrite of "Ross Not Tobogganing," now "Who Was Harold, What Was He?", I managed to fit in perfectly your letter to me about Ross at the wheel. I have absolute confidence that it is the making of this loving and funny chapter, and absolute confidence that you will approve of it. Nevertheless, I'll have Charlie Morton send you a proof of it. I hope you will let me know as soon as possible that you do approve of it, so that my poor thyroid can have some rest. I quote your letter exactly as you wrote it and it fits in smoothly. It is followed by my own experience with Ross in Paris when he wouldn't let me drive him anywhere in my car. "He would as soon have stayed in a room where I was cleaning a shotgun." This is a fine piece, but would be nothing without the heart of it, or the White.

The following explanation is owing to both of us. When I asked Joe Liebling to "bat off for me a couple of hundred words about Ross" he came to me and said, "Jim, it has turned into a piece." From that I got the idea of asking you and a few others to say something, separate and special, about Ross for the book. I ask you to believe that it never crossed my mind or heart to use these, or any of them, for money or publicity, or material profit. The book, which is being published by the Atlantic Press-Little Brown, not by Simon & Schuster, thus took on a generous shape that seemed to everybody in Boston and to several outside editors outsized and unbalanced. The argument that completely convinced me of their rightness was that I parade through sixteen chapters and crowd my friends and colleagues into the back room. That was not my idea, and I quickly began seeing my mistake. I've had to write all the boys, returning their pieces, but yours could be incorporated in the body of the book, and should be, along with Gibbs's "The Theory and Practice of Editing New Yorker Articles." Gibbs knew precisely how I was going to use it in the now abandoned End Papers, but he had also told me twice that I could use it anyway I wanted to and it also fits well into another chapter . . .

There will certainly be no mention of you or anyone else as "contributor" to the book, now that the End Papers have been taken out. I have never leaned on anybody that way, or taken advantage of anybody that way for profit . . .

You are the only person who did not like the chapter on Ross and sex, the only man, anyway. Fadiman found it "enchanting," Gibbs said it was "magnificent," Wilson called it "your most amusing installment," and George Kaufman, who had known Ross since 1919, and "learned to love the man," wrote me in London: "Your current Atlantic installment on Ross is the best piece ever written by anybody about anybody at any time." So it goes. I have had to deal with all kinds of minds and imaginations in the writing of this book, all kinds of temperaments and prejudices, and it is my last project about real persons, living or dead.

I will ask Morton and Weeks, and through them, Little Brown, to avoid the use of your name, if you say so, in connection with promotion and publicity. It is possible that it cannot be avoided, certainly not by critics, since you necessarily sparkle all the way through the book, as one of the makers of the magazine and one of the factors that encouraged Ross to go on, as he put it himself . . .

To paraphrase and extend a thought of George Meredith's: My heart is not made of the stuff that breaks, my mind of the stuff that cheapens, my soul of the stuff that is on sale to the devil. In the same mail with your letter came one from Frank Sullivan that began like this: "You warmed the cockles of my heart and wrung my withers by your message the other day. I have never had a book dedicated to me but of all the books I would like to have dedicated to me, this is the one. Yours is the best Christmas present I could have hoped for and I don't need any other present. Anything else would be anticlimax. Thank you a thousand times." Incidentally, the new dedication goes like this: "To Frank Sullivan, Master of humor, newspaperman, good companion, friend to Ross, this book is dedicated with the love and admiration I share with everybody who knows him."

The same to you, Andy old fellow. God bless you . . .

P.S. You can return the two enclosures when you have a moment. Take it in your stride, and don't let anything get you. You are a great and good man.(15)

But the epistolary attempts at smoothing things over between the two old friends failed. Thurber said to Lewis Gannett that White's letter "is not, however and alas, unsubcommittee,"(16) and the Whites let it be known that Thurber had not written about "their Ross," to which Helen replied that Thurber wrote about "Thurber's Ross" and the Whites ought to write about their own. As for the sex-and-money complaint, the Thurbers answered that those two forces were what makes the world go around. The Whites and Thurbers didn't see much of each other.

"After the *Atlantic* series, we were all up in arms," White said, "but now *The Years with Ross* just seems distasteful, not awful. I objected to the distortions in the book, the sex—just Jim showing off—and the payments for the writers. Also, Jim exaggerated his own administrative duties. He never, as far as I know, scheduled the magazine or attended art meetings regularly. When the book came out, I didn't write Jim about it, and it was the only book of his he never inscribed to us."

Katharine White had marked up her copy of *The Years with Ross* with critical notes, and in looking through that copy several years later she found that almost every page had a mark. "I was very close to Ross," she said, "and at the time Jim's book upset me. Now it doesn't seem so bad. I was upset that he emphasized Ross's lack of literary education. What Jim didn't understand was that Ross spent all his life reading to catch up. Ross was a natural literary man."

White also took offense at Thurber's letters to him over those years. "I thought they were patronizing," he said, "and I resented it. I felt he was jealous of me towards the end, very competitive. There was never a complete break, but we saw practically nothing of each other. Then, when we heard he was so sick, we had a small reconciliation. I felt very bad about it, very sad. When he was well and sober, there was never a kinder, nicer friend."

Thurber's gloom was measurably darkened by the rift with the Whites. And when old *New Yorker* comrades, like Daise Terry, became noticeably colder, the gloom quickly turned to paranoia and fury. He wrote Edmund Wilson that the *New Yorker* "has always dished it out with laughter and taken it back with tears."(17) And to Roger Angell, to whom he was still sending casuals of the wordy variety, he said:

. . . The book has brought me the oddest experiences of my life, and runs the whole gamut of human expression, for the strangest assortment of reasons, appreciation, jealousy, envy, hatred, and even insanity. Of fifty-five books we sent to those mentioned in the book, about forty-six did not even acknowledge them. Many of my closest friends seem to have clammed up, as if the book were somehow a personal affront, but the men and women who knew Ross longer than I did even are uniformly enthusiastic. So also were Edmund Wilson, McKelway, and Pete De Vries. I can't escape the uneasy conviction, probably absurd, that the word went out from somebody somewhere not to mention it to me in writing or in person. One friend said, "Do you know what the dullest pages in the book are?" Seems they are those "written by Ross." Another friend, a famous writer, said, "Do you realize that your book is autobiographical?" I said any child could tell that from the title. It is utterly amazing to me that, even to minds I have considered intelligent, I have to explain how and why the book was planned. I have to say that I am the only person alive or dead, who started out as Miracle Man, personally on bad terms with Ross, then became a copy editor, a holder of the artists' hands, close friend of Ross, and both writer and cartoonist for his magazine, which surely puts me in the position, to quote McKelway, Nunnally Johnson, and Stanley Walker, of being the ideal one to take on the terrific task. "Both as a literary portrait and a history of journalism it will certainly become a classic," Edmund Wilson wrote me. Bob Sylvester in the Daily News wrote, "It is as dull as The New Yorker—almost, that is." One lady reviewer revealed in herself something dark and fanged and malevolent, coiled in her wit. Antipathy to Ross and The New Yorker is awful when it flashes its fangs, and proves Andy's statement: "Whoever puts pen to paper writes about himself, whether he knows it or not." The death pangs of comedy show up, but only here and there, thank goodness, although many miss the basic planned comedy of the book, I don't see how. There is a lot more to the story of its making, but I'll keep that for my memoirs. It is not my best book, and was not intended to be, since it is entirely expository and in no sense creative. Its popularity is that of [a] magnificent freak, the story of the Great Illiterate of Sophisticated Literature. If the president of U. S. Steel were a midget, if the line coach of the New York Football Giants were a pretty girl, we would have the same freak appeal. I have done the same thing only twice before, in the soap opera series and the story of the Loch Ness monster. Critical estimate at its best often shows up abroad, because of perspective, I guess. Fortunately, most reviewers see at once that it is an affectionate appreciation of Ross and the magazine, a tribute, even a Valentine. Never get into biography, it throws too harsh a light on the prevalence of lunacy.

I have got more letters from "Friends, Romans, Countrymen" than from any other piece I ever wrote, excellent letters, one of which I am enclosing. Send it back when you have time. I now get thirty letters a day and wish I were what Ross once called, a "herman," meaning hermit . . .

P.S. Ken Tynan is reviewing the book for The London Observer, Rebecca West for the London Sunday Times.(18)

The reviews by Kenneth Tynan and Rebecca West were unexpectedly bad, and Thurber reacted irrationally and vengefully, disavowing the belief that "critical estimate at its best often shows up abroad." So vengeful was he that he threatened to break off his reciprocal love affair with all of England, as a result. He wrote his British publisher:

. . . Charles Morton sent me the GUARDIAN and SPECTATOR reviews, tagging them as "obtuse and aimless" and I would not read them. We have been chilled by the British reception of the book and the reviews of Rebecca West, Tynan, and Priestley, mindless, arrogant, and outrageous. Many people have been shocked by them, and my love of England and London are cooling. I don't mind attack. I've had it here from Dawn Powell, Granville Hicks, and a few others, but 95% have been from excellent to wonderful. Maybe a truly good and honest book is bound to get a beating from imbeciles and decaying egos. Just why the OBSERVER, the SUNDAY TIMES, and others would pick aging or youthful authors instead of competent critics I don't know. I know that John Davenport likes and understands the book, and would not have given it the goat-blather treatment. Is it the last outpost of Empire? Is it a declining strength no longer able to face vitality?

I saw a desperate decline of humor in "For Adults Only" in London and smelled the decay round about, but didn't realize it had such a strong pathological and psychopathic element. The bald and sick and insulting assumption of West, Tynan, and Priestley that they knew Ross and that I didn't seems infamous to me and somehow menacing. Having heard such crap as "Flowering Cherry" and other signs of the fall of talent in England, I should not have been so startled, I guess.

I am entirely convinced that Britain is coolly dressing for dinner at the outpost of Empire, and I see the butler, Maunders, telling Lord Sagg-Badleigh that humor and truth have arrived in the compound. The last of the Britons says, grimly, "Show them in, Maunders, but it won't *be* humor and truth." They are brought in and he stares at them, and through them, and, seeing nothing, tells Maunders they are not there and then proceeds to describe them, the ape of arrogance on his back, age and decay nibbling at the sour corners of his once noble edifice of intelligence.

While I have no desire to see any of those "critics" again, I cherish the few friends I still have in London, even though my desire to bring out more books there is about gone. I do not think books should be read by a nation that cannot understand them. I have been cheered a little by notes from Frances Crane and others, deploring especially the West attack. Ross did keep up a long correspondence with her, but it long ago began to get him down. All my friends, and even strangers, are at a loss to understand Tynan's review, especially his "proof" that Ross had a sense of humor which I did not bring out. I suppose the fault is really that of Undisestablishmentarianismship, a snarl of ego and psyche for which the human mind can probably find no escape. People over here are cracking up, too, and the end is probably not far off, many of us believe. . . .*(19)

All that anti-British talk came less than a year after he and Helen had stayed in England and France again for five months, a trip made notable, in part, by Thurber's public declaration of love for England. He said then that he had come to prefer England to France, and England repaid the compliment with more gushy publicity and singular honors. Ostensibly, he had travelled to Europe to gain a fresh perspective on Ross for his eternally unfinished play and the Ross book (he still had to add six more chapters to the published *Atlantic* pieces). Rose Algrant came over to visit the Thurbers in France, and she found him in a lighter mood than she had seen him in for some time. "He was very funny," she said. "He imitated the taxi drivers and he could swear beautifully in French."

Earlier in 1958, a television version of *The Male Animal* was presented in America by Playhouse 90. It received, deservedly, poor reviews. But one criticism—specifically one line in one review by John Lardner writing in the *New Yorker*—set Thurber off again. Lardner had described *The Male Animal* as an "already moribund play." When Thurber learned of the comment while he was in London, it elicited a whole new diatribe against the *New Yorker*. He wrote Lardner that he

---

*He did see at least Tynan again. At a large, flashy party given by Tynan at a large, flashy Manhattan restaurant in early 1960 (which this writer attended), Thurber was very much in evidence, careering and careening about, creating a problem for his wife and his friends as he frequently demanded to be led to the men's room through the swirl of other guests. Several people at the party who had never seen him before refused to believe that the strident man was one of their favorite writers, James Thurber.

wanted the magazine's checking department to research the "living truth" about the play's viability; he said he was sending a carbon copy of the letter to the department's head towards that end. "I'm afraid that you have fallen for a sorry *New Yorker* tradition . . . the risking of a fact for the sake of rhythm," he went on, adding that Ross would never have allowed the word "moribund" in such a context. On and on the letter coursed like a brush fire, singeing the magazine's cavalier attitude towards him, its "political timidity," its rejection of certain fables and the uncut *The Wonderful O,* and its editors in general.(20)

Lardner wrote back, explaining that "already moribund" referred to the dated Chic Harley-type worship theme. Thurber answered with another lecture, pointing out in his peroration that Chic Harley "was the toughest guy in the world and the gentlest, and so, I think, are most of us. And that is the figure in the carpet of everything I write, from 'Walter Mitty' through 'The Catbird Seat' to all the fairy tales."(21) He had reached the dangerous point in life where he was attempting to explain himself.

But three exciting events during his 1958 trip to Europe caused Thurber to forget his feelings of not being appreciated back home: He was the first American since Mark Twain (and the second ever) to be called to the *Punch* magazine Wednesday luncheon table; he was the cynosure at an all-night party at harmonica player Larry Adler's London house; and he spent an evening with Adlai Stevenson in Paris.

The *Punch* lunch, perhaps the rarest honor of Thurber's career, was a weekly rite perpetuated by the magazine's editors as an excuse to choose the following issue's political cartoon and pontificate a bit. It was a ceremony full of old-boyisms—the honored guest was invited to write his initials on the *Punch* table, alongside such monograms as "WMT" (William Makepeace Thackeray)—and Thurber, by all accounts, had a marvelous time. He further consecrated the table by writing his famous "Th," the signature for many of his first published drawings. The event amply demonstrated the British esteem for Thurber, equal to that for Mark Twain. (It is interesting to note that Thurber had earlier found *Punch* to be arrogant, especially towards Americans, and found Mark Twain to be overblown. The *Punch* editors, for their part, wanted to honor Thurber and also, if possible, get a piece or two out of him. They got two, "The New Vocabularianism" and "Here Come the Dolphins."

The Larry Adler party ("I never had a finer time," Thurber told Adler)(22) was a high revel featuring Adler's virtuosic harmonica playing and Thurber's holding forth and singing old favorites like "The Tennessee Waltz." When Adler wrote Thurber the next day thanking him for bringing such warmth into his house, Thurber answered that he appreciated the thanks because "I woke up the next morning feeling that I had made some kind of cockeyed idiot of myself . . . Nobody should ever let me sing, for I am almost tone deaf, can't stay on key or pitch or in rhythm . . . and I have shown no progress in music since the fourth grade, when I got my only F in my whole school career, under Miss Ballinger."(23) Thurber was so moved by Adler's musicianship and so outraged by his political persecution (Adler went into exile in England because he was deprived of jobs in America) that he conspired with friends to get Adler a nightclub date in New York. Through the conspirators' intercession, Adler played the Village Gate and even appeared on American television in 1959. At the Village Gate opening, an ecstatic Thurber stood up at midnight and made an impromptu speech, comparing Adler to, among others, Abe Lincoln. It was a vicarious triumph for Thurber, and, to his amazement, he received only one crank letter "out of the dark ages of McCarthy" for his efforts.(24)

His meeting with Adlai Stevenson, in John Duncan Miller's Paris apartment, was an extraordinary experience for everybody present. "Stevenson was also a friend of mine," Miller said, "so when both he and Jim showed up in Paris—Stevenson was addressing some organization or other—it was the most natural thing to get them together. They both were instantly entranced by each other's eloquence and they promised to visit often in America. It was the best evening I ever spent with Jim. Stevenson and Thurber were so rich with ideas and words that the next morning I couldn't remember a thing about it. Except for that evening when he flowered, Jim was very bad and getting worse, it seemed to me. The pattern was ranting, raving, and then apology. He had become incredibly vain."

But even with all the honors, interviews, and Olympian evenings, Thurber managed to finish the last chapters of his Ross book in Europe. It was easier to write in London than in New York, he said.(25)

Not long after they came home from Europe, and just before *The Years with Ross* was published as a book, both Thurber and Helen had another nasty scare. Helen's doctors recommended a second operation to remove a new ovarian cyst, but this time, after the surgery, the doctors thought there was malignancy and that Helen would die. Thurber fell apart when he learned of their suspicions. At the Algonquin in the care of friends (Jap Gude, of course, and Elliott Nugent, in a high manic state), he drank himself into something approaching narcosis, as a defense against the terrors, real and imagined. He figured out that Helen and he had gone through a total of fourteen operations since they were married in 1935. "I have known what the valley and the shade are," he later told Peter De Vries.(26)

For five days, the doctors at Doctors Hospital dodged Thurber, convinced, as they were, that they had only bad news for him and knowing that he was in no shape for more bad news. Then, to the joyous astonishment of one and all, final tests showed that the cyst was benign. Suddenly, the doctors were chatting with Thurber about the overuse of cortisone, the disappearance of phosphorus, and other sunny matters. Helen, resilient as ever, recovered quickly. "It was so strange, though," she recalled. "Jamie was terribly upset when he thought I had cancer, but when he was told I didn't, he was cool, almost uninterested. I had seen a lot of strange reactions from him before but never anything like that."

There were more honors to be gleaned in America, too, but not quite up to the British ones. Thurber was asked to appear on Edward R. Murrow's television interview program "Small World,"* in the course of which he assailed the *New Yorker* once more for not printing enough humor; this latest attack widened the distance between himself and the Whites, who, with other magazine personnel, were growing impatient with his fickleness. Later in 1959, he went to Columbus to receive the Distinguished Service Award of the Press Club of Ohio, using the occasion to reminisce about his old newspaper days. "I was a helluva good newspaperman," he said.(27) (The award dinner, scheduled after the Ohio State–Iowa football game, relaxed its stag rules so Helen could accompany her husband.) And in April of 1960, he travelled to Columbus once again to make the dedicatory speech for a new O.S.U. Arts and Sciences building named after the late Professor Joseph Denney. His truce with Ohio was now a separate peace with honor.

The speech, read by Helen after some prefatory remarks by its author, pulled few punches, however. True, he paid homage to the "importance of the American Middle West to the culture and destiny of the United States" and to his trio of influential Ohio State professors, but he added pointedly about Denney:

... He held the lamp of learning and the torch of freedom high, for the higher you hold them, the smaller become the shadows in which the enemies of learning can lurk and operate . . .(28)

---

*With Siobhan McKenna and Thurber's fancied competitor, Noel Coward.

At a reception after the dedication ceremonies, given by his *Sundial*-affair enemy John Fullen (with whom he had also made a separate peace), Thurber was on the agitated side. He talked and smoked incessantly, according to Professor James Pollard, who sat next to him. Pollard recalled that somebody came up behind Thurber, put his hands on Thurber's shoulders, and introduced himself. Thurber, hardly breaking off his monologue, said, "Take me to the bathroom." He was led away, returned in a few minutes, and picked up his monologue exactly where he had left off.(29) "The women were all at his feet," said his host, Fullen, "and he just held forth for two hours or so. I wish I had a tape recorder on."

Thurber's own view of that particular Columbus experience was slightly more jaundiced. From his hometown, he wrote a friend:

. . . We came out here by train last Wednesday night and, oh, wonder unmixed, we are going back to New York alive tonight. It was a series of ordeals this time all in one day, a luncheon at the faculty club at which I sat on the right of President Novice Fawcett (shake hands with Wragford Novice), and then the dedication of Denney Hall, the new Arts and Science Building, named in honor of one of the truly first rate scholars, teachers and gentlemen of his time, which was my time in the university too. Nugent and I had him in mind when we wrote the part of the Dean in "The Male Animal." Having been sick in bed for a month, I didn't have time to finish my speech and learn it too, so Helen stepped into the breach and read it for me, in a very moving performance, the day was hers. Then came the reception and for some reason there wasn't a dry palm in the damn line of 70 women I shook hands with. My daughter tells me that all girls have moist hands nowadays on account of everything . . .

Your perfect picture and description of Truman Capote was properly chilling. Instant Woollcott is exactly what he is.(30)

As a final gesture of armistice, he sent back to O.S.U. the two-hundred-dollar expenses check.

Yet, withal, Thurber felt ignored and unvenerated. Real honor for him, at this late point in his life, meant something along the lines of the Nobel Prize. Edmund Wilson, in his book *Upstate*, described Thurber as being "haunted" by that idea, once telling Wilson (while having drinks at the Algonquin and "throwing his weight around," as Wilson put it) that the prize should be given to a humorist for a change.(31) There was little chance of that, but Thurber was in no temper then to accept the unhappy fact. He was a very sick man, mentally and physically, and he was fighting for his very existence.

*　　　　*　　　　*

Then, as if dispatched by a benevolent angel, along came Haila Stod-dard. A blond, comely actress with a steady role in a television soap opera (Thurber always was a pigeon for actresses), she had been an avid Thurber fan for years. With the misty aim of becoming a Broadway producer, she dreamed up the idea of a revue consisting of Thurber pieces and drawings, writing an outline based on simple dramatizations of the material she liked best. She showed the outline to Elliott Nugent, who liked the concept and promised to tell Thurber about it. Thurber had been turning down all such revue notions (although one venture, to be produced by Cheryl Crawford, was announced for the 1953 Broad-way season), because he had never been convinced that his casuals and drawings, so dependent on the printed page for their effect, would work on stage. However, Nugent's enthusiasm, the simplicity of the Stoddard concept, and his insatiable need for recognition at the time all conspired to tweak his interest. A meeting was arranged at the Algonquin, and Haila read her outline draft to Thurber, who approved of it in principle.

With the approval and promised dramatic rights, Haila informed her friend Helen Bonfils, the Colorado newspaper heiress who dabbled in theatre, and got all the backing she required. Before long, she had signed Burgess Meredith as the director and Tom Ewell, Peggy Cass, Alice Ghostley, and Paul Ford as half the cast, plus Don Elliott and his jazz quartet for the music. Thurber became truly excited. The slim idea had magically grown into a reality entitled *A Thurber Carnival* (a good index of his celebrity), and Thurber, suddenly revitalized with a bright new spirit, put aside all his depressing projects to become the writer and general consultant for the revue.

However inspiriting the work was for his psyche, it signalled—for Helen, at least—the beginning of the end of his career. "Jamie's deci-sion to redo his old material for *Carnival* showed that he couldn't write fresh things any more," she said. "He always told me he would never rework a finished product; once it was done to his satisfaction, that was it. When his writing for *Carnival* was finished, so was he."

He threw himself into the difficult rehearsal and tryout period with a heedless verve. It was being stage-struck all over again, only more so. "Burgess wanted him to write new material for the show," Haila said, "but I wanted the old material fashioned to work on the stage. I finally won out, but meanwhile Jim had written tons of new stuff, enough for two other revues. The new stuff was not at all like the old. It was cantankerous and definitely not funny. Still, he kept on writing, writing —almost all of it unusable." The only new material that was put into the final production could easily have been discarded with the rest. A sketch called "Gentlemen Shoppers," dealing with a plan by expensive women's department stores to serve drinks to Christmas-shopping men, was predictable and even slightly plagiaristic. Thurber borrowed his favorite Marx Brothers routine for the occasion:

BAILEY: We're going to spend the night at Ovington's.
GIRL: But there isn't any Ovington's.
WESTWATER: Then, by God, we'll build one.(32)

And there was some drastic plastic surgery done in a series of blackouts called "Word Dance," in which the actors danced together between punch lines culled from old cartoon captions but ruined with racy, updated rewriting (e.g., "After all, she has eight children. No wonder every man she looks at seems to be a rabbit"). Indeed, such humiliation of what made Thurber Thurber was, unfortunately, the most memorable aspect of the show; the difficulty, perhaps the impossibility, of transforming written Thurber into acted Thurber was evident throughout.

The more successful sketches were a simple monologue rendering of "The Night the Bed Fell," three of the early fables ("The Wolf at the Door," "The Unicorn in the Garden," and "The Little Girl and the Wolf"), a zesty "If Grant Had Been Drinking at Appomattox," and an effective slide-and-narrator version of *The Last Flower*. But heavily reworked Thurber classics—like "File and Forget," "Mr. Preble Gets Rid of His Wife," "The Secret Life of Walter Mitty" (the last, one hopes, squeezing of that poor tortured little cherub, with dialogue added by Thurber as a fumbling answer to Sam Goldwyn), and even "The Pet Department" (manhandled from its pristine madness into a television-show bit)—were cheapened by their inclusion.

Whatever the revue was or wasn't on the stage, it was good therapy for Thurber. He was working hard at something palpable again, and such was his frame of mind that he agreed to try out the show in Thurber Country, not along the standard New Haven–Boston–Washington–Philadelphia route. On January 7, 1960, *A Thurber Carnival* opened at the Hartman Theater in Columbus, Ohio, the scene of the Scarlet Mask Club triumphs. Of all his homecomings, this one was by far the most spectacular. Governor Mike DiSalle proclaimed "James Thurber Week" in Ohio ("Over my dead body," said Thurber until, as Helen said, the ham in him took over),(33) and Mayor W. Ralston Westlake presented him with Columbus's first Distinguished Son citation.

Thurber ate it all up and declaimed for interviewers as the elder curmudgeon. He damned investigating committees, congressmen, television sponsors and producers, and, with an uneasy eye to possibly poor
reviews, the decline of comedy before a "mythical stupid American
audience."(34)

Opening night, a lavish, social affair at which some men (who checked
with the theatre management beforehand) wore black tie, found the
audience and the critics generally pleased by the gentle, sometimes
almost non-existent humor. Everyone agreed it needed work, the safest
thing to say during a tryout. One woman amused Thurber when he
overheard her saying, after the "If Grant Had Been Drinking at Appomattox" sketch, "Oh, I don't believe in doing that to history."(35) For
Thurber's old Columbus friend Ted Gardiner, it was a painful evening.
"I had to leave the theatre," he said. "I couldn't stand to see what they
were doing to those pieces I loved. But it was good to see Jim fairly
happy, anyway." Another hometown friend felt it "was a bomb,
whether Columbus was sophisticated enough for it or not. Thurber
should be read at leisure."

After a three-night run in Columbus, the show went on a six-week
tour of the Midwest before its Broadway opening at the ANTA Theatre
on February 26, 1960. It was a chaotic tour, with perhaps more script-
tinkering and feuds than most. Elinor Wright, the company's production secretary on the road, was adopted, in effect, by the Thurbers and
was privy to most of the chaos. "There were so many conflicts and
fights," she recalled. "Burgess versus Haila, Ewell versus Haila, and so
on. And in the center of it all was this blind man, sick and old in that
Midwestern winter, trying to keep it going by constant rewriting and
giving out Girl Scout interviews. I somehow could always make him
laugh, though, and he liked me to read his writing back to him. 'You
don't add anything to my writing,' he told me. He would dictate with
punctuation and he'd get furious if I left out even the smallest comma.
Only once he made a small pass at me. It didn't mean anything. It was
Helen who was the great peacemaker for the cast and producers. Everyone came to her with problems. She managed to smooth things over.
She even ran errands when things got very tight."

After Detroit, Cleveland, St. Louis, Cincinnati, and Pittsburgh, the
company slogged into New York with its polished version. Exhausted
and fearful, Thurber wrote a hedging piece for the February 21, 1960,
Sunday *Times* drama section, entitled "The Quality of Mirth." The
quality of mirth was strained, he said, and everybody wanted to save his
show with bad suggestions about how to make it funnier. He was frankly

worried about the lack of boffo laughs in the revue, which seemed to evoke more of an "appreciative smile" than a yuk. He read a great deal into his casuals-turned-sketches (always perfectly capable of standing on their own as pure humor), calling "The Pet Department," for instance, a demonstration of Americans' "hasty and thoughtless lack of observation and perception." And he concluded that if all theatre-goers want is the boffo laugh, then "I shall return to the dignity of the printed page, where it may be that I belong." It took him a long time to realize that sterling truth, but the realization came too late.

Thurber needn't have feared the critics or the theatre-goers. Both were exceedingly generous, with Walter Kerr of the *Herald Tribune* making Thurber's reservations sound silly by mentioning the "belly laughs" in the revue. Most of the critics called it the funniest show of the year, and Brooks Atkinson of the *Times* was impressed by its more cerebral humor than the usual revue offered. Richard Watts of the *Post*, an old Bleeck's friend, was particularly relieved to like the show, finding Tom Ewell a perfect "Thurber man." Only the *Nation*'s critic disapproved. Considering everything, the show did well at the box office, but not as well as the reviews would seem to indicate. Even *A Thurber Carnival* took more effort than the tired businessman was willing to exert after a long day at the office.

As for Thurber himself, he was once again the toast of the town, besieged for favors and interviews. The day after the New York opening, however, he fell ill with a throat infection and the flu, complicated by exhaustion, and went up to Cornwall to rest. Helen caught the flu, also, but still ran the even more hectic household. It was a rerun of their post-*The Male Animal* collapse in 1940. "At least five hundred letters have piled up . . . and life is now three times as crowded as it was," he wrote the Williamses. "It is not easy for a man who will be eighty in a little more than fourteen years."(36) Nevertheless, there was time for more holding forth. Interviewed in Cornwall by Arthur Gelb of the *Times*, he complained of the jet-propelled pace of life and its victims. He announced, for easily the tenth time, his forthcoming play about Ross, and let it be known that he was creating a new revue out of leftovers from *Carnival*. But his imminent project, he insisted, was a thirty-thousand-word satire, *The Nightinghoul*, about the rumored descent on a city of a large, mechanized flying creature, being a tale concerning fear of nonexistent evil. "I don't think anyone should write comedy nowadays that is pure nonsense; it must have meaning," Thurber added. "I'm always astounded when my humor is described as gentle. It's anything but that, and I intend to beat up the next person who says that about me."(37) The truth, of course, was that he was too sick to write gentle pure nonsense any more. He had lost the touch. And that was the real tragedy of James Grover Thurber.

Elinor Wright continued to be, off and on, Thurber's part-time secretary and part-time house guest in Cornwall and New York. "Rose Algrant didn't like the idea of a young girl as his secretary," she said, "so the Thurbers gave a party for me and Rose finally approved. I noticed that he was becoming infatuated with death. We would have lunch in the Algonquin, for instance, and he would talk about Benchley and other dead writers as ghosts sitting and lunching at different tables in the same room. It was eerie."

With the exception of the Denney Hall dedication ceremonies at Ohio State in April, Thurber fell into his old rut of big nights and big talk, especially when he was in New York. It was a way of not writing. One of those nights, in the spring of 1960, almost finished him off for good. His compulsive need for people, even strangers, around him led to one of the most traumatic incidents of his life. A woman had come up to the Thurbers during dinner at Maria's, his favorite small New York restaurant, and invited them to an impromptu party in her apartment on the upper East Side. At two A.M. the Thurbers were the last two persons to leave the party, and while Helen was freshening up in a bathroom and the hostess was in the kitchen, Thurber discovered that a living-room chair was on fire. Flames rapidly separated Helen from him, and each feared the other was lost in the fire. Meanwhile, the hostess had fled downstairs to turn in the alarm. Staving off panic, Thurber groped his way to a second bathroom, where he had the presence of mind to close the door and seal it with towels, open the window, and put a wet handkerchief over his face. At last, the fire department arrived and rescued both the shaken, angry Thurbers. As he later wrote the Williamses:

. . . We got out of this one by the grace of God and the skin of our teeth, and though it was no fault of ours we have paid the woman $2500 to replace her living room furniture and to get her out of our hair and off our backs. Right now we never want to see New York again and we shall never go to strange apartments with strange people . . .(38)

The press picked up the story, finding Thurber at his surliest, especially since he was blamed for starting the fire. When he was asked how he knew he was in a bathroom, he replied, "How does anyone know he's in a bathroom? It has a toilet seat and a basin and a bathtub and you know it's a bathroom, don't you?" Why didn't he panic? "If I didn't panic when I found out I was a human being, I'm never going to." And the state of his blindness? "I'm awfully fed up with the way the press plays up my blindness. It seems to me they're more interested in my blindness than my vision."(39) All his life, Thurber had a terror of fire; it appeared often in his dreams as a consuming menace, undoubtedly magnified by his blindness. "For Jamie," Helen said, "that apartment fire was far more terrible than it would have been for anybody else. It took him a long time to recover from it."

To add to his unhappiness, *A Thurber Carnival*, not all that healthy at the box office after seventeen weeks, fell victim to an actors' strike and was forced to close. After a month off, the company reassembled in Helen Bonfils's home territory of Central City, Colorado, where it played successfully for a month at her opera house, but without Tom Ewell who was lost to a Hollywood commitment. (He was replaced by Eddie Mayhoff, a Burgess Meredith choice Haila Stoddard didn't approve of.) Colorado was a summer diversion for the Thurbers, as he wrote the Williamses, on August 27, 1960:

. . . We went to Central City, Colorado, where our Carnival played all of August at the old opera house. It was a trip into the past. The town has a crier with cowbells and there are not many baths or telephones. It's 8500 feet high, and I was one of the few not affected by the altitude. It got Helen's sinus a little. So we spent our last two weeks at the Brown Palace Hotel in Denver, the most wonderful and luxurious hotel in the world. Denver is full of rich widows who give parties around their swimming pools. The women are most friendly, and instead of shaking hands hug you. One young lady said to me, late at night, "I don't wear any stockings—see?" I told her I couldn't see, and she said, "Well, feel then." The next minute she was in Helen's lap.

We got back to New York August 22, Dorothy Parker's 67th birthday. My first love, Eva Rosebud Prout Barks Geiger, will be 66 in October. On our way back we stopped in Chicago to meet my son-in-law's parents for the first time. We had lunch with them and Rosie and Fred, and Sara, aged six, and Gregory, aged four, but able to take a house apart in half an hour. The youngest, Mark, nine months, is said to be a genius, because he can darn near walk and talk, and looks a little like the Great Quillow. I didn't walk till I was five or talk till I was seven . . .

Helen is fine and she has been the balance wheel of the Carnival company since the beginning, the only one who can deal with all the different egos. When one actor threatened to quit, his wife wrote him, "Don't you do anything till you talk it over with Mrs. Thurber." He didn't quit. The show broke all records out there by selling out for the whole month in advance, and we even had to put on three extra performances. It grossed $164,000, or about twice as much as the next highest, Lillian Hellman's "The Lark." It reopens at the Anta Labor Day matinee . . .

The reopening in New York was not wise. Without Tom Ewell, the show's failure was certain. Thurber was called upon again to write a publicity puff piece for the *Times* drama section, neatly reversing himself by saying that the *Carnival* tours demonstrated the sign of a humor revival all over America.(40) As the box office slipped badly, Thurber asked Haila Stoddard what else he could do to help. "I told him, 'Go into the show,' " Haila said. "He literally jumped at the chance. It was the only way to save the show. He was always performing, anyway—grabbing the mike in nightclubs and making speeches and singing 'Bye Bye, Blackbird'—so what could be more natural than Thurber playing Thurber in the 'File and Forget' sketch? Jap Gude was against the idea; he thought it would kill Jim. Helen didn't know what to recommend. But, as it turned out, he was a born actor and he loved the theatrical experience. He was suddenly a happy man again, full of involvement with the show and in love with being the new star on Broadway. And for the three months he was acting, the box office was fine. He saved his own show."

Thurber must have sensed how much personal good his appearance in *Carnival* would do him. He later told Roger Angell that he agreed to go on stage in order to pull himself out of "grave psychosomatic problems . . . to restore a very shaky balance,"(41) and in yet another puff piece for the *Times* he said that being an actor was a relaxing respite from the real hard world of menaces. Acting was in his blood, he went on. He even planned to write in a part for himself in his ever-forthcoming play about Ross: "I consider myself a professional writer, a semi-professional cartoonist, and an amateur actor." His blindness didn't interfere with his acting, since he was discovered in an armchair in the "File and Forget" scene and he merely had to dictate to an actress playing his secretary, as in real life. It was easier for a blind man to act the part of a sighted man than vice versa, he claimed.(42)

Elinor Wright had been the understudy to the "File and Forget" secretary, as well as Thurber's actual secretary, but during his acting tenure, she played the role opposite him. "He was a real actor with natural timing," she said, "and he was great to work with on stage, although he liked to ad-lib a lot. It was obviously fun for him." Meanwhile, Fritzi Von Kuegelgen, who had left Thurber's employ to teach at a New York City private school, returned to work for him part-time. "It was the most hectic period of his life, I think," Fritzi said. "There were never enough taxis during the holiday season to take us from the Algonquin, where he lived, to the theatre, so finally we had to hire a limousine. But he was so happy."

The ham in him was sizzling. Several critics re-reviewed the show and found something new to praise. There was a parade of cronies coming to see him perform, most of them enjoying what they saw. E. B. White turned up, by way of reconciliation, and even Ann Honeycutt, who had always been amused by Thurber's mimicry talents (if not, of late, by Thurber himself), came to see him. A good part of the fun for Thurber were the visits by friends backstage and the drinks with them after the performance. Constantly talking about the celebrities trekking to his dressing room bored others, but most understood his need to regain self-confidence. Fairly bursting with joy and hope, he wrote the Williamses, offering them a trip to New York from Bermuda, as a Christmas present, to see him in the show:

... Tonight I make my 46th appearance on stage and Helen and I do not intend to have you two miss seeing the play. We shall probably open in London with it in February, or a little later, with an all English cast, except for Thurber as Thurber. Rosie and Fred came on to see the show from Illinois, and we had a fine time with them. In spite of the play and the hundreds of letters I have to answer, Helen and I are putting the final touches on my latest book, "Lanterns and Lances," which contains twenty-four pieces that I somehow managed to write between 1957, when I began the Ross book, and today, when I finished the last piece for the new book. In my spare time next year I hope to become an umpire for the American Baseball League. I've also made countless appearances on radio and television and have given out about eleven hundred interviews. This has left me no time at all to chase girls, my only regret. I will be 66 in December, but feel forty-three years younger . . . I am no longer called "Old Totters," but Junior, or Buster, by the older members of Equity . . .(43)

If he wasn't exactly the good old Thurber, he wasn't exactly the bad old Thurber, either. For eighty-eight performances he basked in the Fresnel beams, until the show ran out of customers willing to pay to see Thurber play himself on stage. It closed at the end of November, not quite sturdy enough to make it through the usual Christmas doldrums. (However, within a year, a bus-and-truck company, starring Imogene Coca and Arthur Treacher, profitably toured the provinces.) Thurber collected a special Antoinette Perry Award (the "Tony") for distinguished writing, and then, all at once, he had nothing to do but return to Cornwall and try to pick up the pieces of his true career. With hardly a moment's pause, he plunged to the bottom of his despair again. It was as if he had used up the very last bit of fun left in his mercurial life.

One day in Cornwall, just after *Carnival* folded, he was working with Fritzi and suddenly became annoyed at something. "His head seemed to grow in size and he became very red," she recalled. "He looked like he'd pop, like a balloon." Neither Fritzi nor Helen nor the doctors he refused to consult knew it then, but he was probably experiencing one of several small strokes that occurred during his last year on earth. In retrospect, those closest to him could pinpoint what they thought were the actual moments of the strokes. "I think the first one was after my cyst operation in 1959," Helen said, "when he reacted so strangely after the doctors told him I didn't have cancer. I should have known something serious was wrong with him then."

So began Thurber's final year. Even his most casual acquaintances sensed that the year would not go well for him. Relatives and friends never knew what to expect from day to day, from minute to minute. Almost everyone became the object of his abuse, with Helen usually receiving the worst of it. As she put it: "The last year was one long nightmare for me."

For Rose Algrant, as his quasi-second wife, the post-*Carnival* change in Thurber was frightful, too. "Maybe being an actor was too much for him," she said, "even though he loved it so much. When he came back to Cornwall, he was no more patient, even with me. Then he started to be violent, with so many fights, throwing glasses on the walls—in my house he broke millions—and soon people would keep away. Helen sometimes asked me to stay over her house because she was afraid. He resented her. He resented that he needed her so bad all the time. Whenever she was sick, he was out of his mind with worry. Every day it got worse. He drank more and more and always demanded people around. He was not working well. Once, he fell asleep in his chair in my living room. That worried me because he never fell asleep before, no matter how much he drank. Nobody suspected strokes then. I was his confessor. I had to listen to his fears of death. He had such bad dreams. One is about a party for his friends of the *New Yorker*, and all the drinks are empty—that is, all the friends are dead. He mentioned death so much and he pretended he wasn't scared. But he was. He was afraid of doctors. All he believed in any more was E.S.P. I told him I had E.S.P. when I called him after a feeling he was in danger, and he was really sick. He believed in my E.S.P. powers."

This ballooning infatuation with the occult brought on one of the

most tragic events of his tragic last year—a fight and consequent breaking of relations with Mark Van Doren, whom Thurber probably loved
and respected more than any other man. The background of the fight
was rather spooky in itself. On September 16, 1923, Thurber had written
in his Columbus *Dispatch* "Credos and Curios" column a dreadful little
short story called "The Plaguey Hundredth Chance," which dealt with
a fictional Professor George H. Van Dreddin, a famous debunker of
ghosts who was startled one day by his father's shade. Thurber's ridicule
of the fictional professor was a weird rehearsal for arguments he had
about the same subject, more than thirty-five years later, with Professor
Mark Van Doren. But they were just arguments between two men of
letters, one eminently rational, the other suffering from spasms of irrationality. Peace was always restored afterwards. Indeed, Thurber had
spoken lovingly of Van Doren at Columbia University's 1958 Hamilton
Medal Dinner honoring the poet–professor, and when Mark's son
Charles had his celebrated television quiz-show difficulties in 1959,
Thurber was among the most loyal and sympathetic friends. But one
night in 1961 at Rose Algrant's house, he blew up. For the plaguey
hundredth time, Thurber was relating the "real" story of "The Night
the Ghost Got In," but with more passion and conviction than ever.

"I thought Jim was putting it on a little thick," Van Doren said, "so
I questioned the ghost story in a kidding way. It turned out he wasn't
just talking this time. He was very serious about that damn ghost. I
should have realized he was sick and therefore offended by my kidding,
but it was too late. He was a wild man, shouting and threatening. I had
to leave. It was too awful. There were no formal apologies exchanged,
and we didn't see each other much after that. It was never the same
again between us."

Thurber's heavy concern with the unexplainable was likely to
emerge anywhere, even in a long cheer-up letter to a depressed, ailing
Ernest Hemingway (a letter never sent, on the good advice of Helen,
who thought it would further deject Hemingway):*

Dear Ernest:

This is what the gals call a chatty letter intended to cheer, and not to be
answered until you and I meet at Tim Costello's,—one, ten or twenty years from

---

*He was fond of writing cheer-up letters during this most despairing year. In some
perverse way, such letters somehow reassured him, especially as he called the sometimes
fanciful roll of his own illnesses.

now, and the sooner the better. Groucho Marx once yelled across the dining room at Ross, "You'll come over to my table if you know what is good for me." . . .

This has been the damndest November and December for friends of mine, and for me, too, in my memory. Everyone of us, though, began to pick up again during the first week of January. I have been doing some research about the cycle of ailments and moods in the human being, and have found out that the medical men, as well as psychiatrists, have become aware of seasonal phases of the body and the mind. It is now known that stomach ulcers increase greatly in November and, as for the mind, "the winter of our discontent", just scratches the melancholy surface. I believe that all of us, especially the men, are manic-depressives, but only a small percentage are malignant ones. My friend, Elliott Nugent, was hard hit by his cycle this November, but he is putting up a good fight. He used to get hit worse in March, which rates second among the bad months.

A few years ago I wrote Ross's Boston doctor, Sarah Jordan, about the cyclical nature of Man and said that I believed that it also affected ability and skill, but that each person had his own timetable. I suggested that there are periods when surgeons should not be allowed to operate. She wrote back that the psychiatrists agreed with me, but the surgeons did not. I never write like an angel, but I have recurrent phases when I write like a charwoman . . .

In 1931 I had a medical examination for insurance at the New Yorker. A few days later I met my insurance agent on the street. He had approached me shaking his head and said, "You have sugar in your urine and a murmur in your heart." "That's not a diagnosis," I said, "that's a song cue."

A few months later another examination showed no sugar and no murmur. My great eye doctor, Gordon M. Bruce, who lost half his hearing but won two silver stars in the South Pacific, told me, "Only the reputation of the greatest doctor could survive you." What he meant was after my left eye was shot out with an arrow, when I was seven, the sight of the other eye was completely destroyed about a year later. "You lost the apparatus of vision," he said, "but you just went on seeing anyway." "You can call it God or E.S.P." Then he said, "I can't believe God wanted you to do those drawings." I reminded him that God had drawn the kangaroo, the human being, to mention only two, which proved that God has a comic sense.

This kind of thing seems to happen more and more often and the baffled doctors are not very crazy about it. When I was nineteen, a Columbus eye doctor told me, very irritably, "I suppose you could play the piano with both hands cut off at the wrists." I talk quite a lot nowadays to doctors I know who are continually puzzled by cases of regression of disease. Two years ago the Herald-Tribune reported fifty-four cases of total regression of incurable cancer. All they need to do now is to find out the secret, and there are many good men working on it.

I still have personal physicians who stick to me when I am down, which I rarely am any more. I guess I got it all over with between forty-five and fifty-seven and, boy, was the scroll charged with punishments. I had five eye operations in eight months, two pneumonias, ruptured appendix with peritonitis, a plus 60 hyper-thyroid, an allergy that made me sneeze about three hours at a stretch and a nervous crack-up during which I pulled out of a castration complex with the psychiatrists. This amazed the psychiatrists I have talked to, none of them professionally, though. One doctor said with a sigh, "We just mark the chart atypical." He had called on me in 1942 when I was running a temperature of 103 and a pulse rate of 122. You name the pulse rate, Ernest, and I have had it. This doctor told my wife, privately, he was sure I had endocarditis. "Nonsense," said Helen. "His temperature and pulse will be normal tomorrow." They were, too.

If all this wasn't so damned reassuring, I wouldn't go into it, but God knows you have pulled out of things, too, and always will. Let's have some drinks together on New Year's Eve, 1980. Your luck, she is always with you, and I know you are not jealous that I share her with you.

One final anecdote about the docs. My appendix ruptured at six a.m. in *November*, 1944, and I wasn't operated on until nine o'clock that night. We were at The Homestead in Hot Springs, Virginia. The assistant surgeon who came to the hotel called my doctor in New York. He told him, "This patient has not been nauseated, but he is hungry!" I don't know what my doctor said, but I can guess. I was taken to a hospital thirty miles away, in the only ambulance available, a hearse. When after three weeks, I got out of bed and dressed and went home, old Dr. Emmett said, "We thought you were gone. How do you account your putting on your clothes and leaving here?" "I always dress before I go out into the street," I told him. "I am romantic."

The other night I dreamed that you and I were walking toward a sunset and suddenly the sun began to rise. Reminds me of a favorite book of mine. But, then, I had the same dream about two other men, when they were down, Carl Sandburg and Robert Frost. Carl was eighty-three on January 6 and Frost is even older. God bless you and keep you. I'll see you in 1980.

As always,

JAMES THURBER(44)

The nightmare year also marked the publication, by Harper & Brothers, of his last collection of new pieces, none of them ever before between book covers. *Lanterns and Lances,* as it was titled, was his first anthology of pieces the majority of which were not previously printed in the *New Yorker,* demonstrating the increasing incidence of his rejections from that magazine. The book was indicative of this dark period in another important way: It reflected his mental state and his inability to write pure humor any more. In the Foreword, Thurber almost apologized for this:

. . . Every time is a time for comedy in a world of tension that would languish without it. But I cannot confine myself to lightness in a period of human life that demands light. . . . Some [pieces] were written in anger, which has become one of the necessary virtues, and, if there is a touch of the "lubugrious" in certain pieces, the perceptive reader will also detect, I like to think, a basic and inde-structible thread of hope . . . let's not look back in anger, or forward in fear, but around in awareness.

The trouble was, what Thurber thought were lantern beams and lance lunges was really just more of the same tedious carping about the decline of language and humor in America. Invention in these pieces deserted him to the point where he couldn't even create new settings or situations for his cavilling essay-casuals; a shocking number of them are set in alcoholic parties with feather-brained matrons stimulating Thurber's dreary sermons. The book leaves the unpleasant impression that its author, knowing he was ill, old, and creatively impotent, wanted to take language and humor down with him. For that unliterary reason alone, the book is his worst.

Lanterns and Lances was dedicated to Rose Algrant—"a lady with a lantern, who lights the pathways of all of us lucky enough to live where she lives, this book is dedicated, with love, wonder, and gratitude." Rose was thrilled with the dedication ("I don't deserve it, I'm embarrassed," she told Mark Van Doren), but even she realized that the pieces in the book were not his best. "He was trying too hard," she said, "and once Helen told him so. He got mad, but I think that deep down he knew she was right."

Yet, he plugged away at his writing—those narrow pieces with titles like "The Future, If Any, of Comedy; Or Where Do We Non-Go from Here?" and "Carpe Noctem, If You Can"; his never-to-be-finished long satiric works and plays; and a whole new hapless opus called, variously, *Autobiography of a Mind, What Happened to Me,* and *Yesterday Upon the Stair.* In the anarchy of his last year, he conceived of *Autobiography of a Mind* as an intensely personal examination of his mental life, dealing in the main with his oft-told claim of total recall ("I was appar-ently born with total recall, even though I can't remember what went on in the womb, but almost everything that was said or done by me or anybody I knew after that"), mental telepathy ("I have proved the existence of this phenomenon beyond the shadow of a doubt, much to the discomfiture of certain intellectual friends of mine who are afraid of the new frontier of the mind, know little or nothing about appercep-tion or the misty mid-region of metaphysics"), and E.S.P. ("I am glad to say that my power in that field has amused me more than it has disturbed me").(45) To these shadowy areas he wanted to add selected ghost stories and his long-planned appreciation of Houdini, which had fallen into dormancy at the *New Yorker*, since Richard Rovere had decided against doing anything with it. (Thurber alerted the *New Yorker* that he was reviving the Houdini idea as a possible piece for the magazine, as well as a chapter in his book.) He would also include the "miracle" of his vision "without the apparatus for sight," his power to cure himself of a castration complex without the aid of psychiatrists, and his ability to analyze dreams—a switch for the old Freud-baiter.

Autobiography of a Mind soon became an autobiography of an obsession. He was possessed by the project and used it to assail and exorcise what he imagined were the devils around him. "This will be the real truth, for the first time," he told Nugent. "I can't hide any more behind the mask of comedy that I've used all my life. People are not funny; they are vicious and horrible—and so is life!"(46) When Helen read the bits and pieces of the disturbing manuscript, she found that "most of it was an attack on me, with the rest about the occult."

Fritzi Von Kuegelgen had to take daily dictation of the mystical work. She was alarmed. "He thought it was his greatest writing," she said, "but I knew it was just terrible. I knew it would never be printed, that it was impossible, but he was desperate to get it all down on paper. It was so discouraging, but I had to go along with him. His memory was operating almost as well as ever, but he wasn't dictating real writing, just disjointed ramblings. He drank all night, sometimes, and I would find empty liquor bottles in the morning. Then he would say to me, 'Don't tell anyone, but Helen is drinking like crazy.' He had lost his gentleness. He was a very different man."

Except for the section on Houdini, Thurber was realistic enough to know that his project was not for the *New Yorker*. But the sorry casuals he continued to hammer out were another matter. The anguished editors had little choice but to turn most of them down. His reaction was predictable: raving, digressive letters, alternating between the I-really-couldn't-care-less pose of the jilted lover and personal assaults on everybody he could think of. After just about every note of rejection from Angell came, by return mail, a blistering answer from Thurber, repeating his anecdotes of the occult and including such statements as "I shall still send an occasional piece to The New Yorker, even though one of us has outgrown the other . . ."(47) and "I am afraid you are all now compulsive collaborators and that only psychiatry could cure it."(48) Angell was by no means the only one to receive these missives. Milton Greenstein, the *New Yorker*'s counsel, was also a prime recipient:

Dear Milt,

I can only conclude from nearly a month's silence since I wrote Shawn, Angell, and Mr. and Mrs. White, that The New Yorker has finally decided, in the tradition begun by Ross, when he would disappear and let somebody else fire a man, that I am being shown the door. This does not depress me at all, for I share Gibbs's feeling during his last years that the Office had become so dreary and humorless that hell wouldn't have it . . .

Since it has become obvious, although both of us have genuinely tried, that the New Yorker and I can no longer see eye to eye on anything at all, I have quite reasonably decided that this [the planned Houdini piece] will be, if taken, the last piece I shall submit. At my age, I no longer have the strength of mind or body to engage in controversy and misunderstanding and recrimination and long silences with editors with whom I seem to share an almost chemical disagreement. They think that I am unreasonable and too outspoken, especially in my criticism of the magazine, inside and outside the Office, and I think that they are, in the great and sad tradition of New Yorker secrecy, anonymity, and easily hurt feelings.

My old relationship really died with Ross and Lobrano, with whom I worked perfectly, as you must know. But the end finally came with the publication of "The Years With Ross' and with Mrs. White's incurable antipathy to that book, an antipathy that White shares completely. I would not have changed a single word in that, or in anything else I write, to please a mouse or a pussycat or a human being. We all have our credos, and that is mine. I want you to know that I spent a great many hours and even days thinking this out, and I know it is the thing to do. Angell has tried to do his best about me, but there is that profound disparity of nature, viewpoint, and belief, and, moreover, he is, after all, Mrs. White's son, and she has said, on the phone, that I no longer regard myself as "a member of the family." The 34-year-old truth is that I never was a member of the family, because everything in me rebelled against our exclusivity and snobbishness and aloofness. Ross, God bless him, was able to take this, in spite of our 24 years of fighting, and Lobrano was wonderful as our go-between when we needed one. I have the ineradicable feeling that I am really not wanted any more, and patronised, whether intentionally or not, and the things I have submitted in recent years have sometimes been treated flippantly or coldly and, in my estimation, without humor.

You must also know that my stuff has often been slashed, changed, and even misunderstood, and the young editors have taken it upon themselves, whatever their intentions may have been, to criticize my knowledge, information, and understanding of life and people in the modern world.

These things happen in any life, and in any career, in one place that has lasted too long, and I am perfectly adjusted and resigned to the inevitable end. In view of all this, Milt, I anticipate with something like distaste any obituary about me that might eventually appear in the New Yorker, and I suggest to you that the best, and most honest tribute, when that day comes, would simply be the reprinting of "The Secret Life of Walter Mitty," with a brief note saying that

I had requested it in my will. This would, of course, involve a radical breaking of precedent in a magazine that has taken on a rigorous form, but I suggest it anyway.

I shall always want to see you, Miss Terry, Miss Jonsson,* Pete De Vries, and McKelway, and a few others. I shall never write another piece about the New Yorker, the editors will be glad to know, but I shall always answer, honestly and fully, any questions about the New Yorker when I am asked . . . I am no longer interested in the petty, the grudge, and the running popgun fight. Ross once wrote me, "Your contribution to this magazine has been enormous," and it was things like that that kept my spirits up; but those men are gone forever, the ones I could love, fight with, and make up with.

Anyway, my last years will be devoted mainly to books and plays . . .

I manage, though, to keep on going.

Helen and I send you our love and best wishes, as always. I hope to have lunch with you when we come back to New York. I should like to have this letter answered by you, and not by anybody else, for reasons that must now be quite plain.

Cordially yours,
JAMES THURBER(49)

Greenstein, who was also the magazine's unofficial handholder for difficult staff members, answered Thurber with a sincere and reassuring letter. It showed the quandary the *New Yorker* was in with its one-time star turned paranoid:

Dear Jim:

I have just (May 2) received your April 26th letter, and am disturbed by it. The idea that a failure by Shawn, the Whites and Angell to reply to recent letters, is evidence of a conspiracy to show you the door, can only be the result of some extraordinary imagining on your part. It is not the fact here. If Shawn hasn't written you, it must be because getting out the magazine is an 80-hour-a-week job. From remarks he has made to me in the last several weeks as to the prospect of future work from you, Shawn for one belies your conclusion. There's a good reason why you haven't heard from the Whites. Katharine has become afflicted with a neurological complaint on the side of her head, painful and incapacitating, that sent her to the hospital twice last month and spoiled what was intended to be a brief vacation in Florida. Andy, not equipped for nursing, has been having a terrible time. Angell has just discarded a set of crutches, after a do-it-yourself accident. There are your conspirators . . .

Put the boys to work on the Houdini house, and when the piece is finished, send it in to us. I don't have to consult anyone to know that all hands here would

---

*Ebba Jonsson, the *New Yorker*'s librarian.

want it that way. Even if there was a feud going on, which God knows is not the case, no one here would turn down a piece that would be good for us to print. And if it turns out that the piece is not for us, we will say so. A rejection can't kill an old pro.

That brings me around to the matter of the obituary. I have filed your suggestion, out of a sense of duty and obligation, but you can't make me discuss it and I'm not going to. Having but just recovered (I think) from an ulcer, I still tend to get confused as to who's dying. Anyway, it's a subject we can safely lay aside for some time.

I honestly think, Jim, that you may be too old for the gypsy life. Come home and settle down to the books and plays you have in mind—and the occasional piece for The New Yorker. You'll never be too old for that.

There's a lot in your letter I want to take issue with but am too wise to be drawn into a *written* debate with you. I'll hold a table at the Algonquin. Until then, my best to Helen and you.

Sincerely,
Milton Greenstein(50)

Greenstein's letter—with its good therapeutic straight talk—worked. Thurber responded with a calm, even understanding, note a few days later, but within two weeks he was lighting epistolary fires again.

Certainly, his worsening paranoia was complicated by an ill-advised and needless trip to London to oversee a possible British production of *A Thurber Carnival.* Because of finances and commitments, the original American cast couldn't be brought over, so an entirely new British cast was necessary, which made the London arrangements less than firm. Nothing was signed, and Haila Stoddard warned Thurber not to go until there was a solid agreement, but Thurber wouldn't listen. "He was in no mood to be reasonable," Haila said. "He decided that the London production had to go on immediately and he wanted to help cast it."

The Thurbers' leave-taking from New York was a grave omen of further disaster. "It was Kennedy's Inauguration Day," Jap Gude recalled, "freezing cold and a terrible snowstorm. I was helping the Thurbers get from the Algonquin to the *Queen Elizabeth's* pier, with their twenty-two pieces of luggage. Of course, no transportation was available, but we finally garnered a limousine. With all the luggage, there was no room for Jim and Helen. Finally, Elinor Wright got hold of a taxi for the principals, which saved the day. While all this was happening, Jim kept up a steady shout—'I'm not going! I'm not going!' We all should have listened to him."

Even at the pier, Thurber insisted that they turn around and head back to the hotel. "We quieted him down," Helen said, "but I think what he was really trying to tell us was that he wanted to go back to Ohio. The hick in him picked that moment to come through. He was tortured by that old contradiction. Also, he wanted to be any place but where he was at the time." But they coaxed him on board the ship.

Somewhat tranquilized at sea, he outlined yet another project—a play or novel to be entitled *The Last Romantic*, which would be an indictment of people "who make love a four-letter word."(51)* But once he realized what was in store for him in London, the new project faded and he was seized with acute depression again. Haila Stoddard and Burgess Meredith flew over for the casting sessions, and it quickly became apparent that a production would not work out with the available British actors. The English producer kept delaying, Haila was chagrinned, Meredith flew home, and Thurber grew frantic. He sent plaintive bulletins to Jap Gude:

... I still feel that my life has ended with a permanent connection with "A Thurber Carnival" and that the two or three books or plays I should love to write may never get done ... What a world, what a species! ...

... For the first time in my life I have begun taking Miltown, three a day, and I feel comparatively calm most of the time. We are both pretty well worn down, however ...

Dear Gudes and dear God,

It must be better on some other planet! ... We have gone through seven stages of hell here, the latest being acute homesickness, and we want to get the hell out of hell. There isn't going to be any Thurber Carnival, since we have

---

*Elliott Nugent had written a novel, *Of Cheat and Charmer*, and Thurber wrote him the day before his departure for England of his intention to read an advance copy on the boat. The letter is an interesting echo of the puritanical Thurber–Nugent letters of their youth.

... I have great expectations for "Of Cheat and Charmer" but I shall probably be severe about four-letter words and what publishers call "frankly sexual scenes." I belong to the unhappy, diminishing company of writers who deplore the fact that we have made love a four-letter word in this country. The decline of the drama and the novel into the lower corridors of bestiality is a sign of our depleted culture and we ought to all help to pull literature and the arts out of the muck and mire. Everybody knows about sex now and it does have, believe it or not, romantic aspects. I am planning a play or novel to be called "The Last Romantic" but I hope I do not become the only survivor of a lost lyrical world. And let us remember what Percy Hammond said, "Just because a thing happened is no reason it's true." ...(52)

not heard a word about auditions . . . Meredith is now in Venus, and Haila is
on Mars, I suppose . . . As ever, or however long, whatever it is, lasts . . .(53)

To Bernard Hollowood, the editor of *Punch* (for which he wrote
another piece), he admitted that "I am no longer as 'Thurberish' as I
used to be,"(54) and indeed he wasn't. With no London *Carnival* in
sight and time a burden, he gave out hours of what Helen called "savage
interviews." ("I would just walk out during them," she said.) John Duncan Miller came over from Paris to visit Thurber and discovered him
"constantly closeted with interviewers, for the single purpose, it
seemed to me, of getting his name in the papers. Jim felt he wasn't
being taken seriously as a philosopher. But he was a humorist who
wasn't writing funny things any more. Money and publicity were ways
for him to get his due. I tried to tell him there were plenty of philoso-
phers around but almost no humorists. He was in too bad shape to
understand."

One of the interviews, published in the *Manchester Guardian* on
February 9, 1961, showed just how savage Thurber was. He slandered
the "female intelligence" and made absurd generalizations about the
United States, England, Russia, and even his own blindness. Then he
added this distinctly un-Thurberish statement: "I don't believe in the
greatest good for the greatest number. I believe in the most good for
the greatest persons, the only ones who have ever made our getting up
off all fours seem worthwhile."

He also attempted to occupy his time with a little work, mostly psy-
chical research for his *Autobiography of a Mind* book. The idea was
taken much more seriously in England, to Thurber's pleasure. But he
did his mental rewriting at dinner parties, to Helen's displeasure. The
Thurbers were still in demand as guests. They saw quite a bit of Bernard
Hollowood, Nunnally Johnson, C.P. Snow, and other friends, but as time
dragged while they waited for the still-promised *Carnival* production,
Thurber's mental state crumbled. "Jamie's paranoia got out of hand,"
Helen said. "He put everybody down, including—especially—me. After
I would go to bed, he'd sit up talking to himself all night, raving on and
on. I decided to drink only water because I was afraid of flying off the
handle if I took anything stronger. After a while, I refused to go to
parties with him, and if he started yelling against me in public, I'd
occasionally slip away."

He developed a complex theory about his own *Angst*, as he termed
it, and the world's. In the spring, he wrote Peter De Vries that "the new
world plague" was spread by "mass mental telepathy." It could only be

cured, he said, by "a new mass frame of mind."(55) On both sides of the Atlantic, those who knew and cared about Thurber were deeply worried.

Again, it was Jap Gude who came to the rescue. "My wife and I were travelling in France that spring," Gude said, "and we had a vague plan to meet the Thurbers in London. But everywhere we went in France we received urgent cables from Jim, saying things like 'HELP HELP HELP PLEASE COME.' So, with some resignation, we went to London. I couldn't believe what I saw there. Each time Jim had something to drink—which was often—he would heap abuse on Helen in the most vicious way. 'You're a stupid woman,' he would suddenly shout at her, 'from a stupid mother and a stupid father!' It was just awful.

"When the *Carnival* production plans collapsed in May,* we booked passage on the *Liberté* from Southampton, the Thurbers in first class and us in cabin class with special permission to visit. From Southampton on it was a nightmare trip. We waited out a delay for hours in a hotel lobby before the Southampton bars opened, and Jim was impossible. Then, on the tender, I had to keep bringing him drinks from the little crowded bar. He was smashed by the time we got on board the *Liberté*. Every evening on the ship there was some new crisis, Helen being his main target. She finally would retire to one room of their suite, and my wife and I would sit up with Jim all night, watching him drink and listening to him rave. He'd sleep through the next day. Somehow, we got to America."

Back in Cornwall, there was a brief respite from *Angst*. Leaving the vagaries of show business and travel behind him, Thurber relaxed a bit and felt better. His letters to friends included more word games than invective ("I still keep making up palindromes . . . Diaper deliverer rereviled, repaid . . . The noon sex alert relaxes no one. HT"),(57) and in one of his last letters to E. B. White, he cheerily wrote:

Dear Andy:

I get the darndest mail, and today there came a letter from a man in England who has a problem completely divorced from politics, nuclear worries, Kennedy's back, and the exchange of men for machines. He is worried because his

---

*In April of 1962, *A Thurber Carnival*, with Tom Ewell in his old role and a company of British actors in new ones, was finally produced in London and ran for three weeks. Most of the critics felt it was not at all good Thurber, one saying it was like "being buttonholed by a bore, which Thurber never was, at least not until reverence turned him into a legend."(56)

son's rabbits do not like carrots! I can deal, a little, with the other problems listed above, but I have no idea what to do about rabbits that won't eat carrots. I also don't know what to do about a phoebe outside my window who keeps calling "Mabel!" instead of "Phoebe!" I hope that what is the matter with all of us human beings, in diet and in sex, is not spreading to the animal world.

It was good talking to both of you the other day. I am pulling out of the deepest Angst I have had since the summer of 1941, when I cracked up after my fifth eye operation. We had one hell of a time in London, but at least there was a blackbird singing outside my window every morning. I am sure he was singing to another blackbird, a female, and that he can still eat what he is supposed to eat . . .

I wonder if the sex life of the bivalve has changed since Benchley died. Love and kisses to you and Katharine . . .

P.S. I have now been listed as a Red by some anonymously printed Hollywood pamphlet, along with Eddie Cantor, Gregory Peck, and Douglas Fairbanks, Jr. This I discovered in several clippings from newspapers that came to my defense. One of the editorials was titled "Poor Jim."

If the United States had had you and G. B. Shaw working together, would the country had had the E.B.G.B.'s? If so, it would have been good for us.(58)

He telephoned Rosemary in Illinois, just after returning from England, and kidded with her so much she almost hung up on him. "Nobody told me there was anything awfully wrong with him," Rosemary said. "They were forever trying to protect me from my father's troubles. I hadn't seen him since he was acting in *A Thurber Carnival*, but he seemed all right on the phone, if a little too talkative. He asked me if I wanted a one-act play for my theatre group. It was called *Cocktails with the Captain*, really a sketch he had written. When he sent it and I read it, I thought it was weird, sort of like Pinter. For some reason, he told me on the phone, 'We mustn't sit around the living room tearing each other apart.' I should have guessed something big was wrong."

In the early summer, the Thurbers threw a large party in Cornwall. To Jap Gude's happy surprise, Thurber behaved quite well in the midst of so many guests and so much liquor. "But the next day," Gude said, "he was off again, following the usual pattern of abuse towards Helen. There was no way of accounting for it them." It was worse than ever for Helen. "We were all trying to talk him into seeing a psychiatrist," Helen said, "but he was convinced *I* was going crazy." To appease him, and to obtain some psychiatric advice indirectly, Helen took the unfinished manuscript of *Autobiography of a Mind* to a psychiatrist a friend recommended. "It was under the pretext of seeing the doctor for myself," she said, "but it didn't work. I don't think the doctor ever read the manuscript."

During this virulent return of *Angst,* Thurber eked out a few pieces, including the last casual he published in the *New Yorker,* "The Manic in the Moon," a boring, humorless piece about space travel and its effect on language. It was a sorry way for him to sign off in the *New Yorker,* and devastating for his readers and editors alike. For the latter, there were more fights. He wrote Hawley Truax, before "The Manic in the Moon" was printed:

... I am determined to finish a play I am writing about a magazine, showing the decline in everything except size since the 1920's. The play is set some time in the 1950's, or after Ross died, but I am frankly and happily patterning the editor after him. The name of the magazine is never mentioned in the play. None of the other characters have any relation to anybody on the magazine, except myself . . .(59)

As the summer wore on, his outgoing letters were largely concerned with death. When Ernest Hemingway took his own life, Thurber was shocked—and slightly intrigued. He wrote Edward P. Morgan:

. . . To paraphrase General Pickett at Gettysburg, I could say, "My noble generation has been swept away." I, too, have been through the deep depression afflicting so many people during the past two years or so. I keep fighting it, though, and I have no shotgun, thank God. I did buy a .38 police revolver a dozen years ago to protect my house in the country, but only Helen knows where it is. Anyway, I do not believe that I am a self-killer . . . But he [Hemingway] regarded me as a man, in spite of the fact that I never shot anything bigger than a sparrow, or caught anything larger than a lake trout . . .(60)

And when Fred Allen's widow, Portland, asked Thurber for his old Allen letters for a book, Thurber complied and also sent along a just-written effort addressed to "Fred in Heaven." It was unabashed treacle, ending with the line: "Make reservations for me up yonder, yeah?"(61)

His theme song, "Bye Bye, Blackbird," whose lyrics mean many things to many people, took on even more of a mystical quality for him during this period. Friends reported that he sang it at every opportunity, and a memorable bright moment in his otherwise unhappy recent London visit was the singing of a blackbird outside his hotel-room window, as he wrote White. In some circuitous way, he identified with the creature; its fortunes were his, its failings his. There is, perhaps, a clue in a scrap of information he passed on to his then soldier son-in-law in 1954: "I was shot at only once myself, by fraternity brothers during my initiation. Their second shot got a blackbird in a cypress tree, which fell at my feet a fifth of a second before I fell at its."(62)

Although Thurber ignored his mental ills, he may well have understood the consequences of his physical ones. People around him noticed that he was crashing into objects he had usually missed before—for instance, tables and chairs in his own living room—but some thought it was because he simply didn't care about his shins any more. Jap Gude was concerned to see that Thurber couldn't find his way around the Algonquin suite he knew as well as his own house. "He had to feel his way with outstretched hands," Gude said, "and he always veered to the left. I suspected something physical, but I believed it was mostly emotional. With hindsight, I'm afraid I know better now."

And Thurber became notoriously incontinent. Long a victim of nervous bladder, he began to wet chairs at social gatherings. He seemed to pay no attention to the problem, and others blamed his incontinence on too much to drink or a compulsion not to miss anything while in the bathroom.

To Edmund Wilson, Thurber complained during the last year of "vastations," a Jamesian word for blackouts. This admission depressed Wilson, since he suspected some brain disease as the cause.(63) Also, Wilson was about the same age as Thurber.

Even with stroke symptoms becoming more obvious every day, Thurber still refused to consult a specialist. In late August, he decided on abstinence from cigarettes and alcohol as a quick panacea for his ailments. Typically, he delivered a temperance lecture to anyone who would listen. Sounding like a W.C.T.U. matron, he wrote Jane Williams:

. . . Only a few of us seem to realize what the hell has happened to this great country, which has now become depressed, apathetic, afraid of shadows, and increasingly full of booze. The sale of strong drink has gone up 800 percent since the war; 5,000,000 cigarettes a second are sold in the nation; 67,000,000 prescriptions for tranquillizers are issued; most people are talking to themselves in the home, at the office, or on the street, and there were 3,800,000 divorces in this country last year. Railroad transportation in the country is in as bad shape as the Broadway theatre, literature, humor, and comedy.

The major cause, the dark shadow behind all this, is the incurable infantilism of a republic, founded by great men, and now peopled by empty-eyed neurotic arrested-development cases, who try to solve everything by facing nothing, who think that the way out is to cloud their personal situation and the world crisis with cigarette smoke and liquor fumes.

We get picked up higher now, and quicker, on liquor, but fall faster, and farther, and hit harder. There are a dozen different kinds of alcoholism, but each person thinks that he is not in bad shape, but that everybody else is. This is brought out in a couple of fairly recent books about heavy drinking, which take up everything from social drinking (that is, sane), habitual, periodic, solitary, secret, public, manic, depressive, and acute. A few years ago there were only 6,000,000 alcoholics in this country, recruited from the ranks of about ten million heavy drinkers, but this is on the increase.

The combination of drinking, fear, and other disturbing factors, has caused some authorities to estimate the number of psychotics in the United States at 72,000,000. We are, of course, not the only people who are drinking too much, thinking too little, and trying to escape by alcohol, nicotine, Miltown, all night parties, sex, and a dozen other dead-end avenues. Wherever and however you fly from yourself, you end up with yourself, only you are worn out by the flight and must have a double Scotch and half a pack of cigarettes.

More than thirty years ago Hendrik van Loon said to me, "You Americans always have to have from two to three pleasures going at once. You are the only people I know who mix sex and alcohol and then have to have a cigarette, and ask some people in for the rest of the night, or go to a movie and eat popcorn."

Why will we never learn that Euphoria is a mirage, and that the only way out of it is the Lonesome Road that leads through Jeopardy and ends up in the Wilderness of Despair.

Inner resources do not mean cocktails or brandy or highballs. A person has to face the fact that what has usually happened to him was himself. In what Fadiman calls the somnolent decades the chafing dish was regarded as more dangerous than the bottle (Welsh rarebit gave you bad dreams,) there was more fudgemaking than fuck, and tea was actually served at tea parties. A woman could go to the ladies' room without being thrown on her way out, by a strange, lurking obstetrician or major-general or waiter or little boy.

The world is in such horrible shape now that it behooves everybody to make the effort of his lifetime to conquer, first of all, the demon in himself. Unless that local battle is won, the world battle will go to the enemy . . . Why do we no longer get older and wiser, but only odder and wider?

As I write this I have not had a drink or a cigarette in two days, even though I have been through, and so has Helen, for more than seven months, the terror of the shade, the valley of the shadow, and the encircling gloom. That last phrase comes from the old hymn, "Lead, Kindly Light." We have replaced that with the new hymn, "Keep 'em Comin'."

Let us then be up and drinking, with a heart for any fight, still pursuing our old grudges, learn to hit, and scratch and bite.

We can never replace, and get anywhere by so doing, a famous old political battle cry, with "Now is the time for all goofy men to come to the aid of their country."

We are coming down in October, but not to drink and stay up all night. I want to get a play finished. Do not rise above the battle, but do rise above the bottle . . .(64)

The abstinence cure lasted just a few more days. And still Thurber shunned medical help. In retrospect, Jap Gude thought that Thurber had guessed the worst and was afraid of knowing the hideous truth— that he was suffering from cerebral accidents. "Before, he was always a man of great courage," Gude said, "but not then. Perhaps part of his fear was of ending his life as his mother did, a vegetable because of a stroke. He watched her die, after all."

At last, after much pleading, wheedling, and bargaining, he consented to see his good friend and trusted doctor, Gordon Bruce. "He was not Jim Thurber any more," Dr. Bruce recalled. "He had lost his humor and practically all he talked about was ghosts and such. There was no logic in his conversation, his faculties were dulled. I suspected arteriosclerosis of the brain—his brain was aging faster than the rest of him was—and it turned out I was right. I didn't mention this to Jim. What would it matter? He wouldn't see a specialist, anyway. It was amazing that he wasn't paralyzed or struck dumb already."

But Helen kept pressing for more medical attention. In September, she convinced her husband to visit a woman psychiatrist who had treated severe war cases. After a few mostly social sessions, the psychiatrist suggested neurological tests, and Thurber exploded with refusals and denials. He did see his old thyroid man, however, but when that specialist also suggested neurological tests, Thurber once again blew his stack. "He banged on the doors and made an awful scene," Helen said. "It was obvious to everyone then that Jamie was paranoid and neurologically ill."

There was nothing to do but wait for the worst to happen. But the worst has a cruel way of taking its own sweet time. In Cornwall, he quarrelled and raged incessantly. His friends found themselves talking to him and even to each other in a different way—"as if we were in church," according to Marc Simont. The raving didn't seem to matter to anybody any more. It was the emperor's clothes. At the last party Thurber attended at Rose Algrant's house, he announced that he hated everyone in Cornwall. "He was very bad and drunk," Rose said, "but when I drive him home, I remember him saying, 'That is my beautiful house but I can't see it.' He wanted his eyes. He wanted to be free, like other people."

The only Cornwall friend, besides Rose, Thurber could tolerate towards the end was Kenneth MacLean, the passive, loyal "listener," as he described himself. "He couldn't stand people then," MacLean said, "but he wanted to see me. His explosiveness never seemed real to me, even when he blew up over real things, like the deterioration of America and language. Right up to our last visit together, he didn't discuss religion. He was an agnostic to the end."

And still, in accord with Thurber's wishes, nobody told Rosemary of the gravity of her father's condition. "There were some phone calls," Rosemary said, "but I was never asked to come to Cornwall. Maybe I could have helped." (It was a mistake not to send for Rosemary, Rose Algrant conceded later.)

The freedom Rose Algrant said Thurber wanted—mainly from Helen and his utter dependence on her—came to a head, like a festering boil. He asked Jap Gude to pick him up and take him away to the city without Helen. In late August, he left Cornwall for the free life in New York.

For about a week, Thurber remained separated from Helen, in the care of his perennial emergency "nursemaid" Jap Gude, who had put aside the greater part of his own life to see to his sick friend at the Algonquin. "Jim had alienated just about everybody by then but me," Gude said. "He was totally irrational and abusive. It was no picnic taking care of him. For instance, the last piece he submitted to the *New Yorker* had been rejected, so, after a couple of drinks, he called Shawn and shouted insults at him and the magazine. 'You're all stupid,' he told Shawn. 'Stupid' was his big insult word. I couldn't stop him from doing things like that. He made me call Ann Honeycutt for him, and he talked to her about their old life together. It was all so sad. One night, we were having dinner at Maria's with a couple he had met on the *Liberté*. He suddenly turned on them, especially the woman, and when I bawled him out, he demanded to be seated at another table by himself. He sat there alone, like an angry little boy, and tried to eat. Finally, I went over to him. He calmed down, but he wouldn't apologize. He just acted as if nothing had happened. Then we went to 21, where we met Burgess. Jim became voluble, then abusive again. It was some evening. But he never got around to attacking me."

In his liberated wandering about the city like a helpless stray, Thurber sought out a few people he still trusted, trying to wring some direction and comfort from them. He telephoned Peter De Vries and asked to see him. "I went over to the Algonquin," De Vries said, "and just talked quietly to him. He swore he hadn't had a drink in four days. At that moment, he wanted some companionship, and there was still a trace of the old Thurber compassion shining through all that sick bitterness."

Elinor Wright met Thurber in the Algonquin lobby and was disturbed when she realized that she couldn't make him laugh. "I always could before," she said. "He just sat there, drinking, without a smile. He drank so much, it never occurred to me his problem was medical. It simply looked like he had too much to drink."

And Nora Sayre met Thurber for lunch at La Bourgogne, a restaurant near the Algonquin. "He looked dreadful," Nora recalled. "When I asked him what was wrong, he said that everything was terrible. Then he said, 'The same is wrong with me as with your mother. You know that.' After I left him, I felt chilled all over. It was the last I saw of him."

After a few days of being wifeless, his freedom was more anguished than jubilant. He telephoned Helen once a day, then several times a day, then, at the end of the freedom week, just about every hour. "He couldn't find anything," Helen said. "When Jap had to go to his office, Jamie was left alone and could only get around with the help of visitors or *New Yorker* office boys." It was clear that he wanted to come home to his wife; however much he resented his dependence on her, he simply couldn't do without her.

So Thurber returned to Cornwall at the beginning of September. He was worse than ever. Helen concluded that, all in all, he would be better off in New York, nearer his doctors, and she took him back to the Algonquin. "He couldn't stay in Cornwall," she said. "He was too jumpy. I thought he might be happier in the city, and that's when I managed to convince him to see the psychiatrist and the thyroid specialist."

The first weekend back in New York, Thurber was driven to Burgess Meredith's house in Rockland County, without Helen. He was very jumpy. At one point late in the evening at Meredith's house, he was nauseated and passed out. Meredith and his other guests assumed it was because of drinking, but when Thurber returned to the city, still dazed and nauseated, Helen knew that it was something more serious. Thurber never passed out because of drinking. (Later, doctors pinpointed this collapse at his first cerebral hemorrhage.) Amazingly, he snapped out of the nausea and fainting spells, but his irrational temperament grew even more frightening. Helen's decades of thick-skinned expertise in nursemaid chores at last failed her. "After a few days," she said, "I moved both of us to a two-bedroom suite in the Algonquin because Jamie would kick me out of our bedroom in the middle of the night, and I'd have to go someplace. Before long, even that didn't work, so I entered Doctors Hospital for bed rest, just to get some peace and quiet."

Thurber was back in the care of Gude again, and anyone else who dropped by for a few hours. An index of his mental state then showed up in a patently psychotic letter to Henry Hewes, the drama critic of the *Saturday Review*. Hewes had earlier written Thurber, asking his opinion of theatrical directors. He reminded Thurber that an interview had previously been cancelled because Thurber had a cold, adding that every time he wanted to arrange an appointment Thurber was sick in bed. Thurber's answer was his last piece of writing:

September 21, 1961

Dear Mr. Hewes:

In the past ten years I have not been down in bed with illness more than twice, so what the hell you are talking about I don't know. The day you called at the Beverley I was down with a virus that had struck quite a few other people in this great City, where eight million people live in peace. Doctors have rated my physical condition as being that of a man in his middle forties and not in his late sixties. In spite of this, in a nation of males who have established a habit of dying young, I have been called "in frail health" by a paper in Colorado, where I spent a month with the "Revue," later returning to New York to make 88 appearances in my own show. Four years ago a woman on the Akron *Beacon-Journal* said in her column that I was bed-bound most of the time! What is with everybody anyway? And no wonder we are supposed to have seventy-two million psychopathic cases in this jumpy country.

I always sign my name to any statements I make, and so I will do it here. From 1940 to 1944 I was my own favorite director, since I directed the principals in four Ohio State musical comedies for which I wrote the book, and I also directed several one-act plays, one of which I had written.

The director with whom I have seen eye to eye most often, and one that I would insist on directing any further plays of mine, is Burgess Meredith. In spite of my frail health we worked smoothly together on "A Thurber Carnival" and for seven weeks during terrible winter weather we traveled to five great big cities in the Middle West, staying up late almost every night, putting in and taking out, and all the rest of it. In spite of all this work, which often began in the morning, I managed to write six new sketches for the play, but we had time to rehearse and stage only one of them.

I hope your present illness doesn't last too long, for it is reassuring to see an elderly gentleman like you still up and about.

Cordially, in spite of the sound of this,

JAMES THURBER.

Somewhat the better for rest, Helen left Doctors Hospital and returned to her husband at the end of September. They tried to resume a normal life, like going to the theatre together. Noel Coward's musical *Sail Away* (Coward was the director, composer, lyricist, and author) was opening on Tuesday evening, October 3rd, and Haila Stoddard, who produced the show with Helen Bonfils, invited the Thurbers to attend the opening and a following party at Sardi's East. Thurber relished the invitation; for Helen, however, it had the earmarks of another painful experience, although she had no way of knowing it would be *Walpurgisnacht*.

Haila and her husband, Whitfield Connor, didn't sit with the Thurbers at the Broadhurst Theatre, but they saw them at the end of the first act. "I asked Jim how he liked the show," Haila recalled, "and he answered, 'It's all radio to me.' That was a strange answer for such a Coward fan." Thurber also said he didn't want to stay for the second act, so he was taken for a drink at Sardi's, across the street. Helen carefully instructed Vincent Sardi to let Thurber have only one drink, since she was returning to the theatre to see the rest of *Sail Away*. After the show, Connor picked up Thurber and took him to the opening-night party across town at Sardi's East. "Jim looked like he had more than one drink," Connor said. "He was quite on the defensive, mostly about Coward and a kind of imagined competition between them."

At the party—a noisy sit-down supper for two hundred and fifty celebrities, at which four hundred showed up—Thurber was unhappy and disoriented. "At first, I thought it was just that his nose was out of joint," Haila said, "but before long, I knew it was more serious. Lauren Bacall was at his table, and I remember Jim telling her and others vituperative things about Coward. He was trying to be funny about it, but he wasn't funny. He was obviously jealous of Coward.* In spite of this, Jim said to Whit that he wished Coward would come over and say hello. Whit immediately asked Coward to greet Thurber, and Coward answered, 'But dear boy, I just did.' We were beginning to get frightened.

"Then, later on, Coward made a charming little speech. When he was through, Jim stood up and demanded the microphone, shouting that he had something to say. Everyone was embarrassed and started to murmur, and Jim bawled them out for not listening to him. But undaunted, he proceeded to sing 'Who' and 'Bye Bye, Blackbird.' Suddenly, he staggered and lurched. My son Christopher helped to hold him up and then get him off. I guess most people thought he was just drunk. Helen asked Whit to take him right back to the Algonquin with her."

They left Sardi's East about 1:30 A.M. in a cab. Till four A.M., Thurber sat in a chair in his Algonquin suite, throwing all his infidelities and affairs in Helen's face. "It was the maddest scene I had ever witnessed,"

---

*Peter Evans of the London *Daily Express* overheard Thurber say at the party, "Coward and I are the last of the great indestructibles."

Connor said. "Helen just took it for hours. Finally, I couldn't stand it any longer and I told him off. It was the only time I was angry with Thurber, and it had to be that night, damn it. I said I had enough and was going home. So I left him alone with Helen."

Thurber and Helen at last went to bed. At six A.M., Thurber collapsed, apparently on his way to the bathroom, and hit his head when he fell. Helen heard a noise and found him on the floor in a pool of blood. He was rushed to Doctors Hospital in an ambulance.

In a blink of consciousness just after the ambulance arrived at the hospital, Thurber asked for Dr. Virgil Damon, his fraternity brother and occasional friend. "They told me Jim wanted me," Dr. Damon said, "so I hurried right over. He was so afraid of doctors. I was the only one allowed in to see him at first, and what I found was bad. It looked like a massive brain tumor or hemorrhage. Jim slipped in and out of consciousness. I was sure that there would have to be an immediate operation."*

During another conscious moment, Helen braced him with that ancient Columbus injunction—"Show your Fisher." Thurber smiled in response. Later that day, a neurological surgeon performed a brain operation on Thurber. A large hematoma, or blood tumor, was discovered near the speech-control center of his brain and was removed. As Dr. Bruce had suspected, there was evidence of arteriosclerosis and several small strokes dating back at least a year. He had a senescent brain. The prognosis was not good. Most likely, he would be a vegetable, as his mother was in her last month, if he lived that long.

Jap Gude, one of the first to come to the hospital, telephoned Rosemary, who flew to New York on the first available flight. "I was taken into my father's room," Rosemary said, "and stood with Helen and some others around the bed, waiting for a sign of recognition. There was none. I started to blabber like an idiot. I felt like an idiot because I knew my father would have hated my blabbering, any blabbering."

While he rallied slightly after the operation, his inert state continued. For almost four weeks (the same length of time of his mother's coma), a deathwatch was set up in the hotellike Doctors Hospital. Rosemary stayed for two weeks before returning to Illinois and her family. Helen was there most of every day and night, in a room next door to her

---

*The tiny rivalry between Thurber's doctor friends, Damon and Bruce (Thurber was going to call his play's Ross character "Walter Bruce" to offset the "Dean Damon" in *The Male Animal*), wasn't in effect at this juncture. Dr. Bruce was himself in a hospital for surgery during Thurber's collapse.

husband. Thurber's brothers were not sent for but were kept informed. Rose Algrant came to visit on weekends, mainly to keep Helen company. ("I saw Thurber in his room only once," she said. "It was too terrible.") Gude was at the hospital constantly, offering his comfort and services, and Nugent was a frequent visitor. The Van Dorens were in Florida during that period, but many of Thurber's *New Yorker* colleagues turned up to pay their respects—except for the Whites, Mrs. White being in a hospital herself, and St. Clair McKelway, who was a patient in Doctors Hospital and was unaware that Thurber was there, too.

Gude handled the press, showing tact and optimism, but there was little reason for the latter. After hearing the news, John Duncan Miller came to New York and sat at the hospital with Helen. Miller never saw Thurber, but from what he knew of the case, he said, "We rather hoped he would die. The alternative was too terrible." Marc Simont agreed: "Anyone could tell that the pain and ugliness were lasting too long."

Helen was intermittently encouraged. "After the operation," she said, "he seemed more conscious than not. He always knew when I was in the room, somehow, even if I didn't touch him or speak to him. He fussed with the nurses, especially one he didn't like, and indicated once that he didn't want Rosemary to see him like that. He moved his left arm in a no gesture, after I told him that Rosemary was in the next room. His right side was paralyzed."

Rosemary, too, was encouraged when her father slowly turned his head towards her at one point and murmured, "God . . . God . . . God." And Helen reported to Gude and Nugent that Thurber had once seemed to whisper, "God bless . . . God damn."

Besides the Lord Jim–Cyrano de Bergerac way of facing death, Thurber had always admired the dog's manner of dying, almost as much as its manner of living. In 1955, he wrote, in a piece about his poodle:

. . . I know now, and knew then, that no dog is fond of dying, but I have never had a dog that showed a human, jittery fear of death, either. Death, to a dog, is the final unavoidable compulsion, the last ineluctable scent on a fearsome trail, but they like to face it alone, going out into the woods, among the leaves, if there are any leaves when their time comes, enduring without sentimental human distraction the Last Loneliness, which they are wise enough to know cannot be shared by anyone . . .(65)

But the quintessentially human James Thurber would not die in solitary majesty. He would be pummelled and punctured by doctors and nurses, who even considered performing the one unspeakable terror for Thurber—a tracheotomy, which Thurber had feared more than anything ever since his brother Robert's life was so altered in his youth by a similar throat procedure for a thyroidectomy. The tracheotomy, mercifully, was not performed, but a bronchoscopy was deemed necessary because, at the beginning of November—the month he so dreaded for its calamities—Thurber developed pneumonia and a blood clot in a lung. He lapsed into a deep coma. Even a shot of brandy was poured into him; what alcohol had done before it could not do now. "We will just have to trust to another Thurber miracle," Helen wrote a friend.(66)

The man who had always been so amused by female behavior was fond of saying about his own wife: "When I'm on my deathbed, Helen will be at the hairdresser's." With Thurberish accuracy, on Thursday afternoon, November 2nd, Helen, while under a dryer, received a call from the hospital informing her that her husband was sinking rapidly. She phoned Jap Gude and asked him to meet her at the hospital right away. "I raced over," Gude said, "and got there just before Helen. In Jim's room, the doctor told me there were only minutes left. I was the last person to see Jim gasping for his life. Then, it was all over. I waited in the room next door to Jim's for Helen to arrive. After I told her, we phoned Rosemary, the brothers, Shawn, Haila, and the press."

Helen returned to the Algonquin to receive friends who stopped by to comfort. "For all of us that day," Marc Simont said, "there was mostly a feeling of tragic relief."

Over the years, Thurber had expressed three different requests for his *New Yorker* obituary: a reprinting of his lovely spot drawing of a Thurber dog staring at a tombstone, a memorial written by E. B. White, or, as he suggested to Milton Greenstein the previous April, a reprinting of "The Secret Life of Walter Mitty" with a brief note stating that the author had requested it in his will. Both White and Shawn set to work on a two-part obituary.

Meanwhile, news stories, editorials, and obituaries appeared all over the world. If there was ever any doubt about Thurber's powerful effect on literate mankind, it was dispelled. He was most often compared to Mark Twain, as a confirmed American original who had lent another dimension to the art of humor. The consensus was, as Red Smith wrote in the New York *Herald Tribune*, on November 5, 1961, that "Jim Thurber was the greatest humorist of his time and probably . . . America's greatest since Mark Twain." The *Times* ran a front-page story and obituary, quoting Shawn as saying that Thurber was "a master among comic artists, one of the great American writers of our time, and one of the few great humorists in all literary history."(67) *Time* printed a full-page tribute, and journals as far removed from each other as the Houston *Chronicle* and *Commonweal* devoted impressive space to Thurber. Some were pedantic paeans tracing his literary ancestry and some missed the point of his talent and his demeanor, a few describing him as shy, slight, and introverted—the very model of the "Thurber man." The British filled their usually stingy pages and airwaves with extensive and telling memorials to the man and his art. They seemed to grasp the peculiar quality of his work, on the whole, better than most Americans and felt the abrupt end of it more ruefully. He was one of their own. The *Times of London* not only likened him to Mark Twain but to Lewis Carroll.

"We are leaving for Columbus tonight and hope to return in a week or so, especially since I do not want to be buried in Green Lawn Cemetery there, in which my once bickering, but now silent, family occupies a good square mile of space." So wrote Thurber to the Van Dorens on November 12, 1959. But the dead have nothing to say in such matters. His ashes were buried in Columbus's Green Lawn Cemetery on a snowy Wednesday morning, November 8, 1961—just two years after he stated his burial request to the Van Dorens and exactly one month before his sixty-seventh birthday. Despite his wishes, it was only fitting. Columbus was his town, for better or for worse, and it was the grander setting for his work, even when he was writing about France or England or New York or Connecticut. There was always the thin Ohio lens through which the Thurber images had to pass.

With the widowed Helen, Rosemary, her husband, Fred, Robert and William Thurber, other Fisher relatives, James Pollard and John Fullen representing Ohio State, George Smallsreed of the *Dispatch*, classmate Tom Meek, the consequential Elliott Nugent, Burgess Meredith, and the faithful Jap Gude in attendance under an awning tent, the Rev. Karl Scheufler, pastor of the First Methodist Church of Columbus, read some brief prayers and a verse from the Methodist hymnal:

> Now the laborer's task is over;
>   Now the battle day is past;
> Now upon the further shore
>   Lands the voyager at last.
> Father, in Thy gracious keeping
>   Leave we now Thy servant sleeping.

There were few flowers (contributions to Fight for Sight were desired in their stead) and few tears. "It was so absurdly short," Rosemary recalled. "He would have wanted it short and to the point, but that service was almost funny. I nearly went to pieces, but Helen was calm and strong through it all, and I just leaned on her."

The bronze urn containing the ashes of Thurber was interred a few yards from his parents' headstones and not far from an enormous block of granite engraved with the mighty legend "FISHER." Thurber also would have been amused by the motto of Green Lawn Cemetery, as it appears in its rules-and-regulations brochure: "Beauty and Dignity Without Extravagance."

The day of the funeral, the *New Yorker* magazine appeared on the newsstands containing the ultimate epitaph for James Thurber. The section of the *New Yorker* obituary that Shawn wrote paid homage to Thurber's part in the magazine's tradition and stated a tremendous truth, that "his work was largely unclassifiable, it was simply Thurber." But it was E. B. White's tribute that made the man and his work settle into place, more than a thousand Methodist ministers or editorialists ever could:

I am one of the lucky ones; I knew him before blindness hit him, before fame hit him, and I tend always to think of him as a young artist in a small office in a big city, with all the world still ahead. It was a fine thing to be young and at work in New York for a new magazine when Thurber was young and at work, and I will always be glad this happened to me.

It was fortunate that we got on well; the office we shared was the size of a hall bedroom. There was just room enough for two men, two typewriters, and a stack of copy paper. The copy paper disappeared at a scandalous rate—not because our production was high (although it was) but because Thurber used copy paper as the natural receptacle for discarded sorrows, immediate joys, stale dreams, golden prophecies, and messages of good cheer to the outside world and to fellow-workers. His mind was never at rest, and his pencil was connected to his mind by the best conductive tissue I have ever seen in action. The whole world knows what a funny man he was, but you had to sit next to him day after day to understand the extravagance of his clowning, the wildness and subtlety of his thinking, and the intensity of his interest in others and his sympathy for their dilemmas—dilemmas that he instantly enlarged, put in focus, and made immortal, just as he enlarged and made immortal the strange goings on in the Ohio home of his boyhood. His waking dreams and his sleeping dreams commingled shamelessly and uproariously. Ohio was never far from his thoughts, and when he received a medal from his home state in 1953, he wrote, "The clocks that strike in my dreams are often the clocks of Columbus." It is a beautiful sentence and a revealing one.

He was both a practitioner of humor and a defender of it. The day he died,

I came on a letter from him. "Every time is a time for humor," he wrote. "I write humor the way a surgeon operates, because it is a livelihood, because I have a great urge to do it, because many interesting challenges are set up, and because I have the hope it may do some good." Once, I remember, he heard someone say that humor is a shield, not a sword, and it made him mad. He wasn't going to have anyone beating his sword into a shield. That "surgeon," incidentally, is pure Mitty. During his happiest years, Thurber did not write the way a surgeon operates, he wrote the way a child skips rope, the way a mouse waltzes.

Although he was best known for "Walter Mitty" and "The Male Animal," the book of his I like best is "The Last Flower." In it you will find his faith in the renewal of life, his feeling for the beauty and fragility of life on earth. Like all good writers, he fashioned his own best obituary notice. Nobody else can add to the record, much as he might like to. And of all the flowers, real and figurative, that will find their way to Thurber's last resting place, the one that will remain fresh and wiltproof is the little flower he himself drew, on the last page of that lovely book.(68)

Back in Cornwall, Rose Algrant continued to have her parties, but they were never quite the same again. For a long time, nobody dared to sit in Thurber's favorite chair in her living room—his throne—and, months later, when a member of the Cornwall circle absently sat on the chair one night, he received cold stares from the entire room. "What I remember of him now is the good times," Marc Simont said. "I remember the great man holding forth and making us laugh and think and feel good. He made us all different in some way, maybe even better people."

God bless . . . God damn.

Afterword

Like any artist of his calibre, Thurber, of course, didn't disappear with his ashes. His pieces and drawings continue to be reprinted in books and magazines with, if anything, increasing frequency. It sometimes seems as if it would be impossible for certain journals to make an elusive point without the aid of an accompanying Thurber cartoon or, at the very least, a reference to Walter Mitty or a Thurber man, woman, or dog. Then, magically, it all becomes clear. His works have been translated into twenty-one languages—from Icelandic to Gujarati—and his widow has brought out two posthumous collections, *Credos and Curios* (Harper & Row, 1962) and *Thurber and Company* (Harper & Row, 1966), with some new work presented in each for the first time. Plays, revues, movies, television shows, readings, recordings, lectures, and new editions of old books are generated every year from the rich source of Thurber. Children, as well as adults, seem to understand and appreciate him more than ever. His name and art are part of the language, a graphic medium, a figure of speech.

What he did was manufacture a unique world with its own creatures, its own mores, its own energy, its own foibles, its own madness—all remarkably similar to the real world, similar enough so we can laugh and then perhaps feel vaguely uncomfortable. It is a creation not to be taken lightly.

As for the man, he passed through with brilliance, cheered the population, suffered and caused some suffering, and then passed on. But most of all, he left something elegant and important behind.

Bridgewater, Connecticut
January 11, 1974

Sources

PART I: CHAPTER 1
1. Op-Ed Page, New York *Times*, April 26, 1972.
2. Ralph McCombs to BB.
3. "Return of the Native," *Credos and Curios.*
4. "Adam's Anvil," *The Thurber Album.*
5. *Ibid.*
6. Helen Thurber to BB.
7. "Man with a Rose," *The Thurber Album.*
8. Helen Thurber to BB.
9. "Conversation Piece," *The Thurber Album.*
10. *Ibid.*
11. "Gentleman from Indiana," *The Thurber Album.*
12. "Daguerreotype of a Lady," *The Thurber Album.*
13. *Ibid.*
14. "Lavender with a Difference," *The Thurber Album.*
15. "The Secret Life of James Thurber," *The Thurber Carnival.*
16. Interview with William Thurber, conducted by Lewis Branscomb, Feb. 14–15, 1972.

PART I: CHAPTER 2
1. "Daguerreotype of a Lady," *The Thurber Album.*
2. *Ibid.*
3. "I Went to Sullivant," *The Middle-Aged Man on the Flying Trapeze.*
4. Donald Ogden Stewart, "Death of a Unicorn," *New Statesman*, Nov. 10, 1961.
5. Ruth Young White, "Early Thurber," *Life*, April 22, 1940.
6. Letter to John and Donia McNulty, Nov. 21, 1937.
7. "James Thurber: In Conversation with Alistair Cooke," *Atlantic*, Aug., 1956.

8. Columbus *Dispatch*, Jan. 5, 1941.
9. Interview with Ruth Young White, conducted by Lewis Branscomb, Aug. 6, 1971.
10. "Gentleman from Indiana," *The Thurber Album.*
11. "University Days," *My Life and Hard Times.*
12. Maurice Dolbier, "A Sunday Afternoon with Mr. Thurber," New York *Herald Tribune* Book Review, Nov. 3, 1957.
13. Letter to Harold Danforth, July 9, 1951.
14. Letter to James Pollard, June 28, 1960.

PART I: CHAPTER 3
1. Interview with Ruth Young White, *op. cit.*
2. Letter to James Pollard, June 28, 1960.
3. "Man with a Pipe," *The Thurber Album.*
4. "The Wings of Henry James," *Lanterns and Lances.*
5. "Man with a Pipe," *The Thurber Album.*
6. *Ibid.*
7. "Length and Shadow," *The Thurber Album.*
8. Nelson Budd, "Personal Reminiscences of James Thurber," *Ohio State University Monthly*, Jan., 1962.

PART I: CHAPTER 4
1. Stephen Vincent and Rosemary Benét, "Thurber: As Unmistakable as a Kangaroo," New York *Herald Tribune* Book Review, Dec. 29, 1940.
2. "Credos and Curios," Columbus *Dispatch.*

PART I: CHAPTER 5
1. "The First Time I Saw Paris," *Alarms and Diversions.*

2. *Ibid.*
3. "Exhibit X," *The Beast in Me.*
4. Letter to R. Henry Norweb, March 25, 1948.
5. *Ibid.*
6. "The First Time I Saw Paris," *Alarms and Diversions.*
7. Letter to Elliott Nugent, April 4, 1920.
8. "The First Time I Saw Paris," *Alarms and Diversions.*

PART II: CHAPTER 6
1. "Credos and Curios," Columbus *Dispatch.*
2. Interview with Ruth Young White, *op. cit.*
3. Letter to Harold Ross, Oct. 19, 1951.
4. "Loose Leaves," *The Thurber Album.*
5. "My Friend McNulty," *Credos and Curios.*
6. *Ibid.*
7. Letter to Dorothy Miller, April 21, 1949.

PART II: CHAPTER 7
1. Letter to Dale Kramer, April 23, 1951.
2. Letter to Helen Mendelson, July 24, 1950.
3. Letter to Frank Gibney, Oct. 31, 1956.
4. *Ibid.*
5. Henry Brandon, *As We Are,* Doubleday and Company, 1961. (Brandon's interview with Thurber was printed, in a shorter version, in the *New Republic,* May 26, 1958.)

PART II: CHAPTER 8
1. Letter to E. B. White, March 1, 1954.
2. Letter to E.B. White, Dec. 22, 1952.
3. "Remembrance of Things Past," *Let Your Mind Alone.*
4. *The Years with Ross.*
5. Malcolm Cowley, ed., *Writers at Work,* Viking, 1959.
6. Letter to John Scott Mabon, March 16, 1946.
7. Letter to Hudson Hawley, July 27, 1954.
8. Letter to E.B. White, Dec. 22, 1952.
9. "La Grande Ville de Plaisir," *My World—and Welcome to It.*
10. *Ibid.*
11. Riviera Edition, Chicago *Tribune,* Feb. 17, 1926.

12. Letter to Frank Gibney, Oct. 31, 1956.
13. *Maclean's Magazine,* May 1, 1951.
14. Letter to Wolcott Gibbs, May 21, 1954.
15. *Newsweek,* Feb. 4, 1957.
16. *Ibid.*

PART II: CHAPTER 9
1. *The Years with Ross.*
2. *Ibid.*
3. *Ibid.*
4. Letter to Jack Goodman, Jan. 15, 1953.
5. Robert Coates, "James Thurber," *Authors Guild Bulletin,* Dec., 1961.
6. Columbus *Dispatch,* Aug. 3, 1958.
7. "Memoirs of a Drudge," *The Thurber Carnival.*
8. *The Years with Ross.*
9. Letter to Ruth Young White, undated.
10. *Ibid.*
11. *The Years with Ross.*
12. *Ibid.*
13. *Ibid.*
14. *Ibid.*
15. *Ibid.*
16. Letter to Frank Gibney, Oct. 31, 1956.
17. *Ibid.*
18. E. B. White to BB.
19. Letter to Frank Gibney, Oct. 31, 1956.
20. Coates, *Authors Guild Bulletin, op. cit.*
21. Letter to Frank Gibney, Oct. 31, 1956.
22. *Writers at Work, op. cit.*

PART II: CHAPTER 10
1. *The Years with Ross.*
2. Letter to Herman Miller, Sept. 22, 1931.
3. Letter to Johnny Parker, Feb. 16, 1956.
4. Letter to E. B. White, Dec. 22, 1952.
5. Columbus *Citizen,* Nov. 13, 1928.

PART II: CHAPTER 11
1. Letter to E. B. White, Jan. 20, 1938.
2. "Christabel: Part One," *Thurber's Dogs.*
3. "And So to Medve," *Thurber's Dogs.*
4. *The Years with Ross.*
5. *Ibid.*
6. Letter to Barbara Kammer, March 5, 1945.
7. "Lo, Hear the Gentle Bloodhound," *Thurber's Dogs.*
8. Letter to Herman Miller, undated (probably 1940).

9. *The Years with Ross.*
10. *Ibid.*
11. E. B. White, Introduction (written in 1950), *Is Sex Necessary?*
12. *Ibid.*
13. *Ibid.*
14. *Ibid.*
15. *Ohio State Lantern*, Feb. 25, 1930.
16. *The Years with Ross.*
17. Letter to John Scott Mabon, March 16, 1946.
18. *The Years with Ross.*

PART II: CHAPTER 12
1. Letter to John McNulty, Oct. 5, 1950.
2. Letter to Thurber from Richard Connell, Jan. 27, 1943.
3. *American Weekly*, 1935.
4. "The Gentleman Is Cold," *The Middle-Aged Man on the Flying Trapeze.*
5. "Salute to Thurber," *Saturday Review*, Nov. 25, 1961.
6. Stewart, *New Statesman, op. cit.*
7. Lillian Hellman, "Julia," *Esquire*, July, 1973.
8. Letter to Malcolm Cowley, Feb. 3, 1951.
9. Letter to Frank Gibney, Oct. 31, 1956.
10. Letter to Malcolm Cowley, Feb. 3, 1951.
11. *The Years with Ross.*
12. Letter to the Thurber family, Dec. 22, 1950.
13. Letter to Helen Thurber from Charles Grant, May 14, 1963.
14. Max Eastman, *Enjoyment of Laughter*, Halcyon House, 1936.
15. Letter to E. B. White, April 24, 1951.
16. "State of the Nation's Humor," New York *Times* Magazine, Dec. 7, 1958.
17. Interview with James Pollard, conducted by Lewis Branscomb, Oct. 18, 1971.
18. New York *Herald Tribune*, Oct. 4, 1949.
19. Interview with William Thurber, *op. cit.*
20. Chronology for *Time*, written by Thurber in 1950.

PART III: CHAPTER 13
1. Letter to E. B. White, Dec. 22, 1952.
2. *Ibid.*

3. Letter to E. B. and Katharine White, Aug. ?, 1935.
4. Letter to Herman and Dorothy Miller, Winter, 1935–36.
6. Letter to E. B. and Katharine White, Spring, 1936.
7. Letter to E.B. White, Summer, 1936.
8. Letter to Herman Miller, Oct. ?, 1936.
9. Helen Thurber, Introduction, *Thurber and Company.*
10. Letter to Thurber from Carl Sandburg, May 14, 1947.
11. Letter to Eugene Reynal, Jan. 5, 1953.
12. Letter to Herman Miller, Oct. ?, 1936.
13. Letter to E. B. White, Winter, 1936–37.
14. Letter to Herman Miller, Oct. ?, 1936.
15. Letter to E. B. and Katharine White, May 29, 1937.
16. Letter to E. B. White, Jan. 20, 1938.
17. Letter to Stanley Walker, May 15, 1959.
18. Letter to Ronald and Jane Williams, July 11, 1937.
19. *Ibid.*
20. *Ibid.*
21. *Ibid.*
22. Post card to the Thurber family, Sept. 10, 1937.
23. Letter to E.B. White, Oct. 6, 1937.
24. Letter to John McNulty, Nov. 21, 1937.
25. Letter to the Thurber family, Dec. 9, 1937.
26. Letter to E.B. White, Dec. 22, 1937.
27. Letter to E.B. White, Jan. 20, 1938.
28. Letter to John Scott Mabon, March 16, 1946.
29. Letter to Katharine White, May 15, 1938.
30. *Ibid.*
31. *The Years with Ross.*

PART III: CHAPTER 14
1. Letter to E.B. White, Sept. 15, 1938.
2. Letter to E.B. White, Sept. ?, 1938.
3. *Ibid.*
4. *Ibid.*
5. Letter to E.B. White, Fall, 1938.
6. Cooke, *Atlantic, op. cit.*
7. *The Years with Ross.*
8. "What Do You Mean It *Was* Brillig?," *My World—and Welcome to It.*
9. Letter to Kenneth MacLean, April 9, 1953.

10. Letter to Mrs. Robert Blake, April 7, 1961.
11. Cooke, *Atlantic, op. cit.*
12. Letter to Thurber from Harold Ross, undated.
13. Stewart Alsop, *Newsweek*, Sept. 25, 1972.
14. Letter to John Gerstad, Sept. 7, 1959.
15. *Ibid.*
16. Elliott Nugent, "Notes on James Thurber the Man, or Men," New York *Times*, Feb. 25, 1940.
17. *Ibid.*
18. Letter to John McNulty, Jan. 18, 194?.
19. Letter to E.B. and Katharine White, Nov. ?, 1939.
20. *Ibid.*
21. *Ibid.*
22. Letter to H.L. Mencken, Nov. 24, 1947.
23. Letter to Thurber from H. L. Mencken, Nov. 29, 1947.
24. Letter to H. L. Mencken, Nov. 24, 1947.
25. Letter to H. L. Mencken, March 10, 1944.
26. Letter to Wolcott Gibbs, Summer, 1950.
27. Letter to Herman and Dorothy Miller, March 19, 1940.

PART III: CHAPTER 15
1. Caption to a Thurber cartoon, printed in the *New Yorker*, Nov. 9, 1940.
2. Letter to Ronald and Jane Williams, ?, 1940.
3. Letter to Ronald and Jane Williams, Aug. 31, 1940.
4. Letter to Dr. Gordon Bruce from Mary Thurber, Oct. 12, 1940.
5. Letter to Brad Darrach, July 17, 1950.
6. Letter to Ronald and Jane Williams from Helen Thurber, May ?, 1941.
7. *Writers at Work, op. cit.*
8. Letter to E.B. and Katharine White, Summer, 1941.
9. Letter to Dr. Gordon Bruce, Aug. ?, 1941.
10. Letter to Frank Gibney, Oct. 31, 1956.
11. "Taps at Assembly," *New Republic*, Feb. 9, 1942.
12. Letter to Ronald Williams, Aug. 18, 1942.
13. Letter to Ruth Porter, March 21, 1953.
14. *Newsweek*, Nov. 22, 1943.

15. Letter to Herman Miller, May 28, 1943.
16. *Newsweek*, Nov. 22, 1943.
17. Letter to E. B. White, June 9, 1943.
18. Letter to E. B. and Katharine White, June 12, 1943.
19. Dorothy Parker, Preface, *Men, Women and Dogs*.
20. "The Lady on the Bookcase," *The Beast in Me*.
21. *The Years with Ross*.
22. *Time*, July 9, 1951.
23. Letter to Peter De Vries, Nov. 19, 1943.
24. Peter De Vries, Introduction, *Lanterns and Lances* (Time, Inc., paperback edition, 1962).
25. *Ibid.*
26. Letter to Peter De Vries, June 14, 1944.
27. *Ibid.*
28. *The Years with Ross*.
29. Letter to Peter De Vries, Sept. ?, 1947.
30. "The Wizard of Chitenango," *New Republic*, Dec. 12, 1934.
31. Letter to E. B. and Katharine White, Sept. 30, 1944.
32. Letter to Herman and Dorothy Miller from Helen Thurber, Nov. ?, 1944.
33. Letter to Joel Sayre and John McNulty, Dec. ?, 1944.
34. Letter to Herman and Dorothy Miller, Dec. 9, 1944.

PART III: CHAPTER 16
1. C. Lester Walker, "The Legendary Mr. Thurber," *Ladies' Home Journal*, July, 1946.
2. *The Years with Ross*.
3. *Writers at Work, op. cit.*
4. Letter to Herman and Dorothy Miller, Jan. 22, 1946.
5. Letter to Herman and Dorothy Miller, March 7, 1946.
6. *The Years with Ross*.
7. *Ibid.*
8. Letter to Thurber from Cyril Connolly, Sept. 17, 1948.
9. Letter to Cyril Connolly, Oct. 30, 1948.
10. Letter to Miss E. Louise Mally, Jan. 7, 1954.
11. Letter to Herman and Dorothy Miller, Dec. 9, 1944.
12. Letter to Katharine White, Summer, 1945.

13. *Radio Times* (B.B.C. journal), Dec. 23, 1949.
14. *New Yorker*, Oct. 27, 1945.
15. Letter to Hamish Hamilton, March 15, 1956.
16. "Such a Phrase as Drifts Through Dreams," *Lanterns and Lances*.
17. Letter to Elliott Nugent, Sept. 13, 1948.
18. Preface, *The Thurber Carnival*.
19. Cooke, *Atlantic, op. cit.*
20. Letter to Joel Sayre, Feb. 11, 1954.
21. Brandon, "As We Are," *op. cit.*
22. Cooke, *Atlantic, op. cit.*
23. Letter to Thurber from John Fullen, Jan. 31, 1946.
24. Letter to Elliott Nugent, April 25, 1946.
25. Letter to Gardner Rea, Jan. 26, 1946.
26. Letter and enclosure to E. B. White, Dec. 3, 1947.
27. Letters to Whit Burnett, Sept. 10, 1948, and Nov. 29, 1949.
28. Letter to John McNulty, Jan. 18, 194?.
29. *Life*, Aug. 4, 1947.
30. *Life*, Aug. 18, 1947.
31. *Life*, Aug. 4, 1947.
32. Letter to Charles Grayson, Jan. 9, 1952.
33. Letter to Herman and Dorothy Miller, March 7, 1946.
34. *Publishers' Weekly*, Oct. 8, 1949.
35. Letter to Lucile Platt, July 27, 1950.
36. Letter to Lucile Platt, Aug. 5, 1950.
37. "The Wings of Henry James," *Lanterns and Lances*.
38. "Soapland," *The Beast in Me*.
39. *The Years with Ross*.

PART III: CHAPTER 17
1. Letter to Frank Gibney, Oct. 31, 1956.
2. Letter to Ann Honeycutt, March 24, 1949.
3. Letter to Dorothy Miller, April 22, 1949.
4. Letter to E.B. White, July 23, 1949.
5. Letter to John O'Hara, Oct. 29, 1949.
6. Letter to E.B. White, July 23, 1949.
7. Letter to Ronald and Jane Williams, Feb. 7, 1950.
8. "Important Authors of the Fall, Speaking for Themselves," New York *Herald Tribune* Book Review, Oct. 8, 1950.
9. Letter to Dr. Russel Voorhees, March 3, 1951.

10. *Writers at Work, op. cit.*
11. Letter to Frank Gibney, Oct. 31, 1956.
12. Harvey Breit, "Talk with James Thurber," New York *Times* Book Review, June 29, 1952.
13. Letter to E. B. White, Dec. 1, 1950.
14. Letter to Dorothy Canfield Fisher, April 11, 1951.
15. Letter to Carey McWilliams, July 21, 1952.
16. "Dark Suspicions," New York *Times*, July 27, 1952.
17. Letter to Gus Lobrano, April 10, 1951.
18. Letter to Gus Lobrano, May 28, 1951.
19. Letter to Gus Lobrano, July 10, 1951.
20. Letter to Gus Lobrano, Aug. 2, 1951.
21. Letter to E. B. and Katharine White, June 12, 1951.
22. Letter to the Thurber family, June 12, 1951.
23. *Ibid.*
24. Letter to the Thurber family, July 10, 1951.
25. Letter to E.B. and Katharine White, July 10, 1951.
26. Letter to E.B. White, April 25, 1952.
27. William Schlamm, "The Secret Lives of James Thurber," *Freeman*, July 28, 1952.
28. Letter to Carey McWilliams, Aug. 13, 1952.

PART III: CHAPTER 18
1. Letter to Ronald Williams, Dec. 15, 1951.
2. Letter to Lester Getzloe, Oct. 26, 1951.
3. Letter to James Pollard, Oct. 25, 1951.
4. Letter to Ronald and Jane Williams from Helen Thurber, June 12, 1950.
5. *Time*, July 9, 1951.
6. Letter to Lester Getzloe, Dec. 8, 1951.
7. *Ibid.*
8. Dayton, Ohio, *Daily News*, June 11, 1967.
9. "Length and Shadow," *The Thurber Album*.
10. New York *Times*, May 1, 1952.
11. "Dark Suspicions," New York *Times*, July 27, 1952.
12. Letter to Hamish Hamilton, April 7, 1952.
13. Letter to Hamish Hamilton, July 23, 1952.
14. *Saturday Review*, Nov. 8, 1952.

15. Letter to Edward R. Murrow, Nov. 11, 1952.
16. Letter to Ronald and Jane Williams, Oct. 15, 1952.
17. Letter to Frank Sullivan, Nov. 3, 1952.
18. Letter to E.B. White, July 18, 1952.
19. Letter to Peter De Vries, Oct. 16, 1952.
20. Letter to Raymond Swing, Nov. 4, 1953.
21. Letter to John McNulty, undated.
22. Letter to Rosemary Thurber, Oct. 3, 1952.
23. Letter to E.B. White, Dec. 22, 1952.
24. Letter to Ronald and Jane Williams, March 14, 1953.
25. *Saturday Review*, Dec. 12, 1953.
26. Letter to Kenneth and Sara MacLean, June 4, 1953.
27. Letter to Jack Goodman, June 11, 1953.
28. Letter to "P. Leslie Woodbine," May 18, 1953.
29. As described fictionally in "Destructive Forces in Life," *Let Your Mind Alone.*
30. Letter to Burrus Dickinson, May 29, 1953.
31. Letter to E.B. and Katharine White, Oct. 7, 1953.
32. Letter to E.B. and Katharine White, Oct. 20, 1953.
33. Letter to George Smallsreed, Sept. 23, 1953.
34. Letter to the Thurber family, May 29, 1953.
35. Letter to Frederick Sauers, Jan. 5, 1954.
36. Letter to William Thurber, Nov. 7, 1956.
37. Letter to Ronald and Jane Williams, June 23, 1955.
38. Letter to Thurber from T.S. Eliot, dated "St. Hortense: 1950."
39. Letter to Malcolm Cowley, July 31, 1952.
40. *Ibid.*
41. Letter to Rose Algrant and Rosemary Sauers, June 18, 1955.
42. Letter to Thurber from Nathaniel Benchley, Sept. 18, 1949.
43. Letter to Peter De Vries, July 2, 1956.
44. Letter to S. J. Perelman, July 5, 1956.
45. Letter to William Maxwell, April 30, 1956.
46. Letter to R. E. M. Whitaker, Feb. 3, 1956.

47. Letter to Wolcott Gibbs, Feb. 8, 1956.
48. Letter to E. B. White, April 16, 1956.
49. Letter to Elmer Davis, May 18, 1956.
50. Letter to Malcolm Cowley, Jan. 18, 1957.
51. Letter to William Maxwell, Oct. 11, 1956.
52. Letter to William Maxwell, Jan. 30, 1957.
53. *The Years with Ross.*
54. Letter to William Shawn, July 31, 1956.

PART III: CHAPTER 19
1. "Conversation Piece," *The Thurber Album.*
2. Brandon, *As We Are, op. cit.*
3. "Thurber—An Old Hand at Humor with Two Hits on Hand," *Life*, March 14, 1960.
4. Letter to Dr. Gordon Bruce, Feb. 4, 1957.
5. Letter to Dr. Gordon Bruce, Jan. 5, 1959.
6. Letter to Dr. Gordon Bruce, Dec. 7, 1960.
7. Letter to Charles Morton, Jan. 18, 1957.
8. Dolbier, *Herald Tribune, op. cit.*
9. Letter to E. B. White, July 26, 1957.
10. Carol Illig, "Hear Your Heroes," *Seventeen*, January, 1960.
11. Letter to Thurber from George Kaufman, undated.
12. Letter to Thurber from Groucho Marx, June 3, 1959.
13. Letter to Thurber from Katharine White, June 2, 1958.
14. Letter to Thurber from E.B. White, Nov. 28, 1958.
15. Letter to E.B. White, Dec. 3, 1958.
16. Letter to Lewis Gannett, Dec. 3, 1958.
17. Letter to Edmund Wilson, May 19, 1959.
18. Letter to Roger Angell, July 2, 1959.
19. Letter to Hamish Hamilton and Roger Machell, July 28, 1959.
20. Letter to John Lardner, July 24, 1958.
21. Letter to John Lardner, Aug. 10, 1958.
22. Letter to Larry Adler, July 30, 1958.
23. *Ibid.*
24. Letter to Donald Ogden Stewart, March 16, 1959.
25. Letter to Donald Ogden Stewart, Aug. 1, 1958.
26. Letter to Peter De Vries, Sept. 21, 1960.

27. Columbus *Dispatch*, Nov. 13, 1959.
28. *Ohio State University Monthly*, May, 1960.
29. Interview with James Pollard, *op. cit.*

30. Letter to Kenneth Tynan, April 5, 1960.
31. Edmund Wilson, *Upstate*, Farrar, Strauss and Giroux, 1971.
32. *A Thurber Carnival*, Samuel French, Inc., 1960.
33. *Newsweek*, Jan. 18, 1960.
34. *Ibid.*
35. Interview with Thurber, conducted by Eugene Gerrard, on radio station WOSU, Columbus, Jan. 8, 1960.
36. Letter to Ronald and Jane Williams, April 29, 1960.
37. Arthur Gelb, "Thurber Intends to Relax Till '61," New York *Times*, March 28, 1960.
38. Letter to Ronald and Jane Williams, June 16, 1960.
39. *Newsweek*, June 13, 1960.
40. "State of Humor in the States," New York *Times* Magazine, Sept. 4, 1960.
41. Letter to Roger Angell, Feb. 29, 1961.
42. "The Thurber Method of Acting," New York *Times* Magazine, Oct. 16, 1960.
43. Letter to Ronald and Jane Williams, Fall, 1960.
44. Unsent letter to Ernest Hemingway, Jan. 11, 1961.
45. Letter to Roger Machell, March 1, 1961.

46. Elliott Nugent, "Events Leading Up to the Comedy," Trident Press, 1965.
47. Letter to Roger Angell, March 13, 1961.
48. Letter to Roger Angell, July 3, 1961.
49. Letter to Milton Greenstein, April 26, 1961.
50. Letter to Thurber from Milton Greenstein, May 3, 1961.
51. W.J. Weatherby, "A Man of Words," *Manchester Guardian*, Feb. 9, 1961.
52. Letter to Elliott Nugent, Jan. 19, 1961.
53. Letters to John Gude, Feb. 13, Feb. 25, April 24, 1961.
54. Letter to Bernard Hollowood, March 8, 1961.
55. Letter to Peter De Vries, May 11, 1961.
56. Robert Muller, London *Daily Mail*, April 12, 1962.
57. Letter to Ted Gardiner, June 22, 1961.
58. Letter to E. B. White, June 19, 1961.
59. Letter to R. Hawley Truax, July 18, 1961.
60. Letter to Edward P. Morgan, July 12, 1961.
61. Letter to Portland Allen Rines, Aug. 29, 1961.
62. Letter to Frederick Sauers, Jan. 5, 1954.
63. Wilson, *Upstate, op. cit.*
64. Letter to Jane Williams, Aug. 26, 1961.
65. "And So to Medve," *Thurber's Dogs*.
66. Letter to Caskie Stinnett from Helen Thurber, Nov. 1, 1961.
67. New York *Times*, Nov. 3, 1961.
68. *New Yorker*, Nov. 11, 1961.

Bibliography

Since the publication of Edwin T. Bowden's exhaustive *James Thurber: A Bibliography* (Ohio State University Press, 1969), it would be redundant to set down another comprehensive bibliography of Thurber's collected and uncollected works. However, there is a complete chronological listing of his published books below, and references are made throughout the text to pertinent pieces and drawings, no matter how obscure. The balance of the following bibliography represents sources of particular importance consulted for the writing of this book.

"Advice from a Blind Writer," *Newsweek*, Feb. 1, 1960.

Allbaugh, Dave. "Time Cooled Thurber Anger at OSU's Gag Rule," Dayton (Ohio) *Daily News*, June 11, 1967.

"Art," *Time*, Dec. 31, 1934.

Arter, Bill. "Thurbertown, Ohio," Columbus *Dispatch* Magazine, April 14, 1957.

Auden, W.H. "The Icon and the Portrait," *Nation*, Jan. 13, 1940.

Baker, Samuel B. "Thurber," *Ohio State University Monthly*, Dec., 1961.

Beizer, James. "The Secret Distractions of James Thurber," Hartford (Conn.) *Courant* Magazine, Aug. 30, 1959.

Benchley, Nathaniel. *Robert Benchley*. McGraw-Hill, 1955.

Benét, Stephen Vincent and Rosemary. "Thurber: As Unmistakable as a Kangaroo," New York *Herald Tribune* Book Review, Dec. 29, 1940.

Benét, William Rose. "Carnival with Spectres," *Saturday Review*, Feb. 3, 1945.

Blair, Walter. *Horse Sense in American Humor*. University of Chicago Press, 1942.

Bohn, William E. *I Remember America*. The Macmillan Company, 1962.

Bowden, Edwin T. *James Thurber: A Bibliography*. Ohio State University Press, 1969.

Brady, Charles A. "What Thurber Saw," *Commonweal*, Dec. 8, 1961.

Brandon, Henry. *As We Are*. Doubleday and Company, 1961.

Breit, Harvey. "Mr. Thurber Observes a Serene Birthday," New York *Times* Magazine, Dec. 4, 1949.

_____. "Talk with James Thurber," New York *Times* Book Review, June 29, 1952.

Budd, Nelson H. "Personal Reminiscences of James Thurber," *Ohio State University Monthly*, Jan., 1962.

Coates, Robert M. "Thurber, Inc.," *Saturday Review*, Dec. 2, 1939.

_____. "James Thurber," *Authors Guild Bulletin*, Dec., 1961.

Cooke, Alistair. "James Thurber: In Conversation with Alistair Cooke," *Atlantic*, August, 1956.

Cowley, Malcolm. "James Thurber's Dream Book," *New Republic*, March 12, 1945.
_____. *The Literary Situation*. The Viking Press, 1954.
_____. "Lions and Lemmings, Toads and Tigers," *Reporter*, Dec. 13, 1956.
_____, ed. *Writers at Work*. The Viking Press, 1959.
De Vries, Peter. "James Thurber: The Comic Prufrock," *Poetry*, December, 1943.
_____. Introduction to *Lanterns and Lances*. Time, Inc. edition, 1962.
Dolbier, Maurice. "A Sunday Afternoon with Mr. Thurber," New York *Herald Tribune* Book Review, Nov. 3, 1957.
Eastman, Max. *Enjoyment of Laughter*. Halcyon House, 1936.
Elias, Robert H. "James Thurber: The Primitive, the Innocent, and the Individual," *American Scholar*, Summer, 1958.
Ernst, Margaret S. *In a Word*. Alfred A. Knopf, 1939. (Illustrated by Thurber; Preface by Thurber added to Channel Press edition, 1960.)
Friedrich, Otto. "James Thurber: A Critical Study," *Discovery*, Jan., 1955.
Gelb, Arthur. "Thurber Intends to Relax Till '61," New York *Times*, March 28, 1960.
"Goldwyn vs. Thurber," *Life*, Aug. 18, 1947.
Goodman, Jack, ed. *While You Were Gone: A Report on Wartime Life in the United States*. Simon and Schuster, 1946.
"Graveside Rites Held for Thurber," Columbus *Citizen-Journal*, Nov. 9, 1961.
Hackett, Francis. *On Judging Books in General and Particular*. John Day Company, 1947.
Hawes, Elizabeth. *Men Can Take It*. Random House, 1939. (Illustrated by Thurber.)
Hellman, Lillian. "Julia," *Esquire*, July, 1973.
Holmes, Charles S. *The Clocks of Columbus*. Atheneum, 1972.
Illig, Carol. "Hear Your Heroes," *Seventeen*, Jan., 1960.
"Important Authors of the Fall, Speaking for Themselves," New York *Herald Tribune* Book Review, Oct. 8, 1950.
"James Thurber, Aphorist for an Anxious Age," *Time*, Nov. 10, 1961.
Jennings, Paul. "James Thurber," *Punch*, March 10, 1965.
Kinney, James R. and Ann Honeycutt. *How to Raise a Dog in the City and in the Suburbs*. Simon and Schuster, 1938. (Illustrated by Thurber.)
Kramer, Dale. *Ross and The New Yorker*. Doubleday and Company, 1952.
Krutch, Joseph Wood. Review of "The Male Animal," *Nation*, Jan. 20, 1940.
McCord, David. "Anatomy of Confusion," *Saturday Review*, Dec. 5, 1953.
McGarey, Mary. "Thurber Kin Gather at Final Rites," Columbus *Dispatch*, Nov. 9, 1961.
MacLean, Kenneth. "James Thurber—A Portrait of the Dog-Artist," *Acta Victoriana*, Spring, 1944.
Manchester, Joe. *The Secret Life of Walter Mitty* (a musical based on the Thurber story). Samuel French, Inc., 1964.
Maney, Richard. *Fanfare, The Confessions of a Press Agent*. Harper & Brothers, 1957.
"Men, Women and Thurber," *Time*, Nov. 15, 1943.
Mian, Mary. *My Country-in-Law*. Houghton Mifflin Company, 1946. (Introduction by Thurber.)

Moates, Alice Leone. *No Nice Girl Swears*. Alfred A. Knopf, 1933. (Illustrated by Thurber.)

Morsberger, Robert E. *James Thurber*. Twayne Publishers, Inc., 1964.

"Movie of the Week," *Life*, Aug. 4, 1947.

Moynihan, Julian. "No Nonsense," *New Statesman*, Dec. 14, 1962.

"Mr. James Thurber," *Times of London*, Nov. 3, 1961.

Murrell, William. *A History of American Graphic Humor*. The Macmillan Company, 1938.

"Newsmakers," *Newsweek*, June 13, 1960.

Nugent, Elliott. "Notes on James Thurber the Man or Men," New York *Times*, Feb. 25, 1940.

_____. "James Thurber of Columbus," *Ohio Valley Folk Publications*, April, 1962.

_____. *Events Leading Up to the Comedy*. Trident Press, 1965.

"Priceless Gift of Laughter," *Time*, July 9, 1951.

Priest, Alan. "Mr. Thurber's Chinese Dog," *Metropolitan Museum of Art Bulletin*, June, 1946.

"Salute to Thurber," *Saturday Review*, Nov. 25, 1961.

Sayre, Joel. *Persian Gulf Command: Some Marvels on the Road to Kazvin*. Random House, 1945. (Introduction by Thurber.)

Schlamm, William. "The Secret Lives of James Thurber," *Freeman*, July 28, 1952.

Seeds, Charme. "Is Sex Necessary?," *Ohio State University Monthly*, April, 1930.

Shawn, William. "James Thurber," *New Yorker*, Nov. 11, 1961.

Smith, Red. "Jim Thurber," New York *Herald Tribune*, Nov. 5, 1961.

Stewart, Donald Ogden. "Death of a Unicorn," *New Statesman*, Nov. 10, 1961.

Taylor, Wilfred. "James Thurber," *Rothmill Quarterly*, Autumn–Winter, 1958.

"That Thurber Woman," *Newsweek*, Nov. 22, 1943.

Thurber, Helen. "Long Time No See," *Ladies' Home Journal*, July, 1964.

Thurber, James. *Is Sex Necessary? or Why You Feel the Way You Do* (with E. B. White). Harper & Brothers, 1929.

_____. *The Owl in the Attic and Other Perplexities*. Harper & Brothers, 1931.

_____. *The Seal in the Bedroom and Other Predicaments*. Harper & Brothers, 1932.

_____. *My Life and Hard Times*. Harper & Brothers, 1933.

_____. *The Middle-Aged Man on the Flying Trapeze*. Harper & Brothers, 1935.

_____. *Let Your Mind Alone! and Other More or Less Inspirational Pieces*. Harper & Brothers, 1937.

_____. *The Last Flower, A Parable in Pictures*. Harper & Brothers, 1939.

_____. *Fables for Our Time and Famous Poems Illustrated*. Harper & Brothers, 1940.

_____. *The Male Animal* (with Elliott Nugent). Random House, 1940.

_____. *My World—and Welcome to It*. Harcourt, Brace and Company, 1942.

_____. *Men, Women and Dogs*. Harcourt, Brace and Company, 1943.

_____. *Many Moons*. Harcourt, Brace and Company, 1943.

_____. *The Great Quillow*. Harcourt, Brace and Company, 1944.

_____. *The Thurber Carnival*. Harper & Brothers, 1945.

_____. *The White Deer*. Harcourt, Brace and Company, 1945.

———. *The Beast in Me and Other Animals*. Harcourt, Brace and Company, 1948.

———. *The 13 Clocks*. Simon and Schuster, 1950.

———. *The Thurber Album*. Simon and Schuster, 1952.

———. *Thurber Country*. Simon and Schuster, 1953.

———. *Thurber's Dogs*. Simon and Schuster, 1955.

———. *Further Fables for Our Time*. Simon and Schuster, 1956.

———. *Alarms and Diversions*. Harper & Brothers, 1957.

———. *The Wonderful O*. Simon and Schuster, 1957.

———. *The Years with Ross*. Atlantic Little, Brown and Company, 1959.

———. *Lanterns and Lances*. Harper & Brothers, 1961.

———. *Credos and Curios*. Harper & Row, 1962.

———. *A Thurber Carnival*. Samuel French, Inc., 1962.

———. *Thurber and Company*. Harper & Row, 1966.

"Thurber Amuses People by Making Them Squirm," *Life*, Feb. 19, 1945.

"Thurber—An Old Hand at Humor with Two Hits on Hand," *Life*, March 14, 1960.

"Thurber and His Humor . . . Up with the Chuckle, Down with the Yuk," *Newsweek*, Feb. 4, 1957.

"Thurber Reports His Own Play, 'The Male Animal,' with His Own Cartoons," *Life*, Jan. 29, 1940.

"Thurber to Hobson to Thurber," *Saturday Review*, Nov. 8, 1952.

Van Doren, Mark. *The Autobiography of Mark Van Doren*. Harcourt, Brace and Company, 1958.

Walker, C. Lester. "The Legendary Mr. Thurber," *Ladies' Home Journal*, July, 1946.

Weales, Gerald. "The World in Thurber's Fables," *Commonweal*, Jan. 18, 1957.

Weatherby, W. J. "A Man of Words," *Manchester Guardian Weekly*, Feb. 9, 1961.

White, E. B. "James Thurber," *New Yorker*, Nov. 11, 1961.

White, E. B. and Katharine S., ed. *A Subtreasury of American Humor*. Coward-McCann, Inc., 1941.

White, Ruth Young. "Early Thurber," *Life*, April 22, 1940.

Wilson, Edmund. Review of *The White Deer*, *New Yorker*, Oct. 27, 1945.

———. *Upstate*. Farrar, Strauss and Giroux, 1971.

"The Years Without Ross," *Time*, May 16, 1960.

Index